# Queensland

**Joseph Bindloss**
**Kate Daly**
**Matthew Lane**
**Sarah Mathers**

LONELY PLANET PUBLICATIONS
Melbourne • Oakland • London • Paris

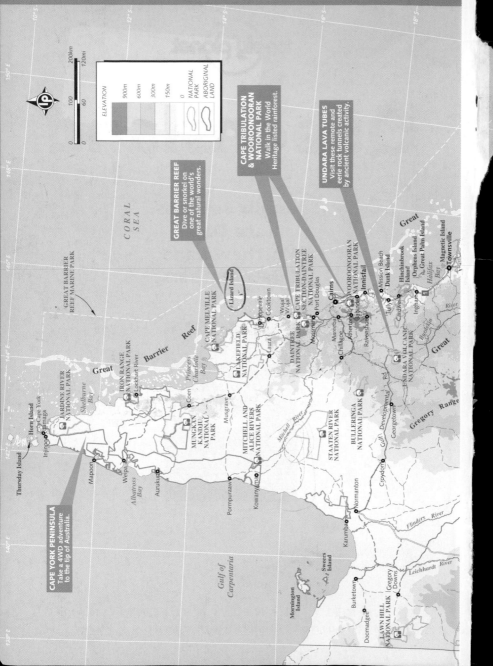

**ELEVATION**

900m
600m
300m
150m
0
NATIONAL PARK
ABORIGINAL LAND

**CAPE YORK PENINSULA**
Take a 4WD adventure to the tip of Australia.

**GREAT BARRIER REEF**
Dive or snorkel on one of the world's great natural wonders.

**CAPE TRIBULATION & WOOROONOORAN NATIONAL PARK**
Walk in the World Heritage listed rainforest.

**UNDARA LAVA TUBES**
Visit these remote and eerie rock tunnels created by ancient volcanic activity.

# The Authors

### Joseph Bindloss
Joe updated Brisbane and Southern Queensland for this edition. He was born in Cyprus, grew up in England and has since lived and worked in the US, the Philippines and Australia, though he currently calls London home. He first developed an incurable case of wanderlust on family trips through Europe in the old VW Kombi. A degree in biology eliminated science from his future choice of careers, and Joe moved through a string of occupations, including mural painting and sculpting, before finally settling on journalism. Joe has previously written for LP in the Philippines, Australia, India, the Indian Ocean islands and London.

### Kate Daly
Born in Sydney, Kate spent several formative childhood years in the remote country town of Wee Waa, in north-western NSW. She dropped out of an arts/law degree in 1985, and turned to travel instead – hitchhiking up the East Coast and through the Northern Territory. Returning to uni she studied writing and has a BA (Communications) from the University of Technology, Sydney. She has travelled widely in North- and South-East Asia and Europe. On the work front, she's done it all, from copywriter in Tokyo to editor in Melbourne. She has written for Lonely Planet's *Out to Eat Melbourne 2000*, and contributed to Lonely Planet's *Queensland*, *Greece* and *Greek Islands* guides.

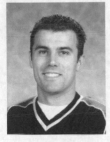

### Matthew Lane
Matthew updated the Outback and Capricorn Coast chapters for this book. Born in England, he grew up in central Victoria, and drifted into the world of journalism at a young age. He started out in newspapers and in the ensuing years tried some television work, studied a bit of graphic design, and interspersed his burgeoning career(s) with some overseas travel. Thinking there must be a way to combine writing, travel and money, he found his way to Lonely Planet. Matthew lives in north-eastern Victoria.

### Sarah Mathers
Sarah grew up in Melbourne, studied history at uni, made gourmet sausages and went on to be an editor at Lonely Planet. On leaving LP Sarah sold vegies at the Queen Victoria market and worked in theatre before returning to freelancing and guidebooks – updating *Queensland* being by far the best gig. Sarah updated the North Coast, Whitsunday Coast and Gulf Savannah for this edition.

## FROM THE AUTHORS

**Joseph Bindloss** Firstly I would like to credit my work on this title to my new baby brother Eddie. As always, the QPWS and Environment Protection Agency deserve huge credit for their assistance and tireless work maintaining Queensland's National Parks. In Brisbane, my thanks to Dennis Bidlake and his family for the low-down on the Brisbane art scene and use of their workshop to customise my campervan. Thanks also to the patient staff of southern Queensland's many tourist offices, and TransInfo and Queensland Rail for assistance with transport information. Thanks to all the readers who wrote in with top tips and timely warnings, particularly regarding Fraser Island.

**Kate Daly** For providing information and tips, thank you to staff at visitors centres, roadhouses, caravan parks, hotels, hostels and B&Bs, and the Queensland Parks and Wildlife Service rangers in Cairns, Mossman, Cape Tribulation and Cape York. Special thanks to Jeannette from the Falls Holiday Park in Millaa Millaa, Rachel at the Esplanade Tourist Information Centre in Cairns, Julie Forbes from the Costa Blanca in Cairns, Terry and Corinne Malony and Richard Knight from the Daintree Eco-Lodge & Spa, Bill from Pam's Place in Cooktown, Kurt Groot from Exploring Oz Safaris and my saviour Sue, from Punsand Bay Safari & Fishing Lodge in Cape York – you are a legend (and so is Gary). Thank you also to Greg Alford, Martin Heng and Jane Hart for giving me a go. And thank you to Mikey for phone calls on the road, and patience, kindness and culinary excellence at home.

**Matthew Lane** My sincere thanks to all the staff at the many helpful information centres along the way, particularly at Birdsville (Susie Van der Linden), Boulia, Hughenden, Richmond, Anakie, Rockhampton and Agnes Water. I also received invaluable assistance from staff at many hostels, hotels, motels and caravan parks throughout the trip, and at several Environmental Protection Agency offices, notably Gladstone, Mt Isa, Birdsville and Carnarvon Gorge. A very big thanks to Butch, who accompanied me (and spurred me on) for the latter half of the trip, and to my partner, Simone, who inspired me to fork out for a sapphire in Rubyvale.

**Sarah Mathers** Thanks to everyone at all the tourist information centres along the way, in particular Amanda Palmer at Townsville Enterprises; Melissa McMahon at the Whitsunday QPWS; Chris Weirman in Croydon, and Britta in Burketown. And John and Kitty, where ever you are; Peter for the long hauls and Ruby for being such a great little travelling companion.

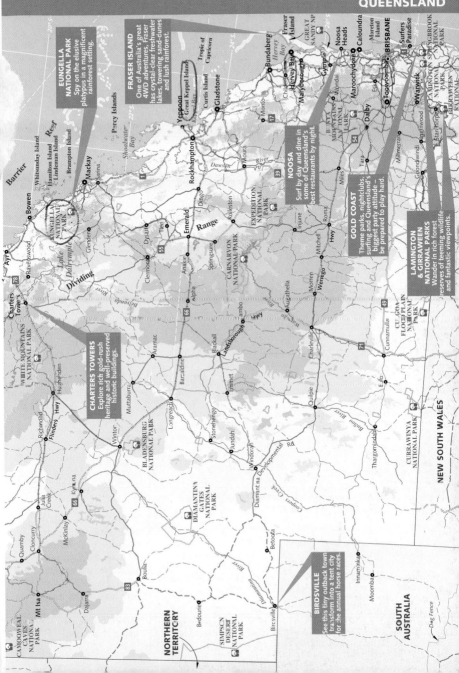

**EUNGELLA NATIONAL PARK**
Spy on the elusive platypus in a magnificent rainforest setting.

**FRASER ISLAND**
One of Australia's great 4WD adventures, Fraser has crystal-clear freshwater lakes, towering sand-dunes and lush rainforest.

**NOOSA**
Surf by day and dine in some of Queensland's best restaurants by night.

**GOLD COAST**
Theme parks, nightclubs, surfing and Queensland's biggest party: be prepared to play hard.

**LAMINGTON & GIRRAWEEN NATIONAL PARKS**
Wander in rich forest reserves of teeming wildlife and fantastic viewpoints.

**CHARTERS TOWERS**
Explore rich gold-rush heritage and well-preserved historic buildings.

**BIRDSVILLE**
See this tiny outback town transform into a tent city for the annual horse races.

Tropic of Capricorn

NORTHERN TERRITORY

SOUTH AUSTRALIA

NEW SOUTH WALES

**Queensland**
**3rd edition** – March 2002
**First published** – January 1996

**Published by**
**Lonely Planet Publications Pty Ltd**  ABN 36 005 607 983
90 Maribyrnong St, Footscray, Victoria 3011, Australia

**Lonely Planet offices**
**Australia** Locked Bag 1, Footscray, Victoria 3011
**USA** 150 Linden St, Oakland, CA 94607
**UK** 10a Spring Place, London NW5 3BH
**France** 1 rue du Dahomey, 75011 Paris

**Photographs**
Many of the images in this guide are available for licensing from
Lonely Planet Images.
W www.lonelyplanetimages.com

**Front cover photograph**
Aerial view of Heron island - Great Barrier Reef, Queensland
(Michael Aw)

ISBN 0 86442 712 3

Printed by SNP SPrint Singapore Pte Ltd

# Contents – Text

## GOLD COAST                                                      154

## DARLING DOWNS                                                   174

## SUNSHINE COAST                                                  193

## FRASER COAST                                                    214

## CAPRICORN COAST                                                 238

## WHITSUNDAY COAST                                               266

# Contents – Maps

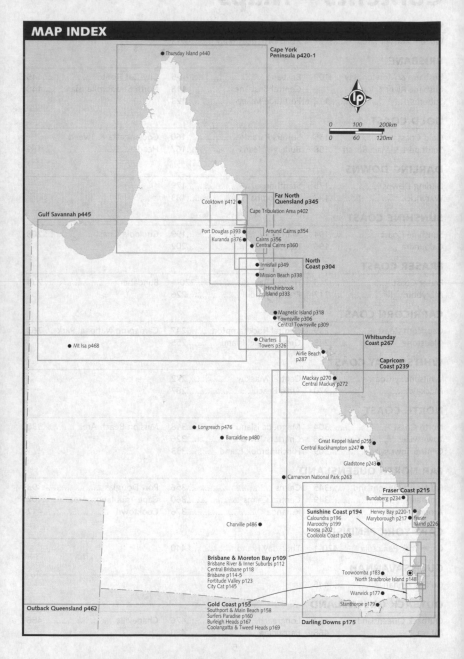

# MAP INDEX

Thursday Island p440

Cape York Peninsula p420-1

0  100  200km
0  60  120mi

Cooktown p412

Far North Quensland p345

Cape Tribulation Area p402

Gulf Savannah p445

Port Douglas p393
Kuranda p376

Around Cairns p354
Cairns p356
Central Cairns p360

Innisfail p349
Mission Beach p338

North Coast p304

Hinchinbrook Island p333

Magnetic Island p318
Townsville p306
Central Townsville p309

Mt Isa p468

Charters Towers p326

Whitsunday Coast p267

Airlie Beach p287

Capricorn Coast p239

Mackay p270
Central Mackay p272

Longreach p476

Barcaldine p480

Great Keppel Island p255
Central Rockhampton p247

Gladstone p243

Carnarvon National Park p263

Fraser Coast p215

Bundaberg p234

Sunshine Coast p194
Caloundra p196
Maroochy p199
Noosa p202
Cooloola Coast p208

Hervey Bay p220-1
Maryborough p217  Fraser Island p226

Charville p486

Toowoomba p183
North Stradbroke Island p148

Brisbane & Moreton Bay p109
Brisbane River & Inner Suburbs p112
Central Brisbane p118
Brisbane p114-5
Fortitude Valley p123
City Cat p145

Warwick p177

Stanthorpe p179

Outback Queensland p462

Gold Coast p155
Southport & Main Beach p158
Surfers Paradise p160
Burleigh Heads p167
Coolangatta & Tweed Heads p169

Darling Downs p175

# This Book

The 1st edition of *Queensland* was researched and written by Mark Armstrong. The 2nd edition was updated by Hugh Finlay and Andrew Humphreys. This 3rd edition was coordinated by Joe Bindloss, who updated the introductory chapters and the Brisbane, Darling Downs, Gold Coast, Fraser Coast and Sunshine Coast chapters. Kate Daly updated the Far North Coast and Cape York Peninsula chapters. Matthew Lane updated the Capricorn Coast and Outback chapters. And Sarah Mathers updated the Whitsunday Coast, North Coast and Gulf Savannah chapters.

## From the Publisher

This edition of *Queensland* was produced in Lonely Planet's Melbourne office. Mapping and design were coordinated by Clare Capell, with additional mapping by Yvonne Bischofberger and mapping assistance from Barb Benson. Matt King coordinated the illustrations, which were produced by Mick Weldon, Kate Nolan, Kelli Hamblett, Martin Harris, Clint Curé and Ann Jeffree. Images supplied by LPI. Clare also drew the chapter end; the climate charts were created by Kusnandar and the fantastic cover was designed by Jenny Jones. Ann Seward coordinated the editing with huge amounts of help from Joanne Newell, Lara Morcombe, Susie Ashworth, Bridget Blair, Pete Cruttenden, Helen Yeates, Victoria Harrison, Jocelyn Harewood, Gina Tsarouhas, Michelle Coxall, Cherry Prior and (of course!) Jane Thompson. Simone Egger, Gina Tsarouhas and Leonie Mugavin did crucial additional research. Mark Germanchis assisted with layout, and artwork checks were done by Corie Waddell, Jane, Errol Hunt, Jocelyn, Brett Moore and Tim Fitzgerald. The 'Great Barrier Reef' colour section was written by Susannah Farfor. Thanks to Ron and Viv Moon for information in the 'Quinkan Art' and 'Lakefield National Park' boxed texts and to Susie Van der Linden for contributing to the 'Birdsville Races' boxed text.

# Acknowledgments

Many thanks to the travellers who used the last edition and wrote to us with helpful hints, useful advice and interesting anecdotes. Your names follow:

Christa Achermann, P W Adams, Richard Adams, Idan Aharon, Jochem Akkermans, Aaron D Albrecht, Tom Allerton, Dave & Julie Arders, Wendy Armbrust, Brad Armstrong, Dale Arvidsson, Jan Ashmore, Vicky Ashworth, Rachel Askham, Tracy Ault, Louise Aylward, Eva Bach Moore, James Bain, Andy Bakx, Rob Barham, Asat Begerano, Julien Benney, Chris Bentley, Ram Bernstein, Gerhard & Nicki Beulke, Nina Beynon, Din Bhumgara, Heather Bingham, Philip Bladon, Ron & Pam Bolzon, Philip Boorer, Fabian Bornefeld, Pat Botham, Dr S J Bourne, Stuart Bowden, Christopher Bowers, Katy Bradbury, Dr Pierre Bradley, Philip Britton, Terri Bromley, Nancy Bronswijk, Melanie Brooks, Russell John Brooks, Janice Brophy, Amanda Brown, Suzanne Brown, Jean Buathier, Steve Buckell, Meike Buhlmann, Bill Busby, Joy Cadelina, Colin Caffrey, Belinda Callow, Marco Camaiti, Ron Campbell, Liam Carey, William Cartwright, Jeff Catherwood, Danielle Cavanagh, Michael Cave, Julia & Eliot Che, Zelmer Chessen, Armand & Godelieve Close, Ursula Collins, Jill Colquhoun, Angela Conroy, Hugh Cookson, V Coombe, Karen Cooper, Donna Corleone, Gary Corrin, Giles Cory, Toby Couchman, Simon Cox, Wendy Crew, Jocasta Crofts, Tine Dandanell, Beverley J Danger, Thea Daubitz, Barbara Davage, Owen Davies, Peter Daw, Karli de Vries, Linda de Vries, Alex Deane, Gil Debeze, Neil Dempsey, Amy Dick, Graham Diplock, Emma Dornan, Joshua A Drew, Duncan Drysdale, Rob Dunakin, Roz Dunk, Jane M Dunn, Karla Duvey, Robet Dwyer, Chris Edwards, Joanne Edwards, Craig Farr, Marvin Feldman, Rachael Fewster, Maria Finlay, Bob Fletcher, Anna Foares, Liliane Foederer, Fiona Fogarty, Esther Forester, J Forsell, Katie Fowler, Jennifer Freeman, Julie French, Claire Frost, Matt Frost, Tove Frykmer, Nick Fullbrook, Andy Gabe, Henry Galgut, Antonella Gallo, Judy-Anne Angelique Galway, Jason Garman, Bill & Julie Gaudin, Tanya Gentry, Andrea Gerber, Patrick Gmuer, Catherine Anna Godfrey, Mark Goff, Calvyn Goldstone, Rae Gordon, Jo Goring, H Gosling, Chris Grantham, James Greed, Chris Greene, Steven Greenleaf, Jon Paul & Sarah Greenman, Ed Griffin, John Groom, Andrea Grossmann, Shala N Gunnells, Adrian Haas, Gerd Haberkern, Anna Hagfeldt, Cheryl Haisch, Hanno Haisch, Ian Hall, R Hall, Frances Hammond, Ben Handley, K Hanks, Eddie Hardy, Jason Harris, Martin Harris, Greg Harrison, Susanne Heckeroth, Klaus Heintel, Denise Hellier, Clotilde Henriot, Marcel Herlaar, Mieke Hermans, Frank Heymenberg, Steve Hill, Di Hinds, Sarah Hine, Bill Hines, Rachel Hirschfeld, Jesse Holliday, Fiona Hollyman, Dave Hopkins, Witold Horbowski, Dawn Horridge, Dennis Howell, Nick Howood, Lee Hubbard, Cristina Huesch, Joel Hughes, Kevin R Hughes, Vickie Hughson, James Hyde, Jan Hyde, Shelley Hynes, Mugs & Paul Jackson, Cheryl Jacques, Nicola James, Paul & Brigitte Janssen, Franki Jay, Karen Jensen, Natalie Johnston, Michael Johnstone, A M Jones, Alan & Ellen Jones, Barnie Jones, Helen Jones, Rob Kaczmarek, Marlene Kagerer, Andrew Kane, Jean Paul Karat, Petra Kaufmann, Alistair Kelly, Ross Kenny, Egan Kerkhof, Adrian Kienast, Rebecca Kirby, James Kirkham, Claudia Klaassen, Michael Klinkenberg, David Koelmeyer, Anke Kotte, Vera Kotz, Mario Kribus, Eric Kuttunen,

James Lacey, Sean Laing, Andrew Lamb, Harriet Lammin, Reto Lamparter, C J Lane, Fredrik Larsen, Vincent Lawrence, Sylvie Leclerc, John Lethbridge, Richard & Fay Lewis, Vered & Udi Linial, Marion Link, Ruth Lipscombe, Louise, Marcus Lucci, Mary Lydon, Rob Lyon, Lisa Macbeth, Izzy Machell, Patricia MacLaurin, Neil Maidment, Darryl Main, Norm and Mary Mainland, Tomas Maltby, Ofri Mann, Reagan Mann, Kaeren Mansfield, Kath & Grant Marriage, Marie-Louise Marten, Anna Martinez, Hanna-Gael Matheson, Michaela Matross, Catherine Mattey, Susi Mattis, Raeleen May, Pater Mayers, Joseph Mayhew, Theresa McCann, Sandy McClean, Stuart Mc-Clelland, Neville McCrostie, Caroline McCullough, Steven McDonald, Steve McGilton, Nicola McGuigan, Liam McGuire, Alex McIlvenna, Nina McKenna, Penny McKenzie, Andy McLean, Keren McSweeney, Lisa Mein-gassner, Liz Mellish, Justin Meredith, Thierry Meyer, Will Middleton, Ferne Millen, Deena Miller, Tom Miller, Catherine Mills, Lindsay Mitchell, Wendy Monger, Gary Moran, Duncan Morgan-Russell, Michael Moritz, Alan Morris, Andrew Mullis, Gail Munro, Eleanor Neiger, Leo & Annemieke No-ordzij, James Norman, Sarah O'Rourke, Heather Oakes, Brenda O'Connell, Victoria Old, Sara Olliff, P A Oppenheim, Linda Oppenmeer, Guylaine Paradis, Neil Parker, Alison Parkin, Julie Parkinson, Reiner Parzefall, Jerry Payne, Tania Perkins, Dave Perry, Terry Perry, Jolene Pestel, Kerstin Peters, Nessie Pham, Mike Plettell, Monica Pokorny, Marcus Pound, Lisa Power, Irena Predalic, Rob Prettejohn, Victoria & Barry Price, Morna Prince, Nikos Prokopiou, Paul Prowting, J Randall, Sarah Rankin, Peter Reeve, Ella Remes, Farinella Renato, Sandra Richmond, Anna Jo Righton, Dennis Rijnbeek, Liza Robertson, Phil Rogers, Darren Rose, Jacqui & David Ross, Jim Royle, Simone Rutishauser, Delia Sala, George Sandilands, Andrew & Pippa Sargent, Todd & Amy SatterstenBuckley, Andrew Savage, Katie Savill, Anna Schaefer, M L Schouten-Hupkes, Anrea Schumacher, Andres Schwerdtle, Eric Scott, Chris Seavell, Jana Seelbach, Sunita Shailam, Jon Shand, Dave Sheppard, Holly Sherman, R Shoesmith, Debs Shorten, Kira Siebert, Andrew Silke, Jane Sinclair, Peter & Gillian Sleight, Maureen Smeaton, Linda Smit, Greg Smith, Ray Smith, Val Smytheman, Rogier Souverein, Mark A Spence, Gary Spinks, Anne Marie Spiritu, Hannah Spungin, Dominique Staehli, Kate Stamps, Vanessa Stewart, Shirley Stockdale, J D Stonham, Paul Storm, Nicolas Stricher, Peter Jon Stubbings, Betsy Stumme, M B Such, Jon Sumby, Lucy Sweetman, Jeremy Tager, Richard Tan, Arlene Tanz, Pauline Teo, David Thomas, Catherine Thomsgard, Philippa Tisdall, Harold Tomanek, Michael Trigg, Simon Trippett, Angus Trumble, Adrian Tschaeppeler, Deon Tucker, Trista Turgeon, Elise Vale, Steef van Berkel, Mike van de Water, Eloi van den Assem, Miranda van der Gronde, Aulije van Gerven, Michiel van Roekel, Gaudia van Sommeren, Isabel van Weel, Amanda Verhoeuen, Cindy Vermue, Rodney Vickers, Claire Vickery, Ludwig Vogler, Ilan Volovitz, Gerald Wagner, Jane Waldron, Mr & Mrs Keith Walker, Patrick Walls, Geoff Walsh, Karen Walsh, Kelly Watson, Alan Weaver, Yvonne Webster, J F Weeks, Torsten Weickert, Samantha Weiss, Sijmen Wesselingh, Dirk Westermann, Ling Weston, Angela Whelan, Alan Whitehead, Andrew Whiteley, Jessica Wiegand, Jo Wilcox, Katie Williams, Andy Wilson, Adrien Wim, Roxanne Winkler, Joanna Wiseman, Erwin Wisman, Greg Woods, Paul Woodward, Ian Woolfenden, Mark Worrell, Paul Wright, Steve Zambuni

# Foreword

## ABOUT LONELY PLANET GUIDEBOOKS

The story begins with a classic travel adventure: Tony and Maureen Wheeler's 1972 journey across Europe and Asia to Australia. There was no useful information about the overland trail then, so Tony and Maureen published the first Lonely Planet guidebook to meet a growing need.

From a kitchen table, Lonely Planet has grown to become the largest independent travel publisher in the world, with offices in Melbourne (Australia), Oakland (USA), London (UK) and Paris (France).

Today Lonely Planet guidebooks cover the globe. There is an ever-growing list of books and information in a variety of media. Some things haven't changed. The main aim is still to make it possible for adventurous travellers to get out there – to explore and better understand the world.

At Lonely Planet we believe travellers can make a positive contribution to the countries they visit – if they respect their host communities and spend their money wisely. Since 1986 a percentage of the income from each book has been donated to aid projects and human rights campaigns, and, more recently, to wildlife conservation.

> Although inclusion in a guidebook usually implies a recommendation we cannot list every good place. Exclusion does not necessarily imply criticism. In fact there are a number of reasons why we might exclude a place – sometimes it is simply inappropriate to encourage an influx of travellers.

## UPDATES & READER FEEDBACK

Things change – prices go up, schedules change, good places go bad and bad places go bankrupt. Nothing stays the same. So, if you find things better or worse, recently opened or long-since closed, please tell us and help make the next edition even more accurate and useful.

Lonely Planet thoroughly updates each guidebook as often as possible – usually every two years, although for some destinations the gap can be longer. Between editions, up-to-date information is available in our free, quarterly *Planet Talk* newsletter and monthly email bulletin *Comet*. The *Upgrades* section of our website (**w** www.lonelyplanet.com) is also regularly updated by Lonely Planet authors, and the site's *Scoop* section covers news and current affairs relevant to travellers. Lastly, the *Thorn Tree* bulletin board and *Postcards* section carry unverified, but fascinating, reports from travellers.

**Tell us about it!** We genuinely value your feedback. A well-travelled team at Lonely Planet reads and acknowledges every email and letter we receive and ensures that every morsel of information finds its way to the relevant authors, editors and cartographers.

Everyone who writes to us will find their name listed in the next edition of the appropriate guidebook, and will receive the latest issue of *Comet* or *Planet Talk*. The very best contributions will be rewarded with a free guidebook.

We may edit, reproduce and incorporate your comments in Lonely Planet products such as guidebooks, websites and digital products, so let us know if you don't want your comments reproduced or your name acknowledged.

**How to contact Lonely Planet:**
**Online**: **e** talk2us@lonelyplanet.com.au, **w** www.lonelyplanet.com
**Australia:** Locked Bag 1, Footscray, Victoria 3011
**UK:** 10a Spring Place, London NW5 3BH
**USA:** 150 Linden St, Oakland, CA 94607

# Introduction

Queensland is an adventure playground of white sandy beaches, tropical island resorts, dry scrub desert, rainforests and the myriad wonders of the Great Barrier Reef. Its fantastic selection of national parks range from the red-sand wilds of the Simpson Desert to the dense greenery of the rainforests at Wooroonooran and Eungella and the oasis-like beauty of Carnarvon Gorge. The Great Barrier Reef, the majestic Fraser Island and the Wet Tropics rainforests of the Far North have all been inscribed on the World Heritage List.

Not surprisingly, the Sunshine State offers plenty of 'islands in the sun', from the wonderful continental islands of the Whitsundays to the 120km-long sandhill of Fraser Island. Divers and snorkellers head straight for the coral cays of the Great Barrier Reef,

and there's a veritable armada of boats offering trips from coastal towns out to the reef and its islands.

Resorts are sprinkled all the way up the eastern coast, and range from laid-back surf centres like Coolangatta to frenetic party places like Surfers Paradise and Queensland's adventure capital, Cairns. If wining and dining is more your thing, there are plenty of sophisticated boutique resorts like Port Douglas and Noosa Heads.

Plenty of people head for Queensland wanting nothing more than a multicoloured cocktail and a tropical beach, but if thrills and spills are what you are after, you can try white-water rafting, scuba diving and snorkelling, bushwalking, rock climbing, horse riding, surfing, bungee jumping, skydiving, abseiling, off-road driving...

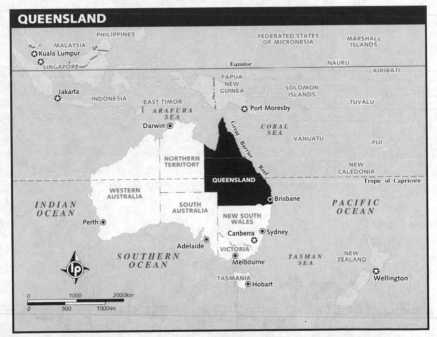

While Queensland hasn't been shy about offering itself at the altar of packaged tourism, you don't have to move far from the big resorts to find the Australia that lies behind the marketing machine. To get away from it all, head inland. Set back from the coast are all manner of wild untouched areas like Cape York Peninsula, the Gulf Savannah and the vast and empty expanses of the mystical outback, where you can go for days without seeing another person.

Whether you want to strap on a backpack and head out into the great unknown, bask in the bright lights of big cities or just recline by the pool, this book should help point you in the right direction.

# Facts about Queensland

## HISTORY
### Indigenous Australians

It is believed that the ancestors of the Aborigines journeyed from South-East Asia to the Australian mainland at least 50,000 years ago, but to this day no-one is quite sure how they managed to reach it. Current theories suggest that the first Aborigines either made the perilous 120km sea journey across the Timor Sea from Indonesia to Australia by some unknown form of boat transport, or island-hopped across to Papua New Guinea and travelled over an ice-age land bridge into northern Queensland.

At the time, Australia was a far lusher and greener continent, with large forests and many inland lakes teeming with fish. The fauna included giant marsupials such as 3m-tall kangaroos, giant koalas and wombats, and huge, flightless birds. With such favourable conditions, the descendants of these first settlers colonised the whole of the continent within a few thousand years.

When the sea levels rose again at the end of the last ice age (around 15,000 to 10,000 years ago), the Aborigines were isolated on the continent. Most of the population congregated on the coasts as the climate became drier and less hospitable. Before the arrival of the Europeans, Aborigines spoke some 250 different languages, and lived in complex tribal groups of between 500 and 1500 people. Queensland was the most populous region, with at least 200 tribes and 100,000–120,000 people.

The settlers viewed civilisation as the advancement from a hunter-gatherer society to an agricultural one, and paternalistically considered the Aborigines to be a backward race. While the idea held some credibility within the social structures of Europe, it held no value in an abundant environment like Australia. In his book *Triumph of the Nomads*, Geoffrey Blainey writes that, at the time of European arrival, the average Aborigine, as far as food, health, warmth and shelter were concerned, probably enjoyed as good a standard of living as the average European in 1800.

The Aborigines had a remarkable skill for adjusting to their environment. With their profound knowledge of the bush and its flora and fauna, Aboriginal people were able to survive quite comfortably in environments that tested European settlers to their limits. More significantly, they existed in harmony with their environment, employing complex rituals for hunting and harvesting that prevented overexploitation of resources.

Aboriginal society was based on family groups with an egalitarian political structure, and so a coordinated response to the European colonisers was not possible; based on the experience of their war-like neighbours in New Zealand, however, it would probably have done little good. The apparent lack of any system of law or land tenure led Captain, then Lieutenant, James Cook to decide that the natives of Australia merely inhabited the land they occupied, rather than owning it, and he claimed possession of the newly discovered land for England in 1788. From that moment forward Australia became the 'property' of the British crown.

By tenuous interpretation of the terms 'ownership' and 'possession' the arriving colonialists proceeded under the principle that the new continent was *terra nullius* – a land belonging to no-one – an interpretation that has affected land rights in Australia to the present day. At a local level, individuals resisted – warriors such as Pemulwuy, Yagan, Dundalli, Pigeon and Nemarluk kept settlers from their lands for a time – but the effect of such resistance was only to postpone the inevitable.

Without any legal right to the lands they once lived on, the Aborigines were driven from their traditional territories by force. Early white Australians behaved with unusual barbarism, even by the standards of the British empire. Aborigines were routinely tortured and shot for sport, or given food laced with strychnine, and soldiers were authorised to shoot any group of more than six Aborigines on sight. It was not until 1838 that a white person was tried and convicted for the murder of an Aborigine.

In 1848 New South Wales (NSW) troopers were brought to Queensland to open up the land for settlement, resulting in huge loss of Aboriginal life. Just as devastating were the diseases brought by the new settlers, such as smallpox, which swept through the territories, destroying whole tribes. Other Aborigines succumbed to the allure of newly arrived commodities like tobacco, opium and, most significantly, alcohol.

Simultaneously, the idea that Aborigines needed to be protected from themselves gained huge popularity among law-makers. In 1865 Queensland passed the Reformatory Schools (Industrial) Act, which decreed that any child born of an Aboriginal or part-Aboriginal mother was considered a 'neglected child' and as such was liable to be sent to a reform or industrial school.

Queensland passed the first Aboriginal Protection Act in 1897, which prohibited non-Indigenous people without permits from entering reserves, but was predominantly concerned with segregating Aboriginal people and restricting the sale of opium. The legislation imposed restrictions on the Aborigines' right to own property and obtain wages for employment, and most significantly, placed the 'care, custody and education' of the children of Aborigines in the hands of the director of any settlement, paving the way for the creation of the Stolen Generations.

For the next 70 years Australia adopted a policy of assimilation of Aboriginal people, based on the bizarre principle that removing Aborigines from the influence of other Aboriginal people and placing them in white custody might cause European ideals to rub off on the natives. It is estimated that between one-tenth and one-third of Aboriginal children were removed from their families to foster homes and state training centres between 1910 and 1970. Incredibly, the principle was reinforced in the 1939 Queensland

Aboriginals' Preservation and Protection Act, which made the director of a settlement the legal guardian of all Aboriginal minors under 21, and was not overturned until 1965.

Aboriginal pastoralists were granted equal pay in 1966 but there was no real social change until 1967, when non-Indigenous Australians voted to give Aborigines and Torres Strait Islanders the status of citizens, and gave the federal government power to legislate for them in all states. The states had to provide them with the same services that were available to other citizens, and the federal government set up the Department of Aboriginal Affairs to identify the special needs of Aborigines and legislate for them.

The assimilation policy was finally dumped in 1972, to be replaced by the government's policy of self-determination, which for the first time enabled Aborigines to participate in decision-making processes. The big engine for change was the 1976 Aboriginal Land Rights (Northern Territory) Act, which was designed as a template for all of Australia and gave Northern Territory Aborigines indisputable title to all Aboriginal reserves (about 20% of the Territory) and a means for claiming other Crown land, including a provision for mineral royalties to be paid to Aboriginal communities. Before it could be implemented, the reformist Labor government of Gough Whitlam was removed by the governor-general (the Queen's representative), backed up by the Australian people in the rush election that followed.

**Mabo & the Native Title Act** Only very recently has the non-Indigenous community begun to come to grips with the fact that a meaningful reconciliation between white Australia and its Indigenous population is vital to the cultural and social wellbeing of all Australians.

In May 1982, five Torres Strait Islanders led by Eddie Mabo began an action for a declaration of native title over Queensland's Murray Islands. They argued that the legal principle of *terra nullius* had wrongfully usurped their title to land, as for thousands of years Murray Islanders had enjoyed a relationship with the land that included a notion of ownership. Aided by a fortunate legal oversight in the original British claim of ownership to the Murray Islands, the High Court of Australia recognised native title to the islands in June 1992, setting a legal precedent for the existence of legal Aboriginal rights to parts of Australia.

The High Court's controversial judgment became known as the Mabo decision, and caused a wave of fear to sweep across Australia as mining and logging companies and pastoralists panicked that their land would be subject to Aboriginal land claims. In fact, the ruling was ambiguous and lacked teeth, but it was hailed by Aborigines and then-Prime Minister Paul Keating as a basis for reparation for Aboriginal Australians.

To define the principle of native title, the federal parliament passed the Native Title Act in December 1993, which, despite huge protest from the mining industry, gave Aboriginal people very few new rights. Native title would be limited to land that no-one else owned or leased and only where Aboriginal people had a continuous physical association with that land. Pivotally, the Act also decreed that existing ownership or leases would extinguish native title, meaning that even if land was successfully claimed by Aboriginal people under the act, they would have no veto over developments, including mining.

**The Wik Decision** Several months before the Native Title Act became law, the Wik and Thayorre peoples had made a claim in the Federal Court for native title to an area of land in Cape York that included pastoral leases but had never been occupied for that purpose. The Wik and Thayorre peoples argued that native title coexisted with the pastoral leases and took the matter to the Federal Court in 1996.

Predictably, the Federal Court decreed that the granting of pastoral leases under Queensland law extinguished native title rights, but the Wik people appealed to the High Court, where the decision was overturned. The High Court ruled that native title rights could continue at the same time that land was under lease, and that pastoralists did not have exclusive right of possession to their leases, but it also ruled that where the two were in conflict, the rights of the pastoralists would prevail.

Despite the fact that lease tenure was not threatened, the Wik decision caused outrage among pastoralists across Australia, who demanded that the federal government step in to protect them by legislating to limit native title rights, as was intended in the original act. Aboriginal leaders were equally adamant that native title must be preserved.

In late 1997 the government responded with its so-called 10 Point Plan, a raft of proposed legislative amendments to the Native Title Act designed to extinguish native title, effectively reinstating the concept of *terra nullius*. After two failed attempts, a watered-down version of the legislation, the Native Title Amendment Act, was passed by Parliament in 1998. Following the ruling, Australia became the first developed nation to be called before the United Nations Committee for the Elimination of Racial Discrimination (CERD). Interpretation of the amended Act is still ambiguous and is likely to keep the lawyers in business for years to come. For now it seems Australia is more prepared to accept Aboriginal ownership of the land as a state of mind, rather than as a state of law.

On the fringes of government, however, the movement for reconciliation has gained ground. Established in 1991, the Council for Aboriginal Reconciliation was instrumental in bringing the Stolen Generations into the limelight, backing a series of high-profile Reconciliation Week festivals that were held from 1998 to 2000, drawing the support of nearly one million non-Indigenous Australians.

In May 2000 the council presented John Howard with a draft document of a formal apology to Aborigines, which Howard famously rejected. The government's refusal to 'say sorry' provoked a political storm, but resulted in no concessions or advancement for the rights of native Australians. In its final report to Parliament, the Council for

Aboriginal Reconciliation recommended the drafting of a treaty between non-Indigenous and Indigenous Australians to move the reconciliation process forward.

In the meantime, Aborigines continue to be the most disadvantaged group in Australian society. Most Aborigines have only limited access to education and primary healthcare, and one in three will fail to finish school. The average life expectancy for Indigenous Australians is still 19 years less than for their non-Indigenous counterparts.

## European Exploration

Historians believe that Portuguese sailors early in the 16th century were the first Europeans to sight the Australian coast, although because of the secrecy that shrouded maritime discoveries of that time there are no records of these voyages.

In 1606 the Spaniard Luis Vaez Torres is known to have sailed through the strait between Cape York and New Guinea that still bears his name, but somehow failed to detect the vast continent to the south. During the same year the Dutch explorer Willem Jansz sailed into the Gulf of Carpentaria and charted part of the Queensland coastline, followed by another Dutchman, Jan Carstensz, in 1623, who also decided Cape York was far too inhospitable for settlement.

This apparently dismal continent was forgotten until 1768, when the British Admiralty instructed Lieutenant James Cook to lead a scientific expedition to Tahiti to observe the transit of Venus across the sun, and then begin a search for the Great South Land. On board his ship *Endeavour* were also several scientists, including an astronomer and a group of naturalists and artists led by Joseph Banks.

On 19 April 1770 the extreme southeastern tip of the continent was sighted and named Point Hicks, and Cook turned north to follow the coast and search for a suitable landfall. It was nine days before an opening in the cliffs was sighted and the ship and crew found sheltered anchorage in a harbour they named Botany Bay.

After leaving Botany Bay, Cook continued north, charting the fertile east coastline,

which seemed far more inviting than the inhospitable land the earlier explorers had seen to the west. He named a number of places as he sailed up the coast of what is now Queensland, including Moreton Bay, the Whitsundays and Cape Tribulation. On 11 June 1770 the *Endeavour* struck a reef off Cape Tribulation and careened onto the banks of the Endeavour River, at the site of present-day Cooktown. During the six weeks needed to repair the ship, Cook and the scientists made studies of the flora and fauna, and encountered Aborigines for the first time. After repairing the *Endeavour*, Cook charted a passage though the Great Barrier Reef and rounded Cape York, landing at Possession Island to raise the Union Jack and claim the continent of New South Wales for King George III.

## Convicts & European Settlement

Following the American Revolution, Britain decided upon Botany Bay as the location for its new penal colonies and the First Fleet sailed into Botany Bay in January 1788 with a cargo of minor felons. The Second Fleet arrived in 1790 with more convicts and some supplies, and the Third Fleet followed up a year later.

The early years were characterised by hardship and disease among both convicts and guards, and it wasn't until 1799 that any serious attempt was made to explore the country. The pioneer of Australian exploration was Matthew Flinders, who left Sydney in the *Norfolk* to explore the northern coast and search for useful ports and rivers; he landed at Bribie Island north of Moreton Bay and sailed as far north as Fraser Island before returning to Sydney.

**Moreton Bay Penal Colony** By 1822 the penal colonies at Norfolk Island and Port Jackson were overcrowded and a new settlement was proposed for the problem inmates at Redcliffe Point on Moreton Bay. A settlement party moved up to Redcliffe Point in 1824, under the command of John Oxley, the surveyor-general of NSW, but the encampment was soon abandoned due to troubles with the local Aborigines and a lack of fresh water. In 1825 a new settlement was established on the site of what is now Brisbane, which offered a safe harbour, fertile land and fresh water from a string of water holes. Although the location was good, the penal colony was considered too far from Sydney and only ever accommodated about 1100 convicts before it was disbanded in 1839.

The colony provided an important base for some of Australia's first settlers, who ventured west from Moreton Bay into the hinterland. In 1827 Allan Cunningham discovered the vast, grassy plains of the Darling Downs and, shortly after, the gap through the mountains of the Great Dividing Range that bears his name. Patrick Leslie and his brothers became the first permanent settlers on the Darling Downs in 1840.

For the natives of the area it was the beginning of the end. Three years later the Moreton Bay area was opened to free settlers, and the slow encroachment inland began.

## Exploration of Queensland

Although Queensland was settled by the 1840s, the vast interior was still mostly unexplored until a series of unlikely explorers moved in to fill in the gaps on the Australian map.

**Ludwig Leichhardt** In 1843 the enigmatic Prussian explorer Ludwig Leichhardt trekked from Sydney to Brisbane before embarking on a 3000km ground-breaking trek inland to Port Essington, near what is now Darwin. Despite his eccentricities and notorious incompetence as an explorer, Leichhardt and his party completed the journey – in 15 months, twice as long as planned.

Leichhardt returned to Sydney in 1846 as a hero. The eager explorer immediately mounted another attempt to cross the continent from east to west, which failed. Undeterred, he mounted yet another expedition with a team of novice explorers, who set out from the Darling Downs in April 1848 and were never seen again.

**Edmund Kennedy** In 1848 assistant surveyor Edmund Kennedy was charged with the mission of trekking overland from Rockingham Bay (south of present-day Cairns) to the top of Cape York Peninsula. The 13 experienced explorers were dropped at Tam O'Shanter Point (at present-day Mission Beach), but had to abandon their heavy supply carts near Tully and failed to find the supplies left by their support ship further up the coast. Before long, most of the party had died from disease, malnourishment or ambushes by hostile Aborigines. Kennedy himself was speared to death only 30km from the end of the fearsome trek. His Aboriginal servant, Jacky Jacky, was the only expedition member to finally reach the supply ship.

**Burke & Wills** In 1860 the stage was set for the greatest act in the exploration of Australia, the journey into the red centre. The Burke and Wills expedition was the largest, most lavish and best equipped, and was fronted by Robert O'Hara Burke, chosen by a committee of the Royal Society of Victoria. Quite why he was chosen was never clear, as Burke was neither an explorer nor a surveyor, had no scientific training, had never led an expedition of any kind and was considered to be an ardent city lover with little experience or knowledge of the bush. He also flatly refused to use Aboriginal guides.

After a farcical journey in which most of their supplies were abandoned, the party proceeded to Menindee (NSW), and then to Cooper Creek, where Burke and his second-in-command, William John Wills, set up a depot. The majority of the party waited here while Burke, Wills, Charles Grey and John King set off for the Gulf of Carpentaria on 16 December 1860.

It says something of their fortitude and sheer guts that they managed to walk 1100km through central Australia in the heat of summer, reaching the Gulf on 11 February 1861. You can still visit their northernmost stop, Camp No 119, near Normanton.

The march north terribly overstretched their resources, and the rush south became a life-or-death race against time. Grey died near Lake Massacre, just west of the Cooper Creek depot, and when Burke, Wills and King staggered into Cooper Creek they were horrified to find that the men there had retreated to Menindee that very morning! The famous 'Dig Tree', arguably the most historic site in inland Australia, still stands on the banks of Cooper Creek in Queensland, near the border with South Australia. Trapped at Cooper Creek the explorers wasted away, dying on the banks of this desert oasis. Only King, who had been befriended by some Aborigines, was alive when the first of the rescue parties arrived in September 1861.

**William Landsborough** In fact, it was the rescue parties, led by experienced bushmen like William Landsborough, that did the majority of the work in opening up Queensland to European settlement. A successful stockman, gold miner and pastoralist, Landsborough travelled south from the Gulf of Carpentaria along the Gregory River in search of Burke and Wills, reaching the Barkly Tableland before returning to his depot on the Gulf. He then followed the Flinders River south to the site of present-day Hughenden, continuing on to Melbourne upon hearing that Burke and Wills were dead. In the process, the party became the first to cross Australia from north to south. Landsborough rather prematurely reported that the interior was full of fine pastoral land, triggering a rush of settlers into an area that quickly dried out in summer.

**The Jardines** In 1863 John Jardine was made the first government magistrate of the settlement of Somerset on the tip of Cape York Peninsula, and promptly commissioned his sons, Frank and Alick, to drive a mob of cattle from Rockhampton to the new settlement. Their epic journey took 10 months, and they arrived at Somerset in March 1865. Along the way they overcame lack of water, skirmishes with Aborigines, flooded rivers, and a maze of swamps and waterways. Frank Jardine later took over from his father as government magistrate at Somerset, where he died in 1919 after building an empire of cattle farming and pearl fishing.

## Separation & Growth

At the end of 1859 Queensland finally won separation from NSW, with Brisbane as the capital of the new colony. The settlers quickly built on their pastoral base in the Darling Downs and huge foreign-backed pastoral companies, such as the Northern Australian Pastoral Company, drove back the frontiers, driving out many smaller operators (and any Aborigines that stood in their way) in the process. The number of sheep and cattle grazing in Queensland increased sixfold, and by the 1890s there were 20 million sheep and six million cattle.

The money filtered back to Brisbane, funding the construction of many handsome public and commercial buildings in the 1880s. Queensland's huge resources attracted some fairly mercenary developers, however, and as pastoralists exhausted the natural grasslands, attention turned to Queensland's forests. Vast swathes of subtropical forest fell to slash-and-burn, and cut timber was either chipped or left to rot. Elsewhere, sawmills chewed through the rainforests, feeding the timber-hungry building, mining and railway industries. As early as the 1880s, many of the cedar and pine species in Queensland's coastal ranges were almost extinct.

In the process, the Aborigines were driven back to the least desirable and least hospitable land. Although some settlers tried to maintain friendly relations with the tribes, the map of settlement in Queensland was painted with Aboriginal blood. Most of the atrocities perpetrated against Aborigines were never recorded, but there are reliable reports of whole tribes being killed with poisoned food and of natives being killed to feed settlers' dogs. A few Aboriginal groups resisted, inflicting minor casualties against the settlers, but this was nothing compared with the numbers of Aborigines killed during the early years of settlement.

Some of the worst massacres were carried out by NSW troops, who were drafted in to facilitate the settling of Queensland, aided by the notorious Native Police force, a death squad made up of Aborigines from disrupted tribes, trained and equipped by the Queensland government.

## Golden Age of Intolerance

During the gold-rush era Chinese prospectors poured into Queensland in their thousands. At one stage of the Palmer River gold rush, there were 11,000 Chinese miners and only 1500 Europeans. The Chinese were diligent workers, but kept largely to themselves and were strongly resented by white Australians. They were stereotyped as immoral and diseased heathens, and subjected to cease-less racist attacks. Leading prospector James Venture Mulligan expressed his anti-Chinese feelings in a letter to the Queenslander in 1874:

They follow up in swarms with odious filth, get the best gold, never give the miner the opening and chance to fall back on old ground where a man could get a little if he did not succeed in other directions.

As the gold ran out, so did the welcome for the Chinese. Workers began to blame the Chinese for taking jobs and lowering wages by working cheaply, and waged a carefully orchestrated campaign of racist attacks, driving most Chinese miners from the goldfields by the 1880s. The government restricted the rights of Chinese workers and then banned Chinese migration altogether at Federation (1901).

Between 1870 and the turn of the century the Chinese presence dropped from 6% of the population to less than 2%, with the majority working in rural industries such as sugar-cane production and banana plantations. These days the Chinese have integrated into mainstream society, and no rural town would be complete without a few Chinese-run businesses.

## Gold & Mining

The discovery of gold in Queensland in the 1860s and '70s brought about the most significant social and economic changes. The first major find was at Gympie in 1867; more than 15,000 diggers rushed the site. In 1872 the rich Charters Towers goldfields were discovered; the town grew so quickly and so dominated life in northern Queensland that it came to be known as 'The World'. Mt Morgan, which became the richest of Queensland's mines, was discovered near Rockhampton in 1882. In 1873 the legendary Palmer River gold rush began.

Extensive deposits of tin were found at Stanthorpe, Herberton and Irvinebank; copper deposits were discovered at Cloncurry, Chillagoe, Mt Garnet and Mt Molloy; and coal-mining provided the main source of energy for the railways, mines and factories.

The industry attracted numerous hard-working Chinese, who flourished in the goldfields until they were driven out by racist gangs. See the boxed text 'Golden Age of Intolerance'.

## Sugar & the Plantation Economy

After early experiments with cotton plantations, sugar-cane production quickly became the colony's major industry. The first plantation was established at Moreton Bay in 1864, and by the late 1860s the plantations had spread to Mackay, the Burdekin River, Bowen and to the Mulgrave and Johnstone Rivers. The growth of the sugar-industry was fuelled by the 1862 Coolie Act, which allowed South Sea Islanders to be employed as cheap labour. Officially, the Kanakas were regarded as volunteers, but in reality workers were frequently obtained by force from isolated atolls. See the boxed text 'Sweat & Molasses' for more on Kanakas.

## Labour vs Capital

The last part of the 19th century was a time of social upheaval in Queensland, characterised by a series of clashes between labour and capital which at times bordered on civil war, but would eventually lead to the election of the world's first (albeit brief) Labor government.

By the 1880s many of the goldfields had been exhausted and the labour markets were flooded with diggers. The industry went into decline and a world-wide recession led to the collapse of the Queensland economy. This created the perfect climate for a militant socialist movement and a number of radical newspapers emerged, including the *Boomerang* and the *Worker*. These targeted working-class audiences and espoused alternative theories of social organisation, leading to the formation of craft and labour unions to represent seamen, factory workers, miners and shearers.

In an attempt to break the hold of the shearers unions, the newly formed Darling Downs Pastoralists' Association employed non-union labour at Jondaryan Station. zThe subsequent strike spread to the waterside workers' and seamen's unions, and their refusal to handle Jondaryan wool won a settlement in favour of the shearers. However, the maritime strike eventually ended in October 1890 with the defeat of maritime workers' unions all along the east coast.

Further major confrontations took place in 1891 and 1894 on the immense pastoral stations of central and western Queensland. During the famous shearers' strike near Barcaldine in 1891, strikers formed armed gangs and went on the rampage, sabotaging property belonging to the pastoralists. The government sent in 1400 soldiers to arrest the strike leaders, and 10 strikers were later convicted of conspiracy and sentenced to three years' hard labour. The strike was broken with the help of the hordes of unemployed workers who filled the shoes of striking shearers.

## Sweat & Molasses

Queensland's early squatters initially relied on Chinese and Indian coolies to do the back-breaking work on their farms, but as the sugar industry took off, a new source of labour had to be found. Robert Towns, the founder of Townsville and a former South Seas trader, had the idea to import Islanders to work on his cotton plantation south of Brisbane, dispatching the *Don Juan* to the Solomon Islands in 1863. The ship returned with 67 Islanders, the first of Queensland's Kanakas (from the Hawaiian word for 'man') who were employed for periods of either six or 12 months at 10 shillings a month.

The first Kanakas were offered almost fair conditions, including three-year contracts and a return passage, but before long Blackbirding – a euphemism for kidnapping – became widespread. Ships sailed out to the Solomons, New Guinea, the New Hebrides and the Torres Strait Islands, trying all manner of brutal tricks to fill their holds with workers.

Once they arrived, the Kanakas were forced to work long hours in appalling conditions, and their mortality rate was up to five times higher than that of Europeans. Public outrage became increasingly vocal and in 1868 the Queensland government passed the Polynesian Labourers Act (incorrectly named – the Kanakas were Melanesian), which required all employers to register their recruits and guarantee to return them within three years, and led to the placement of government agents on all recruiting vessels.

The law did little to improve conditions on the farms. The missionary William Gray travelled to Queensland to inspect the plantations, and later wrote: 'I went to Queensland determined to keep my mind open…I would now say what I would not have said before I went…that the Kanaka Labour Traffic is veiled slavery'. The British government denounced the practice, as did the *Sydney Morning Herald*, but Queensland politicians turned a deaf ear.

The Kanaka population in Queensland swelled to 14,000 by the 1880s and Samuel Griffith won the 1884 election on a platform of abolishing Kanaka labour, bowing to the same pressure from white Australian workers that drove the Chinese from Australia. On the back of this, a few recruiters were charged with kidnapping, but Griffith never delivered his election promise. It wasn't until the newly formed Federal government passed the Pacific Island Labourers Act in 1901 that the workers who built Queensland were freed from virtual slavery, and promptly repatriated to countries most of them had never seen. Only about 1600 Kanakas were allowed to remain in Queensland after 1906. Today, there are about 15,000 Australians of Kanaka descent.

Support for the parliamentary Labor Party, which had formed in 1890, continued to grow throughout the 1890s. In the elections of 1899 disputes between Queensland's governing Liberal and Conservative factions allowed the Labor Party, led by Andrew Dawson, to form the world's first labour government. Dawson's government lasted only six days – he was defeated after the Liberals and Conservatives managed to reconcile their differences.

## Federation to WWII

Queensland voted to join the other states and became part of the Commonwealth of Australia on 1 January 1901, which immediately passed the Immigration Restriction Bill, more commonly known as the White Australia policy. Its express purpose was to prevent the immigration of Asians and Pacific Islanders and allow the removal of unwanted immigrants. Prospective immigrants were required to pass a dictation test in a European language, which could be in as obscure a tongue as the authorities wished. The dictation test was not abolished until 1958.

Like the rest of Australia, Queensland greeted the outbreak of WWI with naive enthusiasm, Queensland-born Prime Minister Andrew Fisher pledged that 'Australians will stand beside our own to help and defend her [England] to the last man and our last shilling'. Many of these volunteered as Anzacs (Australian and New Zealand Army Corps) and formed the front lines in the disastrous Gallipoli campaigns.

In spite of the losses of Anzac soldiers, support for Australia's involvement in the war remained strong until the government attempted to introduce conscription. In Queensland, the radical Labor Party swept to power in 1915 with a platform of anti-conscription policies.

Labor went on to dominate Queensland politics for the next 42 years, instigating a series of social and industrial reforms, including compulsory voting, improved safety and working conditions, workers' compensation and an arbitration court.

There was great economic expansion in the 1920s; in 1923 incredibly rich copper, lead, silver and zinc deposits were discovered at Mt Isa, leading to a new phase in Queensland's resource boom. All this came to a halt with the Great Depression, and by 1931 almost a third of breadwinners were unemployed. Swagmen became a familiar sight, as thousands of men took to the 'wallaby track' in search of work in the country.

## WWII & the Postwar Years

When WWII broke out, Australian troops fought beside the British in Europe, but after the Japanese bombed Darwin, Broome and the New Guinean town of Port Moresby, Australia's own national security finally began to take priority. Prime Minister John Curtin refused to send more troops to Europe, instead engaging the Japanese advancing over the mountainous Kokoda Trail towards Port Moresby.

Fighting a common enemy in the Pacific, Australia and the USA formed close ties, and a string of air bases was built all the way from Brisbane to the top of Cape York. Thousands of American troops were garrisoned in the area and General Douglas MacArthur established his Pacific headquarters in Brisbane before going on to defeat the Japanese in the Philippines.

The shared experience of WWII in the Pacific marked a profound shift in Australia's allegiance, away from Britain and towards the USA. In 1951 the USA and Australia signed the Anzus (Australia, New Zealand and the United States) Treaty, guaranteeing Australian military support for the USA in Asia, a policy that was to drag Australia into the Vietnam War in the 1970s.

The postwar immigration program was expanded to offer assisted passage to refugees from Eastern Europe as well as to British immigrants in the hope that the increase in population would strengthen Australia's economy. 'Populate or perish' became the catch phrase. Between 1947 and 1968 more than 800,000 non-British migrants flocked to Australia, though Queensland received fewer immigrants than other states.

Labor's long rule came to an end in 1957 when internal conflict led to the formation of the breakaway Queensland Labor Party by then-Premier Vincent Gair. Divided, Labor was defeated by the Country and Liberal Parties, which formed a coalition and pooled their votes. The coalition ruled until 1983 when the National Party (formerly the Country Party) won government in its own right.

## The Joh Era & Recent Developments

The Country/Liberal Party's first two premiers were unremarkable, but the death of Jack Pizzey opened the way for Sir Johannes Bjelke-Petersen (universally known as Joh), who went on to become Queensland's most notorious and longest serving premier. During his 19 years' tenure, Joh cynically induced numerous overseas companies to exploit Queensland's natural resources, while targeting every minority group in the state for some kind of persecution.

The ultra-right-wing Country Party took the conservative stance on everything from rainforest clearing and Aboriginal land rights to the public's right to hold demonstrations and even whether condom machines should be allowed in universities. Mining and logging permits were issued with wild abandon and Queensland became almost a rogue state, falling politically out of line with every other state in the country.

In the process, all manner of shady deals passed under the table and everyone from the former commissioner of Queensland police to Joh himself ended up in court at one stage or other over allegations of corruption. By 1987 even the Nationals had decided enough was enough and replaced Joh, though this wasn't enough to save them in the 1989 election.

The incoming Labor government kept things fairly stable with a centre-right set of policies, but the pendulum swung back to the far-right in 1995, when Labor's Wayne Goss administration, who held onto power with a one-seat majority, lost to the Liberals in a by-election when the vote count for that seat was found to be invalid.

In the 1998 election, growing rural insecurity over Aboriginal land rights and rising unemployment led disaffected voters to flock to the extremist One Nation Party led by independent federal MP for Oxley, Pauline Hanson, who gained more than 23% of the vote.

A former fish-and-chip shop owner, Hanson came to prominence for her naive and racist policies, which included banning immigration of Asians, removing benefits for Aborigines and restoring Australia's protectionist trade policies.

Fortunately for the Sunshine State, a coalition between Labor and an independent member took the reins of power. Following the election, Hanson's allies quickly deserted her. Hanson and former One Nation director David Ettridge were recently charged with electoral fraud, but One Nation continues to be a minor player in Australian politics.

Predictably, rural interests dominated the agenda as Premier Peter Beattie strived to win back disaffected rural Queenslanders following Labor's election in 1998. Unusually enlightened was the decision to acknowledge the Kanaka role in the development of Australia as part of the 2001 Federation celebrations.

The Labor government was rocked by accusations of electoral fraud during the first year of its term, but heads rolled in the Beattie administration and the party gained its highest-ever electoral tally in 2001. Among the proposed policies was a new commitment to environment-based tourism. The One Nation and Liberal Parties each gained just three seats.

For a while in 1999 it looked liked like Australia was going to break free of Britain and become a republic, but a small majority of Australians (55%) rejected the proposal in the 1999 referendum, robbing the nation of the chance to celebrate 100 years of Federation with independence. Queensland was the most vocal opponent, while the Australian Capital Territory was the only state with a 'Yes' majority. In retrospect, this was probably more a rejection of the proposed constitution (which provided for a president elected by parliament rather than popular vote) than of the principle of independence. With the various legal obstacles, it may be another 10 years before Australians have another shot at cutting the ties.

# GEOGRAPHY

Australia is the world's sixth-largest country, with an area of 7,682,300 sq km, about the same size as the 48 mainland states of the USA and half as large again as Europe, excluding the former USSR. It represents approximately 5% of the world's land surface, and measures about 4000km from east to west and 3200km from north to south, with a coastline 36,735km long.

Queensland, Australia's second-largest state, has an area of 1,727,200 sq km – about 22% of the Australian continent. At its widest point, it is about 1500km from west to east, and stretches for over 2000km from north to south, with a coastline 5208km long.

Queensland has a series of distinct regions, divided by the appropriately named Great Dividing Range, a mountain range that continues down through NSW and Victoria. The coastal strip is the focus for most of Queensland's booming tourist trade, with beaches, bays, islands and, of course, the Great Barrier Reef. Much of the coastal region is green and productive, with lush rainforests, endless fields of sugar cane and stunning national parks.

The Great Dividing Range is most spectacular in the Far North – at several places the mountains actually run right down to the coastline, and the Bellenden Ker Range, south of Cairns, has Queensland's highest mountain, Mt Bartle Frere (1657m). The McPherson Ranges, in the south-eastern corner, contain some of the state's most spectacular areas, including the pleasant and mountainous Lamington and Springbrook National Parks.

Running to the west of the mountain range are the tablelands – vast areas of flat agricultural land with rich volcanic soils – including the Darling Downs in the south and the Atherton Tablelands in the Far North.

Finally, there's the vast inland area, the barren outback, which fades into the Northern Territory further west. Rain can temporarily make this arid area bloom, but it's a place of sparse population, long, empty roads and tiny, distant settlements.

The Great Artesian Basin lies under much of this region. Water from the Great Dividing Range takes about 2.5 million years to seep westward to any one of the 7500 artesian wells that provide some of the few sources of water for the area's huge sheep and cattle stations.

Extreme climatic conditions prevail in the far northern Gulf Savannah and Cape York Peninsula. Huge, empty regions are cut by countless dry riverbeds that can become swollen torrents in the wet season (January to March). At such times the whole area becomes covered by a network of waterways, which sometimes brings road transport to a complete halt.

# CLIMATE

Australian seasons are the opposite of those in Europe and North America; January is the height of summer and July the depth of winter.

The Queensland seasons are more a case of hotter and wetter, or cooler and drier, than of summer or winter. The tropic of Capricorn crosses Queensland a third of the way up, running through the city of Rockhampton and the outback town of Longreach. The state's northern two-thirds are within the tropics, but only the extreme north lies within the monsoon belt. Although the annual rainfall there looks adequate on paper, it comes in more or less one short, sharp burst.

November/December to April/May is the wetter, hotter half of the year, while the real Wet, particularly affecting northern coastal areas, is January to March. Cairns usually gets about 1300mm of rain in these three months; Tully, 100km south of Cairns, is the wettest place in Australia, with a drenching 4400mm of rain each year!

Summer is also the season for cyclones, and if one hits, the main road north (the Bruce Hwy) can be blocked by the ensuing floods.

By comparison, the south-eastern and inland areas have relatively little rain – though they still have a wet season. Brisbane and Rockhampton both get about 450mm of rain from January to March. Further north, Mackay receives about 1250mm in these months, Townsville 850mm, Innisfail 1800mm and Weipa, on Cape York Peninsula, 1300mm. Just halfway across the

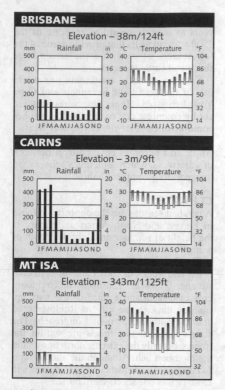

southern part of the state, Cunnamulla receives only 400mm in the whole year, while Birdsville, in the south-western corner, receives the least rain, with only 150mm a year.

From about May to September it rarely gets anything like cold, except inland or upland at night. Temperatures in Brisbane peak somewhere in the 20°C to 29°C range just about every day of the year. In Cairns the daily maximum is usually between 25°C and 32°C, whereas around the Gulf, few days in the year fail to break the 30°C mark. Over at Birdsville you can expect 33°C or more every day from November to March, but rarely more than 20°C from June to August.

## ECOLOGY & ENVIRONMENT

While humans have been living in, and changing, the physical environment in Australia for at least 50,000 years, it is in the 200 years since European settlement that dramatic – and often harmful – change has taken place.

Australia enjoys a reputation as an environmental paradise, but this is more a product of its small population than a sign of a particular environmental sensitivity. Over the last 200 years more than 70% of all native vegetation has been lost or irreversibly altered, including the loss of 40% of total forest area and 75% of rainforests. Land-clearing continues at a rate of more than 5600 sq km per annum (with Queensland clearing a staggering 4250 sq km of that total) placing Australia in the world's top 10 land-clearing nations, ahead of notorious offenders like Malaysia and Brazil.

Sadly, further tarnishing the nation's eco-reputation, Australians are now the world's largest per capita polluters in terms of greenhouse gases. Due to the small population, overall levels are low, but the trend is symptomatic of a widespread belief that Australia is massive enough to absorb any pollutants thrown in its direction. With the difficulty in getting international agreement following the Kyoto conference, it is unlikely that the situation will change in the near future.

Development, often in the name of tourism, has been the cause of numerous battles between developers and environmentalists in Queensland. Foremost among these was the furore that erupted in 1983 when the then National government decided to bulldoze a road through the (now World Heritage–listed) rainforest in the Daintree area of the Far North. Port Hinchinbrook near Cardwell was the scene of another high-profile battle between developers and environmental campaigners.

There have been victories, most notably against the sand miners on Fraser Island (see the Fraser Coast chapter for more details). The Useful Organisations section of the Facts for the Visitor chapter lists details of environmental groups.

## FLORA

Fifty-five million years ago, Australia was covered by cool-climate rainforest, but with the continent's gradual drying, rainforests

## Cane Toads

One of Queensland's most notorious citizens, the cane toad, *Bufo marinus*, was introduced from Argentina by way of Hawaii in 1935 to wipe out the sugar cane beetles that were devastating Australia's sugar cane plantations. Unfortunately, while the Hawaiian cane beetle was a ground dweller and easy prey for the toads, the Aussie variety lived at the top of the cane, far beyond the toads' reach.

Sugar cane beetles turned out to be about the only Australian species that wasn't at some kind of risk from the cane toad. Predators that try to eat the toads are killed by the poison glands on the toads' backs, and the amphibians breed prolifically, devastating populations of native insects. There are even reports of saltwater crocodiles being found dead with stomachs full of toads.

With no real predators, the toads have spread across Queensland like a plague. In recent years they have been found as far afield as northern New South Wales, Cape York Peninsula and Kakadu

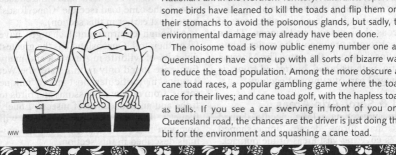

National Park in the Northern Territory. Naturalists report that some birds have learned to kill the toads and flip them onto their stomachs to avoid the poisonous glands, but sadly, the environmental damage may already have been done.

The noisome toad is now public enemy number one and Queenslanders have come up with all sorts of bizarre ways to reduce the toad population. Among the more obscure are cane toad races, a popular gambling game where the toads race for their lives; and cane toad golf, with the hapless toads as balls. If you see a car swerving in front of you on a Queensland road, the chances are the driver is just doing their bit for the environment and squashing a cane toad.

retreated, eucalypts and acacias took over and grasslands expanded. Over a vast period of time eucalypts and acacias adapted to the increased natural occurrence of fire and its later use for hunting and other purposes by Aborigines. Now many species benefit from fire and even rely on it to crack open their tough seed casings.

Queensland's diverse landforms support an incredible variety of plants. Good collections are grown at Brisbane's Mt Coot-tha Botanic Gardens, which features arid-zone plants; Flecker Botanic Gardens in Cairns, which has an interesting Aboriginal plant-use area; and Townsville's Anderson Park, which features rainforest plants and palms from Cape York Peninsula and the tropical north.

### Eucalypts & Acacias

Eucalypts (from the genus *Eucalyptus*, commonly known as gum trees) dominate much of the Australian landscape. Some species grow into huge trees and form extensive forests; others may be stunted by

low rainfall or other climatic factors. Gum trees found in Queensland include river red gums, which have a dangerous habit of dropping large limbs on campers; ghost gums, striking trees of the outback with glossy white bark and bright green leaves; and the coolabah, common along watercourses in the outback. Eucalyptus oil is used for pharmaceuticals and perfumed products; the flowers are valued in honey production; and the gum tree features in folklore, art and literature.

Many of the 660 species of acacia found in Australia are known as wattles. Despite their many differences, all wattles have furry yellow flowers shaped like either a spike or a ball. Mulga, a common acacia which occurs over vast tracts of the outback, is a great drought survivor, but being good fodder for stock puts it at risk from overgrazing.

### Mangroves

Once considered to be swampy wastelands, mangrove forests are now recognised as an essential part of coastal ecosystems. Mangroves grow in dense stands along parts of Queensland's coast and tidal estuaries, where they help to stabilise the shoreline and provide habitat for a huge range of fish, birds, crabs, prawns (shrimp) and other wildlife, including crocodiles.

## Rainforest
Almost all of the remnants of the tropical rainforest that once covered the Australian continent are found in north Queensland. While early settlers cleared most of these forests for farming and timber milling, they ignored some of the less accessible areas of the coastal mountains and ranges. These tropical forests are one of the major drawcards for visitors to the state. The Moreton Bay fig, with its broad, buttressed trunk, is an integral part of rainforest ecology.

## Arid & Semi-Arid Areas
Hardy spinifex is a long, needle-shaped grass that forms dense, dome-shaped masses covering vast areas of the outback. The prickly vegetation harbours rich populations of reptiles, rodents and other small animals. Another well-adapted plant is the dry, shrubby saltbush, which is salt tolerant and helps feed the millions of sheep and cattle living in the arid zone.

Boab trees, or bottle trees, are similar in appearance to the African baobab tree, with small bushy heads and swollen, pregnant-looking bases. During severe drought pastoralists have been known to cut down boab trees and feed their moisture-rich pith to cattle.

After good autumn rains the normally arid inland explodes in a multicoloured carpet of wildflowers. Life in the desert moves into top gear as the ephemerals hurry to complete their brief life cycles and woody plants burst into bloom. Sandhills, plains and rocky ridges come alive with nectar-feeding birds and insects and their predators. This is definitely the best time to tour the outback.

## FAUNA
The Australian land mass broke from the southern supercontinent of Gondwanaland more than 50 million years ago and drifted north to warmer climes. Australia's rich and varied indigenous wildlife is the result of this unusually long period of isolated evolution.

Climatic changes and Aborigines were responsible for a gradual process of vegetation change and wildlife extinction. But since the arrival of Europeans some 17 species of mammal have become extinct. In Queensland this is a result of environmental damage caused by hoofed livestock and feral goats and pigs, and predation by foxes. Perhaps the best-known of Queensland's introduced pests is the cane toad (see the 'Cane Toads' boxed text earlier in this section).

Although environmental changes have taken their toll, Queensland has the greatest diversity of wildlife in Australia and many forms are found only in this state; the Wet Tropics in particular host many unique forms, from rainforest possums and birds to frogs and an abundance of insects. Lonely Planet's *Watching Wildlife Australia* will give you more information about the animals described in this section.

## Mammals
Australia's unique mammals have caused comment and speculation since their discovery by science. Two groups in particular, the marsupials and the monotremes, are remnants of an ancient evolutionary line that has its stronghold in Australia; a high percentage of these are found in Queensland. Most mammals are nocturnal and difficult to see, but several species of kangaroo and wallaby are common and can be seen in any sizeable patch of bush.

Kangaroos are perhaps the most famous inhabitants of the bush; the eastern grey kangaroo is commonly encountered in Queensland woodlands. The family of about 50 species also includes many smaller species such as wallabies and even some adapted to life in the treetops – the tree-kangaroos are agile climbers that feed on leaves, fruits and even small animals in the rainforest canopy.

Kangaroos have an extraordinary breeding cycle: The young kangaroo, or joey, just millimetres long at birth, claws its way unaided to the mother's pouch, and the mother produces two types of milk – one for a joey at heel, the other for the baby in her pouch.

There are now more kangaroos in Australia than there were when Europeans arrived, a result of the better availability of water and the creation of grasslands for sheep and cattle. About three million kangaroos are culled legally each year in Australia, but probably as many more are killed for sport or by farmers who believe the cull is insufficient to protect their paddocks from overgrazing.

Other common native animals are brush-tailed and ring-tailed possums, which can even be found in the heart of big cities, scavenging for household scraps. Much less common, the striped possum is unique to the Wet Tropics, and has an elongated finger for digging into rotten wood for grubs.

Gliders have a membrane stretching between their front and hind legs that acts as a parachute as they jump between trees. Several species are common in woodlands and forests.

On the ground, slow, solid and powerfully built wombats are marsupials adapted to a burrowing life. The female has a backward-facing pouch so she doesn't shovel dirt over her young.

The endearing koala, common along the eastern seaboard, is adapted to life in trees, where it feeds exclusively on eucalyptus leaves. The female carries her young in her pouch until it is old enough to cling to her back. Their cuddly appearance belies an irritable nature, and koalas will scratch and bite if provoked.

The platypus and the echidna are monotremes, a group containing only three species (the third lives in New Guinea). Both lay eggs, as reptiles do, but suckle their young on milk secreted directly through the skin from mammary glands. The shy platypus is rarely seen by the casual observer. One of the best places to look for it is in the forest pools at Eungella National Park (see the Whitsunday Coast chapter). The echidna, or spiny anteater, eats only ants and is protected by stout spines. It hides from predators by digging into the ground or by rolling itself into a bristling ball.

Australia's wild dog, the dingo, first came to Australia from Asia around 4000 years ago and was domesticated by Aborigines. Dingoes can become quite tame around camping grounds. Recently, Fraser Island was the setting for a controversial dingo cull, following the killing of a nine-year-old boy by dingoes in April 2001 (see the boxed text 'Deadly Dingoes' in the Fraser Island chapter).

Whales, dolphins and dugongs can be seen off the Queensland coast. See the Fraser Coast chapter for details on whale-watching. The dugong, also known as the sea cow, is an odd marine mammal that grazes on sea-grass meadows. Good areas to see dugongs include the shallow waters of Moreton Bay and Torres Strait. Take care when boating in these areas – dugongs are slow moving and can be injured by propellers.

## Birds

With more than 600 species, Queensland can boast a greater variety of birds than any other Australian state. The majority can be seen in eastern Queensland, particularly in the tropics, and avid birdwatchers will find an excellent variety of bird habitats within a 100km radius of Cairns.

Two huge, flightless birds are unusual because only the males incubate the eggs and care for the young: the emu, in woodlands and grasslands west of the Great Dividing Range; and the cassowary in dense rainforests. Also unusual are the black brush turkey, with its bald, red and yellow neck and head, and the scrubfowl, with its bright orange legs. These primitive birds of the rainforest incubate their eggs in huge mounds of earth and rotting leaves.

Queensland has a great variety of waterbirds, such as ducks and geese, herons, egrets and smaller species that inhabit the margins of waterways. The best places to see waterbirds are the tropical lagoons of the far north, especially as the dry season wears on and wildlife starts to congregate near permanent water. The black-necked stork, or jabiru, is a striking iridescent black-and-white bird that grows up to 1.2m

The black-necked stork,
or jabiru

tall. The stately brolga – a member of the crane family – performs graceful courtship displays that have been absorbed into Aboriginal legends and ceremonies.

Every year vast flocks of small migratory waders arrive on Queensland's mudflats and waterways from as far away as Siberia and South-East Asia. There are many species, including sandpipers, plovers, curlew, stints and shanks. One of the best places to watch waders is on the Esplanade at Cairns, where high tide pushes them to within a few metres of the shore.

Queensland has all bar a few of Australia's 53 species of noisy, garrulous, colourful parrots. The gorgeous rainbow lorikeet is extremely common along the east coast, the pink-and-grey galah can be seen in any rural area and the sulphur-crested cockatoo is a striking white bird that makes an appalling racket. Queensland is also the former home of the paradise parrot, last seen in the 1920s, now extinct.

The kookaburra's raucous laughter is one of the most distinctive sounds of the bush. Smaller but more colourful kingfishers include the sacred and forest kingfishers and the blue-and-orange azure kingfisher, which is always found near water. During the Wet, Julatten (see the Far North Queensland chapter) is a good place to see the magnificent buff-breasted paradise-kingfisher.

Bowerbirds, unique to Australia and New Guinea, have some of the most remarkable behaviour of any birds. The male constructs a bower of vegetation and decorates it with leaves, flowers and pebbles to attract a mate. The male satin bowerbird is a shimmering blue bird that even uses artificial blue objects, such as pen tops, drinking straws and clothes pegs, to decorate its bower. The golden and tooth-billed bowerbirds are unique to the Wet Tropics

Other birds in Queensland are the Australian magpie, with its beautiful, warbling call; its larger relative, the currawong; and riflebirds, in the rainforests, more often seen than heard. The male riflebird has glossy black plumage and an iridescent gorget that he shows off in a mesmerising display from a tree stump.

## Reptiles & Frogs

The vast majority of Queensland's reptiles are harmless, and all are protected.

Sea turtles are sometimes encountered by divers around islands of the Great Barrier Reef. The females may be seen coming ashore to lay their eggs at Mon Repos Beach near Bundaberg (see the Fraser Coast chapter). The freshwater snake-necked tortoise lives in inland rivers and creeks.

Although the chances of encountering one are not high, many of Queensland's snakes are strikingly beautiful. They include the harmless python; the slender, attractive green tree snake; and the brown snake, a common venomous species in arid areas. Treat all snakes with caution, and see the Dangers & Annoyances section of the Facts for the Visitor chapter for ways of avoiding snakebite.

There is a wide variety of lizards, from tiny skinks and geckos to prehistoric-looking goannas that can grow up to 2.5m long. Goannas can run very fast and when threatened will use their big claws to climb the nearest tree – or leg! The slow-moving bluetongue lizard is sometimes kept as a pet.

Both of Australia's crocodile species are found in Queensland: the large saltwater or estuarine crocodile and the smaller freshwater variety. 'Salties' are found in coastal areas and estuaries north of Mackay, although there have been occasional sightings further south and they may even be found in permanent freshwater more than 100km inland. A large saltie – they can grow to 7m in length – can attack and kill a person. Although very few tourists have been killed by salties, to avoid the possibility stay out of the water whenever you're in croc territory. Observe the guidelines contained in park brochures and you'll be quite safe. 'Freshies' (less than 4m long) can be identified by their narrower snouts and smaller teeth. Though generally harmless to humans, children in particular should be kept away from them.

Queensland has an astonishing diversity of frogs, from the tiny froglets of marshes to the large tree frogs of the tropical rainforests. By walking through rainforest at night with a torch (flashlight) you should be able to pick out the eyeshine of several species.

## Other Wildlife

A dazzling variety of creatures – too many to describe in this space – inhabit the warm waters of the Great Barrier Reef (see the 'Great Barrier Reef' special section later in this chapter). The famous barramundi is a highly prized game fish found in tropical coastal and estuarine waters, and the bizarre lungfish is a rare prehistoric relic found only in a handful of Queensland rivers. There are also a host of butterflies to be found in Queensland, particularly in the tropics, including the birdwing, with a 20cm wingspan, and the electric-blue Ulysses butterfly.

## NATIONAL PARKS & STATE FORESTS

Queensland's magnificent national parks and forest reserves preserve an amazing variety of unique flora, fauna and landscapes and numerous areas of outstanding natural beauty, from the forested peaks of the south-eastern hinterlands to the islands of the Great Barrier Reef.

## National Parks

Queensland has 212 national parks – protected areas of environmental or natural importance. While some cover just a single hill or lake, others are large wilderness areas. Many islands and stretches of the coast are national parks, including Fraser Island, Hinchinbrook Island, Moreton Island, Lizard Island and most of the Whitsundays group.

Cape York Peninsula contains some of the state's best and most remote parks, including the Lakefield, Iron Ranges and Mungkan Kandju National Parks. Along the New South Wales border in the south-east of the state are the spectacular parks of Lamington, on the forested rim of an ancient volcano; and Girraween, with its fascinating landscape of huge granite boulders. Just south-west of Rockhampton, Carnarvon is one of the nation's finest parks, with a 30km gorge; Lawn Hill is an oasis-like river gorge in the remote north-western corner of the state; and rainforested Eungella, near Mackay, is teeming with wildlife.

The international World Heritage List, which includes the Taj Mahal, the Pyramids and the Grand Canyon, currently contains four of Queensland's most significant areas: the Great Barrier Reef, the Wet Tropics Area of the coastal north, Fraser Island and the Riversleigh fossil fields at Lawn Hill. In recent years various bodies have lobbied to have Cape York Peninsula included also.

Until recently, Queensland's national parks were managed by a subdivision of the Department of Environment known as the Queensland National Parks and Wildlife Service, but the department is now the Environment Protection Agency (EPA; **w** www.env.qld.gov.au), and the parks division is the Queensland Parks and Wildlife Service (QPWS), though the two share roles. The EPA operates the following regional information centres (area code ☎ 07):

**Naturally Queensland Information Centre**
(QPWS/EPA Central Office; ☎ 3227 8187)
160 Ann St, Brisbane
**South-West/Central Regional Office**
(☎ 4639 4599) 158 Hume St, Toowoomba
**Central Coast Regional Office** (☎ 4936 0511)
corner of Yeppoon & Norman Sts, North Rockhampton

**North Queensland Regional Office**
(☎ 4721 2399) Reef HQ, Townsville
**Far North Regional Office** (☎ 4046 6600)
10 McLeod St, Cairns
**Whitsundays Regional Office** (☎ 4946 7022)
Shute Harbour Rd, Airlie Beach

It's worth calling in at one of these centres to find out the current status of the various national parks and to pick up the excellent free information sheets on all the parks, which include camping, walking and access information.

There are also information centres and/or ranger stations in many of the parks, as well as EPA offices in many towns. The park rangers themselves are often the best sources of information – they usually know their parks like the backs of their hands.

Public access to the parks is encouraged, so long as safety and conservation regulations are observed. Many parks have camping grounds with water, toilets and showers, and there are often privately run camping grounds, motels or lodges on the park fringes. Sizeable parks usually have a network of walking tracks, ranging from short discovery strolls to longer treks, such as the three- to five-day walk on Hinchinbrook Island.

To camp in a national park – whether in a camping ground or in the bush – you need a permit, which you can either get in advance (by writing or calling in at the appropriate EPA office) or from the ranger at the park itself. Many camping grounds also have self-registration booths, so if the rangers aren't around you can fill in a registration form and drop your permit fee into the box provided.

Camping fees at all national park sites are $3.85 per night per person for anyone over the age of five. Family tickets cover two adults and two children and cost $15.40. On public holidays and long weekends the more popular parks like Carnarvon Gorge and Bunya Mountain may be booked up months in advance. Camp sites are detailed in the EPA/QWPS information sheets. Alternatively, hunt down a copy of the invaluable *Camping in Queensland* ($7, available from EPA offices and most bookshops),

which lists the facilities at every camping ground in the state's national parks.

## State Forests

Queensland has a large number of state forests – timber reserves that are selectively logged – and public reserves around reservoirs and water catchment areas. These areas can be just as scenic and wild as national parks (depending, of course, on how recently the area has been logged). There are plenty of opportunities for recreation in the reserves – scenic drives, camping (free), bushwalking, trail-bike riding, 4WD driving etc.

You can get information on state forest camping sites and facilities from tourist offices or from the Forest Services section of the Department of Primary Industry (☎ 3234 0111), 160 Mary St, Brisbane. Other forestry offices are at Enterprise St, Bundaberg (☎ 4131 5804); 123 Wharf St, Maryborough (☎ 4121 1833); 109 Bolsover St, Rockhampton (☎ 4938 4700); Tennyson St, Mackay (☎ 4967 0724); 52 McIllwraith St, Ingham (☎ 4776 2777); Gregory St, Cardwell (☎ 4066 8804); and 83 Main St, Atherton (☎ 4091 5200).

## GOVERNMENT & POLITICS
### Federal Government

Australia is a federation of six states and two territories, and has a parliamentary system of government based on the Westminster model. There are three tiers of government: federal, state and local. Under the Constitution, which came into force on 1 January 1901 when the colonies joined to form the Commonwealth of Australia, the federal government is mainly responsible for the national economy and Reserve Bank, customs and excise, immigration, defence, foreign policy, and post and telecommunications. The state governments are chiefly responsible for health, education, housing, transport and justice. Federal governments are lead by prime ministers and state governments are lead by premiers, both of whom are chosen by the party who wins the election. There are both federal and state police forces.

[Continued on page 41]

Great Barrier Reef

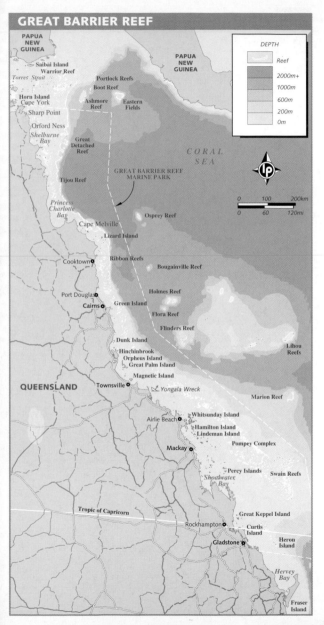

## GREAT BARRIER REEF

PAPUA
NEW
GUINEA

Saibai Island
Warrior Reef
*Torres Strait*

PAPUA
NEW
GUINEA

Portlock Reefs
Boot Reef

Horn Island
Cape York
Sharp Point

Ashmore
Reef

Eastern
Fields

Orford Ness
*Shelburne
Bay*

Great
Detached
Reef

*C O R A L
S E A*

Tijou Reef

GREAT BARRIER REEF
MARINE PARK

*Princess
Charlotte
Bay*

Cape Melville

Osprey Reef

Lizard Island

Cooktown

Ribbon Reefs

Bougainville Reef

Port Douglas

Holmes Reef

Cairns

Green Island

Flora Reef

Flinders Reef

Dunk Island

Hinchinbrook
Orpheus Island
Great Palm Island

*Lihou
Reefs*

Magnetic Island

QUEENSLAND

Townsville

*Yongala Wreck*

Marion Reef

Airlie Beach

Whitsunday Island

Hamilton Island
Lindeman Island

Pompey Complex

Mackay

Percy Islands

*Shodwater
Bay*

Swain Reefs

Tropic of Capricorn

Great Keppel Island

Rockhampton

Curtis
Island

Gladstone

Heron
Island

*Hervey
Bay*

*Fraser
Island*

| DEPTH | |
|---|---|
| | Reef |
| | 2000m+ |
| | 1000m |
| | 600m |
| | 200m |
| | 0m |

| 0 | 100 | 200km |
| 0 | 60 | 120mi |

**Cover:** Carnivores and corals devour each other in competition for space. (Photograph by Leonard Douglas Zell)

**Cover Inset:** One of the Low Isles, off Port Douglas (Photograph by Peter Ptschelinzew)

**T**he Great Barrier Reef is one of Australia's World Heritage Areas and also one of nature's richest realms.

The reef stretches 2000km from just south of the tropic of Capricorn (near Gladstone) to Torres Strait, just south of New Guinea. It is the most extensive reef system in the world, and was made entirely by living organisms. At its southern end the reef is up to 300km from the mainland and is somewhat fragmented, while at the northern end it runs nearer the coast, is continuous for long stretches and up to 80km wide. The lagoon between the outer reef and the coast is dotted with smaller reefs, cays and islands. Drilling has indicated that the coral is more than 500m thick in places. Most of the reef is around two million years old, but there are sections dating back 18 million years.

The Great Barrier Reef is in fact about 2600 separate fringing reefs (off the coasts of islands and the mainland) and barrier reefs (further out to sea). The 'real' Great Barrier Reef, or outer reef, is at the edge of the Australian continental shelf. The channel between the reef and the coast is up to 60m deep. In places, the reef rises straight up from this depth – intriguing, as coral cannot survive below 30m. One theory is that the reef gradually grew as the sea bed subsided, keeping pace with the rate of subsidence. Another theory is that the sea level gradually rose, and again the coral growth was able to keep pace.

**Top:** Pink anemone fish

**Right:** Turret coral

## Formation of the Reef

Coral is formed by small, primitive animals: marine polyps of the phylum Coelenterata, which form a surface by excreting lime. When they die, the hard 'skeletons' remain and gradually build up the reef. New polyps continually add to the reef. The remains of hard corals are white; the colours of reefs come from living polyps.

For healthy coral growth, the water must not be below 17.5°C, and it must be clear and salty. Coral will not grow below depths of 30m because sufficient sunlight does not penetrate. Nor does it grow around river mouths – the Barrier Reef ends near Papua New Guinea because the Fly River's enormous water flow is both fresh and muddy.

One of the most spectacular sights of the Barrier Reef occurs for a few nights after a full moon in late spring or early summer each year, when vast numbers of corals spawn at the same time. The tiny bundles of sperm and eggs are visible to the naked eye, together they look like a gigantic underwater snowstorm. Many other reef organisms reproduce around this time, giving their spawn a greater chance of surviving predators.

COURTESY OF THE NATIONAL LIBRARY OF AUSTRALIA

THE MARINE WONDERS OF THE
GREAT BARRIER CORAL REEF

For particulars & bookings apply
QUEENSLAND GOVERNMENT TOURIST BUREAU, BRISBANE, SYDNEY, MELBOURNE.

## Reef Life

The Great Barrier Reef is home to a plethora of species, including about 400 different types of coral and many equally colourful clams embedded in the coral. Other reef inhabitants include about 1500 species of fish, 4000 types of mollusc (such as clams and snails), 350 echinoderms (sea urchins, starfish and sea cucumbers) and countless thousands of species of crustacean (crabs, shrimps and their relatives), sponges and worms.

**Top:** Starfish (Photograph by Bob Charlton)

**Left:** Early promotional poster for the Great Barrier Reef

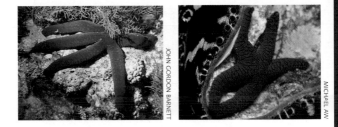

Threatened species, such as the dugong (sea cow), loggerhead turtle, dolphin and humpback whale (which migrates from Antarctica to breed from May to October), are protected in the Great Barrier Reef waters. Minke whales (which can be viewed off the coast from Cairns to Lizard Island in June and July), porpoises, and killer and pilot whales also inhabit these waters. The reef's islands form important nesting colonies for many types of seabird, and six of the world's seven species of sea turtle lay eggs on the islands' sandy beaches in spring or summer.

**Dangerous Creatures** For some people open waters conjure visions of fearsome aquatic menaces. In actual fact, the dangers are slight and in most cases the only precaution needed is simply to avoid touching or picking up things that are best left alone. Some unpleasant creatures that can bite or sting are blue-ringed octopuses, cone shells, crown-of-thorns sea stars, fire coral, moray eels, sea snakes, sea urchins, some sea anemones and stingrays. Others to watch out for include scorpion fish, stonefish and lionfish – all masters of disguise with highly venomous spines. The butterfly cod is a very beautiful scorpion fish that relies on its colourful, slow-moving appearance to warn

**Top Left:** Blue sea star

**Top Right**: Sea star

**Right:** The crown-of-thorns sea star is the only creature that eats living coral.

**Far Right:** Stinging jellyfish are found only along the coast. Although the sting can be lethal, death by sea jelly is a rare occurrence.

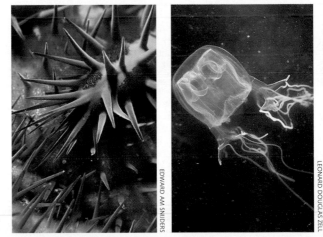

MICHAEL AW

off possible enemies. In contrast, the very poisonous stonefish lies hidden on the bottom, looking just like a rock.

Stinging jellyfish (sea jellies, box jellies and the Portuguese man-o-war) are a danger only in coastal waters from November to April (see the 'Stingers' boxed text in the Capricorn Coast chapter). As for sharks, there has been no recorded case of a visitor to the reef islands meeting a hungry one.

Basic reef safety rules are:

- Avoid touching all marine life.
- Wear shoes with strong soles while walking on or near the reef.
- Don't eat fish you don't know about or can't identify.
- Don't swim in murky water; try to swim in bright sunlight.

MICHAEL AW

**Threats to the Reef** Cyclones, global warming and the effects of El Niño, such as coral bleaching and rising water temperatures, can devastate large areas of the reef. Pollution, sewage and agricultural phosphate runoff (believed to cause cancer in fish) also damage the reef, as do the high impact of development from increased tourist activity, over fishing, damage from boat anchors, and trawling (which accidentally traps animals such as sea turtles and birds). Shipping in the area adds the possibility of oil spills, and in 2000 a section of the reef was blasted to release a ship that had become stuck.

Infestations of crown-of-thorns sea star are notorious because they appear to chew through large areas of coral and occur when the reef ecology is disturbed.

**Top:** Photographing the reef

**Left:** Feather star seascape

MICHAEL AW

LEONARD DOUGLAS ZELL

# Islands

The Queensland islands are extremely variable so don't let the marketing catchword 'reef island' suck you in. There are three types of island off the Queensland coast. South of the Barrier Reef are several large sand islands. Continental islands are strung along the whole coast and have vegetation similar to that of the adjacent mainland; these include Great Keppel Island, most of the Whitsunday Islands, and Hinchinbrook and Dunk Islands.

True coral islands, or cays, such as Green Island near Cairns, the Low Isles near Port Douglas and Heron Island off Gladstone, occur on the outer reef, or between it and the mainland. Cays are formed when a reef is above sea level, even at high tide. Dead coral is ground down by water action to form sand, eventually vegetation takes root. Coral cays are low-lying, unlike the often hilly islands closer to the coast. There are about 300 cays on the reef, 69 of them vegetated. Although most of the popular resort islands are actually continental islands, many still have fringing reefs as well as other attractions that a tiny dot-on-the-map coral cay is simply too small for: hills to climb, bushwalks and secluded beaches.

For more information on individual islands, see the Whitsunday Coast, North Coast and Far North Queensland chapters. Also good is Lonely Planet's *Islands of Australia's Great Barrier Reef* and Pisces' *Diving & Snorkeling Australia's Great Barrier Reef*.

**Top left:** Close-up of fan worm

**Top Right:** Red soft spiky coral can be home to many marine critters.

**Right:** Lady Elliot Island

BOB CHARLTON

# Viewing the Reef

The best way of seeing the reef is by diving or snorkelling – this allows close-up views of jewel-like coral, anemones and tiny fish and a chance to swim with larger creatures, such as turtles. Almost all the diving and snorkelling in the Great Barrier Reef is boat-based, although there are a few good reefs surrounding some of the islands. Otherwise you can reef walk, or view it through the floor of a glass-bottom boat or the windows of a semi-submersible, or descend below the ocean surface inside an 'underwater observatory'. You can also see a living coral reef without leaving dry land, at the Reef HQ aquarium (☎ 4750 0800, Flinders St East) in Townsville.

Innumerable tour operators run day trips to the outer reef and to coral-fringed islands. Cairns and Port Douglas are main ports for reef access; Airlie Beach is the gateway to the Whitsundays and a popular place to learn to dive. The *Yongala* wreck, one of Australia's best dives, is off the coast of Townsville. Trip costs depend on the distance travelled, the type of boat and extras such as lunch and use of dive equipment. Free use of snorkelling gear is usually part of the package. 'Live-aboards' run scheduled trips to offshore reefs from Airlie Beach, Townsville, Cairns and Port Douglas. For further information see the Whitsunday Coast, North Coast and Far North Queensland chapters.

The Great Barrier Reef Marine Park Authority (☎ 4750 0700, W www .gbrmpa.gov.au) is responsible for the reef's welfare. It has an office at Reef HQ. To learn more, check out the slide show and lecture given by a local marine biologist at Reef Teach (☎/fax 4031 7794, e learn@ reefteach.com.au, W www.reefteach.com.au, 14 Spence St, Cairns).

**Top:** Reef walking with the locals – Heron Island

**Left:** Snorkelling off the Low Isles

[Continued from page 32]

In the federal parliament the lower house is the House of Representatives, the upper house the Senate, and the government is led by a prime minister. Elections for the lower house are held at least every three years; senators serve six-year terms, with elections for half of them every three years.

Australia is currently a constitutional monarchy. The head of state is the Queen, represented in Australia by the governor general, and each state also has its own governor. While the governor general and governors are appointed by federal and state governments, their decisions must be ratified by the monarch. The issue of Australia becoming a republic continues to be a hot topic. There are also calls for a new constitution to be drawn up representing the rights of all Australians, not just the Australians of European descent for whom the original document was drafted.

## State Government

Queensland's state government is based in Brisbane. Queensland is the only state without an upper house (it was abolished in 1922). Instead, the decisions of the Legislative Assembly (the lower house) are ratified by the Executive Council, which comprises the cabinet ministers and the governor. Elections for the lower house are held at least every three years; voting is by secret ballot and is compulsory for everyone 18 years of age and over.

Queensland's four main political parties are the Liberal Party, the Australian Labor Party (ALP), the National Party and Pauline Hanson's One Nation Party. The Liberal Party is traditionally conservative, representing the interests of free enterprise, law and order, and family values; the ALP is traditionally socialist (it grew out of the workers disputes and shearers' strikes of the 1890s); and the National Party (known as the Country Party until 1974) is traditionally the party of rural interests, having originally formed to represent conservative farmers unions. One Nation was formed on a platform of intolerance that had a certain historical resonance in

Queensland, but the party succumbed to internal turmoil and its future is uncertain.

## ECONOMY

Queensland is richly endowed with natural resources. Until the mining boom of the 1960s Queenslanders were largely dependent on agricultural and pastoral production for most of their wealth. Agriculture still plays a major economic role, employing just under 10% of the state's workforce. Sugar cane is the major crop; Queensland produces about 95% of Australia's 40-million-tonne sugar crop and exports nearly 5 million tonnes of raw sugar annually. Other major crops include wheat, sorghum, maize, barley and sunflower seed. A thriving fruit industry supplies most of Australia's tropical fruits, such as mangoes, bananas, pineapples and pawpaws; as well as apples, pears, peaches and apricots.

The pastoral industry has always been one of the state's economic mainstays, and raising beef cattle is the largest rural industry. Wool growing is also important, although has been less so in recent years.

Since the 1960s the mining sector has been at the forefront of the Queensland economy. Coal from the huge open-cut mines of central Queensland is the state's major export. North-western Queensland is mineral-rich, and the copper, zinc, silver and lead mine at Mt Isa is one of the world's largest underground mines. On Cape York Peninsula, Weipa has the world's largest bauxite mine. Goldmining has also undergone a resurgence in recent years. The Kidston mine in northern Queensland is the state's richest, and old mines at places like Charters Towers, Ravenswood and Mt Morgan are being reworked successfully.

Recently a number of previously unmineable deposits have been found in south-eastern Queensland, including a huge deposit of mineral silver near Texas, on the NSW border. Sand mining is also big business in Queensland, with several major corporations exploiting the reserves of fine mineral sand (which is used for semiconductors and other engineering components) on Moreton and Stradbroke Islands.

As this book indicates, Queensland is also incredibly rich in natural tourism resources. In recent decades tourism has been the fastest-growing sector of the economy and is now one of the state's major sources of income.

## POPULATION & PEOPLE

Queensland has a population of more than 3.5 million people, making up about 18% of the total Australian population. Its growth rate of 1.7% is well above the national average, though lower than the Northern Territory's. Around 80% of people live in urban areas and the majority of Queenslanders live along the fertile coastal strip between Brisbane and Cairns. The other parts of the state are sparsely populated.

Queensland is notable for being the Australian mainland state with the largest proportion of its people living outside its capital city. The south-eastern corner of the state is Queensland's most crowded region, and more than 60% of the total population lives within 150km of Brisbane. Greater Brisbane has more than 1.5 million residents; the Gold Coast, Toowoomba and the Sunshine Coast are the south-east's other major population centres.

Of the string of cities along the east coast, Maryborough, Hervey Bay, Bundaberg, Gladstone, Rockhampton, Mackay, Townsville and Cairns have populations above 20,000. The mining town of Mt Isa is the only place in the interior to top this figure.

In a 1996 census, around 104,800 people stated they were of Indigenous origin: Aborigines and Torres Strait Islanders, most of whom live in the north of the state or on the islands of Torres Strait, between Cape York and Papua New Guinea.

At one time Queensland was the most multicultural place in Australia, with huge numbers of Indian and Chinese coolies, Melanesians (known as Kanakas) and German contract workers, but the so-called White Australia immigration laws brought in at Federation marked the end of this comparatively enlightened period. Queensland received only 8% of new immigrants after WWII and as a result has a less diverse cultural mix than other states; perhaps the most obvious ethnic group are the Italians, who were brought here to work on fruit and vegetable farms during WWII.

## ARTS & CULTURE

In the epilogue to his 1982 *A History of Queensland*, local historian Ross Fitzgerald lamented 'the cultural wasteland that is Queensland'. Fitzgerald thought the blame for the state's cultural malaise lay with a range of factors, including the authoritarianism and anti-intellectualism of the then National/Liberal Party government, the historically low value that had been placed on education in Queensland and the low levels of immigration.

Fortunately for the arts, the fall of the National Party marked the beginning of a cultural renaissance in Queensland. The new Labor government restored the civil liberties that were taken away by Bjelke-Petersen, such as the right to assembly, and did much to stimulate and encourage artistic and cultural developments. Brisbane in particular has been gripped by a new spirit of creative endeavour, with theatre, opera, alternative cinema, poetry, music and other artistic activities going on every night of the week.

This said, the artistic spirit fades pretty quickly once you leave the capital. There are some interesting regional art galleries, with very 'pioneer' artwork, but for the most part, the arts in rural Queensland are restricted to pub bands and Aboriginal souvenirs.

### Painting

Most of the major developments in the world of Australian visual arts since settlement have taken place in Sydney and Melbourne. Queensland has played only a minor role, although there are a number of excellent galleries that exhibit the works of Australian artists. In particular, the Queensland Art Gallery in Brisbane is well worth visiting and has an excellent Australian collection. Its Web site (W www.qag.qld.gov.au) has links to other Queensland art galleries.

Charles Archer, the founder of Rockhampton, produced some interesting settler paintings in the 1850s. Lloyd Rees is probably the best-known artist to have come out of Queensland and has an international reputation. Others include abstract impressionist John Coburn, Ian Fairweather, Godfrey Rivers, Davida Allen (famous for her obsessive portraits of the actor Sam Neill) and Bill Robinson, who won the 1995 Archibald Prize for portraiture with his quirky *Portrait of the Artist With Stunned Mullet*.

Queensland is a rich centre of traditional and contemporary Aboriginal art. Judy Watson and Gordon Bennett have both won the Moët & Chandon Prize for contemporary artists.

Recently, a number of outback artists have come to prominence, including figurative painter Matthew McCord from Mundubbera in the Darling Downs.

Although Tracey Moffatt is now based in Sydney, her work is also worth looking out for. See the Brisbane chapter for details of galleries featuring Australian art.

## Literature

Two of the most widely acclaimed early Australian writers were AB 'Banjo' Paterson and Henry Lawson. Paterson's classics include the poems *Clancy of the Overflow* and *The Man from Snowy River*. Henry Lawson's greatest legacy is his short stories of life in the bush, published in collections like *While the Billy Boils* (1896) and *Joe Wilson and His Mates* (1901).

Steele Rudd, a contemporary of Paterson's and Lawson's, was born in Toowoomba in 1868. With his classic sketches of the hardships of early Queensland life and the enduring characters he created like 'Dad and Dave' and 'Mother and Sal', Rudd became one of the country's best-loved comic writers.

Rolf Boldrewood's classic *Robbery Under Arms* tells the tale of Captain Starlight, Queensland's most notorious bushranger and cattle thief. Neville Shute's famous novel *A Town Like Alice* is set partly in Burketown, in the Gulf Savannah. Many of Ion Idriess' outback romps were set in Queensland, including *Flynn of the Inland*, the story of the man who created the Flying Doctor Service.

In 1938 Xavier Herbert produced his classic *Capricornia*, an epic tale of the settler existence in the Gulf country. In a similar vein, Kerry McGinnis's *Heart Country* is an evocative autobiography about her life as a cattle drover in the Gulf – Kerry still raises cattle at the Bowthorn Station near Burketown. An interesting play (now also a film) set in Queensland is *Radiance* by esteemed Aussie playwright Louis Nowra.

Queensland has produced plenty of outstanding writers of its own. In particular, Brisbane's University of Queensland has for many years been one of Australia's richest literary breeding grounds.

Lebanese Australian author David Malouf is one of Queensland's most internationally recognised writers, responsible for the evocative tales of an Australian boyhood in Brisbane, *Johnno* and *12 Edmondstone Street*, and *The Great World*, among other titles.

Australia's best-known Aboriginal poet and writer, Oodgeroo Noonuccal (Kath Walker) was born on North Stradbroke Island in 1920, and buried there in September 1993. Her 1964 book *We Are Going* was the first published work by an Aboriginal woman; her other works include *My People*. Herb Wharton, an Aboriginal author from Cunnamulla, has written a series of novels and short stories

**AB 'Banjo' Paterson**

about the lives of the Murri stockmen, including *Unbranded* and *Cattle Camp*.

Thea Astley's 11 published novels include *Hunting the Wild Pineapple*, set in the rainforests of northern Queensland, and *It's Raining in Mango*, a historical saga that traces the fortunes and failures of one pioneer family from the 1860s to the 1980s.

Expatriate writer Janet Turner Hospital was educated in Melbourne and has used the rainforests of Queensland for many of her books, including the wonderful *The Last Magician*.

Ipswich-born Thomas Shapcott is an editor and one of Australia's most prolific writers. His recent books include *The White Stag of Exile*, set in Brisbane and Budapest around the turn of the century.

Brisbane-born journalist Hugh Lunn has written a number of popular books on and about Queensland. They include his humorous two-part autobiography *Over the Top With Jim* and *Head Over Heels*.

In recent years, Brisbane has produced a wave of promising young writers. Andrew McGahan, a university dropout, used the seedy underbelly of the Fortitude Valley scene as the setting for his controversial first novel *Praise*, which was later made into a film. Verano Armanno's *Romeo of the Underworld* is another contemporary novel set in the Valley.

Another prominent young writer is Matthew Condon, whose novels include *The Motorcycle Cafe* and *Usher*. Helen Darville gained notoriety for her novel *The Hand That Signed the Paper*, which won the Miles Franklin Award. Another prominent Brisbane talent is children's author James Moloney, who has picked up lots of awards for his *Swashbuckler* and *A Bridge to Wiseman's Cove* books.

## Architecture
Although Queensland's early settlers lived mostly in crude cabins or tents, it wasn't long before the cash engine of the mining and pastoral industries provided money for some regal public buildings. Post offices, court houses, banks, pubs and town halls were among the first permanent buildings to go up, followed by train stations to welcome the expanding railways. Everything from yellow sandstone to red brick was used in their construction, but far and away the most popular building material was timber, which seemed to be in almost limitless supply.

Before long, no settler's life was complete without a 'Queenslander' home. Built on raised posts to provide ventilation and keep out vermin, hundreds of these distinctive wooden bungalows can be seen throughout the state. With their shady verandas, tin roofs and ornate chimney pots,

**Queenslander house**

Queenslanders have come to represent the country idyll for many Australians. Charters Towers, Ravenswood, Cooktown and Warwick have particularly fine examples of this kind of architecture.

Most of Queensland's impressive public buildings date from the late 19th century, when the gold money was rolling in and there was huge civic pride among the creators of Queensland's first towns. Initially wooden architecture dominated, but this soon evolved into gorgeously ornamental brick and stonework. The Queen St Mall in Brisbane still features many fine shop fronts from the period. By the turn of the century a new movement known as Federation had emerged, which borrowed heavily from the European and American Art Deco movements, and featured simpler, more confident lines and colours.

Much of Queensland's modern architecture is less noteworthy. Rabid developers and a short-sighted obsession with 'progress' have produced such architectural eyesores as the high-rise concrete jungles that engulf the Gold Coast and parts of the Sunshine Coast, and several other booming tourist centres are in danger of following suit.

On a more positive note, Queensland's growing ecotourism industry has led to a trend in resort developments that attempt to blend in with their environments and achieve a degree of stylistic integrity.

## Music

Queensland is the birthplace of Australia's most famous song. Banjo Patterson wrote the lyrics to 'Waltzing Matilda', Australia's unofficial national anthem, early in 1895 while he was visiting his fiancee at an outback station near Winton in central Queensland.

Queensland hosts a wide range of music festivals throughout the year, featuring everything from jazz and blues to chamber music and alternative rock. Two of the best-known music events are the legendary Woodford Folk Festival, held annually between Christmas and New Year, and the Brisbane Biennial International Music Festival, held every odd-numbered year from late May to early June.

Plenty of towns in Queensland host regular bush dances featuring folk and country bands – bush dances are great fun, and an excellent way to meet the locals and gain an insight into Australian music. Country-and-western line dancing has also become incredibly popular in recent years.

Indigenous music is one of the Australian music industry's great success stories of recent years. Yothu Yindi, with its land-rights anthem 'Treaty', is the country's best-known Aboriginal band, but Queensland has produced some outstanding Indigenous musicians of its own. Christine Anu is a Torres Strait Islander who was born in Cairns. Her debut CD *Stylin' Up* blends Creole-style rap, Islander chants and traditional languages with English, and was followed by the interesting *Come My Way* – highly recommended listening. Other regional artists include Torres Strait Islander Rita Mills, and Maroochy Barambah of the Sunshine Coast.

Brisbane's pub-rock scene may not have produced the same wealth of bands that have come out of Sydney and Melbourne, but a couple of Australia's all-time greatest bands had their beginnings in the Sunshine State. The Go-Betweens started out in Queensland, and many of their songs (like 'Cattle and Cane') evoke a strong sense of place. Hunt down the albums *Tallulah* and *Before Hollywood* for a bit of Queensland driving music.

The Saints, considered by many to be one of the seminal punk bands, started out in Brisbane in the mid-1970s before moving on to bigger things in Sydney and, later, London.

More recently, Brisbane's prolific alternative music scene has thrown up prominent bands like Custard and Regurgitator. For the latest on up and coming Brisbane bands, visit the Brispop Web site (W www.brispop.com).

## Cinema

Queensland has a growing film industry based around the Warner Roadshow studios at Movie World on the Gold Coast, and has also become a popular location for foreign productions, although none has so far done much at the box office.

All that is set to change with the Warner Roadshow live-action version of *Scooby Doo*, set in a haunted Gold Coast theme park. Other titles recently filmed in the state include: *Thin Red Line*, Terrence Malick's critically acclaimed tale of soldiers in the Pacific in WWII; *Meteorite*, an end-of-the-world blockbuster; *Komodo*, a killer reptile flick in the *Anaconda* mould; Jackie Chan's *First Strike*, a kung-fu romp partially filmed on the Gold Coast; and of course, *Crocodile Dundee in LA*, the latest instalment of the record-breaking Aussie series (parts one and two were also partly filmed in Queensland).

One of Queensland's most successful location roles was in the hit independent movie *Muriel's Wedding*.

## Alternative Lifestyles

Under the National Party, Queensland considered itself to be one of Australia's great bastions of conservatism. The leader of the Nationals, Sir Joh Bjelke-Petersen, was almost obsessive in his rejection of anything outside the 'hard-working white family' mould. The notorious 1976 raid on the 'hippie commune' at Cedar Bay, in the rainforests north of Cape Tribulation, was one of many examples of Joh's refusal to accept anyone or anything beyond the mainstream.

Attitudes have changed substantially since then, though Queensland still toes a very conservative line. There are several artistic communities in the Sunshine Coast hinterland, such as those at Maleny and

## Aboriginal Land Lore

Early European settlers and explorers usually dismissed the entire Aboriginal population as 'savages' and 'barbarians', and it was some time before the Aborigines' deep spiritual bond with the land, and their relationship to it, was understood by non-Indigenous Australians.

### Society & Lifestyle

Traditionally, the Aborigines were tribal people living in extended family groups or clans, with all clan members descending from a common ancestral being. Tradition, rituals and laws linked the people of each clan to the land they occupied, and were focused on sacred sites to which spirits would return when people died. It was the responsibility of the clan, or particular members of it, to correctly maintain and protect the sites so that the ancestral beings were not offended and would continue to offer protection. Traditional punishments for those who neglected these responsibilities were often severe, as their actions could easily affect the wellbeing of the whole clan – food and water shortages, natural disasters or mysterious illnesses could all be attributed to disgruntled or offended ancestral beings. Even when faced with warlike invaders, the Aborigines had no choice but to protect their sacred sites, allowing whole clan lines to be picked off by settler militias.

Many Aboriginal communities were almost nomadic, but this largely depended on the availability of food. Where food and water were readily available the people tended to remain in a limited area. When they did travel, however, it was to visit sacred places to carry out rituals, or to take advantage of seasonal foods available elsewhere. They did not, as is still widely believed, roam aimlessly and desperately in search of food and water.

Traditionally, men were hunters, tool-makers and custodians of male law; the women reared the children, and gathered and prepared food. There was also female law and ritual for which the women were responsible.

### Environmental Awareness

Wisdom and skills obtained over millennia enabled Aborigines to care for and live well in their environment, abilities sadly lacking in their European successors. An intimate knowledge of the behaviour of animals and the correct time to harvest the many plants they used ensured that food shortages were rare. This ecological savvy allowed wild stocks of food plants and animals to be managed in an almost infinitely sustainable manner.

Eumundi, and several of Brisbane's inner suburbs have a distinctly alternative flavour. The Far North has to make do with Kuranda in the mountains north of Cairns, which has deteriorated into a commercial circus. The rainforests of Far North Queensland are still home to a few members of the state's best-known alternative lifestylers, the Ferals, though the movement is fading quietly into the background.

## RELIGION

A shrinking majority of people in Queensland are at least nominally Christian. Most Protestant churches have merged with each other to become the Uniting Church, although the Anglican Church (Church of England) has remained separate. The Catholic Church is popular, with the original Irish adherents now joined by large numbers of Mediterranean immigrants. American-style evangelist churches are also gaining ground.

Non-Christian minorities abound, the main groups being Buddhist, Jewish and Muslim. Almost 20% of the population describe themselves as having no religion.

## ABORIGINAL CULTURE
### Religion

Traditional Aboriginal cultures are either irreligious or are nothing but religion, depending on how you look at it. Is a belief system that views every event, no matter how trifling, in a nonmaterial context a religion? The

### Aboriginal Land Lore

Although Aborigines in northern Australia had been in regular contact with the farming peoples of what is now Indonesia since at least the 17th century, the farming of crops and the domestication of livestock held no appeal. The only major modification of the landscape practiced by the Aborigines was the selective burning of undergrowth in forests and dead grass on the plains. This encouraged new growth, which in turn attracted game animals to the area and reduced the possibility of major bush fires. Domesticated dingoes assisted in the hunt and guarded the camp from intruders.

#### Hunting & Trading

Technology, such as the boomerang and spear, was used throughout the continent, but techniques were adapted to the environment. In the wetlands of northern Australia, bamboo-and-cord fish traps hundreds of metres long were built to catch fish at the end of the wet season. In what is now Victoria, vast permanent stone weirs were used to trap eels, while in the tablelands of Queensland finely woven nets were used to snare mobs of wallabies and kangaroos. Whatever was hunted, the process was accompanied by strict rituals designed to appease the spirits of the animals and the land they occupied.

The Aborigines were also traders. Goods were dispersed by trade routes that crisscrossed the country. Many of the items traded, such as certain types of stone or shell, were rare and had great ritual significance. Boomerangs and ochre were other important trade items. Large numbers of people would often meet along the trading networks for 'exchange ceremonies', during which not only goods but also songs and dances were passed on.

#### Cultural Life

The simplicity of Aboriginal technology contrasts with the sophistication of their cultural life. Religion, history, law and art are integrated in complex ceremonies that depict the activities of their ancestral beings, and prescribe codes of behaviour and responsibilities for looking after the land and all living things. Totems link Aborigines with ancestral beings, each person has their own totem, or Dreaming. These totems take many forms, such as caterpillars, snakes, fish and magpies. The Dreamtime songs create a physical and spiritual map of the landscape and the movements of the creator ancestors, allowing the people to move through continent along lines of benign rather than malevolent influence. The songs tell of the best places and the best times to hunt, and where to find water in drought years. They can also specify kinship relations and marriage partners.

early Christian missionaries certainly didn't think so. For them a belief in a deity was an essential part of a religion, and anything else was mere superstition.

## Sacred Sites

Aboriginal sacred sites are a perennial topic of discussion. They can lead to headline-grabbing controversy when they stand in the way of developments such as roads, mines and dams. This is because most non-Indigenous Australians still have difficulty understanding the Aborigines' deep spiritual bond with the land.

Aboriginal religious beliefs are based on a belief in the continuing existence of spirit beings that lived on Earth during the Dreamtime, which occurred before the arrival of humans. These beings created all the features of the natural world and are the ancestors of all living things. They took different forms but behaved as people do, and as they travelled about they left signs to show where they passed. Most Australians have heard of rainbow serpents carving out rivers as they slithered from place to place. On a smaller scale is a pile of rocks that marks the spot where an ancestor defecated, or a tree that sprang from a thrown spear.

Despite being supernatural, the ancestors were subject to ageing and eventually they returned to the sleep from which they'd awoken at the dawn of time. Some sank back into the ground and others changed into physical features, including the moon and stars. Here their spirits remain as eternal forces that breathe life into the newborn and influence natural events. Each ancestor's spiritual energy flows along the path it travelled during the Dreamtime and is strongest at the points where it left physical evidence of its activities, such as a tree, hill or claypan. The Dreamtime songs of the Aboriginal tribes form a map of these sacred sites; before the arrival of Europeans, the spiritual and physical landscape of the entire continent of Australia was mapped out by these songs.

The ancestors left strict laws that govern the behaviour of people and animals, the growth of plants, and natural events such as rain and the change of seasons. Every person, animal and plant is believed to have two souls – one mortal and one immortal. The latter is part of a particular ancestral spirit and after death returns to the sacred sites of that ancestor, while the mortal soul simply fades into oblivion. Each person is spiritually bound to the sacred sites that mark the land associated with his or her ancestor. It is the individual's obligation to help care for these sites by performing the necessary rituals and singing the songs that tell of the ancestor's deeds.

However, the ancestors are extremely powerful and restless spirits, and require the most careful treatment. Calamity can befall those who fail to care for their sites in the proper manner. These restrictions often have a pragmatic origin; one site in northern Australia was believed to cause sores to break out all over the body of anyone visiting the area, and was subsequently found to have a dangerously high level of radiation from naturally occurring radon gas.

Unfortunately, Aboriginal sacred sites are not like Christian churches, which can be desanctified before the bulldozers move in. Neither can they be bought, sold or transferred. To damage or destroy a sacred site can bring terrible repercussions to both the living and spiritual inhabitants of the land and, thus far, developers have shown scant respect for Aboriginal traditions. It remains to be seen whether the two maps of Australia, the European's and the Aborigine's, can coexist.

During the settlement of Australia, many Aborigines sought refuge from persecution on missions and became Christians. However, Christianity has not, for most Aborigines, meant renouncing their traditional religion. Many senior Aboriginal law men are also devout Christians, and in many cases ministers, and the two belief systems seem to fit comfortably side by side.

## Language

At the time of contact with Europeans there were around 250 separate Indigenous languages spoken by the 600 to 700 'tribes', and many of these languages were as distinct from each other as English and French.

Often three or four adjacent tribes would speak what amounted to dialects of the same language, but another adjacent tribe might speak a completely different language.

It is believed that all the languages evolved from a single language family as the Aborigines gradually moved out over the entire continent and split into new groups. There are a number of words that occur right across the continent, such as *jina* (foot) and *mala* (hand), and similarities also exist in the grammatical structures.

Following European contact the number of Aboriginal languages was drastically reduced. At least eight separate languages were spoken in Tasmania alone, but none of these were recorded before the native speakers either died or were killed. Of the original 250 or so languages, only around 30 are today spoken on a regular basis and are taught to children.

Aboriginal Kriol is a new language that has developed since European arrival in Australia. It is spoken across northern Australia and has become the 'native' language of many young Aborigines. It contains many English words, but the pronunciation and grammar are along Aboriginal lines, the meaning is often different and the spelling is phonetic. For example, the sentence in English 'He was amazed' becomes 'I bin luk kwesjinmak' in Kriol.

There are a number of generic terms that Aborigines use to describe themselves, and these vary according to the region. The most common of these is Koori, used for the people of south-eastern Australia; Murri is used to refer to the people of Queensland.

# Facts for the Visitor

## HIGHLIGHTS

Queensland sells itself as the 'Sunshine State' and year-round sunny skies and warm temperatures are one of its major draw-cards, followed closely by pristine rain-forests and the wonderful Great Barrier Reef. It's no surprise that most visitors to Australia spend a good portion of their time exploring the idyllic east coast, whether surfing the Gold and Sunshine coasts, div-ing with giant Maori wrasse on the Great Barrier Reef or trekking around the tropical rainforests of Far North Queensland. Add to this great year-round weather and a star-tling array of adventure activities and it isn't hard to see why Queensland features on *everybody's* itinerary.

Tourism in Queensland is more devel-oped than in any other part of Australia, but it doesn't take much effort to escape the crowds and find yourself alone in untouched national parks or historic outback towns. At the other end of the spectrum, Queensland is Australia's entertainment capital, with nu-merous nightlife centres like Cairns and Surfers Paradise where party-people can bop till dawn and still rely on a courtesy bus to take them back to their hostel.

The south-eastern corner of Queensland is the state's most densely populated area, and is home to the state capital, Brisbane, an attractive, cosmopolitan city, with some excellent places to eat and drink and an amazing diversity of attractions within a few hours' drive north or south.

Off-shore from Brisbane is Moreton Bay, which, aside from being home to Queens-land's most delicious resident – the More-ton Bay bug – is also the setting for a number of spectacular sandy islands such as North Stradbroke Island.

Between Brisbane and the New South Wales border is the Gold Coast, the most developed tourist area in Queensland. This glitzy strip of high-rise holiday resorts and American-style theme parks may not be to everybody's taste, but its surf beaches,

restaurants, nightclubs and over-the-top tourist attractions pull in millions of visitors every year.

Inland from the Gold Coast are the spec-tacular Springbrook and Lamington Na-tional Parks, with some great lookouts, plentiful wildlife and excellent bush-walking trails. Further inland, the Darling Downs is the start of Queensland's outback, with big open spaces, old-fashioned rural towns and some fine, rarely visited national parks. Closer to the coast, Stanthorpe is home to Queensland's only winery district.

Heading north from Brisbane, the Sun-shine Coast is a string of friendly resort towns with some good surf, peaking at trendy Noosa Heads. North of Noosa stretches the wild Cooloola Coast, a rain-forest-backed strip of beach that runs up to Fraser Island, the world's largest sand is-land and one of Queensland's most popular traveller destinations. 4WD camping tours and whale-watching cruises run out of nearby Hervey Bay.

The Great Barrier Reef begins at Bunda-berg, and divers and snorkellers can get their first glimpse of the reef on Lady Elliot and Heron Islands. Further north is Rock-hampton, Australia's beef capital, and charming Great Keppel Island, with great beaches, good snorkelling and interesting bushwalks. Inland from Rockhampton are several spectacular national parks, includ-ing rugged Blackdown Tableland and the fantastic Carnarvon National Park.

A world away from the sandbar islands of the south, the wonderful Whitsunday Is-lands have dense mountain forests and idyl-lic blue-green waters, with opportunities for sailing, diving, snorkelling and swim-ming. Eungella National Park, inland from Mackay, is one of the best places to see platypuses in the wild.

The next big population centre is Townsville, an unpretentious coastal town with good diving, the excellent Reef HQ aquarium, and several interesting old gold-mining towns just inland. Offshore is popular Magnetic Island. West of Townsville you enter the real outback, with endless wide-open spaces and dusty open roads. Worth crossing the distance for are outback oddities like Birdsville, with its famous horse races, and Mt Isa, with its enormous mine brooding darkly over the town.

On the north coast between Cairns and Townsville, Hinchinbrook Island is a majestic island national park with a 32km walking trail. Between Townsville and Mission Beach are yet more national parks and island getaways.

Far North Queensland is jam-packed with tourist drawcards. Centred around Cairns, this area has it all – the reef and islands, the rainforests, Cape Tribulation and the Daintree, the Atherton Tablelands – and you don't have to travel far inland to sample the outback. On the coast north of Cairns, Port Douglas is one of the state's most fashionable resort towns.

Right at the top of the state is the truly rugged Cape York Peninsula, one of Australia's last great adventure trips. All the roads through the Cape are dirt and there are numerous river crossings that will test even the most committed 4WD driver. The astounding diversity of wildlife in the remote national parks of Lakefield and Iron Range has to be seen to be believed.

The Gulf Savannah, in the north-western corner of Queensland, is also not for the faint-hearted. This hot, tough and sparsely populated region attracts a small but dedicated band of travellers taking the scenic route across to Darwin in the Northern Territory.

## PLANNING
### When to Go
The winter months are Queensland's busiest time for tourism – it's the place the Mexicans (the Queensland term for anyone from south of the border) head to escape the cold southern winters. The main tourist season stretches from April to November, and the official high-season is from June to September. As with elsewhere in the country, the Easter (April), winter (June to July) and Christmas (December to January) breaks

are also considered to be high season. Australian families swarm into the Sunshine State on school holidays and *everything* is booked out.

Queensland doesn't really have what most of us would call a winter. Even in mid-July, when people in the southern states are snuggling up in front of open fires or heading for the ski slopes, you'll find people swimming at Queensland's beaches. June to August is the perfect time to visit – the extreme heat and stifling humidity of summer have been replaced by warm sunny days and refreshingly cool nights.

In the Far North, January to March (December to April in Cape York) is the wet season and the heat and humidity can make life pretty uncomfortable. Once the monsoonal rains of the Wet arrive, most parts of Cape York Peninsula and the Gulf of Carpentaria, and much of the outback, are often inaccessible except by light aircraft. Deadly 'stingers' (box jellyfish) also frequent the waters at this time (see the 'Stingers' boxed text in the Capricorn Coast chapter).

For more specific climate information, see Climate in the Facts about Queensland chapter.

## Maps
The Royal Automobile Club of Queensland (RACQ) publishes a good series of regional road maps that show almost every driveable road in the state – these are free to RACQ members and to members of affiliated motoring organisations. There are also plenty of road maps published by the various oil companies. These are available from service stations.

Queensland's Department of Natural Resources produces the Sunmap series which, together with commercial maps by companies including Hema, Gregory's and UBD, are available from most newsagents and many bookshops in Queensland. World Wide Maps & Guides (☎ 3221 4330), on the corner of George and Adelaide Sts in Brisbane, has one of the best selections of maps in the state.

For bushwalking and other activities that require large-scale maps, the topographic sheets put out by the Australian Surveying & Land Information Group (AUSLIG) are the ones to get. For more information, or a catalogue, contact AUSLIG (☎ 1800 800 173, ℮ auslig@auslig.gov.au, ☒ www.auslig.gov.au) Dunlop Court, Bruce, ACT 2617.

## What to Bring

With its tropical climate and relaxed attitudes, Queensland's unwritten dress code is 'cool and casual'. This may be one of the few places in the world where a shirt, tie and shorts is common business attire. Bring plenty of light summer gear such as shorts and cotton dresses, plus a smarter outfit if you want to get past the bouncers in Queensland's nightclubs! Thongs (flip-flops) or reef sandals (with good grips and velcro straps) are great for the beach, but unwelcome in bars and restaurants; carry a spare pair of shoes or boots that you can use for both walking and going out.

You are unlikely to need anything warmer than a long-sleeved shirt, although if you're visiting southern Queensland or you're there between June and August, it's worth bringing a light jacket or a fleece top for the occasional chilly evening. An umbrella or light-weight raincoat will prove handy for tropical downpours.

You need to be aware of the dangers of UV radiation in Queensland. Australia has the highest incidence of skin cancer in the world, so sunscreen, sunglasses and a hat are the way to go. Swimming or snorkelling without sun protection is a surefire way to get burnt – a rash-top (a skin-tight, lycra surf shirt) is a sensible investment.

Other essentials, like camping gear, insect repellent and travel medicines, are widely available throughout the state.

## TOURIST OFFICES

There are a number of information sources for visitors to Queensland, and you could easily drown yourself in brochures and booklets, maps and leaflets, although it's worth noting that most of the tourist information places are booking agents and will steer you towards the tour paying them the best commission.

## Local Tourist Offices

The main regional tourist associations in Queensland are found in the following cities: Brisbane, Surfers Paradise (see the Gold Coast chapter), Maroochydore (Sunshine Coast), Toowoomba (Darling Downs), Maryborough, Bundaberg (Fraser Coast), Gladstone, Rockhampton (Capricorn Coast), Mackay, Airlie Beach (Whitsundays), Townsville (North Coast), Cairns (Far North Queensland) and Blackall (Outback Queensland). Each has tourist offices where you can get information on businesses that are paid members of the associations; see individual towns for addresses, phone numbers and opening hours.

## Interstate Tourist Offices

The Queensland Tourist & Travel Corporation is the government-run body responsible for promoting Queensland interstate and overseas. Its offices act primarily as promotional and booking offices, not information centres, but are worth contacting when you're planning a trip to Queensland (☎ 13 88 33, ℮ queensland-travel@tq.com.au, ☒ www.tq.com.au). There are Queensland Government Travel Centres in the following places:

**Australian Capital Territory**
   (☎ 02-6200 1900) 25 Garema Place, Canberra 2601
**New South Wales**
   *Sydney*: (☎ 02-9246 7000) 327–329 George St, Sydney 2000
   *Chatswood*: (☎ 02-9200 8888) 376 Victoria Ave, Chatswood 2067
   *Parramatta*: (☎ 02-9865 8400) Shop 2158, Westfield Shoppingtown, Parramatta 2150
   *Miranda*: (☎ 02-9545 8900) Shop 1110, Kingsway, Miranda 2228
   *Newcastle*: (☎ 02-4960 4900) 97 Hunter St, Newcastle 2300
**Queensland**
   (☎ 3874 2800) 243 Edward St, Brisbane 4000
**South Australia**
   (☎ 08-8401 3100) 10 Grenfell St, Adelaide 5000
**Victoria**
   (☎ 03-9206 4500) 257 Collins St, Melbourne 3000
**Western Australia**
   (☎ 08-9464 3000) 777 Hay St, Perth 6000

## Tourist Offices Abroad

**Australian Tourist Commission** The Australian Tourist Commission (ATC) is the government body intended to inform potential visitors about the country and has little contact with visitors once they are inside Australia. The Australian Tourist Commission maintains a good Web site at W www.atc.net.au which can provide information by email and has a listing of worldwide offices.

**Queensland Tourist & Travel Corporation** The Queensland Tourist & Travel Corporation (QTTC) also has its own overseas representatives, so for information specifically about Queensland, contact one of the following offices:

**Europe** (☎ 089-2317 7177) Herzogspitalstrasse 5, 80331 Munich

**Hong Kong** (☎ 2827 4322) Room 2209, 22nd Floor, Harbour Centre, 25 Harbour Rd, Wanchai

**Japan** (☎ 03-3214 4931) Suite 1301, Yurakucho Denki Building North Wing, 7–1 Yurakucho 1 Chome, Chiyoda-ku, Tokyo 100

**New Zealand** (☎ 09-377 9053) 8th Floor, Krukzeiner Building, 17 Albert St, Auckland

**Singapore** (☎ 253 2811) 101 Thompson Rd, No 07 04, United Square, Singapore 307591

**UK** (☎ 0207-240 0525) Queensland House, 392/3 The Strand, London WC2R OLZ

**USA** (☎ 310-697 0207) 3601 Aviation Boulevard, Suite 2200, Manhattan Beach, Los Angeles, CA 90266

## VISAS & DOCUMENTS
### Visas

All visitors to Australia need a visa. Only New Zealand nationals are exempt, and even they receive a 'special category' visa on arrival.

Visa application forms are available from Australian diplomatic missions overseas and travel agents, and you can apply by mail or in person. There are several different types of visas, depending on the reason for your visit.

**Tourist Visas** The most common tourist visa for European, American and Canadian visitors is the Electronic Tourist Authority or ETA, which is usually arranged by your travel agent when you book your ticket. The whole process is electronic – nothing is stamped into your passport – but there'll be a record of the ETA waiting when you arrive at immigration in Australia. The ETA is free if issued by a travel agent and is valid for a year from the date of issue for a maximum stay of three months. If by some chance your agent hasn't provided you with an ETA, you can apply yourself on the Internet at W www.eta.immi.gov.au (there's a $20 fee that must be paid by credit card). You can extend an ETA within Australia for a further three months if you can provide evidence of sufficient funds and a ticket home; the fee is $180. Apply at any Office of Immigration and Multicultural Affairs.

If you aren't covered by the ETA scheme – if you come from Eastern Europe for example – then you'll need a traditional visa stamped into your passport. Tourist visas are issued by Australian consular offices abroad and are generally valid for a stay of either three (short-stay) or six (long-stay) months. There's a $60 fee and the visa is valid for use within 12 months of the date of issue and will usually allow multiple entries of up to three months within that period.

When you apply for a visa, you need to present your passport and a passport photo, as well as signing an undertaking that you have an onward or return ticket and 'sufficient funds' – the latter is obviously open to interpretation.

**Working Holiday Visas** Young, single visitors from the UK, Canada, the Netherlands, Ireland, Japan, Korea, Malta, Germany, Sweden, Denmark and Norway may be eligible for a working holiday visa. 'Young' is fairly loosely interpreted as around 18 to 30.

A working holiday visa allows for a stay of up to 12 months, but you are only supposed to work for one employer for three months, though there's nothing to stop you from working for more than one employer in the 12 months. This visa can only be applied for from outside Australia (preferably but not necessarily in your country of citizenship), and you can't change from a tourist visa to a working holiday visa.

You can apply for a working holiday visa up to 12 months in advance, and it's a good idea to do so as early as possible as there is a limit on the number issued each year. Conditions attached to a working holiday visa include having sufficient funds for a ticket out, and taking out private medical insurance; a fee of $155 is payable when you apply for the visa.

See the Work section later in this chapter for details of what sort of work is available and where.

**Visa Extensions** The maximum stay allowed to visitors to Australia is one year, including visa extensions.

Visa extensions are made through Department of Immigration and Multicultural Affairs offices in Australia and these days are pretty streamlined, though you should apply a few weeks before your visa expires. There

is an application fee of $180 – and even if they turn down your application they can still keep your money. To qualify for an extension you are required to provide evidence of sufficient funds to cover your stay in Australia and have a ticket out of the country.

If you're trying to stay for longer in Australia the books *Temporary to Permanent Resident in Australia* and *Practical Guide to Obtaining Permanent Residence in Australia*, both published by Longman Cheshire, might be useful.

## Medicare Card

Under reciprocal arrangements, residents of the UK, Ireland, New Zealand, the Netherlands, Finland, Sweden, Malta and Italy are entitled to free or subsidised medical treatment under Medicare, Australia's compulsory national health insurance scheme. To enrol you need to show your passport and health care card or certificate from your own country, and you are then given a Medicare card.

Once you have a card you can get free necessary hospital treatment (provided you are not treated as a private patient), and visits to a private doctor's practice are also claimable under Medicare, although you may have to pay the bill first and then claim the money back. Medicare only covers doctors, consultation fees up to a fixed threshold. Clinics that advertise 'bulk billing' are the easiest to use as they charge Medicare direct and you don't have to pay up front.

For more information you can telephone Medicare on ☎ 13 20 11.

## Driving Licence

You can use your own foreign driving licence in Australia, as long as it is in English (if it's not, a translation must be carried). As an International Licence cannot be used alone and must be supported by your home licence, there seems little point in getting one.

## Copies

All important documents (passport data page and visa page, credit cards, travel insurance policy, air/bus/train tickets, driving licence etc) should be photocopied before

---

### Travel Insurance

A travel insurance policy to cover theft, loss and medical problems is a good idea. Some policies offer lower and higher medical-expense options; the higher ones are chiefly for countries such as the USA, which have extremely high medical costs. There is a wide variety of policies available, so check the small print.

Some policies specifically exclude 'dangerous activities', which can include scuba diving, motorcycling, even trekking. A locally acquired motorcycle licence is not valid under some policies.

You may prefer a policy which pays doctors or hospitals directly rather than you having to pay on the spot and claim later. If you have to claim later make sure you keep all documentation. Some policies ask you to call back (reverse charges) to a centre in your home country where an immediate assessment of your problem is made.

Check that the policy covers ambulances or an emergency flight home.

you leave home. Leave one copy with someone at home and keep another with you, separate from the originals.

It's also a good idea to store details of your vital travel documents in Lonely Planet's free online Travel Vault in case you lose the photocopies or can't be bothered with them. Your password-protected Travel Vault is accessible online anywhere in the world create it at **W** www.ekno.lonelyplanet.com.

## EMBASSIES & CONSULATES
### Australian Embassies & Consulates

Australian diplomatic representation overseas includes:

**Canada**
(☎ 613-783 7665, fax 236 0026) Suite 710, 50 O'Connor St, Ottawa, Ontario K1P 6L2

**France**
(☎ 01 40 59 33 06, fax 01 40 59 35 38) 4 Rue Jean Rey, 75724 Cedex 15, Paris

**Germany**
(☎ 30-8800 880, fax 2248 9294) Philip Johnson House, Friedrichstrasse 200, Berlin 10117

**Indonesia**
*Embassy*: (☎ 021-2550 7111, fax 2550 5695) Jalan HR Rasuna Said Kav C15–16, Kuningan, Jakarta Selatan 12940
*Consulate in Denpasar*: (☎ 0361-235 002, fax 231 990) Jalan Prof Moh Yamin 4, Renon, Denpasar, Bali

**Ireland**
(☎ 01-676 1517, fax 661 3576) Fitzwilton House, Wilton Terrace, Dublin 2

**Israel**
(☎ 03-695 0450, fax 691 5223) Beit Europa (4th Floor), 37 Saul Hamelech Boulevarde, Tel Aviv 64928

**Japan**
(☎ 03-5232 4111, fax 5232 4173) 2-1-14 Mita, Minato-ku, Tokyo 108-8361

**Malaysia**
(☎ 03-246 5642, fax 241 4495) 6 Jalan Yap Kwan Seng, Kuala Lumpur 50450

**Netherlands**
(☎ 070-310 8200, fax 310 8241) Carnegielaan 4, The Hague 2517 KH

**New Zealand**
(☎ 09-303 2429, fax 303 2431) Union House, 132–38 Quay St, Auckland

**Papua New Guinea**
(☎ 325 9333, fax 325 3528) Godwit St, Waigani NCD, Port Moresby

**Singapore**
(☎ 836 4100, fax 735 1242) 25 Napier Rd, Singapore 258507

**Thailand**
(☎ 02-287 2680, fax 213 1177) 37 South Sathorn Rd, Bangkok 10120

**UK**
(☎ 0207-379 4334, fax 465 8218) Australia House, The Strand, London WC2B 4LA

**USA**
(☎ 202-797 3000, fax 797 3100) 1601 Massachusetts Ave NW, Washington DC 20036-2273

### Consulates in Queensland

Canberra is home to most foreign embassies, but many countries maintain consulates in Brisbane as well. If you need to apply for a visa for other countries, you will need to send your passport to Canberra by recorded delivery. Diplomatic missions in Brisbane include:

**Denmark** (☎ 3221 8641) 180 Queen St
**France** (☎ 3229 8201) 10 Market St
**Germany** (☎ 3221 7819) 10 Eagle St
**Japan** (☎ 3221 5188) 12 Creek St
**Malaysia** (☎ 3221 1199) 345 Ann St
**Netherlands** (☎ 3839 9644) 25 Mary St
**Papua New Guinea** (☎ 3221 8067) Level 3, 320 Adelaide St
**Thailand** (☎ 3832 1999) 101 Wickham Terrace
**UK** (☎ 3223 3200) Level 26, 1 Eagle St

It's important to realise what your own embassy – the embassy of the country of which you are a citizen – can and can't do to help you if you get into trouble. Generally speaking, it won't be much help in emergencies if the trouble you're in is remotely your own fault. Remember that you are bound by the laws of the country you are in. Your embassy will not be sympathetic if you end up in jail after committing a crime locally, even if such actions are legal in your own country.

In genuine emergencies you might get some assistance, but only if other channels have been exhausted. For example, if you need to get home urgently, a free ticket home is exceedingly unlikely – the embassy would expect you to have insurance. If you have all your money and documents stolen, it might assist with getting a new passport, but a loan for onward travel is out of the question.

Some embassies used to keep letters for travellers or have a small reading room with home newspapers, but these days the mail holding service has usually been stopped and even newspapers tend to be out of date.

## CUSTOMS

When entering Australia you can bring most articles in free of duty provided that customs is satisfied they are for personal use and that you'll be taking them with you when you leave. There's also a duty-free, per-person quota of 1125mL of alcohol, 250 cigarettes and dutiable goods up to the value of $400.

With regard to prohibited goods, there are two areas that need particular attention. Number one is, of course, drugs. Australia has a massive drug problem and customs is extremely serious when it comes to finding contraband. Most international airports employ very well-trained sniffer dogs and if you get caught and convicted, you'll find it very difficult to travel internationally in the future.

Problem two is animal and plant quarantine – see the boxed text 'Bin It or Declare It' for details.

Weapons and firearms are either prohibited or require a permit and safety testing. Other restricted goods include products (such as ivory and turtle-shell) made from protected wildlife species, nonapproved telecommunications devices and live animals.

There are duty-free stores at the international airports and in their associated cities. Treat them with healthy suspicion: 'duty-free' is one of the world's most overworked catch phrases, and it is often just an excuse to sell things at prices you can easily beat by a little shopping around.

## MONEY

### Currency

Australia's currency follows the decimal system of dollars and cents (100 cents to the dollar). The famous plastic banknotes come in denominations of $100 (green), $50 (yellow), $20 (red), $10 (blue) and $5 (pink) notes. While the bills are fairly indestructible, they do sometimes lose their corners. You can exchange incomplete bills at most banks.

Coins come in $2, $1, $0.50, $0.20, $0.10 and $0.05 denominations. Shop prices are still often set in odd cents, but prices are rounded up (or down) to the nearest five cents on your *total* bill, not on individual items.

There are no notable restrictions on importing or exporting currency or travellers cheques except that you can't take out more than $5000 in cash without prior approval.

### Exchange Rates

The Australian dollar fluctuates quite markedly against the US dollar. Approximate exchange rates are as follows:

| country | unit | | A$ |
|---|---|---|---|
| Canada | C$1 | = | $1.24 |
| Euro zone | €1 | = | $1.76 |
| Hong Kong | HK$10 | = | $2.48 |
| Japan | ¥100 | = | $1.60 |
| New Zealand | NZ$1 | = | $0.82 |
| Singapore | S$1 | = | $1.07 |
| UK | £1 | = | $2.81 |
| USA | US$1 | = | $1.94 |

### Bin It or Declare It

When arriving from overseas you'll be asked to declare all goods of animal or vegetable origin – from ham sandwiches and biscuits to wooden spoons and straw hats – which will be examined by an official. The authorities are keen to prevent pests or diseases getting into the country and they are quite prepared to back this up with on-the-spot fines of up to $110. The fines can be heavier for serious smuggling – in one famous case, three undeclared 1kg tins of ham confiscated from a passenger's luggage at Cairns airport earned a $3100 fine.

Our advice is to declare everything. Searches are thorough and officials come down hard on visitors who knowingly make false declarations. There are also amnesty bins, where you can dump anything you don't wish to get caught with. Objects like wooden souvenirs will usually be returned, though they may have to be treated with pesticides.

## Exchanging Money

Changing foreign currency or travellers cheques is no problem at almost any bank. There are also foreign exchange booths at Brisbane and Cairns international airports that are open to meet all arriving flights.

Thomas Cook and Travelex are the largest and most reliable exchange bureaus, and have foreign exchange booths in the city centres of Brisbane, Cairns and some other major cities. These places have more convenient opening hours than the banks, but their rates generally aren't as good and they charge a commission of around $7 for cash or cheques. Higher rates are usually offered for sums over $2000.

**Travellers Cheques** American Express, Thomas Cook and other well-known international brands of travellers cheques are all widely used in Australia. A passport will usually be adequate for identification; it would be sensible to also carry a driver's licence, credit cards or a plane ticket in case of problems.

Commissions and fees for changing foreign currency travellers cheques seem to vary from bank to bank and month to month. It's worth making a few phone calls to see which bank has the lowest charges. Most charge a flat fee for each cash or travellers cheque transaction, which varies from $5 (National Australia Bank) to $10 (Commonwealth Bank). Fees are usually waived if you have an account with that bank.

Major currencies like pounds sterling, US dollars and Swiss francs can be readily exchanged, but you'll be better off if you buy Australian dollar travellers cheques, which can be exchanged immediately at the bank cashier's window without being converted from a foreign currency so you won't incur commissions or fees.

**Credit Cards & ATMs** The most commonly accepted credit cards in Australia are Visa and MasterCard. American Express, and to a lesser extent Diners Club, are also widely accepted. The Australian-only Bankcard is also common, although less so in recent years.

Credit cards are a convenient alternative to carrying cash or large numbers of travellers cheques. With the advent of electronic banking and the proliferation of automated teller machines (ATMs) throughout the country, a credit card, preferably linked to your savings account, is an ideal way to travel. Visa, MasterCard and American Express cards are most commonly accepted in ATMs – most machines will display the symbols of the credit cards that they accept. Cash advances are also available over the counter from all banks.

If you plan to rent cars while travelling around Australia, a credit card makes life much simpler; they're looked upon with much greater favour by rent-a-car agencies than nasty old cash, and many agencies simply won't rent you a vehicle if you don't have a card.

## Bank Accounts

If you're planning to stay longer than just a month or so, it's worth considering other ways of handling money that give you more flexibility and are more economical.

Most travellers opt for an account that includes a cash card, which you can use to access your cash from ATMs all over Australia. Westpac, ANZ, National and Commonwealth bank branches are found nationwide, and in all but the most remote town there'll be at least one place where you can withdraw money from a hole in the wall.

Many businesses, such as service stations, supermarkets and convenience stores, are linked into the Electronic Funds Transfer at Point Of Sale (EFTPOS) system, and here you can use your Aussie cash card or credit card to pay for services or purchases direct, and often withdraw cash as well.

Opening an account at an Australian bank is easy for overseas visitors if they do it within the first six weeks of arrival. After six weeks (and for Australian citizens) it's much more complicated. A points system operates and you need to score a minimum of 100 points: Passports, driver's licences, birth certificates and other 'major' IDs earn you 40 points; minor ones such as credit cards get you 20 points. Just like a game show really!

## Costs

Australia is generally cheaper than the USA, Canada and European countries, particularly when it comes to cost of living. As a general rule, an Australian dollar will usually get you the same amount of goods as a US dollar would in America or a pound would in the UK. An exception is manufactured goods, which are often marked up to cover the cost of import.

Whether you eat out or self-cater, food in Australia is remarkably cheap because of the buoyant agricultural sector. For fruit and veg, you can often save money by buying at farmers markets or roadside 'fruit barns' and farmers stalls. The cheapest places to eat in the cities are the foodcourts in the main shopping malls. In rural towns, the local pub can almost always rustle up cheap counter meals and grills for less than $10.

Accommodation is also very reasonably priced. In virtually every town where backpackers are likely to stay there'll be a backpackers hostel with dorm beds and double rooms. Another good, cheap option are caravan parks, which offer camp sites and on-site vans. Most pubs in country towns also have cheap accommodation and motels supply most of the mid-range accommodation. See Accommodation later in this chapter for prices.

The biggest cost in any trip to Australia is going to be transport, simply because it's such a vast country. Traditionally, buses are cheaper than trains which are cheaper than planes. If there's a group of you, buying a second-hand car is probably the most economical way to go.

## Tipping

In Australia tipping isn't 'compulsory' the way it is in the USA or Europe. A tip is more a recognition of good service than an obligation, and the amount you tip is usually weighted according to how good the service has been. It's only customary to tip in restaurants, and only then if you want to. If you do decide to leave a tip, 5% to 10% of the bill is considered reasonable by the hospitality industry.

## Taxes & Refunds

In July 2000, the Australian government introduced a 10% goods and services tax (GST). Prices in this book are inclusive of GST, unless otherwise noted.

If you purchase new or second-hand goods with a total minimum value of $300 from any one supplier within 28 days of departure from Australia, you will be entitled to a refund of any GST paid. Contact the Australian Taxation Office (ATO) on ☎ 13 63 20 for details.

## POST & COMMUNICATIONS
### Sending Mail

Post offices are open from 9am to 5pm Monday to Friday, but you can often get stamps from local post offices operated from newsagencies or from Australia Post shops, found in large cities, on Saturday morning as well.

Australia's postal services are relatively efficient and reasonably cheap. It costs $0.45 to send a standard letter or postcard within Australia.

Internationally, aerograms cost $0.78 to any country, air-mail postcards cost $1 to any destination. Airmail letters up to 50g cost $1 to New Zealand, Singapore, Malaysia and other Asia/Pacific destinations and $1.50 to the USA, Canada, Europe and the rest of the world.

The rates for posting parcels are extremely good value. By sea mail a 1–2kg parcel costs $17 to $26 to Canada, the USA, Europe or the UK. Economy airmail rates are only a few dollars more expensive, and straight airmail is a few dollars higher again. To Asia and New Zealand airmail is the only option. A 1–2kg parcel sent by 'economy air' costs $10.50 to $18.50 to New Zealand and $14 to $26 to Asia. For sea mail and airmail, there is a maximum of 20kg.

### Receiving Mail

All post offices will hold mail for visitors and some city GPOs have very busy poste restantes, and some even have a digital database that you can search to see if you have mail. You can also have mail sent to you at the American Express offices in big cities if you have an AmEx card or carry AmEx travellers cheques.

## Telephone

The Australian telecommunications industry is deregulated and there are a number of providers offering various services. Private phones are serviced by the telecom giants, Telstra and Optus, but the expanding mobile phone (cellular phone), pay phone (public phone) and phonecard markets support numerous smaller operators such as Vodafone, Unidial, Global One and AAPT. These companies offer cheap rates, but not long-term security – the biggest of these OneTel, recently collapsed leaving thousands of customers in the lurch.

**Pay Phones & Phonecards** There are a number of different cards issued by the various telecommunications companies, and these can be used in any Telstra pay phones that accept cards (virtually all do these days), or from a private phone by di alling a toll-free access number.

Long-distance calls made from pay phones are generally considerably more expensive than calls made from private phones. If you will be using pay phones to make a large number of calls it pays to look into the various cards available from providers other than Telstra. Explanatory leaflets are available from most card outlets – newsagents are the major vendors – detailing the call charges for the various companies.

Some pay phones are set up to take only credit cards, and these too are convenient, although you need to keep an eye on how much the call is costing as it can quickly mount up.

**Local Calls** Local calls from public phones cost $0.40 for an unlimited amount of time. Local calls from private phones cost $0.30. Calls to mobile phones attract higher timed rates.

**Long-Distance Calls & Area Codes** It's also possible to make long-distance (sometimes known as STD – subscriber trunk dialling) calls from virtually any public phone.

Long-distance calls are cheaper in off-peak hours (basically outside normal business hours), and different service providers have different charges.

Australia is divided into just four STD areas – ☎ 07 covers Queensland, ☎ 02 covers New South Wales (NSW) and the Australian Capital Territory (ACT), ☎ 03 covers Victoria and Tasmania and ☎ 08 covers Western Australia (WA), South Australia (SA) and the Northern Territory (NT). You don't need to use the STD code for calls within the same STD area.

**Toll-Free Calls** Many businesses and some government departments operate a toll-free service, so no matter where you are ringing from around the country, it's a free call. These numbers have the prefix 1800 and we've listed them wherever possible throughout this book. Note that these numbers cannot be called from abroad or from certain mobile phones.

Numbers beginning with 13 or 1300 are charged at the rate of a local call and will often route you to the local branch of the company you are calling. Often these numbers are Australia-wide, or may be applicable to a specific state or STD district only. Unfortunately, there's no way of telling without actually ringing the number.

Calls to these services still attract charges if you are calling from a mobile phone.

To make a collect call dial ☎ 1800 REVERSE (ie, ☎ 1800 738 3773). Directory Inquiries is on ☎ 12455 (☎ 1225 for international numbers).

**Mobile Phones** In recent years Australia has gone mobile phone crazy, and pre-paid mobile phone packages are an excellent idea if you're spending a while in the country. The three main mobile operators are the (mostly) government-owned Telstra, and the two private companies Optus and Vodafone. Phone numbers with the prefix 04 are to mobile phones. The caller is charged mobile rates on calls both to and from mobiles.

Starter kits, which include a phone, SIM card and a starter pre-paid call card, begin at around $169 (with $100 of free calls).

Additional charge-up cards are available from most newsagents. You may also be able to use your own GSM-compatible phone by buying a pre-paid start-up kit, which just includes a SIM card and your first pre-paid call card. The flip side of this is that call charges are higher than for contract-based mobile phone packages.

Bear in mind that coverage runs out quite quickly as you head into the outback.

**Emergency** If you need the police, an ambulance or the fire department in an emergency, dial ☎ 000, ask the operator for the service you need and wait to be connected. This is a 24-hour, free call, which can be traced. To contact these services for other matters, check regional phone books for local numbers.

**International Calls** From most pay phones you can also make ISD (International Subscriber Dialling) calls, although calls are generally cheaper if using a provider other than Telstra.

When making overseas calls, the international dialling code varies depending on which provider you are using – 0011 is the Telstra code.

International calls from Australia are among the cheapest you'll find anywhere, and there are often specials that bring the rates down even further. Off-peak times, if available, vary depending on the destination – see the back of any *White Pages* telephone book for more details. Sunday is often the cheapest day to ring.

Country Direct is a service that gives callers in Australia direct access to operators in nearly 65 countries, to make collect or credit card calls. For a full list of the countries hooked into this system, check any local *White Pages* telephone book or call ☎ 1800 801 800.

### Email & Internet Access

If you want to surf the Internet, there are Internet cafes in most major centres. Typical costs for casual use are $4–$10 per hour. Global Gossip is a well-run state-wide chain that offers loyalty reductions and cheap international calls. If you're staying in a hostel, the chances are that Internet access is provided on site, though you may have to wait in line to get online!

## INTERNET RESOURCES

The World Wide Web is a rich resource for travellers. You can research your trip, hunt down bargain air fares, book hotels, check on weather conditions or chat with locals and other travellers about the best places to visit (or avoid!).

There's no better place to start your Web explorations than the Lonely Planet Web site (W www.lonelyplanet.com). Here you'll find succinct summaries on travelling to most places on earth, postcards from other travellers and the Thorn Tree bulletin board, where you can ask questions before you go or dispense advice when you get back. You can also find travel news and updates to many of our most popular guidebooks, and the sub-WWWay section links you to the most useful travel resources elsewhere on the Web.

The QTTC Web site (W www.tq .com.au) has links to various different departments – most useful of these is the Destination Queensland Web site (W www .queensland-holidays.com.au) with exhaustive information about what to see and do in Queensland. Other good sites include the Far North Queensland Web site (W www .tnq.org.au) and the Backpacker Ultimate Guide (BUG) Queensland site (W www .bugaustralia.com/destinations/au-qld.html).

## BOOKS

In almost any bookshop you'll find a section devoted to Australiana, with books on every Australian subject you care to mention. If you want a souvenir, there are plenty of glossy picture books on Queensland and its various regions – the reef, the outback, the islands, the national parks.

Most books are published in different editions by different publishers in different countries. As a result, a book might be a hardcover rarity in one country while it's readily available in paperback in another. Fortunately, bookshops and libraries search by title or author, so your local bookshop or library is best placed to advise you on the availability of any of our recommendations. Apart from bookshops, it's also worth trying the Australian Geographic Society shops in Brisbane and Cairns, and the Environment Protection Agency's Naturally Queensland office in Brisbane (see the Brisbane and Far North Queensland chapters for their addresses).

## Lonely Planet

If you are travelling further afield after exploring Queensland, Lonely Planet's *Australia* is the book to take. For trips into the outback in your own vehicle, it's worth investing in a copy of *Outback Australia*. Covering the reef, the islands, diving and accommodation, *Islands of Australia's Great Barrier Reef* gives greater detail than the book in your hand.

## Guidebooks

The RACQ publishes a comprehensive *Accommodation Guide* to Queensland that lists caravan parks, motels, resorts and hotels, including facilities and prices, and rates them out of five stars. It also lists some (but not many) pubs and hostels, and is available from all RACQ offices.

In conjunction with the QTTC, the RACQ also publishes a series of motoring holiday guides to Queensland. These large-format paperbacks are well produced and feature colour photos, touring maps, suggested excursions and sights and attractions. *The Queensland Experience* by Jan Bowen covers Queensland region by region, offering historical backgrounds, recommendations and personal anecdotes. It could be a handy primer to read before you go – it lacks hard information but is quite descriptive.

There is a cornucopia of books published that deal with the Great Barrier Reef. For divers, the Pisces *Diving & Snorkeling Guide to Australia's Great Barrier Reef* is an excellent guide to all the dives available on the reef.

## Aborigines

*The Australian Aborigines* by Kenneth Maddock is a good cultural summary. Geoffrey Blainey's award-winning *Triumph of the*

*Nomads* chronicles the life of Australia's original inhabitants, convincingly demolishing the myth that the Aborigines were 'primitive' people trapped on a hostile continent.

For a sympathetic historical account of what's happened to the original Australians since whites arrived, read *Aboriginal Australians* by Richard Broome. *Blood on the Wattle* by Bruce Elder is a new title that sets out to do for Aborigines what *Bury My Heart at Wounded Knee* did for native Americans.

*My Place*, Sally Morgan's prize-winning autobiography, traces her discovery of her Aboriginal heritage. *Don't Take Your Love to Town* by Ruby Langford and *My People* by Oodgeroo Noonuccal (Kath Walker) are also recommended reading for people interested in Aborigines' experiences. For a practical guide to experiencing Aboriginal culture, see Lonely Planet's *Aboriginal Australia & the Torres Strait Islands*.

## Australian History

For a good introduction to Australian history, read *A Short History of Australia*, a most accessible and informative general history by the late Manning Clark, the much-loved Aussie historian (it only runs up to 1984 though!). Robert Hughes' bestselling *The Fatal Shore* is a colourful and detailed account of the history of transportation of convicts. Geoffrey Blainey's *The Tyranny of Distance* is a captivating narrative of white settlement.

*Cooper's Creek*, by Alan Moorehead, is a classic account of the ill-fated Burke and Wills expedition that dramatises the horrors and hardships faced by the early explorers.

Henry Reynolds' challenging *Why Weren't We Told?* explores the whitewashing of Australia's troubled early history in the popular consciousness. His *The Other Side of the Frontier* uses historical records to present the arrival and takeover of Australia by Europeans from an Aboriginal view.

## Queensland History

If you're specifically interested in the history of Queensland, Ross Fitzgerald's *A History of Queensland* is a comprehensive, well-researched and sometimes controversial study. Published in two volumes – *From the Dreaming to 1915: A History of Queensland*, and *A History of Queensland: From 1915 to the 1980s* – it is found in many second-hand bookshops and most Australian libraries.

*River of Gold*, by Hector Holthouse, is a 'factional' account of the wild days of Cooktown and the Palmer River gold rush in the 1870s. Holthouse has used a little artistic licence to fill in the gaps in his research, but the result is a fascinating read and gives an impressive insight into the period.

Glenville Pike is a local writer who has produced more than 20 books based on Queensland's colourful history; most are out of print, but you can find them in second-hand bookshops.

For an insight into the decline and fall of Queensland's National Party, pick up a copy of maverick journalist Hugh Lunn's biography of notorious Queensland premier *Johannes Bjelke-Petersen*.

For something a bit lighter, Bill Bryson applies his trademark mix of humour and history to Brisbane, Cairns and the Gold Coast in *Down Under*. See Literature in the Facts About Queensland chapter for examples of classic and contemporary Queensland works.

## NEWSPAPERS & MAGAZINES

The *Courier-Mail*, Brisbane's major daily newspaper, is available almost everywhere in Queensland. It's a reasonably serious but somewhat parochial broadsheet.

*The Australian*, a Rupert Murdoch-owned paper and the country's only national daily, is also widely available, though it's ultra-conservative and its comment section is almost tabloid. That said, it's the best place to go for country-wide and international news coverage.

The *Sunday Mail* is a bulky broadsheet that's a little short on content, but has a good listings mag. The *Weekend Australian* comes out on Saturday and includes several excellent review sections (Australia really has no Sunday paper tradition).

Many of the larger towns and cities produce their own papers, some daily and some weekly. Major regional dailies include the *Cairns Post*, the *Townsville Bulletin* and the *Gold Coast Bulletin*.

Weekly magazines include an Australian edition of *Time*, and the *Bulletin*, a conservative and long-running Australian news magazine that includes a condensed version of *Newsweek*. International weekly papers are available from larger newsagencies, particularly in the more heavily touristed areas.

## RADIO & TV
### Radio

Australian Broadcasting Corporation (ABC) radio and TV are government-funded, commercial-free and cover most of the country. Radio National can be picked up almost everywhere on AM or FM, while regional/metropolitan services are usually available only around major centres. Fine Music is the ABC's classical music station, and Triple J is its national youth and rock network, which specialises in alternative music and features tons of Aussie bands.

Brisbane has more than 15 AM and FM radio stations, and along the coast you'll usually be able to pick up ABC stations, a local commercial station or two and often a local public station with news of local events and activities. Once you hit the interior, you'll have to make do with non-stop adverts for small businesses on the local FM station or golden hits of country music.

### TV

There are five main TV networks in Queensland: the ABC, the multicultural and multilingual SBS (Special Broadcasting Service, UHF) and the three commercial networks, channels 7, 9 and 10. All of these can be received in Brisbane. Most regional areas receive the ABC and at least one commercial network, but in the more remote areas you might only be able to pick up the ABC. SBS is only available in Brisbane, the Gold and Sunshine Coasts, the Darling Downs, Townsville, Cairns, Mt Isa and Longreach.

The ABC shows some quality current affairs shows and documentaries, among the Aussie dramas of the other stations, and a good selection of educational children's programs during the day. For something a bit more high-brow, SBS has an interesting selection of international and multilingual programs.

The commercial networks all have fairly similar programming formats, with the usual diet of news and current affairs, sport, soap operas and sitcoms, and an overdose of American talk shows during the day.

## VIDEO SYSTEMS

Australia uses the PAL system, and so pre-recorded videos purchased in Australia may be incompatible with overseas systems. DVDs are widely available and are probably the way to go.

## PHOTOGRAPHY & VIDEO

There are plenty of camera shops in all the big cities and standards of camera service are high. Australian film prices are not too far out of line with those of the rest of the Western world. A 36-exposure Kodak or Fuji film costs around $8 for 100 ASA and $9 for 400 ASA. Slide film is widely available in larger towns, but is rare in the interior; stock up before you head inland. Remember that slide film is particularly vulnerable to heat damage. Kodak Elite II is the most widely available film and costs around $12 for a 36-exposure, 100-ASA roll. Developing standards are also high, with many places offering one-hour developing of print film; prices range from $10 to $13.

Video cassettes are widely available at camera and electronics stores.

For the best results, try to take most of your photos early in the morning and late in the afternoon when the light is softer. A polarising filter will help eliminate the glare if you're taking shots of the Barrier Reef or other water locations. Remember that heat, dust and humidity can all damage film; keep film dry and cool and process films promptly to guarantee results. For more information, see Lonely Planet's *Travel Photography: A Guide To Taking Better Pictures* by Richard I'Anson.

Cheap disposable underwater cameras are widely available at most beach towns and resorts. These are OK for snapshots when snorkelling or shallow diving and can produce reasonable results in good conditions, but without a flash the colours will be washed out. These cameras won't work below about 5m because of the water pressure. If you're serious about underwater photography, good underwater cameras with flash unit can be hired from many of the dive shops along the coast.

As in any country, politeness goes a long way when taking photographs; ask before taking pictures of people. Aborigines generally do not like to have their photographs taken, even from a distance.

## TIME

Australia is divided into three time zones. Queensland is on Eastern Standard Time (as are NSW, Victoria and Tasmania), which is 10 hours ahead of UTC (Greenwich Mean Time).

The other time zones in Australia are Central Standard Time (NT, SA), which is half an hour behind Eastern Standard Time; and Western Standard Time (WA), which is two hours behind Eastern Standard Time.

At noon in Queensland it's 2am in London, 3am in Rome, 9am in Bangkok, 2pm in Auckland, 6pm the previous day in Los Angeles and 9pm the previous day in New York.

Lamentably, Queensland is on Eastern Standard Time all year, while most of the rest of Australia sensibly switches to daylight-saving time over the summer months. From roughly October through March, Queensland is one hour behind NSW, Victoria and Tasmania.

## ELECTRICITY

Voltage is 220–240V and the plugs are of the Australian three-pin type, which is not the same as British three-pin plugs. Adaptors for British and other plugs can be found in good hardware shops, chemists and travel agents.

## WEIGHTS & MEASURES

Petrol and milk are sold by the litre, apples and potatoes by the kilogram, distance is measured by the metre or kilometre, and speed limits are in kilometres per hour (km/h). Nevertheless, many people still refer to the old imperial units, especially older folks and people from country areas. For those who need help with metric there's a conversion table at the back of this book.

## HEALTH

Australia is a remarkably healthy country considering that such a large portion of it lies in the tropics. Tropical diseases such as malaria and yellow fever are as yet unknown, although periodic outbreaks of two mosquito-borne diseases, dengue and Ross River fevers, are occurring more frequently due to temperature rises associated with global warming. Diseases of insanitation such as cholera and typhoid are unheard of, and even some animal diseases such as rabies and foot-and-mouth disease have yet to be recorded.

Travel health depends on your predeparture preparations, your daily health care while travelling and how you handle any medical problem that does develop. Few travellers experience anything more than an upset stomach.

### Predeparture Planning

No immunisations are required for entry to Australia and there are few serious diseases. You should still make sure you have adequate health insurance though – see the 'Travel Insurance' boxed text under Visas & Documents earlier in this chapter.

### Environmental Hazards

**Heat Exhaustion** Dehydration and salt deficiency can cause heat exhaustion. Take time to acclimatise to high temperatures, drink sufficient liquids and do not do anything too physically demanding. Salt deficiency is characterised by fatigue, lethargy, headaches, giddiness and muscle cramps; salt tablets may help, but adding extra salt to your food is better.

**Heat Stroke** This serious, occasionally fatal condition can occur if the body's heat-regulating mechanism breaks down and the body temperature rises to dangerous levels. Long, continuous periods of exposure to high temperatures and insufficient fluids can leave you vulnerable to heat stroke.

The symptoms are feeling unwell, not sweating very much (or at all) and a high body temperature (39°C to 41°C or 102°F to 106°F). Where sweating has ceased the skin becomes flushed and red. Severe, throbbing headaches and lack of coordination will also occur, and the sufferer may be confused or aggressive. Eventually the victim will become delirious or convulse. Hospitalisation is essential, but in the interim get victims out of the sun, remove their clothing, cover them with a wet sheet or towel and then fan continually. Give fluids if they are conscious.

**Jet Lag** Australia is a long-haul flight away from anywhere, so jet lag is likely to be a problem that affects most travellers to a varying degree. If you travel by air across more than three time zones (in other words a three-hour time difference), many functions of the human body (such as temperature, pulse rate and emptying of the bladder and bowels) are knocked off their normal 24-hour cycles, leading to fatigue, disorientation, insomnia, anxiety, impaired concentration and loss of appetite. These effects will usually be gone within three days of arrival, but to minimise the impact of jet lag:

- Rest for a couple of days prior to departure.
- Try to select flight schedules that minimise sleep deprivation; arriving late in the day means you can go to sleep soon after you arrive. For very long flights, try to organise a stopover.
- Avoid excessive eating (which bloats the stomach) and alcohol (which causes dehydration) during the flight. Instead, drink plenty of non-carbonated, nonalcoholic drinks such as fruit juice or water.
- Avoid smoking.
- Make yourself comfortable by wearing loose-fitting clothes and perhaps bringing an eye mask and ear plugs to help you sleep.
- Try to sleep at the appropriate time for the time zone you are travelling to.

**Motion Sickness** Eating lightly before and during a trip will reduce the chances of motion sickness. If you are prone to motion sickness try to find a place that minimises movement – near the wing on aircraft, close

## Everyday Health

Normal body temperature is up to 37°C (98.6°F); more than 2°C (4°F) higher indicates a high fever. The normal adult pulse rate is 60 to 100 per minute (children 80 to 100, babies 100 to 140). As a general rule the pulse increases about 20 beats per minute for each 1°C (2°F) rise in fever.

Respiration (breathing) rate is also an indicator of illness. Count the number of breaths per minute: Between 12 and 20 is normal for adults and older children (up to 30 for younger children, 40 for babies). People with a high fever or serious respiratory illness breathe more quickly than normal. More than 40 shallow breaths a minute may indicate pneumonia.

to midships on boats, near the centre on buses. Fresh air usually helps; reading and cigarette smoke don't. Commercial motion-sickness preparations, which can cause drowsiness, have to be taken before the trip commences. Ginger (available in capsule form) and peppermint (including mint-flavoured sweets) are natural preventatives.

**Prickly Heat** Prickly heat is an itchy rash caused by excessive perspiration trapped under the skin. It usually strikes people who have just arrived in a hot climate. Keeping cool, bathing often, drying the skin and using a mild talcum or prickly heat powder, or resorting to air-conditioning may help.

**Sunburn** In the tropics or the outback you can get sunburnt surprisingly quickly, even through cloud. Australians are very aware of the dangers of skin cancer and the old caution, 'slip, slap, slop', always applies: Slip on a shirt, slap on a hat and slop on some sunscreen. The nose and lips are particularly vulnerable. Calamine lotion or Stingose are good for mild sunburn. Aloe vera treatments can provide some relief from more serious burns. Protect your eyes with good-quality sunglasses, particularly if you will be near water and sand.

## Infectious Diseases

**Diarrhoea** Diarrhoea is unlikely to be a major problem when travelling in Queensland. Two potential causes of diarrhoea are drinking mineralised bore water and stopping or camping at places that have been frequented by travellers with a poor understanding of hygiene.

It's always a good idea to carry plenty of safe drinking water in the car, particularly if you have small children in tow – adults can usually cope better with changes in water.

**Fungal Infections** Fungal infections occur more commonly in hot weather and are usually found on the scalp, between the toes or fingers, in the groin and on the body (ringworm). You get ringworm (which is a fungal infection, not a worm) from infected animals or other people. Moisture encourages these infections.

To prevent fungal infections wear loose, comfortable clothes, avoid artificial fibres, wash frequently and dry carefully. If you do get an infection, wash the infected area at least daily with a disinfectant or medicated soap and water, and rinse and dry well. Apply an antifungal cream or powder like tolnaftate (Tinaderm). Try to expose the infected area to air or sunlight as much as possible and wash all towels and underwear in hot water, change them often and let them dry in the sun.

**HIV & AIDS** HIV, the Human Immunodeficiency Virus, develops into AIDS, Acquired Immune Deficiency Syndrome, which is a fatal disease. Any exposure to blood, blood products or body fluids may put you at risk. The disease is often transmitted through sexual contact or dirty needles – vaccinations, acupuncture, tattooing and body piercing can be potentially as dangerous as intravenous drug use. HIV/AIDS can also be spread through infected blood transfusions, although all blood in Australia is screened.

**Worms** Worms are most common in outback animals. Meat bought from a butcher will be fine, but kangaroo or goat that has not been checked by the proper authorities can be suspect, especially if undercooked.

**Sexually Transmitted Infections** Gonorrhoea, herpes and syphilis are all sexually transmitted infections; sores, blisters or rashes around the genitals, discharges or pain when urinating are common symptoms. In some STIs, such as wart virus or chlamydia, symptoms may be less marked or not observed at all especially in women. Syphilis symptoms eventually disappear completely but the disease continues and can cause severe problems in later years.

While abstinence from sexual contact is the only 100% effective prevention, using condoms is also effective. Gonorrhoea and syphilis are treated with antibiotics. Different sexually transmitted infections require specific antibiotics. There is no cure for herpes or AIDS.

**Tetanus** Tetanus occurs when a wound becomes infected by bacteria that live in soil and in the faeces of horses and other animals. The germ enters the body via breaks in the skin. All wounds should be cleaned promptly and adequately and an antiseptic cream or solution applied. Use antibiotics if the wound becomes hot, throbs or pus is seen. The first symptom may be discomfort in swallowing, or stiffening of the jaw and neck; this is followed by painful convulsions of the jaw and whole body. The disease can be fatal, but poses only a small risk to the traveller.

### Insect-Borne Diseases

Dengue and Ross River fevers are two serious diseases, transmitted by mosquitoes, that can be contracted in Queensland, particularly in Cape York and the Gulf of Carpentaria. Neither is normally fatal, but both can be debilitating. There are no vaccines against dengue and Ross River fevers, the best protection is to avoid being bitten. In areas where mosquitoes are common, remember to cover up and/or wear repellent.

**Ross River Fever** Properly known as epidemic polyarthritis, Ross River fever occurs throughout Australia but mostly in the east. Outbreaks are most likely to occur in January and February, but the risk of infection is very low. Ross River fever is characterised by marked joint pains and muscle aches. Joints of extremities (hands and feet) are most commonly affected, but back pains are also common. Loss of appetite, headache, fever and tiredness may also occur. These symptoms are usually accompanied by a rash on the trunk and limbs. The time from the mosquito bite to the development of the illness is anywhere between three and 21 days, but generally the illness takes hold between seven and nine days.

Conventional wisdom has it that the symptoms do not last more than a few months, although there are now serious doubts about this: some people still feel the effects (mainly chronic fatigue) years after contracting the disease.

**Dengue Fever** Small outbreaks of this viral disease have been reported from Far North Queensland, although there is a small risk to travellers. The *Aedes aegypti* mosquito, which transmits the dengue virus, is most active during the day, unlike the malaria mosquito, and is found mainly in urban areas.

Signs and symptoms of dengue fever include a sudden onset of high fever, headache, joint and muscle pains (hence its old name, 'breakbone fever') and nausea and vomiting. A rash of small red spots appears three to four days after the onset of fever. Dengue is usually self-limiting and runs its course within a week or so, but there is no specific treatment for the disease. Paracetamol can be taken to control fever and patients should drink plenty of water. Aspirin should be avoided, as it increases the risk of developing the far more serious haemorrhagic form of the disease. Recovery may be prolonged, with tiredness lasting for several weeks.

Dengue is commonly mistaken for other infectious diseases, including influenza, but infection can be diagnosed by a blood test.

### Cuts, Bites & Stings

Wash well and treat any cut with an antiseptic such as povidone-iodine. Where possible, avoid bandages and Band-Aids, which can keep wounds wet. Bee and wasp stings are usually painful rather than dangerous. However, in people who are allergic to them, severe breathing difficulties may occur and require urgent medical care. See Dangers & Annoyances later in this chapter for information on spiders, snakes and other dangerous wildlife, as well as what to do about coral cuts.

## Women's Health

Sexually transmitted infections are a major cause of vaginal problems. Symptoms include a smelly discharge, painful intercourse and sometimes a burning sensation when urinating. Medical attention should be sought for the infections; male sexual partners must also be treated. Remember, in addition to these infections, HIV or hepatitis B may also be acquired during exposure. After abstinence, the next best thing is to practise safe sex using condoms.

Antibiotic use, synthetic underwear, sweating and contraceptive pills can lead to fungal vaginal infections when travelling in hot climates. Good personal hygiene, and wearing loose-fitting clothes and cotton underwear will help prevent these infections.

Fungal infections, characterised by a rash, itch and discharge, can be treated with a vinegar or lemon-juice douche, or with yoghurt. Nystatin, miconazole or clotrimazole pessaries or vaginal cream are the usual treatment.

## WOMEN TRAVELLERS

Queensland is generally a safe place for women travellers, although it's probably best to avoid walking alone late at night in any of the major cities. Sexual harassment is rare, although the Aussie male culture does have its sexist elements. Don't tolerate any harassment or discrimination. Some women have reported problems at party hostels on the Gold Coast. With intoxicated men stumbling up from the bar, rural pub rooms are probably best avoided.

Female hitchhikers should exercise care at all times. See the section on Hitching in the Getting Around chapter.

## GAY & LESBIAN TRAVELLERS

Historically, Queensland has a poor reputation when it comes to acceptance of gays and lesbians. Homosexuality was only decriminalised in Queensland in 1991, after the fall of the right-wing National Party government.

Brisbane has an increasingly lively gay and lesbian scene centred on the inner-city suburbs of Spring Hill and Fortitude Valley, with quite a few nightclubs, pubs and a couple of guesthouses. See the Brisbane chapter for more information on gay and lesbian culture there. There are also gay- and lesbian-only accommodation places in some of the more popular tourist centres including Brisbane, Cairns and the Gold Coast. Elsewhere in Queensland, however, there's still a strong streak of homophobia and violence against homosexuals is a risk, particularly in rural communities.

Publications such as Brisbane's *Q News* magazine list contact points, accommodation places and other gay and lesbian groups throughout Queensland. They are on the Web at W www.qnews.com.au.

The Gay and Lesbian Welfare Association of Brisbane (on the Web at W www.glwa.org.au) has information about the organisation and some listings of venues, groups and events.

## SENIOR TRAVELLERS

Queensland is a popular retirement destination for Australian seniors and things are generally well set up for senior travellers. Sadly, the generous discounts on rail services (up to 50%) only apply to Queensland residents. Overseas pensioners are entitled to discounts of at least 10% on most express bus fares and bus passes with McCafferty's/Greyhound. Queensland's caravan parks are popular with retired couples touring Australia, so a hire-campervan is a great way to meet people with similar interests.

## DISABLED TRAVELLERS
### Organisations

There are number of organisations that can supply information for disabled travellers visiting Queensland.

NICAN (National Information Communications Awareness Network; ☎ 02-6285 3713, 1800 806 769, PO Box 407, Curtin ACT 2605) has fact sheets on accessible accommodation and recreation facilities.

ACROD (☎ 3366 4366) offers similar services and has its Queensland office at 240 Waterworks Rd, Ashgrove.

The Disability Services Queensland in Brisbane offers telephone information and referral services (☎ 3224 8031, 1800 177 120). Their Disability Information and Awareness Line (DIAL; ☎ 3224 8444, TTY 3224 8021) provides advice and referrals. The Paraplegic and Quadriplegic Association in Brisbane (☎ 3391 2044), corner of O'Connel St and Shafton Ave, is another useful resource.

Queensland Tourism has an Accessible Tourism Web site (W www.tq.webcentral .com.au/accessqld).

## Getting Around

The Brisbane City Council's Disability Access and Services section(☎ 3403 6795), GPO Box 1434, Brisbane, Qld 4001, has an excellent *Access Brisbane* brochure, with information about buildings, services, restaurants, hotels etc. It also produces a *Mobility Map* of the city centre, showing an accessible route, parking and toilets. Queensland Railways (QR), at 305 Edward St in the city, offers disabled assistance on both long haul (☎ 3235 2222) and CityTrain (☎ 3235 5555) services. The *Citytrain Accessibility Guide*, available from the QR offices at Central and Roma St stations, has a list of other disabled accessible stations.

In Cairns, Disability Services Queensland (☎ 4039 8370), 36 Shields St, is a good source of information.

The international wheelchair symbol for parking in allocated bays is generally recognised in Queensland. Car stickers are available from local councils.

Avis and Hertz offer hire cars with hand controls at no extra charge, which can be picked up at major airports; give 24 hours notice. Most taxi companies in the major cities and towns have modified vehicles that take wheelchairs. In Brisbane, try Black & White Taxis (☎ 13 10 08) or Yellow Cabs

(☎ 13 19 24). In Cairns, Black & White Taxis (☎ 13 10 08) has vans with hydraulic lift access at the rear, and a stretch cab.

## Accommodation

Accommodation in Queensland is generally good, and most of the newer places must now include facilities for people with disabilities. Contact tourist information centres for lists of accessible accommodation – see Tourist Offices earlier in this chapter.

The RACQ's *Accommodation Guide* to Queensland includes symbols indicating accommodation that is 'independently accessible' or 'accessible with assistance', but always check with the proprietors to ensure that facilities will be suitable.

A number of YHA hostels have accessible accommodation; contact the YHA Membership and Travel Centre (☎ 3236 1680), at 154 Roma St, Brisbane.

## Attractions & Activities

Movie World, Sea World and Currumbin Sanctuary, on the Gold Coast, encourage disabled visitors and many tour operators can cater for people with disabilities. In Cairns, for example, Great Adventures encourages disabled people to join their trips out to the Barrier Reef by offering a discount to the wheelchair traveller's companion, and they'll take you snorkelling to see the coral. The Kuranda Scenic Railway can accommodate wheelchair passengers, and some of the tour operators to the rainforest areas of the Daintree and Cape Tribulation will take you in their vehicles, although they are not specifically accessible vehicles. Whale watching in Hervey Bay is a hugely popular activity and many boats have disabled access – see Hervey Bay in the Fraser Coast chapter for more information.

Sporting Wheelies has offices throughout Queensland, with information on accessible diving trips, sporting and recreation facilities. Contact their Brisbane office at 60 Edmondstone Rd, Bowen Hills (☎ 3253 3333).

## TRAVEL WITH CHILDREN

Travelling with children presents few unforeseen problems. The Barrier Reef is one of Australia's top family holiday spots so it comes as no surprise that kids are well catered for at most of the bigger places there. This is usually in the form of a Kids Club or something similar, where the children are supervised and distracted for the greater part of the day, leaving the parents free to kick back on the beach or go diving. Most of these services are free, and are generally available between about 8am and 6pm, although this does of course vary from island to island.

During the evening the larger resorts can also arrange for babysitters, and this costs around $15 per hour for one or two children. Most tours and attractions offer discount children's rates and cheap family packages if you ask.

At the other end of the scale are resorts that are resolutely child-free zones. These resorts include Bedarra and Lizard islands, while at Orpheus Island children are 'not catered for', which basically means children are charged full price and there are no special activities.

## USEFUL ORGANISATIONS
## RACQ

The RACQ is the Queensland motoring association – it produces a particularly useful set of regional maps to Queensland, which are free to members. Its offices also sell a wide range of travel and driving products, including good maps and travel guidebooks; book tours and accommodation; and advise on weather and road conditions. The RACQ can also arrange additional motor insurance on top of your compulsory third-party personal liability cover.

The RACQ's head office (☎ 3361 2444) is in Brisbane at 300 St Pauls Terrace in Fortitude Valley (although their office beside the Brisbane GPO in Queen St may be more convenient). There are other offices all around the state and almost every town has a garage affiliated with the RACQ – see the information sections of the individual towns for details on these.

## Environment Protection Agency

The Environment Protection Agency (EPA) is an efficient and well-run organisation

responsible for the management of Queensland's national parks. It maintains information offices and rangers stations throughout the state, and all provide good advice and information about its respective parks. See the National Parks section in the Facts about Queensland chapter for details.

## Australian Trust for Conservation Volunteers

The Australian Trust for Conservation Volunteers (ATCV) is a nonpolitical, nonprofit group that organises practical conservation projects (such as tree planting, track construction and flora and fauna surveys) for volunteers and is an excellent way to get involved with the conservation movement and, at the same time, visit some of the more interesting areas of the country.

Most projects are either for a weekend or a week and all food, transport and accommodation are supplied in return for a small contribution to help cover costs. Most travellers who take part in ATCV join a Conservation Experience Package, which lasts six weeks and includes several different projects. The cost is $966, and further weeks can be added for $161.

Contact the head office (☎ 03-5333 1483, ⓔ info@conservationvolunteers.com.au, ⓦ www.conservationvolunteers.com.au) at PO Box 423, Ballarat, Victoria 3350, or the Queensland office (☎ 3846 0893) at 41 Tribune St on the South Bank.

## Willing Workers on Organic Farms

Willing Workers on Organic Farms (WWOOF) is a relatively new organisation in Australia, although it is well established in other countries. The idea is that you do a few hours' work each day on a farm (usually, though not always, organic) in return for bed and board. Some places have a minimum stay of a couple of days but many will take you for just a night. Some will let you stay for months if they like the look of you, and you can get involved with some interesting large-scale projects. There are about 200 WWOOF associates in Australia, mostly in Victoria, New South Wales and Queensland.

To join WWOOF send $45 to WWOOF, care of the Post Office, Buchan, Victoria 3885 (☎ 03-5155 0218) or pay online at **W** www.wwoof.com.au, and they'll send you a membership number and a booklet that lists WWOOF places all over Australia.

Alternatively, try the following agents:

**Brisbane** Banana-Benders Backpackers
(☎ 3367 1157) 118 Petrie Terrace
**Cairns** Backpackers World
(☎ 4041 0999) 12 Shields St

## National Trust

The National Trust is dedicated to preserving historic buildings in all parts of Australia. The Trust actually owns a number of buildings throughout the country that are open to the public. Many other buildings are 'classified' by the National Trust to ensure their preservation.

The National Trust also produces some excellent literature, including a fine series of walking-tour guides to Brisbane and some of Queensland's more historic towns, which are available from many tourist offices. The National Trust's Brisbane office (☎ 3229 1788) is at Old Government House (in the grounds of the QUT) in George St.

## DANGERS & ANNOYANCES
### Theft

Queensland is a relatively safe place to visit, but it's better to play it safe and take reasonable precautions.

The Gold Coast is notorious for car crime, and more than a few travellers have lost all their belongings from locked vehicles in public car-parks. The golden rule is to never leave valuables in your vehicle. An $8 steering-wheel lock for your steering wheel is also a worthwhile investment.

Cairns also has a reputation for theft from hostels. Other hostel residents are often the culprits, so it's worth putting valuables like wallets and cameras in the safe storage provided by the hostel owners, or keeping it on your person when you sleep.

Most accommodation places have somewhere they can store your valuables, and you won't regret taking advantage of this service. It should go without saying, but don't leave hotel rooms unlocked.

If you are unlucky enough to have something stolen, immediately report all details to the nearest police station. If your credit cards, cash card or travellers cheques have been taken, notify your bank or the relevant company immediately.

## Racism

Many Queenslanders are vocal in their negative opinions of Indigenous Australians, and nonwhite travellers may find themselves targeted for the same kind of racial abuse. Mostly it's low-level stuff, but travellers have reported threats of violence in some areas; if you feel threatened in a rural pub, walk away and spend your tourist dollars somewhere more deserving.

## Swimming

Aside from the obvious – ie, don't swim after drinking alcohol or immediately after eating – there are a few special conditions in Australia to watch out for.

**Surf Beaches** There are surf beaches all along the coast of southern Queensland as far north as Fraser Island and many are patrolled by Surf Life Saving clubs. If possible, always swim between the flags – see the boxed text 'Swim Between the Flags' for more information. If you get into trouble in the water, raise one arm above your head to catch the attention of the life-savers.

If you happen to get caught in a rip (strong current) and are being taken out to sea, the first (and hardest) thing to do is not panic. Raise your arm until you have been spotted, and then swim parallel to the shore – *don't* try to swim back against the rip, you'll only tire yourself.

**Sharks** Shark attacks are extremely rare in Australia, especially in the warm, shallow waters inshore of the Great Barrier Reef. The closest you're likely to come to a shark is in the local fish and chip shop, unless you're scuba diving, and even then, you'll be lucky to see anything more substantial than a harmless black-tipped reef shark.

## Swim Between the Flags

Drownings and swimming-related accidents have been hugely reduced by Queensland's beach patrol program. Patrolled beaches are indicated by a red and yellow flag, one at each end of the patrolled area. Swimming conditions are indicated by single flags:

- Green flag: Safe to swim
- Yellow flag: Dangerous conditions
- Red flag: Do not enter the water

Swimming and surfing outside of these areas is at your own risk. Blue signs around a swimming beach indicate that surfers are using the water beyond the red and yellow flags. In addition, there's a sound you should listen out for, though it almost never sounds, the claxon for a shark in the water.

Further south, where you'll also find the best surf beaches, there is no protective reef and the deep water provides a home to big predatory species such as tiger, hammerhead and whaler sharks. Attacks are still extremely rare, but a number of swimmers and surfers have been bitten over the years, particularly on the Gold Coast and around Fraser Island. Any danger there is will be dramatically reduced if you follow a few simple rules:

- Only swim or surf in areas patrolled by lifeguards.
- Never swim or surf alone.
- Avoid swimming near river mouths.
- Don't swim immediately after rain.

In the incredibly unlikely event that you are bitten, the conventional wisdom is to hit the shark on the nose or in the gills, though it's questionable how well you'll remember that in the event of an attack!

**Crocodiles** In north Queensland, saltwater crocodiles can be a real danger and have killed a number of people (travellers and locals). They are found in river estuaries and large rivers, sometimes a long way inland, so before diving into that inviting, cool water, find out from the locals whether it's croc-free. See Reptiles & Frogs in the Fauna section of the Facts about Queensland chapter for more details.

**Coral Cuts** Coral can be extremely sharp, and you can cut yourself by merely brushing against the stuff. Even a small cut can be very painful, and coral cuts are notoriously slow to heal. If they are not adequately cleaned, small pieces of coral can become embedded in the wound, resulting in serious infections. The best solution is not to get cut in the first place – avoid touching coral. Wash any coral cuts thoroughly and douse them with a good antiseptic.

**Fish Poisoning** Ciguatera poison is a poison that seems to accumulate in certain types of fish due to the consumption of certain types of algae by grazing fish. The poison accumulates up the food chain so it isn't the original algae-eating fish which poses the danger, it's the fish which eats the fish which eats the algae-eating fish! The danger is remote but unpredictable and recovery, although usually complete, is very slow. Chinaman fish, red bass, large rock cods and moray eels have all been implicated. Another fishy no-no is pufferfish which contains a fast-acting, fatal neurotoxin.

**Other Marine Dangers** Between November and April, lethal box jellyfish (aka 'stingers') occur in inshore waters north of Rockhampton and the sea should be avoided at these times. For more information on box jellyfish, see the 'Stingers' boxed text in the Capricorn Coast chapter.

There are quite a few other potential hazards lurking in the waters of the Barrier Reef, which require a little care on the part of beachcombers, swimmers and divers.

Butterfly cod, scorpion fish and stonefish all have a series of poisonous spines down their back. These can inflict a serious wound and cause incredible pain. Blue-ringed octopuses and Barrier Reef cone shells can also be fatal, so don't pick them up. If someone is stung, apply a pressure bandage, monitor breathing carefully and conduct mouth-to-mouth resuscitation if breathing stops.

Also watch out for stingrays, which can inflict a nasty wound with their barbed tails, and sea snakes, which are potentially deadly, although they are more curious than aggressive.

### Snakes

The best-known danger in the Australian outback, and the one that captures visitors' imaginations, is snakes, but in fact only a very few of Queensland's venomous snakes are aggressive. Unless you have the bad fortune to stand on one it's unlikely that you'll be bitten. Taipans and tiger snakes, however, will attack if alarmed.

To minimise your chances of being bitten always wear boots, socks and long trousers when walking through undergrowth where snakes may be present. Don't put your hands into holes and crevices, and be careful when collecting firewood.

Snake bites do not cause instantaneous death and antivenins are usually available. Keep the victim calm and still, wrap the bitten limb tightly, as you would for a sprained ankle, and then attach a splint to immobilise it. Seek medical help, if possible with the dead snake for identification.

Don't attempt to catch the snake if there is even a remote possibility of being bitten again. Tourniquets and sucking out the poison are now comprehensively discredited.

### Spiders

The risk of being bitten by a spider is similarly remote. Queensland does have a selection of dangerous spiders, but they can usually be avoided if you don't go poking around in hollow tree-trunks or sticking your hand into curious-looking webs.

The spider you are most likely to encounter is the huntsman, a large, tarantula-like spider that can administer a painful but harmless nip. Also common in the Daintree area is the harmless golden orb spider, with its distinctive plum-coloured abdomen.

Potentially dangerous species found in Queensland include the black house spider, the whistling spider, the tiny redback and

**Australian nasties**

the white-tailed spider, which has a venom that causes localised skin damage. Funnelwebs rarely occur this far north.

Most spider bites are treated in the same way as snake bite and antivenins are widely available. For redback bites apply ice and seek medical attention.

### Insects

**Flies** In the cities the flies are not too bad; it's in the country that it starts getting out of hand, and the further out you get the worse the flies seem to be. They are such a nuisance that virtually every general store sells the Genuine Aussie Fly Net (made in Korea), which is rather like a string onion bag but is very effective. It's either that or the 'great Australian wave' to keep them away. Repellents such as Aerogard and Rid go some way to deterring the little bastards.

**Mosquitoes** 'Mozzies' can be a problem, especially in the warmer tropical and subtropical areas. Fortunately malaria is not present in Australia, although its counterpart, dengue fever, is a significant danger in the tropics (see the Health section for more information on dengue and Ross River fevers).

Mosquitoes are most active at dusk, and also at night, and there are some precautions you can take to avoid being bitten. The first is to use a good insect repellent such as Rid. Slap it on all over – during the day, at dusk and at night before you go to bed. Wearing long, loose, light-coloured clothes is also advised.

It's also worth considering investing in a mosquito net, stocked by most camping shops. Mosquito coils are another solution, but the smoke they produce is fairly noxious. You'll rarely be bitten if you sleep under a reasonably fast ceiling fan. The default technique is to share a room with someone who is tastier to mozzies than you are!

**Ticks & Leeches**  The common bush-tick (found in the forest and scrub country along the eastern coast of Australia) can be dangerous if left lodged in the skin as the toxin the tick excretes can cause paralysis and sometimes death. Check your body for lumps every night if you're walking in tick-infested areas. The tick should be removed by dousing it with methylated spirits or kerosene and levering it out, but make sure you remove it intact. Remember to check children and dogs for ticks after a walk in the bush.

Leeches are common, and while they will suck your blood they are not dangerous and are easily removed by the application of salt or heat. You'll usually find yourself carrying a few 'passengers' at the end of any walk in the Daintree.

## On the Road

Kangaroos pose a real hazard to drivers in rural areas and collisions with roos contribute to a number of driving fatalities every year. Even if you do walk away from a collision, your car probably won't, and a nocturnal garage call-out to the middle of nowhere can be very expensive. Do as the locals do and avoid driving at dusk or at night, or if you really must drive, keep your speed well below 70km/h.

Kangaroos are most active around dawn and dusk, and usually travel in groups. If one hops across the road in front of you, slow right down – its friends are probably just behind it. If you reach that critical point with a roo ahead of you and not enough road to stop, only swerve if it's safe to do so; avoiding an oncoming truck probably outweighs animal welfare at this point.

Other drivers are also a hazard. Drink-driving is a way of life in rural areas and most calls to the flying doctor service are from alcohol-related motor accidents. Again it's mainly a nocturnal phenomenon, so stay off the roads at night.

If you aren't used to driving long distances, you should heed the advice 'revive and survive'. Rest areas are provided at regular intervals on major roads and it's recommended you take a break of at least 15 minutes every two hours (if nothing else you'll be aware enough to avoid the road-train drivers who fall asleep at the wheel in front of you).

## Bushfires

Bushfires happen every year in Queensland. Don't be the mug who starts one. In hot, dry, windy weather, be extremely careful with any naked flame – don't throw live cigarette butts out of car windows. On a day of Total Fire Ban (listen to the radio, watch the billboards on country roads or front pages of daily newspapers) it is forbidden even to use a camping stove in the open. The locals will not be amused if they catch you breaking this particular law and the legal penalties are severe.

If you're unfortunate enough to find yourself driving through a bushfire, stay inside your car and try to park off the road in an open space, away from trees, until the danger has passed. Lie on the floor under the dashboard, covering yourself with a wool blanket if possible. The front of the fire should pass quickly, and you will be much safer than if you were out in the open. It is very important to cover up with a wool blanket or wear protective clothing, as it has been proved that heat radiation is the big killer in bushfire situations.

Bushwalkers should take local advice before setting out. On a day of Total Fire Ban, don't go – delay your trip until the weather has changed. Chances are that it will be so unpleasantly hot and windy, you'll be better off in an air-conditioned pub sipping a cool beer.

If you're out in the bush and you see smoke, even at a great distance, take it seriously. Go to the nearest open space, downhill if possible. A forested ridge is the most dangerous place to be. Bushfires move very quickly and change direction with the wind.

## BUSINESS HOURS

Business hours are from 9am to 5pm, Monday to Friday. Most shops in Queensland are open on weekdays from around 8.30am or 9am until 5pm and on Saturday morning, and most of the larger towns and cities will have at least one night a week when the shops stay open until 9pm – usually Thursday or Friday. Banks open at 9.30am Monday to Friday and close at 4pm on these days except Friday (5pm).

In the regional centres and tourist resorts – notably Brisbane, the Gold and Sunshine Coasts and Cairns – larger stores stay open later and all day on Saturday. In country towns, many shops close up if things look quiet and on Sunday you still won't find many shops open anywhere. Pub bistros and restaurants in rural areas close promptly at 8pm.

## PUBLIC HOLIDAYS & SPECIAL EVENTS

The Christmas holiday season is part of the long summer school vacation in Australia and the time you are most likely to find accommodation booked out and long queues at attractions. Easter is also a busy holiday time, and there are three other shorter school holiday periods during the year. See the earlier When to Go section in this chapter for details.

The main public holidays in Queensland are:

**New Year's Day** 1 January
**Australia Day** 26 January
**Easter** March/April – Good Friday and Easter Saturday, Sunday and Monday
**Anzac Day** 25 April
**Labour Day** 1st Monday in May
**Queen's Birthday** 2nd Monday in June
**Christmas Day** 25 December
**Boxing Day** 26 December

Queensland's major annual festivals and events include the following:

### January/February
**Australia Day** The nation celebrates the arrival of the First Fleet in 1788 on 26 January.
**Australian Skins** This big-money golf tournament is played over two days at Laguna Quays Resort on the Whitsunday Coast in February.
**International Cricket** One-day internationals, Test matches and Sheffield Shield games are played at the Brisbane Cricket Ground in Woolloongabba.

### March/April
**Surf Life-Saving Events** Life-saving championships are held on the Gold Coast, including the classic Ironman and Ironwoman events.
**Anzac Day** The nation commemorates the landing of the Australian and New Zealand Army Corp (Anzac) troops at Gallipoli in 1915 on April 25. Veterans of both World Wars and the Korean and Vietnam Wars hold marches.

### May/June
**Brisbane Biennial International Music Festival** This biennial (every odd numbered year) festival features just about everything from jazz to indigenous music, from Australia and all over the world.
**Outback Muster Drovers Union & National Outback Performing Arts Show** This major festival is held in Longreach.
**Palmer Street Festival** Townsville's major festival features street theatre and music.
**Gold Coast International Jazz & Blues Festival** The Gold Coast hosts its two-day music event in mid-June.
**Cooktown Endeavour Festival** A festival commemorating Captain Cook's landing in 1770 is held over the Queen's Birthday weekend.
**Wintermoon Festival** Several days of world music are enjoyed in Mackay.

### July
**Gold Coast International Marathon** Queensland's biggest event for distance runners also includes some less superhuman events.

### August
**Brisbane International Film Festival** The festival features films from Australia and the Asia-Pacific region.
**Hervey Bay Whale Festival** Held over a fortnight, it celebrates the annual migration of these magnificent creatures.

**Brisbane Ekka** Held at the RNA Showgrounds in Brisbane, this is Queensland's largest agricultural show.

**Mt Isa Rodeo** This is one of the country's richest rodeos.

## September

**Birdsville Races** The country's premier outback horse-racing event is held on the first weekend in September.

**Brisbane Riverside Festival** Brisbane's annual arts festival is held over two weeks in early September.

**Carnival of Flowers** Toowoomba's gardens are on display for eight days, with a flower show, a parade and a Mardi Gras.

**Capricana Festival** Rockhampton's major festival, held over 10 days in early September, features a street parade, a carnival and daily activities.

## October

**IndyCar** A four-day festival centred around the IndyCar Grand Prix car race around the barricaded streets of Surfers Paradise.

**Oktoberfests** Traditional beerfests with food, plenty of beer and live entertainment for all ages are held in several towns in Queensland.

**Reef Festival** This is Cairns' main annual festival, and features a carnival, street parades and musical events.

## November

**Melbourne Cup** Australia's premier horse race is run in Melbourne, Victoria, on the first Tuesday in November. The whole country shuts down for three minutes while the race is run.

## December

**Woodford Folk Festival** Formerly the Maleny Folk Festival, this huge folk festival is held over five days between 28 December and New Year's Day.

Almost every community in Queensland has at least one annual festival of its own, and these are often unique and quirky celebrations. You might find anything from rodeos and bush race meetings to cooee championships and cockroach races – and these festivals are a great way to meet the locals.

## ACTIVITIES

Queensland is Australia's natural adventure playground, with an incredible range of activities on offer, including scuba diving and snorkelling on the Great Barrier Reef, surfing on the Gold Coast, bushwalking in rainforests, camping on isolated tropical islands, horse riding along coastal beaches, and wildlife spotting throughout the state's numerous national parks and reserves.

## Bushwalking

Bushwalking is a popular activity in Queensland year-round. There are a number of bushwalking clubs and several useful guidebooks. Lonely Planet's *Walking in Australia* describes 23 walks of different lengths and difficulty in various parts of the country, including three in Queensland.

Look for Tyrone Thomas' *50 Walks in North Queensland* (for walks on the beach or through the rainforest areas of the World Heritage-listed Wet Tropics areas, covering from Cape Hillsborough, near Mackay, up to Cape Tribulation and inland as far as Chillagoe), and his *50 Walks: Coffs Harbour & Gold Coast Hinterland* (covering Tamborine Mountain, Springbrook and Lamington National Parks). There's also *The Bushpeople's Guide to Bushwalking in South-East Queensland*, with colour photos and comprehensive walking-track notes.

One of the best ways to find out about bushwalking areas is to contact a local bushwalking club, such as the Brisbane Bushwalkers Club (☎ 3856 4050), at 116 Alderley Ave, Alderley, or look in the *Yellow Pages* under 'Clubs – Bushwalking'. Outdoor shops such as Mountain Designs and Paddy Pallin are also good sources of information.

National parks and state forests are some of the best places for walking. See the contact details in the Facts about Queensland chapter for more information. National parks on the mainland favoured by bushwalkers include Lamington in the McPherson Ranges, Main Range in the Darling Downs, Cooloola just north of the Sunshine Coast, Carnarvon Gorge in central Queensland, Eungella just west of Mackay and Bellenden Ker south of Cairns, which contains Queensland's highest peak, Mt Bartle Frere (1657m). See the individual sections for details.

## Diving & Snorkelling

The Great Barrier Reef provides some of the world's best diving and snorkelling and there are dozens of operators vying to teach you to scuba dive or provide you with the ultimate dive safari. The Queensland coast is one of the world's cheapest places to take your scuba dive certification – a five-day course leading to a recognised open-water certificate costs somewhere between $170 and $500 – and you can usually choose to do a good part of your learning in the warm waters of the Barrier Reef itself.

Every major town along the coast has one or more diving schools – the three most popular places to learn are Airlie Beach, Cairns and Townsville – but standards vary. Diving professionals are notoriously fickle and good instructors move around from company to company – ask around to see which one is currently well-regarded.

When choosing a course, look carefully at how much of your open-water experience will be out on the reef. Many of the budget courses only offer shore dives, which are frequently less interesting. Normally you have to show you can tread water for 10 minutes and swim 200m before you can start a course. Most schools also require a medical which will usually cost extra (around $50).

For certified divers, trips and equipment hire are available just about everywhere. You'll need evidence of your qualifications, and some places may also ask to see your log book. You can snorkel just about everywhere too. There are coral reefs off some mainland beaches and around several of the islands, and many day trips out to the Barrier Reef provide snorkelling gear for free.

During the wet season, usually January to March, floods can wash a lot of mud out into the ocean and visibility for divers and snorkellers is sometimes affected.

## Cycling

There are possibilities for some great rides in Queensland. See the Getting Around chapter for information on long-distance cycling. Available from most bookshops, *Pedalling Around Southern Queensland* by Julia

Thorn, has tour notes and mud maps for numerous bike rides in the south of the state. For longer trips, Lonely Planet's authoritative *Cycling Australia* covers the epic east coast trip and other rides in Queensland.

There are companies that offer cycling tours in various places, including Cairns, Townsville and Brisbane. It might also be worth contacting one of the local cycling clubs like the Brisbane Bicycle Touring Association (☎ 3279 3666), at PO Box 286, Jindalee, Brisbane 4074. For other areas, look under 'Clubs – Bicycle' in the *Yellow Pages*.

## White-Water Rafting, Sea Kayaking & Canoeing

The Tully and North Johnstone Rivers between Townsville and Cairns are the big ones for white-water rafting. You can do day trips for about $145, or longer expeditions. See the Cairns and Mission Beach sections for details.

Sea kayaking is also popular, and there are numerous operations along the coast that offer paddling expeditions through the calm Barrier Reef waters, often from the mainland out to offshore islands. See the Cairns, Mission Beach, Cape Tribulation, Noosa and Maroochydore sections for details.

Coastal Queensland is full of waterways and lakes so there's no shortage of canoeing territory. You can rent canoes or join canoe tours in several places – among them Noosa, Townsville and Cairns.

## Surfing

From a surfer's point of view, Queensland's Great Barrier Reef is one of nature's most tragic mistakes – a 2000km-long breakwater! Mercifully, there are some great surf beaches in southern Queensland. The Gold Coast has some of the best of these, although you have to be prepared for crowds. Near Brisbane, North Stradbroke Island also has good surf beaches, as does Moreton Island. Despite its exposed coast, Fraser Island has a few too many rips and sharks to appeal to surfers.

Further north, Noosa is a popular hangout for long-boarders, with good wave action at Sunshine Beach and the point breaks around the national park, especially during the cyclone swells of summer (December to February) Queensland's most northern surf beaches are at Agnes Water and the Town of 1770, just south of Gladstone.

You can hire second-hand boards from almost any surf shop along the coast, and op shops in surf resorts are usually full of old boards. It's probably best to start off with boogie boarding and work up, as surfing isn't as easy as it looks. If you're keen, there are a couple of learn-to-surf schools in Surfers Paradise and at Noosa Heads.

Surfing enthusiasts will be glad to hear that Mark Warren's definitive *Atlas of Australian Surfing*, is now available in a portable size, as well as the large coffee-table book. You may also find copies of the slim surf guide *Surfing Australia's East Coast* by Aussie surf star Nat Young.

Surfing competitions are held at several locations including North Stradbroke Island and Burleigh Heads on the Gold Coast; there are also numerous surf life-saving carnivals that take place on the beaches of southern Queensland from December, culminating in the championships in March/April.

Visit the Queensland Tourism surfing site ( **W** www.queenslandwavefinder.com) for more information.

## Swimming

The very word 'Queensland' conjures up visions of endless stretches of sun-bleached sand with turquoise-blue waters lapping at the shore, backed by palm trees swaying gently in the breeze. You certainly won't be disappointed in the south of the state, but once you get north of Gladstone, the allure of many of the mainland beaches is spoiled by mudflats and mangroves. Further damaging the illusion are lethal box jellyfish that swarm along the north coast of Queensland every summer (see the boxed text in the Capricorn Coast section). To find your place in the sun, head out to Queensland's islands, which range from sandbars to mountainous continental groups and should provide all the white sand and azure ocean you need.

Inland, there are many magnificent lakes and rivers where you can cool off – as long as it's safe from crocodiles! – and almost every country town has its own Olympic-sized swimming pool.

## Sailing & Other Water Sports

Sailing enthusiasts will find plenty of opportunities to practise their sport, and many places along the coast and inland that hire boats. Airlie Beach and the Whitsunday Islands are probably the biggest centres, but there's also a sizeable scene around Manly, just south of Brisbane. Water-skiing is often available too. There are water sports hire places in all the coastal resorts and on most of the islands where you can hire catamarans, sailboards, jet skis, canoes, paddle boats and snorkelling gear.

## Hang-Gliding, Parasailing & Gliding

Hang-gliding is popular at many places along the Queensland coast, including the Lamington National Park in the south-eastern corner and Eungella National Park near Mackay. You can take tandem flights or enrol in a hang-gliding course. Parasailing outfits can be found at many beach resorts.

There are more than a dozen gliding clubs throughout the state, many of which will take you up to experience this pure form of flying. Contact the Queensland Soaring Association ( ☎ 3878 1672) at PO Box 1324, Milton, Brisbane 4064, to find the nearest clubs.

## Bungee Jumping & Skydiving

There are plenty of opportunities for adrenaline-junkies to get a hit in Queensland. Bungee jumping is big in places like Surfers Paradise, Airlie Beach and Cairns. Tandem skydiving is also big, and for $250 to $350, (depending on the drop height) you can do a tandem jump from around 10,000 feet. Surfers Paradise, Brisbane, Noosa, Cairns, Mission Beach, Airlie Beach and Great Keppel Island all offer tandem jumps.

## Horse Riding & Trekking

Horse riding is another activity available all along the coast, from one-hour strolls, to gallops along the beach, to overnight (or longer) treks. Check with backpackers hostels and tourist offices to find out what's available.

## Rock Climbing & Abseiling

Believe it or not, Brisbane is a good place to learn rock climbing, centred on the Cliffs, a series of 18m rock faces along the southern banks of the Brisbane River. A number of operators offer climbing and abseiling instruction in Brisbane and other popular climbing areas – climbing and outdoor shops are good sources of info. Look under 'Outdoor Adventure Activities' in the *Yellow Pages*.

## Fishing

As you'll soon realise, fishing in all its forms is incredibly popular – surf fishing in places like North Stradbroke Island and Fraser Island, line fishing in the clear tropical waters of the Barrier Reef, big-game fishing at places like Hamilton, Hayman and Lizard islands, and barramundi fishing in the coastal and estuarine waters of Far North Queensland. The 'barra' is Australia's premier native sport fish, partly because of its tremendous fighting qualities and partly because it's delicious! Note that the minimum size for barra is 50cm in Queensland – there are also bag limits, and the barra season is closed from 1 November to 31 January. There are quite a few commercial operators offering sports-fishing trips in the Far North.

There are plenty of reef fish to choose from, but the reef is divided into different zones that impose certain restrictions on what you can and can't do in each area. Zoning maps are available from most tourist offices along the coast, or from offices of the Great Barrier Reef Marine Park Authority or the Environment Protection Agency.

Made famous by the likes of actor Lee Marvin, Lizard Island in the Far North is Queensland's big-game fishing capital. The heavy-tackle season runs from September to December, and the annual Black Marlin Classic on Halloween night (31 October) is a major attraction. Hamilton Island also hosts the Billfish Bonanza each December.

## Fossicking

There are lots of good fossicking areas in Queensland – see the *Gem Fields* brochure, published by QTTC. It tells you the places where you have a fair chance of finding gems and the types you'll find. You'll need a miners right or 'fossickers licence' before you hit the gemfields; most caravan parks in the fossicking areas can sort you out with a licence or you can visit any office of the Department of Natural Resources and Mines. A one-month fossickers licence costs $5.10 for individuals or $7.20 for families

Most of Queensland's gemfields are in fairly remote areas. Visits to these areas can be adventurous, great fun and maybe even profitable, and even if you don't strike it lucky you're bound to meet some fascinating characters. Queensland's main fossicking areas are the gemfields around Sapphire and Rubyvale (about 300km inland from Rockhampton), the Yowah Opalfields (deep in the southern outback, 150km west of Cunnamulla) and the gemfields around Mt Surprise and Georgetown (about 300km south-west of Cairns) – see the Outback, Capricorn Coast and Gulf Savannah chapters for more detailed information.

## WORK

If you come to Australia on a tourist visa then strictly you shouldn't work, though some travellers find low-paid casual work, usually in the tourism industry. If you like Queensland enough to want to work here, you don't want to blow your chances of coming back by being caught working illegally.

There are numerous possibilities with a Working Holiday visa (see the Visas section earlier). Coastal resorts like Cairns may not be as lucrative as larger towns inland, as the competition is greater. Fruit-picking work is available in the hinterland of the Sunshine and Fraser Coasts, and in Ingham, Innisfail, Tully, Bowen and Cardwell in the north, though it's hard work and living conditions in workers hostels can be very basic.

Other good prospects for casual work include doing factory work and bar work, waiting on tables, washing dishes (kitchen hand), working in telesales or as a station hand (jackaroo/jillaroo), and collecting for charities. People with computing or secretarial skills should have little difficulty finding work in the major cities, and for qualified nurses agency work is often available.

The various backpacker magazines, newspapers and hostels are good information sources – some local employers even advertise on hostel notice boards. Try the classified ads in the daily papers under Situations Vacant, especially on Saturday and Wednesday. The government Centrelink offices are of virtually no help.

*Workabout Australia*, by Barry Drebner, gives a comprehensive state-by-state breakdown of the seasonal work opportunities.

## Tax File Number

If you have a Working Holiday visa, it's important to apply for a Tax File Number (TFN) – not because it's a condition of employment, but because without it tax will be deducted from any wages you receive at the maximum rate, which is currently set at 47%! To get a TFN, contact the Australian Taxation Office (☎ 13 28 61) for a form. It's a straightforward procedure, and you will have to supply adequate identification, such as a passport, and show that you have a work visa. Getting a TFN takes about four weeks.

## Paying Tax

Yes, it's one of the certainties in life! If you have supplied your employer with a TFN, tax will be deducted from your wages at the rate of 29% if your weekly income is below $397. As your income increases, so does the tax rate, with the maximum being 47% for weekly incomes over $1153. For nonresident visitors, tax is payable from the first dollar you earn, unlike residents who have a $6000 tax-free threshold, so it's unlikely you'll be entitled to a tax refund when you leave.

If you have had tax deducted at 47% because you have not submitted a TFN, you may be entitled to a partial refund when you lodge a tax return. Your return must include a copy of the Group Certificate all employers issue to salaried workers at the end of the financial year or within seven days of the employee's leaving a job. But before you can lodge a tax return, you must have a TFN.

## Superannuation

As part of the government's compulsory superannuation scheme, employers must make contributions to a superannuation fund on your behalf. These contributions are made at the rate of 8% of your wage, and the money must remain in the fund until you reach 'preservation age' (sounds nasty!), which is currently 55.

The only escape from this is if you earn less than $450 in any calendar month, in which case you can decide to opt out of superannuation and instead receive the payment as part of your regular salary or wages.

## Casual Employment Seasons

The table below lists the main times where casual employment is a possibility.

| time | type of work | region |
| --- | --- | --- |
| Jan–Apr | Grape picking | Stanthorpe |
| Feb–Mar | Apple/pear picking | Warwick |
| March–Dec | Vegetable harvesting | Bundaberg |
| Apr–Oct | Tourism | Cairns |
| May–Aug | Trawler fishing | Cairns |
| May–Nov | Vegetable harvesting | Bowen |
| Aug–Dec | Asparagus harvest | Warwick |
| Dec–Jan | Mango picking | Atherton |
| Year-round | Banana picking | Tully |

## ACCOMMODATION

Queensland is very well equipped with a wide range of accommodation alternatives with everything from backpackers hostels and caravan parks to five-star hotels and island resorts. Arranged from budget to top-end, the options are:

**Camping** $3.85 per person or $15.40 per family in national parks; $10–$22 a double elsewhere.
**Hostels** $13–$22 per person in dorm beds.
**Pub Rooms** From $20/30 a single/double.
**Motels** From $40/50 a single/double.
**B&Bs** From $60/70 a single/double.
**Hotels** From $70 a double.

If you're travelling in a group, you can save money by staying in units or family rooms, which sleep between three and eight, and splitting the costs. The RACQ produces a comprehensive accommodation directory to Queensland – see Guidebooks in the earlier Books section for details.

## Camping & Caravanning

Camping in the bush is for many people one of the highlights of a visit to Australia. The magnificent camping grounds in the state and national parks are a credit to the nation, and nocturnal visits from wildlife add to the bush experience. Payment can either be made in advance when booking, or at self-registration booths at some sites.

You can also pitch your tent in one of the hundreds of caravan parks that are scattered across Queensland; most have pools, toilets, laundry facilities and barbecues, but only a few have camp kitchens. Unfortunately, a curious quirk of council law prohibits caravan parks from convenient central locations; Brisbane is the worst offender in this respect, with a ban on tents within a 22km radius of the centre! Although there are some sites in Brisbane within that radius, they're strictly for caravans – no campers allowed.

Many caravan parks also have on-site vans that you can rent for the night for around $30, and cabins, which are usually self-contained Portacabin units with kitchens and bathrooms, which range from $45 to $90, depending on how motel-like the facilities are.

## Campervans

The advantages of travelling in a Kombi, campervan or station wagon are that it's cheap – you don't have to pay for a bed – and you can sleep wherever you happen to be without worrying about booking. Queensland is one of the few states that allows people to sleep in roadside stops, and these can be found along many of the major highways. Caravan parks mainly exist to cater to caravans and campervans, and all offer powered sites where you can plug in whatever you need to power up, from campervan cookers to mobile phone rechargers. If you're doing things on a shoestring, there are shower blocks in most highway roadhouses, or you could nip into a swimming pool to use the facilities for a few dollars.

## Youth Hostels

Australia has a very active Youth Hostel Association (YHA) but most hostels are actually franchises, and are not run directly by the association. In fact, YHA hostels are little different from other backpackers hostels, but you can normally rely on them to be clean and well run.

Unlike in European YHAs, you don't need to do chores (except your own washing up!) and both single-sex dorms and doubles are usually available. Sheets and cooking utensils are normally provided for a deposit. Many of the hostels are purpose-built, so facilities are often excellent, and include kitchens and laundries. However, the YHA hostels are generally more austere than the mainstream places and tend to attract guests who value a quiet night's sleep over backpacker bars and drinking games.

Members of the Australian YHA, or any of the Hostelling International (HI) or International Youth Hostel Federation (IYHF) associations normally receive around $3 discount on all room rates. Non-members are also welcome, but pay the full rate, which is usually comparable to other backpacker places.

To become a full YHA member in Australia costs $32 a year (there's also a $20 joining fee, although if you're an overseas resident joining in Australia you don't have to pay this). You can join at a state office or at any youth hostel, and your membership card will also get you a discount of up to 10% off most bus tickets and other transport options.

There's also the introductory Aussie Starter Card membership, where you pay no initial membership, but instead pay an additional $3.50 at any hostel. Once you have stayed for ten nights, you get a full membership. The YHA also has vouchers that cover the first $15 for any room in any YHA; these cost $130 for 10 vouchers and $250 for 20 vouchers, giving you a 20% discount.

The annual *YHA Accommodation & Discounts Guide* booklet, which is available from any YHA office in Australia and from some YHA offices overseas, lists all the YHA hostels around Australia, plus handy discounts on things such as car hire, activities and accommodation for YHA members. Individual hostels can book accommodation in other YHAs throughout Australia.

The Queensland YHA Membership and Travel Centre (☎ 3236 1680) is at 154 Roma St, Brisbane.

## Backpackers Hostels

Queensland also has a staggering number of backpackers hostels, and the standard of these places runs from the magnificent to the awful, depending on how they are run. The vast majority are converted motels, which guarantees you a pool but not always adequate cooking facilities or communal spaces.

Many of the best backpackers hostels are small, family-run places in converted wooden Queenslander houses, some are run by former globe-trotters who know what it takes to make a hostel into a home away from home. At the other end of the spectrum are the backpackers resorts, huge, custom-built places with hundreds of beds and a party attitude, which tend to have extensive facilities, but are a little short on that human touch. You'll probably find it easier to meet people at the smaller, more intimate places

With the cut-throat competition, most of the hostels send out minibuses and touts to court backpackers arriving at the bus and train stations or airports, usually with a placard of photos of the hostel and the name in big, bright letters.

Prices at backpackers hostels are generally in line with YHA hostels. Singles and doubles are often available from around $30, though many places charge $50 for plain rooms with shared facilities – some of the most overpriced rooms in Australia!

There's at least one organisation (VIP) that you can join where, for a modest fee (typically $15), you'll receive a discount card (valid for 12 months) and a list of participating hostels. The dollar discounts of accommodation soon add up and there are also discounts of up to 20% on most bus tickets and other transport. Members of the Nomads Backpackers (☎ 08-8224 0919, fax 8232 2911) organisation also get discounts on buses and cheap rates at the Nomads hostels.

A warning for Australian and Kiwi travellers: Many hostels will only admit overseas backpackers, because of problems with drunks and drug users. If you encounter this kind of reception, the best you can do is persuade the desk people that you're genuinely travelling the country, and aren't just looking for a cheap place to crash for a while.

## Pubs

In rural areas, or anywhere away from the beaten tourist track, budget accommodation usually means pub accommodation. There are hundreds of old Federation-era hotels offering wild-west-style rooms on the upstairs balcony, although many are now closing down their pub rooms, or upgrading them to the level and price of motel units.

The standard of accommodation rarely lives up to the architecture outside – facilities are shared, most rooms are pretty old, and the neighbours can be quite boisterous – but they're cheap and within staggering distance of the pub bistro and bar. The disadvantage is that these places aren't really safe for single women. In small rural towns, the pub is often the social centre, and you'll usually get a warm reception if you're staying upstairs.

## Motels

If you want a more modern place than a pub, with your own bathroom and other facilities, then you're moving into the motel bracket. Prices vary, and in motels (unlike hotels), singles are often not much cheaper than doubles. A room in a budget motel usually guarantees you TV and a pool. The more upmarket motels, and those in the busier centres, charge as much as $100 a night.

## Guesthouses & B&Bs

These are the fastest-growing segment of the accommodation market. New places open all the time, and the network of accommodation alternatives throughout the country includes restored miners cottages, converted barns and stables, renovated and rambling old guesthouses, upmarket country homes, romantic escapes and simple bedrooms in family homes. Tariffs range from $60 to $130 (per double).

## Farm- & Station-Stays

Australia is a land of farms (known as 'stations' in the outback), and one of the best ways to come to grips with Australian life is to spend a few days on one. Many farms offer accommodation where you can just sit back and watch how it's done, while others like to get you more actively involved in the day-to-day activities. With the general rural crisis, tourism offers the hope of at least some income for farmers at a time when many are being forced off the land.

The accommodation varies enormously. Some places have just bunged a couple of dongas (transportable huts, often used in mining towns) in the yard and will charge perhaps $20 a night; at others, you can pay $150 a double to stay in a historic country homestead that has been restored to provide a luxurious taste of a bygone era. Most places fall somewhere between these two extremes.

Quite a few farm-stays are included in this guidebook. The QTTC also produces a brochure called *Farm & Station Holidays*, which lists many of the places with accommodation – it's available from regional information offices or from the QTTC.

## Hotels

The top-end of the hotel spectrum is well represented – in Brisbane, on the Gold Coast and in Cairns, at least. There are many excellent four- and five-star hotels and quite a few lesser places. Outside the capitals, quality accommodation is offered by the more expensive motels or beach resorts.

## Holiday Flats

Holiday flats, found mainly in beachside towns, are geared to family holidays, so they fill up at peak times and often have minimum rental periods of a week. Outside peak times you might be able to rent one by the night. Standards and prices vary, but if you have a group they can be very affordable and might even be cheaper than hostels outside the peak season. Local letting agents usually represent dozens of options in their area.

## Resorts

As you would expect, Queensland has all sorts of holiday resorts from five-star places with their golf courses; fleets of windsurfers, catamarans and jet skis; diving schools and

### Clubbing – Queensland Style

Clubs are big business in Queensland, but don't expect techno music and disco lights. Most of the state's clubs are members of the Returned Servicemen's League, a charitable venture set up to provide for veterans of WWI and WWII.

These gathering places are the social linchpin of rural communities, with live music, vaudeville entertainers, pokies, bars, and most importantly ultra-cheap Aussie meals, served from noon to 2pm and 6pm to 8pm.

While the decor can be pretty chintzy – plastic palm trees and portraits of Queen Elizabeth II are still all the rage – the tucker is normally excellent, and at $5 to $10 for a slap-up meal, who's complaining?

Other clubs to keep an eye out for are Surf Life Saving clubs (which normally have excellent sea views), bowls clubs, Irish clubs and sports clubs. In all cases, you'll have to sign in as a temporary member and you may be asked to prove you're a bone fide visitor.

restaurants; to clusters of old-fashioned cabins on lonely islands on the reef. There are hundreds of places to choose from.

## Other Accommodation

In the cities, if you want to stay longer, the first place to look for a shared flat or a room is the classified ads section of the daily newspaper. Wednesday and Saturday are the best days for these ads. Notice boards in universities, hostels, certain popular bookshops and cafes, and other contact centres are good places to look for flats and houses to share or rooms to rent.

## FOOD

Queensland chefs make full use of their cultural influences and the fantastic array of ingredients right on their doorstep. Brisbane and Noosa in particular have risen to prominence as gastronomic centres, boasting some of the best restaurants in Australia. Away from the coast, however, chefs seem to lose a little of their adventurous spirit and menus are still dominated by homestyle Aussie favourites like rump steak, meat pie, fish and chips, and mango chicken.

## Local Food

In recent years there's been a great rise in popularity of exotic local and 'bush' foods, and for the adventurous these dishes offer something completely different. So in a swish Cairns restaurant or Brisbane bistro you might find braised kangaroo tail samosas, emu pate, gum-leaf smoked venison, salt-bush lamb or wattle-seed ice cream.

All major cities also have a selection of cafes and restaurants serving modern Australian (mod Oz) cuisine, which borrows heavily from a wide range of foreign cuisines, but has a definite local flavour. You might find Asian-inspired curry-style dishes sharing a menu with Mediterranean-inspired dishes. It all makes for interesting dining.

Australia also has a superb range of seafood: fish like John Dory and the famous barramundi, or superb lobsters and other crustaceans such as the engagingly named Moreton Bay bugs. Yabbies are freshwater crayfish and can be magnificent.

At the bottom end of the food scale, every takeaway in Australia has a tepid heater cabinet full of various types of meat pies: Four'n Twenty Pies are the most popular brand (no, they're not made of blackbirds). Meat pies are one of the founding blocks of Aussie food culture, and are worth trying, though probably only once. Even more a part of Australian food culture is Vegemite. This strange, dark, salty yeast extract looks and spreads like tar, but remarkably, it's great on toast.

## Fast Food

In Brisbane and the larger cities, or along the highways, you'll find all the major fast-food chains – McDonald's, KFC, Pizza Hut etc – all in prominent positions and blatantly signposted. You may be stuck with these places if you want a meal later than 8pm.

Food courts are found in most shopping malls and offer more wholesome alternatives such as roast meats, kebabs, curries, noodles and sushi. For the ultimate in cheap and cheerful dining, milk bars and takeaways sell meat pies, pasties, sausage rolls, sandwiches and milk shakes. There are also plenty of gourmet sandwich bars, delis and health-food shops that can rustle up more interesting sandwich fillings.

On a less tasty note, on the highways you'll constantly encounter roadhouses and anonymous cafes with stuff they call food sitting under hot lights waiting for unsuspecting travellers – don't eat it, you'll only encourage them. On the other hand, some of the small, remote roadhouses of the outback, the Gulf and Cape York still serve enormous, old-fashioned burgers that will keep you going all day.

## Pub Bistros

Every town in Queensland has at least one pub (there are plenty of 'one-pub towns' consisting of just a pub and nothing else). Most have bistros, a hangover from the days when they were real roadhouses, providing lodging, sustenance and grog for weary travellers.

Pub bistros are usually open from noon to 2pm and from 6pm to 8pm, though some don't serve meals on Sunday. The food on offer is simple, wholesome Aussie fare – steaks, pies, roasts, fish and chips, and lasagne feature on almost every menu – but it's cheap and filling after a long day's drive. Expect to pay between $10 and $17 for a meal. Most pubs also serve basic counter meals at the bar for around $5 to $7.

## Cafes & Restaurants

In Brisbane and the larger centres, you'll find plenty of cafes and restaurants, with Mediterranean, modern Australian and Asian food dominating the scene, but in smaller country towns you might just find an old-fashioned cafe, a pub and a Chinese restaurant. For full-on gourmands, there are world-class eateries in Brisbane, Noosa Heads, Cairns and Port Douglas, but you'll typically pay upwards of $25 for a main course in Queensland's top restaurants.

## DRINKS
## Nonalcoholic Drinks

Tap water is clean and drinkable in most parts of Queensland, with the exception of some of the more remote outback towns. Bottled water is also widely available.

Most shops stock a wide range of plain and flavoured mineral waters, soft drinks, fruit juices and flavoured milk; a milk shake from a local milk bar is a bit of an Aussie institution. Cafes and delis often make smoothies (a milk shake with added fruit, yoghurt, honey, nuts etc) and freshly squeezed fruit juices.

Most cafes and restaurants in places like Brisbane, the Gold and Sunshine Coasts, Cairns and Port Douglas serve cappuccinos, espressos, cafe lattes and macchiatos that will satisfy any caffeine addict. 'Real' coffee is also commonplace in many rural towns due to the sizeable Italian population (in fact, the default coffee in many outback towns is a huge mug of cappuccino, topped by an inch of foam).

## Alcoholic Drinks

Queensland is also the home of Australia's most famous spirit, the distinctive Bundaberg Rum, a dark rum made from raw molasses (which is a by-product of the local sugar industry).

**Beer** There's a bewildering array of beer available in bottle shops, pubs, bars and restaurants; the biggest brewery players in Queensland are Carlton United (brewers of Carlton Cold and the light beer Carlton Mid-strength) and Castlemaine Perkins (brewers of XXXX and the light variation XXXX Gold). Normal beers run to about 5% alcohol, light beers to about 3.6%. Interstate beers are also widely available, from the ubiquitous Victoria Bitter (VB), Fosters, Hahn and Tooheys – available in Tooheys New (lager) or Tooheys Old (black ale). Also worth hunting down are Tasmanian beers Cascade and James Boag's. International faces include Kiwi brew Steinlager, American Budweiser and Guinness (brewed under licence by Foster's).

Beer comes in bottles of 750ml (tallies), or 375ml (stubbies) and 375ml cans (tinnies). Draught beers are usually served up in 'pots' (285ml) and occasionally 'schooners' (425ml), but British-measure pints are increasingly common in Irish pubs and backpacker bars.

**Wine** Queensland's climate is generally too warm to produce good wines, but the town of Stanthorpe in the Granite Belt of the Darling Downs is starting to produce some respected wines in its many boutique wineries. Other wine areas include Atherton Tablelands, the Sunshine Coast Hinterland and around Kingaroy. Of course, the famous wines from further south are available all the way up the coast.

It takes a little while to become familiar with Australian wineries and their styles, but it's worth the effort. There are plenty of books out there to help you out, and most bottle shop owners can point you in the right direction. Queensland has a popular 'bring your own' (BYO) tradition at cafes and restaurants, so you can pick up a bottle of wine you like from any bottle shop and just pay a small corkage charge (typically $1.50 per person) with your meal.

## ENTERTAINMENT
### Cinema

At one time, almost every township in Queensland had its own small cinema, but ultra-modern multiplexes are the mainstay these days. A few independent and art house cinemas cling on in Brisbane and some rural towns, but the Birch, Carroll and Coyle empire dominates, guaranteeing surround-sound, big-screen entertainment, and a fairly homogenous diet of mainstream Hollywood movies. The surviving members of the small Village chain are a bit more daring with their program, offering regular foreign-language films.

City cinemas charge from $13 to $16 per seat, but the prices quickly drop to around $8 once you leave the coast. Cheap Tuesday is an inspired concept, with tickets typically running at half the normal price in most cinemas.

Drive-in cinemas used to be found all over Australia. They're a dying breed now, although there are still quite a few towns in Queensland where you can watch a movie from the comfort of your own car.

## Pubs, Nightclubs & Live Music

There's certainly no shortage of pubs in Queensland, and many of them feature live music or DJs, especially on Thursday, Friday and Saturday nights and Sunday afternoon. Some of the larger cities, including Brisbane, Cairns and Townsville, have free music and entertainment magazines that list local gigs. Otherwise, look in the local papers or inquire at information offices. Cover charges usually apply, especially for well-known bands. Pubs usually stay open until around midnight or 1am.

Most reasonably sized towns also have at least one nightclub. These places vary enormously, from grungy pick-up joints to up-market clubs with dress codes and cover charges. Nightclubs are generally licensed until 5am, although they'll close earlier during the week if there's no one around.

This book provides comprehensive information on lots of pubs, clubs and venues – look under the Entertainment section for each town.

## Gambling

Australians love to gamble, and hardly any town of even minor import is without a horse-racing track or a Totalizator Agency Board (TAB) betting office. You can place a bet on the horses, the trots (harness racing) and the dogs (greyhound racing), and you'll also find TAB agencies inside plenty of Queensland's pubs. Those accursed poker machines can be found inside most pubs and all licensed clubs, while whole legions of them are contained in the casinos at Townsville, the Gold Coast, Brisbane and Cairns.

## SPECTATOR SPORTS

If you're an armchair – or wooden bench – sports fan, Queensland has plenty to offer.

## Football

Australians play at least four codes of football, each type being called 'football' by its aficionados. All are played over winter, with seasons from about March to September.

Rugby is the main game in Queensland, and it's rugby league, the 13-a-side working-class version, that attracts the crowds. The most awaited event in the calendar is the State of Origin series every June/July, where the mighty Maroons take on arch rivals NSW.

Rugby union, the 15-a-side game for amateurs, is growing in popularity, aided by the unparalleled success of the world-champion Wallabies, who defeated the British Lions for the first time ever in Australia in 2001.

Australian Rules, a curious indigenous game based on elements of Gaelic football, is also played throughout the state, although the Brisbane Lions are Queensland's only side in the AFL (Australian Football League). Games are played at the Gabba (the Brisbane Cricket Ground in Woolloongabba, a suburb of Brisbane).

Soccer is widely played on an amateur basis but the national league is only semi-professional and attracts a fairly small (but growing) following. It's gaining popularity thanks to the success of the national team, the Socceroos.

## Cricket

During the other (nonfootball) half of the year there's cricket. International Test and one-day matches are played at the Gabba every summer. There is also an interstate competition (the Sheffield Shield) and numerous local grades.

## Other Sports

Basketball is growing in popularity as a spectator sport and there is a national league. Queensland has three sides in the NBL (National Basketball League) – the Brisbane Bullets, the Townsville Suns and the Gold Coast Rollers.

There's also yacht racing, some tennis and motor racing. The Australian IndyCar Grand Prix is held in Surfers Paradise every October. Major golf tournaments include the Coolum Classic, held on the Sunshine Coast in December, and an international 'skins' tournament at Laguna Quays on the Whitsunday Coast each February.

Rodeos are held at dozens of places throughout the state. Some of the biggest rodeos are held at Mareeba in the Far North, Warwick in the Darling Downs, and Mt Isa and Longreach in the outback.

## SHOPPING
## Aboriginal & Torres Strait Islander Art

Top of the list of real Australian purchases would have to be art and craft items produced by Aboriginal and Torres Strait Islander artists.

Aboriginal art is a symbolic art form, traditionally expressed in the form of rock art and cave painting, but recently Aboriginal artists have begun painting in more portable formats and using Western art materials like canvas and acrylic paints. The paintings depict traditional Dreamtime stories and ceremonial designs, and each design has a particular spiritual significance.

Prices of the best works are way out of reach for the average traveller, but among the cheaper artworks on sale are hand-painted boomerangs, didgeridoos and bull-roarers; ceramics; art works on paper, bark and canvas; and prints, baskets, small wood carvings and some very beautiful screen-printed T-shirts produced by Aboriginal craft cooperatives.

As well, Queensland is flooded with knock-off didgeridoos and dodgy boomerangs produced by cynical companies who put nothing back into the Aboriginal community. It's worth shopping around and paying a few dollars more for the real thing.

Some places worth visiting are Queensland Aboriginal Creations, Southbank Aboriginal Centre and the Fire-Works Gallery in Brisbane, Barambah Emus in Murgon, Flying Arts in Milton, the Dreamtime Cultural Centre in Rockhampton, and the Tjapukai Aboriginal Cultural Park in Cairns. See the brochure *Aboriginal & Torres Strait Islander Holiday Experiences*, available from the QTTC, for more information.

See Shopping under Cairns in the Far North Queensland chapter for what to look for in a didgeridoo.

## Antiques

Many antiques on the Australian market are imported from Europe, especially England. Instead, look for Australian colonial furniture made from cedar or huon pine; Australian silver jewellery; ceramics – early factory pieces or studio pieces (especially anything by the Boyd family); glassware such as Carnival glass; and Australiana collectables and bric-a-brac such as old signs, tins and bottles.

## Opals

The opal is Australia's national gemstone, and opals and opal jewellery are popular souvenirs. They are beautiful stones, but buy wisely and shop around for best quality and price. Some stores will let you pick up a hammer and crack your own opal boulder and then polish up your 'find'.

## Australiana

The term 'Australiana' is a euphemism for souvenirs. These are the things you buy as gifts for the folks back home or to remember your visit by, and are supposedly representative of Aussie culture (they aren't – Australia is far more sophisticated than this!). Some of the more popular items are:

- Stuffed toys, especially koalas and kangaroos
- Wool products such as hand-knitted jumpers
- Animal Crossing road signs
- Sheepskins and kangaroo skins
- Akubra bush hats and straw sunhats
- T-shirts, windcheaters and towels printed with Australian symbols or typical slogans like 'No flies on me, mate!'
- Australia-shaped egg flippers or fly swats
- Any- and everything that can fit onto a keyring from mini boomerangs to perspex dolphins
- Jewellery made from opals and pewter, often in the shape of native animals
- Boomerangs (most of which are decorative rather than of the returning variety)
- Painted didgeridoos
- Local glassware and ceramics
- High-kitsch items like ceramic flying pigs or koalas

PHIL WEYMOUTH

Cane toad purse

## Opportunity Knocks

An Aussie institution, the humble opportunity shop, or 'op shop' is a great place to get kit for everything from camping to scuba diving, and all at rock-bottom prices. Queensland has hundreds of these second-hand stores, ranging from old-fashioned, second-hand clothes shops (keep an eye out for wetsuits) to pawnbroker megastores such as Cash Converters with tents and camp stoves, guitars, bicycles, surf boards and power tools – ideal for that campervan conversion.

The seeds of many of Australia's native plants are on sale all over the place. Try growing kangaroo paw back home, if your own country will allow it in. Australian wines are a great buy; the price of a cheap bottle of Jacob's Creek back home will buy you a top bottle of Rosemount Estate reserve here. Other gourmet items include honey (leatherwood and blue gum honey are two powerful local varieties) and macadamia nuts. We have also heard rumours of tinned witchetty grubs, honey ants and other bush tucker. Among the more dubious export items are zip-up cane toad purses (complete with legs and boggly eyes) and kangaroo scrotum pouches!

### Aussie Clothing

While you're here, fit yourself out in some local clothes – made in Australia for Australian conditions. Start off with some Bonds undies and a singlet, a pair of Holeproof Explorer socks and Blundstone or Rossi boots ($80 to 120). Then there's anything from the RM Williams line (boots, moleskin trousers, shirts), some Yakka or King Gee workwear, a shearer's top or bush shirt, a Bluey (a coarse woollen worker's coat), a Driza-Bone oilskin riding coat (around $130) – and top it off with an Akubra hat ($45 to $100).

### Surf Equipment

Australia produces some of the world's best surfing equipment, and a whole range of fashion 'surf-gear'. Quicksilver, Billabong and 100% Mambo are brands to be seen in, and cost less in Australia than they do abroad.

Think carefully before buying a board; learners will improve far faster on a long board, but it's a hell of a thing to get home. Short boards are harder to master, but more portable. New boards cost from $300 to $700, but second-hand boards can be found for as little as $80.

### Diving & Snorkelling Gear

As one of the world's premier diving destinations, Queensland is well equipped with shops selling all manner of reasonably priced dive gear. If you wear glasses, prescription diving masks are a good idea. If you're looking to put together your own kit, many of the dive companies in Cairns and Townsville sell on their old gear at the end of the season for very reasonable rates; try the dive centres or local op shops.

### Outdoor Gear

With Australians among the world's keenest travellers, Queensland's outdoor and adventure shops carry an excellent range of both Australian-made and imported gear. In many cases, the locally made products are of equivalent quality to (and cheaper than) the imports. Paddy Pallin, Mountain Designs, Kathmandu and Silk Road are reputable local firms.

# Getting There & Away

Getting to Australia from almost anywhere else means flying. If you're already in Australia and heading for Queensland, you have a choice of flying, taking a bus or train, driving, or hitching a ride on a yacht.

## AIR

Australia is a *long* way from Europe or America, and even a long-haul flight away from Asia, so be prepared for plenty of in-flight movies. All flights from Europe make a stop in Asia, usually in Bangkok, Hong Kong, Singapore or Kuala Lumpur; flying from the USA usually involves a stop on one of the Pacific islands. Flights into Australia are heavily booked during the European and US summer holidays and at Christmas time.

Most flights head to Sydney or Melbourne before they fly to Queensland, but Brisbane and Cairns receive direct international flights, and a few flights from New Zealand land at Coolangatta airport on the Gold Coast.

## Airlines

International airlines with offices in Brisbane include:

**Air New Zealand** (☎ 13 24 76) 63 Adelaide St
**Air Niugini** (☎ 1300 361 380) 99 Creek St
**Ansett** (☎ 13 13 00) 63 Adelaide St
**British Airways** (☎ 13 12 23) Level 12,
  313 Albert St
**Garuda Indonesia** (☎ 1300 365 330)
  288 Edward St
**Malaysia Airlines** (☎ 07-3229 7117) Level 17,
  80 Albert St
**Qantas** (☎ 13 13 13 for domestic flights,
  ☎ 13 12 11 for international) 247 Adelaide St
**Singapore Airlines** (☎ 07-3259 0700)
  344 Queens St
**Thai Airways International** (☎ 07-3215 4700)
  Level 4, 145 Eagle St

In addition, the budget airline Freedom Air (☎ 1800 122 000) flies from Coolangatta and Brisbane to Hamilton and Palmerston North in New Zealand. It also flies to Dunedin from Brisbane airport.

## Buying Tickets

**Discount Tickets** Rule number one if you're looking for a cheap ticket is to go to an agency, not directly to the airline. The airline can usually only quote you the full regular fare, while agencies can offer all sorts of special deals, particularly on competitive routes.

Ideally an airline would like to fly all its services with every seat in use and every passenger paying the highest fare possible. However, rather than flying with empty seats, most airlines will release seats to travel agencies at a discount rate, or make one-off special offers on particular routes – watch the travel ads in the press.

Of course what's available and what it costs depends on what time of year it is, what route you're flying and who you're flying with. If you're flying on a popular route (like Hong Kong to Cairns) or one where the choice of flights is very limited (like routes to South America or Africa) then the fare is likely to be higher or there may be nothing available but the official fare.

Dirt-cheap fares tend to be with obscure airlines at inconvenient times with lengthy stopovers.

**Round-the-World Tickets** If you're flying to Australia from the northern hemisphere, round-the-world (RTW) tickets can be a real bargain, and often you won't pay much more than a standard return fare. RTW tickets are put together by the airline alliances, Star Alliance and Oneworld, and are only valid for a limited period of time (usually one year). You can fly to any destination covered by the carrying airlines as long as you stay within the set mileage/number of stops; with some tickets you can't backtrack. The number of stopovers or total number of separate flights is determined before you travel.

An alternative type of RTW ticket is one put together by a travel agency using a combination of discounted tickets, which may

## Warning

The information in this chapter is particularly vulnerable to change: Prices for international travel are volatile, routes are introduced and cancelled, schedules change, special deals come and go, and rules and visa requirements are amended. Airlines and governments seem to take a perverse pleasure in making price structures and regulations as complicated as possible. You should check directly with the airline or a travel agent to make sure you understand how a fare (and ticket you may buy) work, and be aware of security requirements for air travel. In addition, the travel industry is highly competitive and there are many lurks and perks. At the time of writing, many airlines were facing an uncertain future due to a worldwide decline in air travel. Many have reduced schedules and some have gone under, and it seems likely that more will follow. This will only add to pricing uncertainty.

The upshot of this is that you should get opinions, quotes and advice from as many airlines and travel agents as possible before you part with your hard-earned cash. The details given in this chapter should be regarded as pointers and are not a substitute for your own careful, up-to-date research.

allow for more flexibility. Another option is a multiple-destination ticket, which is generally cheaper than a RTW ticket and allows for a couple of stops en route to Australia.

RTW tickets start from around £800 from the UK, and around US$1800 from the USA.

### Departure Tax

There is a $38 departure tax when leaving Australia, but this is incorporated into the price of your air ticket and so is not paid as a separate tax.

### The UK

Discount air travel is big business in London. Advertisements for many travel agencies appear in the travel pages of the weekend broadsheet newspapers, in *Time Out*, the *Evening Standard* and in the free magazine *TNT*.

For students or travellers under 26 years, popular travel agencies in the UK include STA Travel (☎ 020-7361 6262, **w** www.statravel.co.uk), which has an office at 86 Old Brompton Rd, London SW7, and branches across the country; and Usit Campus (☎ 0870-240 1010, **w** www.usitcampus.co.uk), which has an office at 52 Grosvenor Gardens, London SW1, and branches throughout the UK. Both of these agencies sell tickets to all travellers but cater especially to young people and students. Flightbookers (☎ 0207-757 2444) 117 Tottenham Court Rd, London W1P 0LX, is a good budget agency with consistently cheap fares. You can book international flights originating from London and many other European airports on their Web site at **w** www.ebookers.com. Another good agency is Trailfinders (☎ 0207-938 3366) at 46 Earls Court Rd, London W8.

The cheapest 'bucket-shop' (discount ticket agencies) tickets from London to Brisbane via Asia are about £385/585 one way/return. London to Cairns is around £430/745 one way/return. The best prices are usually only available if you leave London in the low season (March to June). In September and mid-December fares go up by about 30%, while the rest of the year they're somewhere in between.

Typical fares from other European cities include 4480/7300FF one way/return from Paris and DM2464/1368 from Frankfurt.

### North America

There is a variety of connections across the Pacific from Los Angeles or San Francisco to Australia. Qantas, Air New Zealand and United Airlines all have direct 14½-hour flights to Australia. There are also numerous airlines offering flights via Asia, with stopover possibilities including Tokyo, Kuala Lumpur, Bangkok, Hong Kong and Singapore and via the Pacific, with stopover possibilities including Nadi (Fiji), Rarotonga (Cook Islands), Papeete (Tahiti), and Auckland (New Zealand).

Discount travel agencies in the USA are known as consolidators (although you won't see a sign on the door saying Consolidator).

San Francisco is the ticket consolidator capital of America, although some good deals can be found in Los Angeles, New York and other big cities.

Council Travel, America's largest student travel organisation, has around 60 offices in the USA. Call it for the office nearest you (☎ 800-226 8624) or visit its Web site at ⓦ www.counciltravel.com.

STA Travel (☎ 800-777 0112, ⓦ www .statravel.com) has offices in Boston, Chicago, Miami, New York, Philadelphia, San Francisco and other major cities.

You can typically get an off-peak return ticket for US$1375/1800 from the west/east coast.

Flight possibilities from Canada are similar to those from the USA, with most Toronto and Vancouver flights stopping in one US city (such as Los Angeles or Honolulu) before heading on to Australia.

Canadian discount air ticket sellers are also known as consolidators and their air fares tend to be about 10% higher than those sold in the USA.

Travel CUTS (☎ 800-667 2887, ⓦ www .travelcuts.com) is Canada's national student travel agency and has offices in all major cities.

Fares out of Vancouver to Sydney or Melbourne cost around C$1800/2200 low/ high season travelling via the US west coast. From Toronto, fares go from around C$2100/2400.

One way/return fares available from Australia include: A$1045/1600 to Los Angeles, A$1220/1330 to New York and A$1020/1320 to Vancouver.

### New Zealand

Air New Zealand and Qantas airlines operate a network of trans-Tasman flights that link Auckland, Wellington and Christchurch in New Zealand with most major Australian gateway cities. There's also Freedom Air (ⓦ www.freedomair.com), a smaller, no-frills airline with services between Coolangatta airport and New Zealand (Auckland, Hamilton, Palmerston North and Dunedin).

From Auckland to Brisbane with Qantas or Air New Zealand it is around NZ$570/820

one way/return. From Auckland to Cairns you're looking at around NZ$670/780 one way/return.

### Asia

Ticket discounting is widespread in Asia, particularly in Singapore, Hong Kong, Bangkok and Penang. Flights to or from Bangkok, Hong Kong and Singapore are often part of the longer Europe-Australia route so they are also sometimes very full. Plan ahead. For more information on South-East Asian travel, and travel on to Australia, see Lonely Planet's *South-East Asia on a shoestring*.

Typical fares to Brisbane from Asia include: around S$1300/1890 one way/return from Singapore; RM1390/2015 from Kuala Lumpur; HK$6420/8880 (HK$5810 return on promotion) from Hong Kong; and 22,640/34,825B from Bangkok. Malaysia Airlines, Cathay Pacific, Japan Airlines and Qantas fly to Cairns from various destinations in Asia; fares are slightly lower than for Brisbane, eg, RM1265/1650 from Kuala Lumpur.

One-way fares from Cairns start from around $715 to Hong Kong, Bangkok or Singapore, and $615 to Kuala Lumpur. Flights from Brisbane to all four destinations start at around $550.

### Within Australia

A few years ago domestic air travel in Australia was revolutionised when several small budget airlines arrived to break the Ansett-Qantas duopoly. Fares plummeted – the Melbourne-Brisbane one-way fare, for example, dropped from $520 to $97 – and air travel became a real alternative to low-cost bus and train travel throughout Australia.

Unfortunately, it doesn't look like this enviable state of affairs will last. Qantas took over the pioneer budget airline Impulse in June 2001. Ansett temporarily took over bankrupt Flight West, before running into trouble itself in September 2001 (see the boxed text 'The Collapse of Ansett' in the Getting Around chapter). Industry pundits predict that fares will creep back up in the near future, though they are unlikely to go as high as in the pre-Impulse days.

Because Qantas flies international and domestic routes, flights leave from the international and domestic terminals. Flights with flight numbers QF001 to QF399 operate from international terminals, and flight numbers QF400 and above from domestic terminals. You don't have to reconfirm domestic flights on Ansett and Qantas, but you should phone on the day of your flight to check the details. For Qantas, call ☎ 13 12 23; for Ansett, call ☎ 13 15 15.

The major domestic carriers all have 'local' reservations numbers:

**Ansett** (☎ 13 13 00) W www.ansett.com.au
**Qantas** (☎ 13 13 13) W www.qantas.com.au
**Virgin Blue** (☎ 13 67 89)
  W www.virginblue.com.au
**Macair** (☎ 13 15 28) W www.macair.com.au

Several smaller regional airlines fly into Queensland, for example, Augusta Airways flies to Birdsville, Boulia and Bedourie from Port Augusta in South Australia.

All airports and domestic flights are non-smoking.

**Fares** Airlines and travel agencies quote the same prices on domestic flights, so you may as well just use whoever is nearest. If you have a credit card and you book more than three days in advance, you can book direct with the airline and they'll forward your ticket to you by express post. Ticketless travel is available on some routes – you'll just need to show your passport or drivers licence when you check in.

Full economy fares are quoted throughout this book, but you'll rarely end up paying the full whack on domestic flights, as there are all sorts of discounts and promos. For the time being you can get some excellent deals on popular routes into Brisbane with Ansett, Qantas or Virgin Blue.

On most other routes, fare discounts will depend on your age, whether you're studying, where you're going, and how far in advance you book your ticket. It's worth noting that you only get one bite at the discount cherry – you can't qualify for an advance purchase discount *and* a student discount off the same fare.

Full-time university or other higher education students under 26 get 25% off the regular economy fare when they show student ID or an International Student Identity Card (ISIC), but fares are often discounted by more than that anyway.

Nonresident international travellers can get up to a 30% discount on domestic Qantas flights simply by presenting their international ticket when booking, but again, the discount fares are often cheaper. The best advice is to ring around and explore the options before you buy.

Many of the smaller regional airlines in Queensland offer cheap deals on minor routes and at certain times of the year, often undercutting the bigger companies – see the individual chapters for more details.

***Advance Purchase Fares*** If you're planning a return trip and you have 14 days up your sleeve, you can save around 55% by travelling Apex (advance purchase excursion). You have to book and pay for your tickets 14 days in advance and you must stay away at least three days or one Saturday night. Flight details can be changed at any time, but the tickets are nonrefundable. Smaller, but still generous, discounts are also available if you book 10 or seven days in advance.

***Air Passes*** With all the discounting these days, air passes do not represent the value they once did, although pre-buying a pass does save you the hassle of hunting around for special deals. If you're flying to Australia with a Oneworld partner airline such as Qantas or British Airways, you can purchase coupons for up to half-price flights within Australia. There is a two coupon minimum and the first two must be purchased outside Australia. Additional coupons can be purchased within Australia.

## LAND

Travelling overland to Queensland from elsewhere in Australia will really give you an impression of just how big this country is.

The journey from Brisbane to the nearest state capital, Sydney, is a tortuous 1030km, and the journey from Brisbane to Cairns, the next biggest city in Queensland, covers 1700km! To give you a sense of scale, Melbourne is 1735km away from Brisbane, Adelaide is 2130km distant, Perth is a mere 4390km away and the shortest route to Darwin covers 3495km.

## Bus

Travelling by bus is usually the cheapest way to get around Australia, and there is now effectively only one national bus company in Australia – McCafferty's/Greyhound Pioneer (☎ 13 14 99, 13 20 30). Services are fully integrated between the two affiliated bus lines, so you can start a multistop journey on McCafferty's and finish it with Greyhound. As a general rule, most services within Queensland are with McCafferty's, while Greyhound covers longer-haul routes to the Northern Territory and elsewhere in Australia, though there is plenty of overlap.

Prices are generally very reasonable considering the distances and you can usually stop off along the route and resume the journey at a later date. The main Queensland service hugs the east coast, but there are inland connections from Brisbane to Adelaide, Melbourne and Sydney, and connections across to Darwin from Townsville, continuing down through Alice Springs to Adelaide.

Several smaller bus companies offer segments of the same routes, and are usually cheaper than McCafferty's/Greyhound, but services are less frequent and they are often heavily booked. The big coastal operators are Premier (☎ 13 34 10), which runs from Brisbane to Sydney and Brisbane to Cairns; and Kirklands (☎ 1300 367 077), which runs from Brisbane to Lismore via Byron Bay. Smaller companies include Suncoast Pacific (Brisbane to the Sunshine Coast) and Coachtrans (Brisbane to the Gold Coast).

The buses for all the companies are pretty similar and all are equipped with air-con, toilets and videos. Big city bus terminals are generally well equipped, with toilets,

showers, accommodation desks, lockers and food courts.

There are basically two types of fare for bus travel – express fares and bus passes. Students (ISIC card holders), backpackers (YHA and VIP card holders) and pensioners get discounts of at least 10% off most express fares and bus passes.

There are also a few interesting alternatives to straightforward bus travel – see the Organised Tours section of the Getting Around chapter for details.

**Express Fares** Express fares are for straight point-to-point travel. Stopover conditions on these tickets vary from company to company – some give you one free stopover or allow you to stopover wherever they have a terminal, and others charge a fee of perhaps $10 for each stopover. If you want to make multiple stopovers, you'll end up paying full fares on each separate segment – in these cases a bus pass may work out to be better value.

Several companies ply the busy Brisbane to Sydney route, including McCafferty's/Greyhound and Kirklands. The Pacific Hwy run along the coast takes around 16 hours; the inland New England Hwy takes a couple of hours less. The fare for both routes is around $89, although these are competitive routes: you'll usually find discounted fares and special backpacker deals if you shop around.

For direct buses from Brisbane to the other capital cities (except Perth), it's McCafferty's/Greyhound all the way.

The Newell Hwy is the most direct route between Brisbane and Melbourne ($164, 25 hours). To Adelaide, the shortest route is via Dubbo ($204, 31 hours). It's a 48-hour trip from Brisbane to Darwin (via Longreach), and the fare is around $371.

**Bus Passes** McCafferty's/Greyhound has a wide variety of passes available. The Aussie Kilometre Pass gives you a specified amount of travel to be completed within 12 months, the shortest being 2000km ($281), going up in increments of 1000km to a maximum of 20,000km ($1975), with a 10%

discount for YHA and VIP members, and ISIC card holders. You can change direction or backtrack and stop as often as you like, and for as long as you like, along the way. As an indication, 2000km will get you from Cairns to Brisbane, 4000km ($477) from Cairns to Melbourne, and 12,000km ($1259) will get you a loop from Sydney to Melbourne, Adelaide, central Australia, Darwin, Cairns and back to Sydney.

Aussie Day Passes are like the Kilometre Pass, except that you are limited by days of travel rather than by kilometres. Passes for seven ($672), 10 ($863) and 15 ($1004) days of travel are valid for 30 days; 21-day passes ($1325) are valid for two months.

Aussie Explorer Passes give you three, six or 12 months to cover a set route. You haven't got the go-anywhere flexibility of the Kilometre Pass, but if you can find a set route that suits you – and there are loads to choose from – it generally works out cheaper. When a pass follows a circular route, you can start anywhere along the loop and finish at the same spot.

The main limitation is that you can't backtrack, except on 'dead-end' short sectors such as Darwin to Kakadu, Townsville to Cairns and from the Stuart Hwy to Uluru. Rates range from $261 for a one-month, unlimited-stop tour from Sydney to Cairns, to $1116 for the Best of the East & Centre ($1288, including Uluru and Kakadu tours), which covers the east coast, Darwin and Uluru/Alice Springs.

**Other Bus Options** Various party tour buses operate up and down the coast, stopping at various sights and pubs along the way and checking into big party hostels every night. These trips are economically priced and will certainly get you from A to B. If you're backpacking around it can be a more fun way to travel – the buses are usually smaller, you'll meet lots of other travellers – but you may not see much of Australia except through the bottom of a glass. Many travellers complain of poor service, missed pickups and poor accommodation along the route. Oz Experience (☎ 1300 300 028, **W** www.ozexperience.com)

and Aussie Magic Bus (☎ 1800 449 444, **W** www.aussiemagicbus.com) are the main players.

## Train

Australia's railway system is less comprehensive than the bus networks, and train services are less frequent and more expensive. Having said that, the trains are much more comfortable than buses, and you certainly see Australia at ground level in a way no other means of travel permits. Interstate trains are as fast or faster than buses and in recent years the railways have cut their prices in an attempt to be more competitive.

The interstate railway booking system is computerised, so all stations (other than those on metropolitan lines) can make a booking for any journey throughout the country. For reservations call ☎ 13 22 32 from anywhere in Australia; this will connect you to the nearest booking agency. See the Getting Around chapter for information on train travel within Queensland.

**Fares & Conditions** There are three standard fare levels for interstate rail travel – economy, 1st class and sleeping berths, although sleeping berths aren't available on all trains. Depending on availability, a limited number of discounted fares are offered on all trains. If you book more than 14 days before you travel, you can save up to 50% on the fare, but smaller discounts apply right up to two days before travel. There are also half-price concession fares available to children under 16, secondary students and Australian tertiary students, but unfortunately not for backpackers.

On interstate journeys you can make free stopovers – you have two months to complete your trip on a one-way ticket and six months on a return ticket.

There are no discounts for return travel – a return ticket is just double the price of a one-way ticket.

**Train Passes** There are a number of passes available that allow unlimited rail travel either across the country or just in one state, but with the exception of the Queensland

Roadrail Pass and Sunshine Rail Pass, these passes are only available to international visitors and must be purchased before arrival in Australia.

With the Austrail Pass you can travel in economy class anywhere on the rail network during a set period ($660/860/1035 for 14/21/30 days). A seven-day extension to any of these passes costs $345.

The Austrail Flexipass allows a set number of economy class travelling days within a six-month period ($550/791/1110/1440 for eight/15/22/29 days). The eight-day pass cannot be used for travel between Adelaide and Perth or between Adelaide and Alice Springs.

**Interstate Services** Interstate railway services basically operate between the capital cities. That means that while there are direct services from Brisbane to Sydney, if you want to go from Brisbane to either Melbourne or Adelaide you have to go via Sydney, and if you want to go from Brisbane to Perth you have to go via Sydney *and* Adelaide.

Countrylink (☎ 13 28 29) has a daily XTP service between Brisbane and Sydney ($110/154 in economy/1st class, $231 in a sleeper, 15 hours). The north-bound service runs overnight, and the south-bound service runs during the day.

Motorail services (with a special carriage for cars) are also available on some interstate trains.

***Great South Pacific Express*** The most luxurious way to get from Sydney to Brisbane or Cairns is the *Great South Pacific Express*, a sumptuously refurbished period train that runs from Sydney to Cairns about 30 times a year. It's more of a tour than a train ride, with luxury accommodation, fine dining and wines and various detours along the route, including trips to the Great Barrier Reef and the rainforest at Kuranda, plus a wine-tasting excursion to the Hunter Valley in New South Wales (NSW). Fares start at a cool $2970 per person for the three-day/two-night trip. Call ☎ 1800 627 655 for more details.

## Car & Motorcycle

See the Getting Around chapter for details of road rules, driving conditions and information on buying and renting vehicles.

The main road route into Queensland from the west is the Barkly Hwy, which leaves the Stuart Hwy at Threeways (about 1000km south of Darwin and 500km north of Alice Springs) and cuts across to Mt Isa. From Mt Isa, you can continue eastward along the Flinders Hwy to Townsville on the coast, or head south-east along the Landsborough (Matilda) Hwy towards Brisbane.

There are a couple of major routes into Queensland from the south. The Pacific Hwy is the coastal route between Sydney and Brisbane and it passes through a number of popular tourist spots on the way as well as some great scenery. The New England Hwy is a quieter, albeit longer, inland route from Sydney to Brisbane, but the road is the undisputed territory of road trains (a string of trailers pulled by a semitrailer), and kangaroos at night.

The Newell Hwy is the most direct route from Brisbane to Melbourne – it's a good road through the heart of rural NSW. The major route from Adelaide to Brisbane is the Barrier Hwy, which takes you across to Dubbo via Broken Hill; from Dubbo, the Newell Hwy takes you up to Brisbane.

The other major route into southern Queensland is the Mitchell Hwy, which links Bourke in outback NSW with Charleville and Barcaldine in outback Queensland. For those wanting to travel further into the outback, have a look at Lonely Planet's *Outback Australia*.

## SEA
### Yacht

It's quite possible to make your way around the Australian coast to Queensland, or even to and from countries like New Zealand, Papua New Guinea or Indonesia, by hitching rides or crewing on yachts. Ask around at harbours, marinas or yacht clubs. It's often worth contacting the secretaries of sailing clubs and asking whether anyone is advertising for crews – look under 'Clubs – Yacht' in the *Yellow Pages* telephone directory.

It obviously helps if you're an experienced sailor, but some people are taken on as cooks (not very pleasant on a rolling yacht). Usually you have to chip in something for food, and the skipper may demand a financial bond as security. A lot of yachties head north for Queensland from south-eastern Australia to escape the winter, so April is a good time to look for a berth in the southern harbours.

# Getting Around

## AIR

Queensland's major regional airline is Sunstate (a subsidiary of Qantas, ☎ 13 13 13, which handles bookings). Sunstate offers daily connections from Brisbane to Bundaberg, Coolangatta (Gold Coast), Emerald, Gladstone, Hamilton Island, Hervey Bay, Mackay, Maroochydore/Sunshine Coast, Proserpine/Airlie Beach, Rockhampton and Thursday Island. Qantas itself offers connections from Brisbane to Townsville.

Macair (☎ 13 15 28) is the outback carrier.

There's also a multitude of smaller airlines operating up and down the coast, over to the islands off the east coast, across Cape York Peninsula and into the outback. During the wet season, such flights are often the only means of getting around the Gulf Savannah or Cape York Peninsula. See the Getting There & Away sections in the individual chapters for details.

In general, the regional carriers fan out from Brisbane, so if you're flying in from Sydney and want to get to Bundaberg, you'll have to change at Brisbane.

## BUS

With the merger of McCafferty's and Greyhound Pioneer, there is now just one major bus company in Australia, McCafferty's/

---

## The Collapse of Ansett

Friday September 14 2001 was a dark day in Australia's aviation history. Their skies already darkened by the September 11 attack on America, Australians woke to find that the nation's second-largest airline, Ansett, had suddenly and dramatically ceased all operations. As many as 30,000 people (including 17,000 directly employed staff) were suddenly out of work, passengers were left stranded, bewildered, clutching tickets for planes that were no longer flying.

The news at first was very bleak: Ansett's owner, Air New Zealand, had cut the company adrift, calling in administrators amid claims that Ansett was losing a staggering $1.3 million a day. Taking a look at the books, Qantas declined to buy out the foundering airline and the federal government initially refused to bail it out – transport minister John Anderson famously described Ansett as a 'carcass'. But with the unions and the public up in arms, a government-backed deal was eventually reached to get some of the planes flying again. At the time of writing, five jets were operational on a three-month trial, flying between Sydney, Melbourne, Brisbane and Perth. Having cobbled together an airline of sorts, administrators were striving to find a suitable buyer for 'Ansett Mark II'.

Ansett's problems began late in 2000 when three planes were grounded by the Civil Aviation Safety Authority (CASA) after cracks were found in the tails. In April 2001, the entire fleet of 767s suffered the same fate, not only costing Ansett millions, but denting consumer confidence in the airline. At the same time Ansett was forced to compete not only with traditional rival Qantas, but with new budget airlines Impulse and Virgin Blue (Impulse was later bought out by Qantas). However, many blame Ansett's collapse squarely on Air New Zealand, which took full control of Ansett between 1996 and 2000, paying more than $1 billion. Lumbered with an ageing fleet and unwieldy staffing levels, Ansett was haemorrhaging money and Air New Zealand seemed unable (some say unwilling) to stem the flow.

Ansett was founded in Victoria by road transport entrepeneur Sir Reginald Ansett in 1935. Over the next 35 years it grew to become Australia's largest domestic airline. It introduced the first jet airliner to Australia in 1964.

After 65 years of aviation history, the airline's fall was swift, sudden and calamitous. It remains to be seen if it is final.

Greyhound (☎ 13 14 99). The affiliated companies now offer an integrated service – you can book with either company and tickets are interchangeable – and offer comprehensive coverage throughout Queensland, linking up with interstate services into the Northern Territory (NT) and New South Wales (NSW) – see the Getting There & Away chapter for details of passes, fares and conditions.

There are also numerous smaller bus companies with more specialised local services, including Premier (☎ 13 34 10); it's the main competitor to McCafferty's/Greyhound on the Melbourne-Sydney-Brisbane-Cairns route along the coast, and is a few dollars cheaper on most routes. See the Getting There & Away headings under individual towns for other operators.

## Bus Services & Fares

McCafferty's/Greyhound offers express fares for straight point-to-point travel. If you don't have a bus pass and want to make stopovers between point A and point B, you'll either have to pay separate fares for each sector or pay a stopover fee of perhaps $10.

The busiest bus route is the coastal run up the Bruce Hwy. The express Brisbane-Cairns fare is $182 (27 hours); individual sector fares are considerably more. Major sectors along the coast are: Brisbane–Hervey Bay ($41, 5½ hours); Hervey Bay–Rockhampton ($69, seven hours); Rockhampton-Mackay ($50, four hours); Mackay–Airlie Beach ($33, two hours); Airlie Beach–Townsville ($47, four hours) and Townsville-Cairns ($49, six hours).

The other major bus route out of Brisbane is the inland service to Mt Isa ($144, 25 hours), and you can continue to either Darwin or Alice Springs in the NT. The individual sectors include: Brisbane-Roma ($53, seven hours); Roma-Longreach ($67, nine hours); Longreach–Mt Isa ($77, eight hours).

The other major services are from Townsville to Mt Isa ($108, 11½ hours) via Charters Towers and from Rockhampton to Longreach ($68, 9½ hours, twice weekly).

Bus trip times may vary depending on what time of day you're travelling. The durations given in this book are approximations.

## TRAIN

Rail services within Queensland are operated by Queensland Rail (QR; ☎ 13 22 32 for reservations, ☎ 13 22 35 for inquiries, **w** www.qr.com.au). There are Queensland Rail Travel Centres throughout the state – these are basically booking offices that can advise you on all rail travel, sell you tickets and put together rail holiday packages that include transport and accommodation. The main Travel Centres are:

**Brisbane** (☎ 3235 1323) Ground floor, 305 Edward St; (☎ 3235 1331) Transit Centre, Roma St
**Cairns** (☎ 1800 620 324, 4036 9250) Cairns train station, Bunda St
**Rockhampton** (☎ 4932 0453) Rockhampton train station, Murray St
**Townsville** (☎ 4772 8358) Townsville train station, Flinders St

You can also buy train tickets through travel agencies. Telephone reservations can be

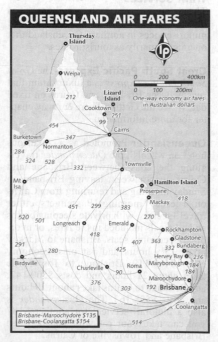

### QUEENSLAND AIR FARES

One-way economy air fares in Australian dollars

Brisbane-Maroochydore $135
Brisbane-Coolangatta $154

made through one of the Travel Centres or through Queensland Rail's centralised booking service from anywhere in Australia. For more information visit the QR Web site.

Rail travel within Queensland is slower and more expensive than bus travel, although some of the economy fares are comparable to bus fares. Depending on your itinerary, a rail pass might also be worth looking into (see Train Passes later in this chapter). The trains are almost all air-con and you can get sleeping berths on most trains for $38.50 extra a night in economy, $60.50 in 1st class. You can break your journey on most services for no extra cost provided you complete the trip within 14 days (single ticket) or two months (return ticket).

Half-price concession fares are available to kids under 16 years of age, students with an International Student Identity Card (ISIC), and Queensland seniors and pensioners.

## Train Services

There are seven major rail services throughout Queensland, as well as three minor services in northern Queensland that operate primarily as tourist routes.

**Great South Pacific Express** The *Great South Pacific Express* is a luxury train that runs between Brisbane and Cairns on fixed dates – see the Getting There & Away chapter for more information.

**Queenslander** Promoted as a 'luxurious hotel on wheels', the *Queenslander* travels along the coast between Brisbane and Cairns once a week, leaving Brisbane on Sunday morning and returning from Cairns on Tuesday morning. Passengers either travel 1st class, with private sleeping berths and all meals included in the fares, or in ordinary economy seats. Brisbane to Mackay takes 15½ hours and 1st class/economy costs $460/119; Brisbane to Townsville takes about 21 hours and costs $509/142; and Brisbane to Cairns takes about 29 hours and costs $558/163. The *Queenslander* is also a motorail service; for another $187 you can take your car with you between Brisbane and Townsville or Cairns.

**Spirit of the Outback** The *Spirit of the Outback* travels the 1326km between Brisbane and Longreach (economy seat/economy sleeper/1st-class sleeper $142/181/273, 24 hours) via Rockhampton ($81/120/190, 10½ hours) twice a week, leaving Brisbane on Tuesday and Friday evenings and returning from Longreach on Thursday and Sunday mornings. A connecting bus service operates between Longreach and Winton.

**Tilt Train & Spirit of Capricorn** The *Tilt Train*, a high-speed economy and business train, does the Brisbane to Rockhampton trip (economy/business $82/174) in just under seven hours, leaving Brisbane at 10.30am from Sunday to Friday. There is also an evening train at 5pm on Friday and Sunday (from Monday to Thursday the 5pm train only runs as far as Bundaberg). In economy/business the one-way fare is $52/119 to Bundaberg.

The *Spirit of Capricorn* covers the Brisbane to Rockhampton route in nine hours on Saturday.

**Sunlander** The *Sunlander* travels between Brisbane and Cairns three times a week, leaving Brisbane on Tuesday, Thursday and Saturday mornings and Cairns on Monday, Thursday and Saturday mornings (economy seat/economy sleeper/1st-class sleeper $163/201/306, 30 hours).

**Spirit of the Tropics** The *Spirit of the Tropics* runs from Brisbane to Townsville (economy seat/economy sleeper/1st-class sleeper $142/181/273, 22½ hours), via Proserpine ($126/164/251, 18 hours), Wednesday and Sunday afternoons, returning from Townsville on Tuesday and Friday mornings.

**Westlander** The *Westlander* heads inland from Brisbane to Charleville every Tuesday and Thursday evening, returning from Charleville to Brisbane on Wednesday and Friday evenings (economy seat/economy sleeper/1st-class sleeper $78/117/184, 16 hours). From Charleville there are connecting bus services to Cunnamulla and Quilpie.

**Inlander** The *Inlander* does what its name suggests, running from Townsville to Mt Isa twice weekly, leaving Townsville on Sunday and Wednesday afternoons and Mt Isa on Monday and Friday afternoons (economy seat/economy sleeper/1st-class sleeper $96/134/204, 20 hours).

**Kuranda Scenic Railway** One of the most popular tourist trips out of Cairns is the Kuranda Scenic Railway – a spectacular 1½-hour trip on a historic steam train through the rainforests west of Cairns. See the Kuranda section in the Far North Queensland chapter for details.

**Gulflander** The *Gulflander* is a strange, snub-nosed little train that travels once a week between the remote Gulf towns of Normanton and Croydon – it's a unique and memorable journey. See the Gulf Savannah chapter for details.

**Savannahlander** Billed as the 'Last Great Train Ride', the historic Cairns to Forsayth service has been resumed after a lull in the mid-1990s, and runs between Cairns and Forsayth once a week – see the Gulf Savannah chapter for more information.

### Train Passes
The Sunshine Rail Pass, available to both international and domestic visitors, gives you unlimited travel on all rail services in Queensland for 14, 21 or 30 days. Fares in economy/1st class are $292/424 for 14 days, $338/521 for 21 days and $424/636 for 30 days. A surcharge is payable if you want to travel on the *Queenslander* (to cover sleeping berths and meals).

Roadrail Passes give you a set number of days of economy-class rail travel and travel on McCafferty's/Greyhound buses within a set period. The cost of these is $286 for 10 days travel in a 60-day period and $374 for 20 days travel within 90 days.

### CAR
Queensland is a big, sprawling state and among the locals the car is the accepted

## Two Wheels Good; Four Wheels Better

You can cover most of Queensland in a standard 2WD vehicle, but there are quite a few places you *won't* be able to visit in your old Ford or Holden station wagon. 4WD vehicles have the clearance to surmount obstacles that would rip the guts out of an ordinary car, and certain conditions like sand driving and river crossings are impossible in a conventional vehicle.

Following are some of the places in Queensland only accessible by 4WD: North Stradbroke and Moreton Islands and parts of Bribie Island (Moreton Bay), Fraser Island, the Cooloola Coast and Burrum Coast National Park (Fraser Coast Area), Deepwater National Park (south of Agnes Water), Byfield National Park (north of Yeppoon), Cape Palmerston National Park (south of Sarina), Sundown National Park (the Darling Downs) and the Bloomfield Track (the coastal route between Cape Tribulation and Cooktown).

Most of Cape York Peninsula is also only accessible by 4WD. A few addled travellers try for the Tip in normal cars, but beyond Weipa, the roads eat normal cars for breakfast. During the Dry, you *could* also tackle most of the Gulf Savannah or the unsealed outback roads to Birdsville in a conventional vehicle, but you'll see the skeletons of plenty of cars that didn't make it rusting in the back of beyond.

means of getting from A to B. More and more travellers are also finding it the best way to see the country – with three or four of you the costs are reasonable and the benefits many, provided, of course, you don't have a major mechanical problem.

In fact, if you want to get off the beaten track – and in parts of Queensland, it's a *very* beaten track – then having your own transport is the only way to go, as many of the destinations covered in this book aren't accessible by public transport.

## Road Rules

Australians drive on the left-hand side of the road just like the UK, Japan and most countries in South and East Asia and the Pacific.

There are a few variations to the rules of the road as applied elsewhere. The main one is the 'give way to the right' rule. This means that if you approach an unmarked intersection, traffic on your right has right of way. Most places do have marked intersections; Mt Isa doesn't!

The speed limit in towns and built-up areas is 50km/h or 60km/h, sometimes rising to 80km/h on the outskirts and dropping to 40km/h in residential areas and school zones. On the open highway it's usually 100km/h or 110km/h, depending on the area.

The police have radar speed traps and speed cameras and are fond of using them. When you're far from the cities and traffic is light, you'll see many vehicles moving a lot faster than 100km/h. Oncoming drivers who flash their lights at you may be giving you a friendly indication of a speed trap ahead (it's illegal to do so, by the way).

Wearing seat belts is compulsory, and small children must be belted into an approved safety seat. Random breath tests are not uncommon in built-up areas. If you're caught with a blood-alcohol level of more than 0.05 then be prepared for a hefty fine, a court appearance and the loss of your licence.

Night driving is a bad idea anywhere in the state. Drink driving is common in the country, and at night, the roads become the undisputed territory of tired road-train drivers and kangaroos – see Dangers & Annoyances in the Facts for the Visitor chapter.

## Road Conditions

Australia doesn't have the traffic volume to justify multilane highways, so most of the country relies on single-lanes, which can be pretty frustrating if you're stuck behind a slow-moving caravan. Passing areas are usually only found on uphill sections, or steep descents, so you may have to wait a long time for an opportunity to pass.

There are a few sections of divided road, most notably on the Surfers Paradise–Brisbane road. Main roads are well surfaced (though a long way from the billiard-table surfaces the Poms are used to driving on) and have regular resting places and petrol stations.

You don't have to get very far off the beaten track to find yourself on dirt roads, though most are quite well maintained. A few useful spare parts are worth carrying – a broken fan belt can be a damn nuisance if the next service station is 200km away. Also look out for the hybrid dirt road: a single, bidirectional strip of tarmac with dirt verges; it's okay to drive down the central strip but be ready to pull into the verges to pass oncoming traffic.

Between cities, signposting on the main highways is generally OK, but once you hit the back roads you'll need a good map – see Maps in the Facts for the Visitor chapter for suggestions.

Cows, sheep and kangaroos are common hazards on country roads, and a collision is likely to kill the animal and seriously damage your vehicle. See Dangers & Annoyances in the Facts for the Visitor chapter.

Flooding can occur with little warning, especially in outback areas and the tropical north. Roads can be cut off for days during floods, and floodwaters sometimes wash away whole sections of road.

## Fuel

Service stations generally stock diesel, super and unleaded fuel; liquid petroleum gas (LPG; Autogas) is usually available at larger service stations along the main highways.

Fuel is generally cheaper in Queensland than in the southern states, although prices vary from place to place and from price war to price war. Some of the service stations in the more remote outback are not above exploiting their monopolies, and distances between fill-ups can be long.

Be cautious of places offering discount fuel, which often has carburettor-clogging impurities.

## RACQ

It's well worth joining the Royal Automobile Club of Queensland (RACQ; ☎ 13 19 05); it offers emergency breakdown cover for $77 per year, which will get you prompt roadside assistance, and a tow to a reputable garage if the problem can't be fixed on the spot. Membership of the RACQ gives reciprocal cover with the automobile associations in other states, and with similar organisations overseas, for example, the AAA in the USA, or the RAC or AA in the UK. Bring proof of membership with you.

The RACQ can also give general guidelines about buying a car and, most importantly, for a fee (around $105) will check over a used car and report on its condition before you agree to purchase it. It also offers discount car insurance to its members.

## Outback Travel

You can drive all the way around Australia without ever leaving sealed road, but if you really want to see outback Australia there are still lots of roads where the official recommendation is that you report to the police before you leave one end, and again when you arrive at the other. That way if you fail to turn up at the other end they can send out search parties.

Many of these roads can be attempted confidently in a conventional car, but you do need to be carefully prepared and to carry important spare parts. Backtracking 500km to pick up a replacement for some minor malfunctioning component or, much worse, to arrange a tow, is unlikely to be easy or cheap.

When travelling to really remote areas it's advisable to travel with a high-frequency outpost radio transmitter that is equipped to pick up the Royal Flying Doctor Service bases in the area.

You will, of course, need to carry a fair amount of water in case of disaster – around 20L a person is sensible – stored in more than one container. Food is less important – the space might be better allocated to an extra spare tyre or spare fuel.

The RACQ can advise on preparation and supply maps and track notes. See the section on Books in the Facts for the Visitor chapter for recommended books that cover preparation for outback travel.

Most tracks have an ideal time of year – in central Australia it's not wise to attempt the tough tracks during the heat of summer (November-March), when the dust can be severe, the chances of mechanical trouble much greater and when water will be scarce. Similarly, in the north travelling in the wet season may be impossible because of flooding and mud. You should always seek advice on road conditions when you're travelling into unfamiliar territory. The local police will be able to advise you whether roads are open and whether your vehicle is suitable for a particular track.

The RACQ has a 24-hour telephone service with a pre-recorded report on road conditions throughout the state – dial ☎ 1300 130 595. For more-specific local information, you can call into the nearest RACQ office – they're listed in the information sections throughout this book.

If you do run into trouble in the back of beyond, *stay with your car*. It's easier to spot a car than a human being from the air and plenty of travellers have wandered off into the wilderness and died of thirst long after their abandoned car was found!

## Rental

Competition between car-hire firms is pretty fierce so rates tend to be flexible and special deals pop up all the time. Whatever your mode of travel on the long stretches, it can be very useful to have a car for some local travel.

The three major companies are Budget (☎ 13 27 27), Hertz (☎ 13 30 39) and Avis (☎ 13 63 33), with offices in almost every town that has more than one pub and a general store. A second-string company that is also represented almost everywhere in the country is Thrifty (☎ 1300 367 227).

The big firms have a number of advantages. Firstly, they have airport branches, so you can get behind the wheel as soon as you arrive, and drop yourself off at the airport when you leave. The second advantage is that they offer one-way rentals – pick up a car in Sydney and leave it in Brisbane, for example. There is usually a minimum hire period and only certain cars may be eligible for one-ways. One-way rentals are generally not available into or out of the Northern Territory or Western Australia.

The major companies offer either unlimited kilometres or a flat charge plus so many cents per kilometre. On straightforward off-the-card city rentals they're all pretty much the same price. Daily rates are typically about $75 a day for a small car (Holden Barina, Ford Festiva, Daihatsu Charade, Suzuki Swift), about $88 a day for a medium car (Mitsubishi Magna, Toyota Camry, Nissan Pulsar) or about $110 a day for a big car (Holden Commodore, Ford Falcon), all including insurance. Keep your eyes peeled for weekend specials – usually three days for the price of two. Rates plummet if you take

a car for more than a week. You must be at least 21 years old to hire from most firms.

There are plenty of smaller operators that often have cheaper rates – typically $30 per day, based on several days' hire – but they rarely offer one-way trips and may not come down as low as the big players on long-term rentals. See individual towns for details of local hire companies. The most common cars are little Korean Kias and Ford Festivas.

Be aware when renting a car (other than a 4WD) in Australia that travel on dirt roads is generally not covered by insurance; if you have an accident you'll be liable for all the costs involved. This applies to all companies, although they don't always point this out.

**4WD Vehicles** Having 4WD enables you to get right off the beaten track and out to some of the natural wonders in the wilderness and the outback that most travellers don't see.

Renting a 4WD vehicle is within range of a reasonable budget if a few people get together. Something small like a Suzuki costs around $110 per day; for a Toyota Land Cruiser you're looking at around $150, which should include insurance and some free kilometres (typically 100km per day).

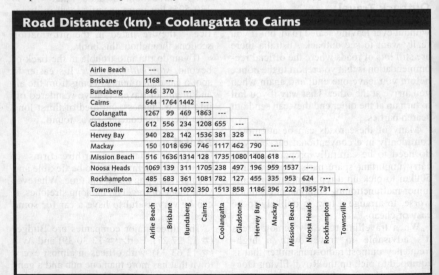

## Road Distances (km) - Coolangatta to Cairns

| | Airlie Beach | Brisbane | Bundaberg | Cairns | Coolangatta | Gladstone | Hervey Bay | Mackay | Mission Beach | Noosa Heads | Rockhampton | Townsville |
|---|---|---|---|---|---|---|---|---|---|---|---|---|
| Airlie Beach | --- | | | | | | | | | | | |
| Brisbane | 1168 | --- | | | | | | | | | | |
| Bundaberg | 846 | 370 | --- | | | | | | | | | |
| Cairns | 644 | 1764 | 1442 | --- | | | | | | | | |
| Coolangatta | 1267 | 99 | 469 | 1863 | --- | | | | | | | |
| Gladstone | 612 | 556 | 234 | 1208 | 655 | --- | | | | | | |
| Hervey Bay | 940 | 282 | 142 | 1536 | 381 | 328 | --- | | | | | |
| Mackay | 150 | 1018 | 696 | 746 | 1117 | 462 | 790 | --- | | | | |
| Mission Beach | 516 | 1636 | 1314 | 128 | 1735 | 1080 | 1408 | 618 | --- | | | |
| Noosa Heads | 1069 | 139 | 311 | 1705 | 238 | 497 | 196 | 959 | 1537 | --- | | |
| Rockhampton | 485 | 683 | 361 | 1081 | 782 | 127 | 455 | 335 | 953 | 624 | --- | |
| Townsville | 294 | 1414 | 1092 | 350 | 1513 | 858 | 1186 | 396 | 222 | 1355 | 731 | --- |

Check the insurance conditions, especially the excesses, as they can be onerous – in Queensland $4000 is typical, although this can often be reduced to around $1000 on payment of an additional daily charge (around $25). Even for 4WDs the insurance of most companies does not cover damage caused when travelling 'off-road', which basically means anything that is not a maintained bitumen or dirt road.

Hertz and Avis have 4WD rentals, with one-way rentals possible between the eastern states and the Northern Territory. Budget also rents 4WDs from Darwin and Alice Springs.

## Brisbane to Charleville

| | Brisbane | Charleville | Dalby | Roma | Toowoomba |
|---|---|---|---|---|---|
| Brisbane | --- | | | | |
| Charleville | 752 | --- | | | |
| Dalby | 218 | 534 | --- | | |
| Roma | 483 | 269 | 265 | --- | |
| Toowoomba | 134 | 618 | 84 | 349 | --- |

## Rockhampton to Cloncurry

| | Barcaldine | Cloncurry | Emerald | Longreach | Rockhampton | Winton |
|---|---|---|---|---|---|---|
| Barcaldine | --- | | | | | |
| Cloncurry | 626 | --- | | | | |
| Emerald | 304 | 930 | --- | | | |
| Longreach | 108 | 518 | 412 | --- | | |
| Rockhampton | 568 | 1194 | 264 | 676 | --- | |
| Winton | 281 | 345 | 585 | 173 | 849 | --- |

## Townsville to Mt Isa

| | Charters Towers | Cloncurry | Hughenden | Mt Isa | Richmond | Townsville |
|---|---|---|---|---|---|---|
| Charters Towers | --- | | | | | |
| Cloncurry | 641 | --- | | | | |
| Hughenden | 245 | 396 | --- | | | |
| Mt Isa | 758 | 117 | 513 | --- | | |
| Richmond | 358 | 283 | 113 | 400 | --- | |
| Townsville | 135 | 776 | 380 | 893 | 493 | --- |

**Campervans** Campervans are a great way to get around Queensland. They'll cut down the cost of accommodation and let you see what you want to see *when* you want to see it. There are hundreds of vans for sale up and down the coast – see Purchase later in this chapter – but a cheaper option is to hire a van with one of the big camper-hire companies. Most have branches in Cairns, Brisbane and other major cities around Australia, and offer one-way hire between certain destinations for a surcharge of around $200. Reliable companies include:

**Backpacker Campervan Rentals**
  (☎ 1800 670 232)
**Britz Australia** (☎ 1800 331 454)
**Campervans for Backpackers**
  (☎ 1800 246 869)
**Travellers Auto Barn** (☎ 1800 674 374);
  one-way on coast only

All these companies offer standard campers, and Britz and Backpacker Campervans also have converted 4WD vehicles. Britz has the best vehicles and the highest prices – typically $81 per day for unlimited kilometres, plus insurance of around $25 to $35 per day – while Campervans for Backpackers charges as little as $33 per day for garishly spraypainted campers.

**Other Vehicles** Motorscooters are available in a number of locations – they're popular on Magnetic Island and in Cairns, for example – and you only need a car licence to ride one. Best of all, in many places you can rent bicycles.

## Purchase
Australian cars are not cheap (a result of the small population) but second-hand prices can be quite acceptable, particularly if split between several travellers. If you're buying a second-hand vehicle reliability is all important. Breakdowns way out in the outback can be inconvenient, expensive and downright dangerous – the nearest mechanic can be a hell of a long way down the road.

What is rather more certain is that the further you get from civilisation the better it is to be in a locally manufactured vehicle, such as a Holden Commodore or Ford Falcon, or one of the mainstream VW, Toyota, Mitsubishi or Nissan campervans. Life gets much simpler if you can get spare parts anywhere from Cairns to Cunnamulla.

Shopping around for a used car involves much the same rules as anywhere in the Western world. Used-car dealers in Australia are of the same mercenary breed you'll find in Los Angeles or London – they'd sell their mother into slavery if it turned a dollar. You'll probably get any car cheaper by buying privately through a newspaper small ad rather than through a dealer. Among other things, dealers are not required to give you any warranty whatsoever when you buy a car in Queensland, regardless of cost.

There's a great deal of discussion among travellers about the best place to buy used cars. It's quite possible that prices vary but don't count on turning it to your advantage. Cairns is a popular spot for travellers buying and selling cars – check the public notice boards in town or in hostels.

In Australia third-party personal injury insurance is always included in the vehicle registration cost. This ensures that every vehicle (as long as it's currently registered) carries at least minimum insurance. You'd be wise to extend that minimum to at least third-party property insurance as well – minor collisions with other cars can be amazingly expensive.

When buying or selling a car in Queensland, the vehicle needs to be re-registered locally (ie, with Queensland Transport) at the time of sale, for which the buyer and seller must complete a Vehicle Registration Transfer Application form, available from Queensland Transport (☎ 13 23 80, **W** www.transport.qld.gov.au) or the RACQ. The seller will usually add the cost of any outstanding registration to the overall price of the vehicle. Before the vehicle can be offered for sale, the seller must also obtain a Safety Certificate (replacing the old Roadworthy Certificate) from a Queensland Transport–approved vehicle inspection station. Stamp duty of $2 per $100 has to be paid when you buy a car and, as this is based on the purchase price, it's not unknown for buyer and seller to agree privately to understate the price. It's much easier to sell a car in the same state that it's registered in, otherwise the buyer will eventually have to reregister it in the new state.

**Buy-Back Deals** One way of getting around the hassles of buying and selling a vehicle privately is to enter into a buy-back arrangement with a car or motorcycle dealer. However, many dealers will find ways of knocking down the price when you return the vehicle – even if a price has been agreed in writing – often by pointing out spurious repairs that allegedly will be required to gain the dreaded RWC. The cars on offer have often been driven around Australia a number of times, often with haphazard or minimal servicing, and are generally pretty tired. The main advantage of these schemes is that you don't have to worry about being able to sell the vehicle quickly at the end of your trip.

## MOTORCYCLE

Motorcycles are a very popular way of getting around; between April and November the climate is just about ideal for biking around Queensland and you can bush camp just about anywhere. The long, open roads are really made for large-capacity machines above 750cc, which Australians prefer once they outgrow their 250cc learner restrictions. Still, a few hardy individuals tackle the length and breadth of the continent on 250cc trail bikes.

If you want to bring your own motorcycle into Australia you'll need a Carnet de Passage, and when you try to sell it you'll get less than the market price because of restrictive registration requirements. Shipping from just about anywhere is expensive.

However, with a little bit of time up your sleeve, getting mobile on two wheels in Australia is quite feasible, thanks largely to the chronically depressed motorcycle market. The beginning of winter (June) is a good time to strike. Australian newspapers and the lively local bike press have extensive classified ad sections where $2500 to

$3000 gets you something that will easily take you around the country if you know a bit about bikes. The main drawback is that you'll have to try to sell it again afterwards.

An easier option is a buy-back arrangement with a large motorcycle dealer in a major city. They're keen to do business, and basic negotiating skills allied with a wad of cash (say, $5000) should secure an excellent second-hand bike with a written guarantee that they'll buy it back in good condition minus $1500 or $2000 after your four-month, round-Australia trip. Popular brands for this sort of thing are BMWs, and large-capacity, shaft-driven Japanese bikes. Harley-Davidsons are very popular in Australia, but no-one is going to buy back a Harley with dings in the chromework.

You'll need a rider's licence and a helmet. A fuel range of 350km will cover most fuel stops. Beware of dehydration in the dry, hot air – force yourself to drink plenty of water, even if you don't feel thirsty – and NEVER ride at night; a road train can hit a kangaroo without stopping but a motorcycle has no chance.

Many roadhouses offer showers free of charge or for a nominal fee. They're meant for truck drivers, but other people often use them too.

It's worth carrying some spares and tools even if you don't know how to use them, because someone else often does. If you do know, you'll probably have a fair idea of what to take. The basics include: a spare tyre tube (front wheel size, which will fit on the rear); puncture repair kit with levers and a pump (or tubeless tyre repair kit with at least three carbon dioxide cartridges); a spare tyre valve, and a valve cap that can unscrew same; the bike's standard tool kit for what it's worth; spare throttle, clutch and brake cables; tie wire, cloth ('gaffer') tape and nylon 'zip-ties'; a handful of bolts and nuts in the usual emergency sizes (M6 and M8), along with a few self-tapping screws; one or two fuses in your bike's ratings; a bar of soap for fixing tank leaks (knead to a putty with water and squeeze into the leak); and, most important of all, a workshop manual for your bike (even if you

can't make sense of it, the local motorcycle mechanic can).

Make sure you carry water – at least 2L on major roads in central Australia, more off the beaten track. And finally, if something does go hopelessly wrong in the back of beyond, park your bike where it's clearly visible and observe the cardinal rule: *Don't leave your vehicle.*

## BICYCLE

Queensland can be a good place for cycling, although you need to choose your areas. There are bike tracks in most cities, but in the country it's variable. Roads such as the Bruce Hwy from Brisbane to Cairns can be long, hot and not particularly safe, as there are limited verges and heavy traffic. The humid weather can be draining too, if you're not used to it. The best areas for touring are probably the Gold Coast hinterland, the Sunshine Coast secondary roads and the area north of Cairns.

Bicycle helmets are compulsory, as are front and rear lights for night riding; a spot fine of $30 applies if you disobey this rule.

Cycling has always been popular in Australia, and not only as a sport: some shearers would ride for huge distances between jobs, rather than use less reliable horses. It's rare to find a reasonably sized town that doesn't have a shop stocking at least basic bike parts.

If you're coming specifically to cycle, it makes sense to bring your own bike. Check with your airline for costs and the degree of dismantling/packing required. Within Australia you can load your bike onto a bus or train to skip the boring bits. Note that bus companies require you to dismantle your bike, and some don't guarantee that it will travel on the same bus as you. Trains are easier, but you should supervise the loading and if possible tie your bike upright, otherwise you may find that the guard has stacked crates of Holden spares on your fragile alloy wheels.

You can buy a good steel-framed touring bike in Australia for about $400 (plus panniers). It is possible to rent touring bikes and equipment from a few of the commercial touring organisations. You can also rent mountain bikes from bike shops in many cities, although these are usually for short-term hire (around $20 a day).

Many towns in the east were established as staging posts, a day's horse ride apart, which is pretty convenient if you want a pub meal and a bed at the end of a day's riding. Camping is another option and it's usually warm enough that you won't need a bulky sleeping bag. You can get by with standard road maps, but as you'll probably want to avoid both the highways and the low-grade, unsealed roads. The government map series is best.

Remember that you need to maintain your body as well as your bike. Exercise is an appetite suppressant, so stock up on carbohydrates at regular intervals, even if you don't feel that hungry. Drink plenty of water; dehydration is no joke and can be life-threatening. Summer in Queensland isn't a great time for cycling – it can get very hot and incredibly humid, and it's no fun at all trying to ride through the torrential downpours that are commonplace during the Wet.

Of course, you don't have to follow the larger roads and visit towns. It's possible to fill your mountain bike's panniers with muesli, head out into the mulga and not see anyone for weeks (or ever again – outback travel is very risky if not properly planned). Water is the main problem, and you can't rely on it being available where there aren't settlements, whatever your map may say.

Always check with locals if you're heading into remote areas, and notify the police if you're about to do something particularly adventurous. That said, you can't rely too much on local knowledge of road conditions – most people have no idea of what a heavily loaded touring bike needs. What they think of as a great road may be pedal-deep in sand or bull dust, and cyclists have happily ridden along roads that were officially flooded out.

Bicycle Queensland (☎ 3844 1144) at 493 Stanley St, Mater Hill, Brisbane (or write to PO Box 8321, Woolloongabba, Brisbane, Qld 4101), is worth contacting for more information on cycling in Queensland. Some of the better bike shops can also be good sources of information on routes, suggested rides, tours and cycling events. For more information on seeing Australia from two wheels, check out *Cycling Australia* (published by Lonely Planet).

## HITCHING

Hitching is never entirely safe in any country in the world, and we don't recommend it. Travellers who decide to hitch should understand that they are taking a small but potentially serious risk. It is safer to travel in pairs and hitchhikers should always let someone know where they are planning to go. A few years back, a number of hitch-hiking backpackers were killed by a murderous truck driver, so the worst-case scenarios can happen.

Never hitch alone, but remember that groups of more than two will struggle to get a ride. A couple hitching will usually have the best luck. The ideal location to pick up a ride is on the outskirts of a town, on the slip road down to the highway in the direction you are travelling. The ideal appearance for hitching is a sort of genteel poverty – threadbare but clean – and don't carry too much gear; drivers aren't going to pull over if they'll have to open the trunk for your bags. The last law of hitching is intuition; if something doesn't feel right, don't get in the vehicle, or if you're already in the cab, make an excuse and get out at the first opportunity.

One last piece of etiquette: Drivers often pick up hitchers for company, so try to provide some conversation if you want to get all the way to your destination.

## BOAT

At any time of the year, there are thousands of yachts and boats travelling up and down the Queensland coast. From time to time the owners of these vessels need to take on extra crew, and if you ask around at marinas and yacht clubs, it may be possible to make your way along the coast by hitching rides or crewing on yachts. Moreton Bay near Brisbane, Rainbow Beach and Tin Can Bay, Hervey Bay, Gladstone, Airlie Beach, Townsville, Cairns and Port Douglas are all good places to try. See the Sea section in the Getting There & Away chapter for more information.

## LOCAL TRANSPORT

Brisbane has a comprehensive public transport system with buses, trains and river ferries. Larger cities like Surfers Paradise, Toowoomba, Mt Isa, Bundaberg, Rockhampton, Mackay, Townsville and Cairns all have local bus services.

At the major tourist centres, most of the backpackers hostels and some resorts and hotels have courtesy coaches that will pick you up from train or bus stations or the airport. Most tour operators include courtesy coach transport to/from your accommodation in their prices. Elsewhere, all of the larger towns and cities have at least one taxi service.

## ORGANISED TOURS

There are all sorts of tours around Queensland, although few that cover much of the state. Most are connected with a particular activity (eg, bushwalking or horse riding) or area (eg, 4WD tours to Cape York). See the Activities section of the Facts for the Visitor chapter and the various chapters of this book for some suggestions. There are also thousands of flyers in hostels and tourist information offices.

Up in the Far North, there are plenty of operators offering 4WD tours of Cape York Peninsula, often with the option of driving

one way and flying or boating the other. See Organised Tours in the Cape York Peninsula chapter for details.

There are all sorts of trips from the mainland out to the Great Barrier Reef. You can fly in a seaplane out to a deserted coral cay; take a fast catamaran to the outer reef and spend the day snorkelling; join a dive boat and scuba dive in a coral garden; or take a day trip to one of the many islands.

There are hundreds of tours operating out of Cairns and Port Douglas – as well as trips to the reef and islands, you can take the Kuranda Scenic Railway up to the Kuranda markets; tour the Atherton Tablelands; visit Cape Tribulation on a 4WD tour; cruise along the Daintree River; go white-water rafting; and visit Aboriginal rock-art galleries in Cape York.

Tours to Fraser Island, organised by the backpackers hostels in Noosa Heads and Hervey Bay, are a convenient way of seeing one of Queensland's natural wonders for those who don't have their own 4WD.

Dozens of operators in the Whitsundays offer cruises around the islands, and if you want to do your own thing you can get a group together and charter a yacht.

From the Gold Coast there are tours to Lamington and Springbrook National Parks, and numerous tours run out of Brisbane to the Sunshine and Gold Coasts and the lovely sand islands of Moreton Bay.

# Brisbane

**postcode 4000 (city central) • pop 1,620,000**

Brisbane has long been viewed by the larger, southern capitals as something of a northern hicksville, little more than an overblown country town, but if this were ever true, it certainly isn't today. Brisbane established its cultural credentials in the 1980s with a string of international sporting and cultural events, and has been on the up and up ever since.

These days Brisbane is one of the most desirable places to live in Australia, with a prosperous, cosmopolitan atmosphere, a great street-cafe scene, beautiful riverside parks, a busy cultural calendar and above-average nightlife (much of it priced out of the backpacker budget).

The first settlement here was established at Redcliffe on Moreton Bay in 1824 as a penal colony for Sydney's more recalcitrant convicts. After struggling with inadequate water supplies and hostile Aborigines, the colony was relocated to the banks of the Brisbane River, the site of the city centre today, but suffered at the hands of numerous crooked warders and was abandoned in 1839. The Moreton Bay area was thrown open to free settlers in 1842, marking the beginning of Brisbane's rise to prominence, and the beginning of trouble for the region's Aborigines.

By the time of Queensland's separation from New South Wales in 1859, Brisbane had a population of around 6000 residents. Huge wealth flowed into the city from the new pastoral and gold mining enterprises in the Darling Downs, and grandiose buildings were thrown up to reflect this new-found affluence. The frontier-town image was hard to shake off, however, and it wasn't until the 1982 Commonwealth Games and Expo '88 that Brisbane was taken seriously as a cultural centre. Today it is the third-largest city in Australia with a population of over 1.6 million.

Central Brisbane is comparatively small and compact, but it is surrounded by a vast

## Highlights

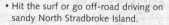

- Buy an Off-Peak Saver pass and spend the day exploring the city from the river on the City Cat.
- Laze about the South Bank Parklands – and take your swimming togs for a splash in the lagoon.
- Hit the Castlemaine Perkins XXXX brewery for a tour followed by a sampling session.
- Take a bus up to Mt Coot-tha lookout for a great Brisbane panorama.
- Feed the wild dolphins at Tangalooma Resort on Moreton Island.
- Hit the surf or go off-road driving on sandy North Stradbroke Island.

expanse of leafy suburbs (before the burbs were reclassified as separate towns, Brisbane was the largest city in the world in terms of geographical area). In recent years, many large corporations have moved their offices here, contributing to the pleasant aura of prosperity.

Brisbane is the undisputed arts capital of Queensland, with dozens of theatres, art-house cinemas, opera and concert halls, galleries and museums. The city is also

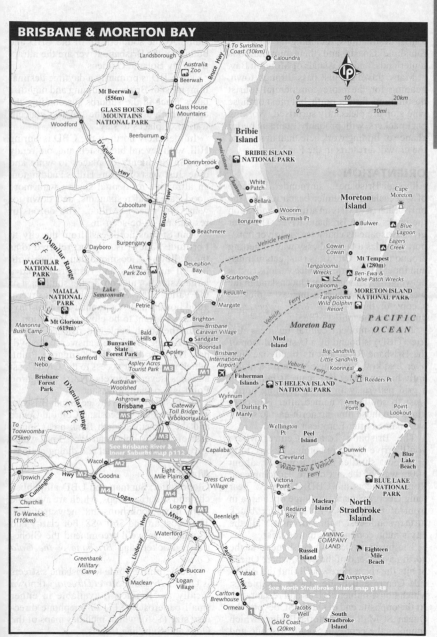

# BRISBANE & MORETON BAY

To Sunshine Coast (10km)
Landsborough
Australia Zoo
Beerwah
Caloundra

Mt Beerwah (556m)
GLASS HOUSE MOUNTAINS NATIONAL PARK
Glass House Mountains

Woodford

Beerburrum

Bribie Island
BRIBIE ISLAND NATIONAL PARK

White Patch
Bellara
Woorim
Skirmish Pt

Cape Moreton

Moreton Island

Caboolture

Bongaree
Beachmere

Bulwer
Blue Lagoon
Eagers Creek

Burpengary
Dayboro

D'AGUILAR NATIONAL PARK

Alma Park Zoo

Deception Bay
Scarborough

Vehicle Ferry

Cowan Cowan
Mt Tempest (280m)

Tangalooma Wrecks
Ben-Ewa & False Patch Wrecks

MAIALA NATIONAL PARK

Lake Samsonvale

Petrie

Redcliffe
Margate

Tangalooma
Tangalooma Wild Dolphin Resort
MORETON ISLAND NATIONAL PARK

PACIFIC OCEAN

Manorina Bush Camp

Mt Glorious (619m)

Bald Hills

Brighton
Brisbane Caravan Village
Sandgate
Boondall

Moreton Bay

Mt Nebo

Samford

Bunyaville State Forest Park

Apsley

Mud Island

Big Sandhills
Little Sandhills
Kooringal

Brisbane Forest Park

Aspley Acres Tourist Park

Brisbane International Airport

Australian Woolshed

Fisherman Islands
ST HELENA ISLAND NATIONAL PARK

Vehicle Ferry

Reeders Pt

Ashgrove

Brisbane

Gateway Toll Bridge
Woolloongabba

Wynnum
Darling Pt
Manly

Amity Point
Point Lookout

To Toowoomba (75km)

See Brisbane River & Inner Suburbs map p112

Wellington Pt
Peel Island

Cleveland

Dunwich

Blue Lake Beach

Wacol

Eight Mile Plains
Dress Circle Village

Capalaba

Water Taxi & Vehicle Ferry

BLUE LAKE NATIONAL PARK

Ipswich

Goodna

Victoria Point

Macleay Island

North Stradbroke Island

Churchill

Logan

Beenleigh

Redland Bay

To Warwick (110km)

Waterford

MINING COMPANY LAND

Greenbank Military Camp

Buccan

Russell Island

Eighteen Mile Beach

Maclean
Logan Village

Jumpinpin

See North Stradbroke Island map p148

Carlton Brewhouse
Ormeau

Jacobs Well

South Stradbroke Island

To Gold Coast (20km)

surrounded by some of the state's major tourist destinations, including the Gold and Sunshine Coasts and their mountainous hinterlands, and the islands of Moreton Bay.

Many travellers just pass through town, heading for the more commercial tourist destinations further north, but most of those who stop are pleasantly surprised. Working backpackers will probably stand a better chance of finding work here than in some of the crowded resorts in the Far North.

## ORIENTATION

Although Brisbane is surrounded by some of Queensland's premier beach resorts, the only beach in town is an artificial sandbar on the banks of the Brisbane River. The river gives Brisbane its character, and river transport provides a fast and easy way of getting around the city. City Cats (fast catamarans) and Inner City Ferries service various routes between the University of Queensland in the west and Bretts Wharf in the east – pick up a copy of the *Brisbane River Experience* guide from the tourist office.

The ultra-modern central business district (CBD) is bound by a U-shaped loop of the Brisbane River, but its small size (just over 1 sq km) gives the city centre a pleasantly human scale. The centre is laid out in a grid pattern, with streets running northwest to south-east named after European kings and those running north-east to southwest named after European queens.

The Brisbane Transit Centre, where you'll arrive if you're coming by bus, train or airport shuttle, is on Roma St, about 500m west of the city centre. Heading east, Roma St meets the CBD at Ann St, near King George Square, the large open area in front of Brisbane's City Hall. One block further south-east is the Queen St Mall, the city's main commercial thoroughfare.

The business heart of Brisbane is at the north-eastern end of the CBD, where Queen St hits the river. Here you'll find the Riverside Centre and Eagle St Pier complexes, which house numerous bars and restaurants. At the opposite end of Queen St, beyond the Queen St Mall, is Victoria Bridge, which connects the centre to South Brisbane and

the cultural development known as South Bank. At the southern tip of the CBD and bound by the Brisbane River are the attractive City Botanic Gardens.

The CBD is primarily a daytime destination; most of Brisbane's dining and nightlife takes place in the suburbs surrounding the city, which also have the greatest concentration of places to stay.

Immediately north of the CBD is Spring Hill, with several big hostels and, on trendy Caxton St, plenty of places to wine and dine. Just west of Spring Hill is Paddington, an attractive residential suburb with more good cafes and restaurants, and down towards the river is Milton, with dozens of restaurants-to-be-seen-in.

Ann St runs north-east from the city to Fortitude Valley (usually just referred to as the Valley) – a cosmopolitan suburb with lots of nightclubs and restaurants and a large Asian population. To the south-east of the Valley is New Farm, which has several good hostels and is a popular base for travellers who want to be close to the action.

On the south bank and reached via the Story Bridge (Brisbane's answer to the Sydney Harbour Bridge) is Kangaroo Point, which is handy for access to the Gold Coast and has several motels. North Kangaroo Point is especially pleasant.

Across the Victoria Bridge, South Brisbane is the site of the Queensland Cultural Centre and the attractive South Bank area. Southeast of here is bohemian West End, which also has plenty of hostel and dining options.

### Maps

Globetrotter, Sunmap and UBD all publish city and suburban maps, which are available from most bookshops and newsagencies. They cost around $6 to $8. For clarity and compact size we'd recommend the Globetrotter Pocket Map *Brisbane & the Gold Coast*.

The definitive guide to Brisbane's streets is UBD's *Brisbane Street Directory* (known locally as 'Refidex'), available in either small paperback ($17) or telephone directory size ($36), which includes maps of the Gold and Sunshine Coasts.

## INFORMATION
### Tourist Offices
Right in the middle of the Queen St Mall is the very convenient Brisbane Tourism information centre (☎ 3229 5918, e enquiries@brisbanetourism.com.au). It opens from 9am to 5pm Monday to Thursday, 9am to 7pm Friday, 9am to 4pm Saturday and 10am to 4pm Sunday. It's a good place to find out about things to see and do in the city.

Also useful is the privately run Brisbane Visitors Accommodation Service (☎ 3236 2020), which opens 7am to 6pm weekdays and 8am to 5pm weekends. On the 2nd floor of the transit centre on Roma St, this place specialises in backpacker travel and can book accommodation and tours up the coast and inland.

In the Stanley Street Plaza in the South Bank Parklands is the South Bank information centre (☎ 3867 2051), open 9am to 6pm, or 10pm on Friday.

### Free Publications
Most cafes and bars have copies of Brisbane's excellent free-listings papers *Scene*, *Time Off* and *Rave Magazine*, all of which offer extensive coverage of live music and clubbing in the city. Rocking Horse Records on Adelaide St in the CBD also has copies of all these papers.

*Brisbane News* is a weekly lifestyle magazine, a little gushing, but useful for picking up on Brisbane's preoccupations of the moment. *This Week in Brisbane* is full of ads but redeemed by a useful map of central Brisbane and the Citytrain network.

### Money
There are foreign-exchange bureaus at Brisbane airport's domestic and international terminals that are open for all arriving flights. There is also an ATM that takes most international credit cards.

Thomas Cook has three foreign-exchange offices in the city centre. Most useful is the kiosk in the Queen St Mall (☎ 3210 6325), on the ground level of the Myer Centre, open 9am to 5.30pm from Monday to Thursday, 9am to 8pm on Friday, 9am to 4pm on Saturday and 9.30am to 4pm on Sunday. There's

another office at 276 Edward St (☎ 3221 9422), open 8.30am to 5pm from Monday to Friday. The office upstairs in the Myer Centre is mainly for business transactions.

Travelex (☎ 3229 8610), in the Queen St Mall in Lennon Plaza, offers currency exchange and Western Union international money transfers from 9am to 6pm on weekdays, 9.30am to 5pm on Saturday and 10.30am to 4.30pm on Sunday.

American Express (AmEx; ☎ 3229 2729) has its office and exchange bureau at 131 Elizabeth St, near Albert St. Opening hours are 9am to 5pm Monday to Friday and 9am to noon Saturday.

For after-hours foreign exchange, the tellers in the Treasury Casino (see under Entertainment later in this chapter) are there 24 hours a day.

### Post
Brisbane's General Post Office (GPO) is in an imposing Victorian building on Queen St, between Edward and Creek Sts. It's open from 7am to 6pm weekdays and has a poste restante counter. There are several smaller Post Shops around, the most useful being on the 2nd level of the Wintergarden Centre on Queen St, open from 8.15am to 5.30pm weekdays and 9am to 4pm on Saturday.

### Email & Internet Access
There are plenty of Internet cafes in the centre, but few in the suburbs. The excellently located Global Gossip (☎ 3229 4033), at 288 Edward St near the Palace Backpackers, has plenty of terminals, cheap-call phone booths and Internet access for $6 per hour.

The Central City Library (call the city council, ☎ 3403 8888), in the basement of the City Plaza complex behind City Hall, has several email terminals for public use at $6 per hour, which can (and should) be booked in advance. There's a one-hour-per-day limit. The library is open from 9am to 6pm Monday to Friday and from 10am to 3pm weekends.

Another option is the State Library of Queensland (☎ 3840 7666), at South Bank, which is open 10am to 8pm from Monday to Thursday and 10am to 5pm from Friday to Sunday. It has a similar setup and charges $4 per hour.

Most of Brisbane's backpackers hostels now offer Internet access to guests.

## Travel Agencies

STA Travel has several branches in Brisbane. In the city, there are offices at 111 Adelaide St (☎ 3221 3722) and 59 Adelaide St (☎ 3229 2499), open 9am to 5.30pm from Monday and Friday and 9am to 3pm on Saturday, plus other offices at the University of Queensland (☎ 3371 2433) and

the Queensland University of Technology (QUT; ☎ 3229 0655).

Trailfinders (☎ 3229 0887), at 91 Elizabeth St, is another good international travel agent, known for its cheap airfares. It's open Monday to Saturday.

The YHA's Membership & Travel office (☎ 3236 1680) is at 154 Roma St, opposite the transit centre; it's open from 8.30am to 5pm weekdays and 9am to 3pm Saturday.

## Useful Organisations

The Department of Immigration and Multicultural Affairs (☎ 13 18 80), on the 13th

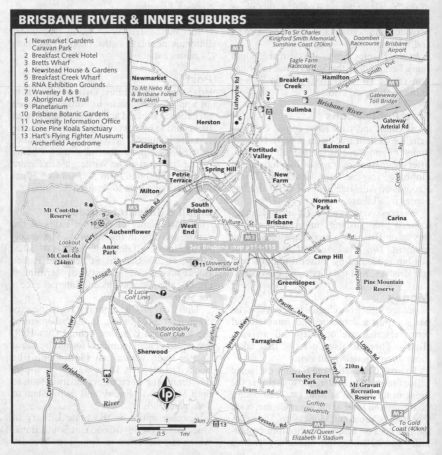

## BRISBANE RIVER & INNER SUBURBS

1  Newmarket Gardens
   Caravan Park
2  Breakfast Creek Hotel
3  Bretts Wharf
4  Newstead House & Gardens
5  Breakfast Creek Wharf
6  RNA Exhibition Grounds
7  Waverley B & B
8  Aboriginal Art Trail
9  Planetarium
10 Brisbane Botanic Gardens
11 University Information Office
12 Lone Pine Koala Sanctuary
13 Hart's Flying Fighter Museum;
   Archerfield Aerodrome

floor at 313 Adelaide St, is the place to come for visa extensions. It's open weekdays from 9am to 4pm (from 10am on Wednesday).

Queensland's motoring association, the Royal Automobile Club of Queensland (RACQ; ☎ 3361 2444), has its head office beside the GPO on Queen St, open 8.30am to 5pm weekdays. Here you can obtain Queensland vehicle registration, insurance and maps. There's a second branch in the Valley at 300 St Pauls Terrace.

The Environment Protection Agency (EPA) runs an excellent information centre called Naturally Queensland (☎ 3227 8186) at 160 Ann St; it's open on weekdays from 8.30am to 5pm. You can get maps, brochures and books on national parks and state forests, as well as camping information and Fraser Island permits.

## Disabled Travellers

Brisbane is commendably wheelchair friendly and Brisbane City Council (BCC) produces a series of useful brochures including *Accessible Brisbane Parks* and the *Brisbane Mobility Map*. These are usually available from the BCC Customer Services Centre at 69 Ann St, behind City Plaza, or call the Disability Services Unit on ☎ 3403 4268.

It may also be worth contacting the Disability Information Awareness Line (DIAL; ☎ 1800 177 120, 3224 8444). See the section on Disabled Travellers in the Facts for the Visitor chapter for more information.

## Bookshops

Brisbane is well stocked with bookshops, though most are national chains and sell quite a mainstream selection of titles. Probably the biggest is Angus & Robertson Bookworld, which has branches in the Myer Centre on the Queen St Mall, the Post Office Square mall in Adelaide St and at 52 Queen St. The largest range of travel guides and maps is to be found at World Wide Maps & Guides (☎ 3221 4330) at 187 George St.

For a fantastic range of second-hand titles try Archives Fine Books (☎ 3221 0491), at 40 Charlotte St in the city centre, which is open till 9pm Monday to Saturday and boasts one million titles. Also worth a look

are Emma's Bookshop (☎ 3844 4973) at 82 Vulture St and Bent Books (☎ 3846 5004) at 205 Boundary St, both in West End.

## Photography

Anderson's Camera Centre (☎ 3221 3133), at 117 Adelaide St, can do repairs for most brands and charges $16 for printing and processing a 36-exposure film ($18 under four hours).

Camera Tech (☎ 3229 5406), at 127 Creek St, is a reliable repair agent and handles most brands.

## Left Luggage

In the transit centre on Roma St there are deep, backpack-sized lockers on the 3rd level that cost $5 for 24 hours, plus $1 each time you want to open and relock the locker within that time. There's a 72-hour limit.

## Medical Services

The Travellers' Medical & Vaccination Centre (☎ 3221 9066), on the 5th floor of the Qantas building at 247 Adelaide St, can handle all vaccinations and medical advice for travellers. Consultation fees depend on the length of visit: A 15-minute consultation will cost $26. The centre is open from 8am to 5pm on Monday and Friday, 10am to 7pm on Tuesday, 8am to 9pm on Wednesday, 8am to 2pm on Thursday and 8.30am to 2pm on Saturday.

The 24-hour Travellers' Medical Service (☎ 3211 3611), on the 1st floor at 245 Albert St, just north of the Queen St Mall, offers travel vaccinations, women's health care and first-aid kits. It's open from 7.30am to 7pm on weekdays, 8.30am to 5pm on Saturday and 9.30am to 4pm on Sunday. The Brisbane Sexual Health Clinic (☎ 3227 8666) is at 484 Adelaide St.

There are numerous chemists (pharmacies) in the centre and the burbs. The Queen St Mall Pharmacy (☎ 3221 4585), 141 Queen St, is open Monday to Saturday until 9pm and Sunday from 10am to 5.30pm.

## Emergency

Dial ☎ 000 for emergency help from the police, ambulance or fire brigade. There's a

# BRISBANE

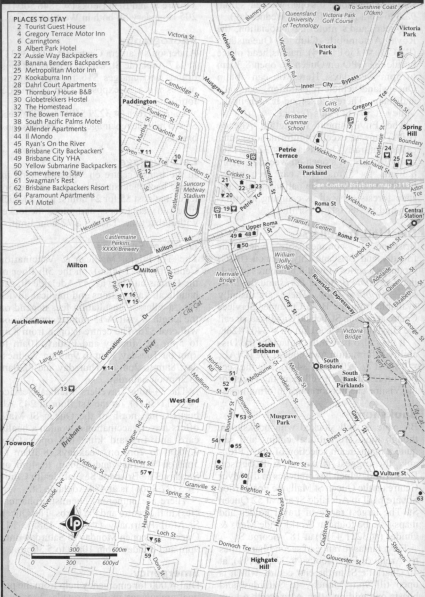

**PLACES TO STAY**
2  Tourist Guest House
4  Gregory Terrace Motor Inn
6  Carringtons
8  Albert Park Hotel
22  Aussie Way Backpackers
23  Banana Benders Backpackers
25  Metropolitan Motor Inn
27  Kookaburra Inn
28  Dahrl Court Apartments
29  Thornbury House B&B
30  Globetrekkers Hostel
32  The Homestead
37  The Bowen Terrace
38  South Pacific Palms Motel
39  Allender Apartments
44  Il Mondo
45  Ryan's On the River
48  Brisbane City Backpackers'
49  Brisbane City YHA
50  Yellow Submarine Backpackers
60  Somewhere to Stay
61  Swagman's Rest
62  Brisbane Backpackers Resort
64  Paramount Apartments
65  A1 Motel

**BRISBANE**

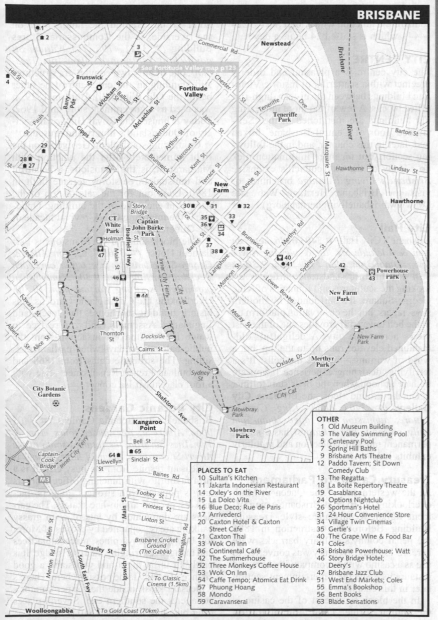

Newstead

Commercial Rd

Hill St

Brunswick St

Fortitude Valley

See Fortitude Valley map p123

Wickham St

Ballow St

Barry Pde

Ann St

McLachlan St

Gipps St

St Pauls Tce

Chester St

Teneriffe Dve

Teneriffe Park

Brisbane River

Barton St

Lindsay St

Hawthorne

Robertson St

Arthur St

Harcourt St

Kent St

James St

Annie St

Macquarie St

Hawthorne

29

28

27

St

Brunswick St

Terrace St

Bowen St

New Farm

Story Bridge

CT White Park

Captain John Burke Park

Holman St

Bradfield Hwy

Main St

Barker St

Tce

City Ferry

Inner City Ferry

30

31

35

36

34

33

Brunswick St

Merthyr Rd

32

37

38

39

40

41

Sydney St

Langshaw St

Moreton St

Lower Bowen Tce

42

43

Powerhouse Park

New Farm Park

Creek St

Edward St

Albert St

Alice St

47

46

45

44

Thornton St

Dockside

Cairns St

Moray St

New Farm Park

Oxlade Dr

Merthyr Park

City Botanic Gardens

Sydney St

Mowbray Park

City Cat

Captain Cook Bridge

Inner City Ferry

Kangaroo Point

Bell St

64

65

Llewellyn St

Sinclair St

Mowbray Park

Baines Rd

Toohey St

Princess St

Linton St

Shafston Ave

Main St

Wellington Rd

Stanley St

Ipswich Rd

Allen St

Merton Rd

South East Fwy

Brisbane Cricket Ground (The Gabba)

To Classic Cinema (1.5km)

Woolloongabba

To Gold Coast (70km)

**PLACES TO EAT**
10 Sultan's Kitchen
11 Jakarta Indonesian Restaurant
14 Oxley's on the River
15 La Dolce Vita
16 Blue Deco; Rue de Paris
17 Arrivederci
20 Caxton Hotel & Caxton Street Cafe
21 Caxton Thai
33 Wok On Inn
36 Continental Café
42 The Summerhouse
52 Three Monkeys Coffee House
53 Wok On Inn
54 Caffe Tempo; Atomica Eat Drink
57 Phuong Hoang
58 Mondo
59 Caravanserai

**OTHER**
1 Old Museum Building
3 The Valley Swimming Pool
5 Centenary Pool
7 Spring Hill Baths
9 Brisbane Arts Theatre
12 Paddo Tavern; Sit Down Comedy Club
13 The Regatta
18 La Boite Repertory Theatre
19 Casablanca
24 Options Nightclub
26 Sportman's Hotel
31 24 Hour Convenience Store
34 Village Twin Cinemas
35 Gertie's
40 The Grape Wine & Food Bar
41 Coles
43 Brisbane Powerhouse; Watt
46 Story Bridge Hotel; Deery's
47 Brisbane Jazz Club
55 West End Markets; Coles
55 Emma's Bookshop
56 Bent Books
63 Blade Sensations

police station in the Queen St Mall, just south of the junction with Albert St (☎ 3224 4444), which is staffed 24 hours a day.

## CITY CENTRE

The city centre is a pleasant and orderly precinct with a scattering of historic Victorian buildings between the hi-tech, high-rise office blocks. A few of the more interesting old buildings are mentioned in the 'Self-Guided Tour of Central Brisbane' boxed text, later in this chapter, and in the following section, but for more information pick up a copy of the city council's extensive *Brisbane's Living Heritage* brochure, or visit the Brisbane Heritage Web site (**W** www.brisbanelivingheritage.org).

### City Hall

Brisbane's City Hall (*☎ 3403 6586, between Ann & Adelaide Sts; lift & viewing tower open 10am-3pm Mon-Fri, 10am-2.30pm Sat*) is a historic sandstone edifice overlooking the sculptures and fountains of King George Square. It's surrounded by modern skyscrapers, but the observation platform up in the bell tower still provides one of the best views across the city. A delightful, old-fashioned elevator runs up to the top, but a word of warning – beware the bells. It's a terrifying, deafening experience if you are up here at noon when the bells start tolling.

On the ground floor, the **Brisbane City Gallery** (*☎ 3403 8888, King George Square; admission free; open 10am-5pm daily, closed public holidays*) has a small, permanent museum collection and regularly exhibits local art.

### Treasury Casino to Parliament

At the western end of the Queen St Mall, overlooking the river, is Brisbane's magnificent Italian Renaissance–style Treasury Building. Before its construction in 1885 the penal colony's military barracks were here. In 1995 the Treasury was converted to use as a casino with accompanying bars and restaurants – see the Entertainment section later in this chapter.

In the block south-east of the casino is the similar former **Land Administration**

**Building**, now taken over by the Conrad hotel group. Behind the hotel, over on the riverside, is the **Commissariat Stores Building** (*☎ 3221 4198, 115 William St; adult/child $4/2; open 10am-4pm Tues-Sun*), one of only two convict-era structures still standing in the city centre (the other being the Old Windmill). Built in 1829, it was used as a government store until 1962. Today it houses the Royal Historical Society of Queensland's library and museum

Continuing south along George St, on the right immediately after the junction with Margaret St, is **the Mansions**, a beautiful and unusual three-storey terrace built in 1890. Look out for the cats on top of the parapet at each end of the building. Opposite is the imposing Greek-revival facade of the **Queensland Club**.

One block south of the Mansions is Parliament House (*☎ 3406 7562, Cnr Alice & George Sts; admission free; 6 free tours each weekday starting from 9.30, 2 only when parliament is sitting starting from 10.30*). Overlooking the City Botanic Gardens, this historic building still houses the Queensland Legislative Assembly, and you're free to watch the law-makers in action from the public balcony on days when parliament is sitting. The structure dates from 1868 and was built in French Renaissance–style with a roof clad in Mt Isa copper.

### City Botanic Gardens

Brisbane's City Botanic Gardens (*☎ 3403 0666, Albert St; free guided tours 11am & 1pm Tues-Sat from the rotunda south of the Albert St entrance; open 24 hours a day*) is a pleasant respite from the busy city. It is a firm favourite with lunching office workers and is popular with strollers, joggers, picnickers, cyclists and in-line skaters. The gardens are dominated by lots of open grassy walking areas, separated by groves of Moreton Bay figs, bunya pines, macadamia trees and mangroves fringing the river's edge. It is partly lit up at night and you stand a good chance of seeing tame possums here. There's a pleasant kiosk inside the former curator's cottage at the southern end. Several places offer bike hire for around $10 per hour.

## Riverfront

The former docks area north-east of the CBD is one of the most attractive and lively areas in the city centre. The only testimony to former maritime commerce is the greenish copper-domed **Customs House** (1886–89) (☎ 3365 8909, 399 Queen St; admission free; open 10am-4pm), where all ships were once required to pay duties. These days the historic building is owned by the University of Queensland and is a venue for fundraisers and private gatherings of distinguished alumni. On the lower level is a free gallery with a small private collection of early Australian paintings, and a very good brasserie (see the boxed text 'The Critics Recommend' under Places to Eat later in this chapter).

Further south are the **Riverside Centre** and the **Eagle St Pier** complexes. Despite some awful plastic kit-architecture this is an attractive riverside site and home to some very fine restaurants. A good time to come here is on Sunday morning, when the area becomes a busy craft market. There are ferry terminals at both complexes.

## MUSEUMS

Brisbane's major museum, the Queensland Museum, is part of the Queensland Cultural Centre – see under South Bank later in this chapter for details.

The excellent **Sciencentre** (☎ 3220 0166, W www.sciencentre.qld.gov.au, 110 George St, City; family/adult/child & student $28/8/6; open 10am-5pm) is a hands-on science museum with interactive displays, optical illusions, a perception tunnel and regular film shows. It's great to visit with kids, but is often packed out by school groups.

**Queensland Maritime Museum** (☎ 3844 5361, Sidon St, South Brisbane; adult/child $5.50/2.80; open 9.30am-4.30pm), at the western end of the South Bank promenade, has a wide range of displays, including artefacts from wrecks along the Queensland coast, and ship models. The highlight here is the HMAS Diamantina, a restored 1945 naval frigate that you can clamber over to indulge your naval-battle fantasies.

Away from the centre, out in St Lucia on Sir Fred Schonell Dr, the **University of Queensland** has anthropology, antiquities and geology museums – see under University of Queensland later in this chapter for details.

By the City Botanic Gardens in the Queensland University of Technology campus is the **QUT Art Museum** (☎ 3864 5370, QUT Campus, George St, City; admission free; open 10am-4pm Tues-Fri, noon-4pm Sat & Sun), which has regularly changing exhibits of contemporary Australian art and work by Brisbane student artists.

**Hart's Flying Fighter Museum** (☎ 3272 9484, Archerfield Aerodrome, Wirraway Ave, Archerfield; admission free; open 9am-5pm Mon-Sat, 10am-2pm Sun), about 12km south of the centre, has a collection of beautifully restored fighter planes all in flying order. Beside the airport freeway is the **Sir Charles Kingsford Smith Memorial**, a hangar holding the famous Southern Cross, in which Sir Charles made the first trans-Pacific flight in 1928

Brisbane City Council is due to open a new museum at the Naval Stores on Amesbury St in Kangaroo Point – ask the Customer Services Centre for more information.

## GALLERIES

Besides the Queensland Art Gallery (see Queensland Cultural Centre under South Bank later in this chapter) Brisbane has a number of smaller art galleries and exhibition spaces, mostly showing paintings and ceramic works for sale. The greatest concentration is in the Valley and New Farm, where you'll find the **Institute of Modern Art** (☎ 3252 5750, Cnr Ann & Gipps Sts; admission free; open 11am-5pm Tues-Fri, 11am-4pm Sat), a noncommercial gallery with an industrial exhibition space and regular showings by local names. Artours (☎ 3899 3686) offers full-day guided tours of Brisbane's galleries with food and wine laid on for $95.

Other interesting galleries in the Valley include:

**Craft on Brunswick** (☎ 3250 1290)
  381 Brunswick St
**Jan Murphy Gallery** (☎ 3254 1855)
  486 Brunswick St
**Philip Bacon Gallery** (☎ 3358 3555)
  2 Arthur St

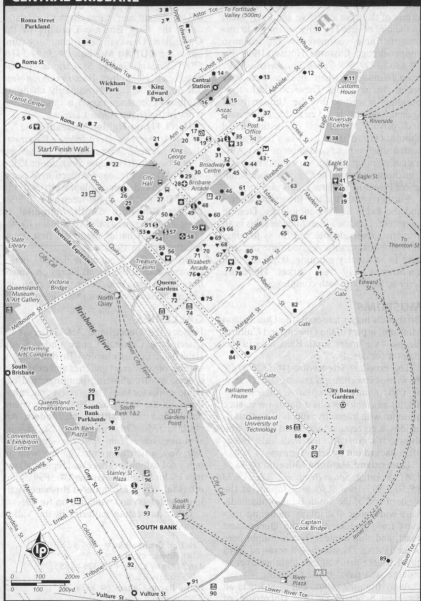

# CENTRAL BRISBANE

Roma Street
Parkland

To Fortitude
Valley (500m)

Wickham Tce

Wickham
Park

King Edward
Park

Roma St

Transit Centre

Start/Finish Walk

King George Sq

Broadway Centre

Brisbane Arcade

City Hall

State Library

Riverside Expressway

North Quay

Treasury Casino

Queens Gardens

Elizabeth Arcade

Queensland Museum & Art Gallery

Melbourne St

Performing Arts Complex

South Brisbane

Brisbane River

Victoria Bridge

North Quay

Inner City Ferry

Queensland Conservatorium

South Bank Parklands

South Bank 1&2

South Bank Piazza

Convention & Exhibition Centre

QUT Gardens Point

Stanley St Plaza

SOUTH BANK

South Bank 3

Parliament House

Queensland University of Technology

City Botanic Gardens

Captain Cook Bridge

River Plaza

Customs House

Riverside Centre

Riverside

Eagle St Pier

Eagle St

To Thornton St

Edward St

Gate

Vulture St

Lower River Tce

River Tce

Inner City Ferry

City Cat

## CENTRAL BRISBANE

**PLACES TO STAY**
1 Acacia Inner-City Inn
3 Dorchester Self-Contained Units
4 Soho Motel
7 Holiday Inn Brisbane; Jazz & Blues Bar
9 Astor Motel
14 Sheraton Brisbane
17 Palace Backpackers; Down Under Bar & Grill
22 Explorers Inn
61 Brisbane Hilton
72 Conrad International
75 Chifley Hotel
82 Royal on the Park

**PLACES TO EAT**
2 Oriental Bangkok
11 Customs House Brasserie
20 Palace Cafe
35 Mekong Chinese Restaurant
38 Michael's
40 Pier Nine; Cha Cha Char
42 Gilhooley's Downtown
45 Jimmy's
54 Malone's
65 Hungry Heart Bistro
67 Pane e Vino
68 Gilhooley's
70 Govinda's
81 F.I.X.
88 Botanic Gardens Kiosk
91 The Ship Inn
93 Capt'n Snapper; Arbour View Cafes
97 Central Cafes
98 Cafe San Marco

**ENTERTAINMENT**
6 The Transcontinental
23 Dendy Cinema
33 Rosie's Tavern; Indie Temple
41 City Rowers; Friday's
47 Hoyt's Regent Theatre
56 Irish Murphy's
59 CBD Wine Bar

64 Metro Arts Centre; Verve Cafe
77 Brisbane Festival Hall
87 QUT Gardens Theatre
94 IMAX Theatre

**OTHER**
5 YHA Membership & Travel Office
8 Old Windmill & Observatory
10 St John's Cathedral
12 Department of Immigration & Multicultural Affairs
13 Camera Tech
15 Cenotaph
16 Queensland Rail Travel Centre
18 Global Gossip
19 Thomas Cook
21 Naturally Queensland (EPA Office)
24 Law Courts
25 City Plaza; Central City Library
26 Brisbane City Council Customer Services Centre
27 Sherry's Disposals
28 Travellers' Medical Service
29 Anderson's Camera Centre
30 STA Travel
31 Coles Express
32 Australia The Gift
34 QTTC
36 Angus & Robertson Bookworld
37 Qantas; Travellers' Medical & Vaccination Centre
39 River Queen Cruises
43 RACQ Head Office
44 MacArthur Chambers
46 Wintergarden Centre; Food Court; Australian Geographic; RM Williams
48 Queen St Mall Pharmacy
49 Brisbane Tourism Information Centre

50 Downtown Duty Free; City International Duty Free
51 Travelex Bureau de Change
52 STA Travel; Ansett; Air New Zealand
53 Angus & Robertson Bookworld
55 World Wide Maps & Guides
57 Thomas Cook
58 Myer Centre; Bus Station; Australian Geographic; Hoyts Cinemas; Greg Grant Country Clothing
60 Greater Union Cinema (Defunct)
62 Nite Owl 24-Hour Convenience Store
63 St Stephen's Cathedral
66 American Express
69 Greater Union Cinema (Defunct)
71 Trailfinders
73 Commissariat Stores Building
74 Sciencentre
76 Archives Fine Books
78 Globetrekker Outdoor Shop
79 Brisbane Bicycle Sales
80 Skatebiz; Mountain Designs; Silk Road
83 Queensland Club
84 The Mansions; Augustine's on George
85 QUT Art Museum
86 Old Government House
89 Kangaroo Point Cliffs (Climbing Area)
90 Queensland Maritime Museum
92 Australian Trust for Conservation Volunteers
95 South Bank Information Centre; Southbank Aboriginal Centre
96 Pauls Breaka Beach (Swimming Lagoon)
99 Nepali Pagoda

## SOUTH BANK

Brisbane's South Bank, formerly the site of Expo '88, has been developed into a very impressive arts and leisure zone, with theatres, museums and galleries; walking and in-line skating tracks; and a landscaped riverside park with streams, canals, fountains, grassy knolls and ornamental gardens.

South Bank was again the centre of attention in August 2001, during the 2001 Goodwill Games.

### Queensland Cultural Centre

On South Bank, just over the Victoria Bridge from the CBD, is the Queensland Cultural Centre, a huge compound that includes a

## Self-Guided Tour of Central Brisbane

The logical starting point for a tour of central Brisbane is the imposing, classical-style **City Hall**, where you should take the lift up to the top of the bell tower for the view over the CBD. It will give you a good idea of the layout of the city centre.

From City Hall, cross King George Square and head south along Albert St until you hit the **Queen St Mall**. This busy pedestrian mall is the commercial centre of Brisbane and is lined with fine facades dating back to Australia's Federation (1901), including the former Carlton Hotel, the former Telegraph Building, the former York Hotel and, a short detour east, the glorious frontage of the old **Hoyts Regent Theatre**.

At the western end of the mall, on the far side of George St, is the unmistakable **Treasury Building**, which has probably seen more money pass through its doors since it was converted into a casino than it ever did when it was the Brisbane city treasury. Turn south along George St and you'll come to another spectacular Italian Renaissance–style building, the **Land Administration Building**, now the Conrad International Hotel. Take the small alley just south of the hotel (Stephens Lane), onto William St; the historic **Commissariat Stores**, one of Brisbane's oldest buildings, sits on the riverbank on the far side of the road.

Head north along William St and take the Victoria Bridge across the Brisbane River to **South Bank**, the focus for Brisbane's cultural energy. The modern complex on the right contains the excellent **Queensland Museum** and **Queensland Art Gallery**, while to the left is the **Performing Arts Complex**, the state's leading venue for concerts and theatre. Spreading south of the Performing Arts Complex is a lovely riverfront park, originally laid out for Expo '88.

Follow the modernist walkway south through the Parklands. Just beyond the Performing Arts Complex, on the left hand side and tucked away among the trees, is an ornate wooden **Nepali pagoda**, created by Nepali craftsmen for the Expo. A little further south you'll find the curious **Pauls Breaka Beach**, a hugely popular artificial beach and swimming lake named after Queensland's favourite milkshake; and **Stanley Street Plaza**, a showy tourist arcade.

Head down to the riverfront and pick up an eastbound Inner City Ferry (adult/concession $1.60/0.80) from the South Bank 3 jetty down the river to the Edward St jetty on the far side of the headland. Just up from the jetty is the entrance to Brisbane's appealing **City Botanic Gardens**, which has a friendly cafe where you can sit with a coffee and watch the world go by. Stroll through the quiet avenues of trees to the far side of the park and enter the Queensland University of Technology (QUT) campus. Check out the impressive columned foyer of the original **Government House**, built in 1860 and now the home of the National Trust. A little further north is the **QUT Art Museum**.

On the edge of the campus, at the corner of George and Alice Sts, is Queensland's regal copper-topped **Parliament House**, which offers regular free tours on weekdays. If parliament is in session, wander up to the public gallery for a peek. Diagonally across from Parliament House is the white colonial **Queensland Club**, where government bigwigs hobnob between debates.

concert and theatre venue, an enormous conference and convention centre and a modern concrete edifice containing the city's main art gallery and museum and the Queensland State Library (a lot of culture to cram into one building!).

At the back of the complex, the **Queensland Museum** (☎ 3840 7555, **w** www.qmuseum.qld.gov.au, Grey St, South Brisbane; admission free; open 9am-5pm) has an interesting collection of exhibits relating to the history of Queensland, from a skeleton of Queensland's own dinosaur *Muttaburrasaurus* to the *Avian Cirrus*, the tiny plane in which Queensland's Bert Hinkler made the first England to Australia solo flight in 1928. Also here is a fantastic selection of Melanesian artefacts and a captured German tank from WWI. There are often interesting temporary exhibitions.

## Self-Guided Tour of Central Brisbane

KH

**Parliament House**

Head north along George St, passing **the Mansions**, an ornate terrace from 1890, and turn right down Charlotte St, opposite the Conrad International Hotel. There are some more old facades on the left-hand side of the street. Take a left turn into Albert St and head north towards the Queen St Mall, passing the Art Deco frontages of the defunct **Greater Union cinemas**.

You can either wrap it up here and continue straight across the mall to King George Square, or hang a right and head north-east along Elizabeth St. On the far side of Edward St on the right-hand side is **St Stephen's Cathedral** (1874) and the more interesting **St Stephen's Chapel** (1850), Brisbane's oldest church, which is attributed to the English architect Augustus Pugin, who designed London's Houses of Parliament.

Across from St Stephen's, an alley leads to the historic **post office building** on Queen St. Cross the road and cut through the Post Office Square arcade to Adelaide St. On the far side is the pretty **Anzac Park**, which is usually full of wild ibises, office workers (at lunchtime) and bicycle couriers. At the far end of the park is the Greek Revivalist **Cenotaph**, where an eternal flame burns in remembrance of Australian soldiers who died in WWI. A short walk south-west along Adelaide St will take you back to King George Square.

For information on more walks in the Brisbane area, hunt down Alison Cotes & Pamela Wilson's *Walking Brisbane*.

The **Queensland Art Gallery** (☎ 3844 8855, W www.qag.qld.gov.au, Melbourne St, South Brisbane; admission free; open 10am-5pm; free guided tours 11am, 1pm & 2pm Mon-Fri, 11am, 2pm & 3pm Sat, 11am, 1pm & 3pm Sun) has an impressive permanent collection and also features visiting exhibitions. As well as some big European names, plenty of Australian artists are represented here, including Sir Sidney Nolan, William Dobell, George Lambert, Charles Blackman, Margaret Preston and Fred Williams.

### South Bank Parklands

The impressive South Bank Parklands owe their existence to Expo '88, but unlike most relics from international shows, South Bank has been extensively redeveloped over the years to keep things fresh and interesting. The Cultural Centre dominates the north of the park, but further south you'll find such oddities as a **Nepali pagoda** left over from the Expo and the curious **Pauls Breaka Beach**, an artificial swimming beach designed to resemble a tropical lagoon – a great spot to kick back and catch some rays.

Behind Breaka Beach is **Stanley Street Plaza**, a renovated section of Stanley St, with shops, cafes and a tourist information centre. On Friday evening and all day Saturday and Sunday, there's a large **craft and clothing market** in the plaza. Heading away from the plaza and river is Ernest St, where you'll find the **IMAX Theatre** (☎ *3844 4222, Cnr Ernest & Grey Sts, South Brisbane; open 10am-10pm*), with a huge surround screen and a regularly changing program. You pay by the dimension: 2-D movies are $14.50/9.50 per adult/child, 3-D movies are $15.50/10.50.

Between late October and early March, an **alfresco cinema** screens family movies on the grassy knoll opposite the South Bank Piazza at 7.30pm on Saturday. The **South Bank Piazza**, an outdoor entertainment venue, has regular concerts and performances, many of which are free. There's usually some kind of child-friendly activity going on here at weekends and on school holidays.

The Parklands are within easy walking distance of the city centre. You can also get there by City Cat or City Ferry (there are three jetties along the river bank) or by bus or train from the transit centre or Central Station.

## INNER SUBURBS

Much of the action in Brisbane goes on in the inner suburbs, where the cafe scene, dining and nightlife are far better than they are in the centre. Arty **West End**, centred on Boundary St, has some good pavement cafes. **Petrie Terrace** and **Paddington** are hilly, leafy suburbs with lots of renovated Queenslander houses and plenty of good restaurants, cafes, art galleries and antique shops.

**Milton** is an up-and-coming area, with chic cafes and restaurants on Park Rd. **Spring Hill**, rising gently to the north of the city, is a transition zone between the city and burbs and has lots of motels and the pleasant King Edward and Wickham Parks, and the new Roma Street Parkland.

The **Old Windmill & Observatory** (1828) on Wickham Terrace, just north-east of the transit centre, is one of Brisbane's earliest buildings. Due to a design flaw, the sails were too heavy for the wind to turn, and a convict-powered treadmill was briefly employed before the whole thing was abandoned. The building was converted to a signal post and later a meteorological observatory.

## Fortitude Valley & New Farm

Fortitude Valley was named after the HMS *Fortitude*, which sailed up the Brisbane River in 1849 with more than 250 immigrants on board. At one time the area was the commercial centre of Brisbane, but it went into sharp decline and until very recently was one of the seediest parts of Brisbane. All that changed in the 1990s, when artists, restaurateurs and various fringe types flooded into the area, attracted by the low rents, transforming the Valley into the buzzing district it is today.

During the day the action is concentrated on **Brunswick St Mall**, an attractive arcade full of pavement cafes. **McWhirter's Markets** at the Wickham St end of the mall is a Brisbane landmark with an impressive Art Deco corner facade. On Saturday from about 8am until mid-afternoon the mall is taken over by an arty-crafty **market** offering the usual import goods plus a few home-spun crafts.

The Valley is also home to Brisbane's small Chinatown, centred on the rather ordinary **Chinatown Mall** in Duncan St. This nonstop strip of Asian restaurants continues around the corner into Wickham St.

Just west of the Valley on Ann St, towards the CBD, is the famously unfinished **St John's Cathedral**. Construction of this classic Gothic cathedral began in 1906 and is still underway after nearly a century of shortfalls in the church restoration fund! There are guided tours at 2pm and 10am daily (2pm only on Sunday).

New Farm, just east of the Valley along Brunswick St, became 'desirable' among young professionals a few years ago and is now chock-a-block with wine bars and restaurants. The streets off Brunswick St have plenty of cheap accommodation including several backpackers hostels. At the eastern end of Brunswick St, **New Farm Park** is a large open parkland with playgrounds, picnic areas with gas barbecues, jacaranda trees and beautiful rose gardens.

On the riverbank at the north-eastern tip of the park is the **Brisbane Powerhouse**, a modernist arts theatre with a buzzing waterfront cafe-bar.

## NEWSTEAD HOUSE

North of the centre on the Brisbane River is Brisbane's best-known heritage site, the lovely old Newstead House *(☎ 3216 1846, Breakfast Creek Rd, Newstead; adult/child $4.40/2.20; open 10am-4pm Mon-Fri, 2pm-4pm Sun)*. Set in attractive forested grounds, the historic homestead dates from 1846 and is beautifully fitted out with Victorian furnishings and antiques, clothing and period displays. You can get here by bus from Adelaide St in the CBD, or Wickham St in the Valley – look for bus No 322, 306 or 300.

## UNIVERSITY OF QUEENSLAND

The University of Queensland occupies a 1.1 sq km site in a loop of the Brisbane River, 7km south of the city. It's an attractive and interesting place to visit, with several museums, good sporting facilities, an excellent bookshop and a cinema. You can ride a bike all the way here from the city along the Bicentennial Bikeway, which follows the western bank of the Brisbane River out of the centre (see Getting Around later in this chapter).

The helpful information office, in a small building beside the main entrance, has a map of the grounds and information about the facilities.

The university centres on the lovely **Great Court**, a spacious area of lawns and trees surrounded by a semicircle of impressive cloistered sandstone buildings. There are several museums open to the general public by appointment including the **Anthropology** *(☎ 3365 3236)*, **Antiquities** *(☎ 3365 2643)*,

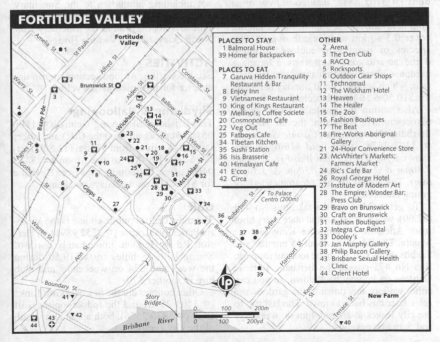

**FORTITUDE VALLEY**

**PLACES TO STAY**
1 Balmoral House
39 Home for Backpackers

**PLACES TO EAT**
7 Garuva Hidden Tranquility Restaurant & Bar
8 Enjoy Inn
9 Vietnamese Restaurant
10 King of Kings Restaurant
19 Mellino's; Coffee Societe
20 Cosmopolitan Cafe
22 Veg Out
25 Fatboys Cafe
34 Tibetan Kitchen
35 Sushi Station
36 Isis Brasserie
40 Himalayan Cafe
41 E'cco
42 Circa

**OTHER**
2 Arena
3 The Den Club
4 RACQ
5 Rocksports
6 Outdoor Gear Shops
11 Technomad
12 The Wickham Hotel
13 Heaven
14 The Healer
15 The Zoo
16 Fashion Boutiques
17 The Beat
18 Fire-Works Aboriginal Gallery
21 24-Hour Convenience Store
23 McWhirter's Markets; Farmers Market
24 Ric's Cafe Bar
26 Royal George Hotel
27 Institute of Modern Art
28 The Empire; Wonder Bar; Press Club
29 Bravo on Brunswick
30 Craft on Brunswick
31 Fashion Boutiques
32 Integra Car Rental
33 Dooley's
37 Jan Murphy Gallery
38 Philip Bacon Gallery
43 Brisbane Sexual Health Clinic
44 Orient Hotel

To Palace Centro (200m)

0   100   200m
0   100   200yd

Geology (☎ 3365 2668) and Zoology (☎ 3365 8548) Museums.

The best way to get here is by City Cat – see Getting Around later in this section.

## MT COOT-THA RESERVE

Mt Coot-tha Reserve is a huge bush parkland a short bus ride or drive from the city. It has an excellent botanic garden and a great lookout over the city. On a clear day you can see all the way to Moreton Bay and the islands, and there's a cafe serving Devonshire teas and snack meals, plus the posh *Summit Restaurant* (☎ 3369 9922), which serves good food (you pay a mark-up for the location).

Just north of the road to the lookout, on Sir Samuel Griffith Dr, is the turn-off to JC Slaughter Falls, reached by a short walking track. Also here is a 1.5km Aboriginal Art Trail, which takes you past eight art sites with work by local Aboriginal artists.

The very beautiful Brisbane Botanic Gardens (☎ 3403 8888; admission free; open 8.30am-5.30pm; free guided walks 11am & 1pm Mon-Sat), at the foot of the mountain, cover 0.5 sq km and include over 20,000 species of plants, an enclosed tropical dome, an arid zone, rainforests, a Japanese garden, a library, and a teahouse and restaurant, which serves a good Sunday barbecue for $10.50/6.50 per adult/child.

Also within the gardens is the largest planetarium in Australia, the Sir Thomas Brisbane Planetarium (Cosmic Skydome; ☎ 3403 2578; adult/child $10/6; 45-min shows 3.30pm & 7.30pm Wed-Fri, 1.30pm, 3.30pm & 7.30pm Sat, 1.30pm & 3.30pm Sun). The shows are not recommended for young children.

To get to Mt Coot-tha take bus No 471 ($2.60), which departs about once every hour from Adelaide St opposite King George Square. The ride takes about 15 minutes and the bus drops you off in the lookout car park. Bus No 471 passes the Brisbane Botanic Gardens on its way back down, so you can either walk or bus down to the gardens and get a later bus back to town. The last trip to the city leaves at around 4pm on weekdays and 5pm at weekends.

## LONE PINE KOALA SANCTUARY

Just a short bus ride south from the city centre, the Lone Pine Koala Sanctuary (☎ 3378 1366; adult/child/VIP or YHA card holder $14.50/9.50/11; open 7.30am-5pm) is an easy half-day trip. The sanctuary is set in attractive parklands beside the river and is home to a variety of Australian wildlife, including kangaroos, possums, wombats, emus and lyrebirds. The star attractions are the 130 or so koalas. They're undeniably cute and most visitors readily cough up the $13 to have their picture taken hugging one. Hand feeding the tame kangaroos is cheaper – $0.50 for a bag of pellets. Talks are given on the animals at set times throughout the day.

Cityxpress bus No 430 ($3.40, 35 minutes) leaves at 30 minutes past the hour from the Koala platform at the Queen St Mall bus station. You can also pick it up at the Cultural Centre busway stop. The MV *Mirimar* (☎ 3221 0300) offers one-way/return trips for $14/22 for adults and $7/12 for children, not including admission to the Sanctuary. Daily cruises at 10am, returning from Lone Pine at 1.30pm, head to the sanctuary from North Quay, next to Victoria Bridge.

## ACTIVITIES

See the Getting Around section later in this chapter for information on cycling.

### Skydiving & Ballooning

The Brisbane Skydiving Centre (☎ 1800 061 555) picks up from the CBD and offers tandem skydives from 3810m (12,500 feet) for $220. Fly Me to the Moon (☎ 3423 0400) offers ballooning trips over Brisbane for $198/218 on weekdays/weekends.

### Golf

The most central public course is the Victoria Park Golf Course (☎ 3252 9891) on Herston Rd in Herston, immediately north of Spring Hill; 18 holes costs $19.50 during the week and $24 on weekends, and club hire is another $20.

Other courses are the St Lucia Golf Links (☎ 3403 2556) and the Indooroopilly Golf Club (☎ 3870 2556), both about 8km south of the city centre.

## In-Line Skating

Skatebiz (☎ 3220 0157), 101 Albert St, City, hires out in-line skates and the necessary protective equipment for $11 for two hours or $16.50 for the day. Blade Sensations (☎ 3844 0606), 493 Stanley St, is just south of the South Bank Parklands and charges $10/25 per hour/day. Some of the best skating areas are the South Bank Parklands, the City Botanic Gardens and the bike paths that follow the Brisbane River.

## Rock Climbing

The Cliffs on the banks of the Brisbane River at Kangaroo Point is a decent rock-climbing venue that is floodlit until midnight or later. Several operators offer climbing and abseiling instruction here, including Jane Clarkson's Outdoor Adventures (☎ 3870 3223). You can join Outdoor Adventures' rock-climbing club every Wednesday night ($15 per person); just make your way to the base of the cliffs. Jane also organises abseiling sessions by appointment ($54 per person) and climbing trips out of Brisbane. The easiest way to get to the Kangaroo Point cliffs is via the South Bank cycle path.

Another good climbing club is K2 Extreme (☎ 3257 3310), based at the K2 outdoor shop at 140 Wickham St, Fortitude Valley.

If you haven't climbed before or just want some indoor practice, Rocksports (☎ 3216 0492), 224 Barry Parade, Fortitude Valley, is an excellent indoor climbing centre with a wide choice of top-roping or leading routes. Entry is $12 and you can hire harnesses for $3.50 and shoes for $4.50.

## Swimming

Aside from the artificial lagoon at the South Bank Parklands, Brisbane has plenty of more-conventional pools. Choices include:

**Centenary Pool** (☎ 3831 2665) 400 Gregory Terrace, Spring Hill. Open 5.30am to 7.30pm weekdays, 6am to 6pm on Saturday and 7am to 6pm on Sunday. This is the best pool in town, with an Olympic-sized lap pool, a kids pool and a diving pool with a high tower.

**Spring Hill Baths** (☎ 3831 7881) 14 Torrington St, Spring Hill. Open morning and evening in the summer. These old-fashioned baths are among the oldest in the southern hemisphere.

**Valley Swimming Pool** (☎ 3852 1231) 432 Wickham St, Fortitude Valley. Open 5.30am to 8pm weekdays, 5.30am to 6pm on Saturday and 7.30am to 6pm on Sunday.

## Tennis

Tennis Queensland (☎ 3871 8555) represents numerous tennis courts around the city; probably the closest to the centre are the courts at the University of Queensland in St Lucia (☎ 3371 7906), which cost $12 per hour before 5pm and $15.40 per hour after 5pm. The courts are just across from the University of Queensland City Cat stop.

## ORGANISED TOURS

There are all sorts of organised tours of Brisbane and the surrounding areas on offer – ask at any of the information centres for brochures and details. Most of the tour bus companies have offices in the Roma St transit centre.

## City Tours

The hop-on, hop-off City Sights bus shuttles around 18 of the city's major landmarks, departing every 45 minutes between 9am and 3.45pm from Post Office Square in Queen St. One-day tickets allow you to get off and on whenever and wherever you want (adult/child $18/12). The tickets also allow unlimited use of other city bus and ferry services. They can be bought on the bus or at the tourism information kiosk in the Queen St Mall.

There are some interesting guided walking tours of Brisbane, mostly devoted to the city's convict history. Brian Ogden's Historical Tours (☎ 3217 3673) offers two-hour walks around central Brisbane, with lots of historical anecdotes (adult/child $11/5.50). Ghost Tours (☎ 3844 6606) offers quirky, entertaining tours of Brisbane on Friday night ($13), with visits to supposedly haunted spots. There are also hearse tours and haunted dinner evenings – call for details.

Numerous operators offer local driving tours, including Mr Day Tours (☎ 3289 8364) and Brisbane City-Trips (☎ 1300 300 242).

## Brewery Tours

There are hugely popular guided tours of the Castlemaine Perkins XXXX brewery (☎ 3361 7597), Milton Rd, Milton. Tours run at 11am, 1.30pm and 4pm Monday to Wednesday and cost $8.50/5.50 for adults/under-18s, including free 'samples' at the end (for over-18s). It's $7.50 for aged pensioners and YHA card holders. There's also a Wednesday night barbecue tour. Most hostels organise trips or you can call and book yourself onto a tour. The brewery is a 20-minute walk west from the transit centre or you can take the Citytrain to Milton station. Wear enclosed shoes.

The Carlton Brewhouse (☎ 3826 5858, corner of Darlington Dr and Pacific Hwy), owned by Carlton and United Breweries, brewers of Foster's and VB among others, also conducts tours of its premises south of the city centre beginning at 10am, noon and 2pm Monday to Friday ($10). There is no public transport to the brewery, but a special bus runs from the transit centre from Tuesday to Thursday (book with the brewery); the cost is $25, which includes beer, snacks and transfers.

## River Cruises

River Queen (☎ 3221 1300) offers cruises of the Brisbane River in the restored wooden paddle-steamers *Kookaburra Queen* and *Kookaburra Queen II* from Eagle St Pier. Cruises last 1½ hours and board daily at 11.45am ($55 with seafood lunch, $35 with buffet lunch and $22 with cookies). There are also dinner cruises ($49 to $65) boarding at 7pm returning 10pm Monday to Thursday, or 10.30pm Friday and Saturday, or boarding at 6pm on Sunday, returning at 9pm.

## Hinterland Tours

Run by a former backpacking globetrotter, Rob's Rainforest Tours (☎ 0409 496 607, W www.powerup.com.au/~frogbus7) offers several day trips out of Brisbane taking travellers to the rainforests at Mt Glorious, Kondalilla Falls and the Glass House Mountains, and Lamington National Park. Several readers have written with high praise for the tours. The price per person is $58, which includes morning tea, a barbecue lunch and pick-up and return to your Brisbane hostel.

Araucaria Ecotours (☎ 5544 1283, e ecotoura@eisnet.au), at Running Creek Rd, 18km east of Rathdowney in the Gold Coast hinterland, offers three-day naturalist-led wilderness tours in the Mt Barney National Park area. The tour picks up in Brisbane every Wednesday morning and calls in at the Daisy Hill Koala Information Centre and the Karawatha Wetlands on the way down to Mt Barney. The cost is $198 including accommodation at the Mt Barney Lodge (self-catering, with stops to buy food), or $264 with meals.

Allstate Scenic Tours (☎ 3285 1777) has day trips from Brisbane to O'Reilly's Guesthouse and Lamington National Park, leaving every day (except Saturday) at 9.30am. The return fare is $44.

## SPECIAL EVENTS
### Summer

The week before Christmas is celebrated with a Christmas Festival at South Bank Parklands. Brisbane joins the rest of the country in celebrating Australia Day each 26 January; the cockroach races at the Story Bridge Hotel in Kangaroo Point are among the more unusual (and popular) events.

The Chinese New Year celebrations – centred on Chinatown in the Valley – run for five days, starting in early February, and feature fireworks, banquets and a temple dragon.

### Autumn

If you're in Brisbane for St Patrick's Day (17 March) head for one of the Irish pubs listed in the Entertainment section. There's also a parade through the city. In March/April, the Paniyiri Festival is a Greek cultural festival with dancing, food and music, centred on Musgrave Park in West End.

The National Trust runs the Heritage Week Festival for two weeks in mid-April to celebrate Brisbane's architectural heritage. There's also an international comedy festival each April. The Bridge to Bay Marathon and the Brissie to the Bay Bike Tour are held at the end of May.

The Brisbane Biennial, an international music festival held every second year (odd numbers), is an outstanding celebration of the world of music. The festival lasts for 10 days in July (call ☎ 3840 7958 for details) and features everything from classical, opera, military bands, world music, jazz and blues to rock, accompanied by fine food and wine.

### Winter
The Winter Racing Carnival stretches from 1 May to 30 June, with major horse-race meetings each weekend at both Doomben and Eagle Farm Racecourses, including the Brisbane Cup in mid-May. Fortitude Valley holds its own festival, the Valley Fiesta, over a weekend in early or mid-July.

Brisbane's annual agricultural show, the Royal National Exhibition (known as the Ekka), is held at the RNA Exhibition Grounds in Spring Hill for a week in early August, and features agricultural and industrial displays, a carnival and various ring events.

The Brisbane International Film Festival runs for 12 days every July/August and includes a diverse range of Australian and foreign films. Special features include films from the South Pacific region and by Indigenous film makers. See the festival Web site at W www.biff.com.au for details.

### Spring
Held over two weeks from late August/early September, the outdoor Brisbane Riverfestival is the city's major festival of the arts; buskers fill the streets and there are concerts and performances every day. Livid, an independent rock festival that attracts international bands as well as local talent, takes place over a weekend in October.

### WORK
Several of the backpackers hostels in Brisbane have job boards with notices of available employment, while many of the bigger hostels have job clubs that aim to find work for guests. Telemarketing, door-to-door sales and table waiting are the most common jobs. The Palace Backpackers in the city centre probably has the biggest job

club. An alternative is the Backpackers Employment Service (☎ 0414 744 575) on the 3rd level of the transit centre.

If you are happy with bar work or waiting on tables the best advice may be to go knocking on doors in Fortitude Valley or New Farm. Be warned that many places want staff for longer than three months, so it may take a bit of footwork to find a willing employer. The *Courier-Mail* has a daily Situations Vacant listing – Wednesday and Saturday are the best days to look.

### PLACES TO STAY – BUDGET
Most of the places listed here are in the inner suburbs, generally within a couple of kilometres of the city centre. The main accommodation clusters are: the city centre (which mainly has the more expensive options); Spring Hill, immediately north of the city; Petrie Terrace, on the western side of the city; Fortitude Valley and New Farm, north-east of the city; and West End in southern Brisbane.

At the transit centre, the Brisbane Visitors Accommodation Service has a free booking service and brochures and information on hostels and other budget options – see Tourist Offices under Information earlier in this chapter.

If you decide to stay longer, there is rental accommodation advertised in the *Courier-Mail* – Wednesday and Saturday are the best days to look – or on the notice boards at hostels and cafes and the university.

Apartments for Backpackers (☎ 1800 110 443) specialises in longer-term apartment rentals for working backpackers, and requires no bonds. Apartments start from $240 a week.

### Caravan Parks & Camping
Most of the camping options are a long way from the centre so any money you save on accommodation may quickly be eaten up by public transport.

***Newmarket Gardens Caravan Park*** *(☎ 3356 1458, fax 3352 7273, 199 Ashgrove Ave, Ashgrove)* Powered sites $20 a double, on-site vans $33, en suite cabins $58. This clean site is just 4km north of the city centre and is connected to town by several bus routes and the Citytrain (Newmarket station).

*Aspley Acres Tourist Park* (☎ *3263 2668, 1420 Gympie Rd, Aspley)* Powered sites from $20.50, on-site vans/cabins from $35/60. This caravan park is 13km north of the centre.

*Brisbane Caravan Village* (☎ *3263 4040, fax 3263 7702, 763 Zillmere Rd, Aspley)* Unpowered/powered sites from $20/22, cabins from $68 per double. This reasonable park is 12km from the centre.

*Dress Circle Village* (☎ *3341 6133, fax 3341 0274, 10 Holmead Rd, Eight Mile Plains)* Unpowered/powered sites from $15/22, cabins around $70. This caravan park is 14km south of the centre.

Alternatively, Globetrekkers Hostel will allow travellers to camp in their vehicles in the backyard – see the following Hostels section.

## Hostels
Brisbane's hostels are concentrated in the city and on the inner suburbs of Petrie Terrace, Spring Hill, Fortitude Valley and New Farm, and south of the city in West End.

**City Centre** There is only one hostel right in the city centre and it is probably the best choice for party people who want to be in the thick of things.

*Palace Backpackers* (☎ *1800 676 340, 3211 2433, fax 3211 2466, Cnr Ann & Edward Sts)* Beds in 7-9–bed dorm/3-bed dorm $17/21, singles/doubles $33/45. The hostel occupies four floors of the huge People's Palace, a lovely old colonial building that (somewhat ironically) was built as a liquor-free hostel for the Salvation Army. There's a huge kitchen, TV lounges, laundries, a tour desk, a job club and a rooftop sundeck. Downstairs is the city's most popular backpackers bar, Down Under (see Entertainment later). The flip side of this is that the halls can be full of drunken revellers at night.

The following three hostels are close to the transit centre, but they can cop quite a lot of traffic noise from busy Upper Roma St.

*Brisbane City Backpackers'* (☎ *1800 062 572, 3211 3221, fax 3236 0474, 380 Upper Roma St)* Dorm beds $15-19, singles/doubles & twins $40/46. This is a modern, neon-orange, 200-bed hostel. Facilities are good – there's a new roof-top pool and a backpackers bar – but it's a little short on character.

*Brisbane City YHA* (☎ *3236 1004, fax 3236 1947, 392 Upper Roma St)* Beds in single-sex 4-6–bed dorm from $21, twins/doubles $51/55. There are also twins, doubles and triples with air-con and en suite for a little more (en suite rooms are $69.50). There are excellent facilities here, including a good cafe, a tour booking desk and facilities for the disabled.

*Yellow Submarine Backpackers* (☎/fax *3211 3424, 66 Quay St)* Beds in 3-bed/6-bed dorm $20/18, twins & doubles $44. One block south of Upper Roma St, this old house is brightly painted – yellow, naturally. It's very homely and friendly, with a pool, small garden terraces and barbecue grills. They'll also help you find work here.

**Fortitude Valley & New Farm** With great nightlife and fine dining right on the doorstep, both Fortitude Valley and New Farm are excellent places to be based. The No 190 and 191 buses run along Brunswick St and down to Adelaide St in the CBD every 15 minutes (half-hourly at weekends).

*Balmoral House* (☎ *3252 1397, fax 3252 5892, 33 Amelia St, Fortitude Valley)* Beds in 3-4–bed dorm $16, singles & doubles with/without en suite $38/50. This very clean, quiet place has good facilities, but it feels a bit institutional. It's just uphill from the Brunswick St Mall.

*Home for Backpackers* (☎ *3254 1984, 515 Brunswick St, Fortitude Valley)* Beds in 4-bed dorm from $11, doubles $30. This old, three-storey timber house has spacious common areas and a small garden, though it still feels a bit claustrophobic.

*Globetrekkers Hostel* (☎ *3358 1251, ℮ hostel@globetrekkers.net, 35 Balfour St, New Farm)* Beds in 5-bed dorm $17, twins & doubles $40, en suite double $44-50. Run by a friendly, arty family, this 100-year-old timber house is small, tranquil and very relaxed, and has a great communal atmosphere. Travellers with campervans can park out the back and use the hostel facilities ($10 per person). There's also a women's dorm.

*The Bowen Terrace (☎ 3254 1575, fax 3358 1488, 365 Bowen Terrace, New Farm)* Singles/twin/doubles $27.50/36/44-53. Like Globetrekkers this is family run and is well maintained, orderly and quiet. The twin and the singles are simple with shared facilities and the pricier doubles have en suite, TV and fridge.

*The Homestead (☎ 1800 658 344, 3358 3538, fax 3354 1609, 57 Annie St, New Farm)* Beds in 6-8–bed dorm $16, doubles & twins $35 with shared facilities. This is a large, lively and modern place. Facilities include a TV room, communal kitchen, small pool and games room. The free bikes are a big plus, and there's a courtesy bus to the city and free trips to Mt Coot-tha lookout. There's a job club and weekly rates are available.

**Petrie Terrace** Just north of the city, Petrie Terrace is slightly run down, but Caxton St in nearby Paddington has plenty of good cates, restaurants and bars.

*Banana Benders Backpackers (☎ 1800 241 157, 3367 1157, fax 3368 1047, e banana_bender@acenet.net.au, Cnr Petrie Terrace & Jessie St)* Beds in 4-bed dorm $18, doubles $42. Painted bright yellow and blue on the outside, this is another good choice; it's small, there's a nice terrace with city views, and the owners offer a great range of activities and can help you find work.

*Aussie Way Backpackers (☎/fax 3369 0711, 34 Cricket St)* Beds in 3-5–bed dorm $17, singles/doubles $29/40. Down the side street past Banana Benders, this small hostel in a beautiful two-storey timber house with a front balcony is very clean and quiet, although the kitchen is quite small and can get crowded at meal times.

**West End** There are a number of budget options in this Bohemian district south of the river

*Brisbane Backpacker Resort (☎ 1800 626 452, 3844 9956, fax 3844 9295, 110 Vulture St)* Beds in 4-bed dorm $19, beds in 6-8–bed dorm $18, beds in 6-8–bed dorm in the older Swagman's Rest building $12. This

is a purpose-built backpackers complex, but it doesn't score highly with backpackers. Although the rooms have TV, fridge and en suite bathrooms and there's a cafe and bar, the atmosphere is quite authoritarian and it's fairly soulless.

*Somewhere to Stay (☎ 1800 812 398, 3846 2858, fax 3846 4584, 45 Brighton Rd)* Beds in 6-bed/4-bed dorm $14/18, singles/ doubles from $23/35. This big, rambling, wooden house has cool balconies and a small pool with an attractive shaded deck. It's set in a decent garden and has a nice atmosphere, though it could be better cared for.

**Spring Hill** This peaceful residential suburb is immediately north of the city.

*Kookaburra Inn (☎ 3832 1303, fax 3822 9735, e accom@kookaburra-inn.com.au, 41 Phillips St)* Singles/doubles $33/50. This quiet old Queenslander houses a relaxed hostel with clean rooms (no dorms), communal bathrooms, kitchens and laundry facilities. It's well located in a quiet, leafy street.

## Guesthouses, Motels & Apartments
Moving up a level from the backpackers hostels, there is a wide variety of budget options around the city centre that variously advertise themselves as B&Bs, hotels or guesthouses. There are also several apartment hotels that work out to be fairly good value, especially if you're in a group.

**Spring Hill** The choice of budget options in Spring Hill includes three places in Upper Edward St that are only a 10-minute (uphill) walk from the transit centre.

*Acacia Inner-City Inn (☎ 3832 1663, fax 3832 2591, 413 Upper Edward St)* Singles/ doubles/doubles with bath $45/55/70, including breakfast. This reasonable, modern motel has OK rooms and a good, central location.

*Dorchester Self-Contained Units (☎ 3831 2967, fax 3832 2932, 484 Upper Edward St)* Single/double/triple units $66/77/88. This is a two-storey block of renovated one-bedroom units, each with a kitchenette, aircon, phone and TV. There are laundry facilities and off-street parking here.

*Dahrl Court Apartments* (☎ 3832 3458, fax 3839 2591, 45 Phillips St) 1-person/2-person apartments from $75/85 nightly, $380/420 weekly. This fantastic complex of bright, airy apartments is tucked away on a quiet residential street, but still close to the CBD. The delightful apartments have a separate kitchen, a small breakfast room, an en suite with a full-sized bath, a phone and a TV. There's also a pool and a small gym.

*Thornbury House B&B* (☎ 3832 5985, fax 3822 7255, 1 Thornbury St) Singles/doubles $85/99. This charming, two-storey Queenslander was built in 1886. It's a friendly place and there's a lovely breakfast courtyard.

*Tourist Guest House* (☎ 3252 4171, fax 3253 2704, 555 Gregory Terrace) Singles/doubles/triples with shared bath $40/55/65, with en suite $50/65/80. Opposite the old museum, but quite a haul from the centre, this is a lovely old Queenslander with lots of heritage features and tidy bright rooms.

**New Farm** There are a few places just south-east of the lively Brunswick St cafe strip.

*Allender Apartments* (☎ 3358 5832, fax 3254 0799, Cnr Brunswick & Moreton Sts) Studios $77, 1-person/2-person suites $99/110. Located in a two-storey, yellow-brick block, these good-value units are large, sumptuously furnished and beautifully maintained.

*South Pacific Palms Motel* (☎ 3358 2366, fax 3358 3489, Cnr Bowen Terrace & Langshaw St) Singles/doubles/triples $64/74/84. This is a neat, modern place with spacious self-contained motel units on a quiet suburban street.

**Paddington** The suburb of Paddington is west of the city centre. *Waverley B&B* (☎ 3369 8973, fax 3876 6655, 5 Latrobe Terrace) Singles/doubles $77/105, self-contained units $425 per week. Situated about 2km from the city centre, this is a good, attractive B&B. It's a renovated two-storey Queenslander with a family home upstairs, two guest rooms and two excellent guest units with well-equipped kitchens.

## PLACES TO STAY – MID-RANGE
### City Centre

Most mid-range hotels cater predominantly for corporate clients and usually have lots of empty beds on weekends. You'll find that most offer good weekend deals.

*Explorers Inn* (☎ 3211 3488, fax 3211 3499, e explorer@powerup.com.au, 63 Turbot St) Doubles & twins $75, 4-person family room $97. One of the best accommodation deals in Brisbane, this modern hotel is right on the edge of the CBD and has a restaurant, bar, laundry and library. The rooms are immaculate and well equipped, each with air-con, fridge, tea- and coffee-making facilities and en suite.

*Holiday Inn Brisbane* (☎ 3238 2222, fax 3238 2288, e reserve@holidayinnbrisbane.com.au, Transit centre, Roma St) Rooms from $119. Right beside the transit centre, this is a four-star hotel with comfortable facilities; look out for special weekend rates.

*Royal on the Park* (☎ 3221 3411, fax 3229 9817, e res@royalonthepark.com.au, Cnr Alice & Albert Sts) Rooms from $135. This very attractive four-star hotel is just across from the Botanic Gardens and offers 150 rooms, a pool, spa, gym, parking and two restaurants.

*Chifley Hotel* (☎ 3221 6044, fax 3221 7474, 103 George St) Standard rooms/suites $131/140. The Chifley has 100 rooms, a pool, spa, restaurant and underground parking. The rooms are small but have been pleasantly refurbished and you can't beat the location.

### Spring Hill

There are numerous motels and hotels just north of the centre in Spring Hill that generally have views of Wickham or Victoria Parks or the new Roma Street Parkland. Quality varies, but as a rule you get what you pay for.

*Albert Park Hotel* (☎ 3831 3111, fax 3832 1290, e albertparkhotel@bigpond.com, 551 Wickham Terrace) Doubles/executive rooms $89/104. Overlooking the Roma Street Parkland, this hotel has extremely comfortable and well-furnished rooms.

*Metropolitan Motor Inn* (☎ 3831 6000, fax 3832 6198, 106 Leichhardt St) Units from

$88. This is a well-run business hotel/motel with a piano bar and restaurant downstairs.

***Gregory Terrace Motor Inn*** (☎ *3832 1769, fax 3832 2640, 397 Gregory Terrace)* Doubles $94, 4-bed family rooms $108-123. Out on Spring Hill's northern edge, this four-star establishment overlooks Victoria Park and is just across from the Centenary Pool.

***Astor Motel*** (☎ *3831 9522, fax 3831 9522,* e *theastor@optusnet.com.au, 193 Wickham Terrace)* Single/double rooms from $89/95, suites from $105/109. Close to the city, near the junction with Upper Edward St, this very attractive place has a variety of tasteful rooms and suites.

***Soho Motel*** (☎ *3831 7722, fax 3831 8050,* e *stay@sohomotel.com.au, 333 Wickham Terrace)* Singles/doubles $64/76. This is one of the better motels in the centre and it's only a short walk uphill from the transit centre. Rooms are comfortable and frequently booked out – reserve early if you want to be sure of a bed.

### Kangaroo Point

North Kangaroo Point is a nice place to be. Although the Story Bridge and its associated highway soars above the streets, it's quiet and leafy and there are frequent ferries across to the city centre.

***Ryan's On The River*** (☎ *3391 1011, fax 3391 1824, 269 Main St)* Rooms $139-159. All rooms have some sort of river view and this place is close to the landing stage for the city ferry.

***Il Mondo*** (☎ *3392 0111, fax 3392 0544, 25 Rotherham St)* Doubles from $65. This quirky, postmodern building has lots of metalwork and angles, and a range of nice, well-appointed rooms. There's also secure parking, a good pool and a very attractive, courtyard cafe-restaurant on the ground floor.

In southern Kangaroo Point there's a cluster of cheaper options, all within 1km of each other on Main St and all pretty similar.

***A1 Motel*** (☎ *3391 6222, fax 3891 0720, 646 Main St)* Units $66-95. This is probably the best of the lot, with friendly staff and tidy, renovated rooms.

***Paramount Apartments*** (☎ *3393 1444, fax 3891 5592, 649 Main St)* Single/double/

twin self-contained apartments from $62/67/73. This is another OK choice, with spacious apartments and a small pool.

### PLACES TO STAY – TOP END

Brisbane has only a handful of five-star hotels and they generally quote prices of over $200 a night for rooms. In practice, you'll find these prices are fairly negotiable – you can often get better package deals through travel agents that might combine airfares with accommodation. Like the mid-range hotels, most of the five-stars offer good weekend deals. These change from time to time, so ring around to see who's offering what.

***Sheraton Brisbane*** (☎ *3835 3535, fax 3835 4960,* e *sheraton.brisbane@sheraton .com, 249 Turbot St, City)* Doubles $320-480. There are 420 rooms in this luxurious hotel, which dominates the northern side of town. You'll rarely pay full rates here – specials usually go for around $168 a double.

***Brisbane Hilton*** (☎ *3234 2000, fax 3231 3199, 190 Elizabeth St, City)* Rooms from $330. Located in the heart of the city, the Hilton also has a good range of weekend packages, including a deluxe double with buffet breakfast for $178 per night.

***Conrad International*** (☎ *3306 8888, fax 3306 8880, Cnr George & Charlotte Sts, City)* Luxury rooms $305-1075. Perhaps the classiest hotel in town, this is part of the Conrad Treasury Casino complex and is housed in one of Brisbane's grandest buildings, the beautifully restored former Land Administration Building. The hotel has 96 rooms and suites, no two of which are the same. Best is the Parkview Gallery Suite ($1075 per night). Special-priced rooms are normally available for around $205 a night.

### PLACES TO EAT

The local restaurant and cafe scene has blossomed in recent years and there's no shortage of good eateries in the city and surrounding areas, including a string of award winners, such as the famous E'cco (see the boxed text 'The Critics Recommend...' for details).

For the cheapest eats, there are surprisingly varied options in the food courts in

Brisbane's shopping malls. Other good cheap options include city cafes and pub bistros. For something better, there are some great areas where you can wander and check out a number of different places before deciding where to eat – places like the Riverside Centre and Eagle St Pier on the riverfront north-east of the city; Chinatown and around Brunswick St in the Valley; the South Bank Parklands; Caxton St and Given Terrace in Paddington; Park Rd in Milton; and Boundary St and Hardgrave Rd in West End.

Brisbane's perfect winter climate makes a significant contribution to the pleasures of eating out and many places take advantage of the weather with open-air courtyards or tables out on the street.

## Restaurants

**City Centre** There are surprisingly few restaurants in the city, as it tends to empty out at night with the homeward migration of office and retail workers. Most city restaurants are top-end places, though there are also mid-range and budget-priced options.

*Pané e Vino* (☎ 3220 0044, Cnr Albert & Charlotte Sts) Mains $13-20. Open 7.30am till late. This good, modern Italian restaurant is a very popular breakfast, lunch or dinner stop for city workers and offers good value for money, with salads and focaccias from $10 and pasta from $13.

*F.I.X.* (☎ 3210 6016, Cnr Edward & Margaret Sts) Dishes $13-20. Open lunch Sun-Fri, dinner daily. Attached to the Post Office Hotel, F.I.X is a trendy restaurant with a bright wooden interior and a menu that stretches to pizzas, pastas, steak, salads and Asian dishes.

*Jimmy's* (☎ 3229 9999, Queen St Mall) Dishes $13-25. Open 24 hours. For all-hours dining, this pavement restaurant in the mall is a good spot for cold beers and hot meals like steak, pasta and gourmet sandwiches. *Malone's* (☎ 3210 0305, Queen St Mall), at the Treasury end of the mall, serves similar food 24-hours a day.

There are plenty of upmarket restaurants clustered together at *Eagle St Pier* and the adjacent *Riverside Centre*.

**Fortitude Valley** The Valley is one of the best eating areas to explore, especially on Friday evening and Saturday when it's bustling with people wandering the streets, eating at outdoor tables and spilling out of the various pubs and bars.

*Enjoy Inn* (☎ 3252 3838, Cnr Wickham & Duncan Sts) Mains $8-20. Open noon-3pm & 5pm-midnight. This very highly regarded Cantonese seafood restaurant has a cheap dining room downstairs and an up-market steamboat restaurant upstairs. Along with the King of Kings, this is where Brisbane's Chinese community comes to eat, so it must be good!

*King of Kings* (☎ 3852 1889, 175 & 169 Wickham St) Dishes $10-18. Open 9.30am-3pm & 5.30pm-midnight. Opposite the Enjoy Inn, this is another classic Cantonese place with a great selection of seafood. At lunchtime, you can help yourself to all you want from the yum cha (dim sum) trolley for $15.

*Vietnamese Restaurant* (☎ 3252 4112, 194 Wickham St) Mains $8-15. Open for lunch & dinner. Over the road from the Enjoy Inn, this place is licensed and BYO and offers very good Vietnamese food at reasonable prices. It gets pretty busy most evenings.

*Garuva Hidden Tranquility Restaurant & Bar* (☎ 3216 0124, 174 Wickham St) Dishes from $9. This highly recommended restaurant offers stylish dining in private screened compartments – great for a romantic dinner. It's very popular so you need to book.

*Sushi Station* (☎ 3216 0568, Central Brunswick Mall, Brunswick St) Plates $2-5. Open noon-2.30pm & 5.30pm-10pm. Part of a popular Japanese chain, this authentic sushi-train restaurant features a miniature train carrying plates of sashimi and freshly rolled sushi.

*Tibetan Kitchen* (☎ 3358 5906, 454 Brunswick St) Dishes $6-14. Open 11.30am-2.30pm & 5pm-9.30pm. This popular Tibetan and Nepali place serves up Nepali curries and less-familiar Tibetan dishes in funky, colourful surroundings.

**New Farm** In the past few years New Farm has become an extremely fashionable place to eat. In particular, the area around the junction of Annie and Brunswick Sts is becoming something of a foodies' Mecca.

*Wok On Inn* (☎ *3254 2546, 728 Brunswick St)* Noodles $8-11. Open lunch daily, dinner Sun-Fri. Part of a popular chain, this place offers freshly prepared noodles that can be cooked in a variety of styles, ranging from Hong Kong fried noodles to laksa, at your request.

*Himalayan Cafe* (☎ *3358 4015, 460-462 Brunswick St)* Dishes $9-15. Open 5.30pm-10.30pm Tues-Sun. This vividly colourful Nepali and Tibetan restaurant is decked out with Tibetan *thangka* paintings and thousands of prayer flags. It's very popular. As well as Nepali curries, you can sample Tibetan dishes like *momo* (steamed dumplings) and *tukpa* (vegetable and noodle soup).

*The Summerhouse* (☎ *3358 1482, New Farm Park)* Dishes $13-20. Open lunch daily, dinner Wed-Sat. This pleasant, open-air restaurant is surrounded by greenery and offers refined alfresco dining in the middle of the park. There's live jazz here on Thursday night.

*Watt* (☎ *3358 5464, 119 Lamington St)* Dishes $8-17. Open 10am-late Tues-Fri, 8am-late Sat & Sun. Further round New Farm Park, this chic waterfront eatery and bar is part of the Powerhouse arts centre and serves up good modern-Australian cuisine.

**Spring Hill** Most people who stay in Spring Hill head into the city to eat, but there are few good choices in Spring Hill itself.

*Oriental Bangkok* (☎ *3832 6010, 454 Upper Edward St)* Mains $7-18. One of Brisbane's better Thai places, Oriental Bangkok is licensed and has authentic Thai food made without MSG or preservatives.

**South Bank** If all the cultural offerings on the South Bank have given you an appetite, there are some good dining choices in the parklands.

*Cafe San Marco* (☎ *3846 4334, South Bank Parklands)* Starters/mains from $11/20. Open breakfast, lunch & dinner daily. You can pay over the odds for food in the South Bank Parklands, but the adven-

turous Mediterranean food is fantastic at this classy riverfront place. It's opposite the South Bank Piazza.

**Petrie Terrace & Paddington** Most of the eateries here are spread out along Caxton St and its western extension, Given Terrace.

*Caxton Thai* (☎ *3367 0300, 47 Caxton St)* Dishes $10-15. Open from 5pm daily. This welcoming little BYO has good food and no pretensions.

*Sultan's Kitchen* (☎ *3368 2194, 163 Given Terrace)* Dishes $12-19. Open lunch and dinner. This excellent BYO Indian restaurant is friendly and popular and set in a pleasant garden; book on weekends.

*Jakarta Indonesian Restaurant* (☎ *3368 1842, 215 Given Terrace)* Dishes $10-16. Open from 6pm Tues-Sun. Reasonably priced rice, noodle, seafood, meat and vegetarian dishes are served up amid evocative bamboo decor.

**Milton** If money is no object, up-and-coming Milton is the place to be seen.

*Arrivederci* (☎ *3369 1407, 14 Park Rd)* Dishes from $20. Open lunch Mon-Fri, dinner Mon-Sat. Our choice in Milton is this upmarket and unpretentious Italian restaurant with a subtle wooden interior and fantastic Italian food.

**West End** There are several good choices around Boundary St in West End.

*Wok On Inn* (☎ *3844 3883, 94 Boundary St)* Dishes $7.50-10.50. Open lunch daily, dinner Sun-Fri. Part of a small chain, this rustic noodle bar offers freshly prepared noodle and soup dishes. Most dishes are $8.30 at lunchtime.

There are several Asian places on Hardgrave Rd, which runs down to the West End jetty.

*Phuong Hoang* (☎ *3225 1610, 59 Hardgrave Rd)* Dishes from $8. Open 9am-10pm Mon-Sat. This simple Chinese and Vietnamese place offers filling fare.

*Caravanserai* (☎ *3217 2617, 1-3 Dornoch Terrace)* Mains $7-14. Open dinner Tues-Sun, lunch Thur-Sun. Close to the West End City Cat stop, this lovely Turkish restaurant has a central open kitchen and offers a broad range of Turkish dishes like kofte kebabs and moussaka.

*Mondo* (☎ *3844 1132, 166 Hardgrave Rd)* Dishes $17.50-22. Open 11.30-late Mon-Fri, 8.30am-late Sat & Sun. This modernist restaurant has a great menu of organic food, including lots of vegetarian choices.

**Breakfast Creek** North of the CBD near the junction of Breakfast Creek and the Brisbane River, this area is famous for its historic pub.

*Breakfast Creek Hotel* (☎ *3262 5988, 2 Kingsford Smith Dr)* Dishes $12-25. Open noon-2.30pm & 5.30pm-9.30pm. This Brisbane institution is in a great rambling building dating from 1889. The pub's open-air Spanish Garden Steak House is a Brisbane legend and serves a fantastic selection of steaks, peaking with the mighty 450g rump. To get to Breakfast Creek, take bus No 322, 306 or 300 from the corner of Adelaide and Edward Sts in the city, or from Wickham St in the Valley. Alternatively, you can take a City Cat to Bretts Wharf and walk back along the river for about 1km.

## Cafes & Canteens

Brisbane loves its cafes, and the choices here run the gamut from cheap indoor canteens for city workers to showy European-style pavement cafes.

**City Centre & South Bank** For a quick meal while you're seeing the heart of Brisbane, try these places.

*Palace Cafe* (☎ *3211 2433 Cnr Ann & Edward Sts, City)* Breakfast $5.50-7.50. Open 7.30am-2pm. Run by the Palace Backpackers, this place offers good cheap breakfasts and sandwiches.

*Hungry Heart Bistro* (☎ *3210 0186, 102-104 Edward St, City)* Dishes $2-8.50. Open 7am-3pm Mon-Fri. This firm office favourite, opposite the Metro Arts Centre, serves up a wide variety of light meals, as well as pasta, casseroles, noodles, roasts and the like served in generous portions.

*Govinda's* (☎ *3210 0255, Upstairs 99 Elizabeth St, City)* All-you-can-eat $7. Open lunch Mon-Sat, dinner Fri. Sunday feast from 5pm ($3). This is a Hare Krishna–run place with tasty vegetarian meals.

*Mekong Chinese Restaurant* (☎ *3236 3766, 197 Adelaide St, City)* All-you-can-eat lunch/dinner $8/9. Open 10.30am-8pm. Just north of Edward St, this is the place to come for a big Oriental-style feed with all-you-can-eat canteen meals.

*Capt'n Snapper* (☎ *3846 4036, Arbour View Cafes, South Bank Parklands)* Dishes $6-15. Open 11am-late. This seafood and steak place is large and constantly crowded. The food may be unadventurous, but it is wholesome.

*Verve Cafe* (☎ *3221 5691, 109 Edward St, City)* Mains from $12. Open noon-5pm Mon & Tues, noon-late Wed-Sat. This arty cafe is in the basement of the Metro Arts Centre and serves up imaginative pasta and salads.

**Fortitude Valley & New Farm** There's a cluster of funky street cafes at the eastern end of the Brunswick St Mall, all of which offer pavement seating, all-day breakfasts and strong espresso coffee.

*Mellino's* (☎ *3252 3551, 330 Brunswick St Mall, Fortitude Valley)* Mains $7.50-17.50. Open 24 hours. This is the cheapest of the street cafes and has a $6.60 big breakfast, and pizzas and pasta for around $10. It's a great place to sip a coffee and watch the Saturday market crowds.

There are several other Fortitude Valley cafes in a similar vein, including *Coffee Societe* (☎ *3252 7140, 332 Brunswick St)* and *Cosmopolitan Cafe* (☎ *3252 4179, 322 Brunswick St)*.

*Fatboys Cafe* (☎ *3252 3789, 323 Brunswick St, Fortitude Valley)* Dishes $11-19. Open 6am-midnight Mon-Wed, 24 hours Thur-Sun. On the far side of the mall next to Ric's Bar, this modern cafe is trendier than most. Salads start at $11, and adventurous pizzas at $13.50.

*Veg Out* (☎ *3852 2668, McWhirter's Arcade, Brunswick St Mall, Fortitude Valley)* Dishes around $6.95. Open 8am-6pm Mon-Wed, 8am-late Thur-Sat, 10am-5pm Sun. This wholesome vegetarian and organic cafe is right on the mall and serves good veggie burgers and hot canteen-style meals.

*Continental Cafe* (☎ 3254 0377, 21 Barker St, New Farm) Dishes $7-22. Open 10.30am-late Mon-Fri, 8.30am-late Sat & Sun. This friendly little cafe has a loyal local following for its broad European menu.

**Milton** The office set flocks to Milton's trendy Park Rd at lunchtime and after work, and there are numerous showy street cafes to choose from.

*Rue de Paris* (☎ 3368 2600, 16/30 Park Rd) and *Blu-Deco* (☎ 3369 5326, 11/30 Park Rd) Dishes $13-22. Open 7am-late. Both are very similar, licensed, pavement cafes with good Italian dishes, focaccia and salads.

*La Dolce Vita* (☎ 3368 1191, 20 Park Rd) Dishes $8-30. Open 6.30am-3am. This vast alfresco cafe features Italian statues and fountains. It sits beneath a giant model of the Eiffel Tower, so you can't miss it.

## The Critics Recommend...

When judging Brisbane's best restaurants, it's probably best to leave things to the professionals. This selection is based on the opinions of a variety of Brisbane's leading food critics. Bookings are advised at all of the following.

*E'cco* (☎ 3831 8344, 100 Boundary St, City) Starters from $16.50, mains from $26.50. Open lunch Tues-Fri, dinner Tues-Sat. Consistently voted Queensland's best restaurant, E'cco serves up treats like quail, duck and seared scallops, and the desserts are legendary. You'll have to book ahead if you want to find out though, as there is usually a waiting list for tables.

*Augustine's on George* (☎ 3221 9365, 40 George St, City) Entrees from $16, mains from $25. Open lunch Mon-Fri, dinner Mon-Sat. This refined restaurant in the historic Mansions building crops up on almost every critic's list of favourite eateries. Elegance is the watchword here, with white-gloved waiters, stylish understated decor and a sophisticated European-influenced menu.

*Circa* (☎ 3832 4722, 483 Adelaide St, City) Entrees $16-18, mains $25-29. Open lunch Tues-Fri, dinner Mon-Sat. This stylish restaurant has won the Visa Best Newcomer award, plus a string of other accolades, and is a fine alternative to E'cco, with a similar game-and-seafood menu.

*Oxley's on the River* (☎ 3368 1866, 330 Coronation Dr, Milton) Mains $25-37. Open lunch & dinner. Oxley's sits on a pontoon on the river in the trendy suburb of Milton, and gathers awards every year for its excellent seafood and modern-Australian dishes. With 400 seats, this is fine dining on a grand scale, but the regular specials make up for the lack of intimacy.

*Isis Brasserie* (☎ 3852 1155, Cnr Brunswick & Robertson Sts, Fortitude Valley) Dishes from $22.50. Open lunch & dinner. This sophisticated brasserie is a great spot for a romantic dinner, with a moody ambience and award-wining cuisine. The imaginative menu features game meats like rabbit and venison.

*Michael's* (☎ 3832 5522, Riverside Centre, 123 Eagle St, City) Dishes $24-50. Open lunch Mon-Fri, dinner daily. This elegant riverside eatery claims to be Brisbane's most awarded restaurant, and specialises in seafood. There is a fantastic array of sea creatures on offer, from oysters to shovel-nosed lobsters. The attached Italian restaurant, *Marco's*, isn't half so impressive.

*Customs House Brasserie* (☎ 3365 8921, 399 Queen St, City) Dishes $19-26. Open lunch Mon-Sun, dinner Tues-Sat. This swish brasserie overlooks the Story Bridge from another Brisbane icon, the historic Customs House, and serves up excellent international cuisine in very refined surroundings.

*Pier Nine* (☎ 3229 2194, Eagle St Pier, City) Mains around $30. Open noon-10pm. Pier Nine is a modern seafood restaurant that bills itself as a *very* upmarket fish-and-chip shop, though oysters and lobster are more likely to grace the menu. A lot of corporate diners come here for the CBD location and river views.

*Cha Cha Char* (☎ 3211 9944, Eagle St Pier, City) Dishes $22-30. Open lunch Mon-Fri, dinner daily. Yet another award winner – does Brisbane have too many good restaurants, or just too many awards? – this modern and upbeat place prides itself on its innovative approach to steaks. The food is excellent.

The menu is Italian all the way, with good focaccia lunches (from $8) and an impressive selection of pasta dishes ($12-30).

**West End** Like the Valley, West End has a fairly cosmopolitan range of cafes, including quite a few budget-priced places.

*Three Monkeys Coffee House* (☎ 3844 6045, 58 Mollison St) Dishes $8-14. Open 10.30am-midnight. Just west of the roundabout, this relaxed place with seductive pseudo-Moroccan decor has good coffee and cakes and a wide range of food.

*Caffe Tempo* (☎ 3846 3161, 181 Boundary St) Dishes $6-13. Open 7am-5.30pm. This is a hip little streetfront eatery with good sandwiches and coffee. A few doors down, *Atomica Eat Drink* (☎ 3844 0333, 173 Boundary St) is another hip sandwich place.

### Fast Food
If you're after cheap eats in Brisbane, you'll probably be reliant on the *food courts* in the major shopping malls. Fortunately there is a fantastic variety of food on offer. The best food courts are between Queen and Elizabeth Sts on the ground floor of the *Wintergarden Centre* and on Level E (the ground floor) of the *Myer Centre*. Both places have hugely popular sushi bars and kiosks selling noodles, curries and kebabs, as well as more familiar Aussie standards like fish and chips, roast meats and gourmet sandwiches. You can eat well for less than $6 in any of these places and the malls are open seven days.

You'll find similar food in a much more pleasant environment at the *Central Cafes* and *Arbour View Cafes* in the South Bank Parklands.

### Self-Catering
Self-caterers generally head for the nearest Coles supermarket; there's a *Coles Express* on Edward St, just west of the Queen St Mall.

For fresh produce, there's a great *farmers market* inside McWhirter's on the corner of Brunswick and Wickham Sts in the Valley, with an excellent range of cheap fruit, veggies, meat and seafood. The *Asian supermarkets* on Wickham St also have an excellent range of fresh vegies and exotic fruit.

### Pub Bistros
Pub meals are as Australian as Aussie Rules Football, and usually as cheap as chips, which are two good reasons to head for Brisbane's pubs. The places listed here are open for lunch and dinner daily.

*Gilhooley's* (☎ 3229 0672, 124 Albert St, City) Dishes $9-20. Most pubs in the CBD have become too trendy to serve meals, but you can rely on this old-style Irish pub. It serves very good basic fare like stew and beef-and-Guinness pie, plus other pricier dishes like steaks. Around the corner is *Gilhooley's Downtown* (☎ 3221 8566, 283 Elizabeth St), with similarly good deals.

*The Ship Inn* (☎ 3846 4321, Cnr Stanley & Sidon Sts, South Bank) Dishes $8-14. This old pub on the southern edge of the South Bank Parklands was a favourite among dock workers in years past, and now does a good trade in reasonably priced bistro meals like fettuccine carbonara, ploughman's platters and T-bone steaks.

*Caxton Hotel* (☎ 3369 5544, 38 Caxton St, Petrie Terrace) Dishes $9-25. Open 11am-late. This flashy renovated hotel has several places to eat: *Caxton Street Cafe* has good sandwiches, and pizzas from $9, while several bistros here offer steaks and other pricier meals.

*Paddo Tavern* (☎ 3369 0044, 186 Given Terrace, Paddington) Dishes from $7. Right in the heart of Paddington, this big, popular pub has a good, cheap bistro that attracts a devoted local crowd; there's a daily $3.50 roast lunch.

*Deery's* (☎ 3391 2266, 200 Main St, Kangaroo Point) Dishes $15-20. At the posher end of the bistro bracket is this popular family bistro in the Story Bridge Hotel, under the bridge on Kangaroo Point.

## ENTERTAINMENT
The *Courier-Mail* has daily arts and entertainment listings and a comprehensive 'What's On In Town' section each Thursday; you can also check out Brisbane's free listings papers – see the Information section earlier in this chapter.

Ticketek (☎ 13 19 31) is a centralised phone-booking agency that handles bookings for many major events, sports and performances. You can pick up tickets from the Ticketek booth on Elizabeth St, at the back of the Myer Centre.

Don't give the bouncers an excuse to not let you in to Brisbane's nightspots; carry proof of age and (especially if you're male) avoid wearing tank-tops, shorts or thongs (flip-flops).

## Pubs & Bars

The backpackers bar scene in Brisbane is extremely limited – to the extent that there's really only one contender.

*Down Under Bar (☎ 3211 9277, 308 Edward St, City)* Tucked underneath the Palace Backpackers, this bar is packed out seven nights a week; there's cheap beer; promotions most nights; and loud, loud music. The general attitude is that anything goes (within reason!) and most patrons have a good time, though there are always a few who take it too far.

Since the early 1990s wine bars have very much taken over as *the* places to drink, especially in the more fashionable parts of town like the Valley and West End, but a few good pubs and bars remain.

*Dooley's (☎ 3252 4344, 394 Brunswick St, Fortitude Valley)* This big, unpretentious Irish pub has loads of pool tables and is a pleasant spot to sip a beer, except on Saturday, when it's positively heaving.

*Press Club (☎ 3852 4000, 339 Brunswick St, Fortitude Valley)* This is a stylish lounge bar with fantastic decor that's become a place to be seen.

*Ric's Cafe Bar (☎ 3854 1772, 321 Brunswick St, Fortitude Valley)* Over in the Brunswick St Mall, Ric's is probably the best bar in the Valley, with live bands downstairs, DJs in the lounge bar upstairs and even the opportunity for a bit of quiet conversation on the tables in the street.

*Irish Murphy's (☎ 3221 4377, Cnr George & Elizabeth Sts, City)* This big, old-fashioned public house is a popular choice for an after-work drink and is refreshingly down to earth compared to most city pubs.

*Gilhooley's* and *Gilhooley's Downtown* (see Pub Bistros under Places to Eat earlier)

are two other popular drinking holes where you can sink a cold one without feeling like you should have gone home and got dressed up first.

Reflecting the tastes of Brisbane's upwardly mobile population, wine bars are all the rage these days. Most offer light meals like tapas and salads accompanied by extensive wine lists, with most wines available by the glass. The following places are stalwarts of the scene.

*Bravo on Brunswick (☎ 3852 3533, 455 Brunswick St, Fortitude Valley)* This stylish wine bar attracts a large crowd of young professionals at weekends, and offers light meals and an enviable wine list.

*Gertie's (☎ 3358 5088, 699 Brunswick St, New Farm)* Open till 1am daily. This imaginatively converted place has windows that open onto the street and a casual Latin atmosphere.

*The Grape Wine & Food Bar (☎ 3358 6500, 85 Merthyr Rd, New Farm)* Open till around midnight daily. Open to the street, this popular wine bar has a very good wine list and a broad menu of tapas and other meals. All wines are available by the glass.

*CBD (☎ 3229 6999, Level E, Myer Centre, Cnr Albert & Elizabeth Sts, City)* Open till 2am daily. This covered, open-air wine bar is in the Myer centre and has a great view out over the street. It's a pleasant spot for a drink, but it attracts a slightly snooty crowd and the food is overpriced.

## Nightclubs

Brisbane has a lively nightclub scene, especially if you know where to look. The alternative scene is centred on the Valley, and attracts a mixed straight and gay crowd.

*The Empire (☎ 3852 1216, 339 Brunswick St, Fortitude Valley)* This huge converted hotel has several rooms featuring different types of music. On Friday and Saturday the *Wonder Bar* upstairs rocks out with a mixture of dance and alternative music.

*Technomad (☎ 3852 1505, 216 Wickham St, Fortitude Valley)* As its name suggests, this dance club is the place for fast bpm and drum and bass.

***Heaven*** *(☎ 3257 3001, 25 Warner St, Fortitude Valley)* Open Wed-Sun. Heaven is a funky techno club in a converted church.

***Orient Hotel*** *(☎ 3839 4625, Cnr Ann & Queen Sts, City)* has a loyal local following for its alternative Friday nights.

***Indie Temple*** *(☎ 3220 1477, 235 Edward St, City)* This central alternative club inside Rosie's Tavern pulls in a younger crowd of students and rock fans at weekends.

The city-centre nightclubs attract a sort of hair-down-once-a-week office set and play a lot of R&B and dance music. Perhaps the most popular are the ***City Rowers*** *(☎ 3221 2888, Eagle St Pier)* and ***Friday's*** *(☎ 3832 2122, 123 Eagle St Pier)*.

***Casablanca*** *(☎ 3369 6969, Cnr Petrie Terrace & Caxton St)* Open till 2am Sun-Thur, till 5am Fri & Sat. Over on Caxton St, this cellar bar has a moody Latin vibe. The dress codes are fairly strict at all the city places.

## Live Music

Plenty of pubs, bars and clubs feature live music, but the following places are dedicated live music venues.

***The Zoo*** *(☎ 3854 1381, 711 Ann St, Fortitude Valley)* More than one band has rated this place as the best small venue in Australia. There are DJs on nights there are no bands booked.

***The Transcontinental Hotel*** *(☎ 3236 1366, 482 George St, City)* Close to the transit centre, this huge, attractively restored pub has live bands and DJs from Wednesday to Sunday.

## Gay & Lesbian Brisbane

The key to Brisbane's gay and lesbian scene is *Q News*, a fortnightly free newspaper that you can pick up at any of the places listed here, or at most of the Valley cafes.

The Gay & Lesbian Welfare Association of Brisbane (GLWA; **w** www.glwa.org.au) operates a gayline (☎ 3891 7377) and a lesbianline (☎ 3891 7388) seven nights a week from 7pm to 10pm. They can offer information on groups and venues and also counselling.

### Places to Stay

There are a couple of good places to stay in Brisbane catering specifically to gay and lesbian travellers. Also check the listings in *Q News*.

***Sportsman's Hotel*** *(☎ 3831 2892, fax 3839 2106, 130 Leichhardt St, Spring Hill)* Singles/doubles $35/45. This place has simple pub-style rooms upstairs exclusively for gay men.

***Carringtons*** *(☎ 3315 2630, **e** info@carringtons.com.au, Gregory Terrace, Spring Hill)* Single rooms with shared bath $75, suites $139. This friendly B&B in a restored colonial home is one of Brisbane's best gay options.

### Entertainment

Brisbane's gay and lesbian scene is centred on Spring Hill and the Valley.

***Sportsman's Hotel*** *(☎ 3831 2892, 130 Leichhardt St, Spring Hill)* This fantastically popular gay venue has a different theme or show for each night of the week; call to find out what's going on.

***Options Nightclub*** *(☎ 3839 1000, 18 Little Edward St, Spring Hill)* Around the corner from the Sportsman's, this predominantly gay and lesbian club also attracts some straights. Every first and third Saturday the club has a lesbian night. There's a cafe and dance room downstairs and a live show every night upstairs.

***Wickham Hotel*** *(☎ 3852 1301, Cnr Wickham Alden Sts, Fortitude Valley)* This is a classic old Victorian pub with good dance music, drag shows, male dancers and Mardi Gras parties. There are also two restaurants here, and a food and wine bar upstairs.

Other good gay and lesbian venues in the Valley include ***The Beat*** *(☎ 3852 2661, 677 Ann St)*, a lively gay dance club, and ***The Den Club*** *(☎ 3854 1981, Cnr Brunswick St & Barry Parade)*.

*Brisbane Festival Hall* (☎ *3229 4250, 65 Charlotte St, City)* This big venue has regular rock gigs and sees plenty of major bands.

*Arena* (☎ *3252 5690, 210 Brunswick St, Fortitude Valley)* Another huge industrial venue, the Arena attracts lots of local and international rock acts.

## Jazz & Blues
*Jazz & Blues Bar* (☎ *3238 2222, Ground floor, Holiday Inn, Roma St, City)* Next to the transit centre, this is the city's major venue for this kind of music, with good local and international acts on stage Wednesday to Saturday.

*Brisbane Jazz Club* (☎ *3391 2006, 1 Annie St, Kangaroo Point)* Admission $8. This is where the jazz purists head on Saturday and Sunday nights, and there are also occasional Thursday shows.

*Story Bridge Hotel* (☎ *3391 2266, 196 Main St, Kangaroo Point)* This soulful pub beneath the bridge on Kangaroo Point has highly recommended jazz and blues sessions on Sunday evening.

*The Healer* (☎ *3852 2575, 27 Warner St, Fortitude Valley)* For smooth R&B, visit this small venue in a converted church.

## Cinemas
There are several mainstream cinemas along the Queen St Mall.

*Hoyts Myer Centre* (☎ *3229 2133, Level A, Myer Centre, Queen St, City)* A dingy multiscreen in the basement of the Myer Centre, this place shows blockbusters nightly.

*Hoyts Regent Theatre* (☎ *3229 5544, 107 Queen St Mall, City).* This lovely old cinema is worth visiting for the building alone. Rates at both Hoyts cinemas drop to $8.50 on a Tuesday.

Brisbane's excellent art house cinemas include:

*The Classic* (☎ *3393 1066, Cnr Stanley & Withington Sts, East Brisbane)* This cinema screens art house and foreign films.

*Dendy Cinema* (☎ *3211 3244, 346 George St, City)* This old-school art house cinema shows first-release and classic movies, and also a lot of home-grown films.

*Palace Centro* (☎ *3852 4488, 39 James St, Fortitude Valley)* This modern, multiscreen cinema shows a good mixture of art house and mainstream films; Tuesday is cheap day.

*Village Twin* (☎ *3358 2021, 701 Brunswick St, New Farm).* Screening a combination of art house and mainstream releases, this cinema has cheap seats on Tuesday. It's worth coming here just for the '70s decor.

For details of what's showing see the daily *Courier-Mail* or the freebie paper *Scene.*

There are also free *open-air movies* (mainly family films) screened several nights a week in the South Bank Parklands from late October until the end of March.

## Concerts, Opera & Theatre
Brisbane is well stocked with theatre venues, most of them located in the South Bank Parklands. The Queensland Cultural Centre has a dedicated phone line (☎ 13 62 46) that handles bookings for all the South Bank theatres. Also keep an eye out for *Centre Stage,* the events diary for the complex, available from tourist offices.

*The Performing Arts Centre* (☎ *3846 4444, Queensland Cultural Centre, Stanley St, South Bank)* The Centre features concerts, plays, dance performances and film screenings in its three venues.

*Queensland Conservatorium* (☎ *12 62 46, 16 Russell St, South Bank)* South of the Performing Arts Centre, this is Brisbane's big opera venue, and plays host to plenty of big international names.

*Metro Arts Centre* (☎ *3221 1527, 109 Edward St)* This is the venue for community theatre, dance and art shows.

*Brisbane Powerhouse* (☎ *3358 8600, 119 Lamington St, New Farm Park)* Housed in a stylish, modernised brick building, this progressive little theatre puts on an ambitious program of plays, music and dance.

*QUT Gardens Theatre* (☎ *3864 4213, Queensland University of Technology, George St, City)* This university theatre plays host to better-than-average amateur theatre.

*Brisbane Arts Theatre* (☎ *3369 2344, 210 Petrie Terrace, Petrie Terrace)* Amateur theatre performances are held here.

*La Boite Repertory Theatre (☎ 3369 1622, 57 Hale St, Petrie Terrace)* This small theatre presents an interesting range of art house theatre in intimate surroundings.

## Comedy

There are a few comedy venues in town, the most prominent being the *Sit Down Comedy Club (☎ 3369 4466, Paddo Tavern, Given Terrace, Paddington)*. Thursday is stand-up night, with a good program of touring acts, and Wednesday is given over to improvisation.

## Gambling

Part of an Australia-wide malaise, pokies (poker machines) are contributing to the demise of live entertainment in most of Brisbane's pubs and clubs.

*Treasury Casino (☎ 1800 506 888, Cnr Queen & George Sts, City)* Open 24 hours. To lose money on a grander scale, head for Brisbane's gaudy casino. It has hundreds of pokies and over 100 gaming tables, with blackjack, roulette, craps, two-up and mini baccarat, as well as a VIP gaming room for those with lots to lose. There are also various places to eat and drink in the complex, including a 24-hour cafe. It has a smart-casual dress code: Shorts, T-shirts or singlets, sandals and work boots aren't allowed. You also have to be over 18 years of age to enter.

Brisbane's two major racecourses are *Doomben (☎ 3268 6800, Hampden St, Doomben)* and *Eagle Farm (☎ 3268 2171, Lancaster Rd, Ascot)* in the north-east of the city. Meets are generally held on Saturday.

## SPECTATOR SPORTS

Like other Australians, people in Brisbane are sports-mad.

## Football

Rugby league is Queensland's premier winter spectator sport. Local heroes Brisbane Broncos, a Superleague team, play their home games at the ANZ/Queen Elizabeth II Stadium (☎ 3403 7511) in Nathan.

Australian Rules football is mainly played in the southern states, but the Brisbane Lions, premiers in 2001, give it their best shot. They play their home games at the Brisbane Cricket Ground (☎ 3435 2222), universally known as the Gabba, in Woolloongabba, south-east of the city, and attract a modest but passionate following.

## Cricket

Each summer you can see interstate Sheffield Shield cricket matches and international Test and one-day cricket matches at the Gabba in Woolloongabba. Check the Gabba Web site (W www.thegabba.org.au) for match schedules.

## Basketball

Australia has a National Basketball League (NBL), which is based on American pro basketball, and the fast-paced NBL games draw large crowds. Brisbane's NBL side, the Brisbane Bullets, is based at the Sports Centre at the Brisbane Entertainment Centre in Boondall (☎ 3265 8111), about 15km north-east of the city.

## SHOPPING

As a capital city, Brisbane is well stocked with shops and boutiques selling everything from designer fashions to 'I Love Australia' fridge magnets.

## Aboriginal Art

*Queensland Aboriginal Creations (☎ 3224 5730, 199 Elizabeth St, City)* Run by the Department of Aboriginal and Torres Strait Islander Affairs, this store stocks a good range of authentic Aboriginal art, crafts and souvenirs, including paintings and prints, didgeridoos, boomerangs, jewellery, clapsticks, bullroarers, woomeras and clothing.

*Southbank Aboriginal Centre (☎ 3844 0255, Southbank House, South Bank)* In Stanley St Plaza, this shop has a good selection of genuine Aboriginal artefacts and is owned and run by Aborigines. The Nunukul Wantamaa dance troupe put on a show of traditional dance from about 11am on Tuesday.

*Fire-Works Aboriginal Gallery (☎ 3216 1250, 678 Ann St, Fortitude Valley)* This place is also worth a look for contemporary and often quite political Aboriginal art.

## Australiana

The Australian marketing machine goes into overdrive in Queensland, and there are numerous emporiums in the city centre selling such treats as kangaroo and merino sheep skins, boomerangs, 'Kangaroo Crossing' road signs, Akubra hats, 'G'day' T-shirts and machine-made didgeridoos.

*Australia the Gift (☎ 3210 0176, 68 Queen St; 136 Queen St; Cnr Adelaide & Edward Sts, City)* This is the biggest vendor of this kind of souvenir in the city and carries extensive stocks of bulk-produced Australiana.

*Australian Geographic Society (☎ 3003 0355, Ground floor, Wintergarden Centre; ☎ 3220 0341, 2nd floor, Myer Centre, City)* Here you can find all manner of imaginative and inspired educational toys and souvenirs relating to Australia.

## Clothing

*RM Williams (☎ 3229 7724, Level 2, Wintergarden Centre, Queen St Mall, City)* One of the best-known makers of Aussie gear, this store stocks an excellent (and expensive) range of boots, oilskins, moleskins, belts, jumpers and flannelette shirts.

*Greg Grant Country Clothing (☎ 3221 4354, Level Q, Myer Centre, Queen St Mall, City)* This shop stocks a wide range of bush gear, including Akubra hats, Driza-Bone oilskin coats and RM Williams boots.

For something a bit more a la mode, there are numerous Australian and international fashion boutiques in the upmarket *Elizabeth Arcade*, between Elizabeth and Charlotte Sts, and in the even plusher, split-level *Brisbane Arcade*, between the Queen St Mall and Adelaide St.

For club fashions and outlandish colours, head to Fortitude Valley. Around Brunswick, Wickham and Ann Sts are dozens of trendy *fashion boutiques* with names like Blonde Venus, BrotherSista and Honor Lulu.

## Outdoor Gear

The best area in Brisbane for outdoor gear is along Wickham St in Fortitude Valley, just south of the intersection with Gipps St. Strung out in a row, and each with different

specialities, are: *Mountain Designs (☎ 3216 1866, 120 Wickham St)*; *Silk Road (☎ 3257 4440, 128-130 Wickham St)*; *Paddy Palin (☎ 3252 4408, 138 Wickham St)*; *K2 Extreme (☎ 3257 3310, 140 Wickham St)*; and *Kathmandu (☎ 3252 8054, 144 Wickham St)*.

In the city, try *Globetrekker (☎ 3221 4476, 142 Albert St)* or the city branches of *Mountain Designs (☎ 3221 6756, 105 Albert St)* and *Silk Road (☎ 3211 8200, 115 Albert St)*. Alternatively, check out *Sherry's Disposals (☎ 3229 3422, 33 Adelaide St)*, a discount camping and outdoor shop with a reasonably extensive range of camping and outdoor gear.

## Duty-Free

Duty-free shops abound in the city centre, the Valley and at the airport. Remember that a duty-free item might not have much duty on it in the first place and may be available cheaper in an ordinary store, so shop around.

In the city centre, try *Downtown Duty Free (☎ 3221 5666, 86 Queen St)* and *City International Duty Free (☎ 3221 0416, 86 Queen St)*.

## Markets

*Crafts Village markets (Stanley St Plaza, South Bank)* Open 5pm-10.30pm Fri, 10am-6pm Sat, 9am-5pm Sun. These popular markets have a great range of clothing, crafts, arts, handmade goods and interesting souvenirs. Stalls are set up in rows of colourful tents.

Every Sunday, the carnival-style *Riverside Centre* and *Eagle St Pier markets* have over 150 stalls, including glassware, weaving, leather work and children's activities. On Saturday, the *Fortitude Valley market*, with a diverse collection of crafts, clothes and junk, is held in the Brunswick St Mall.

## GETTING THERE & AWAY

Brisbane's transit centre on Roma St, 500m north-west of the city centre, is the main terminus and booking point for all long-distance buses and trains, as well as Citytrain services. Airport buses and trains leave from here. The centre has shops, food places, a post office, and an accommodation booking service and backpacker employment agency on the 3rd level, plus some large backpack-sized lockers ($5 per 24 hours).

## Air

Brisbane's main airport is about 16km north-east of the city centre at Eagle Farm and has separate international and domestic terminals about 2km apart, linked by a shuttle bus ($2.70) that runs every 15 minutes from 5am to 9pm. It's a busy international arrival and departure point with frequent flights to Asia, Europe, Pacific islands, North America, New Zealand and Papua New Guinea.

Qantas Airways and Ansett Australia both have downtown offices – see the Getting There & Away chapter for a list of airline offices in Brisbane. Qantas has frequent flights to the southern state capitals and to the main Queensland regional centres.

Standard services and one-way fares from Brisbane with Ansett, Qantas or Macair include Sydney ($317, 1½ hours), Melbourne ($523, 2½ hours), Adelaide ($626, 2½ hours) and Perth ($847, five hours). Within Queensland, one-way fares include Townsville ($451, two hours), Rockhampton ($363, 1½ hours), Mackay ($407, 1½ hours), Proserpine ($418, 1¾ hours), Cairns ($501, 2½ hours) and Mt Isa ($493, 2½ hours). Qantas offers specials to compete with Virgin Blue (☎ 13 67 89), which charges just $119 to Adelaide or Melbourne, $99 to Sydney and $139 to Townsville.

Currently, Sunstate (book Qantas ☎ 13 13 13) runs the coastal services from Brisbane to Maroochy (30 minutes), Hervey Bay (55 minutes) and Bundaberg (50 minutes). Macair also services outback routes.

See the Getting There & Away and the Getting Around chapters for more details on flying to and from Brisbane and around Queensland.

## Bus

Bus companies have booking desks on the 3rd level of the transit centre on Roma St. McCafferty's/Greyhound is the main company on the Sydney to Brisbane run; you can either go via the New England Hwy (17 hours) or the quicker Pacific Hwy (16 hours) for $89. Premier (☎ 13 34 10) often has cheaper deals.

Between Brisbane and Melbourne, the most direct route is the Newell Hwy ($164, 24 hours). To Adelaide, the shortest route (via Dubbo) takes about 31 hours ($211).

North to Cairns, McCafferty's/Greyhound run eight to 10 buses a day. The approximate fares and journey times to places along the coast are as follows:

| destination | duration | one-way fare (A$) |
|---|---|---|
| Noosa Heads | 3 hours | 24 |
| Hervey Bay | 5½ hours | 41 |
| Rockhampton | 10½ hours | 79 |
| Mackay | 15 hours | 121 |
| Townsville | 22 hours | 158 |
| Cairns | 27 hours | 182 (3 free stops) |

There are also daily services to the Northern Territory – it's a 46-hour trip to Darwin ($371) via Longreach ($107; 17 hours) and Mt Isa ($144; 25 hours).

### Airport to the Gold Coast & Beyond

Coachtrans operates the Airporter (☎ 5588 8777) direct services from Brisbane airport to the Gold Coast ($35). Services leave the airport every hour or so from 5.45am to 10.40pm. The buses will drop you anywhere on the Gold Coast between Sanctuary Cove and Palm Beach.

### Airport to the Sunshine Coast

Suncoast Pacific (☎ 3236 1901) is one of several operators with direct services from Brisbane airport to the Sunshine Coast (see the Sunshine Coast chapter for details).

## Train

Brisbane's main station for long-distance trains is the Roma St transit centre. For train reservations and information, telephone ☎ 13 22 32 or call into the QR Travel Centres at the transit centre (☎ 3235 1331) or Central Station (☎ 3235 1323).

For details of interstate and intrastate train services to/from Brisbane, see the Getting There & Away and Getting Around chapters, respectively.

## Car & Motorcycle

There are five major routes into and out of the Brisbane metropolitan area, numbered from M1 to M5. The major north-south route, the M1, connects the Pacific Hwy to the south with the Bruce Hwy to the north, but things get a bit confusing as you enter the city.

Coming from the Gold Coast, the Pacific Hwy splits into two at Eight Mile Plains. From here, the South East Freeway (M3) runs right into the centre, skirting along the riverfront on the western side of the CBD, before emerging on the far side as the Gympie Arterial Rd.

If you're just passing through, take the Gateway Motorway (M1) at Eight Mile Plains, which bypasses the city centre to the east and crosses the Brisbane River at the Gateway Bridge ($2.20 toll). From either direction, the Eagle Farm exit on the northern side of the bridge provides a quick route to the Valley and CBD. Just north is the turn-off to Brisbane airport. The Gateway Motorway and Gympie Arterial Rd meet in Bald Hills, just south of the Pine River, and merge to form the Bruce Hwy.

Heading inland, the Ipswich Motorway (M2) branches off the M1 south of the centre, and crosses the M3 before snaking off south-west to Ipswich and the Darling Downs. For a quick route from the city, pick up Milton Rd at the north-western tip of the CBD and follow it out to the M5, which runs south to meet the Ipswich Motorway at Wacol (this is also the way to Mt Coot-tha).

**Car Rental** All of the major companies – Hertz (☎ 13 30 39), Avis (☎ 13 63 33) and Budget (☎ 13 27 27) – have offices at the Brisbane airport terminals and throughout the city. Other big operators include Thrifty (☎ 1300 367 227), Network (☎ 3252 1599), Europcar (☎ 3868 4755) and National (☎ 3874 8150), all with airport offices.

There are also several local firms that advertise cars from around $30 a day, with free airport pick-ups included. These include Ace Tourist Rentals (☎ 3252 1088), Car-azy Rentals (☎ 3257 1104), Compass (☎ 3208 4288), Letz (☎ 3252 4811) and Roadway Rent-a-Car (☎ 3868 1500).

At 79 McLachlan St, Fortitude Valley, Integra (☎ 3252 5752) offers one-way rentals to Cairns and southern capitals, depending on availability, the season and the hire period. Other companies may offer similar deals.

Several companies also offer campervans for backpackers that you can pick up in Brisbane and drop off elsewhere along the coast – see the Getting Around chapter for details.

## GETTING AROUND

Brisbane boasts a world-class public transport network, and information on bus, train and ferry routes and connections can be obtained from the Trans-Info Service on ☎ 13 12 30; it operates from 6am to 10pm daily. There's also a train information office (☎ 13 22 32) at Central Station, open from 9am to 5pm weekdays.

Bus and ferry information is available at the Queen St Mall information point, and in the Queen St bus terminal beneath the Myer Centre.

Fares on buses, trains and ferries operate on a zone system. The city centre and most of the inner-city suburbs fall within zone one, which translates into a single fare of $1.60.

A Day Rover card (adult/concession $8.40/4.20) allows unlimited travel on bus, ferry and City Cat services for the day. The Off-Peak Saver (adult/concession $4.60/ 2.30) allows similar travel, but only on weekdays between 9am and 3.30pm and after 7pm. The Off-Peak Saver can only be purchased on buses or in shops displaying a yellow and white flag (including most city newsagents). Buy it before you board the City Cat.

South East Explorer tickets ($8.60) allow unlimited travel on buses, ferries and city trains in the metropolitan area.

## To/From the Airport

The easiest way to get to and from the airport is the Airtrain (☎ 3211 2855), which runs every 15 minutes from the Roma St and Central Citytrain stations from 5am to 9pm daily (adult/child one-way $9/4.50, 20 minutes). There are also half-hourly services to the airport from Gold Coast Citytrain stops.

Coachtrans runs the Skytrans (☎ 3236 1000) shuttle bus between the transit centre and the airport, with services about every half-hour between 5.45am and 10pm ($9, 45/55 minutes to the domestic/international terminal). It will also pick-up or drop-off at accommodation in the city centre ($11).

A taxi into the centre from either terminal will cost around $25.

## Bus

Brisbane's bus transport network now includes the Busway, a network of bus-only roads connecting the southern suburbs with South Bank. Unfortunately, most attractions are north of the river, so you'll have to rely on the conventional bus service for now.

The main stop for local buses is in the basement of the Myer Centre, where there's a small information centre. You can also pick up most of the useful buses from the colour-coded stops along Adelaide St, between George and Edward Sts.

Red City Circle bus No 333 does a clockwise loop round the area, stopping at City Plaza, Anzac Square, Riverside, QUT and the Queen St Mall. Buses run every five minutes on weekdays starting at 7am and finishing at 5.50pm.

Useful buses from the city centre include Nos 190 and 191 to Fortitude Valley and New Farm ($1.80), which leave from Adelaide St between King George Square and Edward St. You can pick up Bardon bus No 375 to Paddington ($2.60) from opposite the transit centre or on Adelaide St. In the opposite direction, this bus will take you from the city to the Valley.

Frequent buses to Newstead House and Breakfast Creek leave from the corner of Adelaide and Edward Sts in the city, passing along Wickham St in Fortitude Valley (route Nos 322, 306 and 300). Bus Nos 190 and 191 to West End leave from Adelaide St, opposite City Plaza near the George St corner.

Buses run every 10 to 20 minutes Monday to Friday till about 6pm, and on Saturday mornings. Services are less frequent on weekday evenings, Saturday afternoons and evenings, and Sunday. Bus services stop at 7pm on Sunday, around midnight on Friday and Saturday and on other days at 11pm.

## Train

The fast Citytrain network has seven lines that run as far as Nambour, Cooroy and Gympie in the north (for the Sunshine Coast) and Nerang and Robina in the south (for the Gold Coast). Other useful routes include Rosewood (for Ipswich) and Cleveland (for the North Stradbroke Island ferry). The lines to Pinkenba, Shorncliffe and Ferny Grove are mainly for suburban commuters.

The Airtrain service (see To/From the Airport earlier) integrates with the Citytrain network in the CBD and along the Gold Coast line. All trains go through Roma St (transit centre) and Central Station in the city, and Brunswick St station in Fortitude Valley.

Trains run from around 4.30am, with the last train on each line leaving Central Station between 11.30pm and midnight. On Sunday the last trains run at around 10pm.

The frequency of trains varies; you can expect a train every 10 minutes on weekdays during the rush hour (from 7am to 9.30am and from 3pm to 6pm); once an hour on weekends and after 10pm during the week; and half-hourly at other times.

## Car

There is free two-hour parking on many streets in the CBD, but the major thoroughfares become clearways (ie, parking is prohibited) during the morning and afternoon rush hours. If you do park in the street, pay close attention to the times on the parking signs, as Brisbane's parking inspectors take no prisoners. Parking is free in the CBD during the evening.

Less risky but more expensive are the big commercial car parks dotted around the centre, which charge about $7 per hour, or a flat rate of $5.50 at weekends. King's Parking (☎ 3229 4377) operates at least a dozen multistorey carparks in the CBD.

There is off-street parking at most midrange and top-end places to stay, but at few of the hostels. If you stay at the Palace or any of the hostels along Roma St, you'll have to park in the street or pay for a carpark.

Tropical dome at the Brisbane Botanic Gardens at Mt Coot-tha Reserve

The City Botanic Gardens: a respite from a busy city

King George Square sculpture

The central business district on the Brisbane River

St Stephen's Cathedral

Brisbane's beautiful Mansions terrace, built in 1890

Victoria Bridge, linking the city centre and the Cultural Centre

Leafy Kangaroo Point below busy Story Bridge, Brisbane

South Bank Parklands

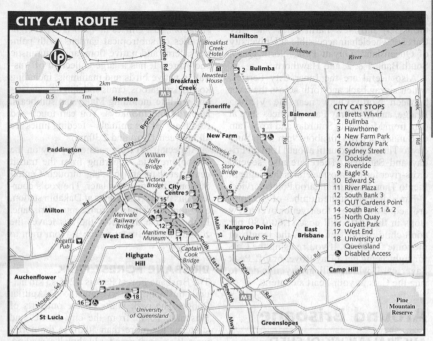

**CITY CAT ROUTE**

CITY CAT STOPS
1 Bretts Wharf
2 Bulimba
3 Hawthorne
4 New Farm Park
5 Mowbray Park
6 Sydney Street
7 Dockside
8 Riverside
9 Eagle St
10 Edward St
11 River Plaza
12 South Bank 3
13 QUT Gardens Point
14 South Bank 1 & 2
15 North Quay
16 Guyatt Park
17 West End
18 University of Queensland
Disabled Access

See the Getting There & Away section earlier for details of car-rental companies.

## Taxi

There are usually plenty of taxis around the city centre, and there are taxi ranks at the transit centre and at the top end of Edward St, by the junction with Adelaide St.

You can book a taxi by phone. The major taxi company here is Black & White (☎ 13 10 08). Rivals include Yellow Cab Co (☎ 13 19 24) and Brisbane Cabs (☎ 13 22 11). Most cabs have Eftpos facilities.

## Bicycle

Brisbane has some excellent bike tracks, particularly around the Brisbane River. Pick up a copy of the city council's *Safe Bikeways* brochure from information centres; it includes good maps of the city's bike routes.

A good way to spend a day is to ride the riverside bicycle track from the City Botanic Gardens out to the University of Queensland. It's about 7km one way and you can stop off for a drink en route at the riverside Regatta pub in Toowong.

There are several places that hire out bikes. Brisbane Bicycle Sales (☎ 3229 2433), at 87 Albert St in the city, hires out mountain bikes for $9 an hour or $20 a day.

Bicycles are allowed on city trains except on weekdays during peak hours (7am to 9.30am and 3pm to 6pm). Bikes must go into the first carriage of the train. You can also take bikes on City Cats and ferries for free, providing there is space.

## Boat

Brisbane has a fast and efficient ferry service along and across the Brisbane River in the form of the zippy blue catamarans known as City Cats. They run every 20 to 30 minutes between 5.50am and 10.30pm from the University of Queensland in the west to Bretts Wharf in the east and back. Stops along the way include North Quay (for the

Queen St Mall), South Bank, Riverside (for the CBD) and New Farm Park. The City Cats are wheelchair accessible at University of Queensland, Guyatt Park, North Quay, South Bank 1 & 2, and Hawthorne.

Also useful are the Inner City Ferries, which zigzag back and forth across the river between North Quay, near the Victoria Bridge, and Mowbray Park. Services start at 6am from Monday to Saturday and from 7am on Sunday, and run till about 9pm from Sunday to Thursday and until about 11pm on Friday and Saturday. There are also several cross-river ferries; most useful is the Eagle St Pier to Thornton St (Kangaroo Point) service.

Fares depend on the number of 'sectors' crossed: a trip across the river or over a few stops in the CBD will cost $1.60/0.80 per adult/child, while you travel the length of the route for $3.60. If you're using the Cats for sightseeing get a Day Rover or Off-Peak Saver card, which will give you a day to ride the Cats to your heart's content.

# Around Brisbane

## AUSTRALIAN WOOLSHED
For an impressive setup celebrating the 'outback experience', visit the Australian Woolshed (☎ 3872 1100, 148 Samford Rd, Ferny Hills; adult/child $15/10; open 7.30am-4pm; shows at 9.30am, 11am, 1pm & 2.30pm). Beyond a large souvenir shop specialising in Australiana, the Woolshed is a spacious and attractive park with free picnic and barbecue facilities, a small fauna park with koalas (available for hugging) and kangaroos (up for feeding), and attractions such as sheep shearing and wool-spinning demonstrations. There's also a one-hour 'ram show', starring eight trained rams and several sheepdogs.

The Woolshed is 15km north-west of the centre. You can drive or come by train – it's 800m from Ferny Grove station to the Woolshed. Some of the commercial bus-tour operators also have day trips here.

## ALMA PARK ZOO
North of the city centre (28km), off the Bruce Hwy, Alma Park Zoo (☎ 3204 6566, Alma Rd, Dakabin; adult/child $17.50/8.75; open 9am-5pm, last entries at 4pm) is set in eight hectares of subtropical gardens, with palm trees, ferns and native flora, and naturalistic enclosures. It has a large collection of Australian native birds and mammals, including koalas, kangaroos, emus and dingoes, and exotic wildlife including Malaysian sun bears, leopards and monkeys. You can touch and feed many of the animals – feeding times are all between 11am and 2.30pm.

A special zoo train runs every day on the Caboolture line, departing from the transit centre at 9am and passing through Central Station a few minutes later. The zoo's courtesy bus meets passengers at Dakabin station, a 50-minute train ride from central Brisbane. In the reverse direction, the bus leaves the zoo at 1.30pm, meeting the 1.47pm train to the city.

## BRISBANE FOREST PARK
The Brisbane Forest Park is a 285 sq km natural bushland reserve in the D'Aguilar Range. The park starts on the outskirts of Brisbane, 10km from the city centre, and stretches for more than 50km to the northwest. It's a great area for bushwalks, cycling, horse riding, camping and scenic drives.

At the entrance to the park in an area called the Gap is the Brisbane Forest Park information centre, which has info about the park and maps of walking trails. Beside the information centre is **Walk-About Creek** (☎ 3300 4855, 60 Mt Nebo Rd; adult/child $3.50/2; open 8.30am-4.30pm Mon-Fri, 9am-4.30pm Sat & Sun), a freshwater study centre where you can see a resident platypus up close, as well as fish, lizards, pythons and turtles. Upstairs, there's the excellent open-sided **Walk-About Creek Restaurant** (☎ 3300 2558, 60 Mt Nebo Rd). The information centre and restaurant are open the same hours as the study centre.

There are good **walking trails** through the park, including the 6km Morelia Track at the Manorina Bush Camp and the 5km Greene's Falls Track at Maiala National Park. Bushwalkers can also **bush camp** at Manorina, although you need a permit ($3.85 per person) from the information centre.

To get to the park from the city, take any bus for the Gap from the corner of Albert and Adelaide Sts in the city (No 385 is an express service). It's a 700m walk to the information centre and Walk-About Creek.

## MORETON BAY

Moreton Bay, at the mouth of the Brisbane River, is reckoned to have some 365 islands. Of these, the two that most people head for are Moreton Island, in particular to participate in the dolphin feeding at the Tangalooma Resort, and North Stradbroke Island, for its great beaches and surfing.

In contrast to the islands, the bayside suburbs are predominantly residential areas and their beaches are mostly shallow and often muddy.

South of Redcliffe, **Brighton** and **Sandgate** are long-established seaside resorts that are now more like outer suburbs of Brisbane. About 25km south-east of the city, the little resort of **Cleveland** is the main access point for North Stradbroke Island. Also here is the interesting **Redland Museum** with displays of local memorabilia. **Cleveland Point**, a narrow peninsula jutting into Moreton Bay, is one of Brisbane's most historic sites, where numerous buildings survive from colonial days.

### Redcliffe

On the bay 35km north of the state capital, the Redcliffe Peninsula is the site of the first white settlement in Queensland. The Aborigines called the place Humpybong (Dead Houses) and the name is still applied to the peninsula. Vehicle ferries to Moreton Island leave from **Scarborough** at the northern tip of the headland. Near the jetty, *Morgans (☎ 3203 5744)* is an excellent seafood restaurant.

### Manly

Lying just a few kilometres south of the Brisbane River mouth, Manly has the largest marina in the southern hemisphere after Fremantle, and is an attractive hangout for yachties. The very helpful tourist information office (☎ 3893 0195), at 43 Cambridge Parade, is open from 10am to 3pm daily.

**Yachting & Cruises** Various sailing companies offer day trips out on Moreton Bay for around $80 per person: the main players are Solo (☎ 3348 6100) and Bay Dolphin Sailing Tours (☎ 3207 9620). Manly Eco Cruises (☎ 3396 9400) has hourly joyrides around the bay in its catamaran ($13/6.50 per adult/child).

The Royal Queensland Yacht Squadron (☎ 3396 8666), south of the centre at 578 Royal Esplanade, has yacht races every Wednesday afternoon, and many of the captains are happy to take visitors on board for the ride. Contact the club secretary for more information. You may also be able to pick up a yacht ride along the coast from here; the club has a notice board where people advertise for crew. Another port of call is the Wynnum-Manly Yacht Club (☎ 3393 5708).

**Places to Stay & Eat** Almost everything in Manly is on Cambridge Parade, which runs inland from the shore-front Esplanade.

*Moreton Bay Lodge (☎ 3396 3020, fax 3396 1355, 45 Cambridge Parade, Manly)* Dorm beds $16.50, singles/doubles $35/48, with en suite $42/60. Upstairs on Manly's main strip, this attractive, terraced guesthouse offers very good rooms and can organise all sorts of activities in the area. Also here is the excellent *Bay Window Restaurant*, open for lunch from Friday to Sunday and dinner from Tuesday to Sunday. Mains start at $12.

*Manly Hotel (☎ 3249 5999, Cambridge Parade, Manly)* Meals from $6. Across from the Bay Window, this friendly, good-value pub has super-cheap bistro meals.

## NORTH STRADBROKE ISLAND
**pop 2300**

Popularly known as 'Straddie', this lovely sand island is just a 30-minute ferry ride from Cleveland. The surf beaches are excellent, there are some good places to stay and eat and the wild south-eastern coast is a playground for 4WD drivers.

North and South Stradbroke Islands (for South Stradbroke see the Gold Coast chapter) used to be joined but a savage storm severed the sand spit between the two in 1896.

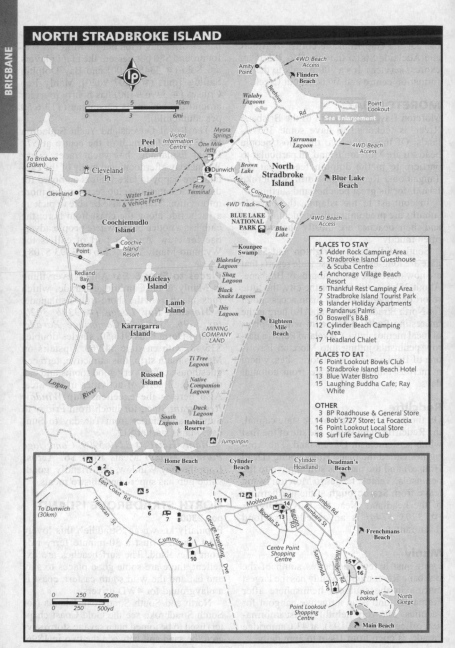

# NORTH STRADBROKE ISLAND

**PLACES TO STAY**
1. Adder Rock Camping Area
2. Stradbroke Island Guesthouse & Scuba Centre
4. Anchorage Village Beach Resort
5. Thankful Rest Camping Area
7. Stradbroke Island Tourist Park
8. Islander Holiday Apartments
9. Pandanus Palms
10. Boswell's B&B
12. Cylinder Beach Camping Area
17. Headland Chalet

**PLACES TO EAT**
6. Point Lookout Bowls Club
11. Stradbroke Island Beach Hotel
13. Blue Water Bistro
15. Laughing Buddha Cafe; Ray White

**OTHER**
3. BP Roadhouse & General Store
14. Bob's 727 Store; La Focaccia
16. Point Lookout Local Store
18. Surf Life Saving Club

Sand mining used to be a major industry here, but these days only the south-west of the island is mined. Elsewhere the vegetation has recovered impressively, creating some beautiful scenery, especially in the middle of the island. It's a popular escape from Brisbane for families and can get pretty busy during the Christmas and Easter holidays.

## Orientation & Information

There are three small settlements on the island, Dunwich, Amity Point and Point Lookout, all grouped around the northern end of the island. Point Lookout, on the main surf beach, is the nicest place to stay. Apart from the beach, the southern part of the island is closed to visitors because of mining.

The Stradbroke Island visitor information centre (☎ 3409 9555) is near the ferry terminal in Dunwich; it's open from 8.45am to 4pm weekdays and until 3pm at weekends.

There are post offices in Dunwich and Point Lookout that can give cash advances on credit cards, and there are Eftpos facilities at the BP Roadhouse, Point Lookout Bowls Club, Stradbroke Island Hotel bottle shop and Bob's 727 store at the Centre Point shopping centre.

With a 4WD you can drive all the way down the eastern beach to Jumpinpin, the channel which separates North and South Stradbroke, a legendary fishing spot. Access is via George St or the Dunwich–Main Beach road. Permits cost $10 for 48 hours or $15 for the week and are available from the Dunwich visitor information centre.

## Things to See

There's a good walk around the **North Gorge** on the headland, and porpoises, dolphins and manta rays and sometimes whales are spotted from up here.

**Dunwich**, on the western coast, is where the ferries dock, but there isn't much here apart from a few cafes and the tiny **North Stradbroke Historical Museum** (☎ 3409 8318) on Welsby Rd, near the post office.

The eastern beach, known as **Eighteen Mile Beach**, is open to 4WD vehicles and campers and there are lots of walking tracks and old 4WD roads in the northern half of the island. Just off the road from Dunwich to the beach, **Blue Lake** is reached by a sandy 4WD track. Much more pleasant is the 2.7km walking trail through the forest, starting from near the junction. The freshwater lake is a beautiful spot for a swim, if you don't mind the spooky unseen depths. There's also good swimming at **Brown Lake**, about 3km along the Blue Lake road from Dunwich.

If you want to hike the 20km across the island from Dunwich to Point Lookout, a number of dirt-track loops break the monotony of the bitumen road. A pleasant diversion is to the **Myora Springs**, which are surrounded by lush vegetation and walking tracks, near the coast about 4km north of Dunwich.

## Beaches & Water Sports

Most people come to Straddie for the beaches, the best of which are the sandy bays around the Point Lookout headland. There are some excellent **surf breaks** at Cylinder Beach and Main Beach, and unpatrolled and exposed breaks all along Eighteen Mile Beach. The Stradbroke Island Guesthouse (☎ 3409 8888) has surfboards or you can hire surfing gear from various places in Point Lookout.

Straddie Adventures (☎ 3409 8414) at Point Lookout offers **sea-kayaking** trips around Straddie including snorkelling stops for $35, and **sand-boarding** (like snowboarding, except on sand) for $25.

The island is famous for its **fishing**, and the annual Straddie Classic, held in August (call the visitor information centre for exact dates) is one of Australia's richest and best-known fishing competitions.

## Diving & Snorkelling

Stradbroke Island Scuba Centre (☎ 3409 8888) at the Stradbroke Island Guesthouse offers snorkelling for $55 inclusive of a two-hour boat trip and all the gear. Open-water courses cost $350, while a trip with two dives for certified divers goes for $116.

## Organised Tours

Stradbroke Island Tours (☎ 3409 8051) based in Point Lookout runs good half-day

4WD tours of the island ($30). It also organises fishing trips to Jumpinpin at the southern tip of the island ($30). Tour de Straddie (☎ 3409 8098) and Straddie Kingfisher Tours (☎ 3409 9502) also offer 4WD trips.

## Places to Stay

Almost all of the island's accommodation is in Point Lookout, strung out along 3km of coastline. Beach camping (no facilities) is permitted on Main Beach south of the cross-island road. Permits cost $5/3 per adult/child and are available from the ranger stations at the camping grounds in Point Lookout. All the places described here are in Point Lookout.

**Places to Stay – Budget** There are seven council-run camping grounds on the island, but the most attractive are grouped around Point Lookout. The *Adder Rock Camping Area* and *Thankful Rest Camping Area* both overlook lovely Home Beach, while the *Cylinder Beach Camping Area* sits right on gorgeous Cylinder Beach. Low-season rates for all the council-run grounds are $5.50 for a tent site (plus $3.30 for each additional adult), $7.70 for a powered site (plus $5.50 for extras). Sites should be booked well in advance through the council's office (☎ 3409 9025).

*Stradbroke Island Tourist Park (☎ 3409 8127, fax 3409 8566, East Coast Rd)* Tent sites $18, self-contained cabins $55-76. This is a big, tidy private park with lots of trees for shade and a nice pool.

*Stradbroke Island Guesthouse (☎ 3409 8888, fax 3409 8588, 1 East Coast Rd)* Beds in 4-bed dorm $20, twins & doubles $48. This large beachside hostel is on the left as you come into Point Lookout and is clean, well kept and has excellent facilities, including a dive school right on the doorstep. Guests can make use of bikes, surf- and boogie-boards and the hostel runs a pick-up bus from opposite the transit centre in Brisbane every Monday, Wednesday and Friday at 2.20pm; you need to book and there's a water transport charge of $8.

*Headland Chalet (☎ 3409 8252, 213 Midjimberry Rd, Point Lookout)* Double & twin cabins $25 per person Sun-Thur, $30 Fri & Sat. An excellent cheap option is this cluster of cabins on the hillside overlooking Main Beach, near the roundabout. The cabins are attractive inside and have good views and there's a pool, TV room and small kitchen.

*Stradbroke Island Beach Hotel (☎ 3409 8188, 3409 8474, East Coast Rd)* Singles/doubles $40/65 Sun-Thur, $80 Fri & Sat. Straddie's only pub sits on a headland above Cylinder Beach and offers comfortable motel-style rooms.

*Boswell's B&B (☎/fax 3409 8875, 26 Cumming Parade)* Doubles from $75 with breakfast. This appealing, family-run B&B is on the hill overlooking Point Lookout.

**Places to Stay – Mid-Range & Top End** There are dozens of holiday apartments and houses for rent on Straddie, ranging from plush beachside resorts like *Whalewatch*, a showy modern apartment complex overlooking Main Beach, and *Claytons on Cylinder Beach*, another flashy complex with beach views, to private holiday houses on the hillside above Point Lookout. These places can be good value for groups, especially outside the holiday season.

There are numerous real estate agents on the island. Ray White (☎ 3409 8255), Mintee St, has an office around the corner from the Laughing Buddha Cafe. Rents vary from $170 to $500 per night, dropping significantly for multiday stays.

There are also several conventional resorts.

*Islander Holiday Apartments (☎ 3409 8388, 3409 8730, East Coast Rd)* Studios $170, 1-bedroom/2-bedroom apartments from $190/260 for 2 nights. This good-value place has well-kept self-contained units and its own pool and tennis court. There's a minimum two-night stay.

*The Anchorage Village Beach Resort (☎ 3409 8266, 3409 8304, East Coast Rd)* Studios $175, 1-bedroom/2-bedroom units $195/245 for 2 nights. This modern place has a pool, laundry and restaurant, plus its own wooden walkway through the palms down to the beach.

*Pandanus Palms (☎ 3409 8106, fax 3409 8339, 21 Cumming Parade)* Self-contained

2-bedroom/3-bedroom units from $160/200 (2-night minimum at weekends). For a bit of tropical luxury, this pleasant resort overlooking Main Beach has tennis courts, a pool and a good restaurant and bar.

## Places to Eat

There are a couple of *general stores* selling groceries in Point Lookout and most also offer Eftpos facilities. There are plenty of dining choices (the ones here are all in Point Lookout), but few restaurants on the island are open after 8pm.

*Point Lookout Bowls Club* (☎ 3409 8182, East Coast Rd) Dishes $4.50-15. Next door to the Masonic Club, the choice of meals here includes a $5 roast on Tuesday evening.

*Stradbroke Island Beach Hotel* (☎ 3409 8188, East Coast Rd) Dishes $6-15. Open for lunch and dinner. This very popular pub has an excellent bistro with a terrace overlooking lovely Cylinder Beach.

*Laughing Buddha Cafe* (☎ 3409 8549, Cnr Mooloomba Rd & Mintee St) Open breakfast & lunch daily, dinner Fri-Sun. A good place for breakfast and snack lunches, this funky licensed cafe has plenty of filled focaccia and similar light eats.

*La Focaccia* (☎ 3409 8778, Meegera Place) Dishes $10-17. Open 6pm-late Mon-Fri, 9am-late Sat & Sun. For good Italian meals, head for this family run licensed and BYO bistro.

*Blue Water Bistro* (☎ 3409 8300, Cnr Endeavour St & Meegera Place) Mains around $21. Open 6pm-late Tues-Sat. Located in the Centre Point shopping centre, this highly reputed restaurant serves up tasty modern-Australian creations.

## Getting There & Away

The gateway to North Stradbroke Island is the seaside town of Cleveland. The best way to get here from Brisbane is by Citytrain; services leave about every 20 minutes from 5am to 11.50pm ($3.70, 50 minutes) and ferry company buses ($0.50) meet the trains at Cleveland Station.

At Cleveland, there are several choices across to Straddie. Stradbroke Ferries (☎ 3286 2666) runs a water taxi to Dunwich

every hour from about 6am to 6pm ($11 return, 30 minutes). It also has a slightly less frequent vehicle ferry ($84 per vehicle, 45 minutes) from 5.30am to 6.30pm (later at weekends).

The Stradbroke Flyer (☎ 3286 1964) also runs an hourly Fast Cat service from Cleveland to One Mile Jetty ($12 return, 30 minutes), 1.5km north of central Dunwich.

## Getting Around

Local buses (☎ 3409 7151) meet the ferries at Dunwich and One Mile Jetty and run across to Point Lookout ($8.40 return). The last bus to Dunwich leaves Point Lookout at about 6pm. The Stradbroke Cab Service is on ☎ 3409 9800.

## MORETON ISLAND
### pop 455

North of Stradbroke, Moreton Island comes a close second to Fraser Island for sand driving and wilderness, and sees far fewer visitors. Apart from a few rocky headlands, it's all sand, with **Mt Tempest** towering to 280m, the highest coastal sandhill in the world. The island's birdlife is prolific, and at its northern tip is a **lighthouse**, built in 1857. Sand-mining leases on the island have been cancelled and 96% of the island is now a national park. Off the western coast are the **Tangalooma Wrecks**, which provide good snorkelling and diving.

Moreton Island has no paved roads, but 4WD vehicles can travel along beaches and a few cross-island tracks – seek local advice about tides and creek crossings. The EPA publishes a map of the island, which you can get from the barge offices or the rangers at False Patch Wrecks (☎ 3408 2710), near the Tangalooma Resort. Vehicle permits for the island cost $30 and are available through the barge operators or EPA offices.

**Tangalooma**, halfway down the western side of the island, is a popular tourist resort sited at an old whaling station. The main attraction is the **wild dolphin feeding** that takes place each evening around sundown. Usually about eight or nine dolphins swim in from the ocean and take fish from the hands of volunteer feeders, but you have to be a guest of the resort to participate (on-lookers are welcome though). Call the Dolphin Education Centre (☎ 3408 2666) between 1pm and 5pm for more details.

The only other settlements, all on the western coast, are **Bulwer** near the north-western tip, **Cowan Cowan** between Bulwer and Tangalooma, and **Kooringal** near the southern tip. The shops at Kooringal and Bulwer are expensive, so bring what you can from the mainland.

Without your own vehicle, walking is the only way to get around the island, and you'll need several days to explore it. Fortunately, there are loads of good **walking trails** and de-commissioned 4WD roads. It's worth making the strenuous trek to the summit of Mt Tempest, 3km inland from Eagers Creek.

About 3km south and inland from Tangalooma is an area of bare sand known as the **Desert**; the **Big Sandhills** and the **Little Sandhills** are towards the narrow southern end of the island. The biggest lakes and some **swamps** are in the north-east, and the western coast from Cowan Cowan past Bulwer is also swampy.

## Organised Tours

Sunrover Expeditions (☎ 3203 4241) is a friendly and reliable 4WD tour operator with good day tours for $120/90 per adult/child, with lunch. Tours depart Brisbane Transit Centre on Friday, Sunday and Monday. There's also a three-day national park safari (adult/child $300/270).

Gibren Expeditions (☎ 1300 343 716) is a new operator offering tours of the island with heaps of activities thrown in, including snorkelling, sand-boarding, sea kayaking and scuba diving. The guides are locals and really know the island, and rates – $189 for two days and $289 for three days – are good value.

## Places to Stay

There are national park *camp sites* with water, toilets and cold showers at Ben-Ewa and False Patch Wrecks, both between Cowan Cowan and Tangalooma, and at Eagers Creek and Blue Lagoon on the island's eastern coast. Sites cost $3.85 per person

per night or $15.40 per family. For information and camping permits contact the EPA (☎ 3227 8186) at 160 Ann St in Brisbane or the ranger at False Patch Wrecks (☎ 3408 2710).

**Tangalooma Wild Dolphin Resort** *(☎ 3268 6333, fax 3268 6299)* Adult/child Wild Dolphin package from $167/61, including transfers, overnight accommodation and dolphin feeding. This is the most desirable locale: a modern resort with plush rooms, nice beaches and tame dolphins. What more could you ask for?

## Getting There & Around

The *Tangalooma Flyer*, a fast catamaran operated by the Tangalooma Resort (☎ 3268 6333), sails to Moreton daily at 10am from a dock at Holt St, off Kingsford Smith Dr; a courtesy bus departs the Brisbane Transit Centre at 9am. You can use it for a day trip (it returns at 3.30pm, which is before dolphin-feeding time) or for camping drop-offs. The fare is $35 for day trippers or $60 return for overnight trips. Bookings are necessary. The trip time is 1¼ hours.

The *Moreton Venture* (☎ 3895 1000) is a vehicle ferry that runs every day except Tuesday from Whyte Island (at the southern side of the Brisbane River mouth) to Tangalooma. The return fare is $120 for a 4WD (including up to four passengers); pedestrians are charged $25 return. The *Combie Trader* (☎ 3203 6399) runs at least once daily except Tuesday, sailing between Scarborough and Bulwer (adult/child foot passengers $26/15, $122 per vehicle). The *Moreton Venture* and the *Combie Trader* take two hours to make the crossing.

You can hire 4WDs to explore the island from Moreton Island 4WD hire (☎ 3410 1338) in Bulwer, which will save you the cost of taking a vehicle over on the ferry. Rates for Suzuki Sierras start at $110 per day. Toyota Troopcarriers are also available.

## ST HELENA ISLAND

Now a national park, little St Helena Island, which is only 6km from the mouth of the Brisbane River, was a high-security prison until 1932. You can now see the remains of several **prison buildings**, plus the parts of Brisbane's first **tramway**, built in 1884. The old trams were pulled by horses, but these days a tractor pulls the coaches as part of the island tour.

AB Sea Cruises (☎ 3396 3994) runs day trips, which include a train ride and a 'dramatised tour' of the prison, to St Helena from Manly Harbour at 9.30am on weekdays and 11am at weekends (adult/child $48/24).

You can reach Manly from central Brisbane in about 35 minutes by train on the Cleveland line.

## COOCHIEMUDLO ISLAND

Tiny Coochiemudlo (or Coochie) Island is a 10-minute ferry ride from Victoria Point on the southern side of Moreton Bay. It's a popular outing from the mainland, with good **beaches**, though it's more built-up than most other Moreton Bay islands you can visit.

*Coochie Island Resort* (☎ *3207 7521, Victoria Parade*) 1-bedroom/2-bedroom unit $150/170 for 2 nights. This relaxed family resort has self-contained units and a licensed *restaurant*, open Thursday to Sunday for lunch and dinner.

Bay Islands Taxi Service (☎ 3409 1145) runs a fast-cat service every 20 minutes until late at night for $4 per passenger. Alternatively, you can use the Coochiemudlo Barge Service (☎ 3820 7227) for $1 per foot passenger or $33 per vehicle.

## BRIBIE ISLAND

postcode 4507 • pop 12,900

This slender sand island at the northern end of Moreton Bay is joined to the mainland by a bridge at its southern tip, where you'll find the small settlements of Woorim, Bellara and Bongaree. The north-western coast of the island is protected as **Bribie Island National Park**, and has some beautifully remote *camping areas* (4WD access only). There's a ranger station (☎ 3408 8451) at White Patch on the south-eastern fringes of the park.

**Woorim**, on the eastern coast, is an old-fashioned holiday township with good, sandy ocean beaches and a range of accommodation. As you cross the bridge onto the island, you'll see the Bribie Island information centre (☎ 3408 9026) on Benabrow Ave in the middle of the median strip. It's open 9am-4pm weekdays, 9am-3pm Saturday and 9.30am-1pm Sunday.

### Places to Stay & Eat

All the options are in Woorim.

*Bribie Island Caravan Park* (☎ *3408 1134, fax 3408 2853, Jacana Ave*) has powered sites for $18.50, on-site vans from $30 and cabins from $39.

*Koolamara Beach Motel* (☎ *3408 1277, fax 3408 1277, Boyd St*) Doubles $77-88. This good mid-range resort is built around a large pool in a landscaped garden setting.

*Bribie Island SLSC* (☎ *3408 2141, Rickman Parade*) Dishes $5.50-12.50. At the southern end of the beach, this surf club overlooking the ocean serves up Aussie tucker.

### Getting There & Away

There are frequent Citytrain services between Brisbane and Caboolture; Bribie Island Bus & Coaches (☎ 3408 2562) provides a Trainlink service from the Caboolture railway station to Bribie Island.

# Gold Coast

Love it or loathe it, the Gold Coast is hard to ignore. This 35km stretch of beach between Surfers Paradise and the New South Wales (NSW) border has some of the most intensive tourist development in Australia – a continuous landfill of ultra-expensive high-rise holiday apartments and cheap motels, punctuated by airport-sized shopping malls and clusters of restaurants and convenience stores.

Yet a mere 50 years ago none of this was here. The Gold Coast's incredible transformation from a string of sleepy seaside towns to modern multiplex was fuelled by some savvy manipulation of the Asian holiday market in the 50s and 60s. These days more than two million visitors descend on the strip every year, drawn by the sand, sea and surf, and a whole host of theme parks and other glitzy artificial attractions.

This is tourism on a grand scale and the commercialism doesn't appeal to everyone. Fortunately, there is a little-visited but beautiful hinterland less than 30km from the beach, with some excellent national parks, including Lamington and Springbrook.

## Orientation

The Gold Coast strip runs from the little resort of Coolangatta/Tweed Heads on the NSW border to the residential high-rise burg of Southport in the north. But the undisputed capital of the Gold Coast is Surfers Paradise, which, depending on your viewpoint, is either the heart of the action or place you'll most want to avoid.

Coolangatta is the quietest and cheapest of the resorts, but prices move along a gradient of increasing cost and luxury as you head north. Mermaid Beach, Broad Beach, Surfers and Southport are all part of the same urban sprawl. An unexpected bit of peace at the northern end of the strip is South Stradbroke Island, the sandbar that extends north from the Broadwater inlet at the mouth of the Nerang and Coomera rivers.

The Gold Coast Hwy runs right along the coastal strip, leaving the Pacific Hwy just

north of Tugun and rejoining it inland from Southport.

Coolangatta airport (actually about 2km north of Coolangatta) receives domestic and international flights.

## Information

There are tourist information centres in Surfers Paradise and Coolangatta, and at

154

Canungra and Tamborine Mountain in the hinterland – see those sections later in this chapter for details.

There are plenty of free glossy booklets available, including *Wot's On*, *Destination Surfers Paradise*, *Today Tonight on the Gold Coast* and *Point Out*. Some have street plans and a bit of useful information, but their main purpose would seem to be to rake in advertising dollars.

**Dangers & Annoyances** Car theft is a major problem all the way along the Gold Coast – cars have even been stolen or raided in national park carparks way up in the hills! Park in well-lit areas and don't leave valuables in your vehicle. A steering-wheel lock is a good idea.

## Activities

**Water Sports & Surfing** Nicks Watersports Hire (☎ 0412 243 111), based on the beach at Southport, opposite Australia Fair Shopping Centre, rents out all types of surfboards ($30), as well as other gear like sea kayaks, windsurfers, catamarans and jet skis. Surfboards can be delivered up and down the Gold Coast.

Aussie Bob's (☎ 5591 7577) at the Marina Mirage in Main Beach offers jet skiing for about $70 per half hour (jet skis normally take two people) and parasailing for $55 per person (you're usually up for about 10 to 15 minutes). XTSea Charters (☎ 0411 493 998) at Fisherman's Wharf also has jet skis and parasailing.

**Horse Riding** Numinbah Valley Adventure Trails (☎ 5533 4137), 30km south of Nerang, and Gum Nuts Horse Riding Resort (☎ 5543 0191), in Carrara, offer half-day rides ($40 to $60), including pick ups from the coast.

**Other Activities** Sea World Helicopters (☎ 5588 2224) at the Sea World theme park offers five-minute flights over South Stradbroke Island for only $46, plus a whole variety of longer, pricier trips. Call for details.

Other adventurous options include ballooning (☎ 5530 3631) and tandem sky diving (☎ 5599 1920).

## Organised Tours

See Organised Tours in the Surfers Paradise section later in this chapter for information on local tours.

**Hinterland Trips** Mountain Trek Adventures (☎ 5536 1700) offers half-day tours that include Springbrook National Park and Tamborine Mountain for $85/50 per adult/child.

Rob's Rainforest Explorer (☎ 3357 7061, 0409 496 607) offers highly recommended day tours of Lamington and Springbrook National Parks from Brisbane.

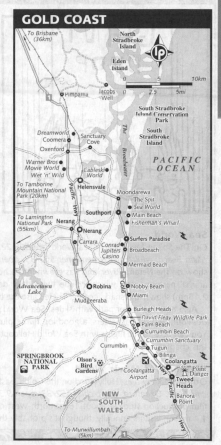

**GOLD COAST**

See Hinterland Tours under Organised Tours in the Brisbane chapter for Details.

There are several large commercial companies operating out of Surfers that offer slightly cheaper trips. Australian Day Tours (☎ 1300 363 436) charges $52/30 for its Springbrook day tour and $58/33 to Lamington National Park. Grayline Tours (☎ 1300 360 776) charges similar rates.

Some companies also offer night tours, but these change regularly – ask at any tourist office for more information.

## Getting There & Away

**Air** Qantas flies direct to Coolangatta airport from Sydney ($180, 1½ hours) and Melbourne ($275, two hours). Qantas has an office at 3047 Gold Coast Hwy in Surfers (☎ 13 13 13).

Budget airline Freedom Air (☎ 1800 122 000) flies from Coolangatta to Hamilton and Palmerston North in New Zealand.

**Bus** Long-distance buses stop at the bus transit centres in Southport, Surfers Paradise

---

## Gold Coast Theme Parks

Immediately north of Surfers Paradise is a string of big, American-style theme parks, all competing for the most thrilling ride or the most entertaining show. These are probably the glossiest theme parks in Australia, and while they aren't cheap, the rides and shows are as good as you'll find anywhere. Discount tickets are sold in most of the tourist offices on the Gold Coast.

If you don't have your own transport, there are plenty of tour operators and bus companies offering transfers. Coachtrans (☎ 5506 9788) picks up from Surfers all the way down to Tweed Heads for $16/10 per adult/child (return).

For a quick transfer from Brisbane, take the Citytrain to Helensvale and pick up a north-bound Surfside bus.

### Sea World
On The Spit in Main Beach, Sea World (☎ 5588 2222, ☎ 5588 2205 for show times, Sea World Dr, Main Beach; adult/child & pensioner $52/33; open 10am-5pm) started out in 1971 as a water-ski show on the Nerang River, and has grown into a huge aquatic theme park. The main draws are the animal performances, which include twice-daily dolphin (10.45am, 3pm) and sea lion (11.30am, 2.15pm) shows, and shark feeding. There's also the twice-daily water-ski spectacular (12.30pm, 4pm).

Also here is a water park with slides, Sea World's famous polar bears, a reproduction of the *Endeavour*, two roller coasters, a good log flume plus tamer options like aquariums and a monorail. You can take scenic flights with Sea World Helicopters (☎ 5588 2224) – see Activities at the start of this chapter.

### Warner Bros Movie World
Otherwise known as 'Hollywood on the Gold Coast', Warner Bros Movie World (☎ 5573 3999, Pacific Hwy, Oxenford; adult/child $52/33; open 9.30am-5.30pm) is next to the Warner-Roadshow film production studios, about 16km north-west of Surfers on the Pacific Hwy. It pulls in around 1.4 million visitors annually, though it's probably the least fun of the parks.

and Coolangatta. Most companies will let you stop off on the Gold Coast if you have a through ticket.

From Brisbane, McCafferty's/Greyhound (☎ 13 14 99) and Coachtrans (☎ 5506 9777) both have frequent services to Surfers ($17, 1½ hours) and Coolangatta/Tweed Heads ($17, two hours). From Surfers to Byron Bay (NSW) you'll pay $28 (two hours), and $89 to Sydney (15 hours).

Kirklands (☎ 1300 367 077) and Premier Motor Service (☎ 13 34 10) undercut the

bigger operators on some of the Gold Coast routes.

**Train** The Gold Coast is served by the train stations at Helensvale and Nerang, both of which have Citytrain links to Brisbane's Roma St and Central stations. Surfside Buses runs regular shuttles from the train stations down to Surfers and beyond, and to the theme parks. The one-way Brisbane-Helensvale (65 minutes) fare is $8, where you can catch the Surfside shuttle to Surfers

---

## Gold Coast Theme Parks

Movie World relies heavily on the appeal of oversized Warner Bros cartoon characters (Daffy Duck, Bugs Bunny etc) wandering around waving. For older kids, there are several thrill rides, including the big Road Runner and *Lethal Weapon* roller coasters. The rest of the park is taken up with re-creations of sets like *Superman*'s Daily Planet building and *Batman*'s Riddler's Lair, plus a *Bonnie & Clyde* bank so you can spend, spend, spend at the pricey eateries and gift stores.

### Wet 'n' Wild

Another Warner Bros project, Wet 'n' Wild (☎ 5573 2255, Pacific Hwy, Oxenford; adult/child $31/20; open 10am-4pm in winter, 10am-9pm in summer) is probably Australia's best water sports park, with an incredible variety of ways to get wet – great raft slides, a twister (in which you pelt down a water-sprayed, tightly spiralled tube), a 70km/h speed slide and Mammoth Falls, a white-water rapids ride that you ride down in a giant rubber ring. If all that sounds too energetic, try Calypso Beach – a slow-moving river on which you can float around in a rubber ring.

Wet 'n' Wild also screens 'Dive-In Movies' every Saturday night from September to April (and every night during January) – you get to watch a film while floating on a rubber tube in the wave pool.

### Dreamworld

Dreamworld (☎ 5588 1111, Pacific Hwy, Coomera; adult/child $52/32; open 9.30am-5pm), on the Pacific Hwy 17km north of Surfers, is a Disneyland-style creation, with 10 themed zones including an Aussie wildlife sanctuary, the Blue Lagoon aquatic playground, re-creations of a gold-rush town and a Bavarian village, all filled with fun rides.

Dreamworld's signature attraction is the Giant Drop, a terminal velocity machine where paying victims freefall from a height equivalent to 38 storeys. Needless to say it's not for the faint-hearted. Other adrenaline-pumpers include the Tower of Terror (like a giant kamikaze slide), Thunderbolt roller coaster, the Gravitron rafting ride and the Wipeout (likened to windsurfing in a washing machine on spin cycle). There are also more sedate options, including an IMAX screen. Dreamworld has been the setting for the Australian version of the hit TV show *Big Brother*.

### Cableski World

Cableski World (☎ 5537 6300, Pine Ridge Rd, Runaway Bay; admission free, water-skiing $35 per day; open 10am-6pm, closed May-Dec) is 12km north of Surfers and offers water-skiing towed by overhead cables, plus other water sports. To get here from Surfers, take Surfside bus No 10, the Sanctuary Cove service.

Paradise, which costs $3.70 and takes 35 minutes.

## Getting Around

**To/From the Airport** Coachtrans (☎ 5506 9747) meets every flight into Coolangatta airport, with transfers to Coolangatta, Burleigh Heads, Surfers and Main Beach ($9 to $12). Gold Coast Tourist Shuttle (☎ 1300 655 655) will take you to the airport directly from your accommodation for $13.

Coachtrans also operates the Airporter bus between Brisbane airport and the Gold Coast (☎ 5506 9777) for $35 one way. Gold Coast Airbus (☎ 5527 4144) charges $33 to $45 depending on how far south you come from Brisbane airport.

**Bus** Surfside Buslines runs a frequent 24-hour service up and down the Gold Coast Hwy between Southport and Tweed Heads, and beyond (routes 1 and 1A). You can buy individual fares, get a Gold Pass (for a day's unlimited travel) for $13, or a weekly pass for $33.

**Car** There are stacks of car rental firms along the Gold Coast, particularly in Surfers – pick up any of the free Gold Coast guides, scan the *Yellow Pages* and see Getting Around in the Surfers Paradise section later in this chapter.

**Taxi** The state-wide taxi number ☎ 13 10 08 will get you a taxi anywhere along the Gold Coast – most services are provided by Regent Taxis.

## SOUTHPORT & MAIN BEACH

postcode 4215 • pop 24,830

Sheltered by the sandbar known as The Spit, Southport was the original town on the Gold Coast, but 50 years of modernisation has produced a fairly nondescript residential centre. There is little to see or do here, but it's an OK alternative to Surfers Paradise for those who want a quiet night's sleep after a hard night of partying. Surfside bus Nos 1 and 1A run to Surfers day and night from outside the Australia Fair Shopping Centre on Scarborough St; the centre is the heart of Southport and has a food court, cinema and Internet cafe.

Immediately south-east of Southport is Main Beach, where the tourist developments begin in earnest. Strung out along The Spit are several luxury resorts and upmarket shopping malls, and the Sea World theme park. The ocean side is, however, unspoiled and is screened off from the tackiness by a strip of parkland – it also sees some good surf.

## Places to Stay – Budget & Mid-Range

*Main Beach Caravan Park* (☎ *5581 7722, fax 5532 0316, Main Beach Parade*) Unpowered/powered sites from $20/23.50,

### SOUTHPORT & MAIN BEACH

1  Sea World Nara Resort
2  Southport Transit Centre
3  Nicks Watersports Hire
4  Trekkers
5  Palazzo Versace
6  Marina Mirage Centre; Saks; Cafe Romas; Aussie Bob's
7  Sheraton Mirage Gold Coast Resort
8  Fishermans Wharf; XTSea Charters
9  British Arms Hostel; Mariner's Cove; Frenchy's
10  Southport SLSC
11  Main Beach Caravan Park

cabins from $90. This attractive, council-run park is just across the road from the beach.

**Trekkers** (*☎/fax 5591 5616, 22 White St*) Dorm beds $19, twins $46. About 1km south of Southport's transit centre, this is one of the best hostels on the eastern coast. The old timber house has been expertly renovated and furnished and there's a lovely garden with a pool. The place has a comfortable, homely feel and the facilities are well above average. There's a courtesy bus to central Surfers every few hours throughout the day, and trips to the nightclubs in Surfers most evenings.

**British Arms Hostel** (*☎ 5571 1776, fax 5571 1747, Mariner's Cove Complex, 70 Sea World Dr*) Dorm beds $21, doubles $50. At the southern end of The Spit, this YHA-affiliated place on the wharf has its own pub and is a short walk from the surf beaches, though it somewhat lacks communal spirit.

### Places to Stay – Top-End
**Sheraton Mirage Gold Coast Resort** (*☎ 5591 1488, fax 5591 2299, Sea World Dr*) Rooms from $290 ($390 with ocean view), suites $515-670. Situated on The Spit in Main Beach, this is a five-star place with over 300 rooms and suites overlooking either the surf beach or the Broadwater.

**Sea World Nara Resort** (*☎ 1800 074 448, 5591 1000, fax 5591 0047, Sea World Dr*) Doubles from $156 ($238 including entry to Sea World). Very popular with families, this place is linked to Sea World by a monorail and has the usual luxury features.

**Palazzo Versace** (*☎ 5509 8000, fax 5509 8888, Sea World Dr*) Doubles from $390. Those who *can*, come to this outrageously glamorous resort owned by Donatella Versace. You can see the hand of Versace in everything from the staff uniforms to the curtains in the sumptuous rooms. The name is reflected in the huge price tag.

### Places to Eat
The cheapest place to eat is the *food court* in the Australia Fair Shopping Centre. Counters here serve up pizza, noodles, roasts, kebabs etc, and there's a McDonald's and KFC.

**Southport SLSC** (*☎ 5591 5083, Mac-Arthur Parade*) Dishes $9-17. Just across from the Main Beach Tourist Park, this Surf Life Saving Club has a great bistro with pasta, roasts, sangers and burgers.

**Frenchy's** (*☎ 5531 3030, Mariner's Cove*) Dishes from $8.50. Opposite the British Arms Hostel, across the wharf, this place serves cheap fish and chips and much pricier seafood main courses. There are more cheap fish and chip places in the little **Fisherman's Wharf** complex just north of Mariner's Cove.

If you're feeling flush, head for the Marina Mirage centre. **Saks** (*☎ 5527 1472*) and **Cafe Romas** (*☎ 5531 3506*) are two extremely popular and lively bar-restaurants with great views across the Broadwater. Both are open from 11.30am till late and serve top-notch food in the $15 to $26 price range.

### Getting There & Away
The Southport Transit Centre is on Scarborough St, between North and Railway Sts. Premier, Coachtrans, Kirklands and McCafferty's/Greyhound buses all stop here.

## SOUTH STRADBROKE ISLAND
This narrow, 20km-long sand island was separated from North Stradbroke Island by a savage storm in 1896. These days, most people cross to the Southport end of the island, which is just 200m away from the northern end of The Spit. Most of the island is undeveloped, and there are some peaceful camping grounds where you can almost forget how close you are to the Gold Coast.

Two-thirds of the way up the island's western coast, the **South Stradbroke Island Resort** (*☎ 5577 3311, fax 5577 3746*) has two restaurants, tennis courts, a pool and spa, and 40 South Sea island–style cabins (double cabins from $95).

The South Stradbroke Island Resort ferry leaves from Runaway Bay Marina at the northern end of the Gold Coast every day at 10.30am and 4pm; the return fare is $25 (20 minutes each way).

## SURFERS PARADISE
postcode 4217 • pop 24,090
In 1965 local entrepreneur Bernie Elsey had the brainwave of employing meter maids in skimpy gold lamé bikinis to feed the parking

meters on the main strip, and Surfers Paradise has never looked back. Imagine Daytona Beach or Miami shifted down under, and you'll have some idea of what to expect.

The place has come a long way since 1936 when there was just the brand-new Surfers Paradise Hotel, a tiny beachfront hideaway for those who found Southport too racy. Some clever marketing in Asia during the 50s and 60s started the boom that turned a little surf town into a beachfront urban jungle. The popularity of Surfers these days rests not so much on the sand and surf (which is better down the coast) but on the shopping, nightlife and its proximity to attractions like the theme parks.

For backpackers it's probably the most partying place in Queensland and hostel staff do their best to ensure the place goes off every night of the week. If you love party nights and lazy days, you're almost guaranteed to have a good time. The partying reaches its peak at the IndyCar races in October. If this isn't your thing, there's always the rest of the Gold Coast to choose from.

## Orientation

The downtown part of Surfers consists of just two or three main streets. The main thoroughfare, Cavill Ave, runs down to the seafront, ending in a pedestrian mall. Orchid Ave, one block back from the Esplanade, is the nightclub and bar strip. The Gold Coast Hwy runs through Surfers one block back from Orchid Ave. It takes the southbound traffic while Ferny Ave, the next road inland, takes the northbound traffic.

## Information

The Gold Coast Tourism Bureau (☎ 5538 4419, ⓔ info@gctb.com.au) on Cavill Ave Mall is open from 8.30am to 5.30pm Monday to Friday, from 9am to 5pm Saturday and from 9am to 3.30pm Sunday. For help with finding somewhere to stay, try the helpful In Transit (☎ 5592 2911) backpackers' accommodation booking desk at the transit centre.

The transit centre has the Backpackers Travel Centre (☎ 5538 0444), which books activities and transport around Australia. There's also lockers here ($4 per 12 hours).

SURFERS PARADISE

## SURFERS PARADISE

**PLACES TO STAY**
1 Marriot Resort
2 Surf & Sun Backpackers
3 Cheers Backpackers
6 International Beach Resort
7 Quarterdeck Apartments
8 Olympus
9 Delilah Motel
10 Chateau Beachside
31 Islander Backpackers Resort
32 Courtyard Marriot
37 Backpackers in Paradise
38 Sleeping Inn Surfers
40 Trickett Gardens Holiday Apartments
41 Mardi Gras International Backpackers Resort
42 Silver Sands Motel
43 Admiral Motor Inn
44 Surfers Paradise Backpackers Resort

**PLACES TO EAT**
12 Sushi Train
14 Costa Dora
16 Centre Arcade; New Seoul; Seafood Village
19 Bavarian Haus
20 Golden Star
36 Bunga Raya

**OTHER**
4 Mopeds City
5 Banzai Bungey; Sling Shot; Flycoaster
11 Nellie Kelly's
13 MP's
15 American Express
17 Cocktails & Dreams; The Party; Shooters; Bourbon Bar; Email Centre, Red Rocket Car Hire
18 Aquabus Booking Kiosk
21 Raptis Plaza; Food Court; Rose & Crown
22 Surfing Monument
23 Surfers Beach Hut Beach Hire
24 Malone's
25 24 Hour Convenience Store
26 Gold Coast Tourism Bureau
27 Thomas Cook Foreign Exchange; Travelex
28 Gold Coast Accommodation Service; Green Bicycle Rentals
29 Melbas on the Park
30 Surfers Paradise Transit Centre; In Transit Booking Desk; Backpackers Travel Centre; Red Back Rentals
33 Paradise Centre
34 Tiki Village Wharf
35 Bus Stop for Southport
39 Qantas

**Money** For foreign exchange, Thomas Cook (☎ 5531 7770) and Travelex (☎ 5531 7917) have foreign exchange offices on the Cavill Ave Mall side of the Paradise Centre. Both are open from around 9am to 9pm daily.

American Express (☎ 1300 139 060) has an office at 16 Orchid Ave that is open from 8.30am to 5.30pm weekdays and from 10am to 6pm Saturday and Sunday.

**Post & Communications** The post office is in the Paradise Centre off the Cavill Ave Mall. For Internet access, try Email Centre (☎ 5538 7500), near Shooters on Orchid Ave, which charges $2 per hour and is open from 8.30am till late.

## Activities

**Surfing** Surfers isn't a bad place to learn to surf, and there are various surf festivals and championships throughout the year.

Surfers Beach Hut Beach Hire (☎ 5526 7077), at the beach end of the Cavill Ave Mall, offers surfing lessons at fixed times throughout the day ($40 per person). You can hire short boards and body boards for $10/25 per hour/day and long boards for $15/30. The kiosk is open from 8am to 5pm daily.

**Bungee Jumping** In Surfers, a former carpark on Palm Ave is home to Banzai Bungey (☎ 5526 7611), with jumps for $75. This place has been slightly upstaged a bit by the nearby Sling Shot (☎ 5570 2700), basically a giant catapult in which you are the projectile ($30 per person), and the Flycoaster (☎ 5570 0474) in which you swing like a pendulum after being released from a hoist 20m up ($39). Photos and video of your facial distortions are available.

## Organised Tours

During the summer months, various cruise companies operate from the Marina Mirage centre on The Spit, or from the Tiki Village Wharf at the river end of Cavill Ave. Most of the cruises include lunch and drinks and meander around the harbour and canals ($34) or go to South Stradbroke Island (about $52). Operators change from season to season; currently the biggest operator is Island Queen Showboat Cruises (☎ 5557 8800).

Semi-aquatic bus tours are all the rage in Surfers, and several operators offer the curious experience of exploring Surfers by road and river in a boat on wheels (about $26), including Aquabus (☎ 5539 0222), which

GOLD COAST

## IndyCar

Since 1991 Surfers Paradise has been host to what has been dubbed Queensland's biggest party – the Australian leg of the IndyCar series (the US equivalent of Formula One motor racing). Each October, the main streets of central Surfers are transformed into a temporary race circuit, around which hurtle some of the world's fastest cars, with drivers who push them up to speeds of more than 300km/h.

On a good year, around a quarter of a million spectators descend on Surfers for the race and the three-day carnival that precedes it, which includes a host of other race events. Surfers is fairly over the top at the best of times, but IndyCar gives the town a chance to *really* let its hair down. It's a great time to be here, or a great time to be anywhere else, depending on how you feel about the place.

Standard admission to the races ranges from $30 to $69 per day, depending on the race day. You'll need a $225 accommodation pass to stay in on-track accommodation, which includes the Surf & Sun hostel.

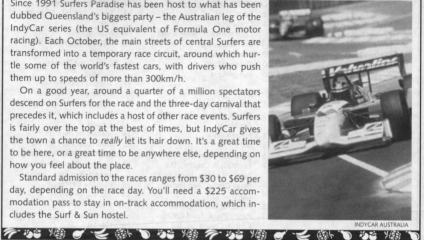

INDYCAR AUSTRALIA

leaves from Orchid Ave, and Adventure Duck (☎ 5557 8800), which leaves from the Tiki Village Wharf. It's certainly an unusual way to explore Surfers Paradise, if you don't mind riding through the town centre in a vehicle that resembles a giant duck!

### Special Events

Surfers is always ready to celebrate something and there are many showy events held throughout the year. The Magic Millions Race Carnival held at the Gold Coast Turf Club (☎ 5538 1599), on Racecourse Dr in Bundall (3km west of Surfers) every July, offers 10 days of horse racing and novelty hats.

Summer is surf life-saving carnival time, while the Gold Coast International Marathon is run in July. October is peak party season, with the lively Tropicarnival Festival and the epic IndyCar races – see the 'IndyCar' boxed text above.

### Places to Stay – Budget

Surfers has several decent hostel options, all of which offer vouchers for the nightclubs in town. Rates for dorms are fairly reasonable, but most doubles are overpriced at $50.

*Islander Backpackers Resort* (☎ 1800 074 393, 5538 8000, fax 5592 2762, 6 Beach Rd) Dorm beds $18, doubles $50. Right in the thick of things, this hostel is annexed to the Islander Resort Hotel. It's a bit of a barracks but the rooms have TV and en suite. The dorms have four to six beds.

*Mardi Gras International Backpackers Resort* (☎ 1800 801 230, 5592 5888, fax 5538 9310, 28 Hamilton Ave) Dorm beds $20, doubles & twins $50. This modern hostel with three- or four-bed dorms is also handy for the beach and clubs and has good facilities. All rooms have a TV, bathroom and balcony.

*Cheers Backpackers* (☎ 5531 6539, fax 5539 0563, e cheers1@fan.net.au, 8 Pine Ave) Dorm beds $21, doubles $50. This big party hostel, with four- to six-bed dorms, is well set up, with a decent pool, a Net cafe, an excellent bar area and large courtyard. It's within staggering distance of most of the clubs, and there are regular events like video nights and karaoke evenings.

*Surf & Sun Backpackers* (☎ 1800 678 194, 5592 2363, fax 5592 2348, e surfnsun@worldlink.com.au, 3323 Gold Coast Hwy) Dorm beds $21, doubles $50.

One of several partying places just north of the centre, this converted motel (with four-bed dorms) earns points for being just 100m from the beach and right on the route of the IndyCar race. It still looks like a motel, but it's comfortable enough and all rooms have en suite. The usual club vouchers are offered.

*Surfers Paradise Backpackers Resort* (☎ *1800 282 800, 5592 4677, fax 5531 5835, 2837 Gold Coast Hwy*) Dorm beds $21, units $25 per person, doubles $25 per person. About 1km north of the centre, this place offers standard dorms and some excellent self-contained apartments with three bedrooms around a large kitchen. The facilities here are very good and there are courtesy buses to and from the transit centre and town.

Just south of the transit centre on Whelan St is another group of hostels.

*Sleeping Inn Surfers* (☎ *1800 817 832, 5592 4455, fax 5592 5266,* e *sleepinginn@ hotmail.com, 26 Whelan St*) Dorm beds $18.50, doubles without/with en suite $48/ 53. A clever conversion of two apartment buildings, this clean, modern hostel is the best choice on Whelan St. It's close to the centre for those who want to party, but offers privacy, peace and quiet for those who don't.

*Backpackers in Paradise* (☎ *5538 4344, fax 5538 2222, 40 Whelan St*) Dorm beds $17.50, twins/doubles $44/46. This backpackers is close to the clubs and has a bar, nightly movies and nightclub vouchers, but it's fairly scruffy. Dorms have four beds.

## Places to Stay – Mid-Range
**Motels** Surfers has a few options in this category.

*Silver Sands Motel* (☎ *5538 6041, fax 5538 6041, 2985 Gold Coast Hwy*) Doubles from $60. This motel is one of the cheapest options in the centre. The rooms are well cared-for and there's a small pool, a barbecue and parking.

*Admiral Motor Inn* (☎/*fax 5539 8759, 2965 Gold Coast Hwy*) Rooms from $55 ($72 on weekends). This is an OK motel with self-contained units.

*Delilah Motel* (☎/*fax 5538 1722, Cnr Ferny & Cypress Aves*) Rooms from $55, self-contained units from $99 (sleeps six).

This place is a little run down, but it's pretty cheap considering the location.

**Holiday Apartments** Surfers is hugely overstocked with beds and there are hundreds of holiday apartments and flats for rent.

*Chateau Beachside* (☎ *5538 788, fax 5570 1449, Cnr Elkhorn Ave & The Esplanade*) Double rooms, studios & suites $119-139. Chateau Beachside is one of the cheapest choices close to the beach and has hotel rooms and units with kitchenettes and bathrooms. There's a great pool and many rooms have excellent views

*Olympus* (☎ *5538 7288, fax 5592 0769, 60 The Esplanade*) Units with 1 & 2 bedrooms from $110 a double. Just 200m north of Elkhorn Ave and opposite the beach, this high-rise block has good apartments.

*International Beach Resort* (☎*1800 657 471, 5539 0099, fax 5538 9613, 84 The Esplanade*) Double units from $80 ($90 with sea view). This seafront high-rise has good one bedroom units.

*Quarterdeck Apartments* (☎ *1800 635 235, 5592 2200, fax 5538 0282, 3263 Gold Coast Hwy*) Single/double/triple units $70/ 80/90. This high-rise contains a variety of comfortable one-bedroom apartments, some of which have great views. There's also an indoor pool.

*Trickett Gardens Holiday Inn* (☎ *5539 0988, fax 5592 0791, 24-30 Trickett St*) 1-bedroom apartments $85 a double, 2-bedroom apartments $148 for 4 people. This friendly low-rise block is great for families, with a central location, a nice pool and well-equipped self-contained units.

For information on other apartments and flats, try the Gold Coast Accommodation Service (☎ 5592 0067) at 1 Beach Rd.

## Places to Stay – Top End
*Courtyard Marriott* (☎ *1800 074 317, fax 5539 8370, Cnr Gold Coast Hwy & Hanlan St*) Rooms $130-212. Right in the centre of Surfers, this plush top-end hotel is attached to the Paradise Centre Mall and offers all the luxury you would expect in this price range, including sea views, and spa baths in the top-price suites.

**Marriott Resort** *(☎ 5592 9800, fax 5592 9888, 158 Ferny Ave)* Doubles from $195 ($230 with ocean view). Just north of the centre, this resort is ridiculously sumptuous, from the sandstone-floored foyer with punkah-style fans to the lagoon-like pool complete with artificial white sand beaches and waterfall.

## Places to Eat

There are plenty of choices in and around the Cavill Ave Mall.

**Golden Star** *(☎ 5592 2484, Raptis Plaza, Cavill Ave)* Lunch & dinner $8.90. This all-you-can-eat Chinese place is one of several in the mall with a pretty good selection of Chinese standards.

The *food court* at the Raptis Plaza Shopping Centre, just off the mall, has plenty of choices, including Italian, burger, Thai places, a carvery and an excellent Japanese place, *Sumo*, which does cheap takeaways.

**Malone's** *(☎ 5592 6066, Cavill Ave Mall)* Dishes $13-25. Open 24 hours. This covered pavement cafe serves up cold beers and pretty good grills.

**Bavarian Haus** *(☎ 5531 7150, Cnr Cavill Ave & Gold Coast Hwy)* Dishes $11-25. This German restaurant offers authentic Bavarian dishes and a tacky-as-you-like dinner show, complete with oompah horns and lederhosen.

**Costa Dora** *(☎ 5538 5203, 27 Orchid Ave)* Dishes $12-22. Open noon-6pm. This is a good, cheap Italian place with pavement seating.

**Sushi Train** *(☎ 5538 6200, Le Boulevarde Centre, Elkhorn Ave)* Sushi plates $2-4. Open 11am-9pm. This fast-food restaurant offers a Japanese-style sushi train with a good variety of sushi and sashimi.

**Chateau Beachside** *(☎ 5526 9994, Cnr Elkhorn Ave & The Esplanade)* Dishes $6-10. Open 7am to 11pm. Right on the seafront, this is a good, cheap brekky option; for a hangover cure, try the all-you-can-eat ($9.50).

Between the Gold Coast Hwy and Orchid Ave is the small Centre Arcade, jam-packed with cheap Asian restaurants.

**New Seoul** *(☎ 5538 6177, Shop 9, Centre Arcade)* Dishes $13-16. This authentic-as-they-come Korean place offers good lunch specials.

**Seafood Village** *(☎ 5592 6789, Shop 28, Centre Arcade)* Dishes $9-15. Open noon-2pm. Try this popular lunchtime place for cheap Chinese and Malay lunches ($9).

**Bunga Raya** *(☎ 5570 3766, 3110 Gold Coast Hwy)* Lunch $7-10, dinner $14-20. This unpretentious Malaysian restaurant serves up big portions of curry, and Malay soups. All dishes are half-price at lunchtime.

## Entertainment

**Bars, Nightclubs & Live Music** Orchid Ave is Surfers' main bar and nightclub strip; most of the clubs are clustered together in The Mark complex. Most of the clubs offer vouchers to backpackers that give free admission and cheap drinks and food – you'll probably get a handful when you check into a hostel.

**Cocktails & Dreams** *(☎ 5592 1955, Orchid Ave)* This is the most popular backpacker club and there are theme nights every night. It's an anything goes kind of place, but the bouncers aren't shy about evicting punters who go too far. Also here is *The Party*, linked to Cocktails by an internal stairway.

**Shooters** *(☎ 5592 1144, Orchid Ave)* This is an American-style saloon with pool tables, big-screen videos and occasional live entertainment. There are plenty of promo nights with drinks specials.

**Bourbon Bar** *(☎ 5538 0668, Orchid Ave)* In the same building as Shooters bar, this gloomy basement bar is a popular starting point because of its cut-price beer. It gets especially busy on Thursday, which is karaoke night.

**Rose & Crown** *(☎ 5531 5425, Raptis Plaza, Cavill Ave)* This new arrival is fast establishing itself as a good place to party at weekends.

**Melbas on the Park** *(☎ 5538 7411, 46 Cavill Ave)* Above the Melbas restaurant, this is a new arrival with a variety of theme nights. It's open all night, so people often congregate here after the other clubs have closed.

**Nellie Kelly's** *(☎ 5526 9455, 9 Elkhorn Ave)* This large, Irish-themed place is good for a drink if you don't have the energy to hit the clubs.

*MP's (☎ 5526 2337, Forum Arcade, 26 Orchid Ave)* This popular gay venue has big-name DJs, shows and partying every night of the week.

**Cultural Centres** For a change of pace, head down to the river.

*Gold Coast Arts Centre (☎ 5588 4008, 135 Bundall Rd)* Located beside the Nerang River, the centre has a 1200-seat theatre that hosts live productions and screens art house movies (all shows $6 on Tuesday). Also here is a restaurant and bar and the *Gold Coast Art Gallery (☎ 5581 6594)*, open 10am to 5pm Monday to Friday, and 11am to 5pm Saturday and Sunday.

## Getting There & Away

The transit centre is on the corner of Beach and Cambridge Rds. Surfers is a major stop on the eastern coast route and all the major bus companies have desks here.

For more information on buses and trains see the Getting There & Away section at the start of this chapter.

## Getting Around

**Car** There are dozens of car rental firms around with fliers in every hostel, motel and hotel. A few of the cheaper ones are Red Back Rentals (☎ 5592 1655) in the transit centre at Surfers; Costless (☎ 5592 4499) at 3269 Gold Coast Hwy; and Red Rocket (☎ 5538 9074) in The Mark complex on Orchid Ave.

Mopeds City (☎ 5592 5878) at 102 Ferny Ave, across from Banzai Bungey, hires out brand new mopeds at $40 for two hours or $95 a day.

**Bicycle & In-Line Skating** Surfers Beach Hut Beach Hire (☎ 5526 7077), at the seafront end of the Cavill Ave Mall, rents out in-line skates for $10/30 per hour/day and bikes for $15/35. There's also Green Bicycle Rentals (☎ 0418 766 880) at 1 Beach Rd, opposite the Hard Rock Cafe, which rents out good mountain bikes for $15 a day.

# BROADBEACH
postcode 4218 • pop 5180

Broadbeach is basically a space filler between Surfers and Burleigh Heads. Its main claim to fame is the temple to Mammon that is **Conrad Jupiters Casino** *(☎ 5592 1133, Gold Coast Hwy; admission free; open 24 hours)*. Hundreds of thousands of optimistic gamblers filter through Conrads every year and leave with their pockets slightly lighter and their addiction briefly sated. This was the first legal casino in Queensland and features more than 100 gaming tables, including blackjack, roulette, two-up and craps, and hundreds of bleeping poker machines. Also here is **Jupiters Theatre** *(☎ 1800 074 144)*, with live music and glamorous dinner shows. You have to be over 18 years of age to enter, and the usual dress codes apply – no thongs, vests or ripped clothes. A monorail runs here from the Oasis Shopping Centre.

## Places to Stay

*Red Emu Motel (☎ 5575 2748, 2583 Gold Coast Hwy)* Doubles from $50. This is one of the cheaper Gold Coast motels.

*Mermaid Beach Motel (☎ 5575 1577, fax 5575 5688, 2395 Gold Coast Hwy)* Units from $39 ($49 Fri & Sat nights). The units here are clean and good value.

*Conrad Jupiters (☎ 1800 074 344, 5592 8130, fax 5592 8219, Gold Coast Hwy)* Rooms from $252, penthouse suites $2026. The penthouse suite at this spectacular hotel is the place to stay if you hit the jackpot at the casino downstairs. The hotel's facilities include six restaurants, four tennis courts, three pools, two spas and a gym.

## Places to Eat

*Kurrawa Surf Life Saving Club (☎ 5527 5660, Old Burleigh Rd)* Dishes $6-16. This typical Surf Life Saving Club on the beachside serves up cheap Aussie grub and breakfasts daily.

There are several restaurants and cafes along the Victoria Ave Mall, beside the Oasis Shopping Centre.

*House of India (☎ 5592 4883, 13 Victoria Square)* Mains $12-16. Open noon-2.30pm &

GOLD COAST

6pm-late. This upmarket restaurant has excellent tandoori dishes and spicy North Indian curries.

There are also plenty of junky options at the *Pacific Fair Shopping Centre*.

## Entertainment

There are two cinemas in the area, *Mermaid 5 Cinemas* (☎ *5575 3355, 2514 Gold Coast Hwy*) and *Pacific Square 12 Cinemas* (☎ *5572 2666, Cnr Hooker Bvd & Gold Coast Hwy*), buried in the huge Pacific Fair Shopping Centre.

## BURLEIGH HEADS

postcode 4220 • pop 8430

Among a certain subset of Australians with the white boards, Burleigh Heads is a legend. In the right weather conditions, the headland here produces a spectacular right-hand point break, famous for its fast and deep barrel rides, but it definitely isn't for beginners. The shore is lined with vicious black rocks, the rip is ferocious and local surfers have an unpleasant habit of swamping visitors they consider unworthy of this revered wave.

For nonsurfers, there's the **Burleigh Heads National Park**, a small but diverse forest reserve with walking trails around the rocky headland. There are also several good commercial wildlife sanctuaries in the area.

## Information

You can get more information on all natural aspects of the area from the Queensland Parks and Wildlife Service (QPWS) information centre (☎ 5535 3032) by the Burleigh Heads National Park entrance on the Gold Coast Hwy. It's open from 9am to 4pm daily.

## Wildlife Sanctuaries

There are three wildlife sanctuaries in the vicinity of Burleigh Heads.

**Currumbin Sanctuary** (☎ *5534 1266, Gold Coast Hwy, Currumbin; Surfside bus stop No 20; adult/child $19/11; open 5pm*). Run by the National Trust, this excellent bushland park is mobbed by technicoloured lorikeets and other birds, with tree kangaroos, koalas, emus and lots more Australian fauna. It runs fascinating

night tours for $45/28, including transfers from Gold Coast hotels.

**David Fleay Wildlife Park** (☎ *5576 2411, West Burleigh Rd; adult/child $13/6.50; open 9am-5pm*) is run with the help of the QPWS. It has a fine collection of native wildlife, and 4km of walking tracks through mangroves and rainforest. The platypus was first bred in captivity here. Take the Tallebudgera-Burleigh exit from the Gold Coast Hwy.

**Olson's Bird Gardens** (☎ *5533 0208, 746 Currumbin Creek Rd; adult/child $8.50/ 4.50; open 9am-5pm*) is interesting – it's an attractive subtropical garden with a collection of over 1000 exotic birds in enclosures. To get here take the first right after crossing Currumbin Creek.

## Surfing

The right-hand point break at Burleigh Heads is the best wave here but it's usually crowded with pro-surfers. There are plenty of other waves to practise on along the beach. The Hot Stuff Surf Shop (☎ 5535 6899) at 1706 Gold Coast Hwy rents out surfboards for $20/35 a half/full day.

## Places to Stay

*Burleigh Beach Tourist Park* (☎ *5581 7755, fax 5535 3127, Goodwin Terrace*) Unpowered/powered sites from $18.50/ 20.50, cabins $95. This good council-run place is set back from the road.

*Tallebudgera Creek Tourist Park* (☎ *5581 7700, fax 5576 4157, 1544 Gold Coast Hwy*) Unpowered/powered sites $18.50/21, cabins $100. On the southern bank of Tallebudgera Creek, this is a good council-run park, and it's just a five-minute walk from a reasonable surf beach.

*Casino Motel* (☎ *5535 7133, fax 5576 8099, 1761 Gold Coast Hwy*) Doubles $45-55 ($55-65 weekends). This is the closest motel to Burleigh Heads and isn't bad for what you pay.

*Burleigh Gardens Holiday Apartments* (☎ *5576 3955, fax 5576 4372, 1849 Gold Coast Hwy*) 1-bedroom/2-bedroom self-contained units from $95/150. This is a well-kept two-storey block of units, close to the beach and the town centre.

*Hillhaven Holiday Apartments* (☎ *5535 1055, fax 5535 1870, 2 Goodwin Terrace)* Units from $200. High on the headland overlooking Burleigh Heads, this 10-storey apartment building has oldish but comfortable two- or three-bedroom units with great views.

## Places to Eat
There are plenty of eatery choices along the seafront.

*The Pantry* (☎ *5576 2818, 15 Connor St)* Dishes $7.50-11. This upbeat and friendly cafe has good salads, focaccias and all-day breakfasts.

*Burleigh Beach Club* (☎ *5520 2972, Cnr Goodwin Terrace & Gold Coast Hwy)* Dishes $7-15. Lunch Mon-Sat, dinner Sun-Thur. This old-style surf club offers good-value steaks and pastas.

*Pagoda Inn* (☎ *5535 1308, 1726 Gold Coast Hwy)* Set lunch $8, dinner $6-10. This cheap and cheerful South-East Asian place serves Chinese and Malay dishes.

The Burleigh Beach Pavilion on Goodwin Terrace is home to a couple of top-notch restaurants.

*Oskars* (☎ *5576 3722, 43 Goodwin Terrace)* Lunch & dinner $19-28. One of the

**GOLD COAST**

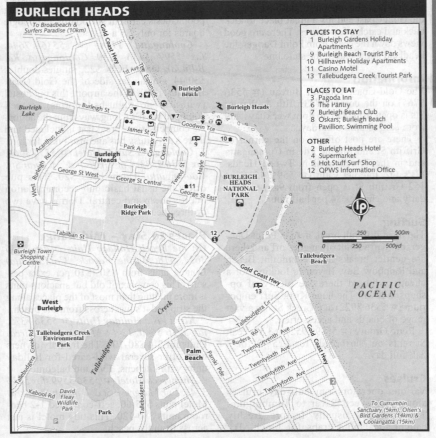

**BURLEIGH HEADS**

PLACES TO STAY
1 Burleigh Gardens Holiday Apartments
9 Burleigh Beach Tourist Park
10 Hillhaven Holiday Apartments
11 Casino Motel
13 Tallebudgera Creek Tourist Park

PLACES TO EAT
3 Pagoda Inn
6 The Pantry
7 Burleigh Beach Club
8 Oskars; Burleigh Beach Pavillion; Swimming Pool

OTHER
2 Burleigh Heads Hotel
4 Supermarket
5 Hot Stuff Surf Shop
12 QPWS Information Office

Gold Coast's top restaurants, this place cooks up plenty of seared, char-grilled and pan-fried Aussie dishes.

## Entertainment

The *Burleigh Heads Hotel (☎ 5535 1000, 12 The Esplanade)* is an OK pub with live bands on Friday and Saturday evenings.

## COOLANGATTA

postcode 4225 • pop 6820

The 'twin towns' of Coolangatta and Tweed Heads straddle the border between Queensland and NSW, but the border between the two is pretty arbitrary. This friendly little surf resort is probably the most laid-back spot on the Gold Coast and it's a great place to kick back and catch a few waves. There are good views down the coast from **Point Danger**, the headland at the end of the state line.

## Information

The Gold Coast Tourism Bureau (☎ 5536 7765) on the corner of Griffith & Warner Sts is open from 8am to 4pm weekdays and from 8am to 3pm Saturday.

There are post offices on the corner of Griffith St and Marine Pde in Coolangatta and in the Tweed Mall in Tweed Heads. PB's OZ Internet Cafe (☎ 5599 4536) at 152 Griffith St is open from 9am to 6pm daily and charges $4 per half hour.

## Surfing

The most difficult break here is Point Danger, but Kirra Point often goes off and there are gentler breaks at Greenmount Beach and Rainbow Bay. If you're looking for a cheap surfboard there are plenty of op-shops in town. The huge Kirra Surf emporium (☎ 5536 3922) at 6 Creek St has a vast range of boards and accessories.

Retro Groove (☎ 5599 3952) at 3 McLean St rents out surfboards for $25/40 for a half/full day.

## Cruises

Various operators run half-day cruises along the Tweed River to Tumbulgum. These cruises usually feature freshly caught local mud crabs for lunch. Try Catch-a-Crab (☎ 5524 2422) or Tweed Endeavour Cruises (☎ 5536 8800).

## Places to Stay – Budget

*Kirra Beach Tourist Park (☎ 5581 7744, fax 5599 3877, Charlotte St, Kirra)* Unpowered/powered sites $17.50/20, cabins $80. This efficient, council-run park is just a short walk to the beach.

*Sunset Strip Budget Resort (☎ 5599 5517, fax 5536 7566, 199-203 Boundary St, Coolangatta)* Beds in 3-4–bed dorms $20, singles/doubles $35/45. This informal resort caters mainly to surfers, and easily offers the best value in town for backpackers. There's a TV lounge, a large, clean kitchen and a big pool. Guests can rent surfboards and boogie boards for only $5 a day.

*Coolangatta YHA (☎ 5536 7644, fax 5599 5436, 230 Coolangatta Rd, Bilinga)*. Dorm beds $22, singles/doubles $30/44. On the far side of the Gold Coast Hwy just north of the airport, this big hostel (with six- to eight-bed dorms) is well equipped but it's a long way from the action. As compensation, breakfast is included and there's a courtesy bus and also bikes for hire.

*Coolangatta Sands Hotel (☎ 5536 3066, fax 5536 2303, Cnr Griffith & McLean Sts, Coolangatta)* Dorm beds $20. This pub offers the usual basic pub accommodation but it's cheap and central. Dorms have two or three beds.

## Places to Stay – Mid-Range

*On the Beach Holiday Units (☎/fax 5536 3624, 118 Marine Parade, Coolangatta)* Double units from $50 ($10 per extra person). This complex of old but spacious units is more inviting than most of the places along the strip and it's just across from the beach.

*Kirra Vista Holiday Units (☎ 5536 7375, fax 5536 5640, 12-14 Musgrave St, Kirra)* Units for 2-4 $80-100. The friendly owners here offer several well-cared-for holiday units with kitchens, TVs and balconies.

*Shipwreck Motel (☎ 5536 3599, fax 5536 3742, Cnr Musgrave St & Winston St, Kirra)* Motel units $55-60, self-contained 1-2 bedroom units $80-120. This tidy motel is just across from the beach.

## Places to Eat

The most pleasant places to eat are the beachfront *Surf Life Saving Clubs* at Coolangatta Beach (☎ *5536 4648*), Greenmount Beach (☎ *5536 1506*) and Rainbow Bay (☎ *5536 6736*). Expect to pay from $7 to $19 for lunch or dinner. These places offer steaks, roasts, pasta and fish and chips on the deck overlooking the ocean.

*Twin Towns Services Club* (☎ *5536 2277, Wharf St, Tweed Heads*) Dishes $7-20. This vast servicemen's club has four restaurants, with prices ranging from $7 for pub-style grills to formal a la carte dining from $15 to $20.

*Farley's* (☎ *5536 7615, Beach House Arcade, Coolangatta*) Dishes $9-21. Open 6am-late Mon-Sat, 6am-2pm Sun. One of several licensed pavement cafes on the main strip, Farley's serves all-day breakfasts, gourmet sandwiches and grills.

*Coolangatta Hotel* (☎ *5536 9311, Cnr Marine Parade & Warner St, Coolangatta*) Lunch from $4.50, dinner $11-16. Here you'll find a bistro with super-cheap lunches and reasonable dinner grills.

There's also an inexpensive food court at the *Tweed Mall*, open seven days.

## Entertainment

Surfies congregate out on the deck at the three surf clubs (Rainbow Bay is the most popular). Alternatively, the *Coolangatta Sands Hotel* has live bands several nights a week, or there are family-oriented shows and regular free movies at the *Twin Towns Services Club* (☎ *5536 1977*) – call for details.

*Coolangatta 6 Cinema Centre* (☎ *5536 8900, Level 2, Showcase on the Beach Centre, Griffith St*) This modern cinema offers six screens of mainstream releases. Tuesday is cheap day ($8).

## Getting There & Away

Golden Gateway Travel (☎ *5536 1700*) at 29 Bay St, south-east of the centre, is the

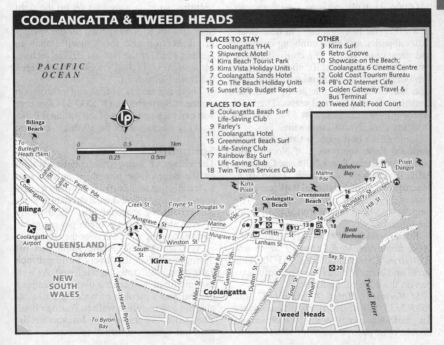

## COOLANGATTA & TWEED HEADS

PACIFIC OCEAN

**PLACES TO STAY**
1  Coolangatta YHA
2  Shipwreck Motel
4  Kirra Beach Tourist Park
5  Kirra Vista Holiday Units
7  Coolangatta Sands Hotel
13  On The Beach Holiday Units
16  Sunset Strip Budget Resort

**PLACES TO EAT**
8  Coolangatta Beach Surf Life-Saving Club
9  Farley's
11  Coolangatta Hotel
15  Greenmount Beach Surf Life-Saving Club
17  Rainbow Bay Surf Life-Saving Club
18  Twin Towns Services Club

**OTHER**
3  Kirra Surf
6  Retro Groove
10  Showcase on the Beach; Coolangatta 6 Cinema Centre
12  Gold Coast Tourism Bureau
14  PB's OZ Internet Cafe
19  Golden Gateway Travel & Bus Terminal
20  Tweed Mall; Food Court

Bilinga Beach
To Burleigh Heads (5km)

0  0.5  1km
0  0.25  0.5mi

Bilinga
Coolangatta Rd
Coolangatta Airport
QUEENSLAND
Charlotte St
Kirra
South St
NEW SOUTH WALES
To Byron Bay
Tweed Heads Bypass

Graham St
Calm St
Pacific Pde
Creek St
Coyne St
Douglas St
Musgrave St
Marine Pde
Musgrave St
Griffith St
Lanham St
Winston St
Appel St
Miles St
Rutledge Rd
Garrick St Sth
Dutton St
Dixon St
Enid St
Wharf St
Bay St

Kirra Point
Coolangatta Beach
Greenmount Beach
Marine Pde
Rainbow Bay
Boundary St
Hill St
Point Danger
Boat Harbour
Tweed River

**Coolangatta**
**Tweed Heads**

terminal for McCafferty's/Greyhound, Kirklands and Coachtrans buses.

# Gold Coast Hinterland

Inland from Coolangatta, the mountains of the McPherson Range stretch back 60km to the NSW border. The national parks here are a paradise for walkers and this unspoiled environment is easily accessible by car or on organised tours from the Gold Coast – a perfect antidote to the noise and clamour of the seaside strip (see Organised Tours at the start of this chapter for Hinterland trips). Expect a lot of rain in the mountains from December to March, and in winter the nights can be cold.

## TAMBORINE MOUNTAIN
Just 45km north-west of the Gold Coast, this 600m-high plateau is on a northern spur of the McPherson Range. Patches of the area's original forests remain in nine small national parks, and offer tumbling cascades and great coast views. The cutesy heritage communities of Mount Tamborine, North Tamborine and Eagle Heights exist to service the Gold Coast tour buses with Devonshire teas and arts and crafts. There's a visitor information centre (☎ 5545 3200) at Doughty Park, North Tamborine.

Some of the best spots are **Witches Falls National Park**, south-west of North Tamborine, and **Cedar Creek Falls** and **Cameron Falls**, north-west of North Tamborine. **Macrozamia Grove National Park** has some extremely old macrozamia palms. The ranger (☎ 5545 1171) has information on all these places.

*Tall Trees Motel* (☎ 5545 1242, fax 5545 0055, Eagle Heights Rd, Curtis Falls, North Tamborine) Singles/doubles $65/70. This small and homely motel has a peaceful garden on the edge of the forest.

*St Bernards Hotel* (☎ 5545 1177, fax 5545 2733, 101 Alpine Terrace, Tamborine) Single/double motel rooms $59/39, single/double/twin pub rooms with shared bath-

rooms $39/59/69 Sun-Thur, $49/69/79 Fri & Sat. This rustic old mountain pub, built in 1911, offers great views out over the forest, good pub meals and cosy pub rooms and motel units, all with breakfast.

## SPRINGBROOK PLATEAU
The forested, 900m-high Springbrook Plateau, like the rest of the McPherson Range, is a remnant of the huge volcano that used to be centred on Mt Warning in NSW. It's an excellent winding drive up from the Gold Coast via Mudgeeraba, with great views over the surrounding countryside.

Much of the area is protected as **Springbrook National Park**, with three sections: Springbrook, Mt Cougal and Natural Bridge. The vegetation is temperate rainforest and eucalypt forest, with gorges, cliffs, forests, waterfalls, and an extensive network of walking tracks and picnic areas.

Each section is reached by a long access road and there are no short cuts between the sections, so make sure you get on the right road. Coming from Nerang, take the Springbrook to Nerang road for the Springbrook section and the Murwillumbah to Nerang road for the Natural Bridge section. Mt Cougal is reached via Currumbin Creek Rd from Currumbin.

There is a ranger's office and information centre at Springbrook (☎ 5533 5147) where you can pick up a copy of the National Parks walking tracks leaflet for all three sections.

### Springbrook
The village of Springbrook is balanced right on the edge of the plateau, with numerous waterfalls that tumble over 100m down to the coastal plain below. Understandably, lookouts are the big attraction here, and there are several places where you can get the giddy thrill of leaning right out over the edge.

At **Gwongorella Picnic Area**, just off Springbrook Rd, the lovely **Purling Brook Falls** drop 109m into the rainforest. As well as a picnic area, there's a pleasant camping ground and a number of walking trails, including a 6km-return walk to Waringa Pool, a beautiful swimming hole. Just south is the national park information centre, and

Canyon Lookout, the starting point for a 4km circuit walk to **Twin Falls** and the 17km **Warrie Circuit**.

At the end of Springbrook Rd, the **Goomoolahra Picnic Area** is another pleasant picnic area with barbecues beside a small creek. A little further on, there's a great lookout point beside the falls, with views across the plateau and all the way back to the coast.

True to its name, the **Best of All Lookout**, which is reached via Lyrebird Ridge Rd, offers spectacular views from the southern edge of the plateau to the flats below. There's a 350m trail from the carpark to the lookout that takes you past a clump of mighty Antarctic beech trees.

**Places to Stay & Eat** You can camp at the *Gwongorella Camping Ground* near Purling Brook Falls. You self-register at the site – fill out the envelope and post your payment into the mailbox provided. It costs $3.85 per head or $15.40 for families. You can book through the ranger at Springbrook (☎ 5533 5147).

Most guesthouses are along or signposted off Springbrook Rd.

*Springbrook Mountain Chalets* (☎ 5533 5205, fax 5533 5156, 2058 Springbrook Rd) Doubles $140-170, $50 per extra person. Just outside Springbrook, these *very* stylish wooden chalets hidden away in the forest can sleep up to six. Rates are $10 higher during the peak season and on Friday and Saturday. A minimum of two nights is preferred.

*Springbrook Mountain Lodge* (☎/fax 5533 5366, 317 Repeater Station Rd, 3km off the Springbrook Rd) Singles/doubles $44/56, plus $22 per extra person, double cabins $132. The highest place on the plateau, this comprises a chalet-style lodge with a large kitchen, recreation areas and great views, and several self-contained cabins; pick-ups from the Gold Coast cost $15 for two people on a two-night stay. There is a discount for YHA members

*Canyon View Guesthouse & Cafe* (☎ 5533 5120, 8 Canyon Parade) Doubles $75. Near the Canyon Lookout, this homely place offers clean guest rooms with bathroom, TV and fridge. Also here is a nice

*restaurant* open for lunch and dinner daily except Monday and Tuesday.

*Mouses House* (☎/fax 5533 5192, fax 5533 5411, Springbrook Rd) Doubles $230 for 2 nights. The alpine-style timber chalets here are very impressive (all have a wood stove), but the Snow White theme is a little tacky. Facilities here include half-court tennis, a spa and sauna, and bikes. There is a minimum two-night stay.

*Tulip Gardens Guesthouse* (☎ 5533 5125, 2874 Springbrook Rd) Doubles $99. This is an attractive timber guesthouse, and lunch and dinners can be provided on request. Breakfast is included in the price.

*Springbrook Homestead* (☎ 5533 5200, 2319 Springbrook Rd) Lunch $6.50-10, dinner around $16. Lunch daily, dinner Fri & Sat. This modern tavern serves ploughman's lunches and steaks.

*Kimba's Kitchen* (☎ 5533 5335, 33 Forestry Rd) Right by the carpark for Purling Brook Falls, this simple tearoom offers sandwiches and light meals.

## Natural Bridge
The Natural Bridge section of the national park is just a couple of kilometres west of Springbrook as the crow flies, but you'll have to drive back up to Numinbah and then down the Murwillumbah road to get here – a total trip of about 35km. A steep 1km walking circuit leads to a rock arch spanning a water-formed cave, which is home to a huge colony of glow-worms, and a small waterfall tumbling into a swimming hole.

About 1km north of the turn-off to Natural Bridge, the *Two Pines Cafe* (☎ 5533 6140) sells fuel and has takeaway meals and Devonshire teas.

## Mt Cougal
The Mt Cougal section is also linked to Springbrook, but to get here, you'll have to go all the way back to the Pacific Hwy and pick up Currumbin Creek Rd at Currumbin. On Currumbin Creek there's a walking trail that passes several cascades and swimming holes, and also a restored sawmill from the wasteful days when the rainforest was felled to make packing cases for bananas!

## CANUNGRA

This small town is 25km west of Nerang. It's at the junction of the northern approach roads to the Green Mountains and Binna Burra sections of the Lamington National Park. The tourist information office (☎ 5543 5156) in the Canungra Library, on the corner of Kidston St and Lawton Lane, is open from 9.30am to 4pm from Sunday to Friday and 9.30am to 2pm Saturday.

If you're heading up to Green Mountains, Canungra Valley Vineyards (☎ 5543 4011) is housed in an old homestead and is open daily for tastings and sales.

*Canungra Hotel (☎ 5543 5233, fax 5543 5617, 18 Kidston St)* Singles/doubles $49.50/55, with en suite $60.50/66. This big old white timber pub has good rooms upstairs, and a bistro with cheap lunches and dinners.

*Canungra Motel (☎/fax 5543 5155, Kidston St)* Single/double units $50/60. This place is an OK choice.

## LAMINGTON NATIONAL PARK

West of Springbrook, the 200 sq km Lamington National Park covers much of the McPherson Range and adjoins the Border Ranges National Park in NSW. The park covers most of the spectacular Lamington Plateau, which reaches 1100m in places, as well as the densely forested valleys below. Much of the vegetation is subtropical rainforest and there are beautiful gorges, caves, waterfalls and lots of wildlife. Commonly spotted animals include satin and regent bowerbirds and the curious Lamington spiny crayfish, and you'll almost certainly see pademelons, a type of small wallaby, on the forest verges in late afternoon. Somewhat incongruously, the park was named for Lord Lamington, a previous governor of Queensland, who visited once, just after the park was founded, to shoot koalas.

The two most popular and accessible sections of the park are **Binna Burra** and **Green Mountains**, both reached via paved roads from Canungra. Binna Burra can also be reached from Nerang. The park has 160km of walking tracks ranging from a 'senses trail' for the blind at Binna Burra and an excellent tree-top canopy walk along a series of rope and plank suspension bridges at Green Mountains, to the 24km **Border Trail**, which links the two sections of the park.

Walking trail guides are available from the ranger stations at Binna Burra (☎ 5533 3584), which is open from 1.30pm to 3.30pm Monday to Friday, and from 9am to 3.30pm Saturday and Sunday, and Green Mountains (☎ 5544 0634), open 1pm to 3.30pm Monday to Friday and 9am to 11am Monday, Wednesday and Thursday.

### Places to Stay & Eat

**Binna Burra** The Lodge is the hub of the Binna Burra area.

*Binna Burra Mountain Lodge (☎ 1800 074 260, 5533 3758, fax 5533 3658, Binna Burra Rd, Beechmont)* Log cabins $159 per person, with en suite $189. This excellent mountain retreat is surrounded by forest, and offers rustic log cabins clustered around a central restaurant that has good views over the national park. The tariff includes all meals, free hiking and climbing gear, and activities like guided walks, bus trips and abseiling. Meals at the *restaurant* start at $11.

*Binna Burra Camp Ground (☎ 5533 3622, fax 5533 3658)* Unpowered/powered

### Life of O'Reilly

*O'Reilly's Guesthouse (☎ 5544 0644, Lamington National Park Rd)* at Green Mountains was established by one of the original settler families who moved into the McPherson Range in 1911. The original wooden lodge was opened in 1926 to cater to hard-core naturalists, and could only be reached by a two-day horse ride from Brisbane.

O'Reilly's became famous across Australia in 1937, when a Sydney-bound Stinson airliner crashed into the rainforest deep inside the national park. Bernard O'Reilly set off alone and located the wreckage after several days' searching, rescuing two passengers, who, miraculously, were still alive 10 days after the crash. You can see photos and relics from the Stinson in the library at the guesthouse, which is still owned and run by the O'Reilly family.

sites $10/13.50, 2-person/4-person on-site safari tents $40/60. Attached to the Binna Burra Mountain Lodge, this very popular camping ground should be booked well in advance. It has a great setting with a laundry, hot showers, shelters with coin-operated barbecues and hotplates.

**Binna Burra Kiosk** Open 8am-5pm Sun-Thur, 8am-8pm Fri & Sat. Next to Binna Burra Camp Ground, this kiosk does good breakfasts as well as sandwiches, rolls, hot dogs, burgers and the like.

**Green Mountains** The Guesthouse is the starting point for visits to this part of the park.

*O'Reilly's Guesthouse (☎ 5544 0644, fax 5544 0638, Lamington National Park Rd)* Singles/doubles $119/195, double units $254-420. This famous guesthouse has been stylishly developed over the years. Tariffs include all meals and activities (eg, bushwalks, spotlighting walks, 4WD bus trips). The library has lots of wildlife books. There's a plush *restaurant* (lunch $26, dinner $37), or the more affordable *Gran O'Reilly's Bistro*, serving light meals from 7.30am to 4pm.

There's a national park *camping ground* close to O'Reilly's, and *bush camping* is permitted in several areas within the park ($3.85 per night or $15.40 per family), but only a limited number of permits are issued. Camping permits must be obtained from the ranger at Green Mountains.

### Getting There & Away
The Binna Burra bus service (☎ 5533 3622) operates daily between Surfers and Binna Burra. The trip takes one hour and costs $22 one way (overnight stay required). The service picks up from the Surfers Transit Centre at 1.15pm and the train station at Nerang at 1.30pm; departures from Binna Burra are at 10.30am daily. Bookings are essential.

Allstate Scenic Tours (☎ 3285 1777) runs a bus service between Brisbane and O'Reilly's from Sunday to Friday, leaving the Brisbane Transit Centre at 9.30am (one-way/return day trip $27.50/$44, 1½ hours).

Mountain Coach Company (☎ 5524 4249) has a daily service from the Gold Coast to Green Mountains via Tamborine Mountain (one hour), costing $35 return or $18 one way.

## MT LINDESAY HIGHWAY
This road runs south from Brisbane, across the Great Dividing Range west of Lamington National Park, into NSW at Woodenbong. About 20km south-west of Tamborine Mountain, **Beaudesert** is a small cattle centre with a pioneer museum-cum-tourist information office (☎ 5541 1284, corner of Brisbane and McKee Sts) and several motels and hotels.

West of Beaudesert is a stretch of the Great Dividing Range, and the gateway to the Darling Downs (see that chapter for information). Further south, **Mt Barney National Park** is undeveloped but popular with bushwalkers and climbers. It's in the Great Dividing Range, just north of the state border, and is reached from the Rathdowney to Boonah road. There's a *camping ground* in the park – call the rangers station at Boonah (☎ 5463 5041).

*Mt Barney Lodge (☎/fax 5544 3233, Upper Logan Rd)* Double cabins $75, with en suite $110. Just off the Rathdowney to Boonah road, this attractively rustic place is a good base for the national park. The cabins are self-contained, and there's a two-day minimum at weekends.

There's a tourist information office (☎ 5544 1222) on the highway at Rathdowney. Araucaria Ecotours runs a three-day tour of the region using the Mt Barney Lodge as a base – see Hinterland Tours under Organised Tours in the Brisbane chapter.

# Darling Downs

West of the Great Dividing Range stretch the rolling plains of the Darling Downs, some of the most fertile and productive agricultural land in Australia. Setting out from Sydney, English botanist Allan Cunningham first explored this region in 1827, describing it as the best piece of country he had ever seen. He named the Downs, after the then governor of New South Wales (NSW).

The Downs was the first part of Queensland to be settled after the establishment of the Moreton Bay penal colony, and towns like Warwick and Toowoomba are among the state's oldest. Almost every town in the region is full of old buildings and some have changed little since the 1950s. There are also some interesting attractions scattered through the region, including the scenic Granite Belt region (near Stanthorpe) with Queensland's only wine-growing district; the excellent Girraween and Sundown National Parks; the historic Jondaryan Woolshed complex west of Toowoomba; and the impressive historical village at Miles.

To the north and west of Brisbane is the South Burnett region with the popular Bunya Mountains National Park and a string of small rural centres along Hwy 17.

## Dangers & Annoyances

The roads through the Downs may seem peaceful and uncrowded, but remember that you're sharing the highway with two of Australia's most lethal inhabitants – the road train and the kangaroo. During one morning drive from Texas to Roma, we saw 35 freshly killed kangaroos and wallabies from the night before. If you have to drive at night, keep your speed well below 70km/h.

## Getting There & Around

**Air** Qantas (☎ 13 13 13) flies from Brisbane to Roma. Macair (☎ 13 15 22) flies between Brisbane, Toowoomba and St George.

**Bus** McCafferty's/Greyhound has two major bus services that pass through the

### Highlights

- There's no better way to experience the Downs than by staying at a traditional homestead like Talgai.
- Hunt down your favourite tipple at the Granite Belt wineries near Stanthorpe.
- Get back to nature among the rugged granite boulders of Girraween National Park.
- Wake up with wallabies: The Bunya Mountains National Park is a great place to camp among friendly, furry and feathered wildlife.
- Visit Miles Historical Village, an accurate re-creation of a turn-of-the-20th-century high street.

Darling Downs. The Brisbane-Longreach service runs along the Warrego Hwy via Toowoomba ($20, two hours), Dalby ($33, four hours), Miles ($39, 5½ hours) and Roma ($53, eight hours), while their inland Brisbane to Adelaide and Brisbane to Melbourne services pass through Warwick ($32, four hours) and Stanthorpe ($39, 4½ hours), or Goondiwindi ($47, five hours), depending on the route.

McCafferty's/Greyhound also has buses between Toowoomba and the Gold Coast ($37, three hours), and between Brisbane and Rockhampton (13 hours) via Toowoomba (two hours) and Miles (five hours).

Crisps' is the biggest local operator, with services from Brisbane to Warwick, Toowoomba, Goondiwindi, Stanthorpe and south to Tenterfield in NSW. See Getting There & Away section for more details of McCafferty's/Greyhound services.

Brisbane Bus Lines has daily services from Brisbane into the South Burnett region.

**Train** The air-con *Westlander* runs from Brisbane to Charleville on Tuesday and Thursday, returning on Wednesday and Friday, stopping in Ipswich (45 minutes), Toowoomba (four hours) and Roma (11 hours). The 777km journey from Brisbane to Charleville takes about 16 hours; there are connecting bus services from Charleville to Quilpie and Cunnamulla.

**Car & Motorcycle** The major route through the Darling Downs is the Warrego Hwy, which runs west from Ipswich to Charleville. There's also the Cunningham

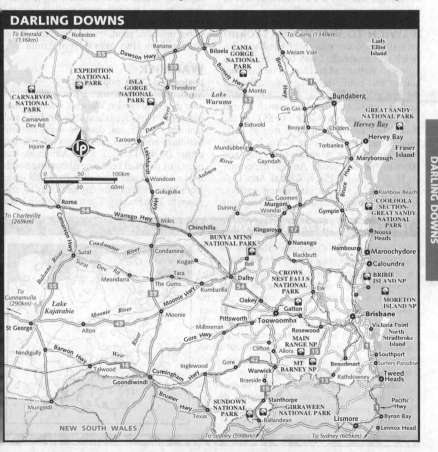

DARLING DOWNS

DARLING DOWNS

Hwy, which runs south-west from Ipswich to Warwick and Goondiwindi.

The two main north-south routes in the Downs are the Leichhardt Hwy, which runs north from Goondiwindi to Rockhampton via Miles, and the Carnarvon Hwy, which runs north from Mungindi on the NSW border to Roma. Hwy 17 runs inland between Brisbane and Rockhampton, passing through the South Burnett region.

The most scenic drives in this region pass through the Great Dividing Range, particularly around Stanthorpe and the Bunya Mountains. West of the mountains most of the highways are pretty dull.

## IPSWICH TO WARWICK (120km)

Virtually an outer suburb of Brisbane, Ipswich was established way back in 1827 as a convict settlement and has some fine, old houses and public buildings, described in the excellent *Ipswich Heritage Trails* leaflets available from the Ipswich tourist information centre (☎ 3281 0555), in the Post Office Building on the corner of Brisbane St and D'Arcy Doyle Place. It's open from 9am to 4pm Monday to Friday and 10am to 3pm weekends. Around the corner on D'Arcy Doyle Place, **Global Arts Link** (☎ *3813 9222*) is an interesting gallery, open from 10am to 5pm. It takes one hour

to get here from Brisbane by Citytrain and costs $6.90.

South-west of Ipswich, the Cunningham Hwy to Warwick crosses the Great Dividing Range at Cunningham's Gap, named for a botanist from London's Kew Gardens, passing through the 1100m-high mountains of **Main Range National Park**. This impressive park covers 184 sq km of dense rainforest and there are numerous walking trails to lookouts over the park. The rangers station (☎ 4666 1133) is west of Cunningham's Gap on the southern side of the highway. There's a small *camping ground* opposite, or a quieter, more secluded *camping area* at Spicer's Gap, reached via a good, unsealed road, which branches off the Cunningham Hwy 5km west of Artula.

## WARWICK

postcode 4370 • pop 20,000

South-west of Brisbane, 162km inland and near the NSW border, Warwick is the second-oldest town in Queensland after Brisbane and is noted for its roses, dairy produce, historic buildings and rodeo. The tourist information centre (☎ 4661 3122), at 49 Albion St, has plenty of material on the neighbouring South Downs towns and a small gallery. It's open from 9am to 5pm Monday to Saturday and 10am to 3pm Sunday. The tourist office has a

## The Fastest Shears in the West

On the corner of the Cunningham Hwy and Glengallan Rd in Warwick is a giant pair of blade shears atop a block of stone. This monument commemorates Jackie Howe, born on Canning Downs Station near Warwick, and acclaimed as the greatest 'gun' (the best in the shed) shearer the country has ever seen. He holds the amazing record of having shorn 321 sheep with a set of hand shears in less than eight hours. Established in 1892, the record still stands today – it wasn't even beaten by shearers using machine-powered shears until 1950.

Jackie had a habit of ripping the sleeves off his shirts when he was working and to this day the sleeveless blue singlets favoured by many Australian workers are known as 'Jackie Howes'.

Another sunny day in Surfers Paradise

Catamarans for hire

Life-saving flags marking the safest spots to swim and surf

Surfboards at Burleigh Heads

The colour of a Gold Coast surf life-saving carnival

MANFRED GOTTSCHALK

Dolphins getting air at Sea World, Main Beach

CHRISTOPHER GROENHOUT

RICHARD I'ANSON

A slick choice of water sports

Kicking back on a Gold Coast beach

MANFRED GOTTSCHALK

Gold Coast: high-rise, multiplex, grand-scale tourism – and great surf

heritage trail map of Warwick's historic buildings, including the 1917 Criterion Hotel and the Abbey of the Roses, south of the centre on Lock St, dating to 1893. Also useful is the *Cultural Heritage & Historic Building Trail* brochure, with scenic drives around Warwick and Stanthorpe.

Well worth a visit is the **Pringle Cottage & Museum** (*☎ 4661 2028, 81 Dragon St; adult/child $3.50/0.50; open 10am-noon Wed-Fri, 2pm-4pm Sat & Sun*), a cottage dating from 1863, stuffed with a collection of old telephones, costumes, photos and assorted historical contraptions.

## Special Events

Warwick's major annual event is the Warwick Rodeo & Campdraft held on the last weekend in October. Also interesting is the Facetors' Guild Meeting every Easter, said to be the country's biggest swap-meet for collectors of precious and semiprecious stones.

## Places to Stay

*Kahler's Oasis Caravan Park* (*☎ 4661 2874, fax 4661 1473, New England Hwy*) Unpowered/powered sites $13/17, cabins from $40, with en suite $55. This tidy caravan park is 1km south of the centre and has a small pool.

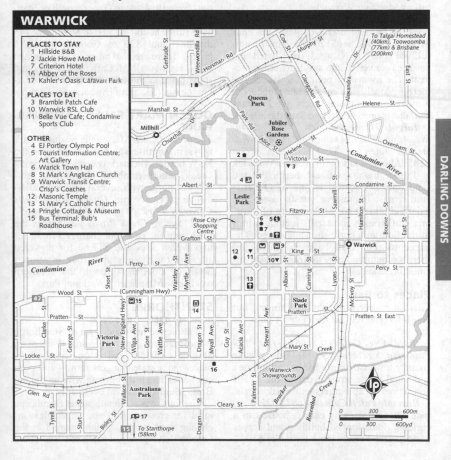

**WARWICK**

PLACES TO STAY
1  Hillside B&B
2  Jackie Howe Motel
7  Criterion Hotel
16  Abbey of the Roses
17  Kahler's Oasis Caravan Park

PLACES TO EAT
3  Bramble Patch Cafe
10  Warwick RSL Club
11  Belle Vue Cafe; Condamine Sports Club

OTHER
4  EJ Portley Olympic Pool
5  Tourist Information Centre; Art Gallery
6  Warick Town Hall
8  St Mark's Anglican Church
9  Warwick Transit Centre; Crisp's Coaches
12  Masonic Temple
13  St Mary's Catholic Church
14  Pringle Cottage & Museum
15  Bus Terminal; Bub's Roadhouse

To Talgai Homestead (40km), Toowoomba (77km) & Brisbane (200km)

Queens Park

Jubilee Rose Gardens

Condamine River

Warwick

Condamine River

Slade Park

Warwick Showgrounds

To Stanthorpe (58km)

0    300    600m
0    300    600yd

*Criterion Hotel* (☎ *4661 1042, fax 4661 1042, 84 Palmerin St*) Rooms from $27. The Criterion is a huge, old country pub with basic but clean rooms opening onto a broad front veranda.

*Jackie Howe Motel* (☎ *4661 2111, fax 4661 3858, Cnr Palmerin & Victoria Sts*) Singles/doubles from $51/61. This budget motel is run by a friendly couple and is fairly close to the centre.

*Hillside B&B* (☎ *4661 2671, fax 4661 7393, 25 Weewondilla Rd*) Rooms from $35 per person. This pleasant B&B is housed in an elegant sandstone former rectory on a hill overlooking Warwick.

*Abbey of the Roses* (☎ *4661 9777, Cnr Lock & Dragon Sts*) Doubles Sun-Thur $100-145, Fri & Sat $120-165. This beautiful, old abbey is National Trust listed and has been converted into a stylish heritage retreat. The rooms are period furnished, and there are lovely rose gardens and cloisters to wander around in, plus a very good *restaurant* that is open Friday and Saturday nights.

*Talgai Homestead* (☎ *4666 3444, fax 4666 3780, Dalrymple Creek Rd*) Deluxe suites Sun-Thur $205, Fri & Sat $285. About 40km north-west of Warwick at Talgai, this magnificent, heritage-listed sandstone homestead is one of Queensland's most impressive guesthouses. The palatial building sits at the centre of a former cattle ranch and tariffs include a tour of the farm in a horse-drawn carriage. The gorgeous rooms all have en suites and there's a sumptuous *restaurant*. Rates include breakfast.

### Places to Eat

There are several lunchtime choices, but you'll have to rely on the clubs or pubs for dinner.

*Belle Vue Cafe* (☎ *4661 1110, 119 Palmerin St*) Meals $5-11. This classic country town cafe–milk bar has a Laminex and vinyl decor straight out of the 1950s and serves cheap burgers and snack meals.

*Bramble Patch Cafe* (☎ *4661 9022, 8 Albion St*) This friendly cafe is housed in a curious, dome-topped building and serves good gourmet sandwiches for under $10.

Warwick's clubs are a good bet for lunch or dinner, but they close at 8pm.

*Warwick RSL Club* (☎ *4661 1229, Cnr Albion & King Sts*) Dishes $6-12. This club serves up cheap and cheerful Aussie tucker.

Other options for cheap meals include the *Condamine Sports Club* (☎ *4661 1911, 131–33 Palmerin St*) and the *Criterion Hotel* (see places to stay earlier).

### Getting There & Away

The Warwick Transit Centre (☎ 4661 8333) is at 72 Grafton St, near the Albion St corner. Warwick lies on the daily Crisps' Coaches runs from Brisbane to Goondiwindi or Stanthorpe. Fares from Warwick are $29 to Brisbane (three hours), $15.50 to Stanthorpe (45 minutes) and $30 to Goondiwindi (2½ hours). There are also buses to Toowoomba ($16, 1½ hours). McCafferty's/Greyhound stops here on the inland Brisbane to Melbourne run ($32 from Brisbane, four hours).

## QUEEN MARY FALLS NATIONAL PARK

The pretty Queen Mary Falls National Park is 43km south-east of Warwick near the NSW border. The park is centred on Spring Creek, which tumbles 40m into a rainforested gorge with several walking trails.

The privately run *Queen Mary Falls Caravan Park* (☎ *4664 7151, fax 4664 7122, Spring Creek Rd*) is just across the road from the park and charges $15.50 for unpowered sites and $17.60 for powered sites. A rough, unsealed road continues north to Boonah, through the southern reaches of Main Range National Park.

## STANTHORPE

**postcode 4380 • pop 9600**

The attractive highland town of Stanthorpe is most famous for being cold – it sits at an altitude of 915m and is one of the few places in the state that gets snow – and even celebrates its chilly climate with an annual Brass Monkey Festival every July.

The four-season climate makes Stanthorpe ideal for growing fruit and vegetables, including wine grapes, which flourish in the Granite Belt region just south of town. There are at least 20 wineries within 20km of Stan-thorpe – pick up a list at the Stanthorpe Visitor Information Office (☎ 4681 2057), at Leslie St just south of the river. It's open from 9am to 3pm Monday, 8.30am to 5pm Tuesday to Saturday and 9am to 4pm Sunday.

There is plentiful work picking fruit here from October to mid-June, if you don't mind the chilly mornings. Stanthorpe holds a popular rodeo in March and a huge Apple & Grape Festival in late February or early March, with street parades, sheep shearing and grape crushing.

Maryland St forms the main thoroughfare.

## Things to See

The **Stanthorpe Heritage Museum** *(☎ 4681 1711, 12 High St; adult/child $3/1; open 10am-4pm Wed-Fri, 1pm-4pm Sat, 9am-1pm Sun)*, on the northern outskirts of town, has a slab-timber jail (1876), an old shire council building (1914), a former school residence (1891), and a meticulously presented collection of local memorabilia.

The **Stanthorpe Regional Art Gallery** *(☎ 4681 1874, Lock St; open 10am-4pm Mon-Fri, 1pm-4pm Sat & Sun)*, north-west of the post office, has exhibitions of works by local artists.

While you're in town, take a stroll through the parkland around Quart Pot Creek, near the visitor information centre. The park is full of trees like the claret ash, which change colour spectacularly during autumn.

## Activities

Red Gum Ridge Trail Rides (☎ 4683 7169) offers various **horse rides** ranging from a one-hour trot ($20) to a tour of the wineries or overnight pub rides – ring for details.

You can **fossick** for topaz at Swiper's Gully, 13km north-west of Stanthorpe – ask about fossicking permits at the visitor information centre.

## Places to Stay

**Caravan Parks & Hostels** The owners of budget accommodation in Stanthorpe specialise in helping backpackers to find work.

*Top of the Town Caravan Village (☎ 4681 4888, fax 4681 4222, 10 High St)*

Powered sites $15.50, workers hostel beds $18.50, cabins from $55. On the northern outskirts, this caravan park mainly caters to seasonal workers, who camp or stay in the bunkhouse ($115 per week). The owners can help you find work, but call ahead to make sure that work is available.

*Summit Backpackers (☎ 4683 2599, Granite Belt Dr)* Dorm beds nightly/weekly $17/115. About 12km north of Stanthorpe at Thulimbah, this place also specialises in finding fruit- and vegetable-picking work for travellers. It's remote, run-down and very basic, but you can make good money picking

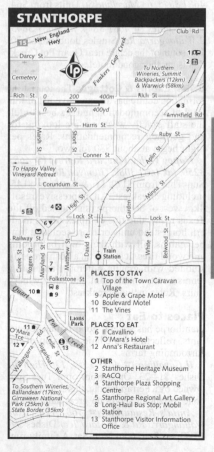

**STANTHORPE**

PLACES TO STAY
1 Top of the Town Caravan Village
9 Apple & Grape Motel
10 Boulevard Motel
11 The Vines

PLACES TO EAT
6 Il Cavallino
7 O'Mara's Hotel
12 Anna's Restaurant

OTHER
2 Stanthorpe Heritage Museum
3 RACQ
4 Stanthorpe Plaza Shopping Centre
5 Stanthorpe Regional Art Gallery
8 Long-Haul Bus Stop; Mobil Station
13 Stanthorpe Visitor Information Office

**DARLING DOWNS**

fruit and there are few places to fritter away your earnings. Buses running between Brisbane and Stanthorpe can drop you at the door – otherwise the owners will pick you up from Stanthorpe. Rates include transfers to work.

**Motels** There are half a dozen motels in town to choose from.

*Boulevard Motel* (☎ *4681 1777, fax 4681 3218, 76 Maryland St*) Singles/doubles from $41/47, with park view $49/55. This is a cheap choice and has rooms overlooking a small park.

*Apple & Grape Motel* (☎ *4681 1288, fax 4681 3855, 63 Maryland St*) Units from $64. This place is central and well maintained.

*The Vines* (☎ *4681 3844, fax 4681 3843, 2 Wallangarra Rd*) Singles/doubles $65/70. Just south of the centre near Quart Pot Creek, this is another good motel.

**B&Bs, Cabins & Cottages** The tourist information centre has an extensive list of this kind of accommodation and it's best to tell the staff exactly what you are looking for and get their recommendations. Rates per night begin at about $80 for two.

*Happy Valley Vineyard Retreat* (☎ *4681 3250, fax 4681 3082, Glenlyon Rd*) Doubles Sun-Thur from $119, Fri & Sat from $145, including breakfast. An impressive resort 4km west of Stanthorpe (signposted off the Texas road), this fine complex offers modern homestead units or more secluded timber cabins, all with their own bathrooms and wood fires. It stands on a bush property studded with granite outcrops, and has a tennis court, a restaurant and daily winery tours. Rates include breakfast.

## Places to Eat

Stanthorpe has several good Italian restaurants, reflecting the ethnic make-up of the surrounding farms.

*Il Cavallino* (☎ *4681 1556, 130 High St*) Dishes $14-23. Open from 5pm Tues-Sun. Owned by a Ferrari fanatic, this slightly overdone restaurant serves up great Italian food.

*Anna's Restaurant* (☎ *4681 1265, Cnr Wallangarra Rd & O'Mara Tce*) Dishes $9-17. Open from 6pm Mon-Sat. A family-run, BYO, Italian restaurant set in a cosy Queenslander, Anna's serves up good, hearty servings of pasta.

*O'Mara's Hotel* (☎ *4681 1044, 45 Maryland St*) Dishes $7.50-16. This friendly little pub has an open fire and good, cheap meals (closed Sunday evening).

## Getting There & Around

McCafferty's/Greyhound and Crisps' coaches stop at the Mobil Garage on the corner of Folkestone and Maryland Sts. There are buses to Warwick (45 minutes), Toowoomba (2¼ hours), Brisbane (4½ hours) and Tenterfield in NSW (1½ hours), where you can pick up the Kirklands bus to Byron Bay. Brisbane to Stanthorpe costs $39 (4½ hours).

For taxi tours of the Granite Belt wineries, try Stanthorpe Taxi Service (☎ 4681 1522).

## SOUTH OF STANTHORPE
## Granite Belt Wineries

The Granite Belt is an elevated plateau of the Great Dividing Range and ranges from 800m to 950m above sea level, creating the only region in the Sunshine State with a climate suitable for viticulture. This modest cluster of vineyards constitutes Queensland's only true wine district, and it's set among some spectacular scenery – there are definitely worse places to sit and sip a glass of 'vino'!

Grapes were first grown in the district in the 19th century but the wine industry really took off during WWII when Italian immigrants were brought into the countryside to work on farms (at the time, Australia was at war with Italy). These forced immigrees flourished, and there are now some 27 wineries dotted around the New England Hwy between Stanthorpe and Ballandean.

Don't expect Hunter Valley-style enterprises though; all the wineries here are boutique places that sell their wines through the cellar doors. The region doesn't have a particular speciality, but its reds are generally stronger than its whites. All of the wineries are open weekends for tasting and sales, and most also open during the week.

Heading south from Stanthorpe, the wineries include:

**Kominos Wines** (☎ 4683 4311) New England Hwy, Severnlea

**Mountview** (☎ 4683 4316) Mt Stirling Rd, Glen Aplin

**Felsberg Winery** (☎ 4683 4332) Townsends Rd, Glen Aplin

**Rumbalara Vineyards** (☎ 4684 1206) Fletcher Rd, Fletcher

**Bungawarra** (☎ 4684 1128) Bents Rd, Ballandean

**Ballandean Estate** (☎ 4684 1226) Sundown Rd, Ballandean

**Bald Mountain Winery** (☎ 4684 3186) Hickling Lane, Wallangarra.

There are also several wineries north of Stanthorpe:

**Old Caves Winery** (☎ 4681 1494) New England Hwy, Stanthorpe

**Boireann Wines** (☎ 4683 2194) Donnellys Castle Rd, The Summit

**Heritage Wines** (☎ 4685 2197) Granite Belt Dr, Cottonvale

**Tours** Several companies run tours of the wineries out of Stanthorpe. Filippo's Tours (☎ 4683 5126) has tours to eight of the 27 wineries from $51 per person, including lunch, plus overnight trips from Brisbane with accommodation in Stanthorpe for $168. Granite Highlands Maxi Tours (☎ 4681 3969) also offers tours out of Stanthorpe.

**Places to Stay & Eat** The most popular base for visits to the wineries is Stanthorpe but there are several choices around Ballandean and Girraween National Park.

*Vineyard Cottages & Café* (☎ *4684 1270,* e *admin@vineyard-cottages.com.au, New England Hwy)* Cottages for 2 people $175-195, for 4 people $310. This interesting place on the northern outskirts of Ballandean, has four comfortable and attractive, heritage-style brick cottages with their own en suites and spas, plus a good restaurant in a converted wooden church.

## Girraween National Park

Wonderful Girraween National Park adjoins Bald Rock National Park over the border in NSW and features the same towering granite boulders surrounded by pristine forests. Wildlife is everywhere and there are 17km of walking trails, which take you to the top of some of the surreal granite outcrops. Shortest is the 3km walk and scramble up the 1080m Pyramids, while the grandaddy of Girraween walks is the 10.4km trek to the top of 1267m Mt Norman.

There are two good *camping grounds* in the park, which also teem with wildlife, and offer facilities like drinking water, hot showers and barbecues. Access is via a paved road from Ballandean, 17km south of Stanthorpe on the New England Hwy.

The visitors centre (☎ 4684 5157) is (usually) open from 1pm to 3.30pm Monday to Friday and all day at weekends. It accepts camp site bookings and usual national park rates apply. Although winter nights here can be cold, it's hot work climbing the boulders, so take plenty of water when you hike.

**Places to Stay** If you aren't up for camping, there are several good places to stay on the access road from Ballandean.

*Girraween Environmental Lodge* (☎ *4684 5138, fax 4684 5148, Pyramids Rd)* Double cabins $170 ($33 for extras). This plush option has very well-appointed cabins in the woods, each with a kitchen, fireplace, TV and veranda.

*Wisteria Cottage* (☎ *4684 5121,* e *wistcott@halenet.com.au, Pyramids Rd)* Cottages per adult/child $70/30 (up to 6 people). This friendly pottery shop has three nice, wooden cabins in the field behind, with kitchens, bathrooms, verandas and fireplaces. Rates include breakfast.

*Girraween Country Inn* (☎ *4683 7109, fax 4683 7203, Eukey Rd)* B&B per couple from $99. On the northern edge of the park, this is a two-storey, chalet-style guesthouse with a restaurant downstairs and a great location beside the national park. Rates include breakfast. To get here, turn off the New England Hwy at Ballandean and follow the Eukey Rd for 9km.

## Sundown National Park

On the Queensland-NSW border, about 80km south-west of Stanthorpe, Sundown

National Park is dominated by the steep, spectacular gorges of the Severn River. There are several ruined mines in the park, but the rugged wilderness and plentiful wildlife are the main attractions. At the southern end of the park, the *Broadwater camping ground* can be reached in a conventional vehicle along a 4km gravel road. The northern section of the park is only accessible by 4WD vehicles from Ballandean. For information and to book camping permits, contact the park rangers at Girraween National Park (☎ 4684 5157).

## GOONDIWINDI
postcode 4390 • pop 4370

West of Warwick, on the NSW border, Goondiwindi (**gun**-doo-windy) is something of a one-horse town, the horse in question being Gunsynd, a remarkably successful racehorse. There's a memorial statue of the 'the Goondiwindi Grey' in MacIntyre St, beside the bridge across the MacIntyre River. There's a Gunsynd memorial lounge in the **Victoria Hotel**, a beautiful old country pub with broad verandas and an eccentric tower. The hotel's on the corner of Marshall and Herbert Sts.

The main thoroughfare, Marshall St, runs parallel to the MacIntyre River.

The municipal tourist office (☎ 4671 2653), at 4 McLean St, is housed in the Goondiwindi-Waggamba Library complex opposite the museum. You can use the Internet here for $4.40 per hour. It's open from 9am to 5pm daily.

'Gundy' is an important cotton centre and visitors can tour the **MacIntyre Cotton Gin** (☎ 4671 2277), 4km east of town, from April to July. Call for appointments.

The **Customs House Museum** (☎ 4671 3041, 1 MacIntyre St; open 10am-4pm Wed-Mon) has a collection put together by the local historical society. There are also a couple of other interesting historical buildings in town; around the corner from the Customs House Museum, on Bowen St, the **Holy Trinity Church** has fine stained glass windows, while 200m east, **Martha's Cottage** is a dwelling constructed of bush timber, and is more than 100 years old.

## Places to Stay & Eat

Goondiwindi is an important staging post between NSW and Queensland, so there are plenty of motels, caravan parks and pubs with accommodation.

*Devon's Caravan Park* (☎ 4671 1383, fax 4671 1383, 3 Delacy St) Unpowered/powered sites $13/16, on-site vans $32, cabins $45. This peaceful caravan park is close to the centre on the MacIntyre River.

Most of the pubs and motels are spread along Marshall St.

*O'Shea's Royal Hotel-Motel* (☎ 4671 1877, fax 4671 3110, 48 Marshall St) Motel-style singles/doubles $60/69, hotel rooms with shared shower $47/57. This place is good value though the sports bar downstairs can get noisy at weekends.

*Binalong Motel* (☎ 4671 1777, fax 4671 1617, 30 McLean St) Singles/doubles from $53/62. North of the tourist office on McLean St, this is another cheap choice.

*The Town House* (☎ 4671 1855, fax 4671 2918, 110 Marshall St) Singles/doubles $85/87. The top place in town, this stylish, modern motel is just east of the junction with McLean and has an extremely good *restaurant*.

*Rustlers Steak House* (☎ 4671 2555) Steaks from $15. Open from 6pm. This upbeat steak place is in an old Queenslander and is a bit more affordable than others in town.

*Goondiwindi RSL Memorial Club* (☎ 4671 1269) Dishes from $8. If you're watching the pennies, this club is good for lunch and dinner.

## Getting There & Away

Brisbane-Melbourne and Brisbane-Adelaide buses stop at the BP Bridge Garage, 1km east of town on the Cunningham Hwy.

## WEST OF GOONDIWINDI

At the junction of the Carnarvon, Moonie and Balonne Hwys, **St George** is 200km west of Goondiwindi. It's at the centre of a major cotton-growing district, and has a petrol station, two *motels* and a *caravan park*. From here it's another long and lonely 290km westward to Cunnamulla, which is well and truly in the outback – see the Outback Queensland chapter for details of this area.

## TOOWOOMBA
postcode 4350 • pop 128,770

On the edge of the Great Dividing Range and the Darling Downs and 138km inland from Brisbane, Toowoomba is the largest town in the region. It has a commanding location, perched 700m above sea level on the crest of the Great Dividing Range, and there are great views from the parks and gardens that fringe the eastern side of town, earning Toowoomba the nickname 'Garden City'. It's a pleasant place to stop for a few days and the centre is graced by some stately old buildings.

## Orientation & Information

The heart of town is loosely centred on Ruthven St (part of the north-south New England Hwy) 1km north of its junction with James St (part of the east-west Warrego Hwy).

The very efficient Toowoomba tourist information centre (☎ 4639 3797, ⓦ www .toowoomba.qld.gov.au) is located south-east of the centre at 86 James St, at the junction with Kitchener St. The staff are thorough, and

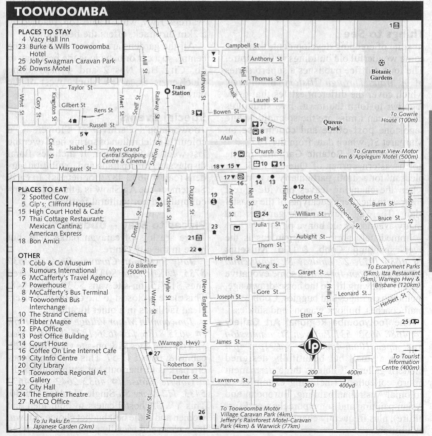

## TOOWOOMBA

**PLACES TO STAY**
4  Vacy Hall Inn
23  Burke & Wills Toowoomba Hotel
25  Jolly Swagman Caravan Park
26  Downs Motel

**PLACES TO EAT**
2  Spotted Cow
5  Gip's; Clifford House
15  High Court Hotel & Cafe
17  Thai Cottage Restaurant; Mexican Cantina; American Express
18  Bon Amici

**OTHER**
1  Cobb & Co Museum
3  Rumours International
6  McCafferty's Travel Agency
7  Powerhouse
8  McCafferty's Bus Terminal
9  Toowoomba Bus Interchange
10  The Strand Cinema
11  Fibber Magee
12  EPA Office
13  Post Office Building
14  Court House
16  Coffee On Line Internet Cafe
19  City Info Centre
20  City Library
21  Toowoomba Regional Art Gallery
22  City Hall
24  The Empire Theatre
27  RACQ Office

it's open from 9am to 5pm. There's also a smaller City Info centre at 476 Ruthven St, open from 10am to 4pm Monday to Friday.

There's an American Express office (AmEx; ☎ 4632 4522) at 172 Margaret St. The Environment Protection Agency (EPA; ☎ 4639 4599) has an office at 158 Hume St, and is open from 8.30am to 5pm Monday to Friday.

The main post office is at 66 Annand St, one block east of Ruthven St. Coffee On Line (☎ 4639 4686), 148 Margaret St, has lots of terminals and charges $6 per half hour ($4 for students). It's open from 9am to 9pm Monday to Friday, 10am to 9pm Saturday and 10am to 7pm Sunday.

## Things to See
In spite of creeping development, there are some wonderful old buildings in the centre. The tourist office publishes a superb series of *A Walk Through History* brochures, which cover the different estates that grew together to form the town. Two structures that you can't miss are the splendid, white sandstone **post office** and **courthouse** on Margaret St, which date from the 1870s.

Toowoomba's **Botanic Gardens**, in the north-eastern corner of Queens Park are pleasant for a stroll, particularly in autumn, when the changing leaves provide a real contrast to the green eucalypts of the coastal plain. There are lawns, rose gardens and shady avenues of old bunya pines.

Immediately north of the gardens is the ever-expanding **Cobb & Co Museum** (☎ *4639 1971, 27 Lindsay St; adult/child $5/3; open 10am-4pm)*, with some evocative displays showing life in the horse-drawn age, including carriages and buggies, Cobb & Co mail coaches, bullock wagons and sulkies.

The **Toowoomba Regional Art Gallery** (☎ *4688 6652, 531 Ruthven St; admission free; open 10am-4pm Tues-Sat, 1pm-4pm Sun)* is a small but beautifully designed modern gallery. It houses three permanent micro collections (including examples of colonial Australian painting, European and Asian painting and some porcelain and furniture), plus frequently changing temporary exhibitions.

The **Ju Raku En Japanese Garden** (☎ *4631 2627, West St; open 7am-dusk)* is a beautiful spot for picnicking and strolling, with 3km of walking trails around a lake, waterfalls and streams. It's several kilometres south of the centre at the University of Southern Queensland in West St.

The Garden City's other great gardens are the **escarpment parks** strung out along the eastern edge of the plateau. These seven separate bushland areas – Jubilee, Redwood, Picnic Point, Table Top, McKnight, Duggan and Glen Lomond – offer great views toward the coast and feature a variety of signposted walking trails. Picnic Point is the most accessible, lying just south of the Warrego Hwy, while Table Top, reached by a 2km dirt track, offers the best views.

All the gardens are a long haul from the centre, so a car or bicycle is the best way to go. City Bus Nos 2 and 4 pass along MacKenzie St, a few blocks west of the parks.

## Special Events
Toowoomba's Carnival of Flowers is a colourful celebration of spring held over the last week in September. It includes floral displays, a grand parade and exhibition gardens (call ☎ 4632 4877 for details). In early September, the Ag Show is a three-day agricultural and horticultural festival.

## Places to Stay – Budget
There are lots of caravan parks here, but none in the city centre.

*Jolly Swagman Caravan Park* (☎ *4632 8735, 47 Kitchener St)* Unpowered/powered sites $13/15, on-site vans $33, cabins $48. This place is closest to the centre and offers clean facilities in a quiet location.

*Toowoomba Motor Village Caravan Park* (☎ *4635 8186, fax 4636 1825, 821 Ruthven St)* Powered sites $18, on-site vans from $29, cabins & units $47-57. This excellent, modern park is further out, but better equipped.

*Gowrie House* (☎ *4632 2642, fax 4632 5433, 112 Mary St)* Singles/doubles $25/40. This YWCA hostel caters to both men and women and is the best budget choice in town. It's a clean and friendly place and it's housed in a nice, old, single-storey Queenslander near Queens Park. Rates include breakfast.

## Places to Stay – Mid-Range

*Vacy Hall Inn (☎ 4639 2055, fax 4632 0160, 135 Russell St)* Doubles $101-187. Just uphill from the town centre this is a magnificent 1880s mansion, which offers heritage-style accommodation of the highest standard – it's like stepping back into another era. All rooms are decked out in period style and the pricier rooms have en suites and verandas.

*Downs Motel (☎ 4639 3811, fax 4639 3806, 669 Ruthven St)* Singles $50-60, doubles $56-65. Not far from the centre, this modern place offers OK budget units and better deluxe units.

*Jeffery's Rainforest Motel-Caravan Park (☎ 4635 5999, fax 4635 9823, 864 Ruthven St)* Powered sites $15, units $49-61. This large complex offers camping and a choice of new or old units, arranged around a nice garden.

There are two more upmarket options opposite the historic Toowoomba Grammar School on the eastern outskirts of town.

*Grammar View Motor Inn (☎ 4638 3366, 39 Margaret St)* Singles/doubles $87/96. This is a no-nonsense business motel with a licensed *restaurant*. Next door, *Applegum Motel (☎ 4632 2088, fax 4639 1334, 41 Margaret St)* has similar facilities and rates.

*Burke & Wills Toowoomba Hotel (☎ 4632 2433, fax 4639 2002, 554 Ruthven St)* Rooms $99-155. Situated in the centre of town, this is a Mercure-owned five-storey hotel with 90 modern rooms. The hotel has several bars and an upmarket conservatory *restaurant*.

## Places to Eat

For budget eating there's a *food court* on the first floor of Myer Grand Central shopping centre at the western end of Margaret St, with all the usual fast-food outlets.

Otherwise, Margaret St has the greatest concentration of restaurants and cafes.

*Bon Amici (☎ 4632 4533, 191 Margaret St)* Light meals $4-10. Open 7.30am-late. This sophisticated licensed cafe serves delectable cakes, breakfasts and, for our money,

the best coffee in the south-east. There's often live music or poetry in the evenings.

*Mexican Cantina (☎ 4638 1888, 164 Margaret St)* Dishes $11-17. Open lunch Tues-Fri, dinner Tues-Sun. Of the many Mexican places in town, this is the most intimate and popular, and it'll spice up the food as hot (or as mild!) as you like it.

*Thai Cottage Restaurant (☎ 4632 2194, 160 Margaret St)* Mains $13-19. For Thai food, lots of locals swear by this central BYO place.

*Spotted Cow (☎ 4632 4393, Cnr Ruthven & Campbell Sts)* Dishes $10-16. This popular, old-fashioned hotel has been nicely restored and has a good upmarket bistro, with steaks and other Aussie dishes. Afterwards, you can pop in for a drink in the *Udder Bar*.

*High Court Hotel & Cafe (☎ 4632 4747, 169 Margaret St)* Dishes $15-20. Another good lunch and dinner choice, this flash pub has steaks and pasta.

*Itza (☎ 4631 5101)* Dishes $13-25. Open lunch Tues-Sun, dinner Tues-Sat. For top-notch cuisine and even better views, try this upmarket place by the Picnic Point lookout. The menu walks a well-trodden Euro-Asian path, but does it with quite a bit of style.

*Gip's (☎ 4638 3588, 120 Russell St)* Dishes $20-28. Open lunch daily, dinner Mon-Sat. The other top-end choice here is this sophisticated place housed in the beautiful old Clifford House. To match the surroundings, the adventurous menu includes treats like pasta with Moreton Bay bugs and asparagus.

## Entertainment

*The Strand Cinema (☎ 4639 3861, Cnr Margaret & Neil Sts)* and *Grand Central (☎ 4638 0879, Myer Centre)* screen predictably mainstream movies.

*Rumours (☎ 4638 3833, 323 Ruthven St)* This big, noisy nightspot is the centre of Toowoomba's club scene.

*Fibber Magee (☎ 4639 2702, 153 Margaret St)* If you fancy a beer without the noise, this agreeable, Irish-themed pub is popular and central.

*The Empire Theatre (☎ 1300 655 299, 56 Neil St)* For something a bit more highbrow, this stylishly restored theatre has regular concerts and cabaret.

Toowoomba's *Chronicle* newspaper has an entertainment section on Thursday, or pick up a copy of the *Time Out* brochure from the tourist information centre.

### Getting There & Away

**Air** Macair (☎ 13 15 28) flies between Toowoomba and Brisbane ($120), St George ($178), Cunnamulla ($277) and Thargomindah ($341).

**Bus** The McCafferty's/Greyhound terminal is at 28–30 Neil St. McCafferty's/Greyhound has numerous daily services from Toowoomba to Brisbane and the Gold Coast. It also has regular services west along the Warrego Hwy to Dalby (1½ hours), Chinchilla (2½ hours), Roma (3½ hours) and Charleville (11 hours).

McCafferty's/Greyhound also acts as the local agent for several other local companies. Crisps' Coaches runs to Warwick twice daily ($16, 1½ hours, once a day Saturday), with connections on to Stanthorpe, Tenterfield, Goondiwindi and Moree. Kynoch Coaches (☎ 4639 1639) runs to St George ($54, five hours, daily except Tuesday and Saturday), Cunnamulla ($81, nine hours, Sunday, Wednesday and Friday) and Lightning Ridge ($81, 8½ hours, Monday and Thursday). Suncoast Pacific runs to the Sunshine Coast on Friday and Sunday (about four hours).

Tickets for all buses can be bought from the McCafferty's/Greyhound travel agent (☎ 4690 9888), at 1 Russell St.

**Train** You can get here on the *Westlander*, which runs between Brisbane and Charleville twice a week. The seat-only fare from Brisbane to Toowoomba is $24. The attractive, old train station is north-east of the town centre, just off Russell St. The ticket office (☎ 4631 3381) is open 9am to 3.45pm Monday to Friday.

### Getting Around

Local bus services depart from the Toowoomba bus interchange on Neil St.

There's an information booth in the terminal where you can find out which bus will take you where.

Bikeline (☎ 4638 2242), at 2 Prescott St, hires out bikes with locks and helmets for about $26 for eight hours.

## TOOWOOMBA TO NANANGO (141KM)

The route north along the New England Hwy travels along the ridges of the Great Dividing Range, passing through a series of small villages. At Highfield there's the **Highfield Orchid Park**, in bloom from April to September.

The pretty little township of **Crow's Nest** is worth a stop for the **Crow's Nest Falls National Park**, an impressive waterfall in an area of eucalypt forest punctuated by craggy, granite outcrops. The park is about 6km east of town and there's a rangers station (☎ 4698 1296), at the park entrance, open from 3.30pm to 4pm Monday to Friday. For accommodation there's the *Crows Nest Caravan Park* (☎ 4698 1269) and *Crows Nest Motel* (☎ 4698 1399), both on the New England Hwy.

Beyond Crow's Nest the road continues 96km north to Nanango, entering the region of South Burnett – see later in this chapter for details.

## TOOWOOMBA TO MILES (211KM)
### Jondaryan Woolshed Complex

Built in 1859, the enormous Jondaryan Woolshed Complex *(☎ 4692 2229, Evanslea Rd; adult/child $11/5.50; open 9am-4pm, tours 1pm Wed-Fri, 10.30am & 1pm Sat, Sun & school holidays)*, 45km north-west of Toowoomba, played a pivotal role in the history of the Australian Labor Party. It was here in 1890 that the first of the great shearers' strikes began. See Labour vs Capital in the History section of the Facts about Queensland chapter for more information.

Today the woolshed is the centrepiece of a large tourist complex with an interesting collection of rustic old buildings, daily blacksmithing and shearing demonstrations. It also has period displays and antique farm and industrial machinery, including a mighty, steam-driven 'roadburner', which applied the first tarmac to many of Australia's roads.

There are several rustic accommodation choices here, all organised through the Woolshed reception. At the Woolshed complex, the **shearers quarters** are basic rooms around an open-sided, sawdust-floored communal cooking and dining shelter and cost $11/5.50 per adult/child. They score top marks for atmosphere, and there are a few comforts like hot showers and toilets. The **Country Hall** in Jondaryan village is an old, wooden house with dorm beds for $11/5.50. You can also **camp** for $9 (up to four people). You need to bring your own linen for all these options.

Jondaryan hosts a number of annual events, including an Australian Heritage Festival over nine days in late August and early September, a New Year's Eve bushdance, an Australia Day celebration, and a Working Draught Horse Expo in June.

## Dalby

Dalby is a dusty rural town in the centre of Queensland's richest grain-growing region. The huge Supastock Feeds factory sets the

### Killer Cactus

According to legend, the prickly pear cactus was introduced to Australia from South America by a young British captain to provide a host for cochineal beetles, which were used to dye the soldiers' red uniforms. Wherever it came from, the troublesome cactus spread like wildfire; it had invaded a staggering 264,000 sq km of rural Queensland by the mid-1920s. Things were looking pretty bleak until 1925, when an Argentine caterpillar, *Cactoblastis cactorum*, was recruited to chew back the infestation.

Today, the caterpillar that saved Queensland is commemorated by the **Cactoblastis Cairn**, next to Myall Creek in Dalby. Somewhat ironically, the success of the prickly pear program inspired naturalists to bring in another South American citizen, the cane toad, initiating one of Australia's worst ecological disasters!

character for the town, but there a few tourist sights that the ladies at the tourist office (☎ 4662 1066), at the corner of Drayton and Condamine Sts, will be glad to tell you about. It's open from 9am to 4.30pm Monday to Saturday and 9.30am to 2pm Sunday.

The **Pioneer Park Museum** (☎ *4662 4760, 3 Black St; adult/child $5/1; open 8am-5pm*), signposted off the Warrego Hwy west of the centre, has a collection of old buildings and farm machinery. The livestock sales at the **Dalby Saleyards** (☎ *4662 2125*) on Yumborra Rd are quite a spectacle – sheep sales are held on Monday, and cattle and pig sales on Wednesday. The Cactoblastis Cairn is beside the creek on Marble St.

There are a number of places to stay and eat should you choose to stop over. **Pioneer Caravan Village** (☎ *4662 1811, fax 4662 3690, 28 Black St*) is opposite the museum on the western outskirts, and has sites for $15 and cabins for $33-44.

**Imperial Hotel** (☎ *4662 2085, 4 Cunningham St*) Singles/doubles $33/44. This friendly, old pub has simple but clean pub rooms.

**Dalby Parkview Motel** (☎ *4662 3222, fax 4662 4997, 31 Drayton St*) Singles/doubles $55/66. Opposite the tourist office, this place has comfortable budget units.

**Dalby RSL** (☎ *4662 2309, 69 Drayton St*) Dishes $6-10. You can't beat this club for a cheap lunch or dinner.

## MILES
### postcode 4415 • pop 1200

This small rural centre at the intersection of the Warrego and Leichhardt Hwys is known as 'The Crossroads of the Golden West' and was established by the eccentric Prussian explorer Ludwig Leichhardt on his 31st birthday on 23 October 1844. Disappointingly, the town was named for a local politician, rather than because it was miles from anywhere!

On the main road at the eastern end of town is the excellent **Miles Historical Village** (☎ *4627 1492, Murilla St; family/adult/child $20/10/2; open 8am-5pm daily*). This is one of the best historical villages in the state and is well worth a visit. The main building houses a collection of glass cabinets crammed with all sorts of bits and pieces, from rocks and gems to tie stretchers and silk-screen printers. There are also numerous historic shop settings, including a boot-maker, a saddlery, a general store and a bank. There's an information centre at the village with the same opening hours.

## Places to Stay & Eat

There are several caravan parks and motels in town.

*Crossroads Caravan Park (☎/fax 4627 2165, 82 Murilla St)* Unpowered/powered sites $9/13, on-site vans $22, cabins $50. Right opposite the Historical Village, this place is well looked after. Alternatively try the *Miles Caravan Park (☎ 4627 1640, fax 4627 2458, 90 Murilla St)*, beside the Ampol service station.

*Hotel Australia (☎/fax 4627 1106, 55 Murilla St)* Singles/doubles $16.50/27.50. The pub offers cheap accommodation in the centre of town and does OK *counter meals*.

*Golden West Motor Inn (☎ 4627 1688, fax 4627 1407, 50 Murilla St)* Singles/doubles $62/73. This is the most central of the motels in town.

## NORTH OF MILES

The Leichhardt Hwy runs north from Miles all the way to Rockhampton. If you're heading this way, see the Banana to Miles – the Leichhardt Hwy section in the Capricorn Coast chapter.

## ROMA

postcode 4455 • pop 6440

An early Queensland settlement, and now the centre of a sheep- and cattle-raising district, Roma also has some curious small industries. There's enough oil in the area to support a small refinery, which produces just enough petroleum for local use. Gas deposits are larger, and Roma contributes to Brisbane's supply through a 450km pipeline.

Tourist attention is focused on the brand-new **Big Rig complex** *(☎ 4622 4355, Mc-Dowall St; adult/child $10/7, combined entry & night show $15.50/10.50; open 9am-5pm, night show at 6pm)*, a museum of

oil and gas exploration centred on the old, steam-operated oil rig at the eastern edge of town. As well as exhibitions and displays on the history of oil exploration, there is a nightly sound and light show at 6pm with plenty of gas-powered pyrotechnics.

Roma's major festival is Easter in the Country, which includes a rodeo, markets, horse races, parades, bush dances and country music.

## Places to Stay

Roma has several caravan parks, and a few motels, which mainly cater to sales reps.

*Big Rig Caravan Park (☎/fax 4622 2538, 4 McDowall St)* Unpowered/powered sites $12/15, on-site vans from $27.50, cabins from $37. Just down the road from the Big Rig, this is a quiet park facing the river.

*Wishing Well Motel (☎ 4622 2566, fax 4622 3606, 77 Quinton St)* Singles/doubles $47/58. This is a clean and friendly establishment.

*Overlander Homestead Motel (☎ 4622 3555, fax 4622 2805, Warrego Hwy)* Doubles from $77. Easily the best motel is this colonial-style place on the eastern outskirts of town, with comfortable rooms and an above-average, licensed steak restaurant.

## Places to Eat

*Club Hotel (☎ 4622 1322, Cnr McDowall & Charles Sts)* Meals $10-17. Open lunch Mon-Sat, dinner daily. For cheap roasts and grills head to this little pub bistro.

*Golden Dragon Restaurant (☎ 4622 1717, 60 McDowall St)* Dishes from $8. Open lunch Mon-Sat, dinner daily. Opposite the post office, this licensed Chinese restaurant makes a nice change from pub meals, with good Chinese food and an extensive menu.

*Bakearoma (☎ 4622 4395, 63 McDowall St)* Snack meals from $4. Open from 7am. This bakery and cafe is good for breakfast, with lots of pastries and cakes.

## Entertainment

*Cinema Roma (☎ 4622 5666, 37 Hawthorne St)* This small cinema alternates between several mainstream releases every day. Tickets are $7.70 on budget Wednesday.

## Getting There & Away

Qantas flies between Roma and Brisbane ($192). McCafferty's/Greyhound has daily buses through Roma on the Brisbane–Mt Isa run; buses stop at Kookas Travel (☎ 4622 1333) on Bowen St. The fare from Brisbane is $53 (eight hours).

The *Westlander* train passes through twice weekly on its way from Brisbane to Charleville. From Roma to Brisbane is 11 hours (economy seat/sleeper $56/95).

## ROMA TO CHARLEVILLE (265KM)

About 40km past Roma, **Muckadilla** is just a service station, a train station and the *Muckadilla Hotel-Motel (☎ 4626 8318, Warrego Hwy)* where you can get a meal or a room.

On the Maranoa River, about 50km further east, **Mitchell** is a relaxed commercial centre with a huge windmill, an artesian well spa, a couple of *pubs* and *supermarkets*, and a small tourist information office (☎ 1800 6482 4355) with brochures on the local area – it's in the library near the windmill. Mitchell is the southern access point for the Mt Moffat Section of the Carnarvon National Park – see the Capricorn Coast chapter for more details – but the park's a rough, mostly unsealed 200km from Mitchell. If you want to stop over, there's a council-run *caravan park* beside the river on the eastern side of town. The *Devonshire Arms Hotel (☎ 4623 1321, Cnr Cambridge & Alice Sts)* has basic pub rooms, and the *Berkeley Lodge Motel (☎ 4623 1666, fax 4623 1304, 20 Cambridge St)* has reasonably-priced motel rooms.

Continuing west from Mitchell, it's another 89km to the small highway town of **Morven**, a drivers water hole with two *pubs* serving meals, a *cafe* and a *general store*, plus the *Morven Hotel-Motel (☎ 4654 8101, Albert St)* with OK motel units.

The junction of the Warrego and Landsborough Hwys is 3km west of Morven. From here, you can continue west to Charleville (90km) or take the Landsborough Hwy north-west to Augathella (90km) – see the Outback Queensland chapter for details of these places.

# South Burnett Region

Stretching north-west from Brisbane, the South Burnett region centres on the Burnett River and its various tributaries. Highway 17 starts near Ipswich and runs north for almost 600km to Rockhampton, providing a popular alternative, inland route for those who want to avoid the much more hectic Bruce Hwy. The highway meanders through a succession of small rural centres, and it's quite a leisurely drive during the day. At night, the road trains and kangaroos come out in force and wise drivers stay off the roads. There are several natural attractions in the region, including the Bunya Mountains National Park and the Cania Gorge National Park.

## Getting There & Away

Brisbane Bus Lines (☎ 3355 0034) operates two services daily from Brisbane to Murgon ($38, four hours). The routes cover a wide area. Buses run via Caboolture (one hour) and Kingaroy (3¼ hours) except on Monday morning when the bus travels to Murgon via the Sunshine Coast, returning via the inland road. The afternoon bus to Brisbane on Saturday also travels via the Sunshine Coast. On Tuesday and Thursday buses continue up the Burnett Hwy to Gayndah (6¼ hours), Mundubbera (6¾ hours), Eidsvold (7¼ hours), Monto (eight hours) and Biloela (nine hours). There are also services from Brisbane to Bundaberg via the Burnett Hwy on Wednesday.

## BUNYA MOUNTAINS NATIONAL PARK

If you really want to see wildlife, Bunya Mountains National Park, 56km south-west of Kingaroy, is a pretty safe bet. Wallabies, crimson rosellas and king parrots are almost guaranteed, and there are plenty of less common beasts in the various environments around the park, which include rainforest, eucalyptus scrub and heathland.

The Bunyas rise abruptly from flat country to over 1000m and have been protected as a national park since 1908, which may explain the confident wildlife. The park is also *extremely* popular, attracting large crowds at weekends and on public holidays. An extensive network of walking tracks zig-zags through the park, from a gentle 500m discovery walk to the 10km trek to the Big Falls Lookout.

The park is named for the curious bunya pine, which every few years produces a crop of huge edible nuts, each the size of a pineapple. Before European settlers came and started logging these forests in the 1860s, Aboriginal tribes used to gather for feasts and ceremonies whenever the bunya nuts were ripe. Beware of falling bunya nuts during the season.

The main access route from the south is via Dalby or Jondaryan on the Warrego Hwy.

### Horse Riding
Bushland Park (☎ 4663 4717) offers guided rides for beginners and experienced riders lasting 1½ to two hours for $33 per person. Accommodation is also available – see the next section.

### Places to Stay & Eat
If you wish to stay in the park, there is a rangers station (☎ 4668 3127) on Bunya Ave in **Dandabah**, near the southern entrance to the park; you can usually catch the rangers between 2pm and 4pm. *Camp sites* can also be booked at the EPA office in Toowoomba. Also at Dandabah is a *general store* including an accommodation booking desk (☎/fax 4668 3131), a small **museum**, and a *snack bar*.

If you don't feel like camping in the park, there are several accommodation options in and around Dandabah.

**Bushland Park** (☎ 4663 4717, Soldiers Rd) Unpowered/powered sites $11/16.50, on-site vans from $38.50, cabins from $44. There are hot showers and toilets at this camping ground, which is 10km south of Dandabah on the road to Dalby.

**Rice's Log Cabins** (☎/fax 4668 3133, Bunya Mountains Rd) Double log cabins from $70 (each additional person $10). This friendly place has a number of self-contained, wooden cabins.

**Dandabah Holiday Units** (☎ 4668 3131, fax 4668 3171, Bunya Ave) Motel-style, self-contained double units $75 (each additional person $10). The units here sleep up to five people.

**Munro's Camp Cabins** (☎ 4668 3150, Just off Bunya Ave) Self-contained double cabins $40 (each additional person $7). Away from Dandabah, on the road south to Dalby, we highly recommend this homey place to anyone looking for peace and solitude, and wallabies! The cabins sleep up to six people.

**Rosella's Restaurant** (☎ 4668 3131, Bunya Ave) Dinner from $8. Open lunch and dinner. For a good sit-down meal, this restaurant is near the rangers station.

## KINGAROY
**postcode 4610 • pop 11,140**
Kingaroy, at the junction of the Bunya Mountains and D'Aguilar Hwys, is the prosperous little capital of the South Burnett region and the centre of Australia's most important peanut-growing area. In fact peanuts dominate almost every facet of life in Kingaroy.

Other than peanuts (and the fact that Queensland's notorious ex-premier, Joh Bjelke-Petersen, comes from here), Kingaroy's main point of note is that it's the northern access point for the Bunya Mountains National Park.

The town's **Bicentennial Heritage Museum** (☎ 4162 4953, Haly St; adult/child $2.50/1; open 9am-4pm Mon-Fri, 9am-2pm Sat & Sun) is devoted to the early days of the peanut industry, with plenty of photos and old machinery. You can tour the **Kingaroy Toasted Peanuts factory** (☎ 4162 2272), at 14 Kingaroy St, from Monday to Friday at 10.30am.

The tourist office (☎ 4162 3199), at 128 Haly St just north of the centre, can arrange accommodation at several farm-stays in the area – you can't miss the place, it's opposite a cluster of enormous, white, peanut silos. It's open from 9am to 5pm daily.

### Places to Stay & Eat
**Kingaroy Caravan Park and Cabins** (☎ 4162 1808, fax 4162 1808, 48 Walter Rd)

Unpowered/powered sites $15/17.50. This neat park is 1.5km out of the town centre, just off the Brisbane-Nanango Hwy.

**Club Hotel** (☎ *4162 2204, 169 Kingaroy St)* Single/double pub rooms $20/30, motel rooms $50/60. This pub has cheap rooms upstairs and good **pub grub** from $8.

There are also a couple of more pricey motels in the centre of town.

**Pioneer Lodge Motel** (☎ *4162 3999, fax 4162 4813, 100 Kingaroy St)* Singles/doubles $64/70. This friendly motel has tidy rooms and a licensed **restaurant**.

**Burke & Wills Motor Inn** (☎ *4162 2933, fax 4162 5131, 95 Kingaroy St)* Singles/doubles $64/75. Across the road from the Pioneer, this is another comfortable option.

## KINGAROY TO MONTO (322KM)

Heading north from Kingaroy the first place you hit is **Murgon**, a pleasant little cattle centre. The tourist information centre (☎ 4168 3864), at Lamb St, is open 9am till 4pm daily. The interesting **Queensland Dairy Industry Museum**, at Gayndah St on the northern outskirts of town, is open 1.30pm till 4pm on the weekend or by appointment.

For accommodation, there's a council-run **caravan park** on Krebs St or the **Australian Hotel-Motel** (☎ *4168 1077, fax 4168 1018, 61 Lamb St)*, with single/double pub rooms for $18.50/28 and motel rooms for $42/52.20.

About 6km south of Murgon the Cherbourg Aboriginal community runs the **Barambah Emu Farm** (☎ *4168 2655, Barambah Rd; adult/child $5.50/2.20; tours at 9.30am, 11am & noon Mon-Fri, 9.30am & 11am Sat)*.

The Burnett Hwy branches north at Goomeri. The next big settlement is **Gayndah**, which was settled in 1852 and is possibly Queensland's oldest town. It's famous for its oranges and mandarins and the lively **Orange Festival**, held in odd-numbered years on the Queen's Birthday weekend in June. The **Gayndah & District Historical Museum** (☎ *4161 2226, 3 Simon St; open 9am-4pm)* has an interesting local history collection spanning three buildings, including a one-teacher school display, war memorabilia and

an 1864 slab-timber hut. For accommodation there's the **River-View Caravan Park** (☎ *4161 1280, 3 Barrow St)* or the **Colonial Motel** (☎ *4161 1999, 58 Capper St)*.

On the banks of the Burnett River, 25km west of Gayndah, **Mundubbera** is another big citrus-growing centre. The river here is home to the rare lung fish, a living fossil step in the journey from fish to amphibian.

There are pleasant riverside walks in **Auburn River National Park**, about 40km west of town. BJ's Packhorse Tours (☎ 4165 4713, 0428 654 713) offers a good range of one- to five-day horse-back tours of the area for around $100 per person per day. If you feel like stopping over, try the **Citrus Country Caravan Village** (☎ *4165 4549, Ann St)*, with sites, vans and cabins, or the **Billabong Motor Inn** (☎ *4165 4410, Gayndah Rd)*.

**Eidsvold**, the next town north, was established as a gold town by two Norwegian brothers and is the centre of an important cattle-rearing area. The **Eidsvold Historical Complex** (☎ *4165 1311, 1 Mount Rose St; open 9am-3pm)* comprises seven heritage buildings housing an extensive and quirky range of displays, including a vast collection of old bottles and various fossicked gems and minerals. You can stay, eat and get tourist information at the **Eidsvold Motel & General Store** (☎ *4165 1209, 51 Morton St)*. The **Eidsvold Caravan Park** (☎ *4165 1168, 1 Esplanade St)*, one block back from the main road, is another alternative.

## MONTO

Monto is near the junction of the Burnett River and Three Moon Creek. According to local legend, the creek was named by a swagman who was boiling his billy on the banks of the creek one night when he saw three moons – one in the sky, one reflected in the creek and another reflected in his billy. The centre of town is just north-east of where the railway line is bridged by the Burnett Hwy. The main drag, Newton St, has three big, old **pubs** with cheap accommodation and meals.

The **Colonial Motor Inn & Restaurant** (☎ *4166 1377, fax 4166 1437, 6 Thomson St)* has single/double motel units for $46/54. Just off the highway at the southern end of town, it's a pleasant place fronted by a 100-year-old timber building, which houses an atmospheric, colonial-style *restaurant*.

For campers, the *Monto Caravan Park* (☎ 4166 1492, Flinders St) is just west of town on the highway.

## CANIA GORGE NATIONAL PARK

About 26km north of Monto, the small Cania Gorge National Park preserves a range of habitats from dry eucalyptus forest and rugged sandstone escarpments to deep gullies filled with mosses and ferns. The scenery is spectacular, wildlife is plentiful and there are numerous walking trails to the most impressive rock formations.

The *Cania Gorge Tourist Park* (☎ 4167 8188, fax 4167 8172, Phil Marshall Dr) has unpowered/powered sites for $8/18, a nine-bed bunkhouse for $36 (each adult/child after the first three people is $12/6.50 extra), on-site vans for $32 and cabins for $46 to $73. You can't camp at the park itself, but Cania Gorge Tourist Park is about 7km beyond the picnic area in the national park. It's well equipped, with a shop, a pool and a campers kitchen.

## MONTO TO ROCKHAMPTON (238KM)

The Burnett Hwy continues north from Monto to Rockhampton via Biloela and Mt Morgan. See the Capricorn Coast chapter for details of this area.

# Sunshine Coast

Tourism has moved at a much slower pace north of Brisbane, and the resorts of the Sunshine Coast, a strip which stretches from the top of Bribie Island to just north of Noosa, are more low-key than on the Gold Coast. That said, the high-rise boom is already beginning at the southern end of the strip, so it may only be a matter of time.

Caloundra, the first place on the strip, is a sleepy beach resort, backed by an interesting area of hinterland, but things start to get pretty Gold Coast-like by the time you reach Mooloolaba. The high-rises don't last long though; it's all pretty relaxed from here to Noosa.

Tucked away beside an excellent national park at the northern end of the strip, Noosa is the most fashionable and exclusive town on the coast, with some lovely accommodation options and a number of extremely good restaurants. North of Noosa is the Cooloola Section of Great Sandy National Park, from where 4WD owners can drive all the way to Rainbow Beach and on to Fraser Island.

## Activities

There are separate Activities sections in the Maroochy and Noosa sections, covering surfing, canoeing, cycling, camel trekking, skydiving, abseiling, tennis and water sports.

**Surfing** The Sunshine Coast is renowned for its great beaches. There are surf beaches all along the coast, ranging from endless stretches of sandy beach breaks to the rocky point-breaks at Alexandra Headland. The most famous (and, unfortunately, most popular) breaks are the series of classic right-hand points around the Noosa National Park.

**Rock Climbing & Bushwalking** The Glass House Mountains have some good bushwalks and are popular with rock climbers. The several small national parks in the hinterland have good bushwalks. The Noosa National Park also has some great short walking tracks.

## Highlights

- Rent a long board and pit yourself against Noosa's famous surfing point breaks.
- Fine dine your way along Hastings St, Noosa's ultra-trendy dining strip.
- Scramble up the sheer slopes of Mt Tibrogargan near Beerburrum for stunning views over the Glass House Mountains.
- Canoe though the beautiful everglades in the Cooloola Section of Great Sandy National Park.
- Find out if crocodile-wrestling is as crazy as it sounds at Steve Irwin's Australia Zoo.

North of Noosa, the Cooloola Section of Great Sandy National Park is another good walking area; the 46km Cooloola Wilderness Trail takes you through the park all the way up to Rainbow Beach, with camp sites along the route.

**Canoeing** The Noosa River is excellent for canoeing; it's possible to follow it up through Lakes Cooroibah and Cootharaba, and through the Cooloola Section of Great Sandy National Park to just south of Rainbow Beach Rd. Canoes can be rented from companies in

SUNSHINE COAST

Noosa or around Lake Cooroibah, and most places will pick you up at the end of your trip.

## Getting There & Away

**Air** The Sunshine Coast airport is on the coast road at Mudjimba, 10km north of Maroochydore and 26km south of Noosa.

Sunstate has daily flights between Brisbane and the Sunshine Coast ($135, one way). Qantas flies to the Sunshine Coast from all major capitals – some flights are direct, others go via Brisbane. The one-way fare from Melbourne is $473 – from Sydney it's $334.

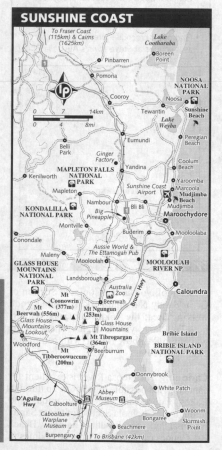

**Bus** Most McCafferty's/Greyhound services travel along the Bruce Hwy, but several of the McCafferty's coaches detour via Maroochydore and Noosa.

Suncoast Pacific (Brisbane office ☎ 3236 1901) runs between Brisbane and Noosa via Brisbane airport, Caloundra and Maroochydore. There are around eight services every weekday and six or seven services on Saturday and Sunday. One-way trips from Brisbane include Maroochydore ($21, two hours) and Noosa ($24, three hours).

The blue minibuses run by Sunbus (☎ 5492 8700) buzz up and down the coast from Caloundra to Noosa ($8, 1½ hours) via Maroochydore ($4.80, 45 minutes) every half hour. Sunbus also has regular buses across from Noosa to the train station at Nambour on the Bruce Hwy ($2.65, one hour), via Eumundi and Yandina.

See the following Getting Around section for details of bus services to and from the airport.

**Train** The main coastal railway line runs well inland from the Sunshine Coast, so it isn't particularly useful for getting around. The most convenient station is Nambour, which has connecting buses to Noosa. There are long-haul services north to Rockhampton and the far north. For getting to and from Brisbane, you're best off using its suburban Citytrain service, which runs from Roma St and Brisbane Central to Nambour approximately half-hourly on weekdays, and every few hours at weekends.

**Car & Motorcycle** The Bruce Hwy runs parallel to the coast, 20 to 30km inland. There are half a dozen roads linking the highway with the coast.

The major coastal road between Maroochydore and Noosa is David Low Way, which is scenic but can be slow going. If you are in a hurry, the newer Sunshine Motorway will whiz you north from Maroochydore. However, a toll is payable.

The Sunshine Coast hinterland offers some outstanding scenic drives – see Organised Tours in that section later in this chapter for details.

## Getting Around

**To/From the Airport** There are two local bus services that meet every flight at Mudjimba airport. Henry's (☎ 5474 0199) has buses going north from the airport and will drop you at the door of wherever you're staying. One-way fares are $8 to Coolum (15 minutes) and $14 to Noosa (45 minutes).

Airport Bus Service (☎ 5443 3678) has airport-to-your-door bus services to the towns south of the airport, including Maroochydore ($12, 20 minutes) and Caloundra ($19, one hour), and can also pick up from Brisbane airport.

Sunshine Shuttle (☎ 0417 196 508) runs back and forth between Brisbane airport and the Sunshine Coast at set times throughout the day, charging $33 to Maroochydore (1½ hours) and $44 to Noosa (2½ hours).

**Taxi** Suncoast Cabs is the biggest company on the Sunshine Coast – call ☎ 13 10 08.

## CABOOLTURE

**postcode 4510 • pop 40,400**

This rural town, just off the Bruce Hwy, 49km north of Brisbane, is worth a stop if you're heading north. A prosperous dairy centre, Caboolture has several museums including the **Caboolture Historical Village** (☎ 5495 4581, Beerburrum Rd; adult/child $8.50/1.50; open 9.30am-3.30pm) and the **Caboolture Warplane Museum** (☎ 5499 1144, Hangar 104, Caboolture airfield; adult/child $5/2; open 10am-4pm), with a collection of restored WWII warplanes, all in flying order.

About 7km east of Caboolture, on the far side of the Bruce Hwy, the **Abbey Museum** (☎ 5495 1652, Just off Bribie Island Rd; adult/child $5/4; open 10am-4pm Mon-Sat) is a world social history museum that has previously been housed in London, Cyprus, Egypt and Sri Lanka before finding its home in Australia.

## GLASS HOUSE MOUNTAINS

About 20km north of Caboolture, the Glass House Mountains are a curious group of volcanic crags sticking up from the coastal plain. Towering to 300m, with sheer rocky sides, Aborigines believed these peaks to be a family of mountain spirits. According to legend, Coonowrin shamed his family by an act of cowardice and was rewarded with a club on the head from his father, Tibrogargan, which broke Coonowrin's neck, giving Mt Coonowrin its distinctive crooked outline. Tibrogargan stares eternally out to sea and away from Coonowrin, unable to contemplate his son's lack of courage.

There are small national parks surrounding Mts Tibrogargan, Beerwah, Coonowrin, Ngungun, Miketeeburnulgrai and Elimbah, with various picnic grounds, walking trails and lookouts, but no camping grounds. The peaks are reached by a series of sealed and unsealed roads known as Forest Dr, inland from Glass House Mountains Rd.

There are walking trails (read: low-grade mountain climbs) on several of the peaks and the views are spectacular. Tibrogargan is probably the best climb, with a steep, rock-cut trail and several amazing lookouts from the flat summit. Allow about two hours for the return trip. Mt Beerwah and Mt Ngungun can also be climbed via steep trails.

The District Forest Office (☎ 5496 0166) at Beerburrum has information on the area. It's open from 8am to 5pm Monday to Friday. The EPA office (☎ 5494 3983) at Maleny also covers the area.

## Organised Tours

The easiest way to see the Glass House Mountains from Brisbane is with Rob's Rainforest Tours, which also includes a trip to Kondilla National Park. See Hinterland Tours under Organised Tours in the Brisbane chapter for details.

## Places to Stay

**Glasshouse Mountains Tourist Park** (☎ 5496 0151, fax 5496 0363, Glasshouse Mountains Rd, Beerburrum) Unpowered/powered sites $12/15.40, on-site vans $35, self-contained double units from $46. This is a good camping ground, 1.5km north of Beerburrum, with a shop and pool, mountain views and plenty of trees for shade.

**Log Cabin Caravan Park** (☎/fax 5496 9338, Glasshouse Mountains Rd, Glass

*House Mountains)* Unpowered/powered sites $13/15, on-site vans $27, self-contained double log cabins from $60. Just off the old highway across from Tibrogargan, this pleasant park has a coffee shop, barbecues, a tennis court and swimming pool, and will pick up from Glass House Mountains railway station.

## AUSTRALIA ZOO

Owned by TV 'Crocodile Hunter' Steve Irwin, Australia Zoo (*☎ 5495 5494, Glasshouse Mountains Rd, Beerwah; adult/child $16.50/8.50, open 8.30am-4pm)* is renowned for its crocodile- and alligator-wrestling shows. You'll have to visit on a public holiday if you want to catch Steve at work, but there are crocodile, snake and bird of prey demonstrations every day, as well as otters, dingoes, kangaroos and camels. To get here take the Landsborough exit from the Bruce Hwy and follow the signs. Various companies offer tours from Brisbane and the Sunshine Coast (see Organised Tours in the Sunshine Coast Hinterland section later in this chapter).

## CALOUNDRA
**postcode 4551 • pop 60,150**

At the southern end of the Sunshine Coast, Caloundra is a quiet little family resort with good fishing and pleasant surf beaches. It sees lots of family groups at weekends, but during the week it can feel deathly quiet. Caloundra is located on a low headland at the northern entrance to the Pumicestone Passage. Bulcock St is the main thoroughfare, with a post office, banks, a cinema and a few takeaway cafes. The best beaches are strung out along the coast north of town.

The Caloundra tourist information centre (*☎ 5491 0202)* is out at 7 Caloundra Rd, on the roundabout at the entrance to town. It's open from 8.30am to 5pm weekdays and 9am to 5pm weekends. Caloundra holds a large Arts & Crafts Festival in August.

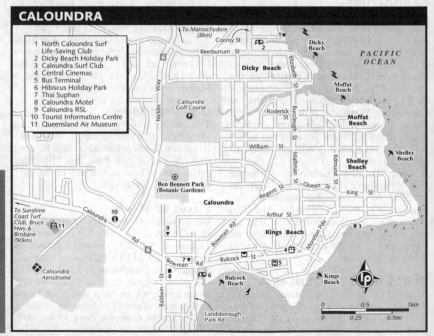

### CALOUNDRA

1 North Caloundra Surf Life-Saving Club
2 Dicky Beach Holiday Park
3 Caloundra Surf Club
4 Central Cinemas
5 Bus Terminal
6 Hibiscus Holiday Park
7 Thai Suphan
8 Caloundra Motel
9 Caloundra RSL
10 Tourist Information Centre
11 Queensland Air Museum

## Things to See & Do

Caloundra's **beaches** are its major attraction. Bulcock Beach, good for windsurfing, is just down from the main street, overlooking the northern end of Bribie Island. Golden Beach Hire (☎ 5492 4344) on the Esplanade in Caloundra rents out windsurfers for $15 per hour. For conventional surfing, you're best off heading north to Moffat's Beach or Dicky Beach.

The **Queensland Air Museum** (☎ 5492 5930, 7 Pathfinder Dr, Caloundra aerodrome; adult/child $5/3; open 10am-4pm) is a community-run museum with lots of aviation displays.

Another attraction in the area is **Aussie World & the Ettamogah Pub** (☎ 5494 5444, Bruce Hwy, Just north of the Caloundra turn-off; admission free; open from 9am). This is a kind of Aussie theme park with a big wheel, camel and pony rides, a snake collection and beer and tucker. Aussie World closes at 5pm and the pub stays open until around 9pm or 10pm.

The Sunshine Coast Turf Club (☎ 5491 6788), west of town on Pierce Ave, has popular race meets on Sundays.

## Places to Stay

**Hibiscus Holiday Park** (☎ 5491 1564, fax 5492 6938, Cnr Bowman Rd & Landsborough Park Rd) Unpowered/powered sites from $17.50/20, on-site vans $27.50, cabins from $30. During school holidays, rates rise by 30%. This is the closest park to the centre of town, and has a nice waterfront location and good facilities.

**Dicky Beach Holiday Park** (☎/fax 5491 3342, Beerburrum St) Unpowered/powered sites $16.50/19.25, cabins from $44. This tidy park is right on the beachfront.

**Caloundra Motel** (☎ 5491 1411, fax 9491 9118, 30 Bowman Rd) Doubles/triples $55/60. This cheap motel is clean and close to the Returned Services League (RSL) club.

## Places to Eat

There are several surf clubs in town where you can pick up simple but filling Aussie lunches and dinners such as steak, fish and chips and lasagne.

**Caloundra Surf Club** (☎ 5491 8418, fax 5492 5730, Ormonde Terrace) at King's Beach, and **North Caloundra SLSC** (☎ 5491 6078, Coochin St) at Dicky Beach, serve up good Aussie favourites for around $12.

**Caloundra RSL** (☎ 5491 1544, 19 West Terrace) Dishes $8-19. This award-winning RSL features two huge restaurants serving hearty meals at lunch and dinner. It's worth a visit just for the flamboyant interior.

**Thai Suphan** (☎ 5491 7899, 61 Bowman Rd) Dishes $5.50-14. Open from 5.30pm Tues-Sun. For good Thai food, try this long-established place on the way to Caloundra.

## Entertainment

**Central Cinemas** (☎ 5492 6077, Cnr Knox & Bulcock Sts) Located on the upper floor of an arcade, this multiscreen complex has budget days on Tuesday and Thursday ($6.50).

## Getting There & Away

Long-distance buses stop at the bus terminal (☎ 5491 2555) on Cooma Terrace. See the Getting There & Away section at the start of this chapter for details of bus services.

## MAROOCHY
### postcode 4558 • pop 44,100

Not so long ago, Maroochydore, Alexandra Headland and Mooloolaba (collectively known as Maroochy) were idyllic little coastal centres, backed by the waterways of the Maroochy and Mooloolah Rivers. Gold Coast syndrome hit a few years ago, and these days more and more high-rise blocks are springing up along the strip.

Mooloolaba is the most pleasant, and most developed, of the three resorts, with a good beach, good surf and some excellent restaurants and nightspots. Also here is The Wharf, a glossy, soulless entertainment and dining complex on the Mooloolah River, with an aquarium and more restaurant and nightlife options.

Alexandra Headland is largely residential, and marred by a busy road along the seafront, while Maroochydore mainly serves as a shopping centre for the region. You may be able to find fruit-picking work in the area – ask at the hostels.

SUNSHINE COAST

## Orientation & Information

The main thoroughfare in Maroochydore is Aerodrome Rd, which becomes Alexandra Parade along the seafront at Alexandra Headland, before turning into Mooloolaba Esplanade at Mooloolaba.

The Maroochy tourist information centre (☎ 5479 1566) is on Aerodrome Rd, near the corner with Sixth Ave. There's a second office in the Sunshine Plaza Mall on the Esplanade in Mooloolaba (☎ 5444 5755). Both offices are open from 9am to 5pm weekdays and from 9am to 4pm weekends.

## Underwater World

Mooloolaba's Underwater World (☎ 5444 8488, The Wharf; adult/child $21.50/11; open 9am-6pm) is the largest oceanarium in the southern hemisphere. It's a bit pricey but there's plenty to see, including a transparent shark tunnel, a variety of touch tanks where you can get up close to marine life and a good performing seal show five times a day. Brave souls can scuba dive with the sharks (ask at reception for details).

## Activities

There are good surf breaks along the strip – probably the best is Pin Cushion near the mouth of the Maroochy River. In the Sunshine Plaza complex in Mooloolaba, Brothers Neilsen (☎ 5444 3545) has long boards for $40 a day and boogie boards for $20 a day (rates drop to half in winter).

Aussie Sea Kayak Company (☎ 5477 5335), in Mooloolaba's Wharf complex, offers a variety of sea kayaking adventures on the Sunshine Coast, from a two-hour evening paddle ($40) to a two-day trip to North Stradbroke or Moreton Island ($245 to $285).

Scuba World (☎ 5444 8596) at The Wharf offers dives for certified divers for $55, and dives with the Underwater World sharks for $95.

Based at The Wharf, Harbour River Canal Cruise (☎ 5444 7477) offers hourlong cruises up the Mooloolah River for $10/4 per adult/child. For longer cruises, Cruise Maroochy (☎ 5476 574) offers full-day cruises for $45/30 and half-day cruises for $25/10. The MV Mooloolah (☎ 5444 7477) offers a daily lunch cruise for $19/6.50, with a tropical buffet.

## Places to Stay – Budget

**Camping** The best camping options are the council-run Maroochy Beach Parks on the foreshore, but none of these places have cabins. All the camping grounds charge $17.60 for unpowered sites, $20.46 for powered sites and $23.50 for shorefront sites.

The best parks are *Cotton Tree Beach Park* (☎ 5443 1253, fax 5443 8807, Cotton Tree Parade) and *Pincushion Beach Park* (☎ 5443 7917, fax 5443 9876, Cnr Cotton Tree & Alexandra Parades), near the mouth of the Maroochy River in Maroochydore.

The other two camping choices are *Seabreeze Beach Park* (☎ 5443 1167, fax 5443 1167, Melrose Parade, Maroochydore) and *Parkyn Parade Beach Park* (☎ 5444 1201, Opposite The Wharf, Mooloolaba).

**Hostels** All the hostels will pick you up from the bus terminal if you phone.

*Cotton Tree Beachouse* (☎ 5443 1755, fax 5451 0978, 15 The Esplanade, Cotton Tree) Dorm beds $16, doubles & twins $32. Only a five-minute walk from the bus terminal, this is a comfortable, rambling old timber guesthouse overlooking the river. It's the most intimate choice in the area and has surfboards and boogie boards free to borrow.

*Suncoast Lodge* (☎/fax 5443 7544, fax 5479 4550, 50 Parker St, Maroochydore) Dorm beds $14, doubles $34. One block south of Aerodrome Rd, this friendly hostel gets good reports. Facilities are above average and there are surf and boogie boards for guests.

*Maroochydore YHA Backpackers* (☎ 5443 3151, fax 5479 3156, 24 Schirmann Dr, Maroochydore) Dorm beds from $18, doubles $40. Buried in a residential estate off Bradman Ave, this place is a bit far from everything, but people seem to like it. Dorms have six to eight beds.

*Palace Backpackers Mooloolaba* (☎ 5444 3399, fax 5477 6455, 75-77 Brisbane Rd, Mooloolaba) Dorm beds $20 ($25 with en suite), doubles $55. This is a big party-style backpackers popular with party-bus tours.

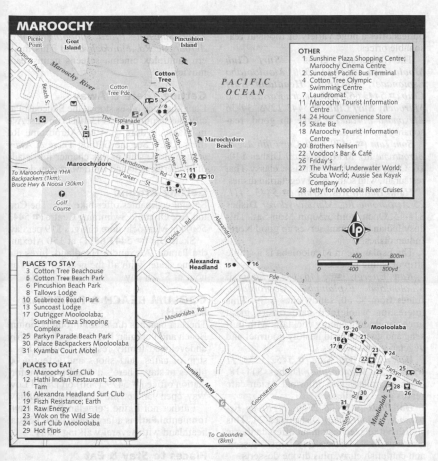

**MAROOCHY**

OTHER
1 Sunshine Plaza Shopping Centre; Maroochy Cinema Centre
2 Suncoast Pacific Bus Terminal
4 Cotton Tree Olympic Swimming Centre
7 Laundromat
11 Maroochy Tourist Information Centre
14 24 Hour Convenience Store
15 Skate Biz
18 Maroochy Tourist Information Centre
20 Brothers Neilsen
22 Voodoo's Bar & Café
26 Friday's
27 The Wharf; Underwater World; Scuba World; Aussie Sea Kayak Company
28 Jetty for Mooloola River Cruises

PLACES TO STAY
3 Cotton Tree Beachouse
5 Cotton Tree Beach Park
6 Pincushion Beach Park
8 Tallows Lodge
10 Seabreeze Beach Park
13 Suncoast Lodge
17 Outrigger Mooloolaba; Sunshine Plaza Shopping Complex
25 Parkyn Parade Beach Park
30 Palace Backpackers Mooloolaba
31 Kyamba Court Motel

PLACES TO EAT
9 Maroochy Surf Club
12 Hathi Indian Restaurant; Som Tam
16 Alexandra Headland Surf Club
19 Fiszh Resistance; Earth
21 Raw Energy
23 Wok on the Wild Side
24 Surf Club Mooloolaba
29 Hot Pipis

## Places to Stay – Mid-Range

There are plenty of motels and hundreds of holiday apartments available for rent here, but few bargains. Most of the apartments have a two-night minimum stay.

*Tallows Lodge* (☎ 5443 2981, fax 5443 7343, 10 Memorial Ave, Maroochydore) Units from $60. At the cheaper end of the scale, this basic apartment complex with self-contained units is one block back from the beach.

*Kyamba Court Motel* (☎ 5444 0202, fax 5444 8336, 94 Brisbane Rd, Mooloolaba) Doubles from $50. This small, inexpensive motel is a short walk from The Wharf and the Mooloolaba seafront.

## Places to Stay – Top End

*Outrigger Mooloolaba* (☎ 5452 2600, fax 5452 2888, Cnr Mooloolaba Esplanade & Venning St, Mooloolaba) 1-bedroom/ 2-bedroom units from $198/$275. The plushest option in Mooloolaba, this high-rise resort has a pool, a spa and a shopping complex.

## Places to Eat

For cheap eating the best option is the *food court* at the Sunshine Plaza Shopping

**SUNSHINE COAST**

Centre in Maroochydore, where about 20 outlets offer a huge variety of foods at reasonable prices.

The three surf clubs – **Surf Club Mooloolaba** (☎ 5444 1300, Mooloolaba Esplanade), **Alexandra Headland Surf Club** (☎ 5443 6677, Alexandra Parade) and **Maroochy Surf Club** (☎ 5443 1298, 34-36 Alexandra Parade) – serve up good, reasonably priced meals.

**Som Tam** (☎ 5479 1700, Cnr Fifth Ave & Aerodrome Rd, Maroochydore) Dishes \$10-16. Open dinner daily. This is a classy Thai restaurant, with some good vegetarian dishes.

**Hathi Indian Restaurant** (☎ 5443 5411, 25 Aerodrome Rd, Maroochydore) Dishes \$11-15. Open from 5.30pm Mon-Sat. This cosy Indian restaurant serves up good North Indian dishes.

The Esplanade in Mooloolaba is a single strip of eating places.

**Raw Energy** (☎ 5446 1444, Shop 3, Mooloolaba Esplanade, Mooloolaba) Juices from \$3.50, sandwiches \$4-9. This interesting wholefood cafe offers great juices (including energy cocktails with ginseng and guarana) and healthy gourmet and vegetarian sandwiches.

**Wok on the Wild Side** (☎ 5452 5255, 11 Burnett St, Mooloolaba) Dishes \$11-18. Open noon-late. This informal Asian cafe serves good noodles.

**Hot Pipis** (☎ 5478 2766, 11 River Esplanade, Mooloolaba) Dishes \$15-24. This stylish but relaxed restaurant offers fantastic creations like Moreton Bay bugs, mussels and cuttlefish curry, plus divine desserts.

Other posh choices include **Fiszh Resistance** (☎ 5452 6699) and **Earth** (☎ 5477 7100), both on the Esplanade near the corner of Venning St in Mooloolaba.

### Entertainment

**Friday's** (☎ 5444 8383, The Wharf, Mooloolaba) This noisy bar, nightclub and grill has live bands at weekends and theme evenings several nights a week.

**Voodoo's Bar & Cafe** (☎ 5477 6877, 17-19 Brisbane Rd, Mooloolaba) This popular drinking hole in Mooloolaba pulls in a mainly thirty-something crowd.

**Maroochydore Cinema Centre** (☎ 5479 2799, Sunshine Plaza Shopping Centre, Aerodrome Rd, Maroochydore) This modern multiplex cinema screens mainstream movies.

### Getting There & Away

Long-distance buses stop at the Suncoast Pacific bus terminal (☎ 5443 1011) on First Ave in Maroochydore, just off Aerodrome Rd (near KFC). See the Getting There & Away section at the start of this chapter for details of bus services to and from Maroochydore.

### Getting Around

Several companies offer bike hire. The Cotton Tree Olympic Swimming Centre (☎ 5443 5601) in Maroochydore charges \$19 per day.

Skate Biz (☎ 5443 6111) at 150 Alexandra Parade, Alexandra Headland, hires out in-line skates with all the gear for \$7.50 an hour or \$22 a day.

## COOLUM BEACH & PEREGIAN BEACH

The surf beaches run north through Coolum Beach and Peregian Beach, which are fairly undeveloped family resorts. Coolum has a strip of cafes, surf shops and a few good places to stay. There's a small tourist information office (☎ 5479 1566) on David Low Way, open 9am to 1pm Monday to Saturday.

Further north, the **Peregian Beach Environmental Park** is a large reserve of coastal heathland with several walking trails.

### Places to Stay & Eat

**Coolum Beach Caravan Park** (☎ 1800 461 475, fax 5448 7157, David Low Way) Unpowered/powered sites \$17/19. This council-run park is on the seafront and has pleasant sites near the beach.

**Coolum Beach Budget Accommodation** (☎ 5471 6666, fax 5446 1968, Cnr David Low Way & Ann St) Dorm beds \$18, singles/twins & doubles \$28/40. Part backpackers, part budget family motel, this place is simple but spotless and has a kitchen, TV room, games room and pool.

**Coolum Beach Surf Club** (☎ 5446 3694, David Low Way) Dishes \$6-17. Beside the beach, this well-run surf club has a good bistro with cheap steaks and seafood.

## NOOSA
**postcode 4567 • pop 41,170**

Surfers started gathering at this quiet cove at the southern end of the Cooloola Coast in the 1960s, lured by the impressive point breaks around Noosa headland. Today, Noosa is a thriving and modern resort, and the boys (and girls) with the boards are joined by throngs of wealthy holidaymakers, who come here to shop for designer clothes and to dine in Noosa's magnificent restaurants. Although it's very developed, Noosa is refreshingly low-rise, and blends neatly into the surrounding Noosa National Park, which covers a number of peaceful coves around the headland.

The area north of the Noosa River is preserved as the Cooloola Section of Great Sandy National Park, and offers great opportunities for 4WD driving, hiking and kayaking.

### Orientation

The name Noosa actually covers a group of small communities around the mouth of the Noosa River. Most of the action is concentrated on Noosa Heads, at the mouth of the Noosa River, where you'll find Hastings St, with most of the upmarket places to stay and eat. Noosa National Park begins at the end of Park Rd, just east of Hastings St.

Heading west along the river, you'll find the residential community of Noosaville, with more places to stay and eat, and Tewantin, the departure point for the Noosa River ferry. Around the headland from Noosa Heads on the eastern coast is the peaceful resort of Sunshine Beach, with some good surf breaks.

### Information

The tourist information centre (☎ 5447 9088) in Hastings St is open from 9am to 5pm daily. There are also several less-useful, privately run tourist information offices. There's a smaller official tourist information centre in the cinema centre on Sunshine Beach Rd (☎ 5474 8400).

The post office is 100m south of Noosa Junction, down Noosa Dr. American Express (☎ 5447 4666) is at 11 Arcadia St, just off Sunshine Beach Rd. Thomas Cook has a foreign exchange bureau (☎ 5447 4077) at Harvey World Travel, 16 Lanyana Way, opposite the Noosa Fair Mall.

There are several Internet cafes in Noosa Junction. Backpacking Round Queensland (☎ 5474 8530) has lots of terminals and fast connections; Net access costs $5 per hour. Over on Arcadia St, Internet Arcadia (☎ 5474 8988) charges $5 per hour.

Written Dimension (☎ 5447 4433) in the cinema centre is an above-average bookshop with lots of paperbacks.

### Noosa National Park

One of Noosa's best features, the small but lovely Noosa National Park extends 2km south-west from the headland that marks the end of the Sunshine Coast. It has fine walks, great coastal scenery and a string of bays on the northern side with waves that draw surfers from all over the country. Alexandria Bay on the eastern side has the best beach, and is also an informal nudist beach.

The main entrance at the end of Park Rd (the eastern continuation of Hastings St) has a carpark, picnic areas and an Environment Protection Agency (EPA) information centre (☎ 5447 3243) where you can obtain a walking track map. It's open from 1pm to 3pm daily. Sleepy koalas are often spotted in the trees in the afternoon and dolphins are commonly seen from the rocky headlands around Alexandria Bay.

For a panoramic view of the park, you can walk or drive up to the **Laguna Lookout** from Viewland Dr in Noosa Junction. From Sunshine Beach, access to the park is via McAnally Dr or Parkedge Rd.

### Activities

**Adventure Activities** Total Adventures (☎ 5474 0177, 0418 148 609) is based at the Noosa Leisure Centre on Eumundi Rd in Noosaville. It runs a good range of adventure activities including abseiling and rock-climbing trips, mountain bike tours and canoeing trips up the Noosa River.

# NOOSA

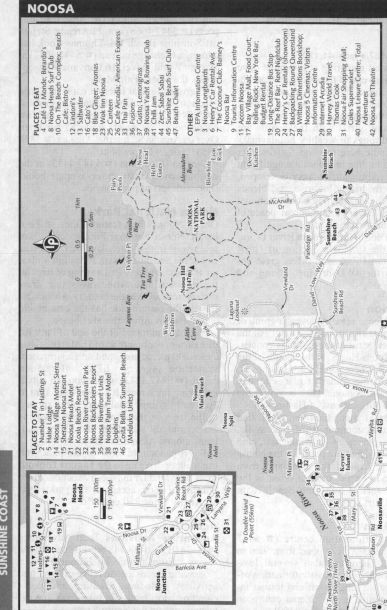

## PLACES TO STAY

2  Number 1 in Hastings St
5  Halse Lodge
14  Noosa Village Motel; Sierra
15  Sheraton Noosa Resort
21  Noosa Heads Motel
22  Koala Beach Resort
32  Noosa River Caravan Park
34  Noosa Backpackers Resort
35  Noosa Riverfront Units
38  Noosa Palm Tree Motel
43  Dolphins
46  Costa Bella on Sunshine Beach (Melaluka Units)

## PLACES TO EAT

4  Café Le Monde; Berardo's
8  Noosa Heads Surf Club
10  On The Beach Complex; Beach Cafe; Bistro C
12  Lindoni's
13  Saltwater
16  Cato's
18  Blue Ginger; Aromas
23  Wok Inn Noosa
25  Canteen
26  Café Arcadia; American Express
33  Thai Pan
36  Fusions
37  Gusto; Lemongrass
39  Noosa Yacht & Rowing Club
41  Chilli Jam
44  Zest; Sabai Sabai
45  Sunshine Beach Surf Club
47  Beach Chalet

## OTHER

1  EPA Information Centre
3  Noosa Longboards
6  Henry's Car Rental: Avis
7  The Coconut Club; Barney's Noosa Bar
9  Tourist Information Centre
11  Accom Noosa
17  Bay Village Mall; Food Court; Rolling Rock; New York Bar; Budget Rental
19  Long-Distance Bus Stop
20  The Reef Bar; Reef Nightclub
24  Henry's Car Rentals (showroom)
27  Backpacking Round Queensland
28  Written Dimentions Bookshop; Noosa 5 Cinemas; Visitors Information Centre
29  Internet Arcadia
30  Harvey World Travel; Thomas Cook
31  Noosa Fair Shopping Mall; Coles Supermarket
40  Noosa Leisure Centre; Total Adventures
42  Noosa Arts Theatre

Noosa Ocean Kayak Tours (☎ 0418 787 577) offers two-hour kayaking tours around Noosa National Park for $45, and along the Noosa River for $40. You can also hire kayaks for $35 a day.

**Golf & Tennis** Golfers should head for Noosa Springs Country Club (☎ 5447 4600) on Links Dr, which has an 18-hole championship golf course ($55/35 for 18/9 holes) and tennis courts from $16 per hour ($3 racket hire). Tewantin Noosa Gold Club on Cooroy-Noosa Rd in Tewantin is cheaper at $30/18 for 18/9 holes.

**Horse Riding & Camel Safaris** South of Noosa at Lake Weyba, Clip Clop Treks (☎ 5449 1254) offers two-hour rides ($40), half-day rides with lunch ($80), and full-day rides for experienced riders ($130). It also has multiday trips across to Fraser Island – call for more details.

The Camel Company Australia (☎ 5442 4402) on Beach Rd in North Shore, on the far side of the Noosa River, offers horse riding and camel safaris – see Lake Cooroibah in the Cooloola Coast section later for details. Across the road, the Noosa North Shore Retreat (☎ 5447 1369) also offers beach rides and bush trail riding.

**Other Activities** Noosa Blue Water Dive (☎ 5447 1300) at the Boatshed cruise terminal on Gympie Terrace offers PADI dive courses for $220 and daily dive trips to local sites. Other activities on offer include paraflying (☎ 0500 872 123), water-skiing (☎ 5474 4548) and tandem skydiving (☎ 0500 555 520) over Coolum Beach. Several places along Gympie Terrace rent out jet skis for around $55 per half hour.

## Organised Tours & Cruises
**Fraser Island** A number of operators offer trips from Noosa up to Fraser Island via the Cooloola Coast.

Fraser Explorer Tours (☎ 5447 3845, 5449 8647) has day trips to Fraser, which last about six hours and take in major sites like Lake McKenzie and the wreck of the *Maheno*. The cost is $99/55 per adult/child, including lunch at Eurong Beach Resort. Multiday tours cost from $170 for two days to $280 for three days, including accommodation. Adventure Tours (☎ 5444 6957) operates interesting day-tours for $130/90 per adult/child.

For the more adventurous, Trailblazer Tours (☎ 1800 626 673) offers good value with three-day camping safaris to Fraser Island ($229 per person). The price covers your driver and guide, all meals and camping gear.

Noosa & Maroochy Flying Services (☎ 5450 0516) offers air transfers to Fraser Island for $99 per person and return flights with a guided 4WD tour for $279 per person.

See the Fraser Coast chapter for more on the island.

**Everglades Tours** Several companies run boats from the Noosa Harbour at Tewantin up the Noosa River into the 'Everglades' area. The Everglades Water Bus Co (☎ 5447 1838) has a four-hour cruise departing 12.10pm daily from $49/35 per adult/child, plus several longer cruises. Noosa River Cruises (☎ 5449 7362) and Everglades Cruises (☎ 5449 9177) offer full-day cruises for around $60. Several pontoon-style boats offer lunch cruises for around $30, including a buffet lunch.

## Special Events
Noosa holds a major jazz festival in late August/early September, with four days of live music at restaurants and other venues.

## Places to Stay
Although Noosa has a reputation as a resort for the rich and fashionable, there are several backpacker hostels and caravan parks in among the resort hotels and apartments. With the exception of backpackers' hostels, accommodation prices can rise by 50% in busy times and 100% in the December to January peak season.

## Places to Stay – Budget
*Noosa River Caravan Park* (☎ *5449 7050, fax 5474 3024, Munna Point, Off Russell St, Noosaville*) Unpowered/powered sites from $14.50/18.50. Situated in Noosaville, this is a neat, well-equipped park on the riverside

and it's understandably popular. Book ahead at weekends.

*Halse Lodge (☎ 1800 242 567, 5447 3377, fax 5447 3371, 2 Halse Lane, Noosa Heads)* Dorm beds $21, doubles $47. Housed in a beautiful 100-year-old heritage-listed building (with six- to eight-bed dorms) with polished wooden floors and big verandas, this excellent hostel has a bar and restaurant and some friendly common rooms. It's just seconds from Hastings St and the national park, and there are free longboards, and bikes for $20 a day. It's not really a party place though – if that's what you're after, head to Koala.

*Koala Beach Resort (☎ 5447 3355, fax 5447 3893, 44 Noosa Dr, Noosa Junction)* 6-bed dorm beds $20, twins & doubles $45 (1 bathroom to 3 doubles). Noosa's premier party hostel, Koala has good facilities including a pool and restaurant, which you'll probably end up using as the backpacker kitchen is tiny. The bar here goes off every night; light sleepers beware!

*Noosa Backpackers Resort (☎ 5449 8151, fax 5449 9408, 9 William St, Noosaville)* Dorm beds $15, doubles $32. This is a pleasantly relaxed place with a good seated courtyard area, a pool and a small bar and restaurant. It has free surfboards and a variety of trips and tours on offer.

*Dolphins (☎ 5447 2100, fax 5473 5392, 14 Duke St, Sunshine Beach)* 4-bed dorm beds $20, twins in 2-bedroom units $55. Just uphill from the main surf beach, this comfortable converted apartment building has good facilities and plenty of kitchens and bathrooms to go round.

*Costa Bella on Sunshine Beach (☎/fax 5447 3663, 7 Selene St, Sunshine Beach)* Apartment beds $22-26. Also known as *Melaluka Units*, this complex of several apartment buildings offers units out to backpackers on a bed-by-bed basis. Kitchens and bathrooms are shared between two to four people and some of the buildings have pools and good sea views.

### Places to Stay – Mid-Range
Most of the Hastings St accommodation is heavily overpriced, but there are a few bargains in town.

*Noosa Village Motel (☎ 5447 5800, fax 5474 9282, 10 Hastings St, Noosa Heads)* Doubles/triples $88/95. This newish motel is right in the thick of things and has bright spacious rooms.

*Noosa Heads Motel (☎/fax 5449 2873, 2 Viewland Dr, Noosa Junction)* Units $80 (plus $10 per extra person). Just under 1km back from Hastings St, you'll find four

---

## Not Drowning, Waving

With a string of excellent breaks around an unspoiled national park, Noosa is a fine place to catch a wave. The best year-round break is probably Sunshine Corner, at the northern end of Sunshine Beach, though watch out for the brutal beach dump. The point breaks around the headland only perform during the summer, but when they do, expect wild conditions and good walls at Boiling Point and Tea Tree on the northern coast of the headland.

There are also gentler breaks on Noosa Spit at the far end of Hastings St, where most of the surf schools do their training. Options include Wavesense (☎ 5474 9076), Surfing Queensland Inc (☎ 5445 4870) and Learn to Surf (☎ 0418 787 577). Two-hour group lessons on long boards cost around $35, and you're guaranteed to stand up first time.

If you just want to rent a board to practise, Noosa Longboards (☎ 5474 2722) at 64 Hastings St has long boards for $40 per day, short boards for $25 a day, and bodyboards for $15 a day.

excellent and comfortable, one- or two-bedroom self-contained units in an attractive and shady garden setting.

One of the best areas for cheaper accommodation is along Gympie Terrace, the riverside main road through Noosaville.

*Noosa Palm Tree Motel* (☎ 5449 7311, fax 5474 3246, 233 Gympie Terrace, Noosaville) Doubles $65, 1-bedroom units from $75. West of Noosa Riverfront Units on Gympie Terrace, this is an OK motel with both rooms and units.

For private units to rent in the area, try Accom Noosa (☎ 5447 3444, fax 5447 2224) at 47 Hastings St, Noosa Heads, which represents a variety of apartments ranging from $80 to $300 per night.

## Places to Stay – Top End
*Sheraton Noosa Resort* (☎ 5449 4888, fax 5449 2230, Hastings St, Noosa Heads) Rooms from $410 ($495 high season). Noosa's only five-star hotel, the Sheraton backs onto Noosa Sound and has four bars, three restaurants, and a gym, pool, sauna and spa. If you purchase 60 days in advance rates can drop as low as $185.

*Number 1 in Hastings St* (☎ 5449 2211, fax 5449 2001, Cnr Hastings St & Morwong Dr, Noosa Heads) 2-bedroom apartments $255, 3-bedroom apartments/penthouses from $285. Marching up the hillside on the edge of the national park and reached by a funky sloping lift, this exclusive complex of stylish apartments and penthouses has great views over Laguna Bay and there's a gym, pool and spa.

## Places to Eat
**Hastings St** For a cheap lunch on Hastings St, the *food court* at the Bay Village Mall has a pizza and pasta bar, a bakery, a Chinese kitchen, a fish bar and a deli. You can eat well here for around $6.

*Beach Cafe* (☎ 5447 2740, Hastings St) Snack meals $5-8.50. Open 7am-4pm daily. On the seafront inside the On the Beach complex, this up-graded fish and chip shop has plenty of good, cheap burgers and snacks.

*Noosa Heads Surf Club* (☎ 5474 5688, Hastings St) Dishes $10-20. By the round-about on Hastings St, this popular surf club has good club grub and a lovely terrace overlooking the beach.

*Café Le Monde* (☎ 5449 2366, Hastings St) Mains $10-25. Open from 6.30am-late daily. This good-value, open-air place serves up a bit of everything from Thai to pasta to steaks in generous portions.

Of course, Hastings St is better known for its upmarket dining, and plenty of places here cater to the café latte and focaccia crowd.

*Blue Ginger* (☎ 5447 3211, 30 Hastings St) Dishes $12-20. Open noon till late. This classy but relaxed restaurant specialises in modern Asian dishes, from Korean to Thai, all of which are available as entrees or mains.

*Lindoni's* (☎ 5447 5111, 18 Hastings St) Dishes from $15. Open 6pm-late daily. With a covered patio, this good Italian place is popular with locals and has great seafood.

*Aromas* (☎ 5474 9788, 32 Hastings St) At the end of an evening, this is a popular place to sit with a cappuccino and watch Noosa go by; all the seats face onto Hastings St.

**Noosa Junction** Self-caterers should head to *Coles supermarket* in the Noosa Fair Mall. There's also a number of restaurant choices.

*Wok Inn Noosa* (☎ 5448 0372, 77 Noosa Dr) Dishes around $9-13.50. Open noon-2.30pm & 5pm-9pm daily. Across from Koala near the junction of Noosa Dr and Sunshine Beach Rd, this place serves up freshly made noodle dishes such as laksa, and Thai stir-fries.

*Canteen* (☎ 5447 5400, 4-6 Sunshine Beach Rd) Sandwiches & light meals $4.50-11.50. Open 8.30am-6pm. This funky little cafe offers truly inspired gourmet sandwiches and breakfasts. You can browse for 30 minutes on one of its Internet terminals if you buy a coffee, tea or juice.

*Cafe Arcadia* (☎ 5474 8833, 5 Arcadia St) Light meals $4-10. Around the corner from Canteen, this is a friendly little pavement cafe with a $10 all-day breakfast.

## Meals for the Well-Heeled

Noosa is home to some of Queensland's finest restaurants, and if money is no object, even the most demanding gourmand should find something here to tease their palate. Most of the upmarket options are on Hastings St in Noosa Heads. Few of these places charge less than $20 for a main course; bring the platinum credit card and be prepared to use it!

*Saltwater* (☎ 5447 2234, 8 Hastings St) Dishes $24.50-31. Open lunch & dinner daily. This superb, minimalist restaurant serves up fantastic creations involving Moreton Bay bugs, lobster, scallops, king prawns and reef fish, cooked up according to your specifications. Highly recommended.

*Cato's* (☎ 5449 4888, Hastings St) Dishes $15.50-25.50. Seafood buffet $52 for 2 people. Open 7am-11pm daily. This elegant cafe offers cool, sophisticated interior design and European-inspired seafood dishes. Cheaper meals and snacks are available in the popular bar area till late. The $21 buffet breakfast here is epic.

*Bistro C* (☎ 5447 2855, On the Beach Complex, Hastings St) Dishes $16-23. Open 8am-late daily. With a terrace on the seafront, this tasteful bistro offers Asian- and Mediterranean-inspired dishes like pot-roasted duck and cuttlefish, and prawn and swordfish antipasto, surrounded by simple Mediterranean decor.

*Berardo's* (☎ 5447 5666, 50 Hastings St) Dishes $23-29. Open lunch & dinner Mon-Sat. This exclusive restaurant is the place for candlelit dining, and even if the conversation runs flat, you can take consolation in the fantastic cuisine. There's plenty of game meat and seafood, including a fine sand-crab linguine, and a *very* sophisticated wine list.

*Chilli Jam* (☎ 5449 9755, Cnr Weyba Rd & Swan St, Noosaville) Dishes $17-24. Open dinner Tues-Sat. It's worth breaking away from Hastings St for this upbeat Thai restaurant. Familiar dishes like red curry are given an injection of life by unusual ingredients like black mussels and Moreton Bay bugs, and all the curry pastes are made in-house.

**Noosaville** Gympie Terrace is Noosaville's own aspiring Hastings St, with dozens of upmarket cafes facing the river.

*Noosa Yacht & Rowing Club* (☎ 5449 8602, Chaplin Park, Gympie Terrace) Dishes $10-14. Lunch & dinner daily. Overlooking the river, this friendly club offers cheap Aussie meals.

*Thai Pan* (☎ 5474 1844, 13 William St) Dishes from $12. Open from 5.30pm Tues-Sun. This restaurant is next to the Noosa Backpackers Resort and serves up good Thai standards. It has a BYO licence, so you bring along your favorite chilled drop.

*Fusions* (☎ 5474 1699, 271 Gympie Terrace) Dishes $13-24. Open 7.30am-late. On the corner of James St, this Mediterranean-inspired bistro offers gourmet pizzas and interesting deli sandwiches and focaccias in the $6-9 range.

*Lemongrass* (☎ 5449 8833, 255 Gympie Terrace) Dishes $16-19. This relaxed but upbeat BYO restaurant has a broad menu of modern Asian dishes, including Chinese, Indian, Thai and Malay.

*Gusto* (☎ 5449 7144, 257 Gympie Terrace) Dishes $16-25. Open dinner Mon-Sat, lunch daily. Gusto is another upmarket riverfront cafe with plenty of pan-seared and char-grilled Aussie treats.

**Sunshine Beach** The cheapest options here are the *takeaways* on Duke St. There are also a few sit-down options.

*Sunshine Beach Surf Club* (☎ 5474 5177, The Esplanade) Dishes $10-20. This is a good surf club with hearty bistro meals, overlooking the main surf beach.

In the Duke St arcade, *Zest* (☎ 5474 5533) and *Sabai Sabai* (☎ 5474 5177) are two trendy restaurants serving modern Australian and modern Asian cuisine respectively.

*Beach Chalet* (☎ 5447 3944, 3 Tingira Crescent) Dishes $6-17. This fun cafe is above a general store and has an open-air balcony overlooking the ocean.

## Entertainment

**Bars, Nightclubs & Live Music** The bar and club scene in Noosa has come on a lot in recent years. Most evenings start at the **Koala Beach Resort** bar in Noosa Junction and then move down to Hastings St.

*The Reef Bar (☎ 5447 4477, Downstairs at the Noosa Reef Hotel, Noosa Dr, Noosa Junction)* This pub has occasional live bands and *very* popular Wednesday karaoke sessions. If you venture downstairs there's *Reef Nightclub*, which is open till 3am Friday and Saturday.

All the other party places are in Noosa Heads.

*The Coconut Club (☎ 5474 9555, 50 Hastings St)* Admission usually free. At the end of an evening, most backpackers end up at this club, upstairs on the corner of Hastings St and Noosa Dr.

*Rolling Rock (☎ 5447 2255, Bay Village Mall, Off Hastings St)* Admission $5-7. This big showy nightclub attracts big name DJs. The dress code is 'smart casual'. In the same complex, *New York Bar* is a sophisticated cocktail bar that appeals to an older crowd.

*Sierra (☎ 5447 4800, 10 Hastings St)* and *Barney's Noosa Bar (☎ 5447 4544, Cnr Hastings St & Noosa Dr)* also score highly with older drinkers.

**Cinema** The movies is a cool alternative to bars and beaches.

*Noosa 5 Cinemas (☎ 1300 366 339, 29 Sunshine Beach Rd, Noosa Junction)* This plush, comfortable cinema screens the latest flicks.

## Getting There & Away

Long-distance buses stop at the bus stop (there's no bus terminal in Noosa) near the corner of Noosa Dr and Noosa Parade, just back from Hastings St. All of Noosa's hostels have courtesy buses that will pick up from the bus stop (except Halse Lodge – it's only 100m away!). See Getting There & Away at the start of this chapter for more information on long-distance bus services.

Sunbus (☎ 5492 8700) runs frequent daily services between Noosa and Maroochydore, and has local services linking Noosa Heads,

Noosaville, Noosa Junction etc. There are regular Trainlink buses from Noosa Heads to Nambour train station (one hour), passing through Eumundi (30 minutes).

## Getting Around

**Car** Henry's (☎ 5447 3777) at 13 Noosa Dr in Noosa Junction is the biggest car rental operator here, with cars from $39 per day. It also rents out a range of 4WD vehicles for trips to Cooloola Section of Great Sandy National Park, from $135 for Suzuki Sierras to $165 for Toyota Landcruisers.

There are several other car rental agencies around Hastings St, including Avis (☎ 5447 5055), opposite the bus stop on Noosa Dr, and Budget (☎ 5447 4588) at the Bay Village Mall.

**Bicycle** Bikes can be hired from a number of places, including Koala Bike Hire (☎ 5474 2733), which has mountain bikes from $17 a day, and delivers and picks up the bikes from accommodation.

**Boat** Noosa Ferry (☎ 0413 548 042) provides a pricey water taxi from the wharf at the Sheraton Hotel to Noosa Harbour. The fare is $6.50/10 one-way/return (15 minutes each way).

## COOLOOLA COAST

Stretching for 50km between Noosa and Rainbow Beach, the Cooloola Coast is a remote strip of long sandy beaches backed by the Cooloola Section of Great Sandy National Park. Although it's undeveloped, the Toyota Landcruiser and tin boat set flock here in droves so it's not always as peaceful as you might imagine. If you head off on foot or by canoe along the many inlets and waterways, you'll soon escape the crowds.

From the end of Moorindil St in Tewantin, the Noosa River ferry (☎ 5447 1321) operates from 6am to 10.30pm daily (5am to 12.30pm Friday and Saturday); cars cost $4 and motorcycles and horses $3.

### Up the Beach

If you have a 4WD you can drive right up the beach to Rainbow Beach (and on up to

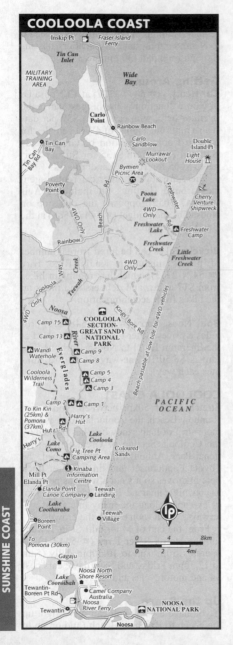

**COOLOOLA COAST**

Inskip Pt
Fraser Island Ferry
Tin Can Inlet
MILITARY TRAINING AREA
Wide Bay
Carlo Point
Rainbow Beach
Tin Can Bay Rd
Tin Can Bay
Carlo Sandblow
Double Island Pt
Murrawar Lookout
Light House
Bymien Picnic Area
Poverty Point
Poona Lake
Beach Rd
Freshwater Rd
Cherry Venture Shipwreck
4WD Only
Freshwater Lake
Freshwater Camp
Rainbow
AWD Only
Freshwater Creek
Little Freshwater Creek
Rainbow Way
Teewah Creek
4WD Only
Noosa
4WD Only Cooloola Way
Kings Bore Rd
Camp 15
COOLOOLA SECTION GREAT SANDY NATIONAL PARK
Camp 13
Camp 9
Wandi Waterhole
Everglades
River
Camp 8
Cooloola Wilderness Trail
Camp 5
Camp 4
Camp 3
Beach passable at low tide for 4WD vehicles
Camp 2
Camp 1
PACIFIC OCEAN
To Kin Kin (25km) & Pomona (37km)
Harry's Hut
Hut Rd
Harry's
Lake Cooloola
Lake Como
Fig Tree Pt Camping Area
Coloured Sands
Mill Pt
Elanda Pt
Kinaba Information Centre
Elanda Point
Canoe Company
Teewah Landing
Lake Cootharaba
Teewah Village
Boreen Point
To Pomona (30km)
Gagaju
Noosa North Shore Resort
Lake Cooroibah
Tewantin-Boreen Pt Rd
Camel Company Australia
Noosa River Ferry
NOOSA NATIONAL PARK
Tewantin
Noosa

0　4　8km
0　2　4mi

Inskip Bay, from where you can take a ferry across to Fraser Island), but check the tide times before setting out. There is talk of closing parts of the coast to traffic due to excessive wear from all the 4WDs thundering up and down the beach.

On the way up the beach you'll pass the Teewah coloured sand cliffs, estimated to be about 40,000 years old, and the rusting *Cherry Venture*, a 3000-tonne freighter swept ashore by a cyclone in 1973.

## Lake Cooroibah

A couple of kilometres north of Tewantin, the Noosa River widens out into Lake Cooroibah. If you take the ferry across the Noosa River, you can drive up to the lake in a conventional vehicle; there are a couple of good camping grounds between the eastern side of the lake and the coast.

Camel Company Australia (☎ 5442 4402), based at the Lake Cooroibah Resort, offers camel rides and safaris ranging from one hour in the bush ($28) to two-hour beach rides ($42) to six-day safaris to Fraser Island ($1100).

There's also a couple of accommodation options.

*Gagaju* (☎ 1300 302 271, ☎/fax 5474 3522, 118 Johns Dr) Camp sites from $10, dorm beds $17, doubles $45. This is a totally laid-back riverside wilderness getaway with a large dorm. It's midway between Lakes Cooroibah and Cootharaba in forest bordering the Cooloola Section of Great Sandy National Park. The whole thing is built from scavenged timber, and there are plenty of bush activities including canoeing trips, mountain biking and bushwalking. Shower and toilet facilities are basic and you're a long way from the shops, so bring your own food. The Gagaju minibus will pick you up from the bus stop in Noosa.

*Noosa North Shore Retreat* (☎ 5447 1225, fax 5447 1266, ⓔ info@noosaretreat .com.au, *East shore of Lake Cooroibah*) Unpowered/powered sites $4.40/5.50 per person, on-site tents $22 (for 2 people), cabins from $88 for 2 nights (4-6 beds), resort rooms from $154 for 2 nights. This large, low-key resort offers almost every kind of accommodation from camping to luxury apartments. It has good facilities including a pub and *restaurant*, store, tennis and squash courts and horse riding.

## Lake Cootharaba & Boreen Point

Cootharaba is the Cooloola Section of Great Sandy National Park's biggest lake, measuring about 5km across and 10km in length. On the western shores of the lake and at the southern edge of the national park, Boreen Point is a relaxed little community with several places to stay and eat. The lake is the gateway to the Noosa Everglades, offering bushwalking, canoeing and bush camping.

From Boreen Point, an unsealed road leads another 5km up to **Elanda Point**, where there's a rangers station (☎ 5449 7364) that's open 9am to 3pm daily, and the headquarters of the Elanda Point Canoe Company (☎ 5485 3165), which charges $35 a day for canoes and kayaks. There is also a river taxi to the Everglades camping grounds for $10 per person.

Everglades Waterfront Holidays (☎ 5485 3164) at Boreen Point Parade in Boreen Point also rents out kayaks, charging $44 per day ($15 for subsequent days).

**Places to Stay & Eat** There are some great choices in Boreen Point.

*Boreen Point Caravan & Camping Area* (☎ 5485 3244, Dun's Beach, Teewah St) Camp sites $10. This remarkably cheap camping ground is right on the foreshore of Lake Cootharaba in a grove of eucalypts. Take a right turn off Laguna St onto Vista St and bear right at the lake.

*Lake Cootharaba Holiday Units* (☎ 5485 3153, 64 Laguna St) Doubles $65 (2-night min). This place has two self-contained units (attached to an art gallery) that sleep up to four people.

*Apollonian Hotel* (☎ 5485 3100, fax 5485 3499, Laguna St) Dorm beds $14, doubles from $35 (shared bathrooms). Originally erected in Gympie during the gold rush and later transported here, this is a really

attractive timber pub with broad, shady verandas. Rooms are in the Queenslander out the back and the meals here are fantastic (Sunday is hog-roast day).

*The Jetty* (☎ 5485 3167, Boreen Promenade) Dishes $14-21, 3-course set menu $49.50. Open lunch daily, dinner Sat. With a lovely setting on the edge of Lake Cootharaba, this is a stylish licensed restaurant with an excellent reputation. The restaurant runs a free courtesy bus from Noosa every day if you book in advance.

## Cooloola Section – Great Sandy National Park

The Cooloola Section of Great Sandy National Park, or the Great Sandy National Park as it's also known, covers over 54,000 hectares from Lake Cootharaba north up to Rainbow Beach. It's a varied wilderness area with long sandy beaches, mangrove-lined waterways, forest, heath and lakes, all of it featuring plentiful bird-life – including rarities such as red goshawk and grass owl – and lots of wildflowers in spring.

The Cooloola Way, which runs from Tewantin all the way up to Rainbow Beach, is open to 4WD vehicles unless there's been heavy rain – check with the rangers before setting out. Most people prefer to bomb up the beach, though you're restricted to a few hours either side of low tide.

Although there are many 4WD tracks running to lookout points and picnic grounds, the best way to see Cooloola is by boat or canoe, along the numerous tributaries of the Noosa River. Boats can be hired from Tewantin and Noosa (along Gympie Terrace), Boreen Point and Elanda Point – see also Gagaju in the Lake Cooroibah section.

There are some fantastic walking trails starting from Elanda Point on the shore of Lake Cootharaba, including the 46km Cooloola Wilderness Trail to Rainbow Beach and a 7km trail to the EPA information centre (☎ 5449 7364) at Kinaba Island.

**Places to Stay** There are around 15 camping grounds in the park, many of them along the river. The most popular (and best equipped) camp sites are **Fig Tree Point**, at the northern end of Lake Cootharaba, **Harry's Hut**, about 4km upstream, and **Freshwater**, about 6km south of Double Island Point on the coast. Standard national park rates ($3.85/15.40 per person/family) apply. Apart from Harry's Hut and Freshwater, all sites are accessible by hiking or river only. For site bookings and information, contact the rangers' offices at Elanda Point, Kinaba information centre or Rainbow Beach.

## EUMUNDI

Just off the Bruce Hwy on the way to Noosa, Eumundi is an appealing little rural township famous for its **Saturday market** that draws in thousands of visitors from all over the region. From roughly 6.30am to 2pm the main street and areas just off it are crowded with more than 200 artsy-craftsy stalls, selling everything from Spice Girls rings to home-made strawberry jam. Eumundi also has a smaller weekly market from 8am to 2pm every Wednesday.

The town's other claim to fame is **Eumundi Lager**, originally brewed in the Imperial Hotel. Nowadays it's made down at Yatala on the Gold Coast, but you can still sample it on tap in the Imperial Hotel. The former brewing room is now an art gallery with glass-blowing displays.

The **Eumundi Historical Museum** (☎ 5442 8762, Memorial Dr; open 10am-4.30pm Wed & Fri, 9am-3pm Sat & 9am-1pm Sun) is worth a visit.

About 10km north-west of Eumundi, the little village of **Pomona** sits in the shadow of looming Mt Cooroora (440m), and is home to the wonderful **Majestic Theatre** (☎ 5485 2330) – one of the only places in the world where you can see a silent movie accompanied by the original Wurlitzer organ soundtrack. The Majestic only plays one film, Rudolph Valentino's last screen performance, The Son of the Sheik, every Thursday at 8.30pm (in fact, the Majestic has shown The Son of the Sheik every Thursday for 13 years!); seats cost $6.

### Places to Stay & Eat

Eumundi has a camping ground and several B&Bs but things are pretty quiet here on nonmarket days, so most people don't stop overnight.

**Eumundi Caravan Park** (☎ 5442 8411, fax 5442 7414, 141 Memorial Dr) Unpowered/powered sites $11/15.40, double cabins from $55. This friendly and clean park has a pool and a quiet, forested location off the Gympie road.

**Eumundi Rise B&B** (☎ 5442 8855, fax 5442 8859, 37-39 Crescent Rd) Doubles

Pomona's Majestic Theatre only shows one movie – The Son of the Sheik, with Rudolph Valentino.

from $110. Housed in an attractive Queenslander just off Etheridge St, this B&B offers pleasant rooms and lovely views from the veranda.

*Taylor's Damn Fine B&B* (☎ 5442 8685, fax 5442 8168, 15 Doonan Rd) Doubles from $121 (with breakfast). True to its name, this damn fine B&B offers accommodation in a lovely country home, or there are rooms in the converted railcar in the garden. It's about 1km from Eumundi on the Noosa road.

Your best option for a meal is the big old *Imperial Hotel* (☎ 5442 8303, Memorial Dr) or *Eats* (☎ 5442 8555, 106 Memorial Dr), a stylish gourmet cafe open for breakfast and lunch.

### Getting There & Away

Henry's (☎ 5474 0199) and Storeyline Tours (☎ 5474 1500) offer trips to the Eumundi markets on Wednesday and Saturday for $12/7 per adult/child (30 minutes). Call them to have them pick you up from your door. The local bus between Noosa Heads and Nambour also stops here.

# Sunshine Coast Hinterland

The Blackall Range rises a short distance inland from the coast, with spectacular countryside, some appealing national parks, and numerous (rather chintzy) rustic villages, full of Devonshire tearooms, antique shops and craft emporiums. There are plenty of tours, but it's worth coming up here with your own transport as the landscape between the villages is the real attraction.

### Organised Tours

Various companies offer guided hinterland tours and will pick up from anywhere along the Sunshine Coast, including Tropical Coast Tours (☎ 5474 9200), Noosa Hinterland Tours (☎ 5474 3366) and Storeyline Tours (☎ 5474 1500). Most combine a trip through the Blackall Range with other attractions like the Glass House Mountains, the Big Pineapple, the Ginger Factory or

Australia Zoo. Prices for the day start at around $50/20 per adult/child.

For something a bit different, Off Beat Rainforest Tours (☎ 5473 5135) offers 4WD tours to the little-visited Conondale National Park for $115/75 per adult/child. Baraka Australia (☎ 5494 4555) offers whole-day gorge treks, mountain biking tours and rock-climbing trips for $95 per person.

## NAMBOUR & YANDINA

Nambour is the main commercial centre in the hinterland, but there's not much here for travellers.

The **Big Pineapple** (☎ 5442 1333, Nambour Connection Rd, Nambour; admission free; open 9am-5pm daily) is one of Queensland's kitschy 'big things'. As well as the 15m-high fibreglass fruit, there's a train ride through the plantation, a macadamia orchard tour and a themed boat ride. It's all set up to encourage you to buy souvenirs.

On the Bruce Hwy about 7km north of the Big Pineapple is Yandina, where you'll find

---

### Are We There Yet?

A vivid memory from my childhood is our yearly trek to the Big Pineapple. It didn't matter that we really wanted to go to Dreamworld – my grandparents were on holiday and determined to visit 'the tropics'.

And we did enjoy ourselves when we got there – the trundling old train ride, racing to the top of the huge (yes, it really is big, especially when you're a kid) pineapple, and deciding what colour pineapple-shaped eraser we'd get *this* year.

But what made the trip worthwhile were the parfaits: magnificent, wobbling edifices of freshly whipped real cream, chunks of glorious fruit, and mounds of creamy ice cream.

But a warning: Parfaits and the windy roads around Esk do not agree. Especially when you are a child prone to car sickness. Let's just say that I don't think my father ever wore his volunteer rural fire brigade helmet again after a trip to the Pineapple in 1983.

**Joanne Newell**

the **Ginger Factory** (☎ 5446 7096, 50 Pioneer Rd; admission free; open 9am-5pm daily), a tacky souvenir store-cum-attraction. There are train rides, factory and plantation tours and, of course, a huge range of ginger products and souvenirs on sale.

*Spirit House Restaurant* (☎ 5446 8994, 4 Ninderry Rd, Yandina) Open lunch daily, dinner Wed-Sat. This very highly esteemed restaurant has spectacular modern Thai food from $23.

Nambour is on the main coastal train line, and is well connected to Brisbane by Citytrain services. Sunbus (☎ 5492 8700) runs regular services from Noosa Heads to Nambour ($2.65, one hour) via Yandina and Eumundi.

## MALENY
Probably the nicest settlement in the hinterland, Maleny has thus far escaped the tacky heritage developments. In place of Devonshire tearooms, you'll find pleasant street cafes, a handful of craft shops selling work by local artists and a relaxed, laid-back community of dairy farmers and craftspeople.

**Mary Cairncross Scenic Reserve** (☎ 5494 2287), south-east of town on Mountain View Rd, is a small nature reserve with wheelchair-friendly walking tracks, picnic areas and a snack kiosk. You can go boating on **Lake Baroon**, signposted 9km north of Maleny.

There's a small information centre (☎ 5499 9033) at the Maleny Community Centre, which is open 10am to 3pm daily. Maleny has a craft market on Sunday morning.

### Woodford Folk Festival
The famous Woodford (formerly Maleny) Folk Festival, which is held on a property near the town of Woodford, runs annually over the five days leading up to New Year's Day. The festival program features a huge diversity of music including folk, traditional Irish, indigenous and world music, as well as buskers, belly dancers, craft markets, visual arts performances and a visiting squad of Tibetan monks. If you want to settle in for the festival, camping grounds are set up on the property with toilets, showers etc.

Tickets cost $66 per day including camping ($82.50 on New Year's Eve) and can be bought on the gate or in advance through the festival office (☎ 5496 1600). Check online at Ⓦ www.woodfordfolkfestival .com for a program of performances.

## Places to Stay
*Maleny Palms Tourist Park* (☎ 5494 2933, fax 5494 3147, 23 Macadamia Dr) Powered camp sites $22, self-contained double cabins from $60. This tidy and well-run park is north-west of the town centre on the road to Kenilworth.

*Maleny Hotel* (☎ 5494 2013, fax 5494 3108, 6 Bunya St) Singles/doubles $55/70. Just south of the centre, this renovated pub offers good hotel rooms.

*Maleny Lodge Guest House* (☎ 5494 2370, fax 5494 3407, 58 Maple St) B&B doubles $132-175 (with breakfast). Right in the centre of town, this is a beautifully restored 1894 timber guesthouse furnished in period style with antiques.

## Places to Eat
There are several good cafes along Maleny's main road, Maple St.

*Up Front Club* (☎ 5494 2592, 31 Maple St) Dishes $6-9. Open 8am-4pm daily, evenings Mon & Fri. This friendly and cosy little cafe and club has pavement seating, good breakfasts and sangers, and dinner with live music on Friday. Musicians are welcome to the blackboard sessions on Monday evenings.

Maleny is known for its fine dining, with several very posh restaurants just south of the centre.

*Malcolm's* (☎ 5494 2825, 124 Mountain View Rd) Mains $17-26. Open lunch Tues-Sun, dinner Fri-Tues. Overlooking the Glass House Mountains, this upmarket place serves fine Australian cuisine.

*The Terrace* (☎ 5494 3700, Mary Cairncross Corner) Dishes $23-27. Open lunch & dinner. This award-winning seafood place is a popular stop for coach tours.

*Perry's* (☎ 5494 2822, 76 Maple St) Perry's serves up imaginative European-influenced cuisine in an old wooden church.

## MONTVILLE

On a ridge midway between Mapleton and Maleny, the historic village of Montville has long since vanished under a mountain of chintzy 'Olde English' developments. Expect fudge emporiums, endless Devonshire tearooms and craft shops shaped like antique German cuckoo clocks. Nearby Flaxton offers more of the same.

More interesting is **Kondalilla Falls National Park**, 3km north. The falls drop 80m into a rainforested valley; there's a 4.8km round-trip walk to the bottom.

There's a helpful information centre (☎ 5478 5544) at 160 Main St, open 10am to 4pm daily, which can help you find B&Bs in the area.

### Places to Stay & Eat

*Montville Mountain Inn* (☎ 5442 9499, fax 5442 9303) Doubles from $77 (Sun-Thur), dinner, B&B packages $99 (Fri & Sat). This mock-Tudor building has comfortable modern rooms.

*Treehouses* (☎ 5445 7650, Kondalilla Falls Rd) Cabins from $110 ($165 weekdays). This retreat at Kondalilla National Park has plush cabins (with spas) tucked away in the forest.

## MAPLETON

Mapleton is a laid-back little township 8km north of Montville. It has a couple of craft and pottery galleries and a good pub that has fine views from the veranda.

West of town on Obi Obi Rd is **Mapleton Falls National Park**, where Pencil Creek plunges 120m down into Obi Obi Valley. There's a lookout point just a couple of hundred metres from the carpark. There are several walking tracks and plenty of colourful bird-life.

*Lilyponds Caravan Park* (☎ 5445 7238, fax 5445 7238, 26 Warruga St) Unpowered/powered sites from $14/17, double self-contained cabins from $43. This park is just north of the friendly *Mapleton Tavern* pub and overlooks the Mapleton Lily Ponds.

# Fraser Coast

The main attraction of the Fraser Coast is majestic Fraser Island, the world's largest sand island. Essentially one long, forest-backed beach, Fraser Island offers stunning scenery, excellent bushwalking and thrilling 4WD driving along its broad beaches at low tide. Most visitors arrive from Hervey Bay, a busy tourist centre further north and a popular spot for whale-watching from late July to October.

Bundaberg, the largest city in the area, is the home of Queensland's favourite spirit, Bundaberg rum, made from local cane sugar, and there are numerous natural attractions in the area, including the southern Barrier Reef Islands and the turtle hatchery at lovely Mon Repos beach. Many travellers stop here to take advantage of plentiful seasonal fruit- and vegetable-picking work.

## Getting There & Around

Sunstate (a subsidiary of Qantas, ☎ 13 13 13) services Hervey Bay and Bundaberg, with daily flights from all major centres. From Brisbane, the fare is $184 to Hervey Bay (55 minutes) and $236 to Bundaberg (one hour).

For bus travellers, the McCafferty's/Greyhound (☎ 13 44 99, 13 20 30) coastal service along the Bruce Hwy detours to Bundaberg and Hervey Bay. Premier (☎ 13 34 10) and Suncoast Pacific (☎ 3236 1901) also service the Brisbane to Rockhampton route. Smaller local companies connect Gympie to Rainbow Beach and Tin Can Bay, and Bundaberg to Maryborough.

The main coastal train line between Brisbane, Rockhampton and Cairns passes through Gympie, Maryborough West and Bundaberg. There is a Trainlink bus from Maryborough West to Hervey Bay.

## GYMPIE
postcode 4570 • pop 15,150

Gympie came into existence in 1867 when a lone gold prospector, James Nash, hit pay dirt in a small gully off the Mary River. As

### Highlights

- Test your 4WD skills on a self-drive tour through wild and beautiful Fraser Island; while there, swim in lovely Lake Wabby and Lake McKenzie.
- Cruise with the whales of Hervey Bay between July and October.
- Sample Australia's most famous rum at the distillery in Bundaberg.
- Hike along the Cooloola Coast to the coloured sand cliffs at Rainbow Beach.

soon as news got out, a town appeared on the site almost overnight. The settlement was named Gympie after *gimpi gimpi*, the Aboriginal name for a local tree. The town is known for its annual Country Music Muster every August.

There's a heritage map of Gympie's old buildings on display at the joint offices of the Cooloola Regional Development Bureau (☎ 5482 5444) and the Environment Protection Agency (EPA; ☎ 5482 4189), beside the Bruce Hwy on the southern outskirts of town (open daily from 8.30am to 3.30pm).

The **Gympie Gold Mining & Historical Museum** (☎ *5482 3995, 215 Brisbane Rd;*

*adult/child $6.60/1.10; open 9am-4.30pm)*, on the southern outskirts of town, has a large and diverse collection of mining equipment and functioning steam-driven engines.

A few kilometres north of Gympie on Fraser Rd (which branches off the Bruce Hwy near the golf course), the **Woodworks Forestry & Timber Museum** (☎ 5483 7691, *Fraser Rd; adult/student $4/2; open 9am-4pm Mon-Fri, 1pm-4pm Sun)* is devoted to Queensland's lucrative, if destructive, timber industry. You can get information here on camping in nearby state forests.

On Sunday and Wednesday morning, the **Valley Rattler** steam train (☎ 5482 2750; *adult/child $27.50/13.75 return)* runs the 40km from Gympie to the tiny township of Imbil and back.

## Places to Stay & Eat

*Gympie Caravan Park* (☎ 5483 6800, *1 Jane St)* Unpowered/powered sites $14/17.50, on-site vans from $35, double cabins

$35-47. This is a small caravan park in an attractive setting.

*Gympie Motel* (☎ *5482 2722, fax 5482 2175, 83 River Rd)* Singles/doubles from $44/52. This old-fashioned motel has OK rooms and a central location.

*Imperial Hotel* (☎ *5482 1706, 170 Mary St)* Pub grub from $6.50. This central hotel offers roasts and pasta for lunch and dinner.

*Kingston House Impressions* (☎ *5483 6733, Cnr Channon Rd & Barter St)* Light lunches $4-13, dinner $17-24. Open for lunch Mon-Sat, dinner Tues-Sat. This posh option is housed in a lovely old Queenslander with broad verandas. It has good lunchtime sandwiches and quiche and an upmarket dinner menu.

## Getting There & Away

McCafferty's/Greyhound and Premier coaches stop at the Polley's Coaches (☎ 5482 2700) terminal in the centre of town, on the corner of Channon Rd and

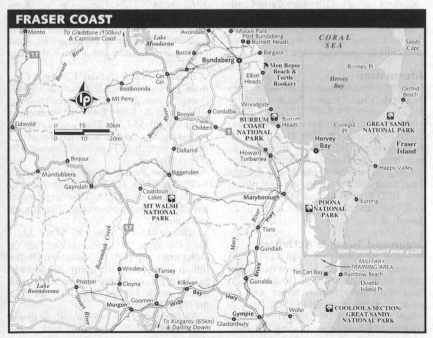

Mary St. Polley's has local buses to Rainbow Beach at 6am and 1.30pm from Monday to Friday ($11.50, 1¾ hours).

Gympie is on the main Brisbane to Rockhampton train line (from Brisbane, $31, 3¼ hours). The train station is 1km east of the centre on Tozer St.

## RAINBOW BEACH
postcode 4581 • pop 900

Famed for its coloured sand cliffs, the sleepy seaside settlement of Rainbow Beach sits in a great location on Wide Bay, 70km northeast of Gympie. To the north is Fraser Island, reached by a vehicle ferry from Inskip Point, 13km north (see under Getting There & Away in the Fraser Island section later in this chapter for details of services). To the south is the Cooloola Section of Great Sandy National Park, with the rusting hulk of the **Cherry Venture**, a Singaporean freighter blown ashore by heavy winds in 1973. With a 4WD it's possible to drive all the way to Noosa.

Closer to town is 120m-high **Carlo Sandblow**, reached via a 600m track along the cliffs at the southern end of Cooloola Dr. A 2km walk along the beach are the **coloured sand cliffs** that gave the town its name.

### Information

For local information and tour bookings try the privately run Rainbow Beach tourist information centre (☎ 5486 3227), at 8 Rainbow Beach Rd. It opens seven days a week.

The EPA office (☎ 5486 3160), also on Rainbow Beach Rd, is open from 7am to 4pm. It provides information and 4WD and camping permits for Fraser Island and the Great Sandy National Park. Several places offer 4WD hire for around $150 per day – try Aussie Adventure (☎ 5486 3599) at 27 Goondi St.

### Organised Tours & Activities

Surf & Sand Safaris (☎ 5486 3131) runs four-hour 4WD trips south down the beach, taking in the lighthouse at Double Island Point, the *Cherry Venture* wreck and the coloured sands (adult/child $55/27.50).

Sun Safari Tours (☎ 5486 3154) offers day trips to Fraser Island costing $71 ($42 for children), including morning tea and lunch. Also on offer are overnight tours with accommodation at the Eurong Resort ($165/105), and trips south to Double Island Point, the *Cherry Venture* and the coloured sands, which include morning tea (adult/child $55/27.50).

Other organised activities include scuba diving at Wolf Rock, paragliding, horse rides along the beach and canoe tours around Tin Can Inlet. You can book all these through the information office or wherever you're staying. There's a good surf break at Double Island Point.

### Places to Stay & Eat

*Rainbow Beach Backpackers (☎/fax 5486 3288, 66 Rainbow Beach Rd)* Dorm beds & doubles $16 per person. Beside the main road on the way into town, this place is fairly cramped and facilities aren't the best, but the owners offer 4WD hire and tours.

*The Rocks Backpacker Resort (☎ 5486 3711, fax 5486 3229, 3 Spectrum Ave)* Dorm beds $18, doubles with shared bathroom/en suite $38/48. This clean, converted motel is a better backpacker choice. There's a good pool, a scuba centre and a bar with cheap meals.

*Rainbow Beach Holiday Village & Caravan Park (☎ 5486 3222, fax 5486 3401, Rainbow Beach Rd)* Unpowered/powered sites from $15.20/17.40, self-contained cabins from $54.50. This well-equipped park is right by the beach and has a pool and units brought here from the Olympic Village in Sydney.

*Rainbow Beach Motor Inn (☎ 5486 3400, fax 5486 3317, 18 Spectrum Ave)* Singles/doubles $45/55. This large motel has good, comfortable rooms, a restaurant and a pool.

*Mikado Motor Inn (☎ 5486 3211, fax 5486 3283, 105 Cooloola Dr)* Double motel units $60 ($70 on Saturday). On the hilltop south-east of the centre, the Mikado has luxury motel suites with balconies and great views and is just down the road from the Carlo Sandblow.

*Nielsen's (☎ 5486 3403, Rainbow Beach Rd)* Dishes $17-20. Round the back of the main shopping arcade on Rainbow Beach Rd, Nielsen's cooks up posh meals featuring fare such as rabbit, kangaroo and duck.

***Rainbow Beach Surf Club*** (☎ *5486 3249, Rainbow Beach Rd)* Lunch $7-11, dinner $13-20. For the usual meals at the usual times, head to this simple club near the track down to the beach.

There are several takeaway-style *cafes* in the arcade.

## Getting There & Away
Polley's Coaches (☎ 5482 2700) in Gympie has buses between Gympie and Rainbow Beach ($11.50, 1¾ hours). On weekdays only, buses leave Gympie at 6am and 1.30pm, returning from Rainbow Beach at 7.30am and 3.45pm.

## TIN CAN BAY
Tin Can Bay is small community at the southern tip of the Great Sand Strait, the body of water separating Fraser Island from the mainland. It's a quiet little place, but growing numbers of tourists are coming here to see the tame dolphins that swim right up to the boat ramp at the Tin Can Bay marina most mornings. Monitored dolphin feeding takes place

from 8am to 10am – you'll have to wash your hands and remove watches and jewellery.

The closest motel to the marina is ***Cosy Cabins*** (☎ *5486 4126, 2 Cod St)* with cheap units from $55. On the other side of the headland are several caravan parks including the ***Kingfisher Caravan Park*** (☎ *5486 4198, The Esplanade)* with sites for $15 and cabins from $33.

## Getting There & Away
The Polleys bus service between Gympie and Rainbow Beach stops in Tin Can Bay on weekdays only. The fare is $9 to Gympie (45 minutes) and $3.30 to Rainbow Beach (one hour). There's one morning and one afternoon bus – for Gympie buses leave at 8.30am and 4.15pm and to Rainbow Beach buses leave at 6.40am and 4.15pm.

## MARYBOROUGH
**postcode 4650 • pop 24,870**
Maryborough came to prominence in the 1860s as the port of entry to Australia for some 21,000 European immigrants. This small timber and sugar centre is known for its fine Victorian architecture, but most visitors just pass through on the way to Hervey

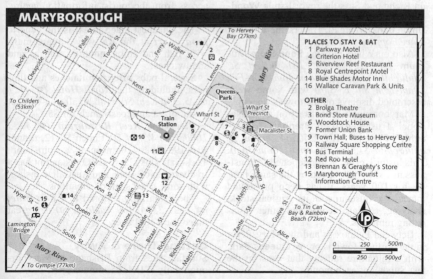

**MARYBOROUGH**

PLACES TO STAY & EAT
1 Parkway Motel
4 Criterion Hotel
5 Riverview Reef Restaurant
8 Royal Centrepoint Motel
14 Blue Shades Motor Inn
16 Wallace Caravan Park & Units

OTHER
2 Brolga Theatre
3 Bond Store Museum
6 Woodstock House
7 Former Union Bank
9 Town Hall; Buses to Hervey Bay
10 Railway Square Shopping Centre
11 Bus Terminal
12 Red Roo Hotel
13 Brennan & Geraghty's Store
15 Maryborough Tourist Information Centre

Bay. Many impressive Federation buildings from the town's heyday still survive in the town centre. Most locals shop in the modern Railway Square mall, giving quiet downtown Maryborough a strange 'ghost town' atmosphere.

It's worth visiting on Thursday for the heritage market, held between 8am and 2pm along Adelaide and Elena Sts.

## Orientation & Information

Kent St is the main shopping street in old Maryborough, but you'll find most of Maryborough's residents at the Railway Square mall near the intersection of Kent St and the Bruce Hwy (Ferry St).

The Maryborough Tourist Information Centre (☎ 4121 4111), at 30 Ferry St, opens from 10am to 2pm Monday to Friday, and is about 1km south of Kent St on the Bruce Hwy. It has stacks of leaflets and brochures on the Fraser Coast region.

## Things to See & Do

There are many fine old buildings in the historic port district along Wharf St. The 1866 Italianate **post office**, on the corner of Bazaar and Wharf Sts, is Queensland's oldest. Over on Richmond St is the revival-style **Woodstock House** and the neo-classical **former Union Bank**, where PL Travers, the author of *Mary Poppins*, was born.

Also on Wharf St is the **Bond Store Museum** (☎ *4123 1523, 101 Wharf St; adult/child $5/1; open 9am-4pm Mon-Fri, 10am-1pm Sat & Sun*) with some well-assembled displays on the town's history.

Maryborough's best attraction is the National Trust–classified **Brennan & Geraghty's Store** (☎ *4121 2250, 64 Lennox St; adult/child $3.30/1.10; open 10am-3pm*). This historic general store opened for business in 1871 and was run by the same family for 100 years. It has been preserved intact as a museum with its original stock, shelving, trading records and other fascinating remnants.

Between Lennox St and the Mary River in the north of town is pretty **Queens Park**, with a miniature railway that runs on the last Sunday of each month.

The **Brolga Theatre** (☎ *4122 6060, 5 Walker St)*, just north of the centre, has regular music and theatrical events.

## Places to Stay & Eat

***Wallace Caravan Park & Units*** *(☎ 4121 3970, fax 4121 5111, 22 Ferry St)* Unpowered/powered sites $11/14, single/double cabins from $26/30, self-contained motel units from $40/50. This is a quiet park right beside the tourist office with a variety of accommodation options.

***Criterion Hotel*** *(☎ 4121 3043, 98 Wharf St)* Singles/doubles $20/30. This old-style pub isn't really flash but the rooms have just been renovated and are OK for the money.

***Royal Centrepoint Motel*** *(☎ 4121 2241, fax 4121 2500, 326 Kent St)* Single/double motel units from $45/50. This old pub offers clean motel rooms in a central location.

***Parkway Motel*** *(☎ 4122 2888, fax 4122 2546, 188 John St)* Singles/doubles from $60/70. This is an excellent modern motel with a range of superior units, a licensed restaurant, and a pool, sauna and spa.

***Blue Shades Motor Inn*** *(☎ 4122 2777, fax 4122 3514, Cnr Ferry & Queen Sts)* Single/double units from $66/71.50. Just across from the tourist information centre, this is a clean, well-maintained motel.

The cheapest place to eat is the generic *food court* at the Railway Square mall, with fish and chips, noodles, kebabs and sandwiches.

Several pubs offer pub lunches and dinners, including the ***Royal Hotel*** *(☎ 4121 6225, 336 Kent St)*, with an all-you-can-eat pasta, pizza and roast lunch for $5.

***Riverview Reef Restaurant*** *(☎ 4123 1000, 106 Wharf St)* Lunch $8-12, dinner $16-19. Open 10am-4pm & 6pm-10pm Tues-Sat. This classy BYO restaurant has a lively menu of Asian and Australian dishes, with some good seafood creations.

The beautifully restored ***Red Roo Hotel*** *(☎ 4121 3586, 100 Adelaide St)* is a great place for a cold beer.

## Getting There & Away

Sunstate flies from Brisbane to Maryborough daily ($184, 45 minutes).

Trains on the Brisbane to Rockhampton line now stop at Maryborough West ($45, 4½ hours), 7km west of the centre, but there's a shuttle bus from the main bus terminal beside the Maryborough train station on Lennox St. This is also the stop for long-haul buses north and south.

Wide Bay Transit (☎ 4121 3719) has nine bus services every weekday and three services on Saturday between Maryborough and Hervey Bay ($5.25, one hour). Buses depart Maryborough from outside the Town Hall in Kent St.

## HERVEY BAY
postcode 4655 • pop 42,390

Hervey Bay consists of five small, linked settlements – from west to east, Point Vernon, Pialba, Scarness, Torquay and Urangan – stretching for 10km along the bay. There isn't a great deal to the town: Everything is geared towards getting tourists over to Fraser Island or onto the whale-watching tours in the bay, and most tourists don't stick around longer than it takes them to organise this.

However, the local council tries to encourage visitors to stay an extra few days. The surf-free beaches are good for swimming and you can go scuba diving, take dolphin-spotting tours and visit the local Aboriginal community. Most accommodation is concentrated in Scarness and Torquay, around the coastal Esplanade, several kilometres from the bus station and the marina.

### Information
The Hervey Bay Tourism & Development Bureau (☎ 1800 811 728, 4124 2912), on

## The Whales of Hervey Bay

Up to 3000 humpback whales (*Megaptera novaeangliae*) enter the waters of Hervey Bay every year, from late July through to the last week of October. They arrive in clusters of two or three (known as pods) and numbers usually peak in early September. Every year these massive creatures (they can grow up to 15m in length and weigh 40 tonnes) swim some 5000km from Antarctic waters up to the warmer waters off eastern Australia, where they mate and give birth before returning south.

No one is quite sure why the whales make the diversion from their homeward leg into Hervey Bay; one theory is that it is a kind of pit stop that gives them a chance to rest up after a stressful period of birthing and mating. A few weeks in the calm, warm waters may also give the new calves more time to develop the protective layers of blubber necessary for survival in the icy Antarctic waters.

Hervey Bay provides an excellent whale-watching opportunity, but the whales' behaviour – they often roll up beside the boats with one eye clear of the water – does raise the question of who's actually watching who.

AJ

the outskirts of town on the corner of the Urraween and Maryborough Rds, opens from 8.30am to 5pm Monday to Friday and 10am to 4pm on weekends. It is the only official tourist office, but there are numerous booking agents in town who also give out tourist information. We can recommend the Adventure Travel Centre (☎ 4125 9288), at 410 The Esplanade, and Fraser Island Backpackers Booking Office (☎ 4124 8444), at 363 The Esplanade.

There are dozens of Internet cafes along the Esplanade. The Adventure Travel Centre is probably the best-equipped and charges $4 per hour. It's open 7am till 10pm daily. The main post office is at 3 Bryant St, Pialba, with branch post offices at 414 The Esplanade, Torquay and 546 The Esplanade, Urangan.

If you need tent pegs, a fuel stove or other camping gear for your trip to Fraser Island, try Torquay Disposals & Camping (☎ 4125 6511).

## Things to See & Do

Hervey Bay itself has a handful of attractions.

**Hervey Bay Natureworld** (☎ *4124 1733, Cnr Maryborough Rd & Fairway Dr, Pialba; all-day admission adult/child $13.50/ 6.50; open 9am-5pm*) has native fauna, including wedge-tailed eagles and koalas, as well as introduced species such as camels and water buffaloes. There's a guided tour at 11.30am, koala shows at noon and 3pm and snake-handling at 12.30pm.

**Vic Hislop's Great White Shark Expo** (☎ *4128 9137, Cnr The Esplanade & Elizabeth St, Urangan; adult/child $12/5; open 8.30am-6pm*) is the brainchild of notorious shark-hunter Vic Hislop and has various gory displays designed to show these predators in the worst possible light. The 'documentaries' on show don't hold much scientific merit, but the displays (including three frozen great whites) hold a certain gruesome fascination.

**Neptune's Reef World** (☎ *4128 9828, Cnr Pulgul & Kent Sts, Urangan; adult/*

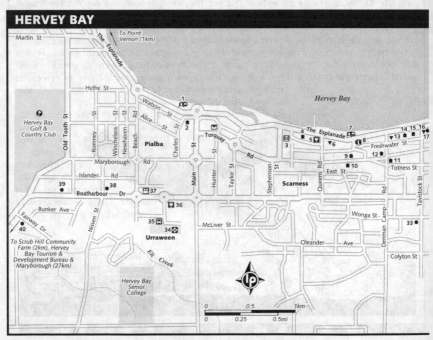

HERVEY BAY

*child $13/7; open 9.30am-4pm)* is a small, old-fashioned aquarium with coral displays. There are touch tanks for petting turtles and stingrays, shark-feeding at 2pm and seal displays at 10.30am and 3pm.

**Hervey Bay Historical Museum** *(☎ 4128 1816, 18 Zephyr St, Scarness; adult/child $2.50/0.50; open 1pm-5pm Fri-Sun)* is a small museum with a collection of old buildings, industrial machinery and local memorabilia.

**Scrub Hill Community Farm** *(☎ 4124 6908, Scrub Hill Rd; guided tours Wed & Thur $16.50/5.50)*, just off the Maryborough Rd, is run by the Korrawinga Aboriginal Community. The self-sufficient community produces organic vegetables, tea tree oil and native artworks. The tours include a guided bush-tucker walk.

## Whale-Watching

Boat tours to watch the humpback whales on their annual migration operate out of Hervey Bay every day, weather permitting, between mid-July and late October. Incredibly, sightings of the mighty cetaceans are guaranteed from August to the end of October (you get a free return trip if the whales don't show). Out of season many boats offer dolphin-spotting tours, with the same free-trip guarantee.

The boats cruise from the Urangan marina out to Platypus Bay and then zip around from pod to pod to find the most active whales. It's not uncommon for inquisitive whales to come right up to the boats, surfacing just a few feet from startled onlookers. Most skippers will also drop a submersible microphone into the water to pick up the haunting song of the whales – it's an awe-inspiring experience.

Most vessels offer two four-hour trips per day, one in the early morning and one in the afternoon, but the whales are just as active in the afternoons as in the mornings. Prices for half-day tours range from $65 to $75, with substantial reductions for children. We can recommend the speedy MV *Seaspray*

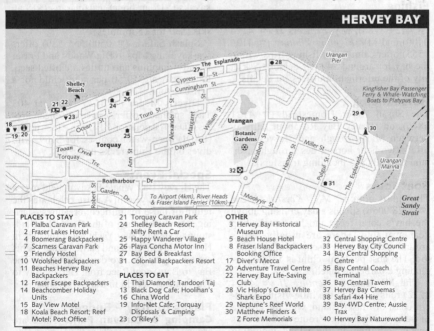

**HERVEY BAY**

| PLACES TO STAY | | |
|---|---|---|
| 1 Pialba Caravan Park | 21 Torquay Caravan Park | OTHER |
| 2 Fraser Lakes Hostel | 24 Shelley Beach Resort; | 3 Hervey Bay Historical |
| 4 Boomerang Backpackers | Nifty Rent a Car | Museum |
| 7 Scarness Caravan Park | 25 Happy Wanderer Village | 5 Beach House Hotel |
| 9 Friendly Hostel | 26 Playa Concha Motor Inn | 8 Fraser Island Backpackers |
| 10 Woolshed Backpackers | 27 Bay Bed & Breakfast | Booking Office |
| 11 Beaches Hervey Bay | 31 Colonial Backpackers Resort | 17 Diver's Mecca |
| Backpackers | | 20 Adventure Travel Centre |
| 12 Fraser Escape Backpackers | PLACES TO EAT | 22 Hervey Bay Life-Saving |
| 14 Beachcomber Holiday | 6 Thai Diamond; Tandoori Taj | Club |
| Units | 13 Black Dog Cafe; Hoolihan's | 28 Vic Hislop's Great White |
| 15 Bay View Motel | 16 China World | Shark Expo |
| 18 Koala Beach Resort; Reef | 19 Info-Net Cafe; Torquay | 29 Neptune's Reef World |
| Motel; Post Office | Disposals & Camping | 30 Matthew Flinders & |
| | 23 O'Riley's | Z Force Memorials |

| | |
|---|---|
| 32 Central Shopping Centre | 37 Hervey Bay Cinemas |
| 33 Hervey Bay City Council | 38 Safari 4x4 Hire |
| 34 Bay Central Shopping | 39 Bay 4WD Centre; Aussie |
| Centre | Trax |
| 35 Bay Central Coach | 40 Hervey Bay Natureworld |
| Terminal | |
| 36 Bay Central Tavern | |

(☎ 4125 3586), the smallest boat here, offering a more intimate experience with the whales.

The larger boats run ¾-day trips, but they take around two hours to reach Platypus Bay. However, the amenities are better, with most boats including a lunch of some kind and all having a licensed bar. The MV *Discovery One* and MV *Islander* (☎ 4125 1700) offer a variety of cruises and have all mod cons. Other well-regarded boats include the MV *Whalesong* (☎ 4125 6222), MV *Mikat* (☎ 4125 1522) and the MV *Spirit of Hervey Bay* (☎ 4125 5131). Fares including lunch are around $75.

Bookings for boats can be made with your accommodation or the information centres. Many vessels are wheelchair accessible – we recommend MV *Whalesong* for its disabled-friendly tours. Take a hat, sunglasses and sunscreen and don't forget your camera – the whales can make spectacular breaches.

### Fishing
Numerous vessels such as the MV *Snapper I* (☎ 4124 3788), MV *Princess II* (☎ 4124 0400) and MV *Fighting Whiting* (☎ 4124 9555) offer calm-water fishing trips within the bay for around $40 per person. Ask at any of the information offices for details.

### Horse Riding
The Susan River Homestead (☎ 4121 6846), on Hervey Bay Rd about halfway between Maryborough and Hervey Bay, offers two-hour horse rides through bushland for $40 ($45 including transfers).

### Boat Tours
The glass-bottom MV *Krystal Klear* (☎ 4128 0066) spends a day cruising above the bay's coral reefs and has snorkelling gear available. There are usually turtles around and quite often schools of dolphins too. The cost per adult/child is $56/38, including a barbecue lunch.

The MV *Tasman Venture II* (☎ 4124 3222) runs across to the little-visited western coast of Fraser Island, with the chance of seeing dolphins en route and various beach activities on the island including

guided snorkelling and walks plus a BBQ lunch. The cost is $60/30 per adult/child.

### Skydiving
Skydive Hervey Bay (☎ 4124 8248) offers tandem skydives over the beach. Rates vary from $219 for 3050m (10,000ft) to $308 for 4270m (14,000ft).

### Scenic Flights
Air Fraser Island (☎ 4125 3600) offers scenic flights over Fraser Island and the Great Barrier Reef for $135. For super-cheap scenic flights, the Sunshine Flying Academy (☎ 4125 2000) charges $25 per person (minimum of three people). All flights leave from Hervey Bay airport.

### Water Sports
There are a couple of places along the waterfront where you can hire water-sports gear. Torquay Jet Ski & Beach Hire (☎ 4125 5528), a beach shed on the foreshore, has kayaks ($15 an hour), catamarans ($18 an hour), windsurfers ($25 an hour) and jet skis ($30 for 15 minutes).

Splash Safaris (☎ 0500 555 580) offers sea-kayaking trips to Big Woody and Fraser Islands; dolphins and turtles are often seen. Rates start at $59/50 per adult/child for a half-day tour.

Diver's Mecca (☎ 4125 1626), at 403 The Esplanade, offers extremely cheap Professional Association of Diving Instructors (PADI) open-water courses for $169, with dives on the shipwrecks in the bay.

### Special Events
The Hervey Bay Whale Festival, held over a fortnight each year in August, celebrates the return of these magnificent creatures, starting with the blessing of the fleet. The Gladstone to Hervey Bay Yacht Race finishes in Hervey Bay in April and participating yachts are on display for two days afterwards. The Bay to Bay Yacht Race from Hervey Bay to Tin Can Bay is held in May every year.

### Places to Stay – Budget
**Camping & Caravan Parks** There are around 27 caravan parks in the Hervey Bay

area. *Pialba Caravan Park* (☎ *4128 1399, fax 4124 3859)*, *Scarness Caravan Park* (☎ *4128 1274, fax 4124 5353)* and *Torquay Caravan Park* (☎/*fax 4125 1578)* are three council-run, tourist parks, along the Esplanade. All offer unpowered/powered sites for $15/18 ($21 powered on the beachfront). It's a good location, but they open onto the beach and security can be a problem.

Most of the private camping grounds are along Truro St in Torquay.

*Happy Wanderer Village* (☎ *4125 1103, fax 4125 3895, 105 Truro St, Torquay)* Unpowered/powered sites $17/20, on-site vans from $29, cabins from $41. This top-notch park has good facilities and a quiet location.

**Hostels** Hervey Bay has a growing number of backpackers hostels, spread between Scarness and Urangan. All do pick-ups from the main bus stop, and most organise trips to Fraser Island as well as booking whale watching tours and other activities. You'll need to pay a deposit for linen and crockery in most of these places.

*Koala Beach Resort* (☎ *4125 3601, fax 4125 3544,* e *koala@whitsunday.net.au, 408 The Esplanade, Torquay)* Beds in 6-bed/3-bed dorm $14/18, beds in 3-bed dorms with bathroom & TV $20. This is the best of the party places, with a central palm-shaded pool, a TV room, and a large bar and restaurant with a terrace overlooking the pool. The rooms aren't quite so hot, but the communal bathrooms are clean and the Fraser Island trips get good reports.

*Reef Motel* (☎ *4125 2744, fax 4125 2998, 410 The Esplanade, Torquay)* Dorm beds $20, doubles & twins $50. Next door to Koala, guests here make use of the TV lounges, kitchen, pool and restaurant at Koala. The rooms are spotless.

*Beaches Hervey Bay Backpackers* (☎ *4124 1322, fax 4124 2727,* e *herveybay@ beaches.com.au, 195 Torquay Terrace, Torquay)* Dorm beds $17, doubles $44. This is another big party place with a very similar set-up to Koala, though it's less appealing. The hostel has a bar and restaurant, self-drive Fraser Island trips and other activities. Again, the rooms could use some attention.

*Fraser Escape* (☎ *1800 646 711, fax 4124 6237, 21 Denman Camp Rd, Torquay)* Dorm beds $12, doubles $35. This new hostel has good facilities and highly regarded self-drive Fraser Island trips with experienced guides. There's a pool, bar and restaurant and campers are welcome to pitch a tent for $5.

*Friendly Hostel* (☎ *4124 4107, fax 4124 4619, 182 Torquay Rd, Scarness)* Dorm beds $17, twins $20 per person. A small, quiet, family-run place, Friendly Hostel is as its name suggests. Accommodation is in units with three bedrooms (two or three beds) that share a TV lounge, kitchen and bathroom.

*Woolshed Backpackers* (☎ *4124 0677, fax 4124 6953, 181 Torquay Rd, Scarness)* Dorm beds $17, doubles & twins $40. Across the road from Friendly Hostel is another friendly, family-run place. Woolshed Backpackers is styled after an Aussie woolshed, and has several cabin-style buildings set in a secluded garden. The facilities are very good and rates include breakfast.

*Colonial Backpackers Resort* (☎ *4125 1844, fax 4125 3161,* e *herveybay@ bigpond.com.au, Cnr Boatharbour Dr & Pulgul St, Urangan)* Beds in 3-bed dorm $18, twins $22.50 per person or $26 (en suite and kitchen). Set in 4.5 hectares of bushland near the marina, this excellent YHA-associate hostel offers accommodation in attractive wood cabins in the bush. Possums and cockatoos are regular visitors. There's a restaurant and bar, tennis courts and one of Queensland's few hostel pools large enough to swim in. This place offers Fraser Island trips and several dollars discount to YHA members.

*Fraser Lakes Hostel* (☎ *4124 5588, fax 4124 7711, 2-4 Charles St, Pialba)* Dorm beds $15, doubles $30, en suite doubles $35. Housed in a beautiful, old Queenslander (formerly the town hospital), this place offers a variety of simple, but good, rooms and a quiet, friendly atmosphere.

## Places to Stay – Mid-Range

Some motels and holiday flats offer fantastic value and can work out much cheaper than a hostel, particularly if you are part of a group. A B&B is a more homey alternative.

*Beachcomber Holiday Units* (☎ 4124 2152, 384 The Esplanade, Torquay) Doubles/triples/quads $40/50/60. This friendly little place offers simple, comfortable, self-contained units that sleep up to four, and is great value for money.

*Bay View Motel* (☎/fax 4128 1134, 399 The Esplanade, Torquay) Singles/doubles $40/45. Close to Beachcomber, this place offers similar facilities, but is a little less homey.

There are some good self-contained units in the $60 to $90 range.

*Playa Concha Motor Inn* (☎ 4125 1544, fax 4125 3413, 475 The Esplanade, Torquay) Motel units $88, self-contained apartments from $110. This is a very comfortable, modern place with good units, a licensed restaurant, a pool and a spa.

*Shelley Beach Resort* (☎ 4125 4533, fax 4125 4878, 466 The Esplanade, Torquay) 1-bedroom/2-bedroom units from $85/105. This well-equipped resort has a pool and tennis courts and sea views from the more expensive units.

*Bay Bed & Breakfast* (☎ 4125 6919, fax 4125 3658, 180 Cypress St, Urangan) Doubles/deluxe/suite $80/90/100. This private house has beautifully well-kept guest rooms, and a pool and deck dining area. All rooms have TV and video player and breakfast is included.

## Places to Eat

The *Colonial*, *Koala*, *Fraser Escape* and *Beaches* hostels have their own cheap restaurants, and in the case of the last at least, nonresidents are welcome to eat there.

*Info-Net Café* (☎ 4125 5011, 417 The Esplanade) Lunch $3-9, dinner $9.50-17. Open 7am-10pm (till 9pm Sun). This friendly little BYO cafe has great, cheap lunches and dinners like quiche, lasagne and steaks, plus a few Internet terminals. The pavement seating is a great spot for breakfast.

*O'Riley's* (☎ 4125 3100, 445 The Esplanade) Dishes $9-22. Open 5pm-9.30pm Mon-Fri, 7.30am-10.30pm Sat & Sun. This is a relaxed BYO pancake, pizza and pasta joint with plenty of main dishes for under $12. There's a delectable range of dessert

pancakes for $5-7 that makes a great weekend breakfast.

*China World* (☎ 4125 1233, 402 The Esplanade) Dishes $9-14. Open 11am-2pm & 5pm-9pm daily. Right in the centre of Torquay, this Chinese place has a great all-you-can-eat deal for $5 at lunch and $11 in the evening. Dishes on the standard menu are also very good.

There are several other Asian places clustered together on The Esplanade in Scarness.

*Thai Diamond* (☎ 4124 4855, 353 The Esplanade) Dishes $13-18. Lunch Tues-Fri, dinner daily. This is a good licensed and BYO Thai restaurant.

*Tandoori Taj* (☎ 4128 2872, 355 The Esplanade) Dishes $12-18. This is a popular Indian restaurant with a good range of vegie and meat curries.

*Black Dog Cafe* (☎ 4124 3177, 381 The Esplanade) Dishes $4.50-13. Open 11.30am-2pm Thur-Sun and 5.30pm-late daily. This upbeat modern Japanese place cooks up treats like yakitori (Japanese satay), teriyaki, sushi and very cheap udon noodle soup, as well as more conventional grills.

## Entertainment

**Bars** Most backpackers rely on the backpackers bars at the *Koala*, *Beaches* and *Fraser Escape* hostels. These bars have loud, loud music and backpacker events and party games; Koala probably has the best atmosphere.

*Hoolihan's* (☎ 4194 0099, 382 The Esplanade, Scarness) This laid-back Irish pub is a quieter choice than the backpackers bars and has big-screen sports.

*Beach House Hotel* (☎ 4128 1233, 344 The Esplanade, Scarness) Probably the nicest spot for a drink is this smart, modern pub and bar that pulls in an older local crowd.

*Bay Central Tavern* (☎ 4124 4111, 115 Boatharbour Dr, Urangan) This old-style pub has live rock bands on Friday and Saturday nights in its Stockman's Bar & Grill.

**Cinemas** For movies, check out *Hervey Bay Cinemas* (☎ 4124 8200, 128 Boatharbour Dr). This big, six-screen cinema is out near the bus station and offers $7 seats on

Going bush at Main Range National Park

Fishing off the coast of Noosa, Sunshine Coast

Parma wallaby

The *Maheno*, wrecked on the coast of Fraser Island by a typhoon in 1935

A cluster of goblet fungi

Volcanic crags of the Glass House Mountains

Colourful cliffs on Fraser Island

Tiny rainforest beauties

Cathedral Beach, Fraser Island

Pandanus palm in Noosa National Park

Tuesday as well as occasional $5 seats for unpopular movies.

## Getting There & Away
**Air** Sunstate has a daily service between Brisbane and Hervey Bay. The one-way fare is $184 (55 minutes). Hervey Bay airport is off Booral Rd, Urangan, on the way to River Heads.

**Bus** Buses depart Bay Central Coach Terminal (☎ 4124 4000) on Boatharbour Dr; hostels run minibuses to meet the coaches. McCafferty's/Greyhound offers the most services on the coastal route, but Premier and Suncoast Pacific are slightly cheaper. It's about 5½ hours from Brisbane (around $41) and about seven from Rockhampton ($69).

Wide Bay Transit (☎ 4121 3719) has nine services between Maryborough and Hervey Bay every weekday, and three on Saturday ($5.25, one hour), but they aren't much use for local transport; most places to stay will pick you up from the bus station.

## Getting Around
**Car** Nifty Rent a Car (☎ 4125 4833) at 463 The Esplanade has small cars from $29 a day (based on several days' hire).

**4WD** Safari 4X4 Hire (☎ 1800 689 819, 4124 4244), at 102 Boatharbour Dr, and Bay 4WD Centre (☎ 1800 687 178, 4128 2981), at 54 Boatharbour Dr, both have good, reliable vehicles costing about $100 a day for a Suzuki Sierra or Jimny up to $150 for a Toyota Landcruiser, based on multiple days. Both companies also hire out camping gear and arrange ferry bookings. Aussie Trax (☎ 1800 062 275, 4124 4433), 56 Boatharbour Dr, Pialba, is the other big player.

All companies require a $500 to $1000 bond, usually in the form of a credit card imprint, that you *will* lose if you drive in salt water – don't even think about running the waves! Most rental agreements involve an excess of $4000, but this can be reduced to $500 for around $25 per day.

You can also hire 4WDs from several places on Fraser Island – see Getting Around in the Fraser Island section for details.

**Bicycle** Rayz Bike Hire (☎ 0417 644 814) dominates the bike-hire business in Hervey Bay. There are various outlets along The Esplanade or Rayz will deliver to your doorstep. Bikes cost $8/12 per half/full day.

## FRASER ISLAND
It is said that all the sand from the eastern coast of Australia eventually ends up at Fraser Island, a gigantic sandbar measuring 120km by 15km, created by thousands of years of longshore drift. Although it's made almost entirely of sand, Fraser Island preserves a remarkable variety of landscapes, from vast, rolling sand dunes, known as sandblows, to dense tropical rainforests and deep, mysterious freshwater lakes. Offshore, whales, dolphins and sharks can often can be seen from high points on the island. Fraser was inscribed on the World Heritage List in 1993 and since 1990 the island has been protected as the Great Sandy National Park.

Fraser Island is one big recreation ground for anyone who loves camping, fishing, walking, off-road driving or simply the exhilaration of the great outdoors. The island boasts nearly 200 freshwater lakes for swimming. That's just as well, as the sea is a definite no-go: There are lethal undertows as well as the odd man-eating shark or 10. Other wildlife is in abundance, including 40 different mammal species and plentiful birds and reptiles. Aggressive dingoes have become a serious problem in recent years. See the 'Deadly Dingoes' boxed text in this chapter.

The island is sparsely populated and, although more than 20,000 vehicles a year pile on to it, it remains wild and rugged. A network of sandy tracks crisscrosses the island and you can drive along great stretches of beach – but it's 4WD only: There are no paved roads. There are several places to stay on Fraser, but most people prefer to get into the outdoor spirit and camp.

Access to Fraser Island is by vehicle ferry from River Heads, about 10km south of Hervey Bay, to Kingfisher Bay or Wanggoolba Creek, or from Inskip Point (near Rainbow Beach) to Hook Point at the southern tip of the island. There is also a Fastcat

# FRASER ISLAND

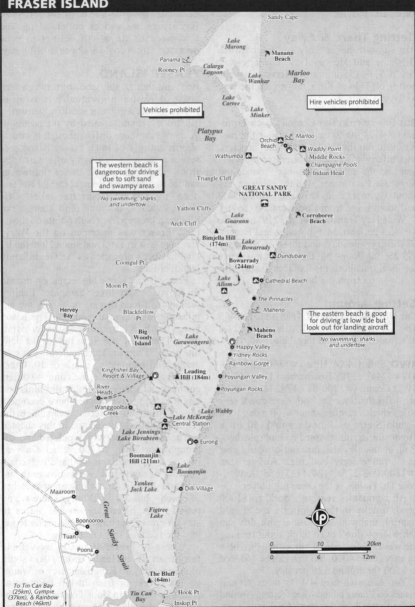

Sandy Cape

Lake Marong

Manann Beach

Panama

Rooney Pt

Calarga Lagoon

Lake Wanhar

Marloo Bay

Lake Carree

Lake Minker

Vehicles prohibited

Hire vehicles prohibited

Platypus Bay

Orchid Beach

Marloo

Waddy Point

Wathumba

Middle Rocks

Champagne Pools

Indian Head

The western beach is dangerous for driving due to soft sand and swampy areas

Triangle Cliff

GREAT SANDY NATIONAL PARK

No swimming: sharks and undertow

Yathon Cliffs

Corroboree Beach

Arch Cliff

Lake Gnarann

Bimjella Hill (174m)

Lake Bowarrady

Coongul Pt

Bowarrady (244m)

Dundubara

Moon Pt

Lake Allom

Cathedral Beach

Eli Creek

The Pinnacles

Hervey Bay

Blackfellow Pt

Maheno

Big Woody Island

Lake Garawongera

Maheno Beach

The eastern beach is good for driving at low tide but look out for landing aircraft

No swimming: sharks and undertow

Happy Valley

Yidney Rocks

Rainbow Gorge

Kingfisher Bay Resort & Village

Leading Hill (184m)

Poyungan Valley

River Heads

Poyungan Rocks

Wanggoolba Creek

Lake Wabby

Lake McKenzie

Central Station

Lake Jennings

Lake Birrabeen

Eurong

Boomanjin Hill (211m)

Lake Boomanjin

Yankee Jack Lake

Dilli Village

Maaroom

Figtree Lake

Boonooroo

Tuan

Great Sandy Strait

Poona

0      10      20km
0      6      12mi

To Tin Can Bay (25km), Gympie (37km), & Rainbow Beach (46km)

Tin Can Bay

Hook Pt

Inskip Pt

The Bluff (64m)

service for pedestrians from Urangan marina in Hervey Bay to Kingfisher Bay.

## History

The island takes its name from Eliza Fraser, wife of the captain of the *Stirling Castle*, which was wrecked on the north-western coast of the island in 1836. The survivors of the wreck began a ragged march south along the coast and would probably have died during their two-month wait for rescue had the Butchulla Aborigines on the island not provided for them until they were rescued.

Fraser Island briefly was a reserve for the Butchulla people, until the land-hungry settlers woke up to the economic value of its timber and shifted the Aborigines to a string of ever-smaller reserves on the mainland.

To the Aborigines, the island was known as K'gari (Paradise) after a spirit who helped the great god Beeral create the earth and other worlds. K'gari loved earth so much she asked Beeral to let her live there and so he changed her into a beautiful island, with trees and animals for company, and limpid lakes for eyes through which she could gaze up at the heavens, her former home.

To the settlers, Fraser Island meant timber, and huge tracts of rainforest were cleared in their search for Fraser Island turpentine (satinay), a rot-resistant wood that was highly prized by ship builders. Logging continued right up until 1991, when the island was taken over by the Queensland Parks and Wildlife Service (QPWS). Native Title to Fraser Island was recognised in 1993 (see the History section in the Facts about Queensland chapter for more information on Native Title).

Sand mining was big business here until local residents formed the Fraser Island Defence Organisation (FIDO) and took that matter all the way to the High Court. The mines were abandoned in 1975, following a High Court injunction.

## Information

There are several ranger stations on the island with information leaflets, tide times, free firewood (one armful per camp) and drinking water:

**Central Station** (☎ 4127 9191) Open 10am to noon.
**Dundubara** (☎ 4127 9138) Open 8am to 9am and 3pm to 4pm.
**Eurong** (☎ 4127 9128) Open 10.30am to 4pm Monday, 7am to 4pm Tuesday to Thursday, 2pm to 4pm Friday to Sunday.
**Waddy Point** (☎ 4127 9190) Open 7am to 8am and 4pm to 4.30pm.

General supplies and expensive fuel are available from stores at Cathedral Beach, Eurong, Kingfisher Bay, Happy Valley and Orchid Beach. Most stores stock some camping and fishing gear, and those at Kingfisher Bay, Eurong and Happy Valley sell alcohol. There are public telephones at these locations and most camping grounds (minimum call charge $0.70).

Walkers can take advantage of the Fraser Island Taxi Service (☎ 4125 5511), which will pick you up from the ferry and drop you

## Deadly Dingoes

The decades-old argument over whether dingoes are dangerous to humans was laid tragically to rest on 30 April 2001, when a nine-year-old Brisbane boy was mauled to death just 75m from his family camp site at Waddy Point. In response to the attack, around 30 of Fraser Island's estimated 160 dingos were culled on the orders of the Queensland government, drawing condemnation from Aboriginal and environmental groups.

Dingoes first came to Australia from Asia around 4000 years ago and are comparatively common on the mainland, but the Fraser population is genetically pure, having never interbred with other dogs. In recent years there have been numerous attacks on humans; most of the blame falls on tourists for feeding the wild dogs and approaching dingoes to take photographs. There is now a minimum fine of $225 for feeding dingoes or leaving food where it may attract dingoes to camping grounds. The Queensland Parks and Wildlife Service provides visitors with a leaflet on being 'dingo smart'. The cardinal rule must be: Keep an eye on your children.

wherever you want to be on the island. There are tow truck services at Eurong (☎ 4127 9188) and Yidney Rocks (☎ 4127 9167).

**Permits** You'll need a permit to take a vehicle onto the island and to camp. The most convenient place to get permits is the QPWS kiosk (☎ 4125 8473) at the River Heads ferry terminal. It opens from 6.30am to 3.30pm. Vehicle permits cost $30, or $40 if you forget and have to buy one from the rangers on the island. You'll need to pay in cash. Camping in any of the national park camping grounds costs $3.85 per person per night. No permit is required for the private camping grounds or resorts.

Permits can also be obtained from the EPA offices in Brisbane, Bundaberg, Gympie, Maryborough and Rainbow Beach.

**Books & Maps** When you get your vehicle permit, you'll receive a Fraser pack with a basic map and leaflets about camping, natural features and walking trails on the island. Hema and other companies produce decent, detailed maps of around 1:130,000 scale that are widely available in Hervey Bay (around $8). The excellent paperback *Fraser Island & Cooloola Visitors Guide* by Ross & Heather Buchanan is the most detailed guide to finding Fraser's hidden gems ($20).

## Organised Tours

While thundering along Fraser's beaches at low tide in your own 4WD is extremely satisfying, a large part of Fraser's allure is the wildlife and wilderness that surround you. Several operators offer one-, two- or three-day tours led by astoundingly well-informed guides. Most tours use comfortable 4WD buses and include buffet lunches and guided walks. Typical stops include the *Maheno* wreck and the Pinnacles, plus a forest walk from Central Station and one or more of Fraser's lakes.

The Kingfisher Bay Resort (☎ 1800 072 555) has superior ranger-guided day tours, including Fastcat transfers from Urangan marina and a buffet lunch at the resort (adult/child $85/45). There are also good two- and three-day tours that include

accommodation at the resort for $198 and $270 per person, based on quad-share (twin share also available for supplement).

Another good operator is the Fraser Island Company (☎ 1800 063 933), formerly Top Tours, with day tours (adult/child $82/49), and two-day (adult/child $170/120) and three-day (adult/child $299/229) trips including meals and accommodation at Happy Valley (bring your own linen). Fraser Venture (☎ 1800 249 122) also offers day trips (adult/child $82/47), and two-day (adult/child $170/115) or three-day ($225/165) trips with accommodation at the Eurong Resort ($280/195 for a three-day trip including Indian Head). Sand Island Safaris (☎ 1800 246 911) has popular three-day tours in its distinctive six-wheel jeeps ($290). Most places will let you split the trip and stay a few days on the island before coming back.

Air Fraser Island (☎ 4125 3600) flies out of Hervey Bay airport and lands on the island's east-coast beach. You can do a day trip for $50 per person (once down you're left to amuse yourself for the day until it's time to fly back) or, for $110 per person, a day's hire of a 4WD is included (permit is extra). Two-day tours with camping gear and 4WD hire cost $190 per person.

For more Fraser Island packages see under Noosa in the Sunshine Coast chapter or under Rainbow Beach in this chapter.

**Backpacker Tours** The cheapest way to experience driving on Fraser Island is one of the self-drive tours organised by the Hervey Bay backpackers hostels. These trips are extremely popular and cost between $125 and $170 per person for a three-day trip, usually with eight people to a jeep. This doesn't include food or fuel, but the vehicles, permits, ferry crossings and camping gear are all organised for you. The payoff is that you have to split the decision making, as well as the cost, eight ways. Koala Beach Resort's tours seem to get consistently good reports, while Fraser Escape offers three-day self-drive tours with an on-hand guide who'll take you to places you wouldn't normally see ($220 per person).

## Around the Island

Starting from the south at Hook Point, where the ferry leaves for Inskip Point on the mainland, the first settlement you reach is **Dilli Village**, the former sand-mining centre. (At the time of research beach access from Hook Point to Dilli Village was proposed for closure. This means that motorists will need to use an old inland mining road, once it's upgraded.) A short drive north brings you to the resort at **Eurong**, with shops, fuel and places to eat. From here, the inland track crosses to Central Station and Wanggoolba Creek (for the ferry to River Heads).

Right in the middle of the island is the ranger centre at **Central Station**, the starting point for numerous walking trails. From here you can walk or drive to the beautiful **McKenzie**, **Jennings**, **Birrabeen** and **Boomanjin** lakes. Most of Fraser Island's lakes are 'perched' lakes, formed by the accumulation of water on top of a thin impermeable layer of decaying leaves and other organic material. Lake McKenzie is spectacularly clear and is ringed by sand beaches making it a great place to swim, but many local people prefer Lake Birrabeen, which sees fewer tour and backpacker groups.

## 4WD Driving Tips

Driving on Fraser Island is 4WD-only for good reason: Even experienced drivers can get into trouble on some of the tracks, and driving on sand requires a good deal of care, to protect not only yourself but also the fragile environment. When planning your trip reckon on covering roughly 20km an hour on the inland tracks and 50km an hour on the eastern beach. Some pointers for safe 4WD driving are:

- Speed kills, and nowhere more so than when driving on sand. Keep to less than 35km per hour inland and well below 80km per hour on the beach.
- Washouts are steep-sided channels in the sand caused by freshwater run-off and can be very hard to spot. Hit one at speed and your 4WD may roll end over end. Drive slowly and cross washouts where they are shallowest.
- 4WD should be engaged at all times, except on the tarmac roads in Kingfisher Bay and Eurong. Remember to lock your front wheels and reduce your tire pressure for driving on sand.
- Away from the beach, you must stick to designated tracks. Most are two-way and there are frequent passing areas. Vehicles coming uphill and anything larger than you should generally be given right of way.
- Do NOT drive in salt water. In a hire car you will automatically lose your deposit (and they *can* tell if you've ignored this advice!). Salt water will damage your car's electrical system, cause corrosion and the water can wash the sand from under the wheels.
- The eastern beach track detours inland around the Yidney and Poyungan Rocks. Do as the locals do and follow these detours – plenty of 4WDs have been lost trying to nip between the rocks and the waves.
- Do NOT drive on the western beach. The sand is treacherous and has swamps and holes. Many vehicles have vanished completely under the rising tide here.
- Make sure you know the tide times. Generally you can drive on the eastern beach two hours either side of low tide.
- Use your indicators to show oncoming vehicles which side you intend passing on, and beware of aircraft landing on the beach at Eurong, Eli Creek and Cathedral Beach.
- If you do get bogged, make your vehicle as light as possible and try to reverse out. If this doesn't immediately work, stop and engage low-gear 4WD, then try again. If you really can't get out of a bog, stop before you dig yourself in any deeper and signal for help – most passing drivers will stop to lend a hand.

MW

About 4km north of Eurong along the beach is a signposted walking trail to the beautiful **Lake Wabby**, the most accessible of Fraser's lakes. An easier route is from the lookout on the inland track. Lake Wabby is surrounded on three sides by eucalypt forest, while the fourth side is a massive sandblow that is encroaching on the lake at a rate of about 3m a year. The lake is deceptively shallow and diving is not recommended – in the past people have been left paralysed after diving into Lake Wabby. There are often turtles and huge catfish in the eastern corner of the lake under the trees.

As you drive up the beach you'll have to detour inland to avoid Poyungan and Yidney Rocks before you reach **Happy Valley**, with more places to stay and a shop and bistro. About 10km north is **Eli Creek**, the largest stream on the eastern coast and a nice spot for splashing around. About 2km from Eli Creek is the rotting hulk of the *Maheno*, a former passenger liner that was blown ashore by a typhoon in 1935 as it was being towed to a Japanese scrap-yard.

Roughly 5km north of the *Maheno* you'll find the **Pinnacles** – an eroded section of coloured sand cliffs – and, about 10km beyond, **Dundubara**, with a ranger station and a very good camping ground. Then there's a 20km stretch of beach before you come to the rock outcrop of **Indian Head**, the best vantage point on the island. Sharks, manta rays, dolphins and, during the migration season, whales, can often be seen from the top of the headland.

Between Indian Head and Waddy Point the trail branches inland, passing **Champagne Pools**, which offer the only safe saltwater swimming on the island. There are good camping areas at **Waddy Point** and **Orchid Beach**, the last settlement on the island.

Hire vehicles are prohibited from the final 30km of beach to **Sandy Cape**, the northern tip, with its lighthouse.

## Places to Stay & Eat

Come well equipped since supplies on the island are limited and only available in a few places. And be prepared for mosquitoes and March flies.

**Camping** The QPWS operates camping grounds with coin-operated showers, toilets and barbecues at Waddy Point, Dundubara, Lake Allom, Lake McKenzie, Central Station, Lake Boomanjin, and Wathumba on the western coast, plus a few remote sites accessible by boat or on foot. You can also camp on designated stretches of the eastern beach. To camp in any of these public areas you need a permit.

*Cathedral Beach Resort & Camping Park* (☎ 4127 9177, fax 4127 9234, *Cathedral Beach*) Sites $20, double/quad cabins $50/75. This privately run park prefers families to backpackers. It's about 34km north of Eurong.

*Dilli Village Recreation Camp* (☎ 4127 9130, *Dilli Village*) Sites $5.50 per person, rooms with shared bathroom $16.50, self-contained units $55 (up to 4 people). This privately run camping ground has good facilities and discourages backpacker groups.

**Other Accommodation** The main settlement on the eastern coast is *Eurong Beach Resort* (☎ 4127 9122, fax 4127 9178, e eurong@fraser-is.com) Beds in 4-bunk cabin $17, cottages $100 for 4 ($6 per extra person, sleeps 8), double motel units from $88, 2-bedroom apartments $210 for 4 ($6 per extra person, sleeps 6). This well-equipped resort has everything from budget cabins to top-notch apartments, along with a good *restaurant* (lunch buffet $12, grills from $15), a bar and a well-stocked shop.

*Fraser Island Beachhouses* (☎ 4127 9205, fax 4127 9207, *Eurong Second Valley*) Double studios $165, 2-bedroom apartments (good for 4) $238. This complex of plush modern units is right by the beach just south of the Eurong resort.

*Fraser Island Retreat Happy Valley Resort* (☎ 4127 9144, fax 4127 9131, e retreat@fraserislandco.com.au, *Happy Valley*) Doubles/triples/quads $150/175/190. The resort has good, self-contained timber lodges, a bar, a popular *bistro* and a shop. Room rates drop to $135 in the low season.

*Sailfish on Fraser* (☎ 4127 9494, fax 4127 9499, *Happy Valley*) Self-contained apartments from $135. This plush and modern complex offers spotless apartments with all mod cons right by the beach at Happy Valley.

***Kingfisher Bay Resort*** *(☎ 1800 072 555, fax 4120 3326, Kingfisher Bay)* Hotel rooms from $119 per person, 2-bedroom villas from $200. This impressive and luxurious resort on the western coast offers accommodation in a variety of upmarket wooden cabins. There are ***restaurants***, bars and shops and a variety of tours on offer, plus a day-trippers' section near the jetty, with the ***Sandbar*** bar and brasserie.

## Getting There & Away

**Air** Air Fraser Island (☎ 4125 3600) charges $50 for a return flight (20 minutes each way) to the island's east-coast beach, departing Hervey Bay airport.

**Boat** Several large vehicle ferries (known locally as barges) connect Fraser Island to the mainland. Most visitors use the two services that leave from River Heads.

The *Fraser Venture* (☎ 4125 4444) makes the 30-minute crossing from River Heads to Wanggoolba Creek on the western coast of Fraser Island. It departs daily from River Heads at 9am, 10.15am and 3.30pm, and returns from the island at 9.30am, 2.30pm and 4pm. On Saturday there is also a 7am service from River Heads that returns at 7.30am from the island. The return fare for vehicle and driver is $82, plus $5.50 for each extra passenger. Walk-on passengers pay $16.50 return.

The Kingfisher Bay Resort (☎ 1800 072 555) also operates two boats. The *Fraser II* does the 45-minute crossing from River Heads to Kingfisher Bay daily. Departures from River Heads are at 7.15am, 11am and 2.30pm, and from the island at 8.30am, 1.30pm and 4pm. The return fare is $82 for a vehicle and driver, plus $5.50 for extras. The *Kingfisher 3* is a Fastcat that crosses from the Urangan marina to Kingfisher Bay every few hours from 8.30am to 10.30pm (adult/child $35/17, 45 minutes).

Coming from Rainbow Beach, the *Rainbow Venture* (white barge) and the *Eliza Fraser II* (orange barge) make the 15-minute crossing from Inskip Point (near Rainbow Beach) to Hook Point on Fraser Island regularly from about 7am to 5.30pm daily. The price is $25 return for a vehicle and passengers, and you can get tickets on board the ferry. Walk-on passengers pay $5. Call ☎ 5486 3120 for reservations.

There's also a service from the Urangan marina in Hervey Bay to Moon Point on Fraser Island, but it isn't a particularly convenient place to land and car-hire companies won't let you use this ferry as it involves a beach landing.

## Getting Around

If you have the money, you'll have more space and more freedom if you go it alone and hire your own 4WD. Hostels will try to steer you away from doing this, but it can work out as quite a cheap option if you get a group together yourself. Camping gear and 4WDs can be hired in Hervey Bay, permits are readily available and you have a choice of catching a ferry or flying to the island (see Getting There & Away earlier in this section).

You can also hire 4WDs on the island through Kingfisher Bay 4WD Hire (☎ 4120 3366), with Landrover Defenders from $195 a day, and Eurong Beach Resort (☎ 4127 9122), with Landcruisers from $165.

## CHILDERS
**postcode 4660 • pop 3400**

Until recently, this historic township was best known for its pretty heritage buildings and fruit-picking work, but the town has been marked indelibly by the devastating fire at the Palace Backpackers Hostel, in which 15 backpackers died (see the 'Childers Tragedy' boxed text in this chapter).

The main street in Childers is classified as a heritage area and is worth a look if you're passing through town. In late July, Childers holds a large Multicultural Festival, with music and food celebrating the region's diverse cultural mix.

## Information

For tourist information, visit the tourist office at the Childers Pharmaceutical Museum & Art Gallery (see under Things to See & Do). The Childers Discount Printshop (☎ 4126

1555) at 56 Churchill St offers Internet access for \$4.40 per hour.

## Things to See & Do

At the **Childers Pharmaceutical Museum & Art Gallery** (*☎ 4126 1994, 90 Churchill St; admission free; open 8.30am-4.30pm Mon-Fri, 8.30am-noon Sat*) all of the old bottles, instruments, potions and prescription books that were used by the town's first pharmacist are on display in their original cedar cabinets. There is also a small gallery upstairs. The museum doubles as the Childers tourist information office.

Other interesting old buildings along Churchill St include the **Federal Hotel**, on the corner of North St, and the historic, wooden **National Bank**, built in 1895 for one of its rivals, the Bank of North Queensland. Also here is the shell of the Palace hostel.

## Places to Stay

North of the centre on the Bruce Hwy is *Sugarbowl Caravan Park* (*☎/fax 4126*

### Childers Tragedy

The historic Palace Backpackers Hostel in Childers was the scene of Australia's worst-ever tourist disaster on 23 June 2000, when 15 backpackers were killed in a devastating fire. At the time of writing, a local man was on trial for arson and murder, but his case was being appealed through the High Court and the trial date adjourned pending the outcome. The hostel owners faced legal action over non-functioning smoke alarms and blocked fire escapes. In the aftermath of the fire, backpackers hostels across Australia have been forced to adopt stringent new antifire measures. The frontage of the Palace miraculously survived the blaze, and the Childers council plans to redevelop the site to incorporate a new hostel at the rear, and an art gallery, visitor information service and open courtyard plaza, which will include remnants of the old building. A monument dedicated to those who lost their lives is hoped to be unveiled on 23 June 2002, the second anniversary of the fire.

*1521, Churchill St)* Sites \$15.50, double cabins from \$44, workers bunkhouse \$90 per week. This park mainly caters to backpackers and fruit-pickers. The owners can help you find work and provide transport to the farms, but farm owners generally demand long hours from their workers. Pickers must leave a \$30 bond.

*Federal Hotel* (*☎ 4126 1438, fax 4126 2407, 71 Churchill St)* Dorm beds nightly/weekly \$16.50/88.50. This pub has basic but OK rooms and friendly owners who can arrange transport to work.

*Motel Childers* (*☎ 4126 1177, fax 4126 2266, 136 Churchill St)* Singles/doubles \$56/64. This motel is rather plain, but it's centrally located at the northern end of the main street.

## Places to Eat

*Federal Hotel* (*☎ 4126 1438, fax 4126 2407, 71 Churchill St)* Dishes \$4-5.50. This relaxed and friendly old pub has a good bistro with a cheap pub-grub menu.

*Tropicana Cafe* (*☎ 4126 1871, 102 Churchill St)* Snack meals \$3-7. This is probably the best of the takeaways on the main road.

*Laurel Tree Cottage* (*☎ 4126 2911, 89 Churchill St)* Dishes \$8.50-11. Open 9am-4pm. At the northern end of town, this boutique cafe offers a wide selection of open sandwiches and other light meals.

## Getting There & Away

Childers is on the main bus run up the Bruce Hwy; long-distance buses stop at the Shell service station just north of the town centre.

## BURRUM COAST NATIONAL PARK

The attractive Burrum Coast National Park covers two sections of coastline, on either side of the little holiday community of Woodgate, 37km east of Childers. The Woodgate section of the park begins at the southern end of the Esplanade, and has nice beaches, good fishing and a *camping ground*, reached by a 4WD-only track (usual QWPS camping rates apply). Several walking tracks start at the camping ground or Acacia St in Woodgate. There are more isolated *bush camping* areas in the Kinkuna section of the park, a few kilometres north of Woodgate, but you'll need a 4WD to reach them. Contact the rangers at the park (☎ 4126 8810) to book camping permits.

## Places to Stay & Eat

*Barkala Caravan Park (☎ 4126 8802, fax 4126 8699, 88 The Esplanade)* Unpowered/powered sites $15.50/16.50, self-contained cabins $33-55. This well-run park is just a short walk to the national park.

*Beach Hotel-Motel (☎ 4126 8988, fax 4126 8793, 195 The Esplanade)* Doubles $55/77 (low/high season). At the northern end of the Esplanade, this modern brick pub has a block of reasonable motel units just across from the beach. It offers *pub meals*.

## BUNDABERG
postcode 4670 • pop 42,840

A small, pretty and prosperous town, Bundaberg lies on the Burnett River at the northern end of Hervey Bay, about 50km east of the Bruce Hwy. 'Bundy', as it's popularly known, attracts large numbers of working backpackers who come here to pick fruit and vegetables on the surrounding farms and orchards. Among Australians, the town is best known as the home of the wildly popular Bundaberg rum – you'll see the Bundy rum polar bear on billboards all over town.

Historically, Bundaberg's fortunes have been tied to sugar cane, and much of the local product still ends up at the Bundaberg Rum Distillery, which offers daily tours and is probably the town's biggest tourist attraction. Growing numbers of people are also using Bundaberg as a jumping-off point for Lady Elliot and Lady Musgrave Islands, at the southern tip of the Great Barrier Reef. The Mon Repos turtle rookery, 15km northeast of town, is another drawcard.

Most of the fruit-picking work in Bundaberg is arranged through the backpackers hostels in town, all of which offer cheap weekly rates, work placements and rides to and from the farms. There is usually something being harvested year round, but the peak harvest season runs from March to August. It's worth calling ahead to make sure there *is* work.

## Information

The main Bundaberg tourist information centre (☎ 1800 060 499, 4152 2333), at 271 Bourbong St, is open 9am to 5pm. It's on the highway at the southern end of town, but there is a more convenient City Council Visitors Centre (☎ 4153 9289) in the council offices at 186 Bourbong St. It opens 8.30am to 4.45pm Monday to Friday and 10am to 1pm Saturday and Sunday.

The EPA office (QPWS; ☎ 4131 1600), at 46 Quay St, is open from 9am to 5pm Monday to Friday for Fraser Island permits.

The post office is the grand building with the clock tower on the corner of Bourbong and Barolin Sts. The Bundaberg Email Centre, at 200 Bourbong St, charges $5 an hour for Internet use.

**Dangers & Annoyances** Car theft is a growing problem in Bundaberg and backpackers' vehicles are popular targets. Park in a well-lit area and don't leave valuables in your car.

## Things to See

There are numerous interesting old buildings in town, including the ornate **Union Bank building** on Targo St, and the lovely **School of Arts Building** on Bourbong St. Pick up a copy of *A Walking Tour of the Bundaberg City Centre* from the City Council Visitors Centre.

Aficionados of Bundy rum can tour the **Bundaberg Rum Distillery** *(☎ 4150 8684, Avenue St; adult/under-18 $5.50/2.20; tours hourly from 10am-3pm Mon-Fri & 10am-2pm Sat & Sun)*, about 2km east of the town centre. The tour includes a video on the distilling process and a visit to the fermentation house, distillery, bottling plant and store, winding up at Spring Hill House, where over-18s can try a free sample of the product. Call ahead to make a booking.

Bundaberg's attractive **Botanic Gardens** are 2km north of the centre on Gin Gin Rd. Within the reserve are rose gardens, walking paths and three good museums. The **Hinkler**

FRASER COAST

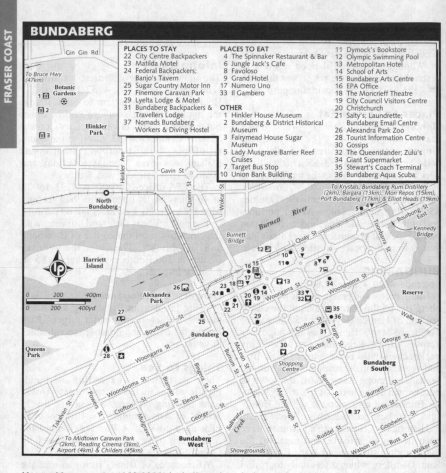

## BUNDABERG

**PLACES TO STAY**
22 City Centre Backpackers
23 Matilda Motel
24 Federal Backpackers;
   Banjo's Tavern
25 Sugar Country Motor Inn
27 Finemore Caravan Park
29 Lyelta Lodge & Motel
31 Bundaberg Backpackers &
   Travellers Lodge
37 Nomads Bundaberg
   Workers & Diving Hostel

**PLACES TO EAT**
4 The Spinnaker Restaurant & Bar
6 Jungle Jack's Cafe
8 Favoloso
9 Grand Hotel
17 Numero Uno
33 Il Gambero

**OTHER**
1 Hinkler House Museum
2 Bundaberg & District Historical
   Museum
3 Fairymead House Sugar
   Museum
5 Lady Musgrave Barrier Reef
   Cruises
7 Target Bus Stop
10 Union Bank Building

11 Dymock's Bookstore
12 Olympic Swimming Pool
13 Metropolitan Hotel
14 School of Arts
15 Bundaberg Arts Centre
16 EPA Office
18 The Moncrieff Theatre
19 City Council Visitors Centre
20 Christchurch
21 Salty's; Laundrette;
   Bundaberg Email Centre
26 Alexandra Park Zoo
28 Tourist Information Centre
30 Gossips
32 The Queenslander; Zulu's
34 Giant Supermarket
35 Stewart's Coach Terminal
36 Bundaberg Aqua Scuba

**House Museum** (☎ *4152 0222*) is dedicated to the life and times of Bundaberg's most famous son, the aviator Bert Hinkler, who made the first solo flight between England and Australia in 1928. The museum is housed in Hinkler's former home, which was shipped over from England.

Nearby is the **Bundaberg & District Historical Museum** (☎ *4152 0101*), with displays of machinery from the local farming and distilling industries.

At the southern end of the park, the **Fairymead House Sugar Museum** (☎ *4153 6786*) has good displays about the sugar industry, including some frank displays on the hardships endured by Kanaka workers in the cane fields. All the museums are open from 10am to 4pm and charge $3/1 for adults/children.

The **Bundaberg Arts Centre** (☎ *4152 3700, 1 Barolin St; admission free; 10am-5pm Tues-Fri, 11am-3pm Sat & Sun*) is a friendly art gallery with changing exhibits of local and national art.

## Island Trips & Tours
Lady Musgrave Barrier Reef Cruises (☎1800 072 110, 4159 4519) offers day trips

to Lady Musgrave Island from Port Bundaberg, 17km north-east of the centre. Cruises leave from Monday to Thursday and on Saturday at 8.30am and cost $130 (children $65), plus another $9 for the return bus trip. The price includes lunch, snorkelling gear and rides in a semi-submersible, glass-bottomed boat. Scuba dives for certified divers are an extra $58.

You can also fly to Lady Elliot Island with Lady Elliot Island Resort (☎ 1800 072 200). Day-trippers pay $219 (children $110) for a deluxe trip that includes the return flight, lunch, snorkelling gear and a guided reef walk.

See the Lady Elliot and Lady Musgrave Island sections in the Capricorn Coast chapter for information about longer stays on the islands. All reef trips incur a $4 environmental management charge.

Bundaberg Coach Tours (☎ 4153 1037) offers a variety of tours to local sights, including a day trip to Town of 1770, with sand-boarding and an amphibious-vehicle ride (adult/child $95/70).

## Whale-Watching
From mid-August to mid-October, Lady Musgrave Barrier Reef Cruises (☎1800 072 110, 4159 4519) runs whale-watching trips from Port Bundaberg. Cruises leave at 9.15am, returning at 3.30pm, and cost $83 (children $42) including lunch, plus $9 for coach transfers. See the Hervey Bay section in this chapter for more details on whale-watching.

## Diving
Salty's (☎ 4151 6422), 208 Bourbong St, and Bundaberg Aqua Scuba (☎ 4153 5761), 66 Targo St next to the bus station, both offer extremely cheap, four-day, PADI open-water diving courses for around $164, but this only includes shore dives.

Salty's offers a three-day, three-night diving package to Lady Musgrave and other islands on the Great Barrier Reef for $495.

## Special Events
Bundy's major festivals include the Country Music Festival at Easter; Bundy in

Bloom, a spring floral festival held in the second week of September; and a week-long Arts Festival each October.

## Places to Stay – Budget
**Caravan Parks** If you're seeking peace and quiet, try one of the town's caravan parks.

*Finemore Caravan Park* (☎ 4151 3663, fax 4151 6399, Quay St) Unpowered/powered sites $10/14, powered permanent tents $16, cabins from $42. Finemore is a tidy riverfront park in a quiet location at the western end of Quay St.

*Midtown Caravan Park* (☎ 4152 2768, fax 4151 2075, 61 Takalvan St) Unpowered/powered sites $11/16, cabins from $33, self-contained villas from $50. This is a good park about 2km south-west of the post office, with a pool, shop and campers kitchen.

**Hostels** All the hostels mentioned here specialise in finding harvesting work for travellers and offer transfers to and from the local farms.

*Bundaberg Backpackers & Travellers Lodge* (☎ 4152 2080, fax 4151 3355, Cnr Targo & Crofton Sts) Beds in 4-bed dorm nightly/weekly $19/120. Diagonally opposite the bus terminal, this is a clean and modern workers hostel with a friendly atmosphere.

*City Centre Backpackers* (☎ 4153 3501, fax 4153 5756, ℮ ccbackpackers@interworx .com.au, 216 Bourbong St) Dorm bunk beds nightly/weekly $17/110, doubles & en suite dorm beds nightly/weekly $19/116. This well-set-up establishment is in the former Grosvenor Hotel and has good facilities and a friendly, industrious atmosphere.

*Federal Backpackers* (☎ 4153 3711, fax 4151 0266, ℮ federalbackpackers@bigpond .com, 221 Bourbong St) Dorm beds nightly/weekly $17/110, doubles & twins nightly/weekly $18/115 per person. Housed in the former Federal pub, Federal Backpackers has improved a lot in recent years. The old building has lots of character and isn't a bad base for farm work in the area.

*Nomads Bundaberg Workers & Diving Hostel* (☎ 4151 6097, fax 4151 7277, 64 Barolin St) Dorm beds $17, doubles nightly/weekly $19/107 per person. A friendly hostel in a converted Queenslander, Nomads has motel units out the back and OK facilities including a pool.

## Places to Stay – Mid-Range

*Lyelta Lodge & Motel* (☎ *4151 3344, 8 Maryborough St*) Singles/doubles with shared bathrooms $28/36, with en suite $35/40. This basic motel seems to have changed little since the 1950s, but the owners are friendly and the price is definitely right.

*Matilda Motel* (☎ *4151 4717, fax 4153 1455, 209 Bourbong St*) Doubles $66. This modern and well-equipped motel has a central location and very good facilities.

*Sugar Country Motor Inn* (☎ *4153 1166, fax 4153 1726, 220 Bourbong St*) Singles/doubles $82/92. One of the better motels on the highway towards Childers, this place is central and has a licensed restaurant and a pool.

## Places to Eat

For good budget grub head to Bundy's pub bistros. All the bistros are open from around noon to 2pm and 6pm to 8pm daily.

*Grand Hotel* (☎ *4151 2441, 81 Bourbong St*) Dishes $9-17. This bright and popular bistro has great steaks and plenty of pavement seating. It's also open for breakfast from 8am daily.

*Zulu's* (☎ *4152 4691, 51-69 Targo St*) Lunch from $5.50, dinner $9-18. For pub favourites in a tropical garden, head to this bistro located at the Queenslander pub.

*Jungle Jack's Cafe* (☎ *4152 8513, 56 Bourbong St*) Lunch $4.50-6.50. Open 7am-5pm Mon-Fri, 7am-2pm Sat. Just east of the junction with Tanotitha St, Jungle Jack's is an above-average canteen-type place with lots of cheap lunch dishes like pasta, fish and chips, and roasts.

*Numero Uno* (☎ *4151 3666, 163 Bourbong St*) Dishes $10-17. Open for lunch & dinner daily. A popular licensed Italian bistro with good pastas for under $12 and pizzas for under $10. Lunchtime pasta specials start at $5.

*Il Gambero* (☎ *4152 5342, 57 Targo St*) Lunch $6-13, dinner $6-20. Open lunch Tues-Fri, dinner Tues-Sun. This friendly and cheap Italian place has a strangely comforting decor straight out of the 1970s and a huge menu of pastas and pizzas, plus random lunch specials like sushi, and beef stroganoff for $6.

*Favoloso* (☎ *4151 0033, 54 Bourbong St*) Lunch $5-7, dinner $9-15. Open lunch Mon-Sat, dinner Thur-Sat. Locals congregate at this bright little Italian cafe for pasta, focaccias and substantial salads.

*The Spinnaker Restaurant & Bar* (☎ *4152 8033, 1A Quay St*) Dishes $17-30. Open 11.30am-2pm Mon-Fri, 5.30pm-late Mon-Sat. This place serves upmarket seafood dishes and grills from a familiar Aussie menu and has a great setting overlooking the river.

## Entertainment

**Bars & Nightclubs** Bundaberg has its share of pubs and discos.

*Banjo's Tavern* (☎ *4151 6010, 221 Bourbong St*) This plain yet popular pub, below the Federal hostel, pulls in a large crowd of backpackers.

*The Queenslander* (☎ *4152 4691, 51-69 Targo St*) One of the nicest places to drink is this upbeat pub with a funky tropical garden. It's *extremely* popular with locals and there are live bands on Thursday, Friday and Saturday nights.

*Metropolitan Hotel* (☎ *4151 3154, 166 Bourbong St*) This surprisingly friendly biker's bar has live bands and specials several nights a week.

*Krystals* (☎ *4152 6388, 58 Princess St*) This popular techno club on the eastern side of town at the East End Tavern attracts plenty of workers on their nights off.

*Gossips* (☎ *4153 4664, 17 Electra St*) An older, upmarket crowd pulls in at this disco at weekends.

**Cinemas & Theatre** Catch a film at *The Moncrieff Theatre* (☎ *4153 1985, 177 Bourbong St*), a grand, old, one-screen cinema showing several films daily for $5.50. It doubles as a theatre and music venue.

There's also *Reading Cinema* (☎ *4152 1233, Takalvan St*), a big, modern complex on the way to the airport that screens big, modern blockbusters.

## Getting There & Away

**Air** Bundaberg's Hinkler Airport is about 4km south-west of the centre on Takalvan St.

Sunstate flies to Bundaberg daily from Brisbane ($236, one hour), Gladstone ($134, 35 minutes), Rockhampton ($250, 50 minutes), Mackay ($375, two hours) and Townsville ($470, 3½ hours).

**Bus** McCafferty's/Greyhound and Premier offer daily services from Brisbane to Bundaberg and north to Cairns, stopping at all major centres. One-way bus fares from Bundaberg include Brisbane ($55, seven hours), Hervey Bay ($25, 1½ hours), Rockhampton ($54, four hours) and Gladstone ($43, 2½ hours). The main stop is Stewart's Coach Terminal (☎ 4153 2646) at 66 Targo St.

Local bus services are handled by Duffy's Coaches (☎ 4151 4226). It has four services every weekday to Bargara (Route 4, 35 minutes) and Port Bundaberg (Route 5, 35 minutes); buses depart from the Target bus stop on Woongarra St (in front of the Target superstore).

**Train** Bundaberg is a stop on the main line between Brisbane and Rockhampton or Cairns. There are daily trains heading both north and south. The one-way fare to Brisbane (5½ hours) is $52 for an economy seat or $119 in business class.

## AROUND BUNDABERG

There are several beaches around Bundaberg but most are fairly ordinary. The sandy strips at **Moore Park**, 20km north of Bundaberg, **Bargara**, 13km east, and **Elliot Heads**, 19km south-east, are popular with families. Local buses run to all these places from the Target bus stop in Bundaberg.

Australia's most accessible mainland turtle rookery is at **Mon Repos**, a lovely curving beach 15km north-east of Bundaberg. Every year between November and February, large numbers of loggerheads and other marine turtles drag themselves up the beach to lay their eggs. The young emerge and make their way to the sea from mid-January to March.

During the laying and hatching seasons, access to the beach is controlled by staff from the EPA information centre (☎ 4159 1652), who allow visitors to see the turtles in action between 7pm and midnight for a fee of $5/2.50 per adult/child. The centre is open 7.30am to 4pm Monday to Friday plus 7pm to 6am nightly in season.

*Turtle Sands Caravan Park (☎ 4159 2340, fax 4159 2737, Mon Repos Beach)* Powered & unpowered sites from $16.50, on-site vans from $27.50, cabins from $41. This pretty park has good facilities and a great location right on the beachfront.

# Capricorn Coast

This central coastal area of Queensland takes its name from its position straddling the tropic of Capricorn. Rockhampton is the area's major centre, and just off the coast lies the popular Great Keppel Island and the other Keppel Bay islands.

South of Rockhampton is Gladstone, one of Queensland's major industrial and shipping centres. Offshore from Gladstone is the Capricornia Marine Park and the southern Reef Islands, the southernmost part of the Great Barrier Reef. Lady Elliot and Heron islands both have resorts popular with divers, and you can take day trips to and camp on Lady Musgrave Island and several others.

On the coast south of Gladstone are the laid-back holiday towns of 1770 and Agnes Water, the focus of a small stretch of coastline known as the Discovery Coast.

Inland, the Capricorn hinterland has the fascinating Gemfields region and the spectacular Carnarvon and Blackdown Tableland National Parks, both of which are well worth a visit.

## Geography

The tropic of Capricorn passes through the centre of this region, just south of Rockhampton and just north of Emerald. The Capricorn hinterland is dominated by the broad, flattened plateaus of the Great Dividing Range, with numerous spectacular outcrops of sandstone escarpments, most notably around the Carnarvon and Blackdown Tableland National Parks.

This Central Highlands region is one of Queensland's richest natural resources; the fertile soils support major pastoral and agricultural industries, and the area's vast coal deposits supply the majority of the state's coal exports. Between the mountains and the coast are the flatter coastal plains.

## Activities

The southern Barrier Reef Islands offer some of the best diving and snorkelling on the entire Great Barrier Reef. The Gemfields

region in the Capricorn hinterland is the best area in Queensland to go fossicking for gemstones, particularly sapphires. For bushwalkers, the Carnarvon and Blackdown Tableland National Parks offer a wide range of walking trails and climbs.

## Getting There & Around

**Air** Rockhampton and Gladstone both have major regional airports. Sunstate (☎ 13 13 13) has flights linking Brisbane with Emerald.

**Bus** The major bus line, McCafferty's/Greyhound, has frequent services up and down the Bruce Hwy and from Rockhampton inland to Emerald, Longreach and Mt Isa. It also has a daily inland run from Rockhampton to Brisbane via Mt Morgan and Miles.

Premier Motor Service (☎ 13 34 10) operates a Brisbane to Cairns service, stopping at Miriam Vale, Gladstone and Rockhampton.

**Train** The major coastal railway line follows the Bruce Hwy. Twice weekly, the *Spirit of the Outback* train services the inland from Rockhampton to Longreach.

**Car & Motorcycle** The Bruce Hwy runs all the way up the Capricorn Coast, although it goes a long way inland and only touches the coast briefly at Clairview. The major inland route is the Capricorn Hwy, which takes you west from Rockhampton through Emerald and the Gemfields. From Gladstone, the Dawson Hwy takes you west towards the Carnarvon National Park and the town of Springsure.

The Burnett Hwy, which starts at Rockhampton and heads south through the old gold-mining town of Mt Morgan, is an interesting and popular alternative route to Brisbane – see the Darling Downs chapter for details of the Burnett Hwy south of Biloela.

CAPRICORN COAST

# Gladstone Area

## MIRIAM VALE

Miriam Vale, 70km south of Gladstone, is a tiny cluster of buildings either side of the Bruce Hwy. Nevertheless, it's the administration centre of the surrounding shire, and the main turn-off point for the coastal towns of Agnes Water and Town of 1770.

The Discovery Coast Information Centre (☎ 4974 5428) is on the Bruce Hwy, across the road from the Shell roadhouse.

*Miriam Vale Motel (☎ 4974 5233, fax 4974 5134, Bruce Hwy)* has singles/doubles for $44/55 and budget rooms for $33/44. The rooms here are slightly dated (and the walls thin), but it's affordable and clean.

A 100m walk away at the roadhouse, *The Big Crab (☎ 4974 5224, Dougall St)* has pretty good steak and seafood.

There is also a *pub* and a straightforward *caravan park* in town.

## AGNES WATER & TOWN OF 1770

postcode 4677 • pop 2000

The coastal towns of Agnes Water and Town of 1770 are among the state's less commercialised seaside destinations, but the world is awakening to their charms. Development is booming in Agnes Water, with shopping complexes and housing estates sprouting seemingly around every corner. Despite that, it's managing to retain its small-town allure, and its pretty surf beach is a major drawcard. Things are less hectic in the beautiful and tranquil Town of 1770, where the surrounding Sir Joseph Banks Conservation Park keeps development at bay. Most people come here for fishing, boating or visiting the neighbouring national parks; at the very least, ensure you catch the stunning sunset over the harbour. Things get a little hectic at Christmas and Easter, so book ahead to secure accommodation.

The Town of 1770, on a narrow and hilly peninsula on the eastern side of the estuary of Round Hill Creek, was named in 1970 in honour of Captain Cook's landing here on Bustard Beach on 24 May 1770 – the second place he landed in Australia, and the first in Queensland.

## Information

The Discovery Centre (☎ 4974 7002), Shop 12, Endeavour Plaza, on the corner of Round Hill Rd and Captain Cook Dr in Agnes Water, is open from 9am to 5pm daily. It's a helpful, privately run information centre.

Queensland Parks and Wildlife Service (QPWS; ☎ 4974 9350), at Captain Cook Dr, has information and brochures on the Eurimbula and Deepwater National Parks. They sell camping permits and take bookings three months in advance for the holiday periods.

For Internet access try Backpackers 1770, which has two terminals and costs $7 an hour – see Places to Stay later for details. Yok Attack has four terminals and also charges $7 an hour – see Places to Eat. At the time of writing a couple of other places were making plans to offer Internet access.

There's a Westpac bank branch in Endeavour Plaza and an ATM that takes all cards at the supermarket next to the Ampol service station on Round Hill Rd. The service station is open from 6am to 9pm daily.

## Things to See

The **Miriam Vale Historical Society Museum** *(☎ 4974 9511, Springs Rd, Agnes Water; admission $2; open 1pm-3pm Wed, 10am-noon Sat & Sun)* has a small collection of artefacts, rocks and minerals, as well as extracts from Cook's journal.

## Activities

Round Hill Creek at the Town of 1770 provides a calm anchorage for **boats**, there's good **fishing** and **mudcrabbing** upstream, and the southern end of the Great Barrier Reef is easily accessible from here, with Lady Musgrave Island about 1½ hours offshore.

Agnes Water is Queensland's northernmost **surf beach**. A Surf Life Saving Club patrols the main beach and there are often good breaks along the coast. The surf beaches south of Agnes Water are only accessible by 4WD.

You can hire myriad water vessels in and around the marina. 1770 Marine Services

(☎ 4974 9227) hires out 3.6m aluminium dinghies for exploring Round Hill Creek at $80/50 for a day/half day. There are also catamarans (☎ 4974 9539) at $15 for 30 minutes; a houseboat (☎ 4974 9643) from $100; and canoes (☎ 4974 9470) at $30 per half day. There are plenty of other activities on offer, including scuba diving, and jet-ski and trail-bike hire; ask at the tourist office for brochures.

There are also charter boats available for fishing trips, including the MV *Spirit of 1770* (see the following Organised Tours section) and the MV *James Cook* (☎ 4974 9422), which sleeps up to nine people. Sport Fish 1770 (☎ 4974 9686) offers sport-, game-, reef- and fly-fishing tours of the Great Barrier Reef at $380/600 for an adult/child.

## Organised Tours

At the marina on Captain Cook Dr, 1770 Environmental Tours (☎ 4974 9422) runs enjoyable full-day tours in its LARCs (large amphibious vehicles), *Sir Joseph Banks* and *Dr DC Solander*. The tours take in Middle Island, Bustard Head and Eurimbula National Park, and operate Monday, Wednesday and Saturday. It costs $88/55/44 an adult/teen/child, including lunch. There are also daily one-hour sunset cruises ($22).

The MV *Spirit of 1770* (☎ 4974 9077), at Captain Cook Dr, has excellent day trips to Lady Musgrave Island. It takes 90 minutes to get there and six hours is spent on the island. It costs $125/65 an adult/child with lunch, snorkelling and fishing gear included. Cruises depart the Town of 1770 on Tuesday, Thursday, Saturday and Sunday – more often during holiday periods. Island camping transfers are also available for $225 per person ($245 in school holidays), which include lunch and reef fishing on the return journey.

## Places to Stay

**Agnes Water** Accommodation ranges from good backpacker facilities to a comfortable B&B.

*Backpackers 1770* (☎/fax 4974 9849, 3 Captain Cook Dr) Dorm beds/doubles $18/38. This new backpackers has been custom built with a large, clean kitchen,

good-sized rooms and Internet terminals. The friendly owner, Richard, does pick-ups from Miriam Vale.

*Hoban's Hideaway* (☎/fax 4974 9144, ⓔ hoban@bigpond.com.au, 2510 Round Hill Rd) Rooms $110. An accommodating and conscientious couple runs this excellent B&B, in tranquil bush 4km west of Agnes Water. The attractive colonial-style timber homestead has three luxurious double bedrooms with en suites, a lounge room, outdoor dining area, barbecue area and a pool. Rates include breakfast, and for an extra $35 you can get dinner.

**Town of 1770** In 1770 you can stay in 'shacks' with a view or camp beside the beach.

*Captain Cook Holiday Village* (☎ 4974 9219, fax 4974 9142, ⓔ cookholidayvillage@ bigpond.com.au, Captain Cook Dr) Unpowered/powered sites $15.40/17.60, dorm bungalows $55, self-contained cabins $77. This excellent and well-equipped caravan and camping park is in a pleasant bush setting and has a good restaurant (see Places to Eat following).

*The Beach Shacks* (☎/fax 4974 9463, ⓔ beachshack@1770.net.au, Captain Cook Dr). Doubles from $135. These are superbly finished self-contained 'shacks' that are decorated in timber, cane and bamboo. They offer grand views and magnificent, private accommodation just a minute's walk from the water.

Both the *Agnes Water Caravan Park* (☎ 4974 9193, 51 Jeffrey Court) and *Town of 1770 Camping Ground* (☎ 4974 9286, fax 4974 9583, Captain Cook Dr) offer good camping near the beach.

## Places to Eat

*Yok Attack* (☎ 4974 7454, Shop 22, Endeavour Plaza, Cnr Captain Cook Dr & Round Hill Rd) Mains $11-16. Open lunch & dinner daily. This place is run by a Thai family and is highly recommended. You can also surf the Net over your noodles.

*Captain's Table Restaurant* (☎ 4974 9469, Agnes Water Tavern, Lot 1 Tavern Rd) Mains $10-20. It's basically just a pub bistro, but the Captain's Table offers delicious seafood and excellent steaks.

*The Deck (☎ 4974 9219, Captain Cook Holiday Village, Captain Cook Dr)* Mains $13-17. This has a pleasant, leafy, outdoor setting, with spectacular views over Bustard Bay. Tasty menu choices include seafood, pasta and curry.

## Getting There & Away
There are no bus or train services into the area, so you'll need your own transport. From Miriam Vale, on the Bruce Hwy, it's 57km east to Agnes Water, about 10km of which is currently unsealed. Alternatively, it's 123km north from Bundaberg to Agnes Water via Rosedale.

## EURIMBULA & DEEPWATER NATIONAL PARKS
There are several coastal national parks around Agnes Water and Town of 1770. For information or to book camp sites, contact the QPWS in either Bundaberg (☎ 4131 1600) or Town of 1770 (☎ 4974 9350). Alternatively, the parks have self-registration stands.

The 78 sq km Eurimbula National Park is on the northern side of Round Hill Creek and has a landscape of dunes, mangroves and eucalypt forest. There's a basic *camping ground* at Bustard Beach with toilets, bore water and rain water. The main access road to the park is about 10km south-west of Agnes Water.

South of Agnes Water, Deepwater National Park is only accessible by 4WD vehicles. The park has an unspoiled coastal landscape with long sandy beaches, freshwater creeks, good fishing spots and a *camping ground*. It's also a major breeding ground for **loggerhead turtles**, which build nests and lay eggs on the beaches between November and February. You can watch the turtles laying and see hatchlings emerging at night between January and April, but you need to observe various precautions outlined in the QPWS park brochure (obtainable at the office in Town of 1770).

The park entrance is 8km south of Agnes Water, then it's another 7km to the *Wreck Rock camping ground* and picnic areas.

## GLADSTONE
postcode 4680 • pop 27,400
About 20km off the Bruce Hwy, Gladstone is one of the busiest ports in Australia, handling agricultural, mineral and coal exports from central Queensland. Scenically challenged industrial plants mar the town's otherwise attractive estuary setting, but there are a few things here to interest diligent visitors.

Gladstone's marina is the main departure point for boats to Heron, Masthead and Wilson islands on the Great Barrier Reef.

## Information
The helpful visitor information centre (☎ 4972 9922), at the marina on Bryan Jordan Dr, is open from 8.30am to 5pm Monday to Friday and 9am to 5pm weekends.

The Environmental Protection Agency (EPA; ☎ 4971 6500), at 136 Goondoon St, can provide information on all the southern Reef Islands here, as well as the area's mainland parks. It's open from 8.30am to 5pm Monday to Friday.

The Gladstone City Library (☎ 4970 1232), at 144 Goondoon St, has free Internet access, and is open from 9.30am to 5.45pm Monday to Friday and 9am to 4.30pm Saturday.

## Things to See
In the old town hall, the **Gladstone Art Gallery & Museum** *(☎ 4970 1242, Goondoon St; admission free; open 10am-5pm Mon-Fri, 10am-4pm Sat)* has a small, permanent collection of contemporary Australian paintings and ceramics, and regularly features theme exhibitions of art and craft.

The **Auckland Point Lookout** has good views over the Gladstone harbour, port facilities and shipping terminals. A brass tablet on the lookout maps the harbour and its many islands.

The beautiful **Tondoon Botanic Gardens** *(☎ 4979 3326, Glenlyon Rd; admission free; open 9am-6pm Oct-Mar, 8.30am-5.30pm Apr-Sept)*, about 7km south of the town centre, is a 55-hectare area of rainforest and Australian native plants, with walking trails. There's a visitor centre and free guided tours.

## Activities

Gladstone Dive (☎ 4972 9185), at 16 Goondoon St, offers PADI dive courses and day trips to the reef. All gear is available for hire.

For wine buffs, the picturesque Gecko Valley Winery (☎ 4979 0400), at Bailiff Rd, welcomes visitors for **tastings**. It's in a bush setting behind the botanic gardens, and is open from 10am to 5pm daily.

## Organised Tours

Gladstone's various industries, including the power station and port authority, open their doors for free industry tours. The one-hour tours run at either 1.30pm or 2pm (depending on the industry) Monday to Friday. Book at the visitor information centre.

## Special Events

The Gladstone Harbour Festival is held every year from the Monday before Easter until Easter Monday. It coincides with the Brisbane to Gladstone yacht race, and features different activities each day, including street parties and an Easter parade.

## Places to Stay

*Barney Beach Caravan Park* (☎ 4972 1366, *fax 4972 7549, Friend St*) Unpowered/powered sites $14/16.50, on-site vans $28, cabins $36, self-contained villas $52.50. About 2km east of the city centre, this is probably the most central of the caravan parks. It's large, tidy, pleasant and not far from the foreshore.

*Gladstone Backpackers* (☎ 4972 5744, *12 Rollo St*) Beds in 3-4–bed dorm $16.50, doubles $38.50. Although it's friendly and pretty clean, this fairly central little hostel needs maintenance in some rooms and wet areas. However, it has a good kitchen, offers free use of bicycles and does pick-ups from the bus and train.

*Metro Hotel & Suites* (☎ 4972 4711, *fax 4972 4940, 22 Roseberry St*) Doubles with city/harbour view $103/119. The Metro

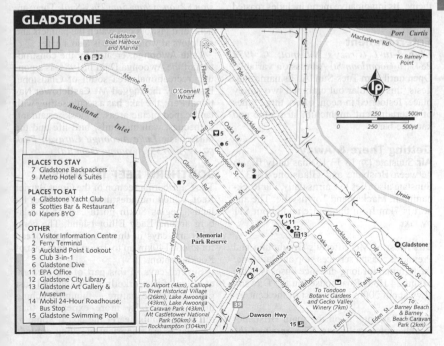

**GLADSTONE**

**PLACES TO STAY**
7 Gladstone Backpackers
9 Metro Hotel & Suites

**PLACES TO EAT**
4 Gladstone Yacht Club
8 Scotties Bar & Restaurant
10 Kapers BYO

**OTHER**
1 Visitor Information Centre
2 Ferry Terminal
3 Auckland Point Lookout
5 Club 3-in-1
6 Gladstone Dive
11 EPA Office
12 Gladstone City Library
13 Gladstone Art Gallery & Museum
14 Mobil 24-Hour Roadhouse; Bus Stop
15 Gladstone Swimming Pool

To Airport (4km), Calliope River Historical Village (26km), Lake Awoonga (43km), Lake Awoonga Caravan Park (43km), Mt Castletower National Park (50km) & Rockhampton (104km)

To Tondoon Botanic Gardens and Gecko Valley Winery (7km)

To Barney Beach & Barney Beach Caravan Park (2km)

Dawson Hwy

is definitely the choice if you're after something more upmarket. The rooms are large and self-contained.

## Places to Eat
*Kapers BYO* (☎ 4972 7902, 124b Goondoon St) Mains $19-30. Open dinner Mon-Sat. The blackboard at the front sports philosophies like 'growing old is mandatory, growing up is optional', which sums up this bright, off-beat little place with hand-painted tables, an amiable hostess and appealing culinary choices.

*Gladstone Yacht Club* (☎ 4972 2294, 1 Goondoon St) Mains $12-18. Open noon-2.30pm & from 6pm. The yacht club is a popular place to dine, and with good reason. The food is tasty, the serves filling and you can eat on the deck overlooking the water.

*Scotties Bar & Restaurant* (☎ 4972 9999, 46 Goondoon St) Mains $18-24. Open from 6pm Mon-Sat, noon Fri. This is a highly recommended place with a decidedly blue theme. Its imaginative menu includes roasted quail, lamb curry and antipasto.

## Entertainment
*Club 3-in-1* (*Crazy's Nitespot;* ☎ 4972 2847, 6 Goondoon St) Admission variable. Open until 3am Tues-Sun. As its name suggests, this popular but cramped two-storey place, festooned in neon, offers three types of entertainment: nightclub, strip club and karaoke bar.

## Getting There & Away
**Air** Sunstate (☎ 13 13 13) has daily flights between Brisbane and Gladstone ($332). Sunstate also flies to Cairns daily, via Rockhampton, Mackay and Townsville. The airport is 7km from the centre and about $11 by taxi.

**Bus** Most of McCafferty's/Greyhound and Premier's coastal services stop at Gladstone; the terminal for long-distance buses is at the Mobil 24 Hour Roadhouse, on the Dawson Hwy about 200m south-west of the centre.

**Train** Gladstone is on the main Brisbane-Rockhampton rail route. The *Spirit of the Tropics,* the *Spirit of the Outback,* the *Queenslander,* the *Sunlander* and the *Tilt Train* all stop here.

## Getting Around
Buslink Gladstone (☎ 4972 1670) runs local bus services on weekdays only, including a service along Goondoon St to Barney Point and the beach, which stops out the front of the caravan park there.

To book a taxi, call Blue & White Taxis (☎ 4972 1800).

## AROUND GLADSTONE
Calliope, on the Calliope River 26km south of Gladstone, has the **Calliope River Historical Village** (☎ 4975 7428, Dawson Hwy; admission $2; open 8am-4pm), with restored heritage buildings including an old pub, church, schoolhouse and a slab hut.

About 7km south of Calliope is an interesting artists' retreat called **Cedar Galleries** (☎ 4975 0444, Lot 100 Bruce Hwy; admission $2; open 9am-5pm Tues-Sun). There are eight slab-hut studios nestled in the gardens here, and visitors can watch the painters and sculptors at work. There is also a cafe.

**Lake Awoonga**, created by the construction of the Awoonga Dam in 1984, is a popular recreational area south of Gladstone. Backed by the rugged Mt **Castletower National Park**, the lake has a scenic setting with landscaped picnic areas, a kiosk/restaurant, barbecues, walking trails, bird-life and the fairly basic *Lake Awoonga Caravan Park* (☎ 4975 0155, Awoonga Dam Rd).

## SOUTHERN REEF ISLANDS
The Capricornia section of the Great Barrier Reef, which includes the southern Reef Islands, begins 80km north-east of Bundaberg around Lady Elliot Island. The coral reefs and cays in this group dot the ocean for about 140km up to Tryon Island, east of Rockhampton.

Several cays in this part of the reef are excellent for snorkelling, diving and just getting back to nature – though reaching them is generally more expensive than reaching islands nearer the coast. Some of the islands are important breeding grounds for turtles and seabirds, and visitors should be aware of precautions to ensure the wildlife's protection, outlined in the relevant QPWS brochures.

*Camping* is allowed on the Lady Musgrave, Masthead, Tryon and North West national park islands, and campers must be totally self-sufficient and abide by certain rules and restrictions. Numbers are limited, so it's advisable to apply well ahead for a camping permit ($3.85 per person). You can book up to 12 months ahead for these islands instead of the usual six to 12 weeks for other Queensland national parks. Contact the EPA in Gladstone (☎ 4971 6500).

Access is from Bundaberg, Gladstone or Rosslyn Bay near Yeppoon.

## Lady Elliot Island

About 80km north-east of Bundaberg, Lady Elliot is a 0.4 sq km vegetated coral cay at the southern end of the Great Barrier Reef. The island has a resort and its own airstrip. It is popular with divers and snorkellers, and has superb diving straight off the beach, as well as numerous shipwrecks, coral gardens, bommies and blowholes to explore.

Lady Elliot Island is not a national park, and camping is not allowed.

*Lady Elliot Island Resort (☎ 1800 072 200, 4125 5344, fax 4125 5778,* e *reservations@ladyelliot.com.au)* has tent cabins/units/suites for $140/185/210 per person. The prices include breakfast and dinner, but are exorbitant for what you get. The resort is a no-frills kind of place, with basic tent cabins for two, three or four people, simple motel-style reef units and more expensive self-contained island suites with two bedrooms.

Whitaker Air Charters flies guests to the resort for $159 return. From Bundaberg or Hervey Bay, you can pay $219 for a day trip, which includes the flight, lunch and snorkelling gear. Book through the resort.

## Lady Musgrave Island

Lady Musgrave Island, a 0.15 sq km cay in the Bunker group, is an uninhabited national park about 100km north-east of Bundaberg. The island sits at the western end of a huge lagoon, which is one of the few places along the Great Barrier Reef where ships can safely enter. Lady Musgrave Island offers some excellent snorkelling and diving opportunities, and the day-trip boats can supply you with gear.

The island has a dense canopy of pisonia forest, which is brimming with terns, shearwaters and white-capped noddies during nesting. The birds nest from October to April, and green turtles nest from November to February.

You can walk around the island in 30 minutes, and there is a trail across the middle to the national park *camping ground* on the western side. Its only facilities are bush toilets, and campers – a maximum of 40 – must be totally self-sufficient. Bring your own drinking water and a gas or fuel stove – open fires are not permitted, and the island's timber and driftwood cannot be burned.

The MV *Lady Musgrave* (☎ 4159 4519) operates day trips from Port Bundaberg marina at 8.30am Monday to Thursday and Saturday. The cost is $130/65 for an adult/child, which includes lunch, snorkelling gear and a glass-bottom boat ride. The trip takes 2¼ hours and you have about four hours on the island. You can also use this service for camping drop offs ($260 return).

There are also day trips and camping drop offs to Lady Musgrave Island from Town of 1770 – see Organised Tours in the earlier Agnes Water & Town of 1770 section.

## Heron Island

Only 1km long and 0.17 sq km in area, Heron Island is 72km east of Gladstone. It's a true coral cay, densely vegetated with pisonia trees and surrounded by 24 sq km of reef. There's a P&O resort and research station on the north-eastern third of the island – the rest is national park.

Heron, famed for superb scuba diving, is a Mecca for divers. Unfortunately, large sections of coral have been killed by silt from dredging for a new jetty. However, there's good snorkelling over the shallow reef and the resort's dive boat runs excursions to the many good diving sites. The dive shop has a full range of diving equipment for hire – a day trip, including equipment, is $160, and six-day certificate courses are $495.

*Heron Island Resort* (☎ 1800 737 678, 4972 9055, fax 4972 0244, ⓔ *resorts _reservations@poaustralia.com)* has bunk rooms for $140 per person and twin-share suites for $210. The resort has simple three- and four-bed bunk rooms and a range of modern, motel-style suites with en suites – the Point Suites have the best views. This is the only place to stay on the island and there are no day trips. Resort guests pay another $126 return in the *Reef Adventurer II* catamaran from Gladstone.

The resort operates day trips for guests to **Wilson Island**, a national park north of Heron. There are excellent beaches and superb snorkelling here, but there is no accommodation.

### Other Islands

There are three other islands in this group worth mentioning, all major nesting sites for **loggerhead turtles** and various seabirds, notably shearwaters and black noddies. The turtles nest between November and February, the birds between October and April. All three islands allow self-sufficient camping with limited facilities.

South-west of Heron Island, uninhabited **Masthead Island** is the second largest of the nine vegetated cays in the Capricorn group. *Camping* is permitted from April to October; there is a limit of 50 campers.

At 106 hectares, **North West Island** is the second biggest cay on the Great Barrier Reef. Formerly a guano mine and turtle-soup factory, it is now a national park popular among campers. *Camping* is closed from Australia Day to Easter, and there's a limit of 150. There are no scheduled services to North West; contact the EPA in Gladstone for details on suitable launches and barges to access the island.

**Tryon Island** is a tiny, beautiful, 11 hectare national park cay north of North West Island. There is a *camping ground*, but the island is currently closed to visitors to allow for revegetation. Check with the EPA in Gladstone (☎ 4971 6500) for the latest details.

# Rockhampton Area

## ROCKHAMPTON
postcode 4700 • pop 64,000

Rockhampton, which sits astride the tropic of Capricorn, is the administrative and commercial centre of central Queensland. Its fortunes are closely linked to the cattle industry, and the city proclaims itself the 'beef capital' of Australia. There are more than two million cattle within a 250km radius of the city, and large statues of Brahman, Braford and Santa Gertrudis bulls mark the northern and southern approaches. Not surprisingly, this is a great place to tuck into a steak.

Queensland's largest river, the Fitzroy, flows through the heart of the city, which has many historic buildings classified by the National Trust. The compact business centre is surrounded by a progressive city of attractive gardens, huge shopping plazas and modern housing estates.

'Rocky' as it's known has a few tourist attractions of its own, including a good art gallery, an Aboriginal cultural centre and some excellent gardens and parklands.

### History

Rockhampton was established as a river trading port in 1853 by the Archer brothers, the first settlers to establish a property in the area. Its growth was boosted by a minor gold rush at Canoona in 1858, but the real development began with the discovery of rich gold and copper deposits at Mt Morgan in 1882. Rockhampton quickly developed into the major trading centre for the surrounding region, and its early-20th century prosperity is evident in the many fine Victorian-era buildings around the older parts of the city.

More recently, sheep and later cattle farming have gradually replaced mining as the region's major income source.

### Orientation

Rockhampton is about 40km from the coast. The Fitzroy River flows through the heart of the city, with the small commercial centre, the oldest part of Rocky, on the southern bank. The long Fitzroy Bridge connects the city centre with the newer northern suburbs.

Coming in from the south, the Bruce Hwy skirts the centre and crosses the river via the Neville Hewitt Bridge.

## Information

The helpful Capricorn Information Centre (☎ 4927 2055) is on the highway beside the tropic of Capricorn marker, 3km south of the centre. It's open from 8am to 5pm daily. The more central Rockhampton Information Centre (☎/fax 4922 5339), at 208 Quay St, is in the historic former Customs House and is open from 8.30am to 4.30pm Monday to Friday and 9am to 4pm weekends.

Rockhampton's post office is a modern rectangular building at 150 East St. It's open 9am till 5pm Monday to Friday.

The Rockhampton library (☎ 4936 8265), at 69 William St, has two Internet terminals available free of charge, but you'll need to book. It's open from 9.15am Monday to Saturday, but 1pm to 8pm Wednesday. Alternatively, Rocknet (☎ 4922 2760), at 238 Quay St, has four terminals at $5 an hour.

The Royal Automobile Club of Queensland (RACQ; ☎ 4927 2255) is at 134 William St. The EPA office (☎ 4936 0511) is on Yeppoon Rd, about 7km north-west of central Rocky.

Angus & Robertson Bookworld has a large outlet inside the City Centre Plaza shopping centre in Fitzroy St. It has a good travel section.

## Things to See

There are many fine old buildings in the town, particularly on **Quay St**, which has grand Victorian-era buildings dating back to the gold-rush days. You can pick up tourist leaflets and magazines that map out walking trails around the town.

The **Rockhampton City Art Gallery** *(☎ 4936 8248, 62 Victoria Parade; admission free; open 10am-4pm Tues-Fri, 11am-4pm*

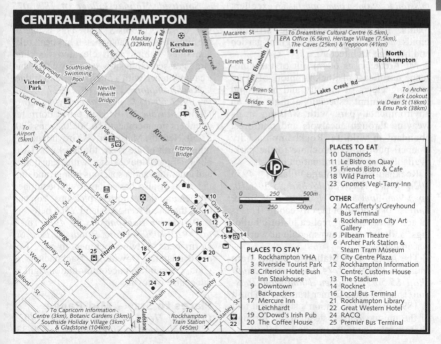

# CENTRAL ROCKHAMPTON

**PLACES TO EAT**
10 Diamonds
11 Le Bistro on Quay
15 Friends Bistro & Cafe
18 Wild Parrot
23 Gnomes Vegi-Tarry-Inn

**OTHER**
2 McCafferty's/Greyhound Bus Terminal
4 Rockhampton City Art Gallery
5 Pilbeam Theatre
6 Archer Park Station & Steam Tram Museum
7 City Centre Plaza
12 Rockhampton Information Centre; Customs House
13 The Stadium
14 Rocknet
16 Local Bus Terminal
21 Rockhampton Library
22 Great Western Hotel
24 RACQ
25 Premier Bus Terminal

**PLACES TO STAY**
1 Rockhampton YHA
3 Riverside Tourist Park
8 Criterion Hotel; Bush Inn Steakhouse
9 Downtown Backpackers
17 Mercure Inn Leichhardt
19 O'Dowd's Irish Pub
20 The Coffee House

*Sat & Sun)* boasts an impressive collection of Australian paintings, including works by Sir Sidney Nolan and Sir Russell Drysdale.

About 7km north of the centre is the **Dreamtime Cultural Centre** *(☎ 4936 1655, Bruce Hwy; adult/child $12/5.50; open 10am-3.30pm daily, tours 10.30am & 1pm)*, a rewarding Aboriginal and Torres Strait Islander heritage display centre, providing a fascinating insight into the region's Indigenous history.

South of the centre are the wonderful **Botanic Gardens** *(☎ 4922 1654, Spencer St; admission free; open 6am-6pm, zoo feeding 2.30pm-3.30pm)*. Established in 1869, this oasis is beautifully landscaped and includes a formal Japanese garden, lagoons covered with lilies and bird-life, and immaculate manicured lawns. There is also a kiosk, attractive picnic area and a small **zoo** with a walk-through aviary.

Just north of the Fitzroy River, **Kershaw Gardens** *(☎ 4936 8254, via Charles St; admission free; open 6am-6pm)* is an excellent botanical park devoted to Australian native plants. Its attractions include artificial rapids, a rainforest area, a fragrant garden and heritage architecture.

**Mt Archer** rises 604m out of the landscape north-east of Rockhampton, offering stunning views of the city and hinterland from the summit, especially at night. It's an environmental park with walking trails weaving through eucalypts and rainforest abundant in wildlife. Rockhampton City Council publishes a brochure to the park, available from the information centres.

Rockhampton's **Heritage Village** *(☎ 4936 1026, Bruce Hwy; adult/child $5.50/1.10; open 9am-3pm Mon-Fri, 10am-4pm Sat & Sun)* is 10km north of the city centre. This is an active museum of replica historic buildings, and even has townspeople at work in period garb.

The **Archer Park Station & Steam Tram Museum** *(☎ 4922 2774, Denison St; adult/child $5.50/3.30; open 10am-4pm Tues-Sun)* is housed in a former train station built in 1899. It tells the station's story, and that of the unique Purrey steam tram, through photographs, soundscapes and displays.

## Organised Tours
Get-About Tours (☎ 4934 8247) offers town tours including the Botanic Gardens and Dreamtime centre, and trips to the Berserker Range, Mt Morgan and the Koorana Crocodile Farm (all $59.40).

## Special Events
Each year the region celebrates the Summer Solstice Light Spectacular at the Capricorn Caves, about 25km north of Rocky. From early December to Christmas, when the sun is directly overhead at midday, the light beams into the caves via fissures in the rock, creating an incredible spectacle.

## Places to Stay – Budget
**Riverside Tourist Park** *(☎/fax 4922 3779, 2 Reaney St)* Single/double sites $11/12, with power $14/16, on-site vans $35/42. For convenience, this is a good choice. It's on the river close to the city centre and has plenty of shaded, grassy sites.

**Southside Holiday Village** *(☎ 1800 075 911, 4927 3013, fax 4927 7750, Lower Dawson Rd)* Sites/cabins $15/36. This is one of the city's best caravan parks. It has neat, self-contained cabins with elevated decking, large grassed camp sites, courtesy coach and a camp kitchen with a microwave and fridge.

**Rockhampton YHA** *(☎ 4927 5288, fax 4922 6040, ℮ peter.karen@yhaqld.org, 60 MacFarlane St)* Beds in 6-bed dorm for members/nonmembers $16.50/20, twins $20/23.50. Near the McCafferty's/Greyhound terminal north of the river, the Rocky YHA is obviously well looked after, with clean dorms and amenities and a spacious lounge and dining area. It also has a large, well-equipped kitchen and does courtesy pick-ups. You can book the Great Keppel Island YHA here.

**Downtown Backpackers** *(☎ 4922 1837, fax 4922 1050, Oxford Hotel, 91 East St)* Dorm beds & twins per person $15. Located upstairs, Downtown Backpackers is good, clean budget accommodation right in the centre of town.

## Places to Stay – Mid-Range
**Criterion Hotel** *(☎ 4922 1225, fax 4922 1226, 150 Quay St)* Singles/doubles $29/33,

with shower, TV & air-con $33/40. The Criterion is perhaps Rockhampton's grandest old pub. Its top two storeys have dozens of good-quality pub rooms, some of which look over the nearby Fitzroy River.

*O'Dowd's Irish Pub* (☎ *4927 0344, fax 4927 0347,* e *info@odowds.com.au, 100 William St)* Single/twin pub rooms $28/40, motel rooms $70/78. O'Dowd's is a beautifully renovated hotel with a strong Irish theme and lively atmosphere. It has superb pub accommodation upstairs with excellent new beds.

*Mercure Inn Leichhardt* (☎ *1800 075 678, 4927 6733, fax 4927 8075, Denham St)* Budget/2-star/4-star rooms $40/66/112. The central Mercure Inn has 105 rooms, ranging from reasonable budget units to plush, comfortable suites with city views. All have aircon and a TV, and downstairs there's a restaurant and bar.

*The Coffee House* (☎ *4927 5722, fax 4927 5186,* e *the_coffeehouse@bigpond.com.au, Cnr William & Bolsover Sts)* Rooms from $104. Despite being crammed into a corner, this offers beautifully appointed self-contained apartments in central Rocky. It also has a restaurant, cafe and bar.

## Places to Eat

*Wild Parrot* (☎ *4921 4099, 66 Denham St)* Breakfast $5-10, mains $11-14. Open breakfast, lunch & dinner. A peaceful little haven with exotic tropical decor, the licensed Wild Parrot serves interesting dishes like moussaka and tandoori chicken, as well as excellent coffee.

*Friends Bistro & Cafe* (☎ *4922 2689, 159 East St)* Meals $7-8.50. Open lunch & dinner. This quaint BYO place offers cheap, tasty feeds in a casual, intimate atmosphere.

*Bush Inn Steakhouse* (☎ *4922 1225, 150 Quay St)* Dishes $10-18. At the Criterion Hotel, the Bush Inn serves some of the best pub food in town and is duly popular. There are big steaks, chicken and fish dishes, and pizzas on the menu.

*Gnomes Vegi-Tarry-Inn* (☎ *4927 4713, 104 William St)* Mains $10.90. Open lunch & dinner Tues-Sat. For vegetarian food, try the excellent Gnomes, where you can dine amid gardens in a charming open-sided courtyard. Its selection includes marinated tofu, curried chick peas and great soups. There's live music here Friday nights.

*Diamonds* (☎ *4922 0855, 179 Quay St)* Lunch $9-13, dinner $10-25. Open lunch & dinner Wed-Sat, lunch Sun. Gastronomically speaking, the relatively young Diamonds is reportedly getting better with age. The service is terrific and the location, in a modern building with a balcony overlooking the river, is unbeatable.

*Le Bistro on Quay* (☎ *4922 2019, 194 Quay St)* Lunch $11-14, dinner around $27. In a charming riverfront building, Le Bistro has a carefully cultivated, intimate atmosphere. Its somewhat pricey menu includes roasted sea perch, Moroccan spiced lamb and roasted duckling.

## Entertainment

*Great Western Hotel* (☎ *4922 1862, 39 Stanley St)* Admission $7.70. Looking like a spaghetti western film set, this saloon is home to Rockhampton's latest craze, a weekly rodeo. There's a big, covered bullring out the back where each Friday night you can watch poor brave fools try to ride a bucking bull. Great entertainment.

*O'Dowd's Irish Pub* (☎ *4927 0344, 100 William St)* You can get your fix of Irish music (and Guinness) here, with bands providing a lively atmosphere on most Friday and Saturday nights.

*Criterion Hotel* (☎ *4922 1225, 150 Quay St)* Easily Rockhampton's favourite pub, the Criterion resonates with a good-time feel in both its front bar and the relaxed Murphy's Irish Bar, and there's live music Wednesday to Sunday in the steakhouse.

*The Stadium* (☎ *4927 9988, 234 Quay St)* Open until late Wed-Sun. This is the place most partygoers head to after the pubs. It's a large, flashy club with a sporty theme (you dance on a mini basketball court), a central bar and pool tables.

*Pilbeam Theatre* (☎ *4927 4111, Victoria Parade)* This plush 967-seat theatre is located in the Rockhampton Performing Arts Complex (ROKPAC) and hosts a range of national and international acts.

## Getting There & Away

**Air** You can fly to Rocky with Qantas from all the major centres along the coast. Its affiliate Sunstate flies from Brisbane to Rockhampton ($363, daily) and Rockhampton to Mackay ($270, daily). There's a Qantas office at the airport.

**Bus** The McCafferty's/Greyhound terminal (☎ 4927 2844) is on the corner of Brown and Linnett Sts, just north of the Fitzroy Bridge. The Premier terminal is at the Mobil roadhouse at 91 George St, although the company also stops at the Mobil station north of the river.

McCafferty's/Greyhound buses all pass through Rockhampton on the coastal route. Destinations include Mackay ($50, four hours), Cairns ($122, 16 hours) and Brisbane ($79, 10½ hours). The company also runs to Emerald ($37, 3½ hours) and Longreach ($68, 9½ hours, twice weekly). Generally cheaper, Premier Motor Service (☎ 13 34 10) runs buses from Rockhampton to Mackay ($31), Cairns ($109) and Brisbane ($70).

Young's Bus Service (☎ 4922 3813) operates a loop service to Yeppoon, Rosslyn Bay, Emu Park and back ($7.30 one way, 11 times daily). Buses depart the Kern Arcade in Bolsover St. Rothery's Coaches (☎ 4922 4320) does the same run ($7.70, thrice daily) from the airport (Canoona Rd), or from motels by arrangement. Young's also has buses to Mt Morgan ($7.30) Monday to Friday.

Yeppoon Backpackers (☎ 4939 4702) runs a free daily bus between Rockhampton and Yeppoon.

**Train** The high-speed *Tilt Train* travels from Brisbane to Rockhampton in under seven hours ($82 economy). The weekly *Spirit of Capricorn* takes nine hours for the same fare on Saturday.

The *Sunlander* and *Queenslander* travel between Brisbane and Cairns via Rockhampton. Economy fares are $81.40 to Brisbane and $162.80 to Cairns. The *Spirit of the Tropics* stops here on route to Townsville.

The slow *Spirit of the Outback* runs between Brisbane, Rockhampton, Emerald and Longreach ($81 economy from Rockhampton, twice weekly). Book with the Queensland Rail Travel Centre (☎ 4932 0453), at the train station, 1km south-east of the centre.

## Getting Around

Rockhampton airport is 5km south of the centre, but there are no bus services – a taxi (Rocky Cabs ☎ 4922 7111) costs about $9.

There's a reasonably comprehensive city bus network operating all day Monday to Friday, and Saturday morning. All services terminate in Bolsover St, between William and Denham Sts.

## AROUND ROCKHAMPTON

The rugged Berserker Range, which starts 26km north of Rockhampton, is noted for its spectacular limestone caves and passages. About 3½ km from the Caves township, **Capricorn Caves** (☎ *4934 2883, Caves Rd; tours $13-45; open 9am-4pm)* is excellent value. Its informative cathedral tour is an easy guided walk leaving hourly, and its highlight is the stone cathedral, where 'Amazing Grace' is played to demonstrate the incredible acoustics. For the more daring, the three-hour adventure tour takes you through tight spots with names like 'Fat Man's Misery'. You must be at least 16 for this tour, and book in advance. There is also a two-hour adventure tour ($55), which includes bus transfers from Rockhampton.

The complex has barbecue areas, a pool and kiosk, and a simple *camping ground* (sites $12, 10-bed chalet $60 a double). There also should be a new 48-bed *backpackers lodge* nearing completion.

Nearby, the **Mt Etna National Park** *(☎ 4936 0511; tours adult/child $7.50/3.50; tours Dec-Feb)* is the habitat of the endangered ghost bat. There are no facilities and access is restricted. The park rangers run night tours of the bat caves (bookings essential).

***Belgamba Cottage** (☎/fax 4938 1818,* **e** *belgamba@rocknet.net.au, Struck Oil Rd)* Double $70, 3-6 people $100. On a hilly 500-hectare property 40km south-west of Rockhampton, this is the place to get off the beaten track. You stay in a spacious self-contained three-bedroom timber cottage, and there are good walking trails to views of the surrounding countryside. You won't find babbling brooks on this predominantly dry property, but it is a nature refuge, so there's plenty of wildlife. Everything is provided except food, and cheaper rates can be negotiated for longer stays. Ring for directions, or to arrange to be picked up from the turn-off if coming by bus.

## MT MORGAN
### postcode 4714 • pop 3200
The historic gold- and copper-mining town of Mt Morgan is 38km south-west of Rockhampton on the Burnett Hwy. William Mackinlay, a stockman, first discovered gold here in 1880. Two years later the Morgan brothers, Thomas, Frederick and Edwin, arrived and started mining, and within a couple of years had made their fortunes.

Thinking the mine's future prospects were limited, the Morgan brothers then sold out to a mining syndicate for £90,000 – a huge sum of money at the time, but nothing compared to what would later come out of the ground. In its first 10 years of operations from 1886, the Mt Morgan Gold Mining Company returned massive dividends on the initial capital, making its major investors some of Australia's richest and most powerful people. Gold yields fell dramatically by 1900, but in 1903 the company began extracting the rich copper deposits deeper in the mine. Open-cut operations continued until 1981.

Mt Morgan has a well-preserved collection of late-19th century buildings, and is registered as a heritage town. There's an interesting historic museum and you can tour the former mine site.

## Information
Mt Morgan's tourist information centre (☎ 4938 2312), at Railway Parade, is in the old train station. It's open from 9am to 4pm daily. The town library (☎ 4938 1169), at 31 Morgan St, has an Internet terminal at $2.50 an hour. It's open from 8.45am to 4.30pm Tuesday to Friday.

## Things to See
The **Mt Morgan Historical Museum** (*☎ 4938 2122, 87 Morgan St; adult/child*

*$4/0.50; open 10am-1pm Mon-Sat, 10am-4pm Sun)* is one of the better country museums you'll see. It has an extensive collection of artefacts, including a 1921 black Buick hearse, old mining equipment, photographs tracing the mine's history and even an old fire engine.

Mt Morgan's lovely old **train station** (*☎ 4938 2312, Railway Parade)* is a focal point for the town. It houses the tourist office and a **market** is held here from 8am on the first Saturday of each month. At the time of writing the **historic train ride** to Cattle Creek and back wasn't operating, but had plans to be in the future – ring the tourist office for details.

The **Running the Cutter** monument, on the corner of Morgan and Central Sts, commemorates the old custom of serving 'cutters' (two-quart billy cans) of beer to the mine workers in Cutter Lane, behind the hotels.

## Organised Tours
Mt Morgan Mine Tours (☎ 4938 1081, @ dinobob@rocknet.net.au, 38 Central St; family/adult/child $50/20/12; tours 9.30am and 1.30pm) runs value-packed two-hour tours that take in the town's sights, the open-cut mine, and a large cave with dinosaur footprints on the roof. Tours depart the tourist office, and there are daily pick-ups from Rockhampton.

## Special Events
The Golden Mount Festival is held every May Day weekend. It features a 'Running the Cutter' event.

## Places to Stay
*Mount Morgan Motel & Van Park* (*☎/fax 4938 1952, 2 Showground Rd)* Unpowered/powered sites $11/13.20, on-site van $22, single/double motel rooms $44/49. Open, grassy and spacious, this is the better of the town's two camping options. It has very clean amenities, a good pool and some small, cheap motel-style units.

*Miners' Rest Motel Units* (*☎ 4938 2350, 44 Coronation Dr)* Cottages $45. These small but comfortable self-contained units are good value. Each has a timber floor, spa, queen-size bed, air-con and a kitchenette. Meals can be supplied if required.

### Getting There & Away
Young's Bus Service (☎ 4922 3813) operates a regular bus from Rockhampton to Mt Morgan and back Monday to Friday. The one-way fare is $7.30.

McCafferty's/Greyhound also passes through Mt Morgan four times a week on the inland route between Rocky and Brisbane.

## ROCKHAMPTON TO BARALABA
*Myella Farm Stay* (☎ *4998 1290, fax 4998 1104,* e *myella@bigpond.com.au, Baralaba Rd*) is a 1040-hectare beef property 120km south-west of Rockhampton popular among travellers looking to experience life on a working station. You stay in a comfortable, renovated four-bedroom homestead with polished timber floors and a wide veranda (two days/one night $143 per person). Guests can relax, choose between leisure activities or help with the daily chores, then eat a large, home-cooked meal around the campfire. Rates include meals and activities.

If you're driving, take the Leichhardt Hwy and turn off towards Baralaba, between Wowan and Banana. The farm is signposted off the Baralaba Rd, 18km west of the Leichhardt Hwy. If you don't have transport, ring the farm to make arrangements.

## YEPPOON
postcode 4703 • pop 8800
Yeppoon is an attractive little seaside township 43km north-east of Rockhampton. Although Great Keppel Island is the area's main attraction, Yeppoon is a popular holiday town with lovely beaches and a pleasant hinterland. Boats to Great Keppel leave from Rosslyn Bay, 7km south.

### Information
The Capricorn Coast Information Centre (☎ 1800 675 785, 4939 4888) is on the Scenic Hwy, beside the Ross Creek Roundabout at the entrance to the town, and has plenty of information on the Capricorn Coast and Great Keppel Island. It's open from 9am to 5pm daily.

Dreamers Coffee Club (☎ 4939 5797), 4 James St, has three Internet terminals at $4 an hour, while the Yeppoon library (☎ 4939 3433), at 78 John St, has one terminal at $3 per 30 minutes.

### Places to Stay
There's a string of decent *motels* and *holiday units* along Anzac Parade facing the beach; most cost around $65/75 for singles/doubles, although there are some cheaper ones, and rates can vary depending on the day.

*Beachside Caravan Park* (☎ *4939 3738, Farnborough Rd*) Unpowered/powered sites $11/15.40. This basic but neat little camping park north of the town centre can boast an absolute beachfront location. It has good amenities and grassed sites with some shade.

*Yeppoon Backpackers* (☎ *4939 4702, fax 4939 8080, 30 Queen St*) Beds in 4-bed dorm for members/nonmembers $17/18, doubles $37/38. This is a friendly and homey backpackers in an attractive old timber house on the hill overlooking the town and beach. It has a big backyard, a pool, good clean facilities, and does free daily pick-ups from Rockhampton.

*Bayview Tower Motel* (☎ *4939 4500, fax 4939 3915, Normanby St*) Doubles $66-105. On the beachfront, the eight-storey Bayview Tower looks luxurious, but all you'll really pay for is the ocean view. It's clean and comfortable, but most rooms are fairly standard. The rates increase the higher up you go.

*Capricorn International Resort* (☎ *1800 075 902, 4939 5111, fax 4939 5666,* e *capricorn@capricornresort.com, Farnborough Rd*) Doubles/suites $130/180, 1-bedroom self-contained apartments $200. This is a large and lavish Rydges resort about 8km north of Yeppoon. Its accommodation ranges from standard hotel rooms to plush self-contained apartments, and there's a huge pool, a gym and several bars and restaurants. As usual, package deals are available.

The resort's two immaculate golf courses are open to the public at $66 for 18 holes, which includes a motorised buggy. Club hire costs another $30.

## Places to Eat

*Dreamers Coffee Club* (☎ 4939 5797, 4 James St) Dishes $5-10. Open breakfast & lunch. Dreamers is a trendy little coffee shop where you can surf the Net over your latte. It sells excellent coffee, as well as 'overstuffed sandwiches', melts, tajitas and salads.

*Spinnaker Bar & Grill* (☎ 4939 9500, Anzac Parade) Lunch $7, dinner $10.50. At the Keppel Bay Sailing Club, this busy place has cheap all-you-can-eat buffet lunches and dinners, and you can dine on the lawn overlooking the beach.

*Cheers Restaurant* (☎ 4939 4666, Anzac Parade) Mains $15-24. Open for dinner. Cheers offers a relaxed dining atmosphere and 'modern Australian cuisine', including 'jumbo' steaks, fish dishes and pastas.

## Entertainment

*Strand Hotel* (☎ 4939 1301, 2 Normanby St) On the corner of Anzac Parade, the Strand looks a bit rundown, but it's a good place for live music. Bands play on Saturday night in the open dining section.

*Bonkers* (☎ 4939 3366, 16 Hill St) Open 8.30pm-late Thur-Sat. Dance till the wee hours at this slightly more upmarket place.

## Getting There & Away

If you're heading for Great Keppel or the reef, some ferry operators will transport you between your accommodation and Rosslyn Bay Harbour. Otherwise, Young's Bus Service (☎ 4922 3813) runs buses from Rockhampton to Yeppoon ($7.30 one way, daily). Rothery's (☎ 4922 4320) does the same run ($7.70) from Rockhampton airport, or accommodation by arrangement.

If you're driving to Rosslyn Bay there's a free day carpark at the harbour, and next door the Rosslyn Bay Inn Resort (☎ 4933 6333) is the closest lock-up car park, at $7 per day under cover.

## YEPPOON TO BYFIELD

The coastal hinterland north of Yeppoon is largely undeveloped, and there are several state forest parks and one national park in the area. You can't get to the coast without a 4WD, but there are some good picnic and camping grounds in the state forests, and you can visit potteries and galleries near tiny Byfield, 40km from Yeppoon. There are also a couple of excellent bush retreats nearby.

The drive north from Yeppoon takes you through the pine plantations of the Byfield

---

## Stingers

The potentially deadly box jellyfish, also known as the sea wasp or 'stinger', occurs in Queensland's coastal waters north of Rockhampton from around November to April, and swimming is definitely not advisable in these places during these times. The lethal jellyfish are usually found close to the coast, especially around river mouths. Fortunately, swimming and snorkelling is usually safe around the reef islands throughout the year.

The sea wasp's stinging tentacles spread several metres away from its body; by the time victims see the jellyfish, they've already been stung. Treatment is urgent: Douse the stings with vinegar (available on many beaches or from nearby houses), and call for an ambulance (if there's a first-aider present, they may have to apply artificial respiration until the ambulance arrives). Do *not* attempt to remove the tentacles.

Some coastal resorts erect 'stinger nets' that provide small areas for safe swimming, but elsewhere, stay out of the sea when the sea wasps are around. If you're in doubt, check with a local, and if you're still in doubt, don't swim – it's not worth the risk.

State Forest, with turn-offs along the way to various other state forest parks and the Upper Stoney Dam.

Just south of Byfield, there are turn-offs to the **Nob Creek Pottery** (☎ *4935 1161, 216 Arnolds Rd; admission free; open 9am-5pm)*, where you can visit the workshop and gallery, and to the **Waterpark Creek Forest Park**. It's 2km east from the main road to the creek crossing, beyond which are an attractive picnic area, with tables and gas barbecues, and a self-registration *camping ground*. From here, a dirt road continues through the pine plantations to the **Byfield National Park**, an undeveloped area of mostly low coastal scrub. If you have a 4WD you can continue to Five Rocks and Nine Mile Beach, which are popular with anglers.

Byfield consists of a *general store* and pottery, a school and a handful of houses. The turn-off to **Wompoo Rainforest Gallery** (☎ *4935 1157, 80 Castle Rock Rd; admission free; open 9am-5pm Fri-Sun)* is 2km north of Byfield. It has a collection of local art, including pottery and paintings.

### Places to Stay & Eat
**Ferns Hideaway** (☎*/fax 4935 1235,* **e** *fernshideaway@bigpond.com, Yaxley Rd)* Camp sites $12, 6-bed cabins $130, double rooms $56. Signposted just north of Byfield, Ferns is a beautiful secluded bush oasis in immaculate gardens. The timber homestead has a quality a la carte *restaurant* open weekends, while nestled among the trees are five cosy, rustic self-contained cabins with wood fires. There are also double rooms with shared facilities; or you can camp, with hot showers included in the tariff.

**Waterpark Cabins** (☎*/fax 4935 1241, Yaxley Rd)* Cabins weekdays/weekends $90/130. Nearby Ferns Hideaway is another little retreat, this one even more secluded. It has four superbly finished log cabins surrounded by bush, offering lovely rustic comfort, along with a log fire, spa and wood-fired barbecue.

### YEPPOON TO EMU PARK
There are beaches dotted all along the 19km coastline running south from Yeppoon to Emu Park.

About 7km south of Yeppoon, **Rosslyn Bay Harbour** is the departure point for trips to Great Keppel Island and other Keppel Bay islands. Further on there are three fine headlands with good views – **Double Head**, **Bluff Point** and **Pinnacle Point**. After Pinnacle Point the road crosses **Causeway Lake**, a saltwater inlet, and further south at **Emu Park** there are more good views and the 'Singing Ship' memorial to Captain Cook – drilled tubes and pipes that emit whistling or moaning sounds in the breeze.

*Emu Park Beach House* (☎*/fax 4939 6111, 88 Pattinson St)* is a friendly backpacker place in a renovated former Baptist retreat camp in an expanse of gardens. There's a range of accommodation (sites/dorm beds/singles/doubles/units $8/15/21/36/45), and a lounge, kitchen and dining room.

The **Koorana Crocodile Farm** (☎ *4934 4749, Coowonga Rd; adult/child $13.50/7; open 10am-3pm, tours 1pm)* is off the Emu Park to Rockhampton road, about 15km from Emu Park. This simple farm has lots of crocs and a tour every day, but the opening hours are short and the owners will turn away latecomers.

Most towns along this stretch of coast have caravan and camping parks, and there are numerous motels and holiday flats.

### GREAT KEPPEL ISLAND
Although it's not actually on the reef, Great Keppel is the equal of most islands up the coast. It's 13km offshore, and big enough to take a few days to explore. It covers 14 sq km, 90% of which is natural bushland, and boasts 18km of fine, white beaches.

Rest and relaxation, although entirely possible, are not a high priority on the island, with a wide range of activities and entertainment to keep guests busy. This is particularly evident at the island's resort, which is due to become a Contiki resort in April 2002, and will only be open to 18- to 35-year-olds. As a result, some of the following information regarding the resort may have changed, including names and prices of the places we list here. Ring the resort (☎ 1800 245 658, 4939 5044) for the latest. An Internet cafe and a gym are planned for the island.

The good news about Great Keppel is that, unlike many resort islands, there are some good budget accommodation alternatives, and it's also one of the cheapest and easiest Queensland islands to reach. It is also a popular destination for day trips; the resort has a separate section for day-trippers, with a small pool, bar, outdoor tables and umbrellas, a restaurant and a cafe – and all sorts of water sports gear for hire.

## Things to See

Great Keppel's beaches are among the best on any of the resort islands. Take a short stroll from the busy main resort area and you'll find your own deserted stretch of white, sandy beach. The water is clear, warm and beautiful, and there is fairly good coral and excellent fish life around, especially between Great Keppel and Humpy Island to the south. A 30-minute walk around the headland south of the resort brings you to **Monkey Beach**, where there's good snorkelling. A walking trail from the southern end of the airfield takes you to **Long Beach**, perhaps the best of the island's beaches.

There are several bushwalking tracks from **Fisherman's Beach**, the main beach.

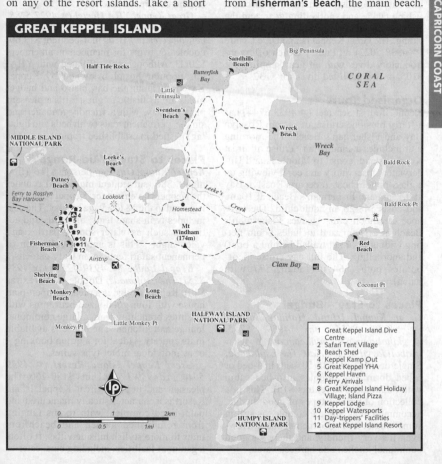

**GREAT KEPPEL ISLAND**

1 Great Keppel Island Dive Centre
2 Safari Tent Village
3 Beach Shed
4 Keppel Kamp Out
5 Great Keppel YHA
6 Keppel Haven
7 Ferry Arrivals
8 Great Keppel Island Holiday Village; Island Pizza
9 Keppel Lodge
10 Keppel Watersports
11 Day-trippers' Facilities
12 Great Keppel Island Resort

The longest, and perhaps most difficult, leads to the 2.5m 'lighthouse' near **Bald Rock Point** on the far side of the island (three hours return).

There's an **underwater observatory** by Middle Island, close to Great Keppel. A confiscated Taiwanese fishing junk was sunk next to the observatory to provide a haven for fish.

## Activities

The Beach Shed on Putney Beach and Keppel Watersports on Fisherman's Beach both hire out sailboards, catamarans, motorboats, fishing tackle and snorkelling gear, and the staff can also take you paragliding or water-skiing. The Great Keppel Island Dive Centre (☎ 4939 5022) on Putney Beach offers introductory dives with all gear supplied for $105, or two qualified dives for $132.

## Organised Tours

Keppel Tourist Services (☎ 4933 6744) has a 'ferry plus one cruise' deal from Rosslyn Bay and Fisherman's Beach. The morning tour includes a commentary cruise of Great Keppel Island, a visit to Middle Island Underwater Observatory and coral viewing on a glass-bottom boat. It departs Rosslyn Bay at 9.15am and Fisherman's Beach at 10am, and costs $48/26 an adult/child. The two-hour afternoon cruise leaves Fisherman's Beach at 2.15pm, and includes boom netting (riding on a net trailed behind a boat) and snorkelling. The full-day cruise incorporates both ($64 per adult, $77 with lunch).

## Places to Stay – Budget

*Great Keppel Island Holiday Village* (☎ 4939 8655, fax 4939 8755, e gkiholidays@ozemail.com.au, w www .gkiholidayvillage.com.au, The Esplanade) Single/double tents $35/50, beds in 4-bed or 6-bed dorm $24, doubles in 4-bed cabin with bathroom $90 (extras $15). This is a collection of various types of good, budget accommodation, and the complex is still in something of a developmental phase. However, it's very friendly, and there's a good communal kitchen and barbecue area.

*Keppel Haven* (Booking office: ☎ 4933 6744, fax 4933 6429, John Howes Dr, Rosslyn Bay) Keppel Haven operates as an umbrella banner for several accommodation facilities. It has a bar and bistro serving breakfast, lunch and dinner, and offers discount packages that include ferry transfers.

*Safari Tent Village* Beds in 4-bed safari tent $17.50, twins $20. The village, part of Keppel Haven, has no-frills, permanent safari tents with beds and lighting set in patchy, poorly-maintained grass. There is a large, covered outdoor dining area adjoining the communal kitchen.

*Great Keppel YHA Hostel* (☎ 4927 5288, 4933 6416, fax 4933 6429, e ktsgki@ networx.com.au) Beds in 4-bed tent $17.60, doubles & twins for members/nonmembers $20/23. Although still affiliated with YHA, this popular hostel is owned by Keppel Haven, meaning the bar, bistro and budget meals are available to guests. It's a pleasant place to stay, with a friendly manager and simple, permanent tents (with beds and lighting) nestled in established tropical greenery.

## Places to Stay – Mid-Range

*Keppel Kamp Out* Per person $116 (first night), $86 (subsequent nights). Also under the Keppel Haven banner, Keppel Kamp Out is geared to the 18 to 35 age bracket. The cost includes twin-share tents, all meals and activities such as water sports, parties and video nights. This is another collection of permanent safari tents set in leafy gardens.

*Keppel Lodge* (☎ 4939 4251, fax 4939 8251, The Esplanade) Doubles $110 (extras $40). Keppel Lodge is a pleasant open-plan house with four good-sized bedrooms with en suites branching from a large communal lounge and kitchen. The house is available in its entirety – ideal for a group booking – or as individual motel-type suites.

*Great Keppel Island Resort* (☎ 4939 5044, fax 4939 1775) Units $180-260. The pleasant and popular Great Keppel Island Resort is a characteristically manicured and palm-lined complex, with rooms ranging from refurbished garden and beachfront units to more stylish hillside villas. It offers a gamut of facilities, including bars, eateries

Marina on Hamilton Island, Whitsundays

Catseye Beach on Hamilton Island

The Whitsunday Islands, once a coastal mountain range

GARETH McCORMACK

Smooth stones and reef rubble

KATE DALY

The colours of the reef for your feet

RICHARD I'ANSON

Yachts under full sail around Hamilton Island

MITCH REARDON

A common Queensland sight, the Major Mitchell cockatoo

RICHARD I'ANSON

Colourful sails

and nightclubs, a golf course, tennis and squash courts, a pool, and water sports from snorkelling to skiing. More than 40 of the activities are free to resort guests. As is the custom, the resort offers a range of package deals to make longer stays cheaper.

## Places to Eat
If you want to cook it's best to bring supplies with you, although the kiosks at *Keppel Haven* and the adjacent *Great Keppel Island Holiday Village* have a few basics like soup and noodles.

*Keppel Haven Bar & Bistro* (☎ 4933 6744) Dishes $5-21. This pleasant, airy eatery is conveniently located for backpackers and budget travellers, but don't expect a budget meal. Moderately pricey, it serves tasty breakfasts, lunches and dinners, but there is a YHA special: fish and chips (or pasta), with salad and a glass of beer ($10).

*Island Pizza* (☎ 4939 4699, *The Esplanade*) Dishes $5.50-27.90. Open dinner Tues-Sun, lunch Sat & Sun. This friendly place prides itself on a unique healthy pizza recipe with plenty of toppings. It also serves hot dogs ($5.50) and pastas ($11), but the pizzas aren't super cheap, ranging from $14.90 to $27.90.

The resort offers a few options.

*Keppel Cafe* Meals $3.90-$15. In the day-trippers' area, Keppel Cafe caters for the 'junk food junkie' offering light lunches and hot food, including sandwiches, pizzas and great (but expensive) burgers.

*Anchorage Char Grill* Mains around $15. Open lunch & dinner. The Char Grill serves reasonably good meals in an open setting near the day-trippers' pool. Options include vegetable samosas and calamari skewers.

*Admiral Keppel Restaurant* 3-course meal $31.50. This more upmarket eatery is upstairs at the resort, where you can eat Thai calamari salad, pumpkin gnocchi and chocolate kahlua cake on the balcony.

## Entertainment
*Wreck Bar* The resort's spacious Wreck Bar, at the day-trippers' area, is the place to party, with pool tables, and a dance floor and live music nightly.

## Getting There & Away
Ferries for Great Keppel leave from Rosslyn Bay Harbour, about 7km south of Yeppoon. Keppel Tourist Services (☎ 4933 6744) operates daily ferries to the island, departing at 7.30am, 9.15am, 11.30am and 3.30pm, and leaving to return at 8.15am, 2pm and 4.30pm. There is an extra service on Friday, departing Rosslyn Bay at 6pm and Great Keppel at 6.40pm. It charges $30/15 per adult/child. Keppel Tourist Services and Rothery's Coaches (☎ 4922 4320) run a daily bus service from Rockhampton to Rosslyn Bay, picking up from the airport ($30 return) and accommodation in Rocky ($15.40 return).

The Freedom Fast Cats (☎ 4833 6244) departs the Keppel Bay Marina in Rosslyn Bay at 9am, 11am and 3pm, and leaving Great Keppel at 10am, 2pm and 4pm. The return fare is $29.

## OTHER KEPPEL BAY ISLANDS
Great Keppel is the biggest of 18 continental islands dotted around Keppel Bay, all within 20km of the coast. You can visit **Middle Island**, with its underwater observatory, or **Halfway** and **Humpy** islands if you're staying on Great Keppel.

Some of the islands are national parks where you can maroon yourself for a few days of self-sufficient *camping*. Most have clean, white beaches and several, notably Halfway Island, have good fringing coral reefs excellent for snorkelling or diving.

## Places to Stay
To camp on a national park island, you need to take all your own supplies including water. Camper numbers on each island are restricted. You can get information and permits from the EPA in Rockhampton (☎ 4936 0511) or Rosslyn Bay (☎ 4933 6608).

The second-largest of the group and one of the most northerly is **North Keppel Island**. It covers 6 sq km and is a national park. The most popular *camping* spot is Considine Beach on the north-western coast, which has toilets and a shower. There are a few small palms and other scattered trees, but shade is limited. Take insect repellent.

Other islands with *camping grounds* include Humpy, Miall and Middle.

**Pumpkin Island** *(☎ 4939 2431, 4939 4413)* Camp sites $10, cabins $130 ($140 for 5 people or more). This is a tiny, privately owned island, just south of North Keppel. It has five simple, cosy cabins with inviting names like 'Sleep Inn'. They have water and solar power, and each has a stove, fridge, barbecue and bathroom. All you need to bring is food and linen. You can also camp here.

### Getting There & Away
The Keppel Bay Marina (☎ 4933 6244) can organise a water taxi for camping drop-offs from Rosslyn Bay to the islands; it costs a minimum of $300 return, so it pays to go as part of a group of 10 or more.

# Capricorn Hinterland

The Capricorn Hwy runs inland from Rockhampton, virtually along the tropic and across the central Queensland highlands to Barcaldine.

The area was first opened up by miners chasing gold and copper around Emerald, and sapphires around Anakie, but cattle, grain crops and coal are its lifeblood today. Carnarvon, south of Emerald, and the Blackdown Tableland, south-east of the coal-mining centre of Blackwater, are two of Queensland's most spectacular and interesting national parks.

The Gemfields region, around the towns of Sapphire and Rubyvale, is a fascinating area to visit and explore, and you can fossick for valuable gemstones here.

At Blair Athol, you can take a free tour of the massive open-cut coal mine.

## ROCKHAMPTON TO EMERALD
It's 261km from Rockhampton to Emerald. On the way, you can take an interesting detour to the spectacular Blackdown Tableland National Park and stay at a popular farm-stay at Dingo.

## Blackdown Tableland National Park
The Blackdown Tableland is an amazing sandstone plateau that rises out of the flat plains to a height of 600m. It features stunning panoramas, great bushwalks to waterfalls and lookouts, Aboriginal rock-art, creeks and eucalypt forests. There's also a good *camping ground* here.

The turn-off to the park is signposted from the Capricorn Hwy, 11km west of Dingo and 35km east of Blackwater. From here, it's 23km to the top, the last 8km of which are steep, winding and often slippery. Caravans are not recommended.

At the top you come to the breath-taking **Horseshoe Lookout**, with picnic tables, barbecues and toilets beside the carpark. There's a walking trail starting here to **Two Mile Falls** (2km).

*South Mimosa Creek camping ground (Dingo rangers ☎ 4986 1964, fax 4986 1325)* Camp sites $3.85 per person. This picturesque self-registration camping area is about 6km on from Horseshoe Lookout. It has pit toilets and fireplaces – you'll need to bring drinking water, firewood and/or a fuel stove, and bookings are advised. Several other walking trails start from the camping ground.

## Dingo
Near Dingo, *Namoi Hills Cattle Station (☎ 4935 9121, fax 4935 9234, e namoi _hills@bigpond.com.au, Namoi Hills Rd* is another popular farm-stay, which caters specifically for backpackers and budget travellers, and has a real focus on fun. It has cheap beds in ranch-style units (rates with/without meals $30.80/17.60) and a special deal for longer stays. The station offers a cross-country tour ($16.50), a make-your-own-didgeridoo trip ($159.50), and excursions to Rubyvale's S'n'S Mine ($154).

## EMERALD
postcode 4720 • pop 9350
At the junction of the Gregory and Capricorn Hwys, Emerald is the gateway of the Capricorn hinterland region. Established in 1879 as a railway siding, it has grown into

a major centre for the surrounding mining and agricultural industries.

Most of the town's older buildings were destroyed in disastrous fires in 1936, 1940, 1954 and 1968. One notable exception is the fine, old **Emerald Railway Station**, on Clermont St in the town centre, built in 1900 and restored in 1987.

The Central Highlands Tourist Information Centre (☎ 4982 4142) is at the western end of Clermont St, next to Morton Park. It's open from 9am to 5pm Monday to Saturday, and 10am to 2pm Sunday.

The town library (☎ 4982 8347), at 44 Borilla St, has two free Internet terminals, and is open varying hours from Monday to Saturday. Alternatively, the Emerald Computer Centre (☎ 4982 4100) is nearby at 3/5 Church Lane, but you'll have to pay.

## Things to See

The **Emerald Pioneer Cottage & Museum** (☎ 4987 6119, 3 Centenary Dr; admission $2; open 2pm-4pm Mon-Fri Apr-Oct) has a collection of historic buildings including the town's first church and jail.

**Kiely's Farm & Animal Sanctuary** (☎ 4987 6700, Weemah Rd; adult/child $7.50/3.50; open 11.30am-5pm daily) is an interesting little place 7km east of Emerald. It has a menagerie of animals enclosed in fairly spacious enclosures, from dingoes and foxes to rats and camels. There's a good canteen and farm tours in season.

If you're into art on a grand scale, Morton Park, on Dundas St next to the tourist office, has a 25m-tall easel sporting an enormous replica of van Gogh's **Sunflowers**, a celebration of the region's reputation as a major sunflower producer. There are plans for a huge interpretive centre to be built in this park, which will be dedicated to Emerald's influences, from Ludwig Leichhardt to the railways, mining and Aboriginal heritage.

## Places to Stay

**Emerald Cabin & Caravan Village** (☎ 4982 1300, fax 4987 5320, 64 Opal St) Unpowered/powered sites $13.30/17.70, vans/cabins $30/45. This large park is only a pitching wedge from the golf course and

has rows of neat cabins and on-site vans, immaculate amenities, and a shaded camping area with a kitchen and barbecue.

**Central Inn** (☎ 4982 0800, fax 4982 0801, 90 Clermont St) Singles/doubles $39/49 ($4 less Fri & Sat). Double-glazed windows and fire doors keep out the highway and railyard noise in this good budget motel with shared facilities and awful green carpet. The tariffs include a continental breakfast.

**Western Gateway Motel** (☎ 4982 3899, fax 4982 3107, Hospital Rd) Singles/doubles $83.50/96.50. The Western Gateway is more upmarket, with big, comfortable rooms in typical motel style, and a good restaurant. Rates include breakfast.

## Getting There & Away

McCafferty's/Greyhound has a terminal at 115 Clermont St. Its buses run daily between Emerald and Rockhampton, and twice weekly between Emerald and Longreach. You can also get here on the twiceweekly *Spirit of the Outback* train, which runs from Rocky to Longreach, or by air on Sunstate from Brisbane ($425).

## AROUND EMERALD

Queensland's second-largest artificial lake, **Lake Maraboon**, is 18km south-west of Emerald. There's a boat ramp, attractive picnic areas and, just 100m from the water, the pleasant *Lake Maraboon Holiday Village* (☎ 4982 3677, fax 4982 1932, Fairbairn Dam Access Rd), where unpowered/powered double sites are $13/16, and cabins are $60.

Tiny **Capella** is midway between Emerald and Clermont. It has a small historic village, and is the starting point for several interesting self-drive tour options, including Scotts Peak, Mt Roper and Bundoora Dam. The town has a pub with budget accommodation, a neat caravan park and a motel.

## CLERMONT

postcode 4721 • pop 2400

Just over 50km north-west of Emerald is Clermont and the huge Blair Athol open-cut coal mine, with the world's largest seam of steaming coal. Clermont is Queensland's oldest tropical inland town, founded on gold, copper, sheep and cattle – influences are commemorated in murals on four train carriages in Herchel St.

In December 1916 a flood virtually destroyed the town and claimed 65 lives. After the disaster, Clermont was moved building by building to higher ground, and the beautiful Hoods Lagoon occupies its former site. A concrete tree stump at the lagoon's southern end shows the high water mark (14 feet 6 inches or 4.35m). Across the road you'll find a replica piano up a tree, another reminder of the flood.

The town's helpful information centre (☎ 4983 3001), at 57 Capella St, is open from 8.30am to 5pm Monday to Friday and until noon Saturday.

The **Historical Society Museum** (☎ 4983 3311, Peak Downs Hwy; adult/child $5/2; open varying hours daily), about 3km north of the centre, has an interesting collection, including a steam traction engine used to relocate the flooded buildings.

Wombat Wanderers (☎ 4983 3292, 6 Kitchener St; free tours 8.45am Tuesday and Friday) takes fascinating four-hour tours of the **Blair Athol Mine**, departing from the information centre. Ring in advance to book.

## Places to Stay & Eat

*Clermont Caravan Park* (☎/fax 4983 1927, 1 Haig St) Unpowered/powered sites $11/15.40, on-site vans from $22, cabins from $38.50. The park is run by a friendly couple, and is obviously well maintained. It has plenty of grass, two big, clean amenities blocks and good vans.

*Peppercorn Motel* (☎ 4983 1033, fax 4983 1679, e peppercorn@cqhinet .net.au, 53 Capricorn St) Singles/doubles $71/79. The Peppercorn is Clermont's best motel, with spacious modern rooms, a pleasant saltwater pool and a good *restaurant*.

## GEMFIELDS

West of Emerald, about 270km inland from Rockhampton, the gemfields around the towns of Anakie, Sapphire, Rubyvale and Willows are known for their sapphires, zircons, rubies, jasper, and even diamonds and gold.

### The Fossicker

The gemfields attract colourful characters as diverse as the difference between a valuable sapphire and an ordinary rock. Out on the fossicking fields you'll find them, hip-deep in holes, swinging a pick in the midday sun. They may have a dog chained up nearby for company, and a battered old thermos for refreshment. If the heat has got the better of them, they may have their shirts off, revealing a sinewy torso baked brown by the sun. Nearby is a primitive and well-worn 'willoughby', the device used to separate the gems from the dirt, and it's here these bounty hunters hope to see 'the big one'. They don't say much, just mumble affably about what's good and what's not in the current batch, slipping anything remotely valuable in their mouths for safe-keeping. When that lot of dirt is washed and thoroughly examined, it's back to the hole and the pick. Such is the life of the gem fossicker.

They are the world's richest sapphire deposits, and it is still possible to find valuable gems in the area, including the 2000-carat Centenary Sapphire found in 1979, and worth more than $1 million. The latest big find was in 2000, when some Bundaberg tourists unearthed the 221-carat Millennium Sapphire, which sold for $87,000.

There are several fossicking parks in the area that sell buckets of dirt that you can wash and sieve by hand – 'doing a bucket' is great fun and a good way to learn to identify raw sapphires. There are also several tourist mines that take underground tours. If you strike it lucky, there are professional cutters who can cut your stones for around $20 per carat.

To go fossicking you need a licence ($5.10) from the Emerald Courthouse or one of the gemfields' general stores or post offices. You can buy *bush camping* permits ($2.20 per night) from the same places, which allow you to pitch a tent anywhere in the fields. Basic fossicking equipment includes sieves, a pick and shovel, water and a container. You can bring this with you, or hire it when you arrive.

The most popular times to visit are the drier, cooler months from April to September – when the population can more than double.

## Information

The Gemfields Information Centre (☎ 4985 4525), at 1 Anakie Rd, has a wealth of information about the area, and conducts tagalong tours ($55) and transported digging tours ($99) to good fossicking sites with all equipment and licences provided.

## Special Events

On the second week in August, Anakie hosts the annual Gemfest Festival of Gems, featuring exhibitions of gems, jewellery, mining and fossicking equipment, art and craft markets, and entertainment.

## Rubyvale

postcode 4702 • pop 600

Rubyvale is the main centre for the gemfields, but don't expect bright lights or hustle and bustle. It's a small, ramshackle place with a scattered collection of dwellings, a pub, a few gem shops and galleries, a general store and a service station.

Rubyvale is 18km north of Anakie. From here, it's another 62km to Capella, about half of which is bitumen.

**Things to See** About 2km north of Rubyvale, **Miners Heritage Walk-in Mine** (☎ 4985 4444, Heritage Rd; adult/child $6.60/2.75; open 9am-5pm) has informative 20-minute underground tours in which you descend into a maze of tunnels 18m beneath the surface. There is also an underground gem shop, and you can 'do a bucket' for $6 in the spacious picnic area up above.

**Bobby Dazzler Mine** (☎ 4985 4170, Main St; adult/child $5.50/2.50; open 9am-5pm) offers similar tours that take half an hour. Again, you can sort through a bucket of dirt ($6), and there's a little museum here.

Unlike the others, the acclaimed **S'n'S Mine** (☎ 4985 4307, Heritage Rd) takes you 17m down a vertical shaft and lets you dig for your own sapphires with a jackhammer.

Unfortunately it's open only for guests of Namoi Hills Cattle Station (see under Dingo in the Rockhampton to Emerald section).

The **Miners Cottage** (☎ 4985 4190, Goanna Flats Rd; open 9am-4pm Apr-Oct) is a small timber cottage with crafts, jewellery and gems on sale. Here you can fill your own wheelbarrow ($35) or 4-gallon drum ($15) with dirt from the surrounding mining claim, wash it, and then realise you've got no-one to blame but yourself if you don't strike it rich.

The **Rubyvale Gem Gallery** (☎ 4985 4388) does educational half-day 4WD tours of the gemfields for $38, while **Fascination** (☎ 4985 4142) conducts self-drive fossicking outings for $30.

**Places to Stay & Eat** Rubyvale offers a small range of accommodation options.

*Taylor's Units* (☎/fax 4985 4518, Heritage Rd) 1-bedroom/2 bedroom units $65/85. If you're looking for some luxury after playing in the dirt, these two brand-new self-contained units, about 1km north of Rubyvale, are as close as you'll get.

*Bedford Gardens Caravan Park* (☎/fax 4985 4175, 10 Vane Tempest Rd) Camp sites/van sites $11/13.20, single/double cabins $55/60.50. There are some excellent camp sites amid the attractive lawns and gardens here, as well as barbecues and a backpackers kitchen. If you'd prefer a bed, there are decent air-con units with kitchens.

*New Royal Hotel* (☎ 4985 4754, fax 4985 4463, 2 Keilambete Rd) Twins $90 (extras $12), groups (6 or more) $20 per person. Counter meals $7-14. The attractive New Royal has four cosy, self-contained log cabins in keeping with the theme of the pub. They sleep eight, and include open fires. There are also good, cheap *lunches* and *dinners* daily, with the usual fare of steak, chicken and pasta.

## Sapphire

About 10km north of Anakie, Sapphire has a petrol station, a post office, and a few houses scattered around the hillside. It also has a unique accommodation option, and several fossicking parks.

**Activities** Pat's Gems (☎ 4985 4544), at 1056 Rubyvale Rd 1km north of Sapphire, has buckets of dirt for $6 each or six buckets for $25. It also has fossicking gear available for hire.

Another 1km north, the Forever Mine (☎ 4985 4616), at 1162 Rubyvale Rd, has a cutting room and jewellery on sale. Again, you can buy a bucket of dirt for $6.

**Places to Stay & Eat** Sapphire offers rustic cabins and alfresco dining.

*Sunrise Cabins (☎ 4985 4281, 57 Sunrise Rd)* Double sites $11, single/double cabins $13/28, doubles in 7-bed cabin $31 (extras $3), single/double self-contained cabins $30/35. In the bush near Sapphire, these cabins are built from 'billy boulders', the smooth, round stones common to the area. They're simple, rustic and homey, and you can choose self-contained units, or larger seven-berth cabins. There are communal toilets and showers, barbecues and a large kitchen.

*Pat's Gems (☎ 4985 4544, 1056 Rubyvale Rd)* Lunch $2-6. Open 9am-4.30pm. This is a pleasant place to regain your strength after a morning's fossicking. It sells sandwiches, burgers, cake and coffee, and you can eat alfresco.

### Anakie

About 1km south of the highway, Anakie has a train station, *caravan park* and a *pub* with units and good counter meals.

*Ramboda Homestead (☎ 4985 4154, fax 4985 4210, Capricorn Hwy)*, just east of Anakie, is an attractive old timber homestead on a working cattle property. It has country-style bedrooms with shared bathrooms on the second storey (singles/doubles $50/100), and the tariff includes both breakfast and dinner.

The turn-off to **Willows Gemfield** is about 27km west of Anakie, and it's another 11km to the village. There are a couple of *caravan parks* here.

### Getting There & Away

You can get to Anakie on a McCafferty's/Greyhound bus or to Emerald on the *Spirit*

*of the Outback* train. Vaughan's Bus Service (☎ 4982 1275) has school buses from Emerald to Rubyvale on weekdays at 3.10pm, returning from Rubyvale at 7.30am ($5 one way).

## SPRINGSURE

Springsure, 66km south of Emerald, has an attractive backdrop of granite mountains and surrounding sunflower fields. The **Virgin Rock**, an outcrop of Mt Zamia on the northern outskirts, was named after early settlers claimed to have seen the image of the Virgin Mary in the rock face.

About 10km south-west at Burnside is the **Old Rainworth Fort** (☎ 4984 1674, Off Wealwandangie Rd; adult/child $6/1.10; open 9am-2pm Mon-Wed & Fri, 9am-5pm Sat & Sun), built following the Wills Massacre of 1861 when Aborigines killed 19 whites on Cullin-La-Ringo Station northwest of Springsure.

*Queen's Arms Hotel (☎ 4984 1533, fax 4984 1150, 14 Charles St)* is on the highway that skirts the town. This old pub is good value, with recently upgraded aircon rooms (singles/doubles $25/45). The tariff includes breakfast.

Springsure also has a couple of midrange *motels* and a *caravan park*.

## ROLLESTON

Rolleston, on the Dawson Hwy 70km south-east of Springsure, is the northern turn-off for Carnarvon National Park. The town has a couple of service stations, and Fulford Tyre Service (☎ 4984 3355) is the local RACQ depot.

The simple and friendly *Rolleston Caravan Park (☎ 4984 3145, fax 4984 3003, Comet St)* has tent sites ($6) and on-site vans ($30), while the *Rolleston Hotel (☎ 4984 4544, fax 4984 3445, Warrijo St)* has basic motel-style units from $55, including breakfast. There are *counter meals* here nightly.

## CARNARVON NATIONAL PARK

Rugged Carnarvon National Park, in the middle of the Great Dividing Range, features dramatic gorge scenery and many Aboriginal rock paintings and carvings. The national park has several sections, but most are virtually inaccessible; most people see the impressive Carnarvon Gorge (the other sections are Mt Moffatt, Ka Ka Mundi and Salvator Rosa).

## Carnarvon Gorge

The Gorge is stunning, partly because it's an oasis surrounded by drier plains and partly because of its scenic variety, which includes sandstone cliffs, moss gardens, deep pools, rare palms and ferns, and lots of wildlife. Aboriginal art can be viewed at three main sites – **Baloon Cave**, **Art Gallery** and **Cathedral Cave**.

About 3km into the Carnarvon Gorge section there's an information centre (☎ 4984 4505, open 8am to 5pm) and a scenic picnic ground. The main walking track starts beside the information centre and follows the Carnarvon Creek through the gorge. Detours lead to various points of interest, such as the **Moss Garden** (3.6km from the camping ground), **Ward's Canyon** (4.8km), the **Art Gallery** (5.6km) and Cathedral Cave (9.3km). Allow *at least* half a day for a visit here and bring lunch and water as there are no shops.

## Mt Moffatt

The more westerly and rugged Mt Moffatt section of Carnarvon National Park has some beautiful scenery, and diverse vegetation and fauna, and **Kenniff Cave**, which is an important Aboriginal archaeological site with stencil paintings on the rock walls. It's believed Aborigines lived here as many as 19,000 years ago.

## Organised Tours

Sunrover Expeditions (☎ 1800 353 717, ☎/fax 3203 4241) runs a six-day camping safari into Carnarvon Gorge. The cost per person is $840, including transport, meals and camping equipment.

CQ Travel Link (☎ 4982 1399), based in Emerald, offers day trips to Carnarvon Gorge, including lunch, for $165 per person.

## Places to Stay

*Takarakka Bush Resort* (*☎/fax 1984 4535,* e *takarakka@telstra.easymail.com.au, Wyseby Rd*) Camp sites per adult/child $8/4, powered sites $22, cabins $65. About 4.6km from the picnic ground, Takarakka is a picturesque bush oasis, with a big open camping area and a ring of simply furnished, elevated

# CARNARVON NATIONAL PARK

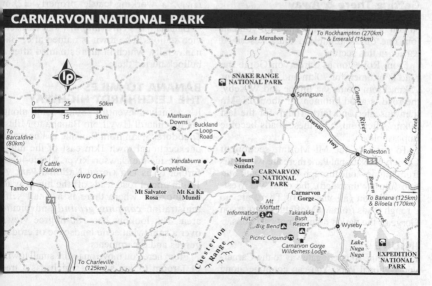

canvas cabins with private verandas. There's a big, modern cooking and eating area, and hot showers in the amenities block.

**Big Bend camping ground** (☎ *4984 4505, fax 4984 4519*) Camping per person $3.85. This isolated national park camping ground is a 10km walk up the gorge, about 500m upstream from Cathedral Cave. Campers require permits, and fires are not permitted. There are toilets here, but no showers.

**Mt Moffatt camping ground** (☎ *Mt Moffatt rangers 4626 3581, fax 4626 3651*) Camping per person $3.85. In the Mt Moffatt section camping with a permit is allowed at four sites, but you need to be completely self-sufficient and a 4WD and extra fuel are advisable. Bookings are a good idea.

**Carnarvon Gorge Wilderness Lodge** (☎ *1800 644 150, 4984 4503, fax 4984 4500,* ⓔ *info@carnarvon_gorge.com.au, Wyseby Rd*) B&B $95 per person, with all meals & activities $190. This upmarket accommodation option is located near the park entrance, offering cosy safari cabins nestled in the bush. There's a **restaurant**, bar and a pool here – the rates drop considerably for longer stays, and between November and April.

### Getting There & Away

No buses travel to Carnarvon National Park so you need your own transport, or you can join one of the organised tours described earlier in this section.

From Rolleston to Carnarvon Gorge the road is bitumen for 70km and unsealed for 25km. From Roma via Injune and Wyseby, the road is good bitumen for about 215km then unsealed and fairly rough for the last 30km. After rain, both these roads become impassable.

To get into the Mt Moffatt section of Carnarvon National Park there are two roads from Injune – one through Womblebank Station (mostly unsealed), the other via Westgrove Station (all unsealed). There are no through roads from Mt Moffatt to Carnarvon Gorge or the park's other remote sections.

### INJUNE

Injune is the southern gateway to the Carnarvon National Park. You can continue along the Carnarvon Developmental Rd to the turn-off to the gorge section of the park 110km north at Wyseby, or turn off here and take the unsealed road that leads 140km north-west into the Mt Moffatt section of the park.

At the **Injune Caravan Park** (☎ *4626 1053, fax 4626 1110, Cnr Station St & Third Ave*) your first two nights are free (after that a site is $5). The **Injune Hotel** (☎ *4626 1205, fax 4626 1453, 31 Station St*) offers basic accommodation (singles/doubles $18/30).

There's also a motel in town, and the Carnarvon Gateway Service Station (☎ 4626 1279) is the local RACQ depot.

### ROLLESTON TO BANANA – THE DAWSON HIGHWAY

**Planet Downs Station** (☎ *3265 5022, fax 3265 3978,* ⓔ *planetd@bloxsom.aust .com, Dawson Hwy*) is a cut above your average farm-stay, with luxury accommodation (including pot-belly stoves, and gold-plated fittings in the en suites), and a hefty tariff that includes all meals and activities (twins $660 per person).

Another, much more affordable farm-stay option is **Cooper Downs Cattle Station** (☎ *4996 5276, fax 4996 5259, Leichhardt Hwy*), a working cattle property 37km north-east of Banana.

Banana has a **caravan park** and two service stations. The town is named after Banana Gully, which in turn is named after a bullock buried there.

### BANANA TO MILES – THE LEICHHARDT HIGHWAY

It's a fairly uneventful 280km south along the Leichhardt Hwy from Banana to Miles. **Theodore**, 59km from Banana, is a neat and unexceptional town 1km east of the highway beside the Dawson River. About 40km further on is **Isla Gorge National Park**. A 1.5km gravel road leads off the highway to the **lookout**, where there is a small self-registration **camping ground** and picnic area. The lookout has 180-degree views over a somewhat eerie landscape of eroded gorges and escarpments.

From here you move on to the small towns of **Taroom** (55km south), which has a tree initialled by Ludwig Leichhardt, and **Wandoan** (59km north of Miles), both of which have *caravan parks*, pubs and *motels*.

*Possum Park* (☎/*fax 4627 1651, Leichhardt Hwy)*, about 50km south of Wandoan, has old RAAF bunkers and troop train carriages that have been converted into simple self-contained guest units (double units $60). This unique and peaceful accommodation complex, in about 3 sq km of bush, also has camping facilities (camp sites $6, caravan sites from $16).

See the Darling Downs chapter for details of Miles and surrounds.

## BILOELA
At the junction of the Dawson and Burnett Hwys, Biloela is a modern commercial centre for the surrounding agricultural, pastoral and coal-mining industries.

The town's small tourist information centre (☎ 4992 2405) is at Callide St, at the junction of the Dawson and Leichhardt Hwys. It's open from 9am to 5pm Monday to Friday and until noon Saturday.

Biloela isn't exactly a tourists' Mecca, but there are some notable diversions here, including **the Silo** (☎ *4992 2400, Exhibition Ave; adult/child $7.50/4.40; open 9am-4pm daily)*, an interesting interactive museum dedicated to the area's primary industries.

The **Greycliffe Homestead** (☎ *4992 1121, Gladstone Rd; admission by donation; open by appointment)* is a National Trust–listed, slab-timber home, built in the 1870s. It's now used as a reminder of how the area's pioneers lived.

In contrast, the huge **Callide B Power Station** (☎ *4992 9329, Callide Mine Rd; admission free; museum open 6am-6pm Mon-Fri, tours 1.30pm Tues-Fri)*, 18km east of town, was built slightly more than 100 years later and is a major supplier of electricity to Queensland. There are tours of the plant and a museum.

There are two good caravan parks in town: The *Boomerang Caravan Park* (☎ *4992 1815, fax 4992 6304, 10 Dunn St)* is the more central. The *Commercial Hotel* (☎ *1992 1603, fax 1992 3554, 61 Kariboe St)* offers tidy single/twin rooms for $20/35.

Biloela's best motel is the modern *Settlers Hotel-Motel* (☎ *1800 105 155, 4992 2933, fax 4992 2627, [e] settlers@tpgi.com.au, Dawson Hwy)*, which has singles/doubles for $75/84.

# Whitsunday Coast

This chapter covers the coastal strip from Sarina to Bowen and the corresponding hinterland. Mackay is the region's major town, and the Whitsunday Islands are the main attraction for travellers.

The chapter is split into two sections: the area around Mackay, including the wonderful Eungella National Park and offshore islands such as Brampton, Carlisle, Newry and Rabbit; and the Whitsunday area, covering the islands themselves as well as the mainland towns and access points for the Whitsundays.

## Activities

There are trips to the outer Barrier Reef from Mackay, as well as a huge range of boat trips and water sports on offer in the Whitsundays. For bushwalkers, the Eungella National Park is a highlight; Cape Hillsborough National Park and Brampton Island also have some excellent walks.

There are a few good golf courses in this area, including those at Mackay and the Laguna Quays Resort; Lindeman, South Molle and Brampton Islands also have courses.

## Getting There & Away

**Air** Mackay has a major domestic airport, and Qantas (☎ 13 13 13) has regular flights to all the major centres. Brampton Island also has its own airport, serviced by Macair (Qantas) from Mackay.

If you're heading for the Whitsundays, Qantas has frequent flights to Hamilton Island, from where there are boat/air transfers to all the other islands. Qantas also flies into Proserpine on the mainland – from there you can take a charter flight to the islands or a bus to Airlie Beach or nearby Shute Harbour.

There's also the Whitsunday airport, a small airfield near Airlie Beach, with regular services to the islands. Lindeman Island has its own airstrip.

**Bus** McCafferty's/Greyhound and Premier bus companies have regular services along the Bruce Hwy with stops at all the major

towns. They also detour off the highway from Proserpine to Airlie Beach.

**Train** The only passenger-carrying railway line in the region is the main coastal line from Brisbane to Cairns.

**Boat** Airlie Beach and Shute Harbour are the main launching pads for boat trips to the Whitsundays – see that section for details.

# Mackay Area

## SARINA
**postcode 4737 • pop 3200**
In the foothills of the Connors Range, Sarina is a service centre for the hundreds of surrounding sugar cane farms. On the town's

# WHITSUNDAY COAST

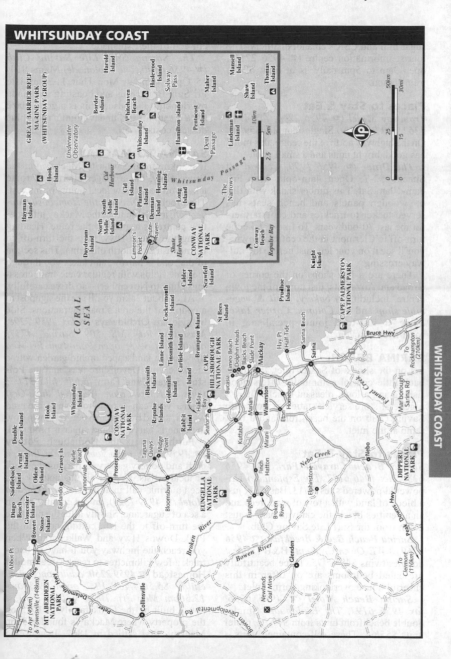

**WHITSUNDAY COAST**

southern outskirts are the huge Plane Creek sugar mill and CSR's ethanol distillery. The tourist information centre (☎ 4956 2251), open 9am to 5pm daily, is in front of the train station.

## Places to Stay & Eat

*Tramway Motel* (☎ *4956 2244, fax 4943 1262, 110 Broad St)* Singles/doubles $59/69. On the highway north of the centre, this motel has good, bright units and a small pool.

*The Diner* (☎ *4956 1990, Central St)* Snacks $2-7. Open 4am-6pm Mon-Fri, 4am-10am Sat. This timber shack with tilt-up wooden panels and bench seats has served tucker to truckies and cane farmers for the last 70-odd years. To find it, take the turn-off to Clermont in the centre of town – you'll see it on your left, just before the railway crossing.

There are a few shops on the corner of Broad and Anzac Sts, just north of the town centre, including a *bakery*, *fruit & vegetable shop* and the *Colonial Corner Takeaway*, a fast-food joint specialising in roast/fried chicken.

## SARINA BEACH

Set on the shores of Sarina Inlet, this laid-back little coastal community offers good fishing and a long, pleasant beach. There's a general store/service station, a Surf Life Saving Club on the beachfront and a boat ramp at the inlet.

## Places to Stay & Eat

*Sarina Beach Caravan Park* (☎ *4956 6130, fax 4946 6197, The Esplanade)* Un-powered/powered sites $7/13. Basically just a block of land with a row of pine trees and an amenities block, the caravan park is just down from the Surf Life Saving Club.

*Sarina Beach Bed & Breakfast* (☎ *4956 6269, 8 WE Owen Crescent)* B&B singles/doubles/twins $48/65/75. Three beautifully presented bedrooms are on offer in this cheerful house overlooking Sarina Inlet.

*Sarina Beach Motel* (☎ *4956 6266, fax 4956 6197, The Esplanade)* Single/double beachfront units from $77/82, motel units $55/64. These self-contained units –

some with beach frontage – are at the northern end of the Esplanade.

*The Sarina Surf Life Saving Club* (☎ *4956 6490, The Esplanade)* Mains $10-15. Open 4pm-late Mon-Thur, 11.30am-late Fri-Sun. Boisterous and boasting a veranda overlooking the beach, this is a good place for a cheap meal; Sunday night's roast plus dessert costs $7.50.

## SARINA TO MACKAY

It's 36km from Sarina to Mackay via the Bruce Hwy, but a longer alternative route takes you past a few local points of interest. The brochure *Discover the Homebush Connection*, available from the Mackay information centre, is a guide to the route. Heading along the Bruce Hwy, take the turn-off to Homebush 2km north of Sarina. This section of the road is narrow, and takes you through the cane fields with regular cane-train crossings (July to November) – so drive carefully.

After about 24km you'll see the signpost to a couple of the area's main attractions. Side by side are **Orchidways** (☎/fax 4959 7298, Masotti's Rd, MS 509 Sarina 4737; adult/child $9/3; open 9am-4pm Fri-Wed Apr-Jan), a landscaped orchid garden with a kiosk serving Devonshire teas, and the **Polston Sugar Cane Farm** (adult/child $14/7; tours at 1.30pm Mon, Wed, Fri, June-Oct) where you can take a tour in a covered wagon, towed by a tractor; you're shown how the cane is harvested and sugar is produced.

Further on is the **Homebush Pottery** (☎ 4959 7339; open 9am-5pm Fri-Tues), a craft and pottery gallery displaying the work of local artists. If, after all this activity you need a drink, call in at the **General Gordon Hotel** (☎ 4959 7324), an old country pub in a sea of sugarcane. Shortly after the pub take the turn-off to the left, cutting north to the Peak Downs Hwy and Walkerston. When you reach the highway you'll have to backtrack a few kilometres to reach **Greenmount Homestead** (☎ 4959 2250; adult/concession/child $5.50/4.40/1.10; open 9.30am-12.30pm Mon-Fri, 10am-3.30pm Sun), a house built by the Cook family in 1915 on the property where Mackay's founder, John Mackay, first settled in 1862. It houses a collection of memorabilia and old farm equipment. To head back to Mackay, return to Walkerston and keep going until you reach the Bruce Hwy.

## MACKAY
### postcode 4740 • pop 73,000

Mackay is surrounded by sugar cane, which has been farmed here since 1865; one-third of Australia's sugar crop is processed here and loaded onto carriers at one of the world's biggest sugar-loading terminals, at Port Mackay.

Mackay is a busy regional city, spread out over a large, flat area. Its attractive town centre has a number of historic buildings, and there are some good beaches a short bus ride away. It's also an access point for the national parks at Cape Hillsborough and Eungella, and there are some interesting islands just an hour or two away, including the popular resort at Brampton Island.

### Orientation

Mackay's city centre is compact, with the main streets laid out in a simple grid on the southern side of the broad Pioneer River. The main thoroughfare is Victoria St, cool and attractive with all its greenery.

The bus terminal is a few hundred metres west of the centre on Milton St, while the train station, airport and tourist information centre are all about 3km south of the city centre.

Sydney St goes across Forgan Bridge to North Mackay, the city's newer suburbs and the northern beaches. Mackay Harbour, 6km north of the centre, is dominated by a massive sugar terminal. The Mackay Marina development, just south of the terminal, is set to be a boon for the town and will provide, at various stages over the next couple of years, shops, restaurants and accommodation.

### Information

Mackay's tourist information centre (☎ 4952 2677, fax 4952 2034, W www .mackayregion.com) is about 3km south of the centre at 320 Nebo Rd (the Bruce Hwy). It's open 8.30am to 5pm Monday to Friday, and 9am to 4pm Saturday and Sunday.

The main post office is in Sydney St, near the corner with Gordon St. There are several places offering Internet access scattered around the city centre.

The office of the Queensland Parks and Wildlife Service (QPWS; ☎ 4944 7800, fax 4944 7811) is on the corner of Wood and River Sts. The Royal Automobile Club of Queensland office (RACQ; ☎ 4957 2918) is on Victoria St in the centre of town.

### Things to See & Do

Despite the effects of several severe cyclones, a number of historic buildings remain around the city centre. The most impressive of these include the neo-Georgian **Court House** (1938), the **Commonwealth Bank** (1880), the impressive **Masonic Lodge** (1925) and the **Old Court House** (1885), which is now the police station. The brochure *A Heritage Walk in Mackay*, available from the tourist centre, guides you around 21 of the town's historic sites.

There are botanic gardens and an **orchid house** *(East Gordon St; admission free; open 10am-11am & 2pm-2.30pm Mon-Fri, 2pm-5pm Sun)* in the attractive **Queen's Park**, about 1km east of the centre. There are good views over the harbour from **Mt Basset**, and at **Rotary Lookout** on Mt Oscar in North Mackay.

In the cane-crushing season, you can visit **Farleigh Sugar Mill** *(☎ 4957 4727, fax 4953 1620; family/adult/child $30/14/8; 2-hour tour departs 1pm Mon-Fri, 7pm Wed)*, 10km north-west of Mackay.

**Beaches & Swimming** Mackay has plenty of beaches, although not all of them are idyllic or even great for swimming. The best ones are about 16km north of Mackay at Blacks Beach, Eimeo and Bucasia (see the Mackay's Northern Beaches section later for accommodation details).

**Town Beach** is the closest to the city centre – to get there, follow Gordon St all the way east from the centre. There is a sandy strip, but the water is very shallow and subsides a long way out at low tides, leaving a long stretch of sand and mud flats – in fact, at low tide you can almost walk across to the

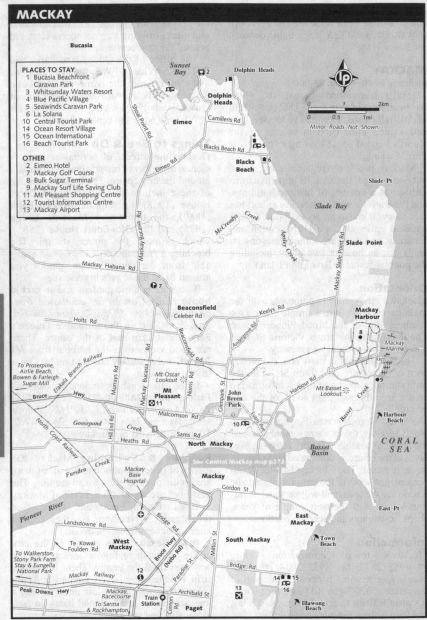

# MACKAY

**PLACES TO STAY**
1 Bucasia Beachfront Caravan Park
3 Whitsunday Waters Resort
4 Blue Pacific Village
5 Seawinds Caravan Park
6 La Solana
10 Central Tourist Park
14 Ocean Resort Village
15 Ocean International
16 Beach Tourist Park

**OTHER**
2 Eimeo Hotel
7 Mackay Golf Course
8 Bulk Sugar Terminal
9 Mackay Surf Life Saving Club
11 Mt Pleasant Shopping Centre
12 Tourist Information Centre
13 Mackay Airport

Minor Roads Not Shown

See Central Mackay map p272

islands 4km offshore. The situation is similar at **Illawong Beach**, a couple of kilometres further south, although the beach here is probably the more attractive of the two.

A better option is **Harbour Beach**, 6km north of the centre and just south of the Mackay Marina. The beach is patrolled by the Mackay Surf Life Saving Club and is backed by a treed foreshore reserve with picnic tables and barbecues.

Back in town, there's an excellent Olympic-sized pool opposite the main bus terminal called the **Memorial Swimming Pool** (☎ 4968 4533, Milton St; adult/child $2.20/1.10).

**Horse Riding** The *Stoney Creek Farm-Stay* (☎ 4954 1177, W www.stoneycreek .webcentral.com.au, Peak Downs Hwy) offers two-hour trail rides from Monday to Saturday for $40. Stoney Creek is 28km south-west of Mackay; trail rides pass through pretty, undulating bush, and you can stay the night in a quaint, hand-hewn cottage (singles/doubles $76/96) or a more basic cabin ($15 per person) with shared facilities. Both types of accommodation are in bush settings – a welcome change to the cane-clad coastal plains. It's possible to get to Stoney Creek by bus; ring ahead for directions.

## Organised Tours

Mackay Adventure Divers (☎ 4953 1431), at 151 Victoria St, offers half-day/full-day snorkelling tours for $95/125, and dive tours for $105/135. This is the only outfit offering dive and snorkelling trips from Mackay; day and night tours take place around the Cumberland Island group.

Jungle Johno Tours (☎ 4951 3728, e larrikin@mackay.net.au) offers day trips for $75/68/40 an adult/YHA member/child. These tours, operating out of Larrikin Lodge YHA, get good reviews and are a great way to see the best bits of Eungella and surrounds in one day. The tour includes pick-up, morning tea, and lunch at the Eungella Chalet.

Reeforest Adventure Tours (☎ 1800 500 353; e adamsonc@tpgi.com.au) has day tours to Cape Hillsborough and Eungella for $85/79/52 an adult/concession/child.

Aboriginal middens, stone fish-traps and a mangrove tour are part of the focus of the Cape Hillsborough trip; and the Eungella tour includes a BBQ lunch at a secluded bush retreat near Finch Hatton Gorge.

## Special Events

Each year around May/June the Wintermoon Festival (☎ 4947 4123, ☎/fax 4958 8390, W www.mockorange.com.au/wintermoon .htm; family/adult/child day tickets $46/18/5) is held at Cameron's Pocket, 70km north of Mackay. This is a great opportunity to hear local and interstate musicians fiddle-strum-sing their stuff; most people make a weekend of it and camp near the festival grounds. Day tickets can be bought from the Mackay Entertainment Centre (☎ 4957 1777) or at the festival.

## Places to Stay

With the exception of the YHA hostel, there's a dearth of good budget accommodation in the city centre. Strung along the southern entry to town, along the Bruce Hwy, there are myriad motels – at night it's one long strip of neon signs – and caravan parks; most of these places have their prices posted out the front. The northern beach suburbs offer a wider choice of accommodation to choose from (see Mackay's Northern Beaches section later).

## Places to Stay – Budget

Good budget accommodation is hard to come by, but there are a few choices.

*Larrikin Lodge* (☎ 4951 3728, fax 4957 2978, 32 Peel St) Beds in 10-bed dorm $17, twin units $30, family room $57. This is a small YHA-associated hostel in an airy, high-ceilinged timber house. It's clean, quiet and friendly. The owners also operate Jungle Johno tours out to Eungella National Park (see Organised Tours earlier).

*Central Tourist Park* (☎ 4957 6141, Malcomson St, North Mackay) Unpowered/powered sites $13/16 per double, cabins $28-40. Row after row of cloned cabins makes this park, about 2km north of the centre, rather boring, but it's an inexpensive option, relatively close to the city.

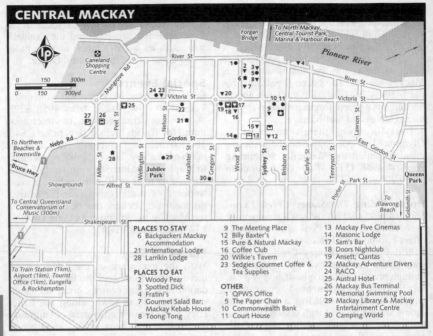

## CENTRAL MACKAY

### PLACES TO STAY
6 Backpackers Mackay Accommodation
21 International Lodge
28 Larrikin Lodge

### PLACES TO EAT
2 Woody Pear
3 Spotted Dick
4 Fratini's
7 Gourmet Salad Bar; Mackay Kebab House
8 Toong Tong

9 The Meeting Place
12 Billy Baxter's
15 Pure & Natural Mackay
16 Coffee Club
20 Wilkie's Tavern
23 Sedgies Gourmet Coffee & Tea Supplies

### OTHER
1 QPWS Office
5 The Paper Chain
10 Commonwealth Bank
11 Court House

13 Mackay Five Cinemas
14 Masonic Lodge
17 Sam's Bar
18 Doors Nightclub
19 Ansett; Qantas
22 Mackay Adventure Divers
24 RACQ
25 Austral Hotel
26 Mackay Bus Terminal
27 Memorial Swimming Pool
29 Mackay Library & Mackay Entertainment Centre
30 Camping World

**Beach Tourist Park** (☎ 4957 4021, fax 4951 4551, 8 Petrie St, Illawong Beach) Unpowered/powered sites $15/21, camp-o-tels $22 per double, cabins $48-70. About 3km south of the centre, this large and modern beachfront caravan park has a shop, a good pool, a campers kitchen and barbecue area.

There's also **Backpackers Mackay Accommodation** (☎ 1800 500 353) at 27 Wood St (singles, twins and doubles are $18 per person).

### Places to Stay – Mid-Range & Top End
There are a couple of reasonable mid-range and top-end selections in the area.

**International Lodge** (☎ 4951 1022, 40 Macalister St) Singles/doubles $46/56. An ordinary motel with small but clean rooms, the International is fairly close to the centre of town.

**Ocean Resort Village** (☎ 1800 075 144, 4951 3200, fax 4951 3246, ℮ info@ oceanresortvillage.com.au, Ⓦ www .oceanresortvillage.com.au, 5 Bridge Rd, Illawong Beach) 2-bedroom units (sleeping up to 6) $125, studio units from $79 a double. This is a good mid-range resort comprising 34 self-contained apartments in a cool, shady setting with a pool and half-court tennis courts.

If you're going to indulge yourself, there's an obvious choice.

**Ocean International** (☎ 1800 635 104, 4957 2044, fax 4957 2636, Ⓦ www.ocean -international.com.au, 1 Bridge Rd, Illawong Beach) Doubles $164, self-contained family unit $193. Mackay's most upmarket hotel is about 3km south of the centre. It's a four-star, four-storey complex overlooking Sandringham Bay, with a restaurant and cocktail bar, pool and spa.

### Places to Eat
**Cafes, Delis & Fast Food** Coffee lovers and snackers are well catered for in Mackay.

WHITSUNDAY COAST

***Sedgies Gourmet Coffee & Tea Supplies***
*(☎ 4957 4845, Cnr Nelson & Victoria Sts)*
Breakfast $4-8, lunch $5-10. Open 9am-3.30pm Mon-Fri, 9am-1.30pm Sat. A popular, friendly place to grab a coffee and read the newspapers, Sedgies offers a huge range of tea and coffee to choose from, as well as sandwiches and salads for lunch.

***Pure & Natural Mackay*** *(☎ 4957 6136, NAB Plaza, Sydney St)* Lunch under $10. Open 7am-4.30pm Mon-Fri, 7am-3pm Sat. Specialising in anything low-fat, this cafe offers a range of healthy looking meals, from quiches and baguettes to salads and juices.

***Gourmet Salad Bar*** *(☎ 4957 5844, 21c Wood St)* Lunch from $4. Open 9am-3.30pm Mon-Fri. Lunches are a bargain at this popular, long-established place serving burgers, sandwiches, salads and cakes.

***Mackay Kebab House*** *(☎ 4944 0393, 27 Wood St)* Kebabs $5-8. Open 9am-4pm Mon-Wed, 9am-9pm Thur & Sat, 9am-4am Fri. Head here for takeaway with Middle Eastern flavours.

***Billy Baxter's*** *(☎ 4944 0173, Cnr Sydney & Gordon Sts)* Breakfast $4-12, lunch $5-9, dinner $12-18. Open 7am-10pm Tues-Sat, 7am-9.30pm Sun & Mon. Pancakes for breakfast, pizzas and grills for lunch, more sophisticated mains in the evening – there's something for all tastes at this central, smart cafe.

***Coffee Club*** *(☎ 4957 8294, 48 Wood St)* Breakfast $6-14, mains $9-19. This big, bustling place offers a range of meals and a licensed bar; try the tapas before heading around the corner to see a movie.

**Pubs** Mackay seems to have a pub on every corner in the city centre, so finding a counter meal is not a problem.

***Wilkie's Tavern*** *(☎ 4957 2241, Cnr Victoria & Gregory Sts)* An attractive old pub, Wilkie's has a long bar, pokies and lots of locals.

***Spotted Dick*** *(☎ 4957 2368, 2 Sydney St)* Pizzas from $7, mains $10-26. This renovated pub comes complete with red-felt pool tables. There's a full a la carte menu – but wood-fired pizzas seem to be the go.

**Restaurants** A variety of cuisines are available in town.

***The Meeting House*** *(☎ 4953 2280, 53 Sydney St)* Mains $8-15. Open noon-2pm Mon-Fri, 6.30pm-late Tues-Sat. You'll find unpretentious and delicious Malay food at The Meeting House. The $6 lunch specials are great value – try the Hokkien Mee – and dinner banquets ($28 per head) are very popular.

***Fratini's*** *(☎ 4957 8131, 8 River St)* Mains $15-25, special dinner menus $35-45. Open noon-2pm Mon-Fri, 6pm-9pm Mon-Sat. Set amid the riverfront warehouses, Fratini's is a big, open restaurant serving delicious, authentic Italian food – with the emphasis on perfectly cooked, fresh seafood. If you're going to feast, do it here – and ask for a table on the veranda.

***Toong Tong*** *(☎ 4957 8051, fax 4957 8504, 10 Sydney St)* Mains $15-20. Open 11.30am-2.30pm & 5.30pm-10.30pm daily. Popular with locals, this cosy Thai restaurant capably serves up all the usual Thai dishes. It's BYO, and there's a busy takeaway service.

***Woody Pear*** *(☎ 4957 4042, 7 Wood St)* Mains $18-22. Open noon-2pm Tues-Fri, 6.30pm-late Tues-Sat. This simple little restaurant serves tried and true favourites like roast duck (with a different sauce for each day of the week) and baked ricotta. It's fully licensed with a good wine list, including a selection from Queensland, and exhibits works by local artists.

## Entertainment
**Nightclubs & Live Music** If you're craving some live music there are a few options.

***Austral Hotel*** *(☎ 4951 3288, Cnr Victoria & Peel Sts)* The Austral has live entertainment – usually someone strumming a guitar – every Friday and Saturday night.

***Sam's Bar*** *(☎ 4957 2220, 83 Victoria St)* Open 8pm-2am daily. On the second floor of a former pub, Sam's is a laid-back meeting place with pool tables and live music on the weekends; enter from Wood St.

***Doors*** *(☎ 4951 2611, 85 Victoria St)* Admission $5. Open 8pm-late Tues-Sun. Doors is a mainstream nightclub above Gordi's Cafe & Bar, where you can take a break from the loud music and fill up on 'macho nachos', steak sandwiches and paninis.

**Classical Music** For a change of pace, try this venue.

*Central Queensland Conservatorium of Music* (☎ 4957 3727, 418 Shakespeare St) The Mackay campus of the conservatorium has regular jazz and classical performances, midday and evening, throughout the year.

**Theatre & Cinema** Find out what's playing at the following venues.

*Mackay Entertainment Centre* (☎ 4957 2255, Gordon St) This is the city's main venue for live performances; phone the box office to find out what's on.

*Mackay Five Cinemas* (☎ 4957 3515, 30 Gordon St) This complex screens all the latest flicks.

## Shopping

There are a couple of places worth browsing through.

*Camping World* (☎ 4957 6658, Cnr Gregory & Alfred Sts) Open 8.30am-5pm Mon-Fri, 8.30am-noon Sat. Happy campers, look no further – this shop has everything you'll need for that national park getaway.

*The Paper Chain* (☎ 4953 1331, 8a Sydney St) Open 8.45am-5pm Mon-Fri, 9am-12.30pm Sat & Sun. This second-hand bookshop and exchange is bursting with character(s).

## Getting There & Away

**Air** Qantas has direct flights most days between Mackay and Brisbane ($407), Cairns ($391), Rockhampton ($270) and Townsville ($276), and you can get to most other cities along the coast with Sunstate and Macair. Macair also flies to Brampton Island for $105.

Qantas is at 105–109 Victoria St.

**Bus** McCafferty's/Greyhound and Premier buses stop at the Mackay bus terminal (☎ 4951 3088) on Milton St. The terminal is open 24 hours, but the booking office's hours are from 7.30am to 6pm Monday to Friday, to 2pm on Saturday.

Typical fares and average journey times are: Cairns ($97, 12 hours), Townsville ($64, six hours), Airlie Beach ($33, two hours) and Brisbane ($121, 15 hours).

**Train** The *Sunlander* and *Queenslander* stop at Mackay on their way between Brisbane and Cairns. A sleeper to/from Brisbane on the *Sunlander* costs $160/240 in economy/1st class, or $120 for an economy seat; to/from Cairns it's $94 for an economy seat, or $132/207 in an economy/1st class sleeper. The *Queenslander* has 1st class (only) sleepers for $461 and economy seats for $120 to/from Brisbane. The train station is at Paget, about 3km south of the centre.

Train bookings can be made at any travel agency, and at the Mackay bus terminal.

## Getting Around

For a taxi, call Mackay Taxis on ☎ 4951 4999. Count on about $12 for a taxi from either the train station or the airport to the city centre. Thrifty, Avis, Budget and Hertz have counters at the airport. Taxi Transit (☎ 4951 4990) connects the city centre with the northern beaches; a one-way ticket will cost around $4.

## MACKAY'S NORTHERN BEACHES

The coastline north of Mackay is made up of a series of headlands and bays. The small residential communities strung along here are virtually outer suburbs of Mackay, despite the distance (up to 15km) from the centre of town. If you're prepared to do a bit of exploring, there are some reasonably good beaches along here.

## Blacks Beach

There's a range of places to stay in Blacks Beach.

*Seawinds Caravan Park* (☎ 4954 9334, 16 Bourke St) Unpowered/powered sites $15/16; caravans $25 a double, extra adults $3; cabin $39 for 2. This rambling beachfront park has lots of shade and plenty of grass.

*Blue Pacific Village* (☎ 1800 803 386, 4954 9090, fax 4954 8385, W www .bluepacificresort.com.au, 26 Bourke St)

Units from $88. All accommodation options at Blue Pacific are fully self-contained and well kept; there's a restaurant, swimming pool and tennis court.

*La Solana* (☎ 4954 9544, fax 4954 9578, 15 Pacific Dr, e lasolana@telstra .easymail.com.au) Studio doubles $65, townhouses $82 a double. These bright and airy flats are in a small establishment a block back from the beach.

## Dolphin Heads
Dolphin Heads is home to the most impressive of the northern beach resorts.

*Whitsunday Waters Resort* (☎ 4954 9666, fax 4954 4740, e dolpmack@ fc-hotels.com.au, W www.whitsundaywaters .com.au, Beach Rd) Studio units $82-156. The 80 modern, motel-style units in garden settings here overlook an attractive (but rocky) bay.

## Eimeo
Beside Dolphin Heads is Eimeo, where the *Eimeo Hotel* (☎ 4954 6105, Mango Ave) crowns a headland. It's open every day, and is a great place for a drink; the food is ordinary but cheap, with lunch specials for $7.

## Bucasia
Bucasia is just across Sunset Bay from Eimeo and Dolphin Heads, but you have to head all the way back to the main road to get up there.

*Bucasia Beachfront Caravan Park* (☎ 4954 6375, fax 4954 6952, 2 The Esplanade, e bucasia@bigpond.com) Unpowered/powered sites $15/20, cabins $40-52. Apart from being in a nice neck of the woods and on the beachfront, this place doesn't have much going for it.

## BRAMPTON ISLAND
About 32km north-east of Mackay, Brampton Island has a popular mid-range resort managed by P&O. Brampton is also the access point for adjacent Carlisle Island, which has a couple of national park camp sites. The island boasts good beaches and walking trails, as well as all the frills associated with a big resort.

Mountainous Brampton is a national park and wildlife sanctuary with lush forests surrounded by coral reefs. It is connected to nearby Carlisle Island by a sand bar that you can sometimes walk across at low tide. In the 19th century, the island was used by the Queensland government as a nursery for palm trees, of which there are still plenty. The Bussutin family, who moved to the island in 1916 to raise goats and horses, established the first resort here in 1932.

## Activities
The resort has two swimming pools, tennis courts and a small golf course, as well as the usual snorkelling gear, catamarans, windsurfers and paddle skis.

The main beach at Sandy Point is very pleasant, and there's good snorkelling over the coral in the channel between Brampton and Carlisle Islands.

There are two excellent walking trails on the island. The 7km walk circumnavigates the central section of the island, and side tracks lead down to Dinghy Bay and Oak Bay. The 2km steady climb to the top of 219m Brampton Peak takes about two hours, and is rewarded with fine views along the way and from several lookout points.

## Places to Stay & Eat
*Brampton Island Resort* (☎ 1800 737 678, 4951 4499, fax 02-9299 2477, W www .poresorts.com) Carlisle Room singles/ doubles $295/205, Palm Room $300/210, Ocean View Room $360/270; extra adults pay $140. This resort is popular with couples, honeymooners and those wanting a relatively quiet island experience; it's not a party island, and children are not catered for.

All meals are served in the *Blue Water Restaurant*; breakfast and lunch are buffet style, while dinner is a more formal affair. As with many of the islands, discounted stand-by rates are often available, so it's worth checking.

## Getting There & Away
**Air** Macair does the 20-minute flight from Mackay to Brampton for $105 one way.

**Boat** The resort has its own launch that leaves Mackay at 11.30am Thursday to Monday; it returns to Mackay at 1.15pm on the same days and a return ticket costs $80.

## CARLISLE ISLAND

Carlisle Island is connected to Brampton Island by a narrow sand bar, and at some low tides it's possible to walk or wade from one island to the other. Carlisle is covered in dense eucalypt forests, and there are no walking trails.

There are national park *camping grounds* at Southern Bay, which is directly across from the Brampton resort, and another site further north at Maryport Bay. Southern Bay has a gas BBQ, rainwater tank and shelter; there are no facilities at Maryport Bay, so you must be totally self-sufficient. Bookings and permits are handled by the QPWS office in Mackay (☎ 4944 7800).

## OTHER CUMBERLAND ISLANDS

If you fancy a spot of Robinson Crusoeing and own a boat, or have chartered a boat or seaplane, most other islands in the Cumberland group and the Sir James Smith group to the north are also national parks.

**Scawfell Island**, 12km east of Brampton, is the largest island in the group. Refuge Bay on its northern side has a safe anchorage, a beach and a *camping ground* with water, BBQs and toilets.

About 3km east of Brampton, **Cockermouth Island** also has a good anchorage and beach on its western side, and a basic *camping ground*.

In the Sir James Smith Group, just northwest of Brampton, **Goldsmith Island** has a safe anchorage on its north-western side, good beaches and a *camping ground* with toilets, tables and fireplaces.

For permits and bookings contact the QPWS in Mackay (☎ 4944 7800).

### Getting There & Away

Transfers out to these islands depend on the weather, how many people are travelling, and so forth. A starting point would be Mackay Adventure Divers (☎ 4953 1431) or the owners of the *Lara Star* (☎ 4959 8148).

## CAPE HILLSBOROUGH NATIONAL PARK

This small coastal park, 54km north of Mackay, takes in the rocky, 300m-high Cape Hillsborough, and Andrews Point and Wedge Island, which are joined by a causeway at low tide. The scenery ranges from cliffs, a rocky coastline, sand dunes and scrub, to rainforest and woodland. Kangaroos, wallabies, sugar gliders and turtles are quite common in the park, and there are remains of Aboriginal middens and stone fish-traps.

There's a rangers office and visitors information centre (☎ 4959 0410) on the foreshore here, and a good picnic and barbecue area nearby.

There are also some good short walking trails through the park, and on the approach to the foreshore area there's a boardwalk leading out over the mangroves.

### Places to Stay & Eat

*Cape Hillsborough Resort* (☎ 4959 0152, fax 4959 0500, W www .capehillsboroughresort.com.au, MS 895 Mackay 4740) Unpowered/powered sites $11/17 a double (extra adults/children $4/2), fishing huts/cabins/motel rooms from $33/66/77. Rates at this pleasant resort vary according to what day of the week you stay, as much as what time of the year; facilities include a swimming pool, bar and *restaurant*. And yes, there really *are* kangaroos on the beach here.

*National Parks camping ground* (☎ 4959 0410, fax 4959 0680, Smalleys Beach) Sites $3.85 per person per night. This is a pretty, grassed camping ground hugging the foreshore and jumping with kangaroos; permits can be obtained on site.

### NEWRY ISLAND GROUP

The Newry Island Group is a cluster of small, little-known islands just off the coast from Seaforth, about 50km north-west of Mackay. They are rocky, wild-looking continental islands with grassy open forests and small patches of rainforest. Five of the islands are national parks. You may spot a dugong along this part of the coast as it's a dugong protection area where net fishing is banned.

The dugong, or sea cow, is an odd marine mammal that grazes on sea-grass meadows. KN

Most of the visitors to these islands are locals (with their own boat transport), here for the good fishing and oystering. Camping permits must be obtained from QPWS (☎ 4944 7800) in Mackay.

The largest of the Newry Island Group is **Rabbit Island**. Its camping ground has toilets and a rainwater tank (which can be empty in dry times). It also has the only sandy beaches in the group along its eastern side, although because of its proximity to the mainland, box jellyfish may be present in summer. From November to January green turtles nest on the beaches here.

**Newry Island** and **Outer Newry Island** each have a *camping ground* with shelter, water and toilets.

## MACKAY TO EUNGELLA

The main access road to the Eungella National Park takes you through the centre of the long and narrow **Pioneer Valley**, which is framed by low mountains on three sides. The first sugar cane was planted here in 1867, and today almost the entire valley is planted with the stuff.

The road takes you through a string of small townships: **Marian** has an enormous sugar mill and **Melba House**, the original house where Dame Nellie Melba and her husband (manager of the sugar mill) lived. It now operates as a tourist information centre (☎ 4954 4299), gallery and home to Melba memorabilia, and is open 10am to 4pm Monday to Sunday. The house is on the right as you approach Marian from Mackay.

The next town is **Mirani**, where there's a **local history museum** (☎ 4959 1100;

*adult/child $3.50/1.25; open 10am-2pm Sun-Fri)*. Behind the library on Victoria St, it displays an interesting collection of relics.

There's a private fauna park at Mirani called **Illawong Fauna Sanctuary** (☎ 4959 1777, fax 4959 1888; adult/child $11/5.50; open daily). Its crocodiles are fed at 2.30pm, and its koalas at 3pm.

The pretty township of **Finch Hatton**, last stop before the climb up to Eungella, has the **Finch Hatton Caravan Park** (☎ 4958 3222, Zamel St), where unpowered/powered sites cost $14/17 a double, and there are on-site vans from $30.

## EUNGELLA

From Finch Hatton, it's another 18km to Eungella. The last section of this road climbs suddenly and steeply, with several incredibly sharp corners – towing a caravan up here is not recommended. At the top of the climb is Eungella, a quiet and old-fashioned mountain village.

### Places to Stay & Eat

*Eungella Chalet* (☎ 4958 4509, fax 4958 4503, At the top of the hill) Singles/doubles & twins $38/59 with shared bathrooms, backpackers twin share/singles $22/28, 1-bedroom/2-bedroom cabins $88/109 a double ($10 per extra adult). This is a great place to stay. It's an old-fashioned, welcoming but slightly musty guesthouse, perched on the mountain edge, with arresting views of the Pioneer Valley below. Upstairs rooms are clean and simple, and there's a lovely big guests' lounge down the corridor. Behind the chalet are the modern

WHITSUNDAY COAST

timber cabins. There's a small and friendly bar downstairs, and the dining room serves breakfast, lunch and dinner.

*Hideaway Cafe* (☎ 4958 4533, *Broken River Rd*) Light meals $4-8. Open 8am-4pm Mon-Sun. Nineteen countries are represented on the menu at this charming, balconied cafe/gallery overlooking the township and run by the wonderfully efficient Suzanne.

*Kelly's Coach House & Gallery* (☎ 4958 4518, *Broken River Rd*) Light meals $5-10. Open 8.30am-8pm Tues-Sun. This stylish Queenslander has broad verandas, Devonshire teas, lunches and local arts and crafts.

## EUNGELLA NATIONAL PARK

Eungella (pronounced **young**-gulla, meaning Land of Clouds) is 84km west of Mackay, and covers nearly 500 sq km of the Clarke Range, climbing to 1280m at Mt Dalrymple. The area has been cut off from other rainforest areas for probably 30,000 years and has at least six life forms that exist nowhere else: the Eungella honeyeater (a bird), the orange-sided skink (a lizard), the Mackay tulip oak (a tall, buttressed rainforest tree) and three species of frog. One of these – the Eungella gastric brooding frog – incubates its eggs in its stomach and then gives birth by spitting out the tadpoles!

Most days of the year you can be pretty sure of seeing a platypus or two – and lots of tortoises – in the Broken River. The best times to see the creatures are the hours immediately after dawn and before dark; you must remain patiently silent and still. Platypus activity is at its max May to August, when the females are fattening themselves up in preparation for gestating their young.

### Broken River

There's a QPWS information office (☎ 4958 4501), picnic area and kiosk near the bridge over Broken River, 5km south of the Eungella township. A **platypus-viewing platform** has been built near the bridge, and bird-life is prolific in this area. There are some excellent walking trails between the Broken River picnic ground and Eungella; maps are available from the information office, which is staffed from 8am to 4pm daily.

There are a couple of **dairies** in the area that welcome visitors. Just before Broken River is the **Riverside Dairy** (☎ 4958 4642), run by the Kerr family. Visitors can watch the milking and bottle-feed the calves if there are any; entry is by donation, which is then passed on to local charities.

**Places to Stay & Eat** You have the choice of camping or cabins at Broken River.

*National park camping ground* (☎ 4958 4552, *fax 4958 4501*) Sites $3.85 per person per night. Sites are about 500m past the information centre and kiosk, along Broken River. This is a lovely place to camp – it's advisable to book in advance, though self-registration sites are usually available if you turn up in the morning.

*Broken River Mountain Retreat* (☎ 4958 4528, *fax 4958 4564*) Double & twin motel-style units from $66, 3-person/4-person/6-person cabins from $77/88/110 ($11 extra person). These self-contained cedar cabins are set in manicured lawns, close to the river. The retreat has a *restaurant* and organises activities for its guests.

### Finch Hatton Gorge

About 27km west of Mirani, just before the town of Finch Hatton, is the turn-off for the Finch Hatton Gorge section of the park. The last couple of kilometres of the 12km drive from the main road are quite rough and involve several creek crossings. At the carpark, there's a good picnic area with barbecues, and a couple of small swimming holes where the creek tumbles over huge boulders. A 1.6km walking trail leads from the picnic area to Araluen Falls, with its spectacular waterfalls and swimming holes. This area is teeming with wildlife – watch where you put your feet!

**Places to Stay** Both these places are near the creek.

*Platypus Bush Camp* (☎ 4958 3204, *Finch Hatton Gorge,* W *www.bushcamp .net*) Camp sites $5 per person, beds in shared hut $15, doubles $45. A true bush retreat, this camp is nestled in a beautiful forest setting just a couple of kilometres from the Finch Hatton Gorge. A creek with platypuses and great swimming holes runs next to the camp, and accommodation is in three slab-timber huts – basically roofed-over sleeping platforms. The communal kitchen/eating area is the heart of the place. There are toilets and hot showers, and you need to bring your own food and linen. Phone in advance; bookings are essential. Both Jungle Johno and Reeforest Adventure Tours do drop-offs from Mackay ($20 per person) to the camp. See Organised Tours in the Mackay section for details.

**Finch Hatton Gorge Cabins (☎ 4958 3281, Road to Finch Hatton Gorge, Finch Hatton)** Self-contained, air-con cabins $77 double (extra person $5.50). There are only two cabins here, and they'll be perfect if you're travelling with young kids: There's a big grassy area and the creek running in front is very shallow and dammed off.

### Getting There & Away
There are no buses to Eungella, but hitching is possible. Reeforest Adventure Tours and Jungle Johno both run day trips from Mackay – see Organised Tours in the Mackay section earlier.

# Whitsundays Area

The 74 Whitsunday Islands are probably the best known of Queensland's islands. The group was named by Captain Cook, who sailed through here on 3 July 1770. They're scattered on both sides of the Whitsunday Passage and are all within 50km of Shute Harbour.

The Whitsundays is a drowned landscape – underwater mountains with only the tips now visible. The actual Barrier Reef is at least 60km out from Shute Harbour, though many of the islands have fringing coral reefs; Hook Reef is the nearest part of it.

The islands and the passages between them are simply beautiful, and while seven are developed with tourist resorts, most are uninhabited and several offer the chance of some back-to-nature beach camping and bushwalking. All but four – Dent, Hamilton,

Daydream and Hayman – are predominantly or completely national park.

### Information
Airlie Beach is the mainland centre for the Whitsundays and there are plenty of travel agents, unofficial 'tourist information centres' and tour operators based here.

The Whitsunday district office of the QPWS (☎ 4946 7022) is 3km past Airlie Beach on the road to Shute Harbour. This office deals with camping permits for the islands, and its staff are generally very helpful and good sources of information on a wide range of topics. This is a good place to visit when you first arrive, particularly for travellers interested in exploring the islands independently rather than joining a packaged tour.

The main Whitsunday Information Centre (☎ 1800 801 252, 4945 3711, W www.whitsundayinformation.com.au) is on the Bruce Hwy on the southern entry to Proserpine.

**Books & Maps** David Colfelt's *100 Magic Miles of the Great Barrier Reef – The Whitsunday Islands* is sometimes referred to as the bible to the Whitsundays. It contains great colour photos, articles on the islands and resorts, features on diving, sailing, fishing, camping and natural history, and an exhaustive collection of charts with descriptions of all boat anchorages around the islands. Colfelt's book costs around $65 and is widely available.

Two of the best maps to this area are the Travelog *Great Barrier Reef* map, which has a *Whitsunday Passage* map on the back, and Sunmap's *Australia's Whitsundays*.

**Zoning** The Great Barrier Reef Marine Park Authority's zoning system divides the waters around the Whitsundays into five different zones, each with certain restrictions on what you can and can't do.

Briefly, most of the waters around the Whitsundays are zoned General Use A and B, with some important exceptions where Marine National Park A and B zoning applies. For the visitor, the main difference is that although both zones are 'look but don't take', Zone A permits limited fishing whereas Zone B permits no fishing at all.

## Activities

**Diving & Snorkelling** There are several companies offering learn-to-dive courses in Airlie Beach (see the Diving section under Airlie Beach later for details), and most of the island resorts also have their own dive schools. For certified divers, there's a huge range of boats offering diving trips to the islands and outer reef areas.

**Fishing Trips** Numerous charter boats offer fishing trips out of Shute Harbour. They include all-inclusive day trips on the 35ft MV *Jillian* (☎ 4948 0999) for $99/55 per adult/child; and the 55ft MV *Moruya* (☎ 4946 6665) for $90/45 per adult/child. Hiring your own boat is also an option; ask at the tourist information centres for details.

**Sail Yourself/Bareboat Charters** Sailing through the Whitsunday Passage in 1770, Cook wrote that 'the whole passage is one continued safe harbour'. In fact, stiff breezes and fast-flowing tides can produce some tricky conditions for small craft but, with a little care, the Whitsundays offer superb sailing, and bareboat charters have become enormously popular. 'Bareboat' doesn't refer to what you wear on board – it simply means you rent the boat without skipper, crew or provisions.

While the charter companies don't actually require potential renters to have any previous sailing experience, it is definitely advisable. As mentioned, conditions can become tricky, especially if the weather turns a bit nasty – chartered boats are run aground on a regular basis (and being rescued is a real hassle and costs money). If you lack experience, it's a good idea to hire an experienced skipper at least for the first day, although even then it's difficult to absorb the amount of instruction you are given in such a short time.

The operators usually require a booking deposit of $600 and a security bond of between $750 and $2000 (depending on the kind of boat), payable on arrival and refunded after the boat is returned undamaged. Bedding is usually supplied and provisions can also be provided if you wish. Most companies have a minimum hire period of five days.

Most of the charter companies have a wide range of yachts and cruisers available. You'll pay around $350 a day in the high season (September, October, December and January) for a Woodwark 28, sleeping two; around $400 a day for a Robertson 31 yacht, with up to five berths; around $600 a day for an Elite 36 sailing catamaran, with up to six berths; and around $480 a day for a Flybridge 35 cruiser, sleeping up to eight.

There are a number of bareboat charter companies around Airlie Beach, including:

**Hunter Yacht Charters Whitsunday** (☎ 1800 351 033, 4948 0033, fax 4946 4943, ℮ wpyc@tpgi.com.au, ⓦ www.hycw.com.au) Abel Point Marina
**Sail Whitsunday** (☎ 1800 075 045, 4946 7070, fax 4946 7044, ⓦ www.rentayacht.com.au) Trinity Jetty, Shute Harbour
**Whitsunday Escape** (☎ 1800 075 145, 4946 5222, ℮ escape@whitsunday.net.au, ⓦ www.whitsundayescape.com) Abel Point Marina
**Whitsunday Rent A Yacht** (☎ 1800 075 111, 4946 9232, fax 4946 9512, ℮ rentayacht@bareboat) Abel Point Marina

## Organised Tours

**Island & Reef Cruises** All boat trips to the Whitsundays depart from either Shute Harbour or the Abel Point Marina near Airlie Beach. There's a bamboozling array of trips on offer, and Airlie is awash with glossy brochures.

Most of the cruise operators do coach pick-ups from Airlie Beach and Cannonvale. You can take a bus to Shute Harbour, or you can leave your car in the Shute Harbour carpark for $8 for 24 hours; or there's Shute Harbour Secured Parking (☎ 4946 9666) a few hundred metres back along the road by the Shell service station, costing $6/11 per day/overnight.

All of the boats and trips are different, so it's worth asking around to find out what trip will suit you. There are leisurely sailing

## Sailing – the Basics

You don't have to be Dennis Connor to hire a yacht on the Whitsundays. Plenty of people who hire yachts here have little or no sailing experience when they start. The bareboat charter companies can teach you all you need to know before you set sail.

Getting the basics of sailing is not so difficult – we're not talking about entering the America's Cup here – and the following will give you insight into what to expect:

### Wind

One thing you'll learn quickly about sailing is that the wind is rarely constant and from the same direction. It requires constant attention. Take note of where the wind is coming from. Look up to the top of the mast, where there should be a flag or some other wind indicator. Good sailors don't need to look, they can feel it on their face – practise that, but look up to make sure.

Also, look for wind changes on the water's surface: a darkening of the water indicates an increase in wind strength.

### Terminology

If this is going to be your only sailing experience then you're not going to need to know all the terminology. The US Navy uses left (port) and right (starboard), so you can do the same. Windward (the side the wind is coming from) and leeward (the opposite) are important to know, and you should know what a mainsail and headsail are. After a few hours with an experienced yachtie you'll learn a sheet is a line (or rope), a shroud is a wire line holding the rigging in place, trimming (the sails) has nothing to do with your waistline, and luff (forward edge of the sail) may have four letters but the kids can safely say it without offending anybody.

### Sails

The boat will come with a basic rig of a mainsail and headsail, and there won't be any need to change these. Usually, the headsail will be self-furling, which means that it doesn't need to be pulled down when not in use (it simply rolls up like a blind).

### Safety

Most of the charter companies require you to report in by radio twice daily. This provides plenty of opportunity to get answers to any questions and also report any problems. There is also an emergency service based at

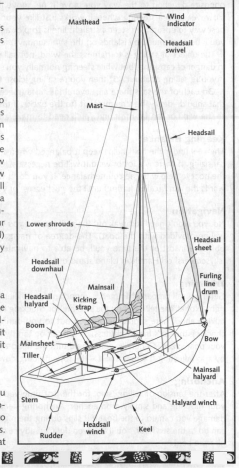

Masthead

Wind indicator

Headsail swivel

Mast

Headsail

Lower shrouds

Headsail sheet

Headsail downhaul

Mainsail

Furling line drum

Headsail halyard

Kicking strap

Boom

Bow

Mainsheet

Tiller

Mainsail halyard

Stern

Halyard winch

Rudder

Headsail winch

Keel

WHITSUNDAY COAST

## Sailing – the Basics

Airlie Beach that you can reach by radio 24 hours a day. When you hire the boat ensure it has appropriate emergency gear and you are familiar with where it is and how to use it.

If somebody falls overboard shout out 'MAN OVERBOARD' straightaway to get all crew on deck. Somebody other than the helmsman (the person steering) should point to the person in the water all the time, never losing sight of them. If you feel confident handling the boat you'll need to tack back around; otherwise drop your sail and turn the engine on to pick the person up.

### Steering

Usually, the smaller/older boats have a tiller (a steering arm attached to the rudder), although the bigger boats will likely have a steering wheel. When steering with a tiller the boat will move in the opposite direction to the way you move it (ie, move it to the right and the boat will move left). However, with a steering wheel it works just like your car (steer right and you go right, etc). The best way to ensure you steer a straight line is to pick an object off in the distance (most of the time you'll be surrounded by islands on the Whitsundays) and aim for it.

The object of sailing is to harness the wind, not sail straight into it. Turn into the wind if you're in danger of capsizing, but while steering normally you should avoid the 45° either side of true wind. If you're sailing at about 45° then you're sailing 'close to the wind' (on the fastest course).

On each of the sails there are several tell-tales (pieces of wool, hanging off it like loose threads) that should, ideally, be streaming aft (to the back). If they aren't, you're pointing the boat too close to the wind or too far off it and you'll need to make a course correction.

### Keeping Balance

The keel under the boat helps keep it balanced when the sails are full of wind and prevents it from capsizing. If there is a lot of wind it will be necessary to position the crew on the windward side of the boat to help with the counterbalance. If you don't want so much wind you can steer slightly towards the wind (called luffing) until the gust eases, or you can limit its effect by easing the mainsail.

### Navigation

No, you won't need to break out the sextant, but you will have to know how to read a map (which will be provided with the boat). The degree of navigational skills you'll need will depend on your objective. Most of the time you'll be able to navigate visually – you'll be amazed how much the 'skyscrapers' on Hamilton Island stand out.

### Trimming

Getting a sail properly trimmed is important for efficiency and can be a complicated business to get right. Not all the tell-tales on the sails are for checking the boat's course – the precise tell-tales we're talking about here should be pointed out to you during your training on the boat – some are for checking the sail's trim (tightness). A sail can be too tight and too loose; getting it right will improve your boat speed. Generally, you should trim the headsail first and adjust the mainsail's trim (possibly by also adjusting the mainsheet – the rope holding down the boom, at the back) to match it.

### Anchoring

After the tension of sailing 'solo' for the first time you shouldn't relax completely when you reach your mooring and simply drop anchor. Anchoring needs to be handled well, both because of the damage you can do to the boat if it slips during the night and because of the potential damage you can do to the sea floor. You'll be given detailed advice on how to do this tricky procedure when you hire the boat.

## Sailing – the Basics

### Tacking

Tacking is how you get a boat upwind, and is achieved by a zig-zagging motion. When setting up for a tack try not to tack into a wave. Instead, look for a flat piece of water – it'll give the least resistance to the turn.

**1** Alert everybody on board about what you're doing and ensure they understand. Push the tiller (slowly at first and more firmly as the boat turns) towards the sails, or turn the wheel away.

**2** Release the headsail sheets (lines) just before turning straight into the wind.

**3** As the boat points into the wind you'll need to trim the mainsail, and then let it out again when you cross the wind.

**4** As the sails cross the centreline, begin to ease the angle of the rudder – although it's better to go beyond the 45° of the tack to get the sails full, before bringing it back closer to the wind – and start to trim the sails. Wait until it's back up to speed before tacking again.

### Gybing

A gybe is essentially the reverse of a tack, although it's a slightly trickier manoeuvre. If you find yourself heading in the wrong direction on a downwind leg you gybe to bring the wind in from the other side.

**1** Alert everybody on board about what you're doing and ensure they understand. Pull the tiller (slowly at first and more firmly as the boat turns) away from the sails, or turn the wheel towards the sails. At the same time start to recover the mainsail, pulling in about half of the mainsheet (mainsail line).

**2** Look out for the boom (and control it) as the sails cross the centre of the boat.

**3** The tiller needs to be centralised – if this is done late it might be necessary to check the boat with some opposite rudder for a second or two. As the wind hits the mainsail, ease the mainsheet out to take some of its force – it's easy to sustain rigging damage if you simply let the mainsail go. Trim the sails.

True Wind

Tacking   45° 45°   Gybing

WHITSUNDAY COAST

---

cruises to uninhabited islands, high-speed diving trips to the outer reef, and cruises that take in several different destinations. You can even spend the night on the outer reef, doing the 'reefsleep' with Fantasea.

Destinations may vary due to weather or tidal conditions, and there's a government Reef Tax of $4 per person per day that must be added to the price of cruise tickets. Most day trips include activities like snorkelling and boom netting, with scuba diving as an optional extra. Children generally pay half fare. Following are some of the day trips on offer (note that substantial discounts are offered by most boats – watch out for standby rates):

**Fantasea** (☎ 4946 5111, W www.fantasea.com.au) 11 Shute Harbour Rd, Jubilee Pocket. Cruises to the outer Great Barrier Reef are on the high-speed catamaran *Fantasea One*, including smorgasbord lunch, snorkelling and rides in a semi-submersible (family/adult/concession/child $336/145/120/75). Overnight 'Reefsleep' trips cost $310 to $370.

*Mantaray* **Charters** (☎ 4946 4321, W www
.mantaraycharters.com) PO Box 839, Airlie
Beach 4802. This tour allows you to spend the
most time on Whitehaven Beach, followed by a
visit to Mantaray Bay (family/adult/child
$200/70/35 without lunch, $230/80/40 with
lunch); the lunch served is delicious.

*Maxi Ragamuffin* (☎ 4946 7777, W www
.maxiaction.com.au) PO Box 1006, Airlie
Beach 4802. *Ragamuffin* visits the beautiful
Blue Pearl Bay and Whitehaven Beach, returning to Shute Harbour at about 4.30pm (family/
adult/concession/child $200/81/73/40). There is
also a Two Cruise Special (ie, two separate
days) if you want to see more...

Both Fantasea and Whitsunday Allover
(☎ 1300 366 494, 4946 6900) offer day
packages, including lunch and use of resort
facilities, to Long, South Molle and Hamilton Islands; these trips range in price from
$30 to $70.

There are also dozens of longer trips
around the islands on offer, often with no
fixed itineraries; a few are covered in the
following list. Meals and snorkelling gear
are usually included, and you either sleep
on board or in tents on an island; most go
out for three days and two nights.

*Derwent Hunter* (☎ 1800 359 554, e tallship@
mackay.net.au) PO Box 407, Cannonvale 4802.
The *Derwent Hunter* is a historic tall ship carrying 21 passengers; accommodation is in private
berths (singles/doubles $352/480). It departs
Abel Point Marina on Thursday and Saturday.

*Jade* **Sailing Safaris** (☎ 1800 677 119, 4946
5435) PO Box 582, Airlie Beach 4802. This 46-
foot catamaran visits Whitsunday highlights,
then anchors at Hook Island each evening for
camping (sleeping bags can be hired) and meals
on shore ($250). It departs from Abel Point Ma-
rina on Tuesday, Thursday and Sunday.

*Prosail* (☎ 1800 810 116, 4946 5433, W www
.prosail.com.au) PO Box 973, Airlie Beach
4802. Prosail runs adventure sailing cruises for
the 18-to-35s market on a range of modern sailing yachts with names like *Matador* and *Hammer* ($370).

*Providence V* (☎ 4948 2337) Abel Point Marina.
Schooner or later you'll long to sail a boat like
this: a modern, timber replica of a much older
vessel. You can try your hand at climbing the
rigging, or just sit back and watch other people
do it ($350).

**Tallarook Sail & Dive** (☎ 1800 331 316, 4946
4777) Beach Plaza, The Esplanade, Airlie
Beach. Free introductory dives are offered on
*Tallarook II* and *Freedom* trips ($240 to $320).
Boats depart from Abel Point Marina.

**Flights** Air Whitsunday Seaplanes (☎ 4946
9111) offers the only day trips to exclusive
Hayman Island for $180/120 an adult/child;
day-trippers have use of all the resort facilities and get a $30 credit towards their
lunch. Other tours include a three-hour trip
to Hardy Reef ($225/150) and 1½-hour
trips to the dazzling Whitehaven Beach
($190/130).

Helireef (☎ 4946 9102) offers tours to
Reefworld (on the outer reef), either
fly/cruise for $290, or return flight for $400.
The trip takes 45 minutes, with three hours
to enjoy the reef before heading back; the
fare includes snorkelling gear, rides in the
glass-bottom boat and semi-submersible.
The fly/cruise option involves returning to
Shute Harbour on one of Fantasea's boats.

## Places to Stay

**Camping** QPWS manages national parks
*camp sites* on several islands for both independent and commercial campers. There's
also a privately run camping ground at
Hook Island – see that section for details.

You must be self-sufficient to camp in the
national park sites. You're advised to take
5L of water per person per day, plus three
days' extra supply in case you get stuck.
You should also have a fuel stove – wood
fires are banned on all islands.

There's a national parks leaflet that describes the various sites, and provides detailed information on what to take and do.

Camping permits are available from the
QPWS office (see the Information section
earlier) and cost $3.85 per person per night.

Get to your island with a day cruise boat
(use the sail-around ones rather than the resort boats). Island Camping Connection
(☎ 4946 5255, fax 4946 5794) can drop you
at Long, North or South Molle, Planton or
Tancred Islands for $35 return (minimum of
two people). The booking offices in Airlie
Beach are helpful and can advise which
boats are best to go where.

## Whitsunday Islands Camping Grounds

| island | camping ground | maximum number of permits issued | toilet facilities | commercial camping |
|---|---|---|---|---|
| Armit | south-western side | 12 | pit | all year |
| Denman | | 4 | bush | none |
| Gloucester | Bona Bay | 36 | pit | all year |
| | East Side Bay | 8 | bush | none |
| Henning | Northern Spit | 24 | pit | all year |
| | Geographers Bay | 12 | bush | all year |
| Hook | Maureens Cove | 36 | pit | all year |
| | Bloodhorn Beach | 12 | bush | all year |
| | Crayfish Beach | 12 | bush | all year |
| | Curlew Beach | 12 | bush | all year |
| Lindeman | Boat Port | 12 | pit | all year |
| Long | Sandy Bay | 12 | pit | all year |
| North Molle | Cockatoo Beach | 48 | pit | all year |
| Olden | | 12 | bush | all year |
| Planton | | 4 | bush | none |
| Saddleback | western side | 12 | bush | all year |
| South Molle | Paddle Bay | 12 | pit | peak season |
| | Sandy Bay | 36 | pit | all year |
| South Repulse | western beach | 12 | bush | all year |
| Tancred | northern end | 4 | bush | all year |
| Thomas | northern side | 12 | bush | all year |
| | Shaw/Neck Bay | 12 | bush | all year |
| | Burning Point | 12 | bush | all year |
| Whitsunday | Dugong Beach | 36 | pit | off peak |
| | Sawmill Beach | 24 | pit | off peak |
| | Joe's Beach | 12 | pit | off peak |
| | Whitehaven Beach | | pit | all year |
| | peak season | 60 | | |
| | off peak | 24 | | |
| | Turtle Bay | 12 | bush | all year |
| | Chance Bay | 12 | bush | all year |
| | Peter Bay | 12 | bush | all year |
| | Nari's Beach | 6 | pit | none |

Northern islands like Armit, Gloucester, Olden and Saddleback are harder to reach since the water taxi and cruises from Shute Harbour don't usually go there. Gloucester and Saddleback are best reached from Earlando, Dingo Beach or Bowen.

Independant campers can stay on the islands at all times of the year provided they have a permit.

The possibilities for camping in national parks in the Whitsundays are summarised in the table above. Note that some sites are subject to seasonal closures because of bird nesting.

**Resorts** There are resorts on seven of the Whitsunday Islands. Most were built during the tourism boom of the 1980s, and with the exception of the Hook Island resort they are all recently refurbished and reasonably expensive. Each resort is quite different from the next, ranging from Hayman's five-star luxury to the simple beach-front huts of the eco-friendly Long Island Wilderness Lodge, and from the high-rise development of Hamilton to basic cabins on Hook.

The rates quoted in this chapter are the standard rates, but hardly anyone pays these. Most travel agents can put together a range of discounted package deals that combine air fares and/or transfers to the resort with accommodation and, in most cases, meals.

It's also worth noting that, unless they're full, almost all of the resorts offer heavily discounted stand-by rates. The limiting factor is that you usually have to book less than five days in advance. All the tourist agents in Airlie Beach can provide information on the resorts.

### Getting There & Around

**Air** The two main airports for the Whitsundays are Hamilton Island and Proserpine. Qantas flies to both these places. See those sections for more details.

The Whitsunday airport also has regular flights from the mainland to the islands – light planes, seaplanes and helicopters. See Getting There & Away in the Airlie Beach section for details. Lindeman Island also has its own airstrip.

**Bus** McCafferty's/Greyhound and Premier buses detour off the Bruce Hwy to Airlie Beach. Local bus services operate between Proserpine, Airlie Beach and Shute Harbour.

**Boat** The Whitsunday Sailing Club is at the end of Airlie Beach Esplanade; check the noticeboards here and at the Abel Point Marina for possible rides or crewing opportunities on passing yachts.

The services to the islands all operate out of Shute Harbour or Abel Point Marina near Airlie Beach. Blue Ferries (☎ 4946 5111) and Whitsunday Allover (☎ 1300 366 494, 4946 6900) provide water taxi and ferry transfers to the islands – see Getting There & Away under the individual islands for details.

### LAGUNA QUAYS

Two-thirds of the way from Mackay to Proserpine, Laguna Quays is an elaborate and upmarket tourism resort and residential development, centred on a marina and **Turtle Point golf course**, home of the rich Australian Skins Tournament, held every year in February. The course is open to the general public, and 18 holes costs $55 (club hire $33, shoe hire $11).

*Laguna Quays Resort (☎ 4947 7777, fax 4947 7770, Kunapipi Springs Rd, Whitsunday 4800)* Rooms from $275. This resort offers restaurants, bars and pools, though it's hard to figure out why you would stay here unless you're an absolute golf nut; for these prices, you could be out on one of the island resorts.

### PROSERPINE

The turn-off point for Airlie Beach and the Whitsundays, Proserpine is pretty typical of the numerous sugar-mill towns strung along the Bruce Hwy in northern Queensland. The Whitsunday Information Centre (☎ 4945 3711, fax 4945 3182, W www .whitsundayinformation.com.au), on the Bruce Hwy on the Mackay side of town, is the main source of information about the Whitsundays and surrounding region. It's open 10am to 6pm daily.

Sunstate (Qantas) has direct flights between Proserpine and Brisbane ($431). The airport is 14km south of town. In addition to meeting all planes and trains, Whitsunday Transit (☎ 1300 655 449) has four scheduled bus services daily from Proserpine to Airlie Beach; tickets from the airport/train station cost $13/7.

### AIRLIE BEACH
#### postcode 4802 • pop 4000
Airlie Beach, 25km north-west of Proserpine, is the gateway to the Whitsunday Islands. The whole town revolves around tourism and pleasure boating, and it attracts a diverse bunch of boaties, backpackers, tourists and divers, all here for a good time. Apart from being the main access point for the Whitsundays, Airlie has a wide range of accommodation, some good cafes and

restaurants, a lively nightlife and lovely lagoon – a huge swimming area open 24 hours, year round, on the foreshore.

Activities loom large in Airlie: It's got a reputation as a centre for scuba dive instruction; whales come to the area for calving between July and September, so whale-watching tours are popular; the hinterland offers all sorts of earthy pursuits like horse riding and hiking; or for loftier thrills, you can jump out of a plane. Despite massive development, Airlie maintains a relaxed air. And with its new, stinger-free lagoon, you can swim all year round.

## Information

**Tourist Offices** The main drag is stacked with privately run tour-booking and ticket agencies, all able to answer queries and organise tours. They include the Airlie Beach Tourist Information Centre (☎ 4946 6665), opposite Beaches Backpackers; and Destination Whitsundays (☎ 4946 6846), upstairs

on the corner of Shute Harbour Rd and the Esplanade. All of the places to stay can also give advice and book tours, boat trips and transport to the islands.

The QPWS office (☎ 4946 7022, fax 4946 7023, **W** www.env.qld.gov.au) is on the corner of Shute Harbour and Mandalay Rds, 3km past Airlie towards Shute Harbour. It's open 9am to 5pm Monday to Friday, and should be your first port of call if you need information and permits for camping in the Conway and the Whitsunday Islands national parks. The staff here are very helpful and can advise you on which islands to camp on, how to get there, what to take etc. (See the general Camping section in the Whitsundays section earlier.)

**Post & Communications** The post office is on Shute Harbour Rd, and open Monday to Friday from 9am till 5pm, and Saturday from 9am till 12.30pm. Internet access is widely available; many of the bigger hostels

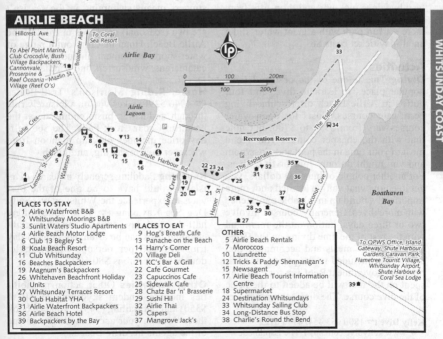

**AIRLIE BEACH**

**PLACES TO STAY**
1 Airlie Waterfront B&B
2 Whitsunday Moorings B&B
3 Sunlit Waters Studio Apartments
4 Airlie Beach Motor Lodge
6 Club 13 Begley St
8 Koala Beach Resort
11 Club Whitsunday
16 Beaches Backpackers
19 Magnum's Backpackers
26 Whitehaven Beachfront Holiday Units
27 Whitsunday Terraces Resort
30 Club Habitat YHA
31 Airlie Waterfront Backpackers
36 Airlie Beach Hotel
39 Backpackers by the Bay

**PLACES TO EAT**
9 Hog's Breath Cafe
13 Panache on the Beach
14 Harry's Corner
20 Village Deli
21 KC's Bar & Grill
22 Cafe Gourmet
23 Capuccinos Cafe
25 Sidewalk Cafe
28 Chatz Bar 'n' Brasserie
32 Sushi Hi!
35 Capers
37 Mangrove Jack's

**OTHER**
5 Airlie Beach Rentals
7 Moroccos
10 Laundrette
12 Tricks & Paddy Shennanigan's
15 Newsagent
17 Airlie Beach Tourist Information Centre
18 Supermarket
24 Destination Whitsundays
33 Whitsunday Sailing Club
34 Long-Distance Bus Stop
38 Charlie's Round the Bend

**WHITSUNDAY COAST**

have terminals, and there are several dedicated Internet cafes.

**Bookshops** The newsagency on Shute Harbour Rd stocks interstate and overseas newspapers and has a large selection of holiday reading and beach literature, as well as a small travel section with a range of books on the Whitsundays. There's also a small, second-hand bookshop in the arcade next to Capuccinos Cafe

**Laundry** There's a laundrette on Shute Harbour Rd, it's next to Club Whitsunday backpackers.

## Things to See & Do
The **Wildlife Park** (*☎ 4946 1480, Shute Harbour Rd, Cannonvale; adult/child $20/ 10; open 9am-4.30pm Mon-Sun)* has a large collection of Australian mammals, birds and reptiles, with the usual 'feed the croc/pat the koala' show every day. A courtesy bus does pick-ups and drop-offs from wherever you're staying. Right next door there's a **fun park** with a giant water slide; an all-day ticket costs $6.

## Activities
**Diving** This is one of the best and most popular places to learn to dive, and four outfits in Airlie Beach offer scuba-diving certificate courses. Costs for open-water courses vary from $350 to $700, but note that with the cheaper courses you spend most of your time in the pool and classroom and you might do only four or five dives. For another couple of hundred dollars, you get to enjoy what you've learned and, more importantly, build up invaluable experience with more dives. Generally, courses involve two or three days' tuition on the mainland with the rest of the time diving on the Great Barrier Reef – meals and accommodation are usually included in the price. An additional $4 government Reef Tax for each day spent on the reef will be added to the price of the dive course. The dive companies are:

**Kelly Dive** (☎ 1800 063 454, 4946 6122,
  W www.kellydive.com.au) 1 The Esplanade

**Oceania Dive** (☎ 1800 075 035, 4946 6032,
  W www.oceaniadive.com)
  257 Shute Harbour Rd
**Pro-Dive** (☎ 1800 075 035, 4948 1888,
  W www.prodivewhitsundays.com)
  344 ShuteHarbour Rd
**Reef Dive** (☎ 1800 075 120, 4946 6508,
  W www.reefdive.com.au)
  277 Shute Harbour Rd

The same companies also offer a good range of diving trips for certified divers, from day trips to overnighters that combine the reef with the islands.

**Swimming & Water Sports** The construction of a huge lagoon on Airlie's foreshore has provided year-round, safe swimming – as well as an attractive and popular public space. While there are some reasonable beaches at Airlie Beach and Cannonvale, low tide means you'll have a long walk before you get more than your knees wet, and the presence of marine stingers means swimming in the sea isn't advisable between October and May. There are two (seasonal) operators in front of the Airlie Beach Hotel that hire out a range of water-sports equipment, including jet skis, catamarans, windsurfers and paddle skis.

**Horse Riding** Morrison's Trail Rides (☎ 4946 5299) takes you on a leisurely ride through undulating bush, ending up at the beautiful Cedar Creek Falls. The $66 half-day price includes pick up at noon from wherever you're staying, and lunch.

**Kayaking** Paddling serenely in search of an island would have to be one of the best ways to experience the Whitsundays. Salty Dog Sea Kayaking (☎ 4946 1388) offers half-day/full-day tours, and overnight camping trips can be arranged. Guided day trips are $80 per person, while single/ double kayak hire is $80/100.

**Other Activities** Other action possibilities include tandem skydiving ($250 to $350) and parasailing ($45) – you can book these through your accommodation or one of the agents in Airlie Beach.

## Organised Tours

**Cruises & Fishing Trips** A huge range of cruisers, yachts and boats offer trips out to the Whitsundays from the Abel Point Marina and Shute Harbour. See Organised Tours earlier in the Whitsunday Area section for details of some of these.

**Rainforest/National Park Tours** Fawlty's 4WD Tropical Tours (☎ 4948 0999) departs daily at 10.30am, and returns at 4pm. This tour is a great way to see the beautiful (when they're running, that is) Cedar Creek Falls and some rainforest close up. Lunch and pick-ups are included in the price ($42/25 per adult/child).

Reeforest Adventure Tours (☎ 4948 2455), at 7 The Esplanade, offers day trips to Eungella National Park ($99/94/65). Eungella National Park and its platypuses shouldn't be missed. The tour is full day and includes pick-ups, morning and afternoon tea, and a big lunch. The BBQ lunch on the Eungella trip is at a secluded bush camp, not far from the beautiful Finch Hatton Gorge.

## Special Events

Airlie Beach is the centre of activities during the annual Whitsunday Fun Race Festival (for cruising yachts) each September. The festivities include a Miss Figurehead competition where the contestants traditionally compete topless.

## Places to Stay

**Camping** There are no caravan parks in Airlie Beach itself, but on the road between Airlie and Shute Harbour there are several parks to choose from.

*Island Gateway Holiday Resort* (☎ 4946 6228, fax 4946 7125, Shute Harbour Rd, Jubilee Pocket) Unpowered/powered sites $17/20 a double, camp-o-tels $25, on-site vans $35, en suite cabins $63. This is a big park about 1.5km east of Airlie Beach, making it the closest camping ground to the town centre. Facilities are good and include a campers' kitchen, pool, shop and half-court tennis.

*Shute Harbour Gardens Caravan Park* (☎ 4946 6483, fax 4948 1978, Shute Harbour Rd) Unpowered/powered sites $16/19, en suite cabins $61. This small park set on a hillside is 1.75km from Airlie Beach.

*Flame Tree Tourist Village* (☎ 4946 9388, fax 4946 9501, W www.flametreevillage .com.au, Shute Harbour Rd) Unpowered/powered sites $17/20, on-site vans $44, en suite units $60. Spacious sites are scattered through lovely, bird-filled gardens in this park 6km west of Airlie.

**Hostels** Backpackers are spoiled for choice in Airlie, with countless budget alternatives.

*Magnum's Backpackers* (☎ 4946 6266, fax 4946 5980, Shute Harbour Rd) Beds in 8-bed dorm with/without dinner $15/12, twins & doubles $37. Magnum's has rebuilt itself as a mini-city within the heart of Airlie. Purpose-built, double-storey blocks of double and twin rooms are surrounded by gardens; everything's got the modern corrugated iron/plywood look, and it's clean and airy. Dorm accommodation is in older-style huts, but these too are scheduled for a make-over. The pub at the front of the complex is very popular, and there's live music there most evenings.

*Airlie Waterfront Backpackers* (☎ 1800 089 000, 4948 1300, e awbpack@airlie .net.au, W www.airliewaterfrontbackpackers .com.au, The Esplanade) Beds in 6-bed/4-bed dorm $20/25, doubles $55. There's a good feel to this hostel tucked under a big A-frame roofline. Fresh, balconied rooms share bathrooms, and the communal areas are bright and clean.

*Beaches Backpackers* (☎ 4946 6244, fax 4946 7764, W www.beaches.com.au, Shute Harbour Rd) Beds in 6-bed, air-conditioned dorm $17, doubles $35-45. This big, converted motel with a party attitude and its own bar and restaurant is popular with travellers and locals alike. All rooms (of varying sizes) share en suites, there's a pool and the communal kitchen is well set up.

*Club Habitat YHA* (☎ 1800 247 251, 4946 6312, fax 4946 7053, 394 Shute Harbour Rd) Beds in 6-8–bed dorm with bathroom $17, singles & doubles $45 (extra $3.50 for non-members). This is a friendly hostel in a converted motel at the end of the main drag.

**Koala Beach Resort** (☎ 4946 6001, fax 4946 6761, e backpackers-info@koalaresort .com.au, W www.koala-backpackers.com, Shute Harbour Rd) Beds in 6-bed dorm $18, doubles & twins $45. Koala's units are fully self-contained; there's plenty of open space and a good-sized swimming pool. Nearly everything here demands a deposit, so come prepared.

**Club 13 Begley St** (☎ 1800 633 945, 4946 7376, e club13@net-lynx.net, W www.whitsundaybackpackers.com.au, 13 Begley St) Beds in 4-6–bed dorm $18, doubles with shared/private en suite $45/50, including breakfast. This place has seen better days, though the views of the sea are impressive. The doubles with en suites are the best option, and there's a small pool and several small kitchen and communal areas.

**Club Whitsunday** (☎ 1800 678 755, 4946 6182, fax 4946 6890, 346 Shute Harbour Rd) Beds in 4-bed dorm $17, air-conditioned twins & doubles $44. This is a small hostel at the lagoon end of town. Rooms are basic, and bathrooms are shared between two or three bedrooms/dorms. Breakfast is thrown in for free.

**Backpackers by the Bay** (☎ 1800 646 994, ☎/fax 4946 7267, e bythebay@ whitsunday.net.au, Lot 5, Hermitage Dr) Beds in 4-bed dorm $18, doubles & twins $44; air-conditioning $0.50 per person. Smaller and probably quieter than some of the other hostels, this relaxed place is about a 10-minute walk from the centre of town. The atmosphere is friendly, and double rooms are some of the best around.

**Bush Village Backpackers Resort** (☎ 1800 809 256, 4946 6177, fax 4946 7227, 2 St Martin's Lane, Cannonvale) Beds in 4-bed standard/deluxe dorm $17/20, standard/deluxe doubles & twins $45/52; air-conditioning $1 for 90 minutes. West of Airlie by 1.5km (there's a courtesy bus into town), this is comfortable accommodation just off Shute Harbour Rd in Cannonvale, close to shops and services. Two-bedroom cabins, all with share bathrooms, some freshly refurbished (deluxe), have cooking facilities, fridge and TV. All rates include breakfast and bed linen.

**Reef Oceania Village** (☎ 1800 800 795, 4946 6137, fax 4946 6846, W www .reeforesort.com, 147 Shute Harbour Rd, Cannonvale) Beds in 4-8–bed dorm $6-14, doubles & twins $50, breakfast included. Known as Reef O's, this big, bustling backpackers resort is about 3km west of Airlie; there's a courtesy bus into town, and you can organise everything from the reception desk.

**Hotels & Motels** The following motel/ hotel options are all good.

**Airlie Beach Motor Lodge** (☎ 1800 810 925, 4946 6418, fax 4946 5400, 6 Lamond St) Singles/doubles $85/89. Tucked away in a residential area of Airlie, this is a neat, quiet motel just a short walk from Shute Harbour Rd action.

**Coral Point Lodge** (☎ 4946 9500, fax 4946 9469, 54 Harbour Ave, Shute Harbour) Singles/doubles from $70/82, with kitchenettes $80/90. This is the place if you want to be out of the hubbub of Airlie. Clinging to the ridge overlooking Shute Harbour, the views are superb; some rooms are refurbished and have polished wooden floors. There's a small pool and the cafe serves good meals and snacks, and is open to nonguests.

**Airlie Beach Hotel** (☎ 1800 466 233, 4964 1999, fax 4964 1988, W www .airliebeachhotel.com.au, Cnr The Esplanade & Coconut Grove) Refurbished motel singles/doubles $77/88, new beachfront hotel rooms from $130/140. Slick and new, this hotel offers all the mod cons as well as having nonsmoking rooms and facilities for disabled guests.

**Holiday Flats & Apartments** There are quite a few blocks of older-style holiday flats and apartments in and around Airlie Beach that can be good value, especially for a group of friends or a family.

**Whitehaven Beachfront Holiday Units** (☎ 4946 5710, fax 4946 5711, 285 Shute Harbour Rd) Singles/doubles $77/88. Smack in the centre of Airlie Beach, these six well-presented apartments have balconies overlooking the foreshore park. As they're set back from the main road, noise is not a problem.

*Sunlit Waters Studio Apartments* (☎/fax 4946 6352, 20 Airlie Crescent) Studio apartments $65-85 a double ($10-15 for each extra person). On a rise overlooking Airlie Beach, these studios sleep up to five people and have stunning views over the sea. The pool, with its great position, is another plus for this friendly, casual place.

**Resorts** Most of the resorts here have package deals and stand-by rates that are much cheaper than their regular rates.

*Club Crocodile* (☎ 1800 075 151, 4946 7155, fax 4946 6007, Ⓦ www.clubcroc .com.au, Shute Harbour Rd, Cannonvale) Singles/doubles from $88/108, including breakfast. Club Crocodile is a popular, midrange resort 1.5km west of Airlie Beach. Motel-style units are built around an attractive central courtyard featuring fountains, a pool, tennis court, restaurants and bar.

*Coral Sea Resort* (☎ 4946 6458, fax 4946 6516, Ⓦ www.coralsearesort.com, 25 Ocean View Ave) Single/double suites $160-280, 1-bedroom/2-bedroom apartments $220/270. At the end of a low headland overlooking the water, Coral Sea Resort has the best position around. The excellent swimming pool is large and flanked by ocean on one side and a bar/restaurant on the other. On the resort's private jetty sits *The Jetty Trattoria*, open each evening.

*Whitsunday Terraces Resort* (☎ 1800 075 062, 4946 6788, fax 4946 7128, Golden Orchid Dr) Studios/suites $110/120. This huge, dominating resort overlooks Airlie Beach and the ocean, and has modern studio-style and one-bedroom apartments with cooking facilities and all mod cons.

**B&Bs** There are a couple of quality B&Bs to choose from.

*Whitsunday Moorings B&B* (☎/fax 4946 4692, Ⓦ www.whitsundaymooringsbb.com .au, 37 Airlie Crescent) At this stylish B&B, well-appointed rooms open up onto a terrace and swimming pool, overlooking the bay. The main road is just below.

*Airlie Waterfront B&B* (☎ 4946 7631, ⓔ awbb@mackay.net.au, Cnr Broadwater & Mazlin Sts) Singles/doubles $99/140

($25 per extra person). Beautifully presented and furnished with antiques, this is a lovely alternative to the busy places right in the town centre.

## Places to Eat
If you're preparing your own food, there's a small *supermarket* open daily on Shute Harbour Rd, in the centre of town, and another, large one in Cannonvale.

**Cafes, Delis & Fast Food** If you're looking for a quick coffee, breakfast or light lunch, Airlie has plenty of places to go.

*Village Deli* (☎ 4964 1121, Opposite Australia Post) Light meals $6-10. Open 7am-5.30pm daily. This casual, funky cafe/deli serves tasty light meals – and they know how to make coffee. The mixed salad plate is great value, and big, healthy breakfasts, gelati and juices are on the go all day. Takeaway provisions and picnic boxes are a speciality.

*Sushi Hi!* (☎ 4948 0400, 390 Shute Harbour Rd) Light meals $6-14. Open 10am-9pm daily. Sushi, sashimi and other Japanese delicacies are complemented by fresh fruit salads and juices and great flat-bread rolls.

*Harry's Corner* (☎ 4946 7459, 273 Shute Harbour Rd) Breakfasts around $7, lunches $12. Open 7am-6pm daily. This small, popular cafe cooks up tasty breakfasts: The 'Big Bavarian' (fried eggs, potatoes, bacon and tomatoes) will keep you going all day.

*Cafe Gourmet* (☎ 4946 6172, 289 Shute Harbour Rd) Sandwiches & light lunches $4-10. Open 7am-5pm daily. You'll get sandwiched in the crowd at this deservedly popular lunch joint offering light lunches and fresh juices.

*Sidewalk Cafe & Cantina* (☎ 4946 6425, The Esplanade) Dishes $6-15. Open 7am-2pm Mon-Sun, 6pm-late Thur-Mon. Serving breakfasts and light lunches, the Sidewalk Cafe transforms into the Sidewalk Cantina at night, and serves up Mexican-influenced dishes.

*Cappuccino's Cafe* (☎ 4946 5033, Pavilion Arcade) Light meals $4-15. Open 8am-8pm Mon-Sun. In a bustling, breezy arcade off the main drag, this busy cafe serves up focaccias, pasta, smoothies and fresh juices.

**WHITSUNDAY COAST**

**Restaurants** It's not hard to find a good restaurant in Airlie.

*Panache on the Beach* (☎ *4946 5541, Mango Terrace, 263 Shute Harbour Rd)* Mains $12-30. Open 11am-10pm daily. With a lovely position opening out onto the lagoon and foreshore, Panache offers both brasserie-style meals (until 6pm) and a more formal menu reflecting the chef's French origins.

*KC's Bar & Grill* (☎ *4946 6320, 282 Shute Harbour Rd)* Mains $11-26. Open 3pm-3am daily. KC's happy hour(s) are followed by dinner between 6pm and 9pm, then there's live music every night. It's lively, licensed and the menu's mostly seafood and grills.

*Chatz Bar'n'Brasserie* (☎ *4946 7223, 390 Shute Harbour Rd)* Mains $16-23. Open 11am-2am daily. There's a popular front bar, while the cosy restaurant section up the back offers vegetarian, seafood and Italian-style main courses.

*Airlie Thai* (☎/fax *4946 4683, 1st floor, Beach Plaza, The Esplanade)* Mains $8-20. Open noon-2pm Mon-Sat, 5pm-late Mon-Sun. This pleasant, licensed restaurant is upstairs in the new Beach Plaza complex; sit out on the veranda and tuck in to the delicious pad thai, among other traditional Thai dishes.

*Capers* (☎ *4946 1777, The Esplanade)* Lunch $10-15, dinner $20-25. Open 7am-late Mon-Sun. On the ground floor of the new Airlie Hotel complex, this is a big restaurant/bar offering the usual breakfasts and slightly more imaginative lunches and dinners; you can escape the game machines by sitting out on the pleasant patio.

*Mangrove Jack's* (☎ *4946 6233, 297 Shute Harbour Rd)* Mains $12-23. Open 11.30am-9.30pm daily. You can watch the results of any kind of race Australia-wide in this lively bar/restaurant. The wood-fired oven pizzas ($18) are a popular choice.

*Hog's Breath Cafe* (☎ *4946 7894, 261 Shute Harbour Rd)* Mains $12-20. Open 11.30am-9.30pm daily. The Hog's Breath is one link in a sausage chain of bar-cum-restaurants serving all things meaty.

## Entertainment

Airlie Beach has a reputation for partying hard. The bars at *Magnum's* and *Beaches*, the two big backpackers resorts in the centre of town, and *Moroccos*, next to the Koala Beach Resort, are usually pretty crowded, and good places to meet travellers. Drinks tend to be cheaper here than elsewhere. Several of the bar/restaurants along Shute Harbour Rd also have regular live music.

*Charlie's Round the Bend* (☎ *4946 6250, Cnr Shute Harbour Rd & Coconut Grove)* Open 4pm-2am Sun-Thur, 4pm-3am Fri & Sat. This is a popular sports bar featuring live music every night.

*Paddy Shenanigans* (☎ *4946 5055, 352 Shute Harbour Rd)* Open 5pm-2am daily. A friendly bar, Paddy's has fiddles playing and Guinness on tap.

*Tricks* (☎ *4946 6465, 354 Shute Harbour Rd)* Open 11pm-5am daily. Tricks is upstairs, and popular with the local crowd; it's a friendly kind of bar and the music is varied.

## Getting There & Away

**Air** The Whitsunday airport, a small airfield midway between Airlie Beach and Shute Harbour, is 6km east of Airlie Beach. Half a dozen different operators are based here, and you can take a helicopter, light plane or seaplane out to the islands or the reef.

Island Air Taxis (☎ 4946 9933) flies to Hamilton ($45) and Lindeman ($55) Islands; Helireef (☎ 4946 9102), Air Whitsunday Seaplanes (☎ 4946 9111) and Island Air Taxis all offer joy flights out over the reef.

**Bus** Premier and McCafferty's/Greyhound buses that travel along the Bruce Hwy detour to Airlie Beach. (If you're reading this while sitting on a bus that doesn't make the detour, you'll have to get off in Proserpine and catch a local bus from there.)

There are buses between Airlie Beach and all the major centres along the coast, including Brisbane ($137, 18 hours), Mackay ($33, 2½ hours), Townsville ($47, 4 hours) and Cairns ($79, 11 hours).

Long-distance buses currently stop on the Esplanade, halfway between the Sailing Club and Airlie Beach Hotel. Any of the booking agencies along Shute Harbour Rd can make reservations or sell bus tickets.

Whitsunday Transit (☎ 1300 655 449) has services from Proserpine/Proserpine airport to Airlie Beach ($7/13) and Shute Harbour ($8/13). Buses operate from 6am to 7pm daily.

**Boat** The Whitsunday Sailing Club is at the end of Airlie Esplanade. There are notice boards at the Abel Point Marina showing when rides or crewing are available. Ask around Airlie Beach or Shute Harbour.

## Getting Around
Airlie Beach is small enough to cover by foot, and all of the cruise boats have courtesy buses that will pick you up from wherever you're staying and take you to either Shute Harbour or the Abel Point Marina.

Several car-rental agencies operate locally; Avis, Budget and National all have agencies on Shute Harbour Rd. Airlie Beach Rentals (☎ 4946 6110) has cars from $46 a day.

To book a taxi, call Whitsunday Taxis on ☎ 13 10 08; there's a taxi rank on Shute Harbour Rd, opposite Magnum's.

## CONWAY NATIONAL PARK
The mountains of this national park and the islands were once part of the same coastal mountain range, but rising sea levels after the last Ice Age flooded the lower valleys and cut off the coastal peaks from the mainland.

Most of the park is composed of rugged ranges and valleys covered in rainforest, although there are also areas of mangroves and open forest. Only a small area of the park is accessible by road.

The road from Airlie Beach to Shute Harbour passes through the northern section of the park. Several walking trails start from near the picnic and day use area, including a 1km circuit track to a mangrove creek. About 1km past the day use area and on the northern side of the road, there's a 2.4km walk up to the Mt Rooper lookout, which provides good views of the Whitsunday Passage and islands. Further along the main road, and up the hill towards Coral Point (before Shute Harbour), there's a pleasant 1km track leading down to Coral Beach and

The Beak lookout. This track was created with the assistance of the Giru Dala, the traditional custodians of the Whitsunday area; a brochure available at the start of the trail explains how the local Aborigines used plants growing in the area.

There's bush camping on the coast at Swamp Bay and access is only on foot.

## Cedar Creek Falls & Conway Beach
To reach the beautiful Cedar Creek Falls, turn off the Proserpine to Airlie Beach road on to Conway Rd, 8km north of Proserpine. It's then about 15km to the falls – the roads are well signposted. This is a popular picnic and swimming spot – when there's enough water, that is!

At the end of Conway Rd, 20km from the turn-off, is Conway Beach. A small coastal community on the shores of Repulse Bay and at the southern end of the Conway National Park, it consists of a few old houses, pleasant picnic areas along the foreshore and the *Black Stump Caravan Park* (☎ 4947 3147) – not exactly the belle of the ball, but there's no alternative.

## LONG ISLAND
postcode 4741
The closest of the resort islands to the coast, Long Island is mostly national park, with three resorts on offer. The island is about 11km long but no more than 1.5km wide, and a channel only 500m wide separates it from the mainland. There are 13km of walking tracks and some fine lookouts, and day-trippers to the island can use the facilities at the Club Croc or Palm Bay resorts.

## Activities
The beaches on Long Island are quite attractive, but severe tidal variations mean that low tide at Happy Bay is time to head for the swimming pool. The two northern resorts have a range of water-sports equipment. Club Croc has a wider selection, hiring out dinghies ($99 a day) and jet skis ($40 for 15 minutes), and offering water-skiing ($28 for 10 minutes). Day-trippers and guests at Palm Bay can also use these facilities.

Sea kayaking is a featured activity at the Whitsunday Wilderness Lodge on the southern side of the island (guests only).

## Places to Stay & Eat

**Camping** There's a national parks *camp site* at Sandy Bay, midway along the western side of the island. There is space here for just six people, and there are no facilities. Permits are available from the QPWS office in Airlie Beach.

**Resorts** Long Island has one big mainstream resort, and two smaller, quieter resorts.

*Club Croc (☎ 1800 075 125, 4946 9400, fax 4946 9555,* **W** *www.clubcroc.com.au, PMB 26 Mackay 4740)* Single/double Lodge units $130/180, Beachfront units $251/410, Garden rooms $281/360. Sitting on Happy Bay in the north of the island, Club Croc is a modern mid-range, well-used resort with three levels of accommodation. It's popular with families and couples – and there are plenty of activities to keep all age groups busy. The Lodge units are small and austere, and bathroom facilities are shared; for the price, you're better off spending the extra to stay in the beachfront or garden rooms. The pleasant, motel-style Beachfront units overlook Happy Bay; and the similar-standard Garden Rooms are in the garden! The resort has two swimming pools, tennis courts, a gym and mini golf; guests also have free use of all the nonpowered water-sports gear.

All meals are included in the tariff, and there are two eating options. *The Palms* is big and rather old-fashioned in a nice kind of way, and it's where breakfast, lunch and dinner are served. *Cafe Paradiso* is the more casual of the two, serving up snacks and light meals throughout the day.

*Palm Bay Hideaway Resort (☎ 1800 095 025, 4946 9233, fax 4946 9309,* **W** *www .palmbay.com.au)* B&B packages $95-260 per person. As far as resorts in this price range go, this one stands out for the fact that it's lovely and *quiet* – there are no phones, televisions or powered water-sports equipment. Veranda'd cabins, all with en suite and some with kitchenettes, sit around the

pretty, sandy sweep of Palm Bay. At the heart of the resort is a large building that serves as the main dining area, bar and lounge. A buffet dinner/a la carte menu is available for $20/30.

*Wilderness Lodge (☎ 3839 7799* **e** *info@southlongisland.com.au,* **W** *www .southlongisland.com.au)* All-inclusive 4-7 night packages $1600-2800 per person. This isolated lodge on Paradise Bay consists of just 10 spacious, waterfront cabins; there's no fan or air-conditioning, but the cabins are positioned to make the most of the sea breezes. The lodge runs on solar power, and is staffed by a friendly crew of just three – informality is the name of the game. Meals are buffet style, and most are cooked over a campfire. There's a four-night minimum stay; with a maximum of 20 guests, no day visitors or kids under 15, and no motorised water sports, you're almost guaranteed some peace.

## Getting There & Away

Long Island is frequently connected to Shute Harbour by ferry service, with Whitsunday Allover and Blue Ferries providing 12 return transfers between them daily. The direct trip takes about 15 minutes (50 if it's via South Molle Island), and costs $25/16 per adult/child.

It's 2km between the Club Croc and Palm Bay resorts and you can walk between them in about 25 minutes. Whitsunday Allover connects Shute Harbour to Palm Bay at 7.15am, 9.15am, 4pm and 5.15pm; it returns at 7.45am, 9.45am, 4.30pm and 5.45pm.

## HOOK ISLAND

The second largest of the Whitsundays, the 53 sq km Hook Island rises to 450m at Hook Peak. There are a number of good beaches dotted around the island, and Hook has some of the best diving and snorkelling locations in the Whitsundays.

The southern end of the island is indented by two very long and narrow fjord-like bays. Beautiful Nara Inlet is a popular deep-water anchorage for visiting yachts, and Aboriginal wall paintings have been found in the inlet. Hook has a small and low-key resort and *camping ground*. You can also learn to dive here; the five-day open-water certificate course (with Prosail Dive, ☎ 4946 7533, 4946 5433) costs $450 including accommodation and transfers.

## Places to Stay & Eat
There's a *national park camping ground* at Maureen Cove on the northern side of the island.

*Hook Island Wilderness Lodge* (☎ 4946 9380, fax 4946 4970, W www .hookislandresort.com.au) Camp sites (unpowered) adult/child $14/8, double/child in cabin with communal bathroom facilities $76/18, in a cabin with en suite bathroom $115/22 ($27 per each extra person in each unit). While it's basic and a bit shabby, this is also the cheapest resort in the Whitsundays – its other advantage is that there's good snorkelling just offshore. The 12 simple, adjoining units each sleep up to six or eight people; the en suite bathrooms are *tiny*, and rates include linen but not towels. Tea, coffee and polystyrene cups are supplied in each room. There are no self-catering facilities, except for a couple of BBQs around the small camping areas at either end of the lodge.

Food is not a priority at the resort. The casual *restaurant* serves pizzas and pasta at night, while snacks are available the rest of the day; there's also a small bar.

## Getting There & Away
Transfers to the island are organised when you book your stay on Hook Island. Jade Sailing Safaris also arranges overnight camping on the Island. See Organised Tours earlier in the Whitsundays Area section in this chapter.

There are only two ways to get out to Hook Island on a day trip.

The *Voyager* does a three-island cruise (Hook Island, Whitehaven Beach and South Molle Island) for adult/child $69/35, lunch $9 extra. This cruise can be booked by calling (☎ 4946 5255). Prosail Dive is responsible for all island transfers (for guests) but people can also travel with them just for a day trip – adult $36 return. These trips can be booked by calling ☎ 4946 9380.

# DAYDREAM ISLAND
postcode 4741
Daydream, the closest of the resort islands to Shute Harbour, is just over 1km long and only a couple of hundred metres across at its widest point. It's a popular day-trip destination, with a wide range of water-sports gear available for hire (free for resort guests); water-skiing is also big here.

A steep and rocky path, taking about 20 minutes to walk, links the southern and northern ends of the island. There's another short walk to the tiny but lovely Sunlovers Beach, and a concreted path leads around the eastern side of the island. And once you've done these walks, you've just about covered Daydream from head to foot.

## Places to Stay
*Daydream Island Resort* (☎ 1800 075 040, 4948 8488, fax 4948 8499, W www .daydream.net.au) Garden room $290 a double, Garden Balcony rooms $320, Ocean Balcony rooms $390, Reef suites $440, Daydreamers suites $650. In 2001 the island underwent a $35 million dollar refurbishment, under the management of Novotel. Surrounded by beautifully landscaped tropical gardens, the resort has tennis courts, a gym, catamarans, windsurfers and three swimming pools – all of which are included in the tariff. Kids under 14 are free, and there's a club with constant activities to keep them occupied. This is a large resort on a small island, so it's not the place to head if you're seeking isolation.

## Places to Eat & Drink
At the time of research, menus for the four new restaurants at the resort had not been finalised. Breakfast, served at the *Waterfall Restaurant*, can be buffet-style ($25 per person), and cheaper a la carte options will also be available. The Waterfall is open all day, serving buffet style meals. More formal is *Mermaids* on the beachfront, or the *Boathouse* bakery/deli will provide sandwiches and other lunchy options during the day. The casual menu at *Castaways* will include snacks as well as more substantial meals. Lunch can be bought for $10 to $20.

In addition, the resort's three bars, **Splash**, **Sunset Bar** and **Lagoon Bar** offer nightly entertainment.

### Getting There & Away
Whitsunday Allover services Daydream from Shute Harbour (for adult/child house guests $30/20 return). A day-trip package costs adult/child $70/35 and includes lunch.

## SOUTH MOLLE ISLAND
postcode 4741

Largest of the Molle group of islands at 4 sq km, South Molle is virtually joined to Mid Molle and North Molle Islands – you can actually walk across a causeway to Mid Molle. Apart from the resort area and golf course at Bauer Bay in the north, the island is all national park. There is some forest cover around the resort, but because of overgrazing in the years before it was declared a national park the rest of the island is mainly rolling grasslands. The island is crisscrossed by numerous walking tracks, and has some superb lookout points. The highest point is Mt Jeffreys (198m), but the climb up Spion Kop is also worthwhile.

The island is known for its prolific birdlife. The most noticeable birds are the dozens of tame, colourful lorikeets; currawongs and the endangered stone curlews are also common. The beaches are reasonably good at high tide but, once again, severe tidal shifts tend to reveal unattractive mud flats. The resort has a big pool, a nine-hole golf course, a gym, and tennis and squash courts. There is also a wide range of water-sports gear available for day-trippers to hire (nonpowered water-sports equipment is free for resort guests).

### Places to Stay & Eat
**South Molle Island Resort** (☎ 1800 075 080, 4946 9433, fax 4946 9580, **W** www .southmolleisland.com.au) Golf rooms $171, Reef rooms $195, Whitsunday rooms $215, Beachcomber rooms $240. In 2000 this resort was refurbished. Tariffs are per person twin share per night and include three buffet meals a day in the **Island Restaurant**, use of the golf course, tennis courts, nonmotorised

water-sports equipment and nightly entertainment. South Molle is a popular resort with families, as children are well catered for. There's a great pool – Mexico meets the South Pacific – and at high tide the jetty is one of the prettiest around.

Breakfast and lunch buffets are served in the main **Island Restaurant**; bistro-style dinners – steak, chicken and seafood dishes – are also served here. Most nights there is the alternative of a barbecue beside the pool, and Friday is Island Feast Night, with an extensive spread and live entertainment.

If you want a break from the Island Restaurant, you can try the smaller **Coral's**.

### Getting There & Away
South Molle is *very* well connected. Ferries frequently stop off en route between Hamilton and Long Islands and Shute Harbour. In addition, there are direct connections with Shute Harbour ($21/12 per adult/child return). Whitsunday Allover's Shute to Molle departs at 10.15am and 2.15pm, returning at 2.45pm and 4.45pm; and Blue Ferries from Shute departs at 10.15am, 11.45am and 2.45pm, returning at 9.30am, 10.30am, 11.30am, 4.30pm and 5.45pm, with an 11pm returning ferry on Friday only.

## HAMILTON ISLAND
postcode 4803

The most heavily developed resort island in the Whitsundays, Hamilton is more like a town than a resort, with its own airport, a 200-boat marina, shops, restaurants and bars, and accommodation for more than 2000, including three high-rise tower blocks.

Hamilton was originally the creation of Gold Coast entrepreneur Keith Williams, who somehow managed to convince the Bjelke-Petersen state government to convert his 'deer farming' lease into a tourism one in the early 1980s. Williams' bulldozer-driven transformation of the island was not only ambitious but somewhat controversial, but by the end of 1986 the resort was up and running. Eventually Williams moved on to an equally controversial development, the Hinchinbrook Marina, now well and truly a fixture on the Cardwell coast. Hamilton

Island is now managed by the Holiday Inns international hotel chain.

Hamilton isn't everyone's cup of tea, but it does have an extensive range of accommodation, restaurants, bars and shops, plus plenty of entertainment possibilities including helicopter joy rides, game fishing and a hilltop fauna reserve. It can make an interesting day trip from Shute Harbour and you can use all the resort facilities.

## Things to See & Do

The resort has tennis courts, squash courts, a gym, a golf-driving range and a mini-golf course. From **Catseye Beach**, in front of the resort, you can hire windsurfers, catamarans, jet skis and other equipment, and go paragliding or water-skiing.

A dive shop by the harbour organises dives and open-water certificate courses; you can take a variety of cruises to other islands and the outer reef. Half-day fishing trips cost $80 per person, with fishing gear supplied.

There are a few **walking trails** on the island, the best being from Catseye Bay up to 230m Passage Peak on the north-eastern corner of the island. Hamilton also has a Day Care centre and a free Fun Club, with activities for kids from five to 18 years old.

## Places to Stay

On Hamilton Island Resort (☎ 1800 075 110, 4946 9999, fax 4946 8888, W www.hamiltonisland.com.au) options range from hotel rooms to self-contained apartments to penthouses. Rates listed are for one night, twin-share accommodation only; meals are not included. All bookings need to be made through the central reservations number listed first here.

***Palm Bungalows*** $277. These attractive, individual units behind the resort complex are closely packed but buffeted by lush gardens. Each has a double and single bed and small patio.

***Palm Terraces*** $232. All new and timber, these rooms are in low-rise complexes with big balconies.

***Reef View Hotel*** Rooms from $350. The large 20-storey hotel has 386 large rooms, mostly balconied.

***Whitsunday Apartments*** $330-400. These serviced one- to four-bedroom apartments are on the resort side of the island.

***Marina Village***, ***Acacia Heights*** and ***North Point Apartments & Villas*** From $490. These fully self-contained units are on the marina side of the island.

***The Beach Club*** $486. Flanking the main resort complex with its reception area, restaurants, bars, shops and pools, these 55 five-star rooms all enjoy absolute beachfront positions.

## Places to Eat

**Resortside** The following restaurants are to be found within the main resort complex. Alternatively, you can head down the harbour where there are several other options to choose from.

***Toucan Tango Cafe & Bar*** *(☎ 4946 8562)* Mains around $17. Open 11am-10pm daily, closed 5pm-6pm Fri & Sat. This large, casual eatery serves breakfast and lunch, including some of Australia's most expensive burgers.

***Beach House*** *(☎ 4946 8580)* Mains $30-35. Modern Australian cuisine forms the basis of the menu at Beach House. The set lunch ($35) comprises six courses; and the evening menu changes daily.

***Outrigger Restaurant*** *(☎ 4946 8582)* Mains $30-52. Outrigger's modern menu includes dishes such as eye fillet, spatchcock and salmon.

**Harbourside** These restaurants, all along the harbour waterfront in what is known as Marina Village (or simply Harbourside), are independently run though you can charge all bills to your room and pay for the lot on departure. There's also a ***supermarket*** for those in the apartments preparing their own meals.

***Turtles*** *(☎ 4946 8224)* Dishes $4-10. Open 7am-5pm daily. This is a busy and understaffed little cafe serving tasty lunches – gourmet pies, lasagne, sandwiches – and coffee.

***Mariners Seafood Restaurant*** *(☎ 4946 8628, fax 4946 8886)* Mains $27-36. Open 6pm-late Mon-Sat. In a big, enclosed veranda overlooking the harbour, Mariners is both licensed and BYO. While the emphasis is on seafood, grills are also available; it's a stylish restaurant with a menu to match.

*Spinnakers Bar & Grill (☎ 4946 8019)* Mains $18-30. Open 6pm-late Thur-Tues. Located upstairs, Spinnakers boasts great views over the marina; mains range from lighter meals like warm chicken salad to steaks or bug tails with garlic butter.

*Romano's (☎ 4946 8212)* Entrees $4-13, mains around $30. Open 6pm-late Thur-Tues. This is a formal Italian restaurant, with white-clothed tables in a large enclosed deck built right out over the water. The menu includes pasta dishes such as gnocchi.

*Manta Ray Cafe (☎ 4946 8213)* Breakfast $9-20, lunch & dinner mains $15-25. Open 10am-10pm daily. If you come to Hamilton on a day trip that includes lunch, this cafe is one of the choices you have. The other choice is the *Yacht Club* (see later in this section).

*Tang Dynasty Chinese Restaurant (☎ 4946 8215)* Mains $18-32. Open noon-2pm Mon-Sat, 6pm-10pm daily. A tank with swimming lobsters awaits you at the top of the stairs – this is a typical Chinese restaurant with a large menu ranging from tofu to Peking duck. There's also takeaway.

*Harbourside Eatery (☎ 4946 8610)* Light meals & takeaways $5-15. Open 8am-9pm daily. This basic fish'n'chip and burger place has tables outside on the footpath (*don't* feed the birds!).

*Hamilton Island Bakery (☎ 4946 8281)* Open 7am-5pm daily. The bakery has cabinets and fridges filled with fresh bread, sandwiches, great-looking pastries and delicious punnets of fresh fruit salad.

*Yacht Club Tavern (☎ 4946 8803)* Mains $13-20. Open 11am-late daily. At the end of the line, the Yacht Club has a big outdoor eating area overlooking the – you guessed it – yachts. Try a 'mug of prawns' with your beer at the bar.

## Entertainment

The bars in the resort, and harbourside, offer nightly entertainment. The *Toucan Tango* has a pianist, or you can head to the harbourside *Boheme's Bar*, which opens from 9pm, with a disco from 11pm till late.

## Getting There & Away

**Air** The Hamilton Island airport is the main arrival centre for the Whitsundays and takes both domestic flights and international charter flights.

Qantas flies from Hamilton to Cairns ($367) and Brisbane ($418). Island Air Taxis (☎ 4946 9933) connect Hamilton with Mackay ($120), Shute Harbour ($60) and Lindeman Island ($60).

**Boat** Blue Ferries have at least eight departures from Shute Harbour to Hamilton Island daily; the trip takes 30 minutes.

With regular daily flights to and from the major capital cities, Hamilton is also the main arrival point for Long, South Molle, Daydream, Hayman and Lindeman Islands. Whitsunday Allover and Blue Ferries meet all incoming and outgoing flights, and connect Hamilton to the other islands. Blue Ferries transfers to South Molle and Long Islands cost $40 return; Whitsunday Allover leaves directly from the airport (and therefore incurs an airport tax), and the return ticket costs $77. Transfers to Lindeman Island are usually included in accommodation packages.

Blue Ferries transfer from the airport (adult/child $33/17) to Shute involves a shuttle bus pick-up from the airport terminal to the Hamilton island marina then the boat to Shute Harbour. From the Marina (only) to Shute it costs $27/15 per adult/child. A return Hamilton Island Marina–Shute Harbour ticket costs $42/23.

## Getting Around

On arrival and departure there's a free bus service for guests between the airport or marina and the resort.

Hamilton is big, no question about it, and there are a few alternatives to walking. One is the island shuttle, which connects all points around the island on an hourly (or better) basis between 8am and 10pm. The cost is $5 for a 24-hour pass, although this is usually included in package deals.

Next are the taxis, which charge $2 per person regardless of distance. Or you can scuttle around like Mr McGoo in a golf-course buggie, available from the office near reception or from the Charter Base at harbourside (two hours/three hours/all day/ 24 hours for $35/40/50/66).

## HAYMAN ISLAND
postcode 4801
The most northern of the Whitsunday Group, Hayman has an area of 4 sq km, and rises to 250m above sea level. It has forested hills, valleys and beaches. It also has one of the most luxurious resorts on the Barrier Reef. The resort is fronted by a wide, shallow reef that emerges from the water at low tide.

Hayman is closer to the outer reef than the other islands, and there is good diving around its northern end and at nearby Hook Island. There are several small, uninhabited islands close to Hayman, and you can walk out to Arkhurst Island at low tide. Langford Island, a couple of kilometres south-west, has some good coral around it, as do Black and Bird Islands nearby.

### Activities
Resort guests have free use of catamarans, windsurfers and paddle skis, but must pay for just about everything else, including tennis and squash. There's also a golf-driving range, putting green and a well-equipped gym.

Hayman has a free Kidz Club that keeps children entertained, and a creche. The resort has a dive shop, and the *Reef Goddess* offers a range of diving and snorkelling trips to the Barrier Reef. Dinghies can be hired for $95 a day, including fishing and snorkelling gear.

Bushwalks include an 8km island circuit, a 4.5km walk to Dolphin Point at the northern tip of the island, and a 1.5km climb up to the Whitsunday Passage lookout.

### Organised Tours
Coral Air Whitsunday (☎ 4946 9111) offers a variety of seaplane tours for resort guests. Destinations include Whitehaven Beach ($195; a 2½-hour stop) and Blue Lagoon at Hardy Reef ($295; 2¾ hours of snorkelling)

### Places to Stay
*Hayman (☎ 1800 075 175, 4940 1234, fax 4940 1567, W www.hayman.com.au)* Tariffs $560-1800. This private island resort

is a member of the exclusive 'Leading Hotels of the World' group, and is the most luxurious big resort on the Great Barrier Reef. If you're looking for a five-star hotel dripping with style and sophistication, look no further.

An avenue of stately 9m-high date palms leads to the main entrance, and with its 245 rooms, five restaurants, four bars, a hectare of swimming pools, landscaped gardens and grounds, an impressive collection of antiques and arts, and exclusive boutiques, Hayman is certainly impressive.

The rooms and suites have all the usual five-star facilities. There are also 11 individually styled penthouses if you really feel the need to spend up big.

If you don't have to plan ahead, remember to keep an eye out for stand-by rates (they can be as low as $200 per person – check the newspapers in Airlie Beach and Mackay).

### Places to Eat
Breakfast is served buffet-style in *Azure*, a relaxed indoor/outdoor restaurant with a great outlook over the beach.

Other restaurants include: the casual open-air *Beach Pavilion* where there's a choice of lunchtime grills, salads, sandwiches and desserts (dishes $19 to $25); *La Fontaine*, the most formal of the restaurants, with a Louis XIV-style dining room and French cuisine (dinner only; mains around $40; a jacket is required for this restaurant); *The Oriental*, in a beautiful Japanese garden setting (mains around $35); and *La Trattoria*, specialising in Mediterranean cuisine (mains around $30).

The Hayman wine cellar numbers over 20,000 bottles of Australian and European wine, and La Fontaine has an additional 400 vintages.

### Getting There & Away
Coral Air Whitsunday (☎ 4946 9111) has seaplane transfers to Hayman from Hamilton Island and the mainland. For information on the only day tour to Hayman from the mainland, see the earlier Organised Tours section.

The resort's luxury cruisers transfer guests to the resort from Hamilton Island. Whitsunday Allover operates transfers from Shute Harbour and there are twice daily services that cost $86 return if your package does not include transfers (most do).

## LINDEMAN ISLAND

postcode 4741

One of the most southerly of the Whitsundays, Lindeman covers 8 sq km, most of which is national park. In 1992, Lindeman Island became the site of Australia's first Club Med resort.

The island has 20km of walking trails and the highest point is Mt Oldfield (210m). With plenty of little beaches and secluded bays, it's no hassle at all to find one to yourself. There are also a lot of small islands dotted around, and some are easy to get to.

### Activities

The resort's daily activities sheet lists an array of things to do, although nothing is compulsory or too regimented. There's a good golf course, as well as tennis courts, an archery range, a gym, beach volleyball, bingo etc. You can even take lessons on the resort's impressive flying trapeze set-up.

The usual range of water-sports equipment is available, and a diving school offers various dive courses and snorkelling trips. Children are also kept busy with all sorts of organised activities.

### Places to Stay

*Club Med Resort* (☎ *1800 258 2633, 4946 9333, fax 4946 9776,* W *www.clubmed.com)* Packages $235-280 per person per night. The internationally famous Club Med style is evident here, with plenty of activities, nightly entertainment and young, friendly staff to help you enjoy yourself and get the most out of your stay.

The main resort complex, with its pool, dining and entertainment areas, is flanked by three-storey accommodation blocks looking out over the water; all the motel-style rooms have their own balcony.

Rates include all meals and most activities. There are also five-night packages available from major cities, which include airfares and transfers; and one- and two-night deals from Mackay and Airlie Beach. Phone the resort for details.

### Places to Eat

All meals and beer, wine and juices are included in the tariffs. The *Main Restaurant* serves buffet-style breakfasts, lunches and dinners; the casual *Top Restaurant*, by the pool and tennis courts, has barbecued steaks and chicken, salads and fruit; and *Nicholson's*, a smaller a la carte restaurant, opens nightly for dinner.

### Entertainment

Every night at 9.30pm there's a live show in the main theatre, and you're just as likely to find yourself up on stage at some time. Later in the evening *Silhouettes* nightclub opens.

### Getting There & Away

Island Air Taxis (☎ 4946 9933) has flights to Lindeman from Shute Harbour (one way/return $60/75) and Mackay ($105 one way).

Whitsunday Allover (☎ 1300 366 494, 4946 6900) has an early morning (about 5am) ferry day trip from Shute Harbour to Lindeman. The adult/child ticket costs $121/60 and includes lunch and use of all of the resort's facilities – but it's a *very* long day.

Club Med has its own launch that connects with flights from the airport at Hamilton Island.

## WHITSUNDAY ISLAND

The largest of the Whitsunday group, this island covers 109 sq km and rises to 438m at Whitsunday Peak. There's no resort, but it has some fine bushwalking; 6km-long **Whitehaven Beach** on the south-eastern coast is the longest and best beach in the group (some say in the country), with good snorkelling off its southern end. Many of the day-trip boats visit Whitehaven. The pure-white silicon sand can be dazzling on a sunny day, so make sure you have sunglasses!

There are *national parks camping grounds* at Dugong and Sawmill Beaches in the west, and at Joe's Beach.

## NORTHERN WHITSUNDAY ISLANDS

The northern islands of the Whitsundays group are undeveloped and seldom visited by cruise boats or water taxis. Several of these – Gloucester, Saddleback, Olden and Armit Islands – have *national parks camping grounds*, and the QPWS office (☎ 4946 7022) in Jubilee Pocket, 3km south of Airlie Beach, can issue camping permits and advise you on which islands to visit and how to get there. The northern islands are best reached from Earlando, Dingo Beach, or Bowen on the mainland.

## OTHER WHITSUNDAY ISLANDS

There's a *camping ground* on **North Molle Island** at Cockatoo Beach, on the island's southern end, with tables, toilets and water. **Henning Island**, just off the western side of Whitsunday Island, also has a *camping ground* at Northern Spit.

Between Cid and Whitsunday Islands, **Cid Harbour** was the anchorage for part of the US Navy before the Battle of the Coral Sea, the turning point in the Pacific theatre of WWII. Today, visiting cruise liners anchor here.

## EARLANDO

*Earlando Tourist Resort* (☎ *4945 7133, fax 4945 7108, Dingo Beach Rd*) Unpowered/powered sites $16/18 a double, double self-contained cabins $74-83 (plus $17/11 per extra adult/child). About 15km south of Dingo Beach, there's a turn-off that takes you to the attractive Bay of Earlando. There's a bar with a shady beer garden and a casual, licensed restaurant, and you can hire dinghies for fishing or getting to the islands for $33/55 a half-day/full day.

## DINGO BEACH

Dingo Beach is a quiet little place set on a long sandy bay backed by low, forested mountains. Nothing much happens here, but it's a popular spot with the fishing fraternity and there's a pleasant foreshore reserve with shady trees, picnic tables and barbecue facilities.

The only facilities are at the *Dingo Beach General Store* on the foreshore, which sells fuel, booze, takeaway meals, a small range of groceries and bait. Next door is the *Dingo Beach Resort* (☎/fax 4945 7153, Deicke Crescent), where self-contained units cost $70 a double ($10 for each extra person).

There are two islands a little way off both ends of the bay, both with small *national parks camping grounds*: **Gloucester Island** is to the north-west and **Saddleback Island** sits to the north-east. Dingo Bay Watersports (☎/fax 4945 7215) offers transfers to these islands for $30 return; they also rent out dinghies for $75 a day.

## BOWEN

**postcode 4805 • pop 8000**

Bowen, founded in 1861, was the first coastal settlement to be established north of Rockhampton. Although soon overshadowed by Mackay to the south and Townsville to the north, Bowen survived, and today it's a thriving fruit and vegetable-growing centre that attracts hundreds of people for seasonal picking work between April and November. Bowen is spread out over a large area, with beaches, resorts and some lovely bays to the north of the older town centre.

### Information

The main tourist information centre (☎ 4786 6222) is about 5km south of Bowen on the Bruce Hwy. It's open 8.30am to 5pm daily. There's also a tourist office (☎ 4786 4494), at 34 Williams St, by the long-distance bus stop in the town centre. The local RACQ depot is Brazil's Auto Service (☎ 4786 1412, 0408 180941) at 28 Don St.

### Things to See & Do

The town's early history is depicted in displays at the **Bowen Historical Museum** (☎ *4786 2035, 22 Gordon St; adult/child $3/1; open 10.30am-4pm Mon-Fri, 10.30am-noon Sun)*.

Several walls and buildings around the centre are decorated with terrific **murals**, depicting different phases in the town's history. Painted by Queensland artists, there are currently 22 mural sites, most within the block made by Gregory, Powell, Herbert and George Sts.

Mullers Lagoon, in the centre of town, is being developed into parkland.

A couple of kilometres north of the town centre are Bowen's **beaches**. At Queens Beach you can catch a movie at the 1948

Bowen Cinema – where you'll sit in the original canvas seats. Driving east around the sandy sweep of Queens Bay you come across a series of secluded coves and bays, including the picturesque **Horseshoe Bay**. There's a **coastal walking track** linking Horseshoe and Rose Bays.

## Places to Stay

*Harbour Lights Caravan Park* (☎ *4786 1565, fax 4786 1770, 40 Santa Barbara Parade*) Sites $16, on-site vans from $28, cabins from $45. Right opposite the harbour, this caravan park has friendly staff and is a few minutes walk to the centre of town.

Out in the beach suburbs there are several other caravan/camping grounds. You could try *Coral Coast Caravan Park* (☎ *4785 1262, fax 4785 1428, Horseshoe Bay Rd*) or *Tropical Beach Caravan Park* (☎/*fax 4785 1490, Argyle St*).

Bowen's hostels specialise in finding seasonal picking work for travellers: It's a competitive scene, so it's worth ringing around before you arrive to find out what's available. Some are described here.

*Whitsunday Sands Resort* (☎ *4786 3333, fax 4786 3388, Horseshoe Bay Rd, Horseshoe Bay*) Singles/doubles $58/68. Out on the headland of Cape Edgecumbe, this midrange resort is in a pleasant setting, with access to several coves and beaches. The complex has a bar, a kiosk and a restaurant.

*Horseshoe Bay Resort* (☎ *4786 2564, fax 4786 3460, Horseshoe Bay*) Unpowered/powered sites $14/18, cabins $45 a double, self-contained units $60-75. This resort is right on Horseshoe Bay and has good facilities including a camp kitchen and pool.

There's also *Barnacles Backpackers* (☎ *4786 4400, fax 4786 4890, 16 Gordon St)*, with beds in four- to 12-bed dorms ($15), as well as twins and doubles ($16.50 per person); or *Trinity's Backpackers* (☎ *4786 4199, fax 4786 4570, 93 Horseshoe Bay Rd*) with beds in self-contained, two-bedroom, eight-bed units ($16).

## Places to Eat

*Horseshoe Bay Cafe* (☎ *4786 3280, Horseshoe Bay*) Mains $10-19. Open 10am-10pm daily. If you've got a car it's worth heading around to this airy, friendly cafe. There's a wide menu to choose from, or you could just have coffee and cake at an outdoor table and admire the pretty beach through the she-oaks and palm trees.

*Club Hotel* (☎ *4786 1006, Cnr Herbert & Powell Sts*) This hotel is a popular watering hole for pickers, packers and backpackers. It also has reasonably good bistro meals.

*Fellows Fish Bar* (☎ *4786 2462, 19 Gregory St*) Open 10am-2pm & 4.30pm-8pm daily. Fellows is a popular little takeaway fish and chip place.

*The Hot Wok* (☎ *4786 3404, 23a Gregory St*) Open 11am-2pm & 5pm-9pm Mon-Sat, 5pm-8.30pm Sun. The Hot Wok is a busy Chinese takeaway with the usual, extensive range of dishes.

*Fullagan's* (☎ *4786 1783, 37 Herbert St*) Mains $11-18. Open 5pm-midnight daily. This small, popular restaurant has an Irish theme, and serves up inexpensive meals like Guinness & beef pies, Irish Stew and steaks. There's a also small bar at the front where the staff serve a wide variety of beers, and you can probably strike up a conversation at any time.

## Getting There & Away

**Bus** Long-distance buses stop outside the Traveland travel agency (☎ 4786 2835), which is in Williams St, between Herbert and Gregory Sts.

McCafferty's/Greyhound both have frequent bus services to and from Rockhampton ($90, eight hours), Airlie Beach ($25, 1½ hours) and Townsville ($35, three hours).

**Train** The *Sunlander* and *Queenslander* trains both stop here, but note that they stop at Bootooloo Siding, 3km south of the centre, *not* at the Bowen train station.

The fare from Brisbane is $170/130 for an economy sleeper/seat.

## Getting Around

Bowen Services (☎ 4786 4414) runs local buses to Queens Beach and Horseshoe Bay Monday to Friday and Saturday morning from near the post office.

# North Coast

This chapter covers Queensland's north coast – from the Cape Upstart National Park to the Mission Beach area, and inland as far as the Gregory Developmental Rd.

At the centre of the north coast is Townsville, the largest city in northern Queensland. As the point of departure for Magnetic Island and some of the best parts of the Great Barrier Reef, Townsville has much to offer. Inland are the former gold-mining centres of Ravenswood and Charters Towers, from where the Flinders Hwy continues its run clear across outback Queensland.

There are some wonderful national parks along this stretch of the coast. The majestic Hinchinbrook Island is one of Queensland's great natural wonders; pack your tent and walking boots and tackle the 32km Thorsborne Trail.

Further north is Mission Beach, a cluster of settlements scattered along a scenic strip of coastline, with the resort islands of Dunk and Bedarra just offshore.

## Geography & Climate

The south-western corner of this region is dominated by the massive Burdekin Falls Dam and the valleys of the Burdekin River – some of the richest farming areas in the state. Sugar cane and rice are the major crops.

The mountain ranges of the Great Dividing Range run parallel with the coast, and become higher and move closer to the coast the further north you go. Blanketed with thick rainforests, these mountains are part of the Wet Tropics World Heritage Area, stretching from just north of Townsville almost as far as Cooktown.

The region's climate is tropical: Summer (December to March) is hot, wet and humid; the rest of the year you can expect predominantly warm, sunny weather with no great extremes. The northern section of this coast, from Ingham to Innisfail, is the wettest part of Queensland – and Tully is the wettest place in Australia, receiving over 4000mm of rain annually.

## Highlights

- Mosey on down Townsville's Strand to Reef HQ and check out who you'll be swimming with.
- Take a trip back in time to the gold-mining towns of Ravenswood and Charters Towers.
- Walk the Thorsborne Trail on Hinchinbrook Island, one of Queensland's best wilderness experiences.

## Activities

White-water rafting trips on the Tully River operate out of Mission Beach. You can get to the outer Barrier Reef from Mission Beach, Magnetic Island and Townsville, and dive courses are offered at all three places.

Highlights for bushwalkers include Hinchinbrook Island, Magnetic Island, the Mission Beach area, Jourama Falls and Mt Spec in the Paluma Range National Park (south of Ingham), and the Bowling Green Bay National Park (south of Townsville).

## Getting There & Away

**Air** Townsville is the major airport for the north coast, with flights to/from all major centres and capital cities.

NORTH COAST

# NORTH COAST

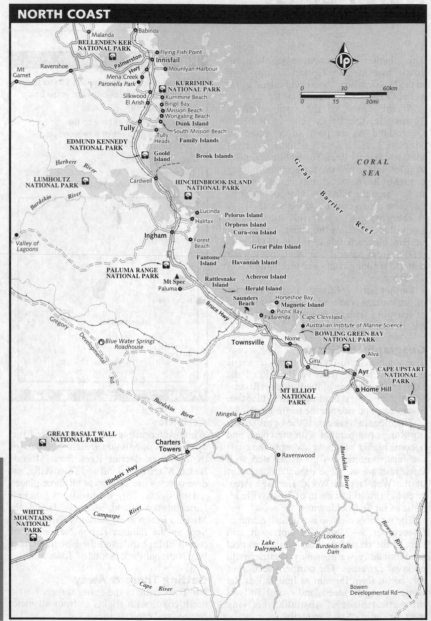

Dunk Island has its own airport, with regular flights to/from Townsville and Cairns.

**Bus** Bus services in this area are almost identical to the routes covered by the trains. McCafferty's/Greyhound and Premier have frequent services up the Bruce Hwy on the Brisbane Cairns run, with detours off the highway to Mission Beach. Brisbane to Townsville takes 22 hours and costs $158.

Inland services operate from Townsville to Mt Isa, via Charters Towers, continuing onto Threeways in the Northern Territory (from where you can either head north to Darwin or south to the Alice).

**Train** The main Brisbane-Cairns train line runs alongside the Bruce Hwy, with stops at all the major centres including Ingham, Cardwell and Tully. The Brisbane-Townsville trip takes around 22 hours and the one-way fare is $148 for an economy sleeper or $226 for a 1st-class sleeper.

The *Inlander* runs between Townsville and Mt Isa twice a week (Sunday and Wednesday); the trip from Townsville to Charters Towers takes three hours and costs $20.

**Car & Motorcycle** The Bruce Hwy is the major route up the coast, while the Flinders Hwy from Townsville is the major inland route. If you have a little time, the detour off the Bruce Hwy to the mountain village of Paluma is one of the most spectacular scenic drives along this section of the coast.

The Gregory Developmental Rd runs parallel with the coast, on the inland side of the Great Dividing Range, passing through Charters Towers to the Lynd Junction. From here, the Kennedy Hwy continues north to the Atherton Tableland.

**Boat** The major ferry services along this coast are from Townsville to Magnetic Island, from Cardwell to Hinchinbrook Island, and from Mission Beach to Dunk Island.

## AYR TO TOWNSVILLE

At Home Hill, a small highway town 9km south of Ayr, there's one of the largest souvenir shops you're ever likely to see.

Besides selling everything from teaspoons to T-shirts, **Ashworth's Tourist Centre** (☎ 4782 1177) also houses the 'Treasures of the Earth' exhibition (adult/child $2.50/1), an impressive collection of fossils, gemstones and rocks. Ashworth's is open 8.30am to 5pm Monday to Friday and from 8.45am to noon on Saturday.

**Ayr** is on the delta of one of the biggest rivers in Queensland, the Burdekin, and is the major commercial centre for the rich farmlands of the Burdekin Valley.

There's a tourist information office (☎ 4783 5988) in Plantation Park, on the southern side of town. The **Ayr Nature Display** (☎ 4783 2189) on Wilmington St, signposted off the main road, has a huge collection of butterflies and other insects. It's open 8am to 5pm daily (adult/child $2.50/1).

If you're interested in marine biology, you can visit the **Australian Institute of Marine Science** (AIMS; ☎ 4778 9211), a marine research facility at Cape Ferguson between Ayr and Townsville. Free tours are conducted every Friday at 10am. The turn-off to AIMS is on the Bruce Hwy about 53km north-west of Ayr or 35km south-east of Townsville.

The turn-off from the Bruce Hwy to the beautiful **Bowling Green Bay National Park** is at Alligator Creek, 28km south of Townsville. Alligator Creek tumbles down between two rugged ranges that rise steeply from the coastal plains. The taller range peaks with Mt Elliot (1234m), whose higher slopes harbour some of Queensland's most southerly tropical rainforest.

A sealed road heads 6km inland from the highway to the park entrance, from where a good gravel road leads to pleasant picnic areas. Further on there's a *camping ground* with toilets, showers and barbecues; the 23 self-registration sites can be booked through the ranger (☎/fax 4778 8203).

Alligator Creek has some superb swimming holes, and there are two walking trails, one to Hidden Valley and the Alligator Falls (17km, five hours return), the other (8km, six hours return) following Cockatoo Creek south, starting from the camping ground. The park gates are closed from sundown to 6.30am.

**NORTH COAST**

## TOWNSVILLE
### postcode 4810 • pop 150,000

The third-largest town in Queensland and the main centre in the north of the state, Townsville is the port for the agricultural and mining production of the vast inland region of northern Queensland. It's also a major armed forces base, the site of James Cook University, and the start of the main route from Queensland to the Northern Territory.

In 1999 huge amounts of money were poured into Townsville: The 2.2km-long foreshore area known as the Strand was completely revamped and now provides a slick, colourful public space enjoyed around the clock. The city also boasts a superb aquarium and museum, designed around the life-size model of an 18th-century boat.

Townsville has a wide selection of accommodation and a lively restaurant and cafe scene. It's the access point for the lovely Magnetic Island, and is only a couple of hours away by fast catamaran from some of the best parts of the Great Barrier Reef.

### History
Townsville was founded in 1864 by the work of a Scot, John Melton Black, and the

TOWNSVILLE

1  Rowes Bay Caravan Park
2  Jezzine Military Museum
3  Coral Sea Memorial Rock Pool
4  Stinger Enclosure
5  Shoredrive Motel
6  Townsville Seaside Apartments
7  Stranded Kiosk
8  Aquarius on the Beach Hotel
9  Beach House Motel
10  Townsville Reef International
11  Castling St Heritage Centre

See Central Townsville map p309

money of Robert Towns, a Sydney-based sea captain and financier. Together these two owned pastoral lands in the high country – but their sheep and cattle farms couldn't survive without a boiling-down works for animal carcasses on the coast. Towns aimed to build this at Bowen, but residents there objected and instead the pair set up the works on Cleveland Bay to the north of Bowen. Towns wanted it to be a private depot for his stations but Black saw the chance to make his fortune by founding a settlement and persuaded Towns to part with £10,000 for the project.

Despite a cyclone in 1867, Black persisted and was elected Townsville's first mayor the same year. The town developed mainly due to Chinese and Kanaka labour; European attitudes at the time were such that there was more alarm when a horse rather than a Kanaka was snatched from the banks of the creek by a crocodile. Eventually a road was forged up to Towns' stations inland, contributing to both their survival and Townsville's.

By the start of WWII, Townsville was a busy port town with a population of around 30,000, shooting to more than 100,000 when it became one of the major bases for Australian and US armed forces.

## Orientation

Townsville's sprawl is extensive, but the centre's a fairly compact area that you can easily get around on foot.

The city is flanked by Ross Creek to the south-east and Cleveland Bay to the north-east. Towering over the lot is the 290m-high Castle Hill to the west. Reef HQ (the aquarium) and the museum are at the northern end of Flinders St East. Out on the breakwater sit the casino and Entertainment Centre, with a marina along the western side. Ferries to Magnetic Island leave from two terminals along Ross Creek: one on Flinders St East and one on the breakwater.

The transit centre, the arrival and departure point for long-distance buses, is on the corner of Palmer and Plume Sts in South Townsville, on the southern side of Ross Creek. The train station is south of the centre

near the corner of Flinders and Blackwood Sts, and the Bruce Hwy bypasses the lot.

## Information

**Tourist Offices** Townsville Enterprises' main tourist information office (☎ 4778 3555) is on the Bruce Hwy, 8km south of the city centre. It's open 9am to 5pm daily, though there's also a convenient information booth (☎ 4721 3660), open 9am to 5pm Monday to Friday and 9am to 12.30pm Saturday and Sunday, in the middle of Flinders St Mall, between Stokes and Denham Sts.

**Post & Communications** The main post office is on the corner of the Flinders St Mall and Denham St. The poste restante section is a small window around the back. There's also a post office shop, open seven days, at Reef HQ.

The Internet Den (☎ 4721 4500), at 265 Flinders Mall, offers Internet access for $5.50 per hour. It's open 8am to 10pm daily. At the Townsville City Library (☎ 4727 9666) Internet access is free to everyone; the library is open 9.30am to 5pm Monday to Friday and 9am to noon on the weekends.

**Useful Organisations** There's a Reef & National Parks information centre (☎ 4721 2399), open 9am to 5pm Monday to Friday and 10am to 4pm Saturday and Sunday, in the Reef HQ building.

The Royal Automobile Club of Queensland (RACQ; ☎ 4775 3999) is at 202 Ross River Rd, in the suburb of Aitkenvale, about 7km south of the centre.

**Bookshops** The Mary Who Bookshop (☎ 4771 3824), 155 Stanley St, is small but bountiful with an eclectic range of books and music. QBD's Bumble Bee Bookshop (☎ 4771 6091) on the Flinders St Mall is a larger mainstream bookshop that includes a large travel section.

The Ancient Wisdom Bookshop (☎ 4721 2434), in Shaw's Arcade off the Flinders St Mall, stocks New Age books; in the same arcade is Jim's Book Exchange (☎ 4771 6020), which sells a wide range of second-hand books.

## Reef HQ & Museum Complex

Townsville's top attractions are clustered together at the end of Flinders St East beside Ross Creek. The main highlights are the aquarium and museum; there's also an IMAX cinema, shops, a national parks information office and the Great Barrier Reef Marine Park Authority office. A special combined ticket (adult/concession/child/family $50/38/24/ 120) for the museum, Reef HQ, the IMAX theatre and the Billabong sanctuary (see Wildlife Sanctuary later in this section) can be bought at any of these places.

**Reef HQ** The highlight of the complex is the aquarium (☎ 4750 0800, W www.reefHQ .org.au; adult/student/child/family $16/ 13.80/7/38; open 9am-5pm daily). The huge main tank, replete with living coral reef, is home to a vast array of fish, sharks, rays and other marine life; to maintain the natural conditions essential for the survival of such a complex ecosystem, a wave machine simulates the ebb and flow of the ocean, circular currents keep the water in motion and marine algae are used in the purification system. The aquarium also has several smaller tanks, displays on the history and life of the reef, and a theatrette where slide shows on the reef are shown. Apart from the 'discovery trail' guided tours at 11am and 2pm every day, other activities, eg diver shows and turtle-feeding, take place each day; on weekends only there's a special program for kids at 11am and 3pm.

**Museum of Tropical Queensland** While the focus of this purpose-built museum (☎ 4726 0600, W www.mtq.qld.gov.au; adult/student/child/family $9/6.50/5/24; open 9am-5pm daily) is the reconstruction of the bow of the Pandora, wrecked in the Torres Strait in 1791, and associated exhibits – relics and some interesting video presentations – this terrific museum also has an extensive natural history collection and a fascinating exhibition of Aboriginal and Torres Strait artefacts and culture.

**IMAX Dome Theatre** Four, hour-long films alternate on the hour through the day at this large-screen cinema (☎ 4721 1481, Flinders St East; adult/student/child/family $12.65/10.45/7.15/31.90; open 10am-4pm).

## Other Museums & Galleries

The **Townsville Museum** (☎ 4772 5725, Cnr Sturt & Stokes Sts; adult/child $2/0.50; open 10am-3pm Mon-Fri, 10am-1pm Sat & Sun), housed in the historic 1877 Magistrate's Courthouse, is an interesting collection of old photographs of what Townsville used to look like, some Aboriginal artefacts, and general memorabilia.

The **Jezzine Military Museum** (☎ 4771 1043; admission by donation; open 9am-12.30pm Mon-Fri, 10am-2pm Sat & Sun) is in an 1890s fort and command post atop Kissing Point, in the grounds of the Jezzine Army Barracks beyond the northern end of the Strand. The museum has a collection of military paraphernalia dating back to the 1880s.

Beside Ross Creek in South Townsville, the **Maritime Museum** (☎ 4721 5251, 42-68 Palmer St; adult/child & student/family $6/4/15; open 10am-4pm Mon-Fri, 1pm-4pm Sat & Sun) has exhibits on northern Queensland's maritime history, in particular on the wreck of the Yongala, and photographs of Port Townsville's golden olden days.

The **Perc Tucker Regional Gallery** (☎ 4727 9011, fax 4772 3656, e ptrg@townsville .qld.gov.au, Cnr Denham St & Flinders Mall; admission free; open 10am-5pm Mon-Fri, 10am-2pm Sat & Sun) is a regional art gallery with a wide range of contemporary and historical exhibitions, by local and interstate artists. Well worth a look.

The National Trust has saved and relocated three historic houses (1878, 1888, 1921) to the **Castling St Heritage Centre** (☎ 4272 5195, 5 Castling St, West End; admission $3; open 10am-2pm Wed, 1pm-4pm Sat & Sun). Two are fully furnished according to their time and open to the public. Castling St is 2km from the city centre, along Ingham Rd. A block east is the West End Cemetery, with graves dating back to the 1880s.

## Parks & Gardens

The **Queens Gardens**, on Gregory St, 1km north-west from the town centre, contain

# CENTRAL TOWNSVILLE

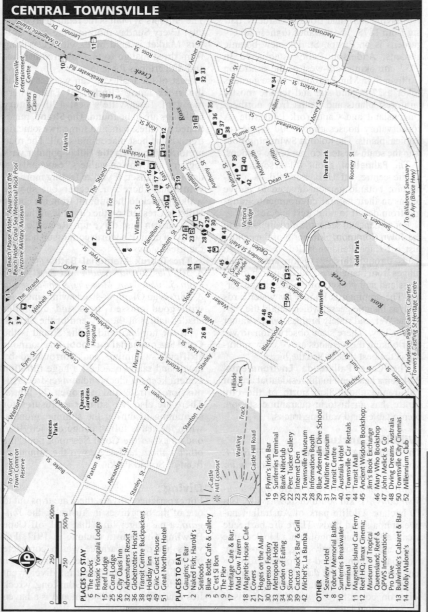

**PLACES TO STAY**
6   The Rocks
7   Historic Yongala Lodge
15  Reef Lodge
25  Coral Lodge
26  City Oasis Inn
32  Adventurers Resort
36  Globetrotters Hostel
38  Transit Centre Backpackers
43  Holiday Inn
49  Civic Guest House
51  Great Northern Hotel

**PLACES TO EAT**
1   Gaugins; C Bar
2   Naked Fish; Harold's
    Seafoods
3   Blue Bottle Cafe & Gallery
5   C'est Si Bon
9   The Pier
17  Heritage Cafe & Bar;
    Mad Cow Tavern
18  Magnetic House Cafe
21  Covers
27  Hoges on the Mall
30  Espresso Factory
33  Metropole Hotel
34  Garden of Eating
35  Sirocco
39  Cactus Jack's Bar & Grill
42  Michel's; La Bamba

**OTHER**
4   Seaview Hotel
8   Tobruk Memorial Baths
10  Sunferries Breakwater
    Terminal
11  Magnetic Island Car Ferry
12  Reef HQ; Imax Cinema;
    Museum of Tropical
    Queensland; Reef &
    QPWS Information;
    Pro Dive
13  Bullwinkle's Cabaret & Bar
14  Molly Malone's
16  Flynn's Irish Bar
19  Sunferries Terminal
20  Bank Niteclub
22  Perc Tucker Gallery
23  Internet Den
24  Townsville Museum
28  Blue Adrenalin Dive School
29  Information Booth
31  Maritime Museum
37  Transit Centre
40  Australia Hotel
41  Townsville Car Rentals
44  Transit Mall
45  Ancient Wisdom Bookshop;
    Jim's Book Exchange
46  Mary Who Bookshop
47  John Melick & Co
48  Diving Dreams Australia
50  Townsville City Cinemas
52  Millennium Club

**NORTH COAST**

sports-playing fields, tennis courts and Townsville's original Botanic Gardens, dating from 1878. The entrance to these lovely gardens is on Paxton St. The new botanic gardens, **Anderson Park**, established in 1932, are 6km south-west of the centre on Gulliver St in Mundingburra. These gardens cover a 27-hectare site and feature mostly rainforest plants and palms from northern Queensland and Cape York Peninsula. A conservatory houses almost 500 species of tropical plants. The **Kokoda Swimming Pool** is in the south-western corner of the gardens.

The **Palmetum**, about 15km south-west of the centre, off University Rd, is a 25-hectare botanic garden devoted to native palms in their natural environments, ranging from desert to rainforest species.

For a chance to see some bird-life, head to the **Town Common**, 5km north of the centre, just off Cape Pallarenda Rd. A 7km road leads through this 32 sq km area, which ranges from mangroves and salt marsh to dry grassland and pockets of woodland and forest. The common is known for water birds such as magpie geese, which herald the start of the Wet, and stately brolgas, which gather in the Dry. There's an observation tower overlooking the wetlands area – early morning is the best time to see the birds.

The **Cape Pallarenda Environmental Park**, on a headland in the residential area of Pallarenda about 8km north of the city centre, has an historic quarantine station, picnic tables and walking tracks.

## Wildlife Sanctuary

The **Billabong Sanctuary** (☎ *4778 8344, fax 4780 4569,* W *www.billabongsanctuary .com.au/, Bruce Hwy; adult/student/child/ family $19.80/15.40/9.90/47.30; open 8am-5pm daily),* 17km south of Townsville, is a 10-hectare wildlife park of Australian native animals and birds. There are barbecue areas, a swimming pool and a kiosk in the park, and various shows (eg, hold-a-koala/wombat/python, feed-a-crocodile/dingo/eagle) throughout the day. There's no public transport to the sanctuary, although daily tours do come here – see the Organised Tours section, later.

## Other Attractions

The **Flinders St Mall** is the retail heart of the city. Every Sunday morning, the busy **Cotters Market** is held here, with everything from dried mango to embroidered hankies and didgeridoos for sale.

East of the mall you can wander beside the creek along **Flinders St East**, where many of Townsville's best 19th-century buildings are to be found. **The Strand**, punctuated by cafes, bars and some awesome fig trees, is the best place for a stroll. The road up to the top of **Castle Hill** is popular with joggers and power-walkers, especially at dawn and sunset; if you're feeling more adventurous, there's a steeper but shorter walking track to the summit from the end of Hillside Crescent on the city side of the hill. Or, you can just drive up. Regardless of how you do it, it's worth coming up here for the great views.

The **Tobruk Memorial Baths** (☎ *4772 6550, The Strand; adult/child $2.20/1.10; open 5.30am-7pm Mon-Fri, 7am-6pm Sat & Sun)* is an Olympic-sized swimming pool with good grassed areas and umbrella-shaded tables at the city end of the Strand.

At the northern end of the Strand is the **Coral Sea memorial rock pool**, an enormous artificial swimming pool surrounded by lawns and sandy beaches; a huge filtration system keeps it clean and stinger-free. Admission is free, and it's open 24 hours. There are also two **stinger enclosures** for swimming in during the summer months, when the sea is full of dangerous jellyfish: one's next to the Coral Sea rock pool, the other's about halfway down the Strand, in front of Strand Park.

## Diving

For experienced divers, there are trips out to one of the best dives in Australia, the *Yongala*, a passenger liner that sank off Cape Bowling Green in a cyclone in 1911. For years her disappearance was a complete mystery. During WWII the ship's location was discovered and the first diver went down to it in 1947. The 90m-long wreck lies intact on the sea bottom and is a haven for a huge variety of marine life.

Diving Dreams, Pro Dive and Blue Adrenalin all offer trips out to the *Yongala* (from $165).

The wreck of the *Yongala* is more of an attraction than the John Brewer Reef, the destination for many day trips. The reef has been damaged by cyclones and the crown-of-thorns sea star, and parts of it have little live coral.

**Courses** Townsville has several diving schools to choose from, and you can get cheap or free accommodation at some hostels if you book a dive course from that hostel. You'll need to get a dive medical certificate (about $60) before enrolling for any course.

Diving Dreams Australia (☎ 4721 2500, ℮ resv@divingdreams.com, ⓦ www .divingdreams.com, 252 Walker St) offers three PADI certificate courses: the five-day 'Liveaboard Adventure' course, which includes nine dives and three days and nights on board the vessel *Divemaster*, starts every Saturday and costs $495; the four-day 'Reef Experience' course includes two days and four dives on the reef plus three nights' accommodation; it starts every Saturday and Thursday and costs $418; and on Tuesdays for $330 you can do the 'Island Getaway', which includes three nights' accommodation, two dives on the reef and two dives off Magnetic Island.

Pro Dive (☎/fax 4721 1760, ℮ prodivet@ ultra.net.au, Reef HQ), another well-regarded diving school, also runs courses in Townsville. Its weekly five-day certificate course costs $545 and includes two nights and three days on the reef, with a total of eight dives.

Blue Adrenalin (☎ 4721 3001, ℮ info@ blueadrenalin.com, ⓦ www.blueadrenalin .com, Shop 21, Metway Arcade, 390 Flinders Mall) offers two-night trips with six dives, leaving Friday, for $368; three-night trips with up to 10 dives, leaving Tuesday, for $475; and five-night trips with up to 16 dives, leaving Tuesday, for $795.

## Fishing Charters

A number of charter boats operate fishing trips out of Townsville. Operators include True Blue Charters (☎ 4771 5474) and Coral Sea Fishing Charters (☎ 018 778 524). The tourist information centre has a full list of fishing and yacht charter operators.

## Other Activities

Right Training (☎ 4725 4571, ℮ climbing@ ozemail.com.au) offers abseiling ($54) and half/full-day ($98/160) climbs of either Castle or Stewart Hill. Coral Sea Skydivers (☎ 4772 4889, 14 Plume St) will let you throw yourself out of a plane ($240 to $340); two-day free fall courses cost $490.

## Organised Tours

**Reef Trips** Pure Pleasure Cruises (☎ 4721 3555, ℮ ppccv@bigpond.com, 4 The Strand) has day trips to Kelso Reef, east of the Palm Island group, where it has a large floating pontoon. The cost is $126 (children $65), which includes lunch, viewing from a glass-bottom boat and snorkelling equipment; scuba dives cost extra.

**Cruises** The *Coral Princess* (☎ 4721 1673, ⓦ www.coralprincess.com.au) does a four-day cruise between Townsville and Cairns every week – see Cruises in the Cairns section of the Far North Queensland chapter for more details.

**Day Tours** Detour Coaches (☎ 4728 5311, 4 Jackson St, Garbutt) offers a two-hour, weekday City Sights tour (adult/child/family $27/8/60); trips to the Billabong Sanctuary at 12.45pm each weekday ($32/16/88 including entry); and day trips to Charters Towers, Mt Spec and Paluma ($77/32/180).

Birds & Bush Tours (☎ 4721 6489, ℮ bbtours@austarnet.com.au, ⓦ home .austarnet.com.au/bbtours) has a range of specialised bird-watching tours ($130). It also offers trips to Charters Towers ($130), the rainforests of Paluma Range National Park ($110) and the spectacular Wallaman Falls ($130).

## Special Events

Townsville's major annual event is the Palmer St Festival. Held each year in May, it features street theatre and other activities.

The Australian Festival of Chamber Music (W www.afcm.com.au), featuring both international and Australian ensembles, is held each July.

## Places to Stay – Budget

*Rowes Bay Caravan Park* (☎ *4771 3576, fax 4724 2017, Heatley Parade, Rowes Bay)* Powered/unpowered sites $21/16 a double, cabins from $48, self-contained villas $67. These leafy grounds with a pool and shop are opposite Soroptomist's Park and the Rowes Bay foreshore, about 3km north of the city centre.

Quite a few other *caravan parks* are strung along the Bruce Hwy to the north and south of Townsville.

There are three hostels on Palmer St, along the southern side of Ross Creek, close to the transit centre, restaurants and cafes; it's a short walk across the river to the city centre.

*Adventurers Resort* (☎ *4721 1522, fax 4721 3251, 79 Palmer St)* Beds in 4-bed dorm $19.50, singles/twins & doubles $33.50/49.00. Some of the rooms in this huge multilevel complex are positively cell-like, though facilities are good and include a shop, car parking and swimming pool. There's a discount for VIP card-holders.

*Transit Centre Backpackers* (☎ *1800 628 836, 4721 2322, fax 4721 2328, Cnr Palmer & Plume Sts)* Dorm beds $13.50, singles/twins/doubles $28.50/35.50/37.50, doubles with en suite $45. Above the transit centre and convenient for bus departures and ferry terminals it may be, but that's about it, with a maze of dank corridors leading to scruffy rooms.

*Globetrotters Hostel* (☎ *4771 3242, 45 Palmer St)* Beds in 4-6–bed dorm $18, twins & doubles with/without en suite $48/42, singles (no en suite) $32. This is a clean, small hostel, with rooms in an old house and a newer building behind it. Rooms are simple (and very low-ceilinged in the older building), and the communal areas are pleasant.

Townsville's other hostels are on the northern side of Ross Creek, in and around the city centre.

*Reef Lodge* (☎ *4721 1112, fax 4721 1405, 4 Wickham St)* Beds in 4-bed dorm $16,

singles & doubles & twins $36. This is a small, rather ramshackle place with rooms spread over several buildings, positioned within a stone's throw of Reef HQ and the ferry terminals. Air-con here is of the coin-in-the-slot variety.

*Civic Guest House* (☎ *1800 646 619, 4771 5381, fax 4721 4919,* e *civic@ultra .net.au, 262 Walker St)* Beds in 4-6–bed dorm with fan/air-con $17/18.50, singles/ doubles with shared bathroom from $38/40, air-con singles/doubles & twins with en suite $50/55. Certainly the pick of the bunch in this range, this is a breezy, easy-going hostel with clean, pleasant rooms and amenities. Friday night sees a free barbecue for guests.

*Great Northern Hotel* (☎ *4771 6191, fax 4771 6190, 496 Flinders St)* Singles/twins $25/35. Rooms with en suites cost an extra $10 and need to be booked well ahead. A wonderful looking old pub opposite the train station, this place offers basic pub rooms, most of which open out onto a broad veranda.

## Places to Stay – Mid-Range

*The Rocks* (☎ *4771 5700, fax 4771 5711,* e *therocks@ultra.net.au, 20 Cleveland Terrace)* Single/double B&Bs $79/99. The Rocks is a beautifully restored historic home, replete with period furnishings and a veranda providing great views over the bay. Built in the 1880s for a prominent local banker, it was later used as a hospital, then occupied by the US navy command during WWII – there's a concrete bunker in the back yard to prove it! Jennie and Joe, the guesthouse's owners, have created a relaxed yet sophisticated ambience; staying here is a lovely experience.

*Beach House Motel* (☎ *4721 1333, fax 4771 6893, 66 The Strand)* Singles/ doubles/triples $71/77/88. This is a neat, renovated budget motel with good units. The *Regatta restaurant* at the front of the motel is quite good and overlooks a small pool.

*Coral Lodge B&B* (☎ *4771 5512, fax 4721 6461, 32 Hale St)* Singles/twins & doubles from $50/60, self-contained units $65 & $75. This quaint old Queenslander has two self-contained units upstairs and eight guestrooms with shared bathrooms, and communal kitchen, downstairs. It's a good-value, quiet place with lots of character and helpful, friendly managers, and is only a short walk from the centre of town. (If you're driving, enter Hale St from Stokes St.)

*Shoredrive Motel (☎ 4771 6851, fax 4772 6311, 117 The Strand)* Singles/doubles/triples $68/78/88. This 3½-star motel is right opposite the Coral Sea memorial rock pool.

*Historic Yongala Lodge Motel (☎ 4772 4633, fax 4721 1074, 11 Fryer St)* Singles & doubles from $85, self-contained apartments from $95 a double. The modern motel units here sit behind a lovely 19th-century building that houses a Greek restaurant (see Places to Eat).

*Townsville Seaside Apartments (☎ 4721 3155, fax 4721 3089, 105 The Strand)* 1-/2-bedroom units from $77/110 a double (2-night minimum). In a two-storey strip of renovated 1960s apartments, these units don't win any interior design prizes, but they're comfortable and fully equipped with good kitchens and air con. Prices vary according to the season and the number of people.

## Places to Stay – Top End
*Townsville Reef International (☎ 4721 1777, fax 4721 1779, 63-64 The Strand)* Doubles with/without sea views from $104/115. This four-star, three-storey motel, with restaurant and pool, overlooks the waterfront at the city end of the Strand.

*City Oasis Inn (☎ 4771 6048, 1800 809 515, fax 4721 5076, e cityoasis@140 .aone.net.au, 143 Wills St)* Singles & doubles/family rooms from $95/113, self-contained 2-bedroom units $159 (4 people). Recently renovated and a stone's throw from Flinders St Mall, the neat-as-a-pin City Oasis has a pool, cafe, barbecue area and laundry.

*Aquarius on the Beach (☎ 4772 4255, fax 4721 1316, e aquariushotel@beyond .net.au, W www.aquarius-townsville.com.au, 75 The Strand)* Studio doubles $127, 4-person studios $193. The tallest building on the Strand has over 130 self-contained units, all with great views, air-con, mod cons and kitchenettes. There's a pool and a restaurant on the 14th floor.

*Holiday Inn (☎ 4772 2477, fax 4721 1263, e reservations@holidayinntownsville.com*

*.au, 334 Flinders St Mall)* Singles & doubles from $160. You can't miss this one – 'the sugar shaker' – the prominent 20-storey circular building in the Flinders St Mall. It has four stars and 159 air-con rooms, two gyms, a rooftop pool, piano bar and restaurant – all smack in the middle of Townsville.

## Places to Eat
With restaurants lining Palmer St on one side of the river and the Strand on the other, there's now a great choice of places to get a feed in Townsville. There are also quite a few takeaways and casual eateries tucked away in the arcades off the Flinders St Mall.

**Cafes, Delis & Fast Food** For light meals and takeaways, the choices abound.

*Blue Bottle Cafe Gallery (☎ 4771 2121, 58 The Strand)* Mains $9-21. Open 10am-10pm Tues-Fri, 9am-10pm Sat, 9am-5pm Sun. There's a nice vibe to this relaxed, licensed cafe/gallery serving breakfasts, tasty bruschettas, good coffee and inventive mains.

*C'est Si Bon (☎ 4772 5828, 43 Eyre St, North Ward)* Breakfast & lunch mains from $6. Open 7am-5pm Mon-Fri, 7am-3pm Sat & Sun. This is an excellent gourmet deli and takeaway, opposite the Townsville Hospital, about 1km north of the centre, specialising in home-made pies, bagels and baguettes.

*Espresso Factory (☎ 4772 6388, Northtown Flinders Mall)* Light lunches around $6. Open 8am-4.30pm Mon-Fri, 8.30am-1pm Sat & Sun. Tucked away in an arcade, the small and slick Espresso Factory does really good sandwiches and tortilla wraps and some of the best coffee in Townsville.

*Magnetic House Cafe (☎ 4771 2172, 145b Flinders St East)* Mains $9-14. Open 11.30am-3.30pm & 6.30pm-late Tues-Sat, closed Wed night. The walls of this low-key, friendly place are covered in pictures; tables are covered in white paper and jars of crayons invite you to draw. Most meals are vegetarian, some vegan – a good place if the meaty menus of other places are getting you down.

*Harold's Seafood (☎ 4724 1322, Cnr The Strand & Gregory St)* Fish boxes $6.50. Weekend queues say it all at this corner takeaway joint selling fish and chips and burgers.

NORTH COAST

**Stranded Kiosk** (☎ *4724 4844, Strand Park*) Takeaways $4-10. With a fabulous location and delicious takeaways, this is a great place to get a meal on the foreshore. The Thai fish curry is particularly good.

**La Bamba** (☎ *4771 6322, 3 Palmer St*) Light meals $6-14, mains $12-17. Open 8am-2pm daily, 6pm-2am Mon-Sat. La Bamba is a busy cafe/bar with live music Tuesday and Thursday nights.

**Pubs** Many of the pubs do decent counter meals.

**Blarney Bar Bistro** (☎ *4771 6191, Great Northern Hotel, 496 Flinders St*) Mains $12-15. Lunch noon-2pm, dinner 6pm-8pm daily. This is an excellent bistro serving steaks the size of dinner plates.

**Metropole Hotel** (☎ *4771 4285, 81 Palmer St*) Mains $8-19. Pasta, seafood and steaks are served in the covered beer garden/bistro out the back or the small dining room; daily lunch specials ($6) are served in the bar.

**Flynns Irish Bar** (☎ *4721 1655, 101 Flinders St East*) Lunch mains $7-13. Open 11am-stumps, Mon-Sat. This is a grand old dame of a Victorian pub, faithfully restored; specials go for $6.50 or you could try the Irish stew or beef and Guinness pies.

**Restaurants** Townsville makes the most of the abundance of fresh fish and produce in the area.

**Covers** (☎ *4721 4360, 209 Flinders St East*) Cafe mains $12-15, restaurant mains $18-25. Covers has a licensed cafe downstairs and a formal restaurant upstairs serving more expensive meals; a meaty menu includes eye fillet, seared native camel and baked buffalo tenderloin.

**Hoges on the Mall** (☎ *4772 6244, Flinders St Mall*) Breakfast from $6, mains $13-16. This bustling family restaurant churns out inexpensive meals.

**The Pier** (☎ *4721 2567, Sir Leslie Thiess Dr*) Mains $14-40. Open noon-2pm Mon-Fri, 6pm-late Mon-Sat. Light-flooded and surrounded by water, this is a stylish, licensed restaurant specialising in seafood.

**Historic Yongala Lodge** (☎ *4772 4633, 11 Fryer St*) Mains $20-22, banquet $35 per person. Greek fare is served in a lovely old building filled with period furniture and *Yongala* wreck relics, and live bazoukis on Friday and Saturday nights.

**Naked Fish** (☎ *4724 4623, fax 4724 4627, 60 The Strand*) 11.30am-2.30pm, 6pm-10pm Wed-Mon. Entrees $13 to $16, mains $18-23. This is a trendy newcomer to the scene, serving mostly fishy dishes, like red emperor with macadamias, honey and wasabi, under a starry ceiling.

**Gaugins** (☎ *4724 5488, Gregory St Headland, The Strand*) Open 11.30am-3pm, 6pm-9pm daily. Entrees $7-15, mains $19-30. There's nothing too adventurous on this menu, though linen-covered tables and walls painted with Gaugin-inspired colours create a lovely ambience. Outside seating – where you can smoke Cuban cigars ($5 to $25) – provides panoramic views of the harbour and Magnetic Island.

**C Bar** (☎ *4724 0333*) Open 8.30am-11pm daily. Breakfasts $4-9, lunch & dinner mains $7-15. C Bar is a casual, lively cafe/bar right on the waterfront. Well-priced, good food is served efficiently, and there's live music out on the deck some nights.

**The Garden of Eating** (☎ *4772 2984, 11 Allen St*) Entrees around $12, mains $20. Open 6.30pm-late Mon, Wed-Sat, 11am-3pm Sun. Tucked behind the Palmer St restaurant precinct, this is a long-time local favourite. It's BYO, the menu is adventurous (and oh so witty) and tables are in a lovely outdoor setting.

**Sirocco** (☎ *4724 4508, 61 Palmer St, South Townsville*) Mains $16-21. Open 10am-2pm & 6pm-late Tues-Sat, 6pm-late Sat, 10am-3pm Sun. With the emphasis on Asian flavours and deft service, this is a top choice; the Thai beef salad is one of the best.

**Cactus Jack's Bar & Grill** (☎ *4721 1478, 21 Palmer St*) Mains $10-14. Lively Mexican: Sangria and margaritas flow fast and furious. You'll need to book on weekends.

**Michel's** (☎ *4724 1460, 7 Palmer St*) Mains $14-22. Open 11.30am-2pm Tues-Fri, 5.30pm-late Tues-Sun. Popular Michel's puts a tasty twist on the usual suspects, eg, grilled barra becomes coconut-crusted barramundi with banana chutney.

Other inexpensive and popular options include *Tim's Surf & Turf*: there's a huge one on Ogden St, down by Ross Creek, and another at the far end of the Strand, overlooking the rock pool.

## Entertainment

Townsville's nightlife ranges from pub bands to flashy clubs, chamber music festivals to the casino. The main nightlife area is along Flinders St East, with a couple of other places along the Strand.

**Pubs & Live Music** As it is in most of Australia, a night at the pub is always a popular option here.

*Flynn's Irish Bar* (☎ 4721 1655, 101 Flinders St East) This Irish bar has live music from 9.30pm on Friday and Saturday nights.

*Molly Malone's* (☎ 4771 3428, 87 Flinders St East) *Vera* is Molly's nightclub next door; open 9pm-late Wed-Sun. At both the pub and the nightclub there are usually drinks specials to lure thirsty punters.

*Seaview Hotel* (☎ 4771 5005, Cnr The Strand & Gregory St) Open 10pm-late daily. Big, loud and popular, the Seaview has three different sections: there's *Coconuts Garden Bar*, *Stage 2 Nightclub* (open 8pm-5am Fri-Sun) and *Francine's* (open 8pm-3am Fri & Sat), an over-28s nightclub upstairs. Before drinking yourself under the table, you can grab a bite at *Arizona's stone grill restaurant*.

*Australia Hotel* (☎ 4771 4339, 11 Palmer St) The Australia has live music on Friday night and karaoke on Saturday; it's a relaxed, friendly pub – and famous for its prize-winning kangaroo pie.

*The Heritage Cafe & Bar* (☎ 4771 2799, 141 Flinders St East) Open 5pm-late daily. This bar has plenty of style and offers a good alternative to the other places playing more mainstream music. Here it's jazz on Wednesday night.

**Nightclubs** Get yourself off the bar stool and onto the dance floor.

*Bank Niteclub* (☎ 4771 6148, 169 Flinders St East) Admission $6. Open 9pm-5am Tues-Sat. This grand old bank building now throbs to the Top 40 – though different nights do have different 'themes'; it's a popular venue, and dress regulations apply.

*Mad Cow Tavern* (☎ 4771 5727, 129 Flinders St East) Open 8pm-late daily. Mad Cow's a bit more laid back than some of its peers; TVs show the sports of the moment, and the music played is probably recognised by most people.

*Bullwinkle's Cabaret & Bar* (☎ 4771 5647, Cnr Flinders St East & Wickham St) Admission $6. Open 8pm-5am daily. This popular club targets the 18–25 market.

*Millennium Club* (☎ 4772 4429, 450 Flinders St West) Admission $5. Open Tues-Thur & Sat 8pm-5am, Fri 5pm-5am. The latest edition to Townsville's nightclub scene, this place has three floors offering different entertainment: a piano bar, a retro bar, and another doing the mainstream thang.

**Casino** At Jupiters, pokies rule, though you can also try your luck at roulette, blackjack and two-up.

*Jupiters Townsville* (☎ 4722 2333, fax 4772 4741, Sir Leslie Thiess Dr) Admission free. Open 9am-3am Sun-Thur, 9am-4am Fri & Sat. A dress code applies – so no T-shirts, runners, thongs or bare feet.

**Theatre & Cinema** Townsville has three main movie venues.

*Townsville City Cinemas* (☎ 4771 4101, Cnr Sturt & Blackwood Sts) Mainstream current releases are shown here.

*Townsville Entertainment Centre* (☎ 4771 4000, Sir Leslie Thiess Dr) This impressive 5000-seat centre is Townsville's main venue for concerts, the performing arts and other major events.

*Civic Theatre* (☎ 4727 9797, 41 Boundary St, South Townsville) The Civic is a smaller venue for performing arts and various other cultural pursuits.

## Shopping

For souvenirs, try *John Melick & Co* (☎ 4771 2292, 481 Flinders St). This is the place to go for a good range of camping and bushwalking gear, Driza-Bone oilskins, Akubra hats, boots and work wear.

## Getting There & Away

**Air** Qantas (☎ 13 13 13) has regular flights between Townsville and the major destinations in Australia. One-way fares include Cairns ($258) and Brisbane ($451). Qantas is at 345 Flinders Mall.

Sunstate (Qantas) has services between Townsville and Mackay ($276), and Rockhampton ($383).

Macair (☎ 13 15 28) flies to Mt Isa ($332).

**Bus** Townsville is on the main Brisbane to Cairns coastal run, and both McCafferty's/Greyhound and Premier have frequent daily services to and from here. All the long-distance buses operate from the Townsville transit centre on Palmer St. Average fares and times from Townsville include Brisbane ($150, 22 hours), Rockhampton ($98, 11 hours), Mackay ($64, six hours), Airlie Beach ($47, four hours), Mission Beach ($45, four hours) and Cairns ($49, six hours).

Townsville is also the start of the main inland route from Queensland across to Darwin and Alice Springs. If you're heading west, the trip to Charters Towers costs $25 and takes 1¾ hours; to Mt Isa the trip costs $108 and takes 11½ hours.

**Train** The train station and Queensland Rail Travel Centre (☎ 4772 8358) is south of the centre on Flinders St.

The Brisbane-Cairns *Sunlander* travels through Townsville three times a week. The trip from Brisbane to Townsville takes 24 hours ($180/273 for an economy sleeper/1st-class sleeper). From Townsville, Proserpine ($36/57 economy/1st-class seat) is a four-hour journey, Rockhampton ($77/122) is 12 hours and Cairns ($41/65) 7½ hours.

The *Queenslander* does the Brisbane-Cairns run once a week (leaving Brisbane on Sunday morning and Cairns on Tuesday morning). The train is fast and luxurious, and you can take a plush sleeping compartment and have all your meals served up to you on the train. There are also economy seats. Townsville-Brisbane is $142/509 economy seat/1st-class sleeper and takes 21 hours; Brisbane-Cairns is $163/558 and takes around 29 hours.

The *Inlander* operates twice weekly from Townsville to Mt Isa ($96/134/204 economy seat/economy sleeper/1st-class sleeper, 20 hours). Townsville to Charters Towers takes three hours ($20).

The *Spirit of the Tropics* runs from Brisbane to Townsville, via Proserpine, on Wednesday and Sunday afternoons, returning from Townsville on Tuesday and Friday morning. In economy/economy sleeper/1st-class sleeper, the fares are $126/164/251 to Proserpine and $142/181/273 to Townsville.

## Getting Around

**To/From the Airport** Townsville airport is 5km west of the city centre at Garbutt; a taxi to the centre costs $15. Airport Transfers & Tours (☎ 4775 5544) operates a shuttle servicing all main arrivals and departures. The cost one-way/return is $7/11, or $11/17 for two people travelling together, and it will drop off/pick up anywhere within the central business district.

**Bus** Sunbus runs local bus services around Townsville. Route maps and timetables are available in the Transit Mall (near the Flinders St Mall tourist office).

**Car** The larger car-rental agencies are all represented in Townsville. Thrifty (☎ 4725 4600), Avis (☎ 4721 2688), Budget (☎ 4725 2344) and Hertz (☎ 4775 4821) all have rental desks at the airport.

Townsville Car Rentals (☎ 4772 1093) is a smaller operator at 12 Palmer St, South Townsville; and if you're after a 4WD you could try Four Wheel Drive Hire Service (☎ 4779 2990) at 39 Duckworth St, Garbutt.

**Taxi** There's a taxi rank at the Transit Mall on the corner of Stokes St and the Flinders St Mall. To book a taxi call ☎ 13 10 08.

## MAGNETIC ISLAND
postcode 4819 • pop 2100

Magnetic Island is one of Queensland's oldest resort islands, with the first tourists arriving from the mainland more than 100 years ago. It's a large (52 sq km) and scenic continental island, with the main attractions being its fine beaches, bushwalks and wildlife. Known locally as 'Maggie', it's a popular, somewhat old-fashioned destination with a welcoming and laid-back atmosphere.

Four small townships, offering a wide range of accommodation, are spread along the eastern coast. About 70% of the island is national park, with 500m Mt Cook in the centre of the island the dominant point. Only 8km offshore, the island is almost an outer suburb of Townsville, with many people commuting to the mainland daily by ferry.

## History

The island was named by Captain Cook, who thought his ship's compass went funny when he sailed by in 1770.

Aborigines were frequent visitors to the island, which they could easily reach from the mainland. The first European settlement was established by timber cutters in the early 1870s. In 1887 Harry Butler and his family settled at Picnic Bay and started putting up visitors from the mainland in thatched huts, and thus the Magnetic Island tourist business was born. In 1899, Robert Hayles saw the potential of the island as a holiday destination for the booming gold-mining centre of Charters Towers. The Hayles family built a hotel and dance hall and started up the first ferry service, and remained involved in the Magnetic Island tourist industry for the next 90 years.

## Orientation & Information

Magnetic Island is roughly triangular in shape, with the main road running up the eastern side of the island linking Picnic Bay to Horseshoe Bay, and a few small settlements in between. There's also a rough track along the uninteresting western coast. Along the northern coast it's walking only.

There's a tourist information booth (☎ 4778 5155) for booking tours and accommodation, right of the pier as you approach Picnic Bay Mall. Queensland Parks and Wildlife Service (QPWS; ☎ 4778 5378) has an office on Hurst St in Picnic Bay.

In an arcade off the mall, there's a small Internet cafe (☎ 4778 5407), open 8.30am to 5pm daily. There are no banks or ATMs on the island, although most of the supermarkets have Eftpos facilities.

**Zoning** Geoffrey Bay, Arcadia and Five Beach Bay on the northern coast of the island are all zoned Marine Park B – in other words fishing is not permitted.

**Warning** Box jellyfish are found in the waters around Magnetic Island between October and April. There are netted swimming enclosures at Picnic and Horseshoe Bays; for some unknown reason, Alma Bay is usually safe for swimming, but in other areas swimming is not recommended during the danger months.

**Picnic Bay** The main settlement on the island, and where the passenger ferries dock, is Picnic Bay. The waterfront mall has a selection of shops and eateries, and you can hire bikes, mokes and scooters here. A lookout above the town provides great views, including down to the wreck of the *City of Adelaide*. In the other direction is **Rocky Bay** where you can take a short but steep walk down to a beautiful sheltered beach.

**Nelly Bay** Next around the eastern coast is Nelly Bay, with a good beach with shade, and a reef at low tide. At the far end of the bay are some pioneer graves. The Nelly Bay Harbour, a source of controversy between those resisting development on the island and developers, dominates one end of the bay.

**Arcadia** Round the next headland you come to **Geoffrey Bay**, overlooked by the town of Arcadia. This is where the vehicle ferry stops, and just around the next headland is pretty **Alma Bay Beach**.

**Radical Bay & The Forts** Midway between Arcadia and Horseshoe Bay, there's a turn-off to Radical Bay: rental vehicles aren't covered by insurance while on this road. Walking tracks lead off to the old **Searchlight Station** on a headland between the secluded **Arthur Bay** and **Florence Bay** – there are fine views from up here. Radical

# MAGNETIC ISLAND

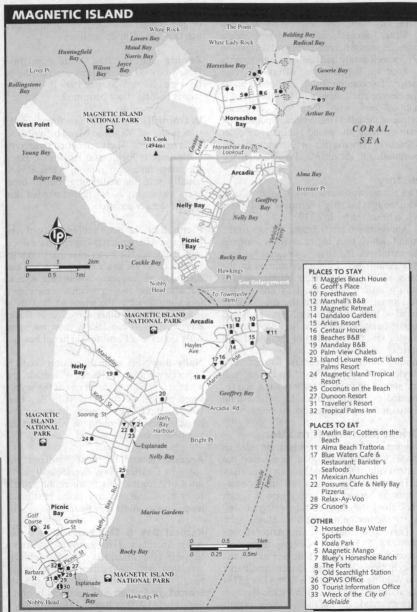

**PLACES TO STAY**
1 Maggies Beach House
6 Geoff's Place
10 Foresthaven
12 Marshall's B&B
13 Magnetic Retreat
14 Dandaloo Gardens
15 Arkies Resort
16 Centaur House
18 Beaches B&B
19 Mandalay B&B
20 Palm View Chalets
23 Island Leisure Resort; Island Palms Resort
24 Magnetic Island Tropical Resort
25 Coconuts on the Beach
27 Dunoon Resort
31 Traveller's Resort
32 Tropical Palms Inn

**PLACES TO EAT**
3 Marlin Bar; Cotters on the Beach
11 Alma Beach Trattoria
17 Blue Waters Cafe & Restaurant; Banister's Seafoods
21 Mexican Munchies
22 Possums Cafe & Nelly Bay Pizzeria
28 Relax-Ay-Voo
29 Crusoe's

**OTHER**
2 Horseshoe Bay Water Sports
4 Koala Park
5 Magnetic Mango
7 Bluey's Horseshoe Ranch
8 The Forts
9 Old Searchlight Station
26 QPWS Office
30 Tourist Information Office
33 Wreck of the *City of Adelaide*

Bay has a lovely beach, though access to it is limited. From the carpark here a walking trail leads across the headland to Horseshoe Bay, with a turn-off halfway to the beautiful and secluded **Balding Bay**, an unofficial nude-bathing beach.

Back at the junction of the road to Radical Bay, there's also a 1.4km walking track leading to The Forts, an old WWII command post and signal station with gun sites and an ammunition store.

**Horseshoe Bay** On the northern coast, Horseshoe Bay has the longest, most sheltered, though not necessarily the best, beach on the island. **Magnetic Mango** is a working mango plantation with an outdoor eatery that serves Devonshire teas and lunches (see Places to Eat later). There's also a desultory **Koala Park** – but you're better off looking for koalas in the national park areas. At the beach there are boats, jet skis and sailboards for hire, and you can walk to Maud Bay, around to the west, or east to Radical Bay.

### Bushwalking
The QWPS produces a leaflet for Magnetic Island's excellent bushwalking tracks. Possible walks, with distances and one-way travel times, include:

| from | to | km | time |
|---|---|---|---|
| Nelly Bay | Arcadia | 6 | 2 hrs |
| Picnic Bay | West Point | 8 | 2½ hrs |
| Horseshoe Bay Rd | Arthur Bay | 2 | ½ hr |
| | Florence Bay | 2.5 | 1 hr |
| | The Forts | 2 | ¾ hr |
| Horseshoe Bay | Balding Bay | 3 | ¾ hr |
| | Radical Bay | 3 | ¾ hr |

### Diving
At Ocean Dive Australia (☎ 4758 1391, Coconuts Resort, Nelly Bay) you can learn to dive from $66, or a four-day reef open-water course will cost $300.

Pleasure Divers (☎/fax 4778 5788, e pleasure.divers@ultra.net.au, w www.magnetic-island.com.au, Shop 2, Arkies Resort) offers a three-day PADI open-water course for $180, or a four-day reef course for $280. You could also try Magnetic Island

Dive Centre (☎ 4758 1399, e mag.is.dive@ozstarnet.com.au); a four-day open-water PADI course costs $175 on the island, and $275 out on the reef.

### Golf
The Magnetic Island Country Club (☎ 4778 5188, fax 4758 1189, Hurst St, Picnic Bay) rents clubs and all equipment for $14, and nine/18 holes cost $11/16.

### Water Sports
At Horseshoe Bay, the centre for a wide range of water sports, you can rent aquabikes and canoes ($8 per half-hour), catamarans ($20 per hour) and jet skis ($65/120 half/full hour); go weight boarding ($25), tube riding ($10) and water-skiing ($25 for 15 minutes).

### Horse Riding
Bluey's Horseshoe Ranch (☎ 4778 5109, 38 Gifford St, Horseshoe Bay) offers two-hour rides ($50) taking you through bush to the beach, where you can swim on horseback. Half-day rides are also available.

### Organised Tours
**Reef Trips** Pure Pleasure Cruises (☎ 4721 3555, 4 The Strand) does a day trip out to Kelso Reef on the outer Barrier Reef, usually stopping at Magnetic on its way out from Townsville. See Townsville's Organised Tours section for details.

**Cruises & Fishing Trips** Barnacle Bill (☎ 4758 1237) provides all gear and bait on its two-hour, $40 per person fishing trips from Horseshoe Bay. Dinghies can be hired for $30 for the first hour, $20 thereafter – maximum $100 per day.

**Sea Kayaking** Kayaking is a great way to experience Magnetic Island's beautiful coastline – and it's quiet.

Magnetic Island Sea Kayaks (☎ 4778 5424, 93 Horseshoe Bay Rd) has half-day tours for $35.

**Jet Skiing** Adrenalin Jet Ski Tours (☎ 4778 5533, Horseshoe Bay) offers a half-day tour for $115. Blast your way around the island...

## Places to Stay – Budget

Camping facilities on the island are limited, and camping isn't allowed in the national park. Two of the backpackers hostels, *Geoff's Place* and *Coconuts on the Beach*, have areas set aside for campers – Geoff's Place is the better set-up.

There's no shortage of backpacker accommodation: It's a competitive scene, and hostels send vehicles to meet the ferries at Picnic Bay. In the quieter months and for longer stays most places offer cheaper rates; accommodation and transport package deals are not uncommon. Most hostels offer discounts of a dollar or two to VIP, HI/YHA members.

*Travellers Resort* (☎ 1800 000 290, 4778 5166, e travellers@ultra.net.au, w www .travellers-on-maggie.com, 1 The Esplanade, Picnic Bay) Beds in 8-bed dorm $19, doubles & twins with/without en suite $46/44. A range of accommodation is situated in several buildings behind the Picnic Bay Hotel. *The Shed* nightclub kicks off here on Friday and Saturday nights from 10pm; there's bullet-proof glass between the dance floor and resident croc Rin Tin Tin, though how he feels about pub life is anyone's guess. For die-hard punters, cane toad races are held in the bar on Wednesday evenings.

*Magnetic Island Tropical Resort* (☎ 4778 5955, fax 4778 5601, e tropres@ byte-tsv.net.au, 56 Yates St, Nelly Bay) Beds in 4-bed dorm with en suite $17, standard cabins $55 a double, with air-con $90 ($11 per extra person). A short walk from the main road, this is a secluded, low-key but pleasant resort providing accommodation in A-frame, louvre-windowed chalets, all set amid lovely gardens with birds galore; there's a swimming pool, lawn tennis courts and the Lattice Bar & Bistro (open to non-guests, too).

*Coconuts on the Beach* (☎ 1800 065 696, 4778 5777, fax 4778 5507, e infococonuts@ bakpakgroup.com, w www.bakpakgroup.com, Nelly Bay Rd, Nelly Bay) Tent sites $8 per person, beds in 8-bed dorm $12-18, camp-o-tel twin-share $35, doubles $60. When we visited there was a lot of construction under way, so the 'new' Coconuts will probably be much fresher than before. Choices range from camp-o-tels (semi-permanent tents with

beds and lights, called 'smurfs' here), high-density dorm accommodation in wooden A-frame huts, and a few new cabins, with wonderful views, on the headland. Coconuts promotes itself as a party place (Full Moon parties etc), which is fine if that's what you're after. There's a beach bar, restaurant, night-club and Internet facilities, and dive courses can be organised through Ocean Dive, which is based here.

*Centaur House* (☎ 1800 655 680, ☎/fax 4778 5668, e centaurhouse@email .com, 27 Marine Parade, Arcadia) Dorm beds $18, singles/doubles $33/39. This is a small, relaxed hostel, full of atmosphere and opposite the beach. It's a quiet and friendly place with behammocked garden and barbecue. Rooms, all upstairs, are small but stylish, and have fans.

*Foresthaven* (☎/fax 4778 5153, 11 Cook Rd, Arcadia) Dorm beds $16.50, singles/ doubles $35/38, units from $66 a double ($11 per extra person). This hostel has seen better days, and the buildings and facilities are basic, although the peaceful bush setting is nice. Accommodation is spread across several buildings, with units with two- or three-bed rooms sharing rather drab kitchen/dining areas. You can hire bikes here for about $13 a day.

*Arkies* (☎ 1800 663 666, 4778 5177, e arkies_magnetic@bigpond.com, 7 Marine Parade, Arcadia) Beds in 6-bed dorm $12, 1-5 night dorm packages $15-40, twins & doubles $45-55. What used to be the Arcadia Hotel Resort, Arkies is a lively back-packers on the main road just opposite Arcadia beach. A party atmosphere is helped along by two bars with pokies; there's a bistro, a communal kitchen and two swimming pools. The local bus service will get you here from Picnic Bay; the ticket price is subsidised if you stay at Arkies.

*Maggies Beach House* (☎ 4778 5144, fax 4778 5194, e maggies@maggiesbeachhouse .com.au, w www.maggiesbeachhouse.com .au, Pacific Dr, Horseshoe Bay) Beds in 6-bed dorm $21, doubles with en suite $75. Maggies is a newcomer to the backpacking scene on Magnetic Island. Rooms are bright, clean and fully air-conditioned,

MATT FLETCHER

Spectacular, unspoiled Hinchinbrook Island wilderness

JOHN HAY

Custard apple – ugly but irresistible

RICHARD I'ANSON

Eyecatching geometry in a palm frond

LAWRIE WILLIAMS

Sugar cane harvesting

Cool, green, shady fan palms

Secluded Arthur Bay on Magnetic Island

View to Dunk Island from Mission Beach

Castle Hill towering over boats on Ross Creek, Townsville

there's a small pool (but just over the street there's a beautiful beach with a stinger enclosure), a pleasant cafe and Internet facilities. And a bar, of course. A shuttle bus links Maggies with the rest of the island.

*Geoff's Place* (☎ *1800 285 577, 4778 5577, fax 4778 5781, e geoffsplace@ beyond.net.au, 40 Horseshoe Bay Rd, Horseshoe Bay)* Tent sites $9 per person, dorm beds with fan/air-con $20.50/21.50, cabins with air-con & en suite $52 a double, cabin with fan $44 a double 1st night, $40 thereafter. With its party atmosphere and nightly activities, this popular hostel draws a crowd. There are extensive grounds, and most of the A-frame cedar huts are a decent distance from one another. The eight-bed dorm cabins have their own bathroom, while the four-bed dorms don't. There's a communal kitchen, pool, a bar and a cheap restaurant. Mountain bikes are for hire, and the hostel has a bus linking up with ferries and Picnic Bay.

## Places to Stay – Mid-Range & Top End

Besides B&Bs, resorts and hostels, self-contained flats – some of which are pretty old-fashioned – are popular. Rates for all accommodation vary with the seasons and demand, and most have cheaper stand-by rates; holiday flats are cheaper if you rent by the week.

*Tropical Palms Inn* (☎ *4778 5076, fax 4778 5897, 34 Picnic St, Picnic Bay)* Singles & doubles $83. These air-con self-contained motel-style units are one street back from the Travellers Resort hostel, in the thick of Picnic Bay.

*Dunoon Resort* (☎ *4778 5161, fax 4778 5532, W www.dunoon.au.com, The Esplanade, Picnic Bay)* Singles & doubles $108, (extra adult/child $16.50/7.50). These older, though renovated, self-contained units are set in lush, landscaped gardens. There's a good pool area, and you're right on the waterfront.

*Island Palms Resort* (☎ *4778 5571, fax 4778 5599, e islandpalms@telstra.easymail .com.au, W www.islandpalms.homestead .com, 13 The Esplanade, Nelly Bay)* Doubles $110. Although this is a timeshare resort,

some of the bright, refurbished, two-bedroom units are usually available. Accommodation is set back from the waterfront, and there are two swimming pools.

*Island Leisure Resort* (☎ *4778 5000, fax 4778 5042, e islandleisure@bigpond .com, W www.islandleisure.com.au, 4 Kelly St, Nelly Bay)* Singles & doubles $110, (extra person $5). The spacious, self-contained units here (all with a double bed and three bunks) are in a cool garden setting. Close to the beach, this small resort has good facilities including a pool, floodlit tennis court, and a games room.

*Palm View Chalets* (☎ *4778 5596, fax 4778 5154, 114 Sooning St, Nelly Bay)* Singles/doubles $60/70 ($5 per extra person). Nestled amid trees opposite the Nelly Bay Marina development, these self-contained, A-frame timber chalets sleeping up to six people offer excellent value.

*Mandalay B&B* (☎ *4758 1943, fax 4758 1444, e nicholsonmandalay@telstra .easymail.com.au, 56 Mandalay Ave, Nelly Bay)* Double & twin $85. This new and stylish fully self-contained unit contains a bedroom, bathroom, kitchenette and sitting room.

*Marshall's B&B* (☎ *4778 5112, 3 Endeavour Rd, Arcadia)* Singles/doubles $40/60. About a five-minute walk from Arcadia Bay, Marshall's has four pleasant bedrooms in a quiet (though bird-filled) garden setting. Stella and Paul, the owners, are founts of knowledge regarding the island.

*Dandaloo Gardens* (☎ *4778 5174, fax 4778 5185, 40-42 Hayles Ave, Arcadia)* 1-bedroom units from $69 ($462 weekly). Older-style units and newer ones are nestled here amid tropical gardens; bed configurations vary from unit to unit.

*Beaches B&B* (☎/fax *4778 5303, e beaches@tpgi.com.au, 39 Marine Parade, Arcadia)* Singles/doubles & twins $60/75. On the Arcadia waterfront, this is a modern timber cottage with a separate B&B section with two air-con bedrooms. There's a good pool out the back and a front veranda overlooking the bay.

Two other good options are *Magnetic North Holiday Units* (☎ *4778 5647,*

e  *magneticnorth@iprimus.com.au, 2 Endeavour Rd, Arcadia)*, where two-bedroom
units go for $110 (plus $10 per extra person) or $595 a week; and the one-/
two-bedroom units at **Magnetic Retreat**
*(☎ 4778 5357, 11 Rheuben Terrace, Arca-
dia)*, which cost $95/104. The **Magnetic Is-
land Tropical Resort** also has a good range
of cabins – see the Budget section earlier.

## Places to Eat

There are **supermarkets** or **minimarts** open
seven days a week in each of the townships.
*Crusoe's (☎ 4778 5480, The Esplanade,
Picnic Bay)* Open 7.30am-9pm Fri, Sat &
Mon, 7.30-4pm Tues-Thur. This is a casual
little takeaway place doing breakfasts,
burgers and fish and chips. There's also a
small restaurant section.
*Relax-Ay-Voo (☎ 4778 5911, Picnic Bay
Mall, Picnic Bay)* Mains $15-20. Open 5pm-
late Mon-Fri. Bistro meals – pastas, steaks
etc – sometimes complimented by local musicians and karaoke are the go at this busy
bar/restaurant at the far end of the mall.
*Mexican Munchies (☎ 4778 5658, 37
Warboy St, Nelly Bay)* Mains $15-20. Open
6pm-late Thur-Tues. Enjoy the usual suspects, like enchiladas and burritos, with a
glass of sangria (BYO other alcohol) at this
small, friendly eatery tucked away in a side
street.
*Alma Beach Trattoria (☎ 4778 5757, 11
Olympus Crescent, Arcadia)* Mains around
$16. Open 11.30am-3pm, 6pm-late Wed-
Sun. Dishes like Tunisian hotpot (tofu, vegies, ginger) or lamb with herbs and fetta are
served at tables set on a patio overlooking
pretty Alma Beach. Pasta and seafood are
also available – as is delicious home-made
ice cream. To get to the restaurant cross the
little bridge below the Surf Life Saving Club.
*Banister's Seafood (☎ 4778 5700, 22
McCabe Crescent, Arcadia)* Mains $5-22.
Open 8am-8pm daily. From simple, delicious fish and chips to 'crumbed bugs', this
is a good place for an inexpensive fishy
meal. It's basically a takeaway, with an
open-air BYO dining area.
*Cotters on the Beach (☎ 4778 5786, Pa-
cific Dr, Horseshoe Bay)* Mains $9-20.

Open lunch from noon, dinner from 6pm
Fri-Wed. This licensed indoor/outdoor
restaurant offers bagel-ish lunches and
more substantial evening meals, with the
emphasis on seafood and steaks.
*Marlin Bar (☎ 4758 1588, 3 Pacific Dr,
Horseshoe Bay)* Mains $10-20. Open for
lunch daily, dinner Tues-Sat. The Marlin has
a long and thriving bar and windows looking
out to Horseshoe Bay with 'the best sunsets
on the planet'. The usual pub fare is on offer,
with specials like sweet-chilli bugs for $15.
*Magnetic Mango (☎ 4778 5018, Apjohn
St, Horseshoe Bay)* Snacks & mains $7-17.
Open 10am-5pm Wed-Sat. Everything here
is home-made – from bread and cakes to
lasagne. After your meal you can have a go
at mini-golf, or *boules* on a Saturday.
A couple of casual options in Nelly Bay
include: **Possums**, a small cafe serving,
among other things, good open sandwiches,
frittata, and smoothies; and the **Nelly Bay
Pizzeria & Takeaway St** *(☎ 4758 1400)*,
which takes phone orders. In Arcadia,
**Michaels on Magnetic** *(☎ 4778 5645, 5
Bright Avenue)* is a restaurant/takeaway that
serves Mediterranean-inspired meals.

## Getting There & Away

Sunferries (☎ 4771 3855) operates about 10
services a day between 8.15am and 8.15pm
from the terminal on Flinders St East,
Townsville. The trip takes about 20 minutes, and costs $15.70/8 adult/child return.
There's another terminal, and a large (unsu-
pervised) carpark, on the breakwater; next
to the Flinders St terminal there's a small
carpark, but otherwise finding a place for
your car might be tricky in the city area.
The Magnetic Island Car Ferry (☎ 4772
5422) runs to Arcadia from the southern
side of Ross Creek six times a day Monday
to Friday, three times on Saturday and four
on Sunday. It's $115 return for a car and up
to six passengers, $37 return for a motor-
bike and $16 return for walk-on passengers.
Bicycles are carried free on all ferries.

## Getting Around

**Bus** The Magnetic Island Bus Service
(☎ 4778 5130) operates up and down the

island between Picnic Bay and Horseshoe Bay at least 14 times a day, meeting all ferries and dropping off at all accommodation places. It takes about 45 minutes all the way from Picnic Bay to Horseshoe Bay, 30 minutes from Picnic Bay to Arcadia. A ticket to get you from one end of the island to the other costs $4.30; it's $1.90 from one bay to the next, $3.10 for two bays.

**Scooter & Trailbike** At Road Runner (☎ 4778 5222, Shop 3, Picnic Bay Arcade) hiring a 50cc scooter for a day/24 hours will cost $28/$38; no motorcycle licence is required, just a valid car driving licence. You certainly don't need anything larger to explore Magnetic. Trailbike hire – for which you'll need a motorcycle licence – costs $45 a day.

**Moke & Car** For something bigger than a bike, Moke Magnetic (☎ 4778 5377, fax 4778 5660), at Shop 4, The Esplanade, Picnic Bay, charges $44 a day plus $0.44 per kilometre and a deposit of $100 per day.

**Taxi** Taxis meet arriving ferries at Picnic Bay.

**Bicycle** Magnetic Island is ideal for cycling: mountain bikes can be hired for $14/20/24 a day/24 hours/48 hours from the Kodak booth (☎ 4778 5411) at the mall in Picnic Bay. Various places to stay, eg, Foresthaven in Arcadia and Geoff's at Horseshoe Bay, also rent out bikes.

**Hitching** You could also hitch around, observing the precautions in the Getting There & Away chapter. Plenty of people do hitch; just start walking – if you don't get a lift you'll soon end up in the next town.

# Townsville to Charters Towers

The Flinders Hwy heads inland from Townsville and runs virtually due west for its entire length – almost 800km from Townsville to Cloncurry. The first section of the highway takes you 135km south-west from Townsville to the gold-mining town of Charters Towers, with a turn-off at the halfway mark to Ravenswood, another gold-mining centre.

Refer to the Charters Towers to Camooweal section in the Outback chapter for details of the Flinders Hwy west of Charters Towers.

## RAVENSWOOD

At Mingela, 88km from Townsville, a paved road leads 40km south to Ravenswood, a former ghost town from the gold-rush days, somewhat reinvigorated in recent years. The town is spread across a series of hills of rough red earth, and although most of the buildings were demolished or fell down years ago, two pubs, a church, a school and a couple of hundred people linger on amid the old, and new, mines.

Ravenswood is an interesting and friendly little town – almost a living museum – and is well worth the detour off the main highway.

### History

Gold was first discovered in this area in 1868. In October 1869 a rich deposit of alluvial gold was found at Top Camp, north of Ravenswood, and the first rush was on. The first crushings in 1870 were incredibly rich, and the field prospered until 1872, when the 'brownstone' (surface ore that had been oxidised and was easily crushed) was exhausted. The deeper ore proved almost impossible to work, and the field suffered a steady decline over the next 20 years.

In 1893 mine manager Laurence Wilson travelled to London and convinced a number of British investors to invest in the mines. Using new crushing and processing techniques, the mines again proved to be viable and people returned to the area. During Ravenswood's boom years, from 1900 to 1912, the area produced an 'ore-some' 12,500kg of gold, and the population peaked at around 4000. But by 1912 the gold was gone, and operations ceased in 1917.

Ravenswood became a virtual ghost town, until 1987 when the Carpentaria Gold company established a new open-cut mine here, successfully extracting gold using the heap-leaching process. In 1994 and again in 2000, new mines opened, breathing new life into Ravenswood.

## Things to See
The **post office** (1878) is a lovely timber building which now houses a general store. The courthouse, police station and lock-up, up on the hill between the two pubs, have been restored and house a **mining and historical museum** (☎ 4770 2047; adult/child $2.20/1.10; open 10am-3pm Wed-Mon), and the gregarious Woody, the keeper of the keys, will show you around.

A series of **old photos** mounted in steel boxes along the main street shows Ravenswood in its boom years. A visit to the town **cemetery**, with its graves dating back to the 1880s, is somewhat sobering; it's soon evident just how low life expectancy was in those early days.

## Places to Stay & Eat
The *council camping ground,* which charges $5.70 per vehicle per night, is more like a sports oval than a camping ground, with some old, shady trees around the periphery.

*Imperial Hotel (☎ 4770 2131, Macrossan St)* Singles/twins/doubles $45/50/55. This two-storey Victorian-era hotel is a real gem. Virtually unchanged from 100 years ago, and built in the extravagant style known as

KH

**The Imperial Hotel – goldfields brash**

'goldfields brash', it has an ornate, solid red-brick facade and iron-lace-trimmed veranda. The public bar features a magnificent red-cedar bar with leadlight inserts. The timber-lined bedrooms upstairs, some with old brass beds and opening out onto the veranda, are clean and well presented. Breakfast is included in the tariff and meals are available from the bar; on Saturday night there's usually a barbecue out under the front veranda.

*Railway Hotel (☎ 4770 2144, Barton St)* Single/double B&Bs $26/43. This is another big, solid, red-brick pub, built in 1871. A great old staircase leads up to basic, plain bedrooms, mostly opening onto the big front veranda. Evening meals are also available here, though it's probably a louder pub than its buddy down the road.

## CHARTERS TOWERS
### postcode 4820 • pop 10,000
The busy town of Charters Towers, 135km inland from Townsville, was Queensland's fabulously rich second city in the gold-rush days. Many old houses, imposing public buildings and mining structures remain. It's possible to make a day trip here from Townsville and get a glimpse of outback Queensland on the way. At 336m above sea level, the dry air of Charters Towers makes a welcome change from the humid coast.

The town is very proud of its history, gold heritage and historic buildings, and even the local police station was renovated in heritage style following lobbying by concerned residents.

### History
The gleam of gold was first spotted in 1871, in a creek bed at the foot of Towers Hill, by an Aboriginal boy called Jupiter Mosman. Within a few years, the surrounding area was peppered with diggings and a large town had grown. In its heyday (around 1900) Charters Towers had a population of 30,000, nearly 100 mines, and even its own stock exchange. Mosman St, the main street in those days, had 25 pubs.

When the gold ran out in the 1920s, the city shrank, but survived as a centre for the beef industry. Since the mid-1980s, Charters

Towers has seen a bit of a gold revival as modern processes have enabled companies to work deposits in previously uneconomical areas. It is now a prosperous, lively country town with five gold mines being worked in the area.

## Orientation & Information

Gill St, which runs from the train station to Mosman St, is Charters Towers' main street. Towers Hill stands over the town to the south. Lissner Park, a couple of blocks north of the centre, is the town's best park and the swimming pool is at its northern end.

The helpful tourist office (☎ 4752 0314, Gill St), between the historic City Hall and Stock Exchange buildings, is open daily from 9am to 5pm. The National Trust of Queensland office (☎ 4787 2374), where you can buy a special ticket (adult/child $7.70/3.85) for entry into the Assay Room and Zara Clark museums and Venus Gold Battery, is in the Stock Exchange Arcade on Mosman St.

## Things to See & Do

On Mosman St, a few metres up the hill from the corner of Gill St, is the picturesque **Stock Exchange Arcade**, built in 1887 and restored in 1972. At the end of the arcade is the **Assay Room & Mining Museum** *(adult/child $2.20/1.10; open 8.30am-1pm & 2pm-4.30pm Mon-Fri, 9am-3pm Sat & Sun)*, a former metallurgical laboratory for smelting gold and silver and determining the content of ore and minerals. The **Zara Clark Museum** *(36 Mosman St; adult/child $4.40/2.20; open 10am-3pm daily)* has an extensive and fascinating collection ranging from old photos to farming equipment, Royal Doulton toby jugs to period costumes. It also includes the small **Charles Wallis military museum**, dedicated to a local hero who was killed in WWI.

The former **ABC Bank Building** (1891) on Mosman St, just up from the Stock Exchange, houses the World Theatre and cinema. The facade is a magnificent mixture of Doric and Corinthian styles.

Probably the finest of the town's old houses is **Frederick Pfeiffer's** on Paull St. It's now a Mormon chapel, but you can walk

around the outside. Pfeiffer was a gold-miner who became Queensland's first millionaire.

Another fine old mansion is **Ay Ot Lookout** *(admission $2.50; open 8am-noon & 1pm-3pm Mon-Fri)*, a restored house now owned by the local shire. The timber building is one of many around town (and, in fact, throughout northern Queensland) built using a method known as 'balloon framing', where the walls lack external cladding, and so do not have a cavity that can lead to vermin problems.

About 5km from town is the **Venus Gold Battery** *(Millchester Rd; admission $3; open 9am-3pm Mon-Fri; guided tours 10am & 2pm)*, where gold-bearing ore was crushed and processed from 1872 until as recently as 1973. The huge dimensions and silence of the place, which has been restored to working order, give it a rather surreal atmosphere; it's well worth a look.

Or, you could catch a movie at the **cinema** *(☎ 4787 4337)* behind the World Theatre on Mosman St or the **Tors Drive-In** *(☎ 4787 1086)*, on the western side of town.

## Organised Tours

Gold Nugget Scenic Tours (☎ 4787 4115; adult/concession/child/family $22/20/11/55) offers half-day city tours, departing from outside the tourist information centre, at 9.30am and 2.30pm Monday to Saturday.

If you'd like to get a taste of real outback living, consider a farm-stay. There are a couple of options.

**Bluff Downs** *(☎ 4770 4084,* e *Bluff_Downs@hotmail.com)*, 110km north-west of Charters Towers, which costs $70 a double including dinner and breakfast; or **Plain Creek** *(☎ 4983 5228,* e *plaincrk@cqhinet.net.au)*, between Clermont and Charters Towers on the Clermont Rd, which is $95 per person including dinner and breakfast (powered sites $16.50).

## Special Events

During the Australia Day weekend in late January, more than 100 cricket teams and their supporters converge on Charters Towers for a competition known as the Goldfield Ashes, and a major rodeo is held here

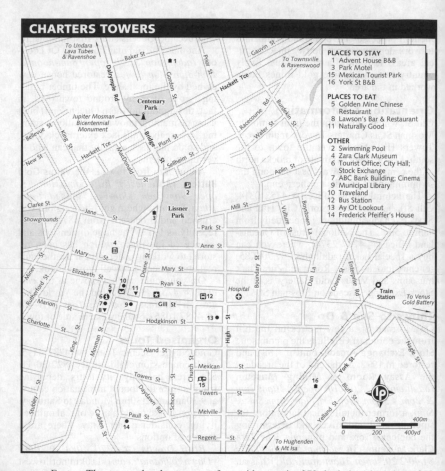

**CHARTERS TOWERS**

PLACES TO STAY
1 Advent House B&B
3 Park Motel
15 Mexican Tourist Park
16 York St B&B

PLACES TO EAT
5 Golden Mine Chinese
  Restaurant
8 Lawson's Bar & Restaurant
11 Naturally Good

OTHER
2 Swimming Pool
4 Zara Clark Museum
6 Tourist Office; City Hall;
  Stock Exchange
7 ABC Bank Building; Cinema
9 Municipal Library
10 Traveland
12 Bus Station
13 Ay Ot Lookout
14 Frederick Pfeiffer's House

every Easter. The town also hosts one of Australia's biggest annual country music festivals (☎ 4787 4500) on the May Day weekend each year.

## Places to Stay
*Mexican Tourist Park* (☎ *4787 1161, fax 4787 4929, Cnr Church & Towers Sts)* Unpowered/powered sites $10/15, on-site vans $28 double, self-contained units $50. While its sites are cramped, this is the most central of the town's three caravan parks.

*York St B&B* (☎ *4787 1028, 58 York St)* Singles/doubles $27/45, heritage-style double

with en suite $72, beds in 4-bed dorm $20. This renovated 1880s timber house includes five lovely, heritage-style bedrooms, each with en suite; the cheaper accommodation is in a relatively drab building behind the main house. There's a small swimming pool and pleasant, breezy verandas. It's 1.5km south of the town centre; the owners will pick you up from the bus stop if you ring.

*Advent House* (☎ *4787 3508, fax 4787 3163, 29 Gordon St)* Singles/doubles $67/84 with en suite, $56/73 with shared bathroom. Advent House, built in the 1880s, is a spacious, beautifully restored and decorated house, with a wide veranda wrapping around three sides. Comfortable communal areas, formal gardens, a swimming pool and gregarious hosts make it a great place to stay.

*Park Motel (☎ 4787 1022, fax 4787 4268, Cnr Mosman & Deane Sts)* Single/double motel units & 'heritage style' rooms in original hotel $69/79. From the street this is an impressive, attractive old hotel with its own restaurant; the more recent motel units hide behind it.

### Places to Eat
*Naturally Good (☎ 4787 4211, 23 Gill St)* Open 8am-4pm Mon-Fri, 8.30am-noon Sat. This is a bright and friendly cafe serving sandwiches, pita pizzas, smoothies, burgers and other snacks.

*Lawson's Bar & Restaurant (☎ 4787 4333, 82 Mosman St)* Lunch $7-14, dinner $11-22. Open 11.30am-2.30pm Wed-Sat, 6pm-late Wed-Sun. Serving home-made cakes and hearty daily specials, Lawson's is a casual eatery in a heritage-lookalike building next to the ABC Bank. It's licensed, and the menu includes some vegetarian options.

*Golden Mine Chinese Restaurant (☎ 4787 7609, 64 Mosman St)* Open 11.30am-2pm Mon-Fri, 5pm-9.30pm daily. Set dinner $7.60, set lunch $6.40. Besides the set meal deal – self-serve from 24 dishes – there's also an a la carte menu to choose from.

### Getting There & Away
McCafferty's/Greyhound has daily buses from Townsville to Charters Towers ($25, 1¾ hours) and on to Mt Isa (Townsville to Mt Isa $108, 11½ hours). Buses arrive and depart at the Catholic church on Gill St.

The twice-weekly *Inlander* service takes three hours to travel from Townsville to Charters Towers and costs $20. The *Inlander* continues on to Mt Isa, taking another 17 hours. Townsville to the Isa costs $96/134/204 economy seat/economy sleeper/1st class sleeper. The train station is on Enterprise Rd, about 1.5km east of the town centre.

# Townsville to Mission Beach

## PALUMA RANGE NATIONAL PARK
About 60km north-west of Townsville, straddling the 1000m-plus high Paluma Range on the inland side of the Bruce Hwy, this region (7200 hectares) includes open eucalypt forests on the lower slopes and rainforests in the upper, wetter areas. Bower birds are relatively common here.

## Mt Spec–Big Crystal Creek Section
There are two roads into the park, both leading off a bypassed section of the Bruce Hwy. To get to these, turn off the new highway either 62km north of Townsville or 47km south of Ingham.

The southern access route, known as the Mt Spec Rd, was built by relief labour during the Depression years from 1931 to 1935. It's a narrow and spectacular road that twists its way up the mountains to the village of Paluma. After 7km you come to **Little Crystal Creek**, where a pretty stone bridge (built in 1932) arches across the creek. This is a great swimming spot with waterfalls and a couple of deep rock pools, and there's a small picnic area opposite the carpark. From here it's another steep 11km up to Paluma.

The northern access route is a 4km dirt road into Big Crystal Creek, which has a picnic area with barbecues and a good camping ground with toilets, hot showers, firewood and water. Sites cost $3.85 per person per night: a gate key and permit must be obtained from either the QPWS (☎ 4776 1700) at 49 Cassady St Ingham, or the Reef Wonderland Office (☎ 4721 2399) at Reef HQ in Townsville; the key must be returned to the point of pick up, where the $25 deposit will be refunded. Just before the camping ground is **Paradise Waterhole**, a good swimming and picnic area.

## Jourama Falls Section
Access to this part of the park is via a 6km dirt road, 91km north of Townsville. Centred

on Waterview Creek, this small but beautiful park has good swimming holes, several lookouts, a picnic area and a camping ground with toilets and barbecues. Sites cost $3.85 per person per night, and you can self-register or book with the Paluma Range National Park ranger (☎ 4777 3112, fax 4777 3278).

Shortly before the Paluma turn-off at Mutarnee is *Frosty Mango* (☎ 4770 8184, fax 4770 8103, Bruce Hwy), a roadside restaurant serving everything and anything to do with mangoes – the icy mango juice is delicious and well worth the stop.

## PALUMA

The Mt Spec Rd, which follows the southern boundary of the Paluma Range National Park up to the mountain village of Paluma, leaves the Bruce Hwy 62km north of Townsville. It's a scenic and winding 18km drive, with panoramic views down to the floodplains of Big Crystal Creek and the ocean beyond. From **McClelland's Lookout**, just before Paluma, several walking trails lead off to delightful lookouts and creeks.

Paluma, founded in 1875 when tin was discovered in the area, is a sleepy little top-of-the-mountain place – Townsville's answer to a hill station – with cool, clear air, mountain streams and dense forest.

There are a handful of houses, *Paluma Pottery* (☎ 4770 8530), specialising in domestic ware, and *Ivy Cottages Tea Room* (☎ 4770 8533), where you can get great Devonshire teas. Other places to stay and eat include:

*Mt Spec Cottage* (☎ 4770 8520, fax 4770 8522) Doubles $75 ($5 per extra person, maximum 4). This is a small but comfortable timber cottage on the main road.

*Misthaven Units* (☎ 4771 5964) 1-bedroom units $65 a double ($5 per extra person). These old-fashioned, self-contained holiday flats are adjacent to McClelland's Lookout.

*Heaven at Camp Paluma* (☎ 4770 8616, 7 Lookout Rd) Open 8am-7pm daily. Light lunches from $6, dinner mains $10. Diagonally opposite McClelland's Lookout carpark, this is a small restaurant serving takeaways and home-made meals.

About 4km beyond Paluma is the turn-off to **Paluma Dam**, a popular boating and water-skiing spot. Another 20km past this turn-off you come to **Hidden Valley**, where you can stay in a log cabin ($66 a double plus $5.50 per extra person, maximum four) or motel-style backpacker units (singles/doubles $19/$39) at the *Hidden Valley Cabins* (☎ 4770 8088, e hvc@austarnet .com, w www.hiddenvalleycabins.com.au). There's also a fully licensed restaurant and a swimming pool.

## INGHAM

**postcode 4850 • pop 5000**

Ingham is the centre of a large sugar cane–growing district. The first sugar cane farms were established in this area in the 1880s, and from early in its history the region attracted a large number of Italian immigrants; each May there's a big festival celebrating the town's Italian heritage.

Ingham is a busy commercial centre and a pleasant enough town with all the usual services. The **Memorial Gardens**, signposted off the main highway from the centre of town, are the town's botanical gardens and a good place for a stroll or a picnic lunch.

### Information

There's a helpful tourist information centre (☎ 4776 5211, fax 4776 3039, e ceo@ hinchinbrook.qld.gov.au) at 21 Lannercost St. It's open 8.45am to 5pm Monday to Friday and 9am to 2pm Saturday and Sunday. The QPWS (☎ 4776 1700, fax 4776 3770, 49 Cassady St), open 9am to 5pm Monday to Friday, deals with information for the Paluma Range and Lumholtz (Wallaman Falls) National Parks.

### Places to Stay & Eat

*Royal Hotel* (☎ 4776 2024, 46 Lannercost St) $11 per person. While the downstairs areas are dominated by pokies, the upstairs bedrooms are pretty much in original condition – basic but the cheapest in town.

*Herbert Valley Motel* (☎ 4776 1777, fax 4776 3646, 37 Townsville Rd) Singles/doubles $50/55. These standard motel units are set back from the main truck route.

*The Olive Tree Coffee Lounge* (☎ *4776 5166, 45 Lannercost St)* Mains around $8.50. The coffee's good here and traditional pasta dishes, prepared by the Sicilian owners, look great.

## Getting There & Away

McCafferty's/Greyhound and Premier buses stop in the centre of town on Townsville Rd, close to the corner of Lannercost St (and the information centre). Ingham is also on the main Brisbane to Cairns train line.

## AROUND INGHAM

There are a number of places worth visiting around Ingham, including **Wallaman Falls** in Lumholtz National Park. The falls are 50km west of Ingham, where a tributary of the Herbert River cascades 305m and creates the longest permanent single-drop falls in Australia. The falls are much more spectacular in the wet season, after good rains. You can normally reach them by conventional vehicle along an unpaved road; drive with care in this area as cassowaries sometimes wander onto the roads. There's a camping ground with a swimming hole nearby.

Only 7km east of Ingham is the **Victoria Mill** (☎ *4776 1722)*, the largest sugar mill in the southern hemisphere. Tours ($8.80/4.50 adult/child) are given during the crushing season, between July and December.

About 25km north-east of Ingham is lovely **Lucinda**, a port town at the southern entrance to the Hinchinbrook Channel. Most visitors come here for the fishing, or to have a look at the town's amazing 6km-long jetty, used to get the huge amount of sugar produced in the area out to the ships. Lucinda is also the access point for the southern end of Hinchinbrook Island.

Hinchinbrook Wilderness Safaris (☎ 4777 8307, fax 4777 8436, 48 Patterson Parade) provides ferry and coach connections for those doing the Thorsborne Trail, as well as eco-cruises across to the island.

## Places to Stay & Eat

*Lucinda Point Hotel-Motel* (☎ *4777 8103, Keast St)* Motel units with/without bathroom & air-con $55/50 double. This is a friendly pub with pleasant motel-style units behind it; *meals* are available.

*Wanderer's Holiday Village* (☎ *4777 8213, fax 4777 8131,* e *stay@wanderers -lucinda.com.au, Bruce Parade, Lucinda)* Unpowered/powered sites $11/14 per person, on-site units $30. Sites are shaded by big trees and there's a shop selling the important things in life like fishing bait.

## ORPHEUS ISLAND

Lying about 20km off the coast east of Ingham, Orpheus is a continental island about 11km long and less than 1km wide. It has some of the best fringing reef to be found on any of the Great Barrier Reef islands. The second largest of the Palm Islands group, it's a quiet, secluded island good for camping, snorkelling and diving. Orpheus is mostly national park and is heavily forested, with lots of bird-life; turtles also nest here.

There is a fairly expensive resort on the island, as well as three national park camping grounds and a giant clam research station.

During the 1800s goats were released on the island as part of a madcap scheme to provide food for possible shipwreck survivors. There obviously weren't enough Robinson Crusoes washed ashore here – the goats thrived to the extent that at one stage they numbered over 4000. As the result of a national parks 'control program', there are now less than a dozen left on the island.

## Zoning

Most of the water around the island is zoned Marine Park B – 'look but don't touch'. From the top of Hazard Bay to the southern tip is zoned 'A', which allows limited line fishing. Collecting shells or coral is not permitted.

## Things to See & Do

Orpheus is a great island for snorkelling. It also has some pleasant sandy beaches, including those at Mangrove Bay and Yank's Bay, south of the resort, and at Pioneer Bay north of the resort. Some of the beaches are quite shallow, which rules out swimming at low tide.

The island also has a great reputation as a diving resort. The dive centre caters exclusively to resort guests, and conducts dive courses and a range of diving and snorkelling trips.

At Pioneer Bay, north of the resort, James Cook University owns and operates a marine and terrestrial research facility (☎ 4777 7336), known for its mariculture and giant clam research. The station is private property; however, tours can be organised with prior arrangement and for a small donation.

### Places to Stay

There are *bush camp sites* at Yank's Jetty, South Beach and Pioneer Bay. All sites have toilet facilities and a picnic area but there is no regular fresh water supply and a fuel stove should be used. You must be totally self sufficient. Bring your own food, water and fuel. Yank's Bay offers the best low-tide swimming and snorkelling. Applications to camp on Orpheus should be made to QPWS (☎ 4066 8601) in Cardwell.

The resort has a great reputation for its food – though the restaurant is only open to house guests.

*Orpheus Island Resort (☎ 1800 077 167, 4777 7377, e orpheus@t140.aone.net.au, w www.orpheus.com.au)* Single/double beachfront units from $635/510 per person, double/quad villas $715/485 per person. Established in the 1940s, this resort is these days one of the most exclusive; and with no nightclub or day-trippers, nor phones or TVs in the units, the atmosphere is one of calm. The cheapest accommodation is in the beachfront terraces, and ranges up in price and size to six two-bedroom Mediterranean villas. Tariffs include all meals and snacks, tennis, water-skiing, and use of non-powered water sports gear (including snorkelling equipment). The resort doesn't cater for anyone under 15 years of age.

### Getting There & Away

The resort has a seaplane that handles transfers from Townsville (one way/return $175/350) and Cairns ($285/565) to Orpheus.

There are no regular boat services to Orpheus, but both MV *Scuba Doo* (☎ 4777 8220) ex-Dungeness, and Orpheus Island Diving, Fishing & Transfer Services

(☎ 4777 9652) ex-Taylor's Beach, near Ingham, will transfer campers out to the island (and Pelorus, too).

## OTHER PALM ISLANDS

Orpheus is part of the Palm Island group, which consists of 10 main islands. Apart from Orpheus, which is predominantly national park, and nearby council-run Pelorus, all of the islands are Aboriginal reserves and permission must be obtained from the Palm Island Aboriginal Council (☎ 4770 1177) before you can land on them. Speak to the Shire Clerk or the Chairperson. You'll need to declare the purpose of your visit, and when and how long you're planning to stay.

The main islands of the Palm Islands group (and their Aboriginal names) are Orpheus (Goolboddi), Pelorus (Yanooa), Brisk (Culgarool), Cura-cao (Inoogoo), Eclipse (Garoogubbee), Esk (Soopun), Falcon (Carbooroo), Fantome (Eumilli), Havannah and Great Palm (Bukaman) Islands.

## CARDWELL

**postcode 4849 • pop 1400**

South of Cardwell, the Bruce Hwy climbs high above the coast with breathtaking views down across the winding, mangrove-lined waterways known as the Mangroves, which separate Hinchinbrook Island from the coast.

Cardwell's main claim to tourism fame is as the access point for Hinchinbrook Island, but it is also a popular fishing spot and there are quite a few interesting sights in the immediate area. Cardwell itself is a fairly old-fashioned holiday town, sprawled along a 3km length of the Bruce Hwy; it's the only town on the highway between Brisbane and Cairns that is actually right on the coast.

### History

Cardwell is one of northern Queensland's earliest towns, dating from 1864, though there's little evidence of its origins now. It predates Townsville and was intended as a port and supply centre for pioneer cattle stations in the Valley of the Lagoons, on the upper Burdekin River. Its beginnings were shaky, however, since finding a decent route over the forested ranges proved very difficult and the early settlement suffered from disputes with local Aborigines. It was the determination of Cardwell's founder George Elphinstone Dalrymple, who also established Bowen, that eventually saw the establishment of a rough track through to the Valley of the Lagoons. Unfortunately for Cardwell, it was out-developed by Townsville from where an easier route was found to the high country.

## Orientation & Information

The Bruce Hwy is the town's main street, along which almost all facilities and services are located.

QPWS's Reef & Rainforest Centre at Cardwell (☎ 4066 8601), beside the main jetty in the middle of town, is a great source of information, and where you should go to organise camping permits and bookings for Hinchinbrook Island and the other national parks in the area. It's open 8am to 4.30pm, Monday to Friday.

## Boating

For boat and fishing information your best bet is to ask around town or at the tourist information operators in Cardwell. There's also Hinchinbrook Rent-A-Yacht (☎ 4066 8007, W www.hinchinbrookrentayacht.com .au), which has yachts, motor cruisers and houseboats for cruising around Hinchinbrook, Dunk and Brook Islands; a houseboat sleeping up to 12 costs $430 per day, while a six-berth yacht can cost up to $800 per day.

## Places to Stay

*Kookaburra Holiday Park* (☎ 4066 8648, fax 4066 8910, 175 Bruce Hwy) Tent sites $16.50, on-site vans from $37, cabins from $45. This well-set-up and attractive caravan park, 800m north of the centre, is also a great source of information about anything local.

*Hinchinbrook Hostel* (☎ 4066 8648, fax 4066 8910, e kookaburra@znet.net.au, 175 Bruce Hwy) Camp sites $7, dorm beds $14, doubles $30 (YHA members $1 less). Located within the grounds of the Kookaburra Holiday Park, this small YHA hostel has good facilities and can store your luggage while you're on the island.

*Cardwell Sunrise Village* (☎ 4066 8550, fax 4066 8941, 43a Marine Parade) Unpowered/powered sites $15/18, cabins $50, single/double/twin rooms $55/69/75. Further north, this is a large accommodation complex with a motel and restaurant.

## Development vs Conservation – the Oyster Point Experience

The Hinchinbrook Marina development at Oyster Point, just south of Cardwell, has caused controversy ever since its inception in 1994. The project of Queensland developer, Keith Williams, this massive development – to include a resort, golf course, airstrip and plenty of private housing – is well under way, with the marina and a bevy of managers already in place. But opposition to the project is far from over.

On one side are the environmental activists and protesters, who claim the development will destroy mangrove areas vital to the coastal ecosystem and bring unsustainable numbers of tourists to Hinchinbrook Island. Keith Williams' previous record also works against him from the conservationists' point of view: after starting the Sea World theme park and playing a major role in developing the Gold Coast, in the 1980s he transformed Hamilton Island from an untouched continental island into a concrete jungle of high-rise hotels and apartments. Pro-development lobbyists argue that the resort will be the economic lifeblood that will save a dying town, create employment and finance badly needed development in Cardwell.

The Cardwell dispute typifies the dilemmas that Queensland faces as its tourism industry grows and provides an increasing proportion of the state's income. The questions being asked – such as whether the Gold Coast-style develop-at-all-costs mentality should be allowed to spread along the coast, and to what extent Queensland's natural resources should be exploited to take advantage of the current boom in ecotourism – are as relevant in the rest of Queensland as they are in Cardwell.

*Hinchinbrook Hop* (☎ *4066 8671, 186 Victoria St)* Unpowered/powered camp sites $11/14, dorm beds $12, on-site vans from $15. Another camping ground on the main drag, this place has two small but bright dorms.

## Places to Eat

*Annie's Kitchen* (☎ *4066 8818, 107 Victoria St)* Breakfasts $8, lunch grills $9. This cafe on the main street does seriously good fish and chips and sandwiches.

*Marine Hotel* (☎ *4066 8662, 59 Victoria St)* Mains around $10. The Marine has passable pub meals. There's a casual bistro out the back and a concrete beer garden.

*Cardwell Muddies* (☎ *4066 8907, 221 Victoria St)* Mains $11-22. This licensed cafe about 1km north of the centre specialises in seafood – watch out for the giant crab-on-a-stick (in true Queensland fashion) out the front of the restaurant. Takeaways are available.

*Edmund Kennedy Restaurant* (☎ *4066 8550, Sunrise Village Leisure Park, 43 Marine Parade)* The Thursday night seafood smorgasbord for $8.50 is popular with the locals.

## Getting There & Away

All McCafferty's/Greyhound and Premier buses between Townsville and Cairns stop at Cardwell. The fare is around $30 from either place. Cardwell is also on the main Brisbane to Cairns train line. Buses stop by the BP station and the Seaview Cafe.

## AROUND CARDWELL

The **Cardwell Forest Drive** starts from the centre of town and is a 26km round trip, taking you to some excellent lookouts, swimming holes, walking tracks and picnic areas. Turn off the highway beside the BP service station in the centre of town – the drive is signposted from the other side of the train station.

Most of the coastal forest north of Cardwell is protected as the **Edmund Kennedy National Park**, named after the ill-fated explorer who was killed by Aborigines at Cape York. At the southern end of the park, there's

an interesting boardwalk through the mangroves – turn off the highway 4km north of Cardwell to reach it. Don't swim or cross any of the creeks in the park – the mangroves here are home to estuarine crocodiles.

The **Murray Falls** have fine rock pools for swimming, a walking track, camping ground and a barbecue area. They're 22km west of the highway, signposted about 27km north of Cardwell. Take care when swimming, as the rocks are incredibly slippery – there have been several drownings here.

Just off the Bruce Hwy, 7km south of Cardwell, the **Five Mile Swimming Hole** is another good swimming spot with picnic facilities.

The **Dalrymple Gap Walking Track**, originally an Aboriginal trail that was upgraded by George Dalrymple in the 1860s as a stock route to the Valley of Lagoons, passes through the **Lumholtz National Park**. The track is 9km long and takes eight hours return, although you have the option of a two-hour 3km walk to an old stone bridge that is registered by the National Trust. The turn-off to the track is off the highway, 15km south of Cardwell.

## HINCHINBROOK ISLAND

Hinchinbrook Island is a spectacular and unspoiled wilderness area, with granite mountains rising dramatically from the sea and a varied terrain – lush tropical forest on the mainland side, thick mangroves lining the shores, towering mountains in the middle and long sandy beaches and secluded bays on the eastern side. All 635 sq km of the island is a national park and rugged Mt Bowen, at 1141m, is the highest peak. There's plenty of wildlife, especially pretty-face wallabies and the iridescent blue Ulysses butterfly.

Hinchinbrook Island has some excellent walking tracks, the highlight being the Thorsborne Trail, a 32km walking track from Ramsay Bay to Zoe Bay and on to George Point at the southern tip. There is a limit of 40 people allowed on the trail at any one time and booking is essential – see following.

Walkers are warned to take plenty of insect repellent – the sandflies and mossies on

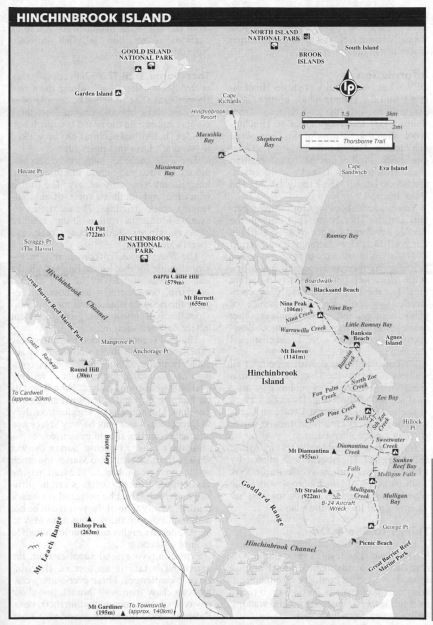

# HINCHINBROOK ISLAND

NORTH ISLAND
NATIONAL PARK

BROOK
ISLANDS

South Island

GOOLD ISLAND
NATIONAL PARK

Garden Island

Cape
Richards

Hinchinbrook Resort

Macushla
Bay

Shepherd
Bay

Cape
Sandwich

Eva Island

Hecate Pt

Missionary
Bay

0        1.5        3km
0        1        2mi

----- *Thorsborne Trail*

Mt Pitt
(722m)

Scraggy Pt
(The Haven)

HINCHINBROOK
NATIONAL
PARK

Ramsay Bay

Barra Castle Hill
(579m)

Boardwalk
Blacksand Beach

Mt Burnett
(655m)

Nina Peak
(106m)

*Nina Creek*

*Nina* Bay

*Warrawilla* Creek

Little Ramsay Bay

Banksia
Beach

Agnes
Island

Mangrove Pt

Anchorage Pt

Mt Bowen
(1141m)

*Banksia Creek*

Hinchinbrook
Island

*Fan Palm
Creek*

*North Zoe
Creek*

Zoe Bay

Round Hill
(30m)

To Cardwell
(approx. 20km)

*Cypress Pine Creek*

Zoe Falls

*Silt Zoe
Creek*

Hillock
Pt

Mt Diamantina
(955m)

*Diamantina
Creek*

*Sweetwater
Creek*

Sunken
Reef Bay

*Falls*

Mulligan Falls

Mt Straloch
(922m)

*Mulligan
Creek*

Mulligan
Bay

*Goddard Range*

B-24 Aircraft
Wreck

George Pt

Bishop Peak
(263m)

Picnic Beach

*Hinchinbrook Channel*

Great Barrier Reef
Marine Park

Mt Gardiner
(195m)

To Townsville
(approx. 140km)

Hinchinbrook can be a real pest. You'll also have to learn how to protect your food from the native bush rats, and there are estuarine crocodiles in the mangroves.

## Information

QPWS has two useful leaflets on Hinchinbrook and the islands to the north. Those planning to walk the coastal track from Ramsay Bay to George Point on Hinchinbrook should get a copy of the *Thorsborne Trail* leaflet. The *Hinchinbrook to Dunk Island* guide is full of fascinating information about Hinchinbrook Island, Goold Island, the Brook Islands, the Family Islands and Dunk Island.

You can make bookings for camping permits and the Thorsborne Trail through the Reef & Rainforest Centre (☎ 4066 8601) in Cardwell. Don't leave arranging your permit until the last minute: try to ring in advance to make sure there is a vacancy, and arrive at the office well before the ferry departure time. For the Thorsborne Trail it's recommended you book one year in advance for public holidays and school holidays, other times at least six months in advance. However, it *is* possible to score a cancellation if you turn up in Cardwell ready to go.

Before being issued with a permit, all walkers must view the 15-minute *Without a Trace* video, which gives guidance on minimal impact bushwalking. It can be viewed at the Reef & Rainforest Centre in Cardwell, or call them for information on where you can view it interstate.

*Hinchinbrook Island,* with text by Arthur and Margaret Thorsborne and photos by Cliff and Dawn Frith, is a coffee-table book on the wonders of Hinchinbrook with some superb photos and an engrossing text revealing a real love for the island.

## Things to See & Do

There are some fine beaches on Hinchinbrook Island. The resort's main beach, **Orchid Beach**, is an idyllic little stretch of sand framed by granite beaches at either end. Also near the resort is **Turtle Bay**, a rocky inlet further west. There are several **walking trails** starting from the resort.

It's worth noting that Hinchinbrook is close enough to the mainland for you to be cautious about box jellyfish between November and April.

**Thorsborne Trail** This 32km coastal track is the finest island walk along the Great Barrier Reef. The walk *can* be completed in two hard days but allowing at least three nights camping on the island is a much better idea. Individual sections can be walked if you don't have that much time.

The walk includes long sandy beaches, mountain streams, humid rainforests and magnificent mountain scenery. The trail is ungraded and includes some often challenging creek crossings. The maximum elevation along the trail is 260m, reached between Upper South Zoe Creek and Sweetwater Creek.

The *Thorsborne Trail* brochure is an essential guide for those intending to walk the trail. It gives you advice on how to plan your trip, book permits and how to conserve the delicate island environment. It divides the walk into stages, giving pertinent advice for each section.

The trail is recommended for moderately experienced bushwalkers who should be adequately prepared and carry a map, compass and drinking water. Water is reliably available year-round only at **Nina Bay**, **Little Ramsay Bay** and at the southern end of **Zoe Bay**. During the dry season, from July to December, water may be very scarce and adequate supplies should be carried.

At the opposite extreme, during the wet season, from December to March, too much water can pose problems. The trail may be very slippery, creek crossings can be difficult and you should be prepared for heavy rainfall. At any time of the year it can be hot and humid during the day but from May to September the nights can be cold enough to require a sleeping bag.

Protecting your food supplies from the native bush rats is another of Hinchinbrook's challenges. These ever-hungry critters can chew their way through just about any type of container, including metal ones. Rat-proof food boxes are provided at some camp sites. Check with the park rangers for advice on ways of protecting your food. Open camp fires and cooking fires are not allowed; you must carry your own fuel stove. A hand trowel is also handy for digging toilet holes.

## Places to Stay
There are six *national parks camping grounds* along the Thorsborne Trail, plus ones at Macushla Bay and Scraggy Point in the north.

The Thorsborne Trail camping grounds are at Little Ramsay Bay, Zoe Bay, Sunken Reef Bay, Mulligan Falls, Mulligan Bay and George Point. Numbers for each camping ground are limited and depend on the total number of walkers on the island.

Apart from the camping, the only accommodation is at an excellent and unobtrusive resort at Cape Richards, the northernmost tip of the island.

*Hinchinbrook Island Resort* (☎ 4066 8585, fax 4066 8271, ⓦ www .hinchinbrookresort.com.au) Self-contained, 4-bed beach cabins $150, single/double cabins $225/430 (plus $95 for children), 1- & 2-bedroom tree-houses $315-355 single, $590-640 double (plus $120 for children). Built into the steep hillside behind Orchid Beach, and linked by boardwalks, each timber 'tree-house' cottage here has its own bathroom and separate lounge area, ceiling fans, fridge, and tea and coffee-making facilities. The older cabins, while fairly basic and straightforward, are comfortable enough with two bedrooms, a bathroom and ceiling fans. The cheaper beach cabins are ideal if you're coming off the walk. There is no radio, TV or phone in the rooms; rates include all meals and use of most equipment.

The resort's facilities include a bar, restaurant (only open to resort guests), an excellent swimming pool, canoes, snorkelling gear, jet skis and fishing equipment.

## Getting There & Away
Hinchinbrook Island Ferries (☎ 4066 8270) at Port Hinchinbrook Marina has a ferry departing at 9am and returning at 5pm daily June through November; and on Wednesday,

Friday and Sunday in December, April and May. Day cruises and camper/hiker return transfers cost $85; if you're walking the Thorsborne Trail the one-way cost from Cardwell to the northern end is $59. Hinchinbrook Wilderness Safaris (☎ 4777 8307) do the pick-up from the southern end of the island; the cost is $57, including transport back to Cardwell. The resort transfers its guests between Cardwell and Hinchinbrook for $85 return.

## ISLANDS NEAR HINCHINBROOK
There are two small island groups just north of Hinchinbrook Island. Both are national parks, and both are accessible by ferry from Cardwell. The 8.3-sq km, granite **Goold Island**, just 4.5km north-west of Cape Richards and 17km north-east of Cardwell, has a *camp site* on its western side. There are toilets, picnic tables and a gas barbecue, but you'll need to bring your own drinking water. There is a limit of 50 campers, and permits are available from the QPWS in Cardwell.

Just south of Goold Island is tiny **Garden Island**, with a recreation reserve controlled by the local council. There are no restrictions on camping here, but permits ($3.85 per person per night) are required; get them at the Cardwell Newsagency (☎ 4066 8622). The island has a good sandy beach but no fresh water.

Hinchinbrook Island Ferries can drop campers at Goold Island on request.

About 8km north-east of Cape Richards are the four small islands of the **Brook Islands group**. South Island has a Commonwealth lighthouse but the other three – Middle, Tween and North – are national parks and covered in thick vegetation. The fringing reef around the three northern islands offers fine snorkelling and North Island's beach is a good picnic spot, but there are no facilities and camping is not permitted.

## TULLY
postcode 4854 • pop 2800
Tully, green and ringed by mountains, is the wettest place in Australia, averaging over 4000mm of rain a year. With the main street's quaint 1930s and '50s shop facades,

## Imperial Pigeons

The Brook Islands are a nesting place for the thousands of pigeons that migrate from New Guinea every summer to breed in Australia. Known by various names, including nutmeg pigeon, Torresian imperial-pigeon and pied imperial-pigeon, they are large, striking birds – pure white with black tail and wing tips.

The pigeons arrive each September, establish large nesting colonies on the islands and depart with their offspring in February. They fly to the mainland each day to feed on fruit trees before returning to the islands each afternoon. Farmers on the mainland used to consider the birds pests, and regularly shot them on the islands in their thousands. But thanks to the efforts of Margaret and Arthur Thorsborne (authors of the book *Hinchinbrook Island*) in the 1960s and '70s, the birds are now protected and numbers have increased to well over 30,000. The Brook Islands are also a breeding place for black-naped terns over summer. If you're visiting the islands, you should be extremely careful not to disturb the birds or their nests. Nesting areas are indicated by signs on the beach. Visits are prohibited from October through February.

LPP

---

and friendly, small-town feel, Tully provides a glimpse of what Queensland country towns would have once looked like. There's a Commonwealth Bank, several pubs and, being in the heart of a large fruit-growing area, a bustling hostel.

It's the cheapest place to start from if you're doing a white-water rafting trip on the Tully River – though most people stay at nearby Mission Beach.

The Tully Information Centre (☎ 4068 2288, fax 4068 2858, Bruce Hwy), on the highway just south of the Tully turn-off, is open 8.30am to 4pm Monday to Friday, and 9am to 1pm on Saturday and Sunday, May through to November.

You can see the **Tully Sugar Mill** (☎ 4068 1222) in action during the crushing season, mid-June to late October. Adult/family tickets cost $7/18 and are obtainable from the tourist information centre; the 1½-hour tours leave at 10am Monday to Friday.

About 8km north of Tully is **Alligator's Nest**, a great swimming spot with picnic tables and barbecues. To get there, take Murray St from the town centre and head north.

### Places to Stay & Eat

**Banana Barracks** (☎ 4068 0455, fax 4068 0466, 50 Butler St) Dorm beds $16, doubles

& twins $17. Rooms in this relatively new and funky hostel are cramped. There's a small pool, a busy bar and meals for $5. Banana Barracks seems to cater mostly for people employed picking bananas.

**The Savoy** (☎ 4068 2400, 4 Plumb St) Beds in 3-bed/6-bed dorm $15.50/14.50. Relatively small and quiet, this is another workers' hostel west of the town centre.

**Tully Motel** (☎ 4068 2233, fax 4068 2751, Bruce Hwy) Singles/doubles with en suite $55/60.50, with shared bathroom $33/40. On the highway but not noisy, this place offers pleasant motel units or plain 'budget' accommodation. There's a *restaurant* attached to the motel.

If you're camping, the **Green Way Caravan Park** (☎ 4068 2055, fax 4068 0681, Murray St), near the centre of town, is a good option (unpowered/powered sites $10/15, cabins $42); or you could head down to Tully Heads, 10km away on the coast, to the **Tully Heads Caravan Park** (☎ 4066 9260), where unpowered/powered sites cost $14/16, on-site vans $25 and air-con cabins $42.

### Getting There & Away

Tully is on the main Brisbane to Cairns train line. McCafferty's/Greyhound and Premier buses also stop here on demand.

## AROUND TULLY

At **El Rancho del Rey** (☎ 4066 7770, fax 4066 7824, e elrancho@znet.net.au, David-son Rd), about 30km south of Tully, you can stay in the Jackaroos' quarters for $66 per person, including all bedding and meals. Aboriginal guided tours over the Echo Creek Falls walking trail and traditional homelands of the Jirrbal people are organised through El Rancho del Rey. You'll need to book ahead.

## MISSION BEACH

postcode 4852 • pop 1050

The name Mission Beach actually covers a string of small settlements along a 14km coastal strip east of Tully. Mission Beach is in the centre; Wongaling Beach and South Mission Beach are to the south, and Bingil Bay and Garners Beach are to the north.

The coastal strip is surrounded by large areas of dense rainforest, which in places hugs the foreshore. The area has a wide range of accommodation, from beachfront camping grounds and backpackers hostels to exclusive and expensive resorts. The area is a good base for a number of activities, including visits to Dunk Island and the reef, and white-water rafting trips on the Tully River.

### History

On 21 May 1848 the barque *Rattlesnake* dropped the explorer, Edmund Kennedy, and his companions at Tam O'Shanter Point, south of South Mission Beach; this was the start of their ill-fated overland expedition towards Cape York. All but three of the party's 13 members died, and Kennedy himself was speared to death by Aborigines a little way south of Cape York. There's a memorial to the expedition at Tam O'Shanter Point.

Pioneers at the first white settlement in the area planted mangoes, bananas, coconuts, tea and coffee, and a timber mill was also built to process the locally cut cedar.

In 1914 the Queensland government established an Aboriginal mission to house the remainder of the local Aboriginal population. The site of the old mission, from which the area takes its name, can still be seen at South Mission Beach.

One of Queensland's worst cyclones struck this stretch of coast in 1918, with winds of over 150km/h, floods and tidal waves destroying the mission and many other buildings and claiming a number of lives.

### Information

The Mission Beach Tourist Information Centre (☎ 4068 7099) is on Porters Promenade at the northern end of Mission Beach. It's well set up with a small library with books on the environment and local history. It's open 9am to 5pm daily.

Right next door is the **Wet Tropics Environment Centre** (☎ 4068 7179, e c4@iig .com.au), an interpretative centre focusing on cassowary conservation and the Mission Beach environment. The centre is open 10am to 5pm daily.

Mission Beach proper is a compact little holiday village with cafes, restaurants, a chemist and a bookshop with Internet access – but no banks.

Wongaling Beach to the south has its own shopping centre.

### Bushwalking

The Tam O'Shanter State Forest, which covers the area behind Mission Beach, provides some impressive walking trails; it's also a haunt of cassowaries – though unfortunately the population has been depleted by road accidents and the destruction of the forest by logging and cyclones. Information on the various walks can be obtained from the tourist information centre.

### White-Water Rafting & Sea Kayaking

Raging Thunder (☎ 4030 7990) and R'n'R (☎ 1800 079 039) charge $145 from Mission Beach for trips on the Tully River. These are the same as the trips on offer in Cairns, but you'll save money and hours on a bus by doing them from here.

Sunbird Adventures (☎ 4068 8229, e sunbird@znet.net.au) offer a full-day kayak trip out to Dunk Island for $80 or a half-day coastal paddle for $48. These tours get rave reviews. Snorkelling gear and lunch

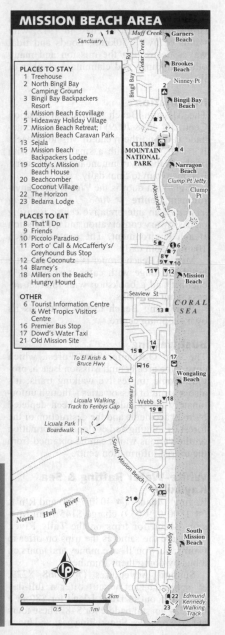

**MISSION BEACH AREA**

To Sanctuary

Muff Creek

Garners Beach

Cedar Creek

Bingil Bay Rd

Brookes Beach

Ninney Pt

Bingil Bay Beach

PLACES TO STAY
1 Treehouse
2 North Bingil Bay Camping Ground
3 Bingil Bay Backpackers Resort
4 Mission Beach Ecovillage
5 Hideaway Holiday Village
7 Mission Beach Retreat; Mission Beach Caravan Park
13 Sejala
15 Mission Beach Backpackers Lodge
19 Scotty's Mission Beach House
20 Beachcomber Coconut Village
22 The Horizon
23 Bedarra Lodge

PLACES TO EAT
8 That'll Do
9 Friends
10 Piccolo Paradiso
11 Port o' Call & McCafferty's/ Greyhound Bus Stop
12 Cafe Coconutz
14 Blarney's
18 Millers on the Beach; Hungry Hound

OTHER
6 Tourist Information Centre & Wet Tropics Visitors Centre
16 Premier Bus Stop
17 Dowd's Water Taxi
21 Old Mission Site

CLUMP MOUNTAIN NATIONAL PARK

Narragon Beach

Clump Pt Jetty

Clump Pt

Alexander Dr

Mission Beach

Seaview St

CORAL SEA

To El Arish & Bruce Hwy

Wongaling Beach

Licuala Walking Track to Fenbys Gap

Cassowary Dr

Webb St

Licuala Park Boardwalk

South Mission Beach Rd

North Hull River

Kennedy St

South Mission Beach

Edmund Kennedy Walking Track

0        1        2km
0    0.5    1mi

**NORTH COAST**

– all organic food – are provided on the day tour, morning tea on the half-day tour.

Coral Sea Kayaking (☎ 4068 9154, W www.coralseakayaking.com, 2 Wall St, South Mission Beach) organises two- and three-day trips out to the Family Islands.

## Other Activities

Jump the Beach (☎ 4031 1822, Pacific Dr, Mission Beach) offers dual skydives for $228. Tandem free fall and hope for a soft, and dry, landing on the beach.

Bush'n'Beach horse rides (☎ 4068 7893, corner of Bingil Bay and Frizelle Rds, Bingil Bay) has 1½-hour/half-day rides for $50/88. Both rides cover rainforest and beach; swimming on horseback can be part of the longer ride.

## Cruises

Two boat services leave from the Clump Point jetty, just north of Mission Beach.

Dunk Island Ferry & Cruises (☎ 4068 7211) does a return trip to Dunk Island (adult/child/under-10 $26/13/free), or a day trip to Dunk, Bedarra and the Family Islands (adult/child $63/23) with lunch included. The MV *Lawrence Kavanagh*, an old Tasmanian passenger ferry, plies the waters daily at a leisurely pace – keep a look out for dolphins.

The *Quick Cat* (☎ 4068 7289) is a fast catamaran that will get you out to Dunk Island in 20 minutes for $26 return (child $13). You can also combine this trip with a cruise to the outer Barrier Reef for $134 (child $67).

## Places to Stay – Budget & Mid-Range

Hostels all have courtesy buses that pick up from the main bus stops.

*Mission Beach Caravan Park (Mission Beach)* Unpowered/powered sites $9/12. These are council-run grounds with beach frontage, good grassy areas and shade, close to the shops.

*North Bingil Bay Camping Ground (Alexander St, Bingil Bay)* Sites $7.70. There's no power at this small, shady, council-run camping ground – but it's in a lovely, quiet position tucked away on the foreshore at the end of the road.

*Hideaway Holiday Village* (☎ *4068 7104, fax 4068 7492,* e *hideaway@internetnorth .com.au, 58-60 Porters Promenade)* Unpowered/powered sites $19/21, cabins with/without en suite $64/54 a double. Grassy and treed, this big, formal holiday park is right in the heart of Mission Beach.

*Beachcomber Coconut Village* (☎ *1800 008 129, 4068 8129, fax 4068 8671, Kennedy Esplanade, South Mission Beach)* Unpowered/powered sites $18/20, cabins from $55. This is another extensive, manicured camping ground with a great beach location.

*Treehouse* (☎ *4068 7137, fax 4068 7028,* e *treehouse.yha@znet.net.au, Frizzel Rd, Bingil Bay)* Camp sites $10, beds in 6-bed dorm $16, doubles $40. Secluded, relaxed and earthy, this YHA-associate hostel at Bingil Bay, 6km north of Mission Beach, is one of the most popular along the coast. Accommodation is in an impressive, timber stilt house; there's a pool and lovely views of the surrounding rainforest and coast.

*Sanctuary* (☎ *4088 6067, 1800 777 012, fax 4088 6071,* w *www.sanctuaryatmission .com, Holt Rd, Bingil Bay)*. Singles/doubles $45/50, singles in a twin share $23. Pole-huts nestled in the rainforest canopy, with only fine mesh between you and the forest, make for an unforgettable experience. In the stylish communal area with its huge deck a *cafe-bar* serves good food (self-catering is an option); bathroom facilities are shared. There's a small pool, and if you're quiet you might well see a cassowary or two. Note that the terrain here is *very* steep. (Sanctuary can't accommodate kids under 11 years old.) If you're on public transport, ring the day before to arrange a Sanctuary pick-up from Mission Beach.

*Mission Beach Backpackers Lodge* (☎ *4068 8317, fax 4068 8616* e *mblodge@ znet.net.au, 28 Wongaling Beach Rd)* Dorm beds $18, doubles $39-47. This is an easygoing, well-equipped hostel with garden surrounds and a pool; there are two buildings, one with dorms, the other with double rooms (shared bathroom).

*Scotty's Mission Beach House* (☎ *4068 8676, fax 4068 8520,* e *scottys@znet.net .au, 167 Reid Rd)* Dorm beds $18-20, doubles

$36 ($49 with air-con & bathroom). Stay here two nights and you'll get a beer and an ice cream. But it ain't quiet: Walls in the cheaper doubles don't make it to the ceiling, and the Hard Banana Bar is loud.

*Mission Beach Retreat* (☎ *1800 001 056, 4088 6229, fax 4088 6111, 49 Porters Promenade)* Dorm beds $19. This small, quiet and friendly hostel is in the heart of Mission Beach. Dorms have air-con.

*Bingil Bay Backpackers Resort* (☎ *4068 7208, fax 4068 7226, The Esplanade via Cutten St, Bingil Bay)* Beds in 4-bed dorm $18, doubles with fan/air-con $38/55. Overlooking Bingil Bay from high on a hillside, this ex-motel has clean, austere rooms, a restaurant and swimming pool.

## Places to Stay – Top End
*Sejala on the Beach* (☎/fax *4068 7241,* e *sjegger@onaustralia.com.au, 1 Pacific St, Mission Beach)*. Singles/doubles from $99/130. Three self-contained, stylish and colourful beach huts, secluded in landscaped gardens with the beach right in front. There's a pool and maximum of nine guests, and breakfast is served on the beach.

*Mission Beach Ecovillage* (☎ *4068 7534, fax 4068 7538,* e *coralsea@ecovillage .com.au, Clump Point Rd)* Singles/doubles $98/141. Here there are self-contained timber bungalows set amid lush gardens (and a great pool) on the foreshore at the northern end of Mission Beach.

*The Horizon* (☎ *4068 8154, fax 4068 8596,* e *info@thehorizon.com.au, Explorer Dr, South Mission Beach)* Doubles from $220. Think glossy magazines. Oozing luxury, million-dollar vistas and one-on-one service make this one of the most exclusive options in Mission Beach.

*Bedarra Lodge* (☎ *4068 8400, fax 4068 8586, 18 Explorers Dr, South Mission Beach)* All-inclusive packages from $198 per person per night. This place had just changed hands when we visited, but the cabins and location will ensure that it remains a luxury choice. The buildings rest on a steep, rainforested hillside, with decks providing beautiful views over the ocean and islands.

## Places to Eat

**Mission Beach** For self-caterers, there's also a *supermarket* in town.

*Port o' Call Cafe* (☎ *4068 7390, Shop 6, Porters Promenade*) Breakfast special $7, lunches $4-7. Open 8am-late afternoon daily. This is a popular eatery serving home-made meals like (*big* serves of) pancakes and good pies, next to the Mission Beach bus stop.

*That'll Do* (☎ *4068 7300, Shop 1, Porters Promenade*) Open 11am-8pm Thur-Tues. Delicious fish and chips are standard at this friendly takeaway joint on the main drag.

*Piccolo Paradiso* (☎ *4068 7008, David St*) Mains around $11, pizzas $9-19. Open 8am-9pm daily. Tucked away at the beach end of the pedestrian-only David St, this lively, licensed Italian bistro dishes out pasta and delicious pizzas.

*Cafe Coconutz* (☎ *4068 7397, Porters Promenade*) Mains $14-20. Open 10am-late daily. Cafe Coconutz is a busy, colourful bar serving juices, smoothies and cocktails, with outside seating for a quieter meal. The menu includes a wide range of Asian noodle dishes.

*Friends* (☎ *4068 7107, Porters Promenade*) Mains $17-25. Open noon-2pm & 6pm-late Mon-Sat. Friends is dark and cosy, with an intimate atmosphere; its simple, classic menu includes a seafood platter for $25.

**Other Areas** There are also options in other parts of the area.

*Millers On the Beach* (☎ *4068 8177, Cnr Banfield & Webb Sts, Wongaling Beach*) Mains $10-20. Open noon-midnight Tues-Sun, 5pm-midnight Mon; lunch noon-2pm, dinner 6pm-late. The menu here offers both small and large serves. Dishes include the 'no hunger burger' for $11. Millers also incorporates the *Hungry Hound* bar, a lively, open-air space with a happy hour and occasional live music.

*Blarney's* (☎ *4068 8472, 10 Wongaling Beach Rd, Wongaling Beach*) Mains average $24. Open 6.30pm-late Tues-Sat, lunch Sun from noon. With timber lattice screens pushed aside to create a big, open space, the licensed Blarney's has a lovely ambience

and old-time favourites like beef Wellington and roast duck.

## Getting There & Away

McCafferty's/Greyhound makes the detour into Mission Beach, stopping outside the Port o' Call Cafe on Porters Promenade. Premier buses stop at the Mission Beach Resort in Wongaling Beach. The average bus fare is $16 from Cairns and $45 from Townsville.

## Getting Around

Mission Beach Bus & Coach (☎ 4068 7400) connects the settlements of the area; buses run on the hour, and each leg (eg Mission Beach to Wongaling, Wongaling to South Mission Beach) costs $3.

Many of the hostels rent out mountain bikes for about $12 per day. Phone ☎ 4068 8155 if you need a taxi.

## DUNK ISLAND

The Family Islands group, offshore from Mission Beach, consists of (Aboriginal names in parentheses): Dunk (Coonanglebah), Thorpe (Timana), Richards (Bedarra), Wheeler (Toolghar), Coombe (Coomboo), Smith (Kurrumbah), Bowden (Budjoo) and Hudson (Coolah). Dunk is about three-quarters national park, and of the other islands, five – Wheeler, Coombe, Smith, Bowden and Hudson Islands – are national parks. Timana and Bedarra are privately owned and now known by their Aboriginal names.

There is a large resort and an area with day-trippers' facilities on Dunk, a small and very exclusive resort on Bedarra, and you can camp on Dunk, Wheeler or Coombe islands. All of the islands are cloaked in dense rainforest, and most have excellent beaches.

The islands were named by Captain Cook, who sailed through the group on 8 June 1770. Lord Montague Dunk was at that time the First Lord of the Admiralty.

Just 4.5km off the coast, Dunk offers a steep terrain with some fine walking trails and good sandy beaches. The island's large resort is owned by P&O; there's also a camping ground and separate day-trippers' section with kiosk, showers, toilets and a water sports shop with windsurfers and jet skis for hire.

From 1897 to 1923 EJ Banfield lived on Dunk and wrote *The Confessions of a Beachcomber* and several other books describing life on Dunk; the island is remarkably little changed from his early descriptions. Dunk is noted for its prolific bird-life (nearly 150 species) and many butterflies. There are superb views over the entrances to the Hinchinbrook Channel from the top of 271m Mt Kootaloo, and around 13km of **walking tracks** lead to headlands and beaches.

There is a small **artists' colony** *(admission $4; open 10am-1pm Mon & Thur)* where pottery, ceramics, jewellery and tapestries are for sale.

Dunk is an easy and affordable day trip from the mainland, with boats running regularly between Mission Beach and the island. A day pass to the resort costs $27.50, including lunch.

## Places to Stay
*National parks camping ground (☎ 4068 8199)* $3.85 per person per night. While it's not exactly in a secluded area, the setup here is good: toilets, showers, barbecues, picnic tables and drinking water are supplied. There's a limit of 30 campers and a maximum stay of five days; permits can be booked through the resort reception.

*Dunk Island Resort (☎ 4068 8199, reservations 1800 737 678, fax 4068 8528,* W *www.poresorts.com.au)* Single/double Banfield Units $310/220 per person, Garden Cabanas $350/260, Beachfront Units $390/300, Bayview Villas $440/350; child 3-14 yrs $70, extra adult $130. Tariffs include breakfast and dinner, and most activities. The resort is on Brammo Bay, at the northern end of the island, and can accommodate up to 400 guests – though it doesn't feel *too* 'mass market'. Architecturally it's all pretty bland, but certainly comfortable, and the lush Dunk greenery provides camouflage and cool.

All rooms have en suite, air-con, ceiling fan, a veranda, TV and telephone, a fridge and tea- and coffee-making facilities.

Activities include squash, tennis, golf, horse riding, clay-target shooting and, of course, diving and snorkelling trips to the Barrier Reef. The resort has two terrific swimming pools.

## Places to Eat
*Beachcomber* Open breakfast & dinner daily. This is the main restaurant in the resort, where the guests obtain the meals included in their tariffs. It's large and tropical-style. Breakfast and dinner are fairly elaborate buffets, with a good range of fresh fruit, cereals, hot foods, salads, cold meat and seafood.

*EJ's on the Deck* This is a casual, open-air lunchtime cafe with an interesting menu. Inevitable focaccias ($10) are supplemented by dishes such as laksa ($10) and gulf prawn wontons ($15).

*BB's by the Beach* Located in the day-trippers' area, this is a fast-food cafe with burgers, sandwiches, salads and fish and chips. A day ticket from Mission Beach can include lunch at either EJ's or BB's

## Getting There & Away
Macair (Qantas) has regular flights to and from Cairns for $165.

From Clump Point the *Quick Cat* (☎ 4068 7289) departs at 10am and costs $26/13 per adult/child; the MV *Lawrence Kavanagh* (☎ 4068 7211) leaves at 8.45am and 10am. Adult/child tickets cost $26/13 (child under 10 years free).

## BEDARRA ISLAND
Bedarra Island is just 6km south of Dunk and about 5km offshore. The island is rocky, hilly and cloaked in rainforest, and fringed with some fine, sandy beaches, a short stretch of mangroves and wildly tumbled collections of giant boulders.

*Bedarra Island Resort (☎ 4068 8233, fax 4068 8215,* W *www.bedarraisland.com, PO Box 268 Mission Beach, 4852)* $840-950 per person per night. This resort, operated by P&O, is one of Australia's best. With a maximum of 30 guests, it is exclusive as well as being expensive; if you can afford that sort of money, Bedarra is about the best resort island on the Great Barrier Reef, perhaps only matched by Lizard Island (see the Far North Queensland chapter).

## OTHER FAMILY ISLANDS

The other five small national park islands of the Family group are Wheeler, Coombe, Smith, Bowden and Hudson Islands. With a permit from QPWS's Reef & Rainforest Centre at Cardwell (☎ 4066 8601), you can camp on Wheeler or Coombe Islands. There are picnic tables at the camp sites on these islands, but no toilet facilities. Wheeler Island has fresh water during the cooler months. The maximum number of campers is limited to 20 on Wheeler Island, and only 10 on Coombe Island.

Charter boats to the islands operate from the Clump Point jetty at Mission Beach or from Cardwell.

## MISSION BEACH TO INNISFAIL

The small township of **El Arish**, just off the highway 17km north of Tully, is the main turn-off point to Mission Beach. In the town is the El Arish Tavern, an historic timber pub draped in hanging baskets and assorted greenery – it's a popular watering hole.

About 8km north of El Arish there's a turn-off to **Kurrimine Beach**, another quiet little beachfront community 10km from the highway. From the beach here you can sometimes wade through knee-deep water all the way out to **King Reef**, which is about 1km offshore. The walk takes about 45 minutes and can *only* be done at low tide during winter – check local advice before attempting the walk, as people have been stranded out here in the past.

You could stay at the *Kurramine Beach Camping Area*, a council-run camping ground right on the foreshore, or the *King Reef Hotel* (☎ 4065 6144), with its range of camp sites, motel rooms and holiday units.

At **Mourilyan**, 7km south of Innisfail, the **Australian Sugar Industry Museum** (☎ 4063 2306, Bruce Hwy; adult/child $5/3; open 8.30am-4.30pm Mon-Fri, 8.30am-2.30pm Sat & Sun) has a collection of old tractors, harvesters, steam-driven crushing engines and back-lit displays depicting the sugar production process. The museum complex also houses the Innisfail Tourist Office (☎ 4063 2306).

## Old Bruce Hwy

An interesting alternative route to Innisfail is to turn off the Bruce Hwy and take the Old Bruce Hwy north through **Silkwood**, **Mena Creek** and South Johnstone. This route leaves the highway 8km north of El Arish, meeting up with the main highway again at the southern outskirts of Innisfail. It's a slower but much more scenic drive, taking you through banana plantations and cane fields surrounded by densely forested mountains on either side. It also takes you to the fascinating Paronella Park, one of the weirdest and most interesting attractions in this area.

After turning off, you drive through the small and old-fashioned Silkwood, from where the road frequently crosses cane railways, so take care if you're here during the harvesting season (June to December).

It's 22km to Mena Creek, where you can get a counter meal or stay at the pleasant, shady *Mena Creek Hotel* (☎ 4065 3201).

## Paronella Park

The unusual, eccentric Paronella Park was the dream-child of José Paronella, a Spaniard who came to Australia from Catalonia in 1913. After working as a cane cutter and farmer for 13 years, he returned to Spain; then with his new wife, Margarita, he returned to Australia a year later, bought a block of land and started building a house in 1929. Next they built a castle, the Grand Staircase down to the river, a Lovers' Tunnel and a hall, all out of poured concrete reinforced with old train tracks. They also planted thousands of trees and commissioned a hydroelectric plant to supply power.

Paronella Park (☎ 4065 3225, fax 4065 3022, ⓦ www.paronellapark.com.au, Japoonvale Rd (Old Bruce Hwy); adult/student $14/12; open 9am-5pm daily) was opened to the public in 1935, and was an instant success and became one of the most popular tourist attractions in northern Queensland. José died in 1948, but his family continued running the park until 1977, when it was sold.

It's still a fascinating and quite bizarre place to visit. Many of the buildings are in ruins, but large parts remain and you can walk through the remains of the castle, down the Grand Staircase to the river and stroll through Lovers' Tunnel. Trails lead through the lovely gardens, and you can swim in the river and walk the suspension bridge across the falls.

***Paronella Park camping & caravan park*** (☎ 4065 3225, fax 4065 3022, ⓔ info@ paronellapark.com.au) Unpowered/powered sites $14/16 a double. Campers also pay the entry fee for the park, but you are then allowed 24-hour access for the duration of your stay.

# Far North Queensland

The geographically small region of Far North Queensland (FNQ) contains the richest pockets of biodiversity in Australia, if not the world. It continues to fascinate travellers, not to mention scientists, with its unique combination of reefs, rivers and rainforests, encompassed by the Wet Tropics World Heritage Area and the Great Barrier Reef Marine Park.

The 8994 sq km Wet Tropics Area stretches from Townsville to Cooktown and includes Cape Tribulation – its meeting of rainforest and fringing reefs is found nowhere else in Australia, and rarely found elsewhere in the world. The rainforest trails and waterfalls of Wooroonooran National Park are also a special example of intact coastal upland rainforest.

The Great Barrier Reef is an amazing kaleidoscope of colour and movement. The Coral Sea reefs of the area are easily accessible, although getting to the far northern reefs may take a little more planning.

Cairns and Port Douglas are the main tourist centres, and both offer an exhausting range of possibilities. An armada of fast catamarans, some able to seat up to 350 passengers (more than the population of some small towns in FNQ!), cruises out on snorkelling and diving trips to the reefs, islands and coral cays of the Great Barrier Reef. While on the land, convoys of minibuses, troop carriers and 4WDs drive north to Cape Tribulation (or Cape Trib, as it's known) and Cooktown, or inland to the high plateau of the Atherton Tableland.

North of Port Douglas are the rainforest-cloaked mountains of the Cape Tribulation Section of Daintree National Park. Further north again is the remote town of Cooktown, which is refreshingly unaffected by the hype of tourism – just getting there can be an adventure.

A few hours' drive inland from the coast, the great Australian outback begins, stretching clear across to the other side of the continent. You can get a taste of the bush by

## Highlights

- Snorkel, dive and swim the outer reef.
- Bushwalk in the World Heritage–listed rainforests of Wooroonooran National Park.
- Spend a night in one of the Tableland's dreamy B&Bs.
- Journey west to the remote towns of Chillagoe and Irvinebank.
- Camp at the untouched Frankland Islands or remote Lizard Island.
- Head to Cooktown, via Cape Tribulation and Bloomfield, and see the pristine Endeavour River, unchanged since Cook's impromptu stopover in 1770.

visiting the historic mining areas of Tyrconnel, Mt Mulligan Station or Chillagoe. Or you can head south-west beyond Mt Garnet on your way to the Undara lava tubes.

## History

The gold and tin discoveries of the 1870s were primarily responsible for opening up Far North Queensland to non-Indigenous settlement. Cooktown was hastily established as a port town for the Palmer River

# FAR NORTH QUEENSLAND

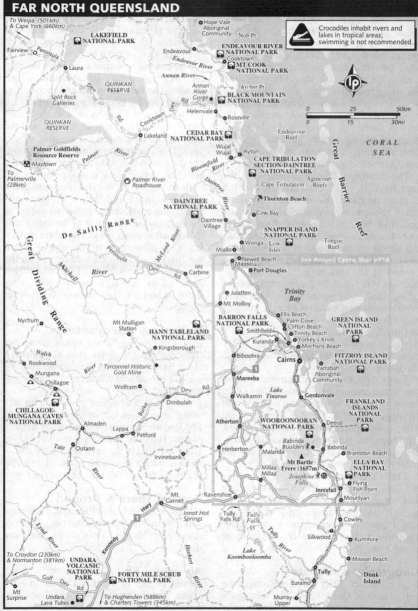

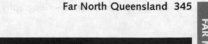
Crocodiles inhabit rivers and lakes in tropical areas; swimming is not recommended.

To Weipa (501km) & Cape York (660km)

Fairview

Peninsula Dev Rd

Laura

LAKEFIELD NATIONAL PARK

Hope Vale Aboriginal Community
Nob Pt

Endeavour
Endeavour River

Cooktown
ENDEAVOUR RIVER NATIONAL PARK
MT COOK NATIONAL PARK

Annan River

Archer Pt

QUINKAN RESERVE

Split Rock Galleries

QUINKAN RESERVE

Annan River Gorge
BLACK MOUNTAIN NATIONAL PARK

Helenvale
Rossville

CORAL SEA

Lakeland

CEDAR BAY NATIONAL PARK

Endeavour Reef

Palmer Goldfields Resource Reserve

Maytown

To Palmerville (28km)

Palmer River

Palmer River Roadhouse

Wujal Wujal
Bloomfield River

Ayton

CAPE TRIBULATION SECTION-DAINTREE NATIONAL PARK

Cape Tribulation

Agincourt Reefs

Great Barrier Reef

De Saiily Range

Daintree River

DAINTREE NATIONAL PARK

Daintree Village

Thornton Beach

Cow Bay

Peninsula Dev Rd

McLeod River

Mt Carbine

Miallo

Wonga

SNAPPER ISLAND NATIONAL PARK

Low Isles

Tongue Reef

Great Dividing Range

Mitchell River

Julatten

Mt Molloy

Newell Beach
Mossman
Port Douglas

See Around Cairns Map p354

Nychum

Mt Mulligan Station

HANN TABLELAND NATIONAL PARK

Kingsborough

Biboohra

BARRON FALLS NATIONAL PARK

Smithfield
Kuranda

Ellis Beach
Palm Cove
Clifton Beach
Trinity Beach
Yorkey's Knob
Machans Beach

Trinity Bay

GREEN ISLAND NATIONAL PARK

Walsh River

Rookwood

Mungana

Chillagoe

Tyrconnel Historic Gold Mine

Wolfram

Dimbulah

Burke Dev Rd

Mareeba

Cairns

Yarrabah Aboriginal Community

FITZROY ISLAND NATIONAL PARK

CHILLAGOE-MUNGANA CAVES NATIONAL PARK

Almaden

Lappa
Petford

Walkamin

Lake Tinaroo

Gordonvale

FRANKLAND ISLANDS NATIONAL PARK

Tate River

Ootann

Atherton

WOOROONOORAN NATIONAL PARK

Deeral

Irvinebank

Herberton

Malanda

Babinda Boulders

Babinda

Bramston Beach

Millaa Millaa

Mt Bartle Frere (1657m)

ELLA BAY NATIONAL PARK

Mt Garnet

Ravenshoe

Josephine Falls

Innisfail

Flying Fish Point

Mourilyan

Innot Hot Springs

Tully Falls Rd

Tully Falls

Cowley

Lynd River

Kennedy Hwy

Herbert River

Tully River

Lake Koombooloomba

Silkwood

Kurrimine

To Croydon (230km) & Normanton (381km)

Gulf Dev Rd

UNDARA VOLCANIC NATIONAL PARK

FORTY MILE SCRUB NATIONAL PARK

Mission Beach

Tully

Dunk Island

Mt Surprise

Undara Lava Tubes

To Hughenden (588km) & Charters Towers (345km)

Euramo

Murray Upper

0   25   50km
0   15   30mi

goldfield in 1873, and became the first major township in FNQ. Cairns was established in 1876 and Port Douglas the following year, as port towns for the Hodgkinson River goldfields in the Mt Mulligan area. Many of the area's mines, such as Herberton, had short life spans, and the diggers drifted from one rush to the next. The port towns, on the other hand, prospered and soon became the main centres for life in the region. As the initial flurry of mining activity gradually waned, timber cutting, sugar cane and dairy farming became the mainstays of the region.

The rainforest Aboriginal people of the area lived in small clan groups, and the Dreamtime stories that survive today accurately relate geographical changes that occurred in the area thousands of years ago. They fought aggressively to keep their land, but ultimately the power of the bullet held sway. Christie Palmerston, an explorer who opened up the area, referred to this in his diary as 'the power of the resistance of the white man'. Dispossessed, the Aboriginal people continued to survive on the margins and, after 1897, many were forcibly moved to Christian missions at Mona Mona, Palm Island, Yarrabah and Wujal Wujal. Today there are over 18,000 Aborigines living in the Wet Tropics Area.

These days, tourism has eclipsed agriculture as the economic life force of the region, much of it the result of the 1988 World Heritage listing of the Wet Tropics Area. The region's population has also increased, with high numbers moving from the southern states and overseas, attracted by the lifestyle and the tourist dollar.

The real challenge for FNQ is to manage the environmental impact of the huge growth in tourism and population in the area. If you take the example of the cassowary, now endangered due to land clearing and introduced predators, the challenge is not being met.

## Geography & Climate
Geographically, FNQ is a microcosm of the entire state of Queensland. The mountains of the Great Dividing Range (known locally

as the coastal range) run parallel with the coast, dividing the region into two distinct zones: a green and fertile coastal strip; and a harsher, drier outback region, which stretches west of the mountains.

The coastal mountain ranges are densely forested; large areas of these rainforests are protected as national parks and included in the Wet Tropics World Heritage Area.

Climatically, FNQ has two distinct seasons – the Wet, or summer months, and the Dry, which lingers on for the rest of the year. This is something of a simplification, but the summer months (January to March) are characterised by high temperatures and high humidity. Tropical downpours are a regular feature and, when cyclones approach the coast, rain depressions can set in for days on end. The rest of the year tends to be what summer is like elsewhere in Australia – plenty of sunshine and warm weather. It seldom gets cold here, with the exception of the Atherton Tableland, which is one of the few areas where you may require warm clothes during the winter months.

## Dangers & Annoyances
If you're heading for the beach, remember that deadly sea wasps, known as 'stingers', are a hazard between October and May – see the boxed text 'Stingers' in the Capricorn Coast chapter.

Saltwater crocodiles also inhabit the mangroves, creeks, rivers and estuaries of FNQ, so avoid swimming or wading in these places. Heed all warning signs. Crocodiles are also found in the open sea around Cooktown and care should be taken when walking along the banks of the Endeavour River.

## Getting There & Around
Cairns is the main link for air, bus and train services in FNQ. See the Getting There & Away entry in the Cairns section for more detail.

**Air** Cairns is FNQ's major airport, with domestic flights to all major cities in Australia, and international flights to major Asian destinations.

**Bus** McCafferty's/Greyhound (☎ 13 14 99, 13 20 30) plies the coastal route up the Bruce Hwy as far as Cairns.

Coral Coaches (☎ 4031 7577) continues the run up the coast from Cairns to Cooktown, and beyond to the Gulf Savannah. In addition, White Car Coaches (☎ 4091 1855) services some of the Atherton Tableland from Cairns.

**Train** Cairns is the end of the main coastal railway link from Brisbane, and the main rail link for services to Kuranda and the region west of the Atherton Tableland.

**Car & Motorcycle** The Bruce Hwy ends in Cairns. From Cairns, the Captain Cook Hwy (complete with a classy 'big' Captain Cook) continues along the coast as far as Daintree Village: the Cairns–Port Douglas

stretch is one of the most scenic coastal drives in Australia.

Just south of Daintree Village is the turn-off to the cable ferry across the Daintree River. The Cape Tribulation Rd, which starts on the other side, is sealed and well maintained. Beyond Cape Trib, the unsealed Bloomfield Track (known as the 'coast road') is 4WD territory all the way to Cooktown. There's also an inland route from Cairns to Cooktown, via Mareeba and Mt Molloy on the Peninsula Developmental Rd, which veers north-east on to the Cooktown Developmental Rd at Lakeland. Conventional vehicles can tackle this road, although the second half is unsealed, rough and bumpy.

There are two major routes heading inland to the Atherton Tableland from Cairns. At Smithfield, just outside Cairns, the Kennedy Hwy climbs up to Kuranda and

---

## World Heritage Listing – What Does It Guarantee?

Far North Queensland's Wet Tropics Area contains amazing pockets of biodiversity. The area covers only 0.01% of Australia's surface area, but has 36% of the continent's mammal species, 50% of its bird species, around 60% of its butterfly species and 65% of its fern species.

Among travellers and even Australians, there's a widespread misconception that the Daintree, the accessible coastal lowland rainforest between Daintree River and Cape Tribulation, is the Wet Tropics World Heritage Area. In fact, the Daintree is but a small part of the World Heritage–listed area that stretches from Townsville to Cooktown, and covers 8944 sq km of coastal and hinterland. Within the area's 3000km boundary are diverse habitats of swamp and mangrove forests, eucalypt woodlands and tropical rainforest.

The Daintree is renowned for good reason though. In 1983 the controversial Bloomfield Track was bulldozed through coastal lowland rainforest from Cape Tribulation to the Bloomfield River, and attracted international attention to the fight to stop land clearing and save the lowland Daintree rainforests. The conservationists lost that battle, but the publicity generated by the blockade indirectly led to the federal government's moves in 1987 to nominate Queensland's wet tropical rainforests for World Heritage listing. Despite strenuous resistance by the Queensland timber industry and state government, the area was inscribed on the World Heritage List in 1988 and one of the key outcomes was a total ban on commercial logging in the area.

Today, the Daintree area remains controversial. The Daintree rainforest reaches as far as the Bloomfield River and much of it is upland rainforest on steep forested slopes and protected as part of Daintree National Park. However, the Cow Bay area that most travellers visit, an area of unique and threatened plant species, is a 1000-block real estate subdivision on freehold private land – look around and you'll see 'for sale' signs aplenty. World Heritage listing unfortunately doesn't affect land ownership rights or control.

Established in 1994, the Daintree Rescue Program, a buy-back scheme, has attempted to consolidate and increase public land ownership in the area, lowering the threat of land clearing and associated species extinction. Check out **W** www.austrop.org.au for more information.

across to Mareeba. From Mareeba you can head north to Cooktown and Cape York, continue west to Chillagoe, or head south into the heart of the Atherton Tableland. The second route, the Gillies Hwy, leaves the Bruce Hwy at Gordonvale, south of Cairns, and climbs up to the Tablelands via Yungaburra and Atherton.

# Innisfail to Cairns

## INNISFAIL
**postcode 4860 • pop 9000**
The deluge of tourists found to the north and south has bypassed Innisfail completely. Its small, quiet harbour, at the confluence of the North and South Johnstone Rivers, is moored with a line of sturdy working fishing boats – there's no fancy marina in sight here.

The area was first explored in 1872 and in 1880 two sugar plantations were established. As the town grew it became known as Geraldton, although in 1910 this was changed to Innisfail when a ship bound for Geraldton in Western Australia to pick up timber mistakenly arrived at the port – just slightly off course! Chinese settlers, tired of scratching a living on the Palmer River goldfields, established the area's banana plantations. Early in the 20th century, Italians arrived to work the cane fields and in the 1930s there was even a local branch of the Mafia, the Black Hand. The town, like many bordering the World Heritage Wet Tropics Area, has survived fire, flood and vicious cyclones.

### Orientation & Information
Innisfail sprawls around the banks of the Johnstone Rivers, with the arrestingly steep streets of the town centre just west of where the two rivers meet. The Bruce Hwy passes through the centre of town, meeting Edith St. Innisfail's Warrina Lakes and Botanic Gardens are north-west of the town centre.

The tourist office, the Cassowary Coast Development Bureau (☎ 4061 7422, fax 4061 7655, e ccdb@oznet.net.au), at 1 Edith St, is a good source of local information. The

Queensland Parks & Wildlife Serve (QPWS; ☎ 4061 4291) is in the Rising Sun complex on Owen St.

There are several banks in town, including the ANZ and National Australia. The post office is on Edith St, near the tourist office. For Internet access head to the Flexi Cyber Cafe (☎ 4061 6250), 38 Rankin St, next to the National Bank. It's open from 9am to 6pm weekdays.

If you're interested in fruit-picking work, your best bet is to check the local Yellow Pages under 'Banana Growers' and contact the plantation directly. Work is available year-round.

### Things to See & Do
The **Local History Museum** (☎ 4061 2731, 11 Edith St; admission $3; open 10am-noon & 1pm-3pm Mon-Fri) is in the old School of Arts building. Its highlights are the See Poy portraits, two early 20th-century paintings of the children of a local Chinese merchant. Another reminder of FNQ's once-extensive Chinese diaspora is a small red and gold **temple**, the Lit Zing Khuong (Temple of the Universal God), on Owen St. The original temple was built in the 1880s, but was razed by a cyclone in 1918. Admission is by donation.

Barrajack Encounters (☎ 4061 3790) runs guided fishing tours of the Johnstone River, as well as Koombooloomba and Tinaroo Dams.

### Places to Stay
**Mango Tree Van Park** (☎ 4061 1656, Access via Couche St off the Bruce Hwy) Camping $10, single/double vans $20/25, en suite caravan $25, cabins $40. Planted with tropical fruit trees on the banks of the South Johnstone River, Mango Tree offers good-value accommodation options.

**Codge Lodge** (☎ 4061 8055, fax 4061 8155, 63 Rankin St) Dorm beds $17, singles/double $20/35. Set on Innisfail's high ground in a renovated house, it has a spacious back balcony with views across to the river. It's one of the best budget places in FNQ.

**Walkabout Motel & Backpacker** (☎ 4061 2311, fax 4061 4919, e motelwalkabout@

*bigpond.com, Ernest St)* Dorm beds $15, motel doubles $55. Dorms have TV, fans and en suite, while the motel rooms have all the standard facilities. It's a friendly place with a comfortable TV area and a good kitchen.

***Barrier Reef Motel*** *(☎ 4061 4988, fax 4061 2896, Bruce Hwy)*. Singles/ doubles $70/78. At the top-end of the range, this motel has a licensed bar and restaurant.

## Places to Eat & Drink

If you're self catering, for fresh seafood head to ***Innisfail Fish Depot*** on Fitzgerald Esplanade. There's also a ***supermarket*** in the Central Arcade on Edith St.

***Oliveri's Continental Deli*** *(☎ 4061 3354, 41 Edith St)*. Rolls from $5.50. Running for 78 years, it's one of the few remaining authentic Italian delis in Innisfail and makes delicious filled panini rolls (perfect to eat by the river).

***Innisfail RSL*** *(☎ 4061 1601, 18 Fitzgerald Esplanade)* Meals from $3.80. It not only has the best river views in town, but it's one of the cheapest places to eat. It's typical RSL food of meat and three veg.

***Ultra Lounge Innisfail*** *(☎/fax 4061 9490, 2 Edith St)* Meals from $9.80. If you want something a little more sophisticated but still alfresco, head to Ultra Lounge. It has a good mod Oz menu, and a changing gallery of work by local artists lines the walls.

***Roscoe's Piazza*** *(☎ 4061 6888, 3B Ernest St)* Open 5pm-10.30pm. Pizza from $10. A popular local pizzeria, it also has an all-you-can-eat buffet on weeknights for only $12.90.

If you're feeling thirsty, head to the renovated ***Queen's Hotel*** on Rankin St in the centre of town, or the ***Canecutter's Hotel*** on the Esplanade.

## Getting There & Around

Innisfail is on the main north-south railway line. Mission Beach Bus & Coach (☎ 4068 7400) runs from Mission Beach to Innisfail ($12, three daily) and from Innisfail to Cairns

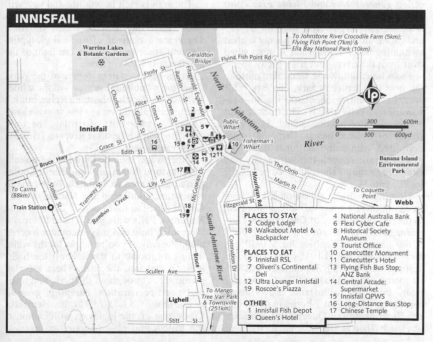

**INNISFAIL**

To Johnstone River Crocodile Farm (5km); Flying Fish Point (7km) & Ella Bay National Park (10km)

Warrina Lakes & Botanic Gardens
Geraldton Bridge
Flying Fish Point Rd
Emily St
Rankin St
Charles St
Alice St
Owen St
Gladys St
Ernest St
Fitzgerald Esplanade
North Johnstone
Innisfail
Public Wharf
Grace St
Edith St
Fisherman's Wharf
River
Bruce Hwy
Lily St
McGowan Dr
The Corso
Banana Island Environmental Park
To Cairns (88km)
Station St
Tramway St
Bamboo Creek
Martin St
Mourilyan Rd
To Coquette Point
Train Station
Fitzgerald St
Webb
Sullen Ave
South Johnstone River
Bruce Hwy
Coronation Dr
To Mango Tree Van Park & Townsville (251km)
Lighell
Stitt St

| PLACES TO STAY | | 4 National Australia Bank |
| 2 Codge Lodge | | 6 Flexi Cyber Cafe |
| 18 Walkabout Motel & Backpacker | | 8 Historical Society Museum |
| | | 9 Tourist Office |
| PLACES TO EAT | | 10 Canecutter Monument |
| 5 Innisfail RSL | | 11 Canecutter's Hotel |
| 7 Oliveri's Continental Deli | | 13 Flying Fish Bus Stop; ANZ Bank |
| 12 Ultra Lounge Innisfail | | 14 Central Arcade; Supermarket |
| 19 Roscoe's Piazza | | 15 Innisfail QPWS |
| | | 16 Long-Distance Bus Stop |
| OTHER | | 17 Chinese Temple |
| 1 Innisfail Fish Depot | | |
| 3 Queen's Hotel | | |

0    300    600m
0    300    600yd

($19, three daily). McCafferty's/Greyhound run services between Mission Beach and Cairns, which stop at Innisfail at the bus centre opposite King George V Park on Edith St ($16, one hour, four daily).

Hasties Bus Service (☎ 4061 2043) runs between Innisfail (from outside the ANZ Bank on the corner of Rankin and Edith Sts) and Flying Fish Point ($2.50, seven daily).

## AROUND INNISFAIL

Head east over the Geraldton Bridge to Flying Fish Point Rd and the **Johnstone River Crocodile Farm**, (☎ *4061 1121,* W *www .crocfarm.com, Flying Fish Point Rd; adult/ child $13/6; open 8.30am-4.30pm daily, feeding times 11am & 3pm)*. Tours run frequently, but the testosterone-addled guides seemingly provoke the crocs. A walk around on your own might be a more adult experience! The park also has wallabies and cassowaries.

North-east of Innisfail (7km), the sleepy community of **Flying Fish Point** has a post office, *general store* and *Flying Fish Point Van Park (☎ 4061 3131, fax 4061 8533)* with unpowered/powered sites for $17/19 and cabins from $45 to $70. It's not a great swimming beach – the water is often silted over from the river – but it's a pretty spot.

From here, follow the signs 5km north to the gem of a national park, **Ella Bay**. This area has a small concentration of **cassowaries**, so drive slowly. The track ends at a locked gate, beyond which is a long stretch of isolated beach. Camping is not permitted within the national park, but there's a basic council-run self-registration *camping ground* a short distance before the locked gate ($7.70).

Heading north along the Bruce Hwy from Innisfail, there's a turn-off after about 8km to the tiny community of **Garradunga**. *Garradunga Hotel (☎ 4063 3708, fax 4063 3708)* has singles/doubles for $20/30 and meals for around $14. It's open noon to 1.30pm and 6pm to 8.30pm. Built in 1888, its rooms are good value. 'The Garra', like many pubs in Queensland, crows about serving up the biggest T-bones in the Southern Hemisphere (all Queensland publicans obviously shop at the same butcher!).

## WEST OF INNISFAIL

The Palmerston Hwy leaves the Bruce Hwy 4km north-west of Innisfail and winds westward up to the Atherton Tableland, passing through organic tea plantations, gently sloping farming land and **Wooroonooran National Park**, part of the Wet Tropics World Heritage Area. The highway follows the original route taken by the bushman, gold prospector and explorer Christie Palmerston.

The Palmerston section of Wooroonooran National Park is one of the richest biological regions in Australia. Its fertile soil and super-wet climate (3500mm annually) support some of the oldest continually surviving rainforest in Australia. There are some gorgeous walking trails through the park, leading to waterfalls and creeks, and linking the picnic and camping grounds. There's a rangers station (☎ 4064 5115) at the eastern entrance to the park, 33km from Innisfail, where you can pick up a copy of the self-guided trail brochure.

The area is rich in wildlife and you will probably cross paths with quite a few creatures, including Boyd's forest dragons. There are a number of marked **platypus-viewing areas**, with first or last light of the day the best viewing time.

At the south-eastern corner of the park, **Crawford's Lookout** has views of the white-water of the North Johnstone River, but it's worth the walk down to view it at a closer distance. At the time of writing, the walk from the North Johnstone River to Tchupala Falls was closed.

Other walks include **Crawford's Lookout to Johnstone River** (one hour, 2km), **Goolagan's picnic area to Tchupala Falls** (one to two hours, 3km) and the **Nandroya Falls Circuit** (three to four hours, 7.2km). On the Nandroya Falls walk you'll need to cross a swimming hole and may encounter leeches along the way. If you're not up for the walk, there's a lookout to the falls off the highway, further into the park. There are also picnic areas throughout the park, and a superb self-registration *camping ground (adult/family $3.85/15.40)* at **Henrietta Creek**, just off the highway, with composting toilets and coin-operated barbecues.

Water is available from the creek. A big downside is that March flies are in full force from September to March, so wear insect repellent and avoid wearing blue-coloured clothes – they're attracted to blue!

The Palmerston Hwy continues west to Millaa Millaa, passing the entrance to the 'waterfalls circuit' just before the town (see the Atherton Tableland section later in this chapter).

## JOSEPHINE FALLS

About 19km north of Innisfail there's a turn-off to Josephine Falls, 8km inland from the highway. It's an 800m walk from the carpark along a mossy creek to the falls, which offer swimming (though only if you're a reasonable swimmer) in a circle of natural, clear pools, fringed by the massive roots of towering trees. The smooth rocks connecting the pools are slippery and can be treacherous, and the flow can be powerful after rain, so observe the signs warning of the dangers – people have drowned here.

The falls are at the foot of the Bellenden Ker Range, which includes Queensland's highest peak, Mt Bartle Frere (1657m). The **Mt Bartle Frere Summit Track** leads from the Josephine Falls carpark to the summit. Don't underestimate this walk: the ascent is for fit, experienced and well-equipped walkers only – it's a 15km, 1500m vertical rise, two-day return trip, and rain and cloud can close in suddenly. There's also an alternative 10km return walk to Broken Nose.

You can self-register at the start of the walk ($3.85 per person), but it's advisable to get more information first from the rangers at the QPWS office in Innisfail (☎ 4061 4291) or Josephine Falls (☎ 4067 6304, fax 4067 6443).

## BRAMSTON BEACH & EUBENANGEE SWAMP NATIONAL PARK

On the Bruce Hwy a couple of kilometres north of the turn-off for Josephine Falls is the turn-off to the small community of Bramston Beach (with only a small *general store*). It's a 17km drive along a road hemmed in by seemingly impenetrable cane fields.

### Rainforest Nasties

As you're walking through the rainforest, watch out for a couple of plants to avoid. The gympie-gympie, also known as the stinging tree, can cause severe and long-lasting pain if you so much as brush against it, and this is easy to do because it grows best along cleared walking trails where there's plenty of sunlight. It has large, hairy, heart-shaped leaves with serrated edges and can grow up to 6m high.

Another is the lawyer vine, a fish-barbed climbing palm that trails from rainforest ferns. Once you're hooked, you'll have to patiently unhook – hence the plant's nickname of 'wait-a-while'.

MW

Bramston Beach is somewhat silted so you won't find the crystal-clear waters of Port Douglas, but it's still worthy of a dip (there's a marine stinger net in place during the stinger season) and there are views of the Frankland Islands from the shore; if you ask around, you may find a local willing to take you over to them for a cheaper price than you'll pay in Cairns.

If you're into fishing, one operator runs out to the Mulgrave, Russell and Johnstone Rivers – Bramston Beach Fishing Charters (☎ 4067 4186), which charges $65/110 for half-day/full-day trips.

There are some good places to stay.

***Bramston Beach Camping Ground*** (☎ *4067 4121, 96 Evans Rd*) 2-person tent sites $11.40. Right on the foreshore, the camping ground has hot showers and free gas barbecues.

***Bramston Beach Holiday Motel*** (☎ *4067 4139, fax 4067 4279, 1 Dawson St*) Motel singles/doubles $52/62, family room (sleeps 6) $95. Just by the water, the comfy rooms overlook a lush garden, and there's a nice camp kitchen and outdoor eating area. Take the first left as you enter town.

About 8km after you leave the highway to head to Bramston Beach, there's a turn-off just before the Alice River crossing to **Eubenangee Swamp National Park**. A 1.5km trail follows the Alice River (a waterway with a healthy croc population) through the mangroves and leads to an elevated grassy knoll overlooking a wetland that resembles Kakadu.

## BABINDA

Hidden behind a huge sugar mill that fronts the Bruce Hwy, Babinda is a small town of veranda-fronted buildings and old timber pubs, shadowed by the Bellenden Ker Range. The Yidinyji tribe occupied the land before white settlement, and the town's name is said to come from the Aboriginal *boorabinda* meaning 'valley of rain'. Its main road leads to the Babinda Boulders Wildland Park.

The Babinda Information Centre (☎ 4067 1008, corner of Munro St and Bruce Hwy) has information on Babinda and Bramston Beach. The town has the usual *takeaway* places if you want to stop for a bite.

You can take a trip back in time at the old-fashioned **Munro Theatre** (☎ *4067 1032, Munro St; movies 7.30pm Fri-Sat*). The cinema dates back to the 1950s and still has hessian-slung seats and a canvas-covered ceiling (to achieve the best acoustics). It's the only cinema in the area and people come from far and wide to see a flick.

Formerly known as the State Hotel, **Babinda Hotel**, an imposing Federation-style pub on Munro St, was built in 1917 as Queensland's only state hotel and, between 1917 and 1930, it controlled the sale of alcohol, which was otherwise prohibited within the Babinda Sugar Works Area! Its bars were once regularly flooded with cane cutters at the end of their shift.

## BABINDA BOULDERS & THE GOLDFIELD TRACK

Seven kilometres inland from Babinda, the Boulders is a truly lovely spot where a fast-running creek rushes between blocks of 4m-high textured granite. Grassy areas and a gentle clear-water swimming hole make it a perfect picnic spot. Walking trails lead to **Devil's Pool Lookout** (470m) and the **Boulders Gorge Lookout** (600m). There's a fierce undertow between these sections and signs warn of the danger of swimming – many people have lost their lives here. A suspension bridge takes you across the river to an 850m circuit through the rainforest.

The free ***Boulder Camping Area***, run by Cairns City Council, is a picturesque camping ground, with toilets and cold showers, right by the reserve.

Closer to the Boulders than to the town is ***Eden Springs*** (☎ *4067 2096, Boulders Rd*) with rooms for $60.50 including breakfast. Run by a French couple, this 20-hectare B&B has fine views of both Bellenden Ker and Bartle Frere.

From the Boulders you can walk the **Goldfield Track** – first opened up in the 1930s when there was a minor gold rush. It leads 10km to the Goldsborough Valley, across a saddle in the Bellenden Ker Range. The track ends at a causeway on the Mulgrave River, where a forestry road leads 8km to a *camping ground* in the **Goldsborough Valley State Forest**. From there it's 15km on to the Gillies Hwy between Gordonvale and Atherton. Expect leeches and a fairly difficult trek. Wooroonooran Safaris (☎ 4051 2708) in Cairns offers a one-day trek from $95.

## GORDONVALE

Back on the Bruce Hwy, Gordonvale is a small town overshadowed not only by the worn steel structures of its sugar mill, but also by the remarkable symmetry of **Walshs Pyramid** (922m). The town sits near the base of the mountain, at the northern tip of

A flock of Australian pelicans

Lotus flower, Keatings Lagoon

Cape Tribulation and Daintree National Park rainforest, Far North Queensland

Chillagoe-Mungana Caves NP

A Far North Queensland sunset

Trinity Inlet, Cairns, named by Captain Cook on Trinity Sunday 1770

Papaya – great with a squeeze of lemon

Fan palm detail, Cape Tribulation National Park

Peninsula Development Rd, near Cooktown

Wooroonooran National Park. It has all the usual facilities and there's an ATM on Norman St, opposite the park.

During the cane cutting season (July to December), you can take a two-hour tour of the **Mulgrave Central Mill** (*☎ 4033 6103, Gordon St; adult/child $17/8; tours 2pm & 7.30pm Mon-Fri*). There's also a half-day tour of a working cane farm (11.15am). Close by is the small **Settlers' Museum** (*☎ 4056 1810, Gordon St; adult/child $3/1; open 10am-3pm Mon-Sat*). It has a display on the European settlement of the Mulgrave Valley, including conflict between the settlers and the local Yidinyji tribe.

The ***Gordonvale Hotel*** (*☎ 4056 1131, fax 4056 3013, 82 Norman St)* has rooms for $22 per person. This pub is the best place to stay in town. An old Queenslander, its balcony has dreamy views across to Walshs Pyramid and it offers ***meals*** ( $6 to $10).

McCafferty's/Greyhound stops here and Sunbus runs to/from Cairns hourly.

## GORDONVALE TO YUNGABURRA

The winding Gillies Hwy leads up onto the Atherton Tableland. It's 43km from here to Yungaburra (one hour). The first section twists and climbs steeply as you head up into the mountains, and you can feel the temperature drop as you climb higher.

Just near the turn-off to Yungaburra is the ***Mountain View Hotel*** (*☎ 4056 1723, Gillies Hwy)*. It's open for lunch and dinner from Monday to Saturday and its beer garden facing the Mulgrave River is a great spot for a meal. Try the Cane Cutter's lunch, the Mountain View's version of a Ploughman's lunch.

## YARRABAH ABORIGINAL COMMUNITY & AROUND
postcode 4871 • pop 1978

Midway between Gordonvale and Edmonton is a turn-off to the Yarrabah Aboriginal community. It's a scenic 37km drive through cane fields and mountains to Yarrabah, offering glimpses of Cairns across the inlet. Yarrabah was established in 1892 as a Christian mission by John Gribble, who was determined to establish a 'sanctuary' for the

dispossessed Gungganyji and Yidinyji tribes of the Cairns and Tableland area.

Unlike many Aboriginal communities, permission to visit is not necessary, although as a courtesy, please drop by the Yarrabah Aboriginal Council (☎ 4056 9120) on Sawmill Rd and let them know that you're visiting. It's the large building on the right as you enter town.

The Yarrabah community is set on Mission Bay, a pretty cove backed by palm trees and decorated with the rusting hulls of two ships. In town visit the **Yarrabah Menmuny Museum** (*☎ 4056 9145, Back Beach Rd; adult/child $5.50/3.30; open 8.30am-4.30pm Mon-Fri)*, which has a collection of Aboriginal artefacts and cultural exhibits. It also has spear throwing demonstrations and a guided boardwalk tour ($13.20/9.90, including admission). To reach the museum turn right at the police station. It's down the road opposite the high school.

About 3km after you leave the highway to head to Yarrabah, there's another turn-off to the **Cairns Crocodile Farm** (*☎ 4056 3095, Redbank Rd, via Gordonvale; adult/child $12.10/6.60; open 9am-4.30pm)*, a further 5km down the road. This place is very different from most croc farms – it's not here to entertain tourists, it's a commercial breeding and hatching farm with over 10,000 crocs housed in its enclosures. Feeding time is at 2pm, and it's worth a visit.

# Cairns

postcode 4870 • pop 106,000

Cairns has the somewhat mythical position as one of Australia's top destinations. While the city's bedrock culture and economy is tourism, many travellers who arrive after the trek or drive up the eastern coast are bound to be disappointed: Cairns is surrounded by mangrove swamps to the south and north – not turquoise-blue beaches. The sea in front of the town is shallow and at low tide it becomes a long sweep of mud. The waterbirds and the surrounding mountains are certainly picturesque, but going for a splash isn't an option.

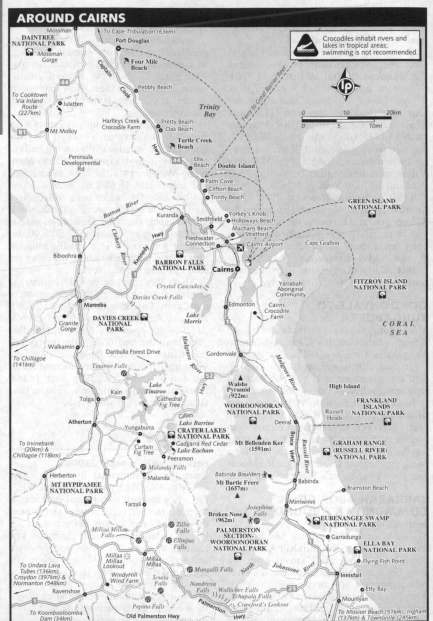

# AROUND CAIRNS

Crocodiles inhabit rivers and lakes in tropical areas; swimming is not recommended.

DAINTREE NATIONAL PARK

Mossman

Mossman Gorge

To Cooktown Via Inland Route (227km)

Julatten

Mt Molloy

Peninsula Developmental Rd

Port Douglas

To Cape Tribulation (63km)

Four Mile Beach

Pebbly Beach

Captain Cook

Hartleys Creek Crocodile Farm

Pretty Beach
Oak Beach

Turtle Creek Beach

Ellis Beach

Double Island

Trinity Bay

Ferry to Great Barrier Reef

GREEN ISLAND NATIONAL PARK

Palm Cove
Clifton Beach
Trinity Beach

Barron River

Kuranda

Smithfield

Yorkey's Knob
Holloways Beach
Machans Beach
Stratford

Cairns Airport

Cape Grafton

FITZROY ISLAND NATIONAL PARK

Freshwater Connection

BARRON FALLS NATIONAL PARK

Cairns

Yarrabah Aboriginal Community

Biboohra

Clohesy River

Kennedy Hwy

Crystal Cascades

Davies Creek Falls

Mareeba

DAVIES CREEK NATIONAL PARK

Granite Gorge

Walkamin

Lake Morris

Edmonton

Cairns Crocodile Farm

CORAL SEA

To Chillagoe (141km)

Danbulla Forest Drive

Tinaroo Falls

Gordonvale

Malgrave River

High Island

Tolga

Kairi

Lake Tinaroo

Cathedral Fig Tree

Gillies

Walshs Pyramid (922m)

WOOROONOORAN NATIONAL PARK

Russell Heads

FRANKLAND ISLANDS NATIONAL PARK

Atherton

Yungaburra

Lake Barrine

CRATER LAKES NATIONAL PARK

Deeral

To Irvinebank (20km) & Chillagoe (118km)

Curtain Fig Tree

Gadgarra Red Cedar
Lake Eacham

Mt Bellenden Ker (1591m)

GRAHAM RANGE (RUSSELL RIVER) NATIONAL PARK

Peeramon

Herberton

Malanda Falls

Malanda

Babinda Boulders

Mt Bartle Frere (1657m)

Babinda

Bramston Beach

MT HYPIPAMEE NATIONAL PARK

Tarzali

Mirriwinni

Broken Nose (962m)

Josephine Falls

EUBENANGEE SWAMP NATIONAL PARK

Millaa Millaa Falls

Zillie Falls

Ellinjaa Falls

PALMERSTON SECTION-WOOROONOORAN NATIONAL PARK

Garradunga

ELLA BAY NATIONAL PARK

Flying Fish Point

To Undara Lava Tubes (136km), Croydon (397km) & Normanton (548km)

Millaa Millaa Lookout

Millaa Millaa

Mungalli Falls

North Johnstone River

WindyHill Wind Farm

Souita Falls

Ravenshoe

Pepina Falls

Old Palmerston Hwy

Nandroya Falls

Wallicher Falls

Tchupala Falls

Crawford's Lookout

Palmerston Hwy

Innisfail

Etty Bay

Mourilyan

To Koombooloomba Dam (34km)

To Mission Beach (51km), Ingham (137km) & Townsville (245km)

0   10   20km
0   5   10mi

A swimming area is something that has created conversation since Cairns was established. In 1901 the Baths Committee was keen to establish netting baths, commenting that, 'a seaport town without baths, or any place for a dip, is an anomaly which requires removing'.

Today the local government has ambitions to remove the anomaly – plans are afoot to build a 4000 sq metre saltwater swimming lagoon on the Esplanade, with sandy beaches and picnic and barbecue facilities.

So while you can't go for a dip (except in your hotel pool), the city does make an excellent base for exploring the Great Barrier Reef and nearby areas of FNQ. The city is also an adventurer's paradise. It's a centre for scuba diving, white-water rafting, canoeing, horse riding, sky diving, bungee jumping and the jungle swing craze 'minjin'. Anything is possible here, and tourism operators will bend over backwards to make sure visitors have a great holiday.

Lots of international travellers start or finish their Australian odyssey in Cairns and, with or without 'a place for a dip', wild celebrations seem to be in order.

## HISTORY
Trinity Bay was named by Captain Cook, who sighted the bay on Trinity Sunday in 1770. Cairns began life in 1876 as a beachhead among the mangroves, intended as a port for the Hodgkinson River goldfield 100km inland. Initially it struggled under rivalry from Smithfield, 15km to the north, and Port Douglas, founded in 1877 after Christie Palmerston discovered an easier route to the goldfield. Fortunately for Cairns, a flood blithely washed Smithfield away in 1879 and Cairns was chosen as the starting point for the railway line through the Atherton Tableland to Herberton during the 1880 'tin-rush'. Its supremacy was consolidated as the Tableland was opened up for agriculture and timber.

By 1947 Cairns had a population of just 16,000, but fuelled by a booming sugar industry it grew rapidly through the 1950s and 1960s. The tourist floodgates opened in 1984 when the airport opened, and Cairns has never looked back.

## ORIENTATION
The centre of Cairns is quite compact and most places of interest are contained in the area between the Esplanade and Wharf, McLeod and Aplin Sts. The main departure points for reef trips are Great Adventures Wharf, Marlin Jetty and the Pier Marina, all just off Wharf St (the southern continuation of the Esplanade). Further south along Wharf St is Trinity Wharf, with a cruise-liner dock and transit centre for long-distance buses.

Back from the waterfront is City Place, a pedestrian mall at the meeting of Shields and Lake Sts, which has free lunch-time concerts every day. Cairns train station is hidden inside Cairns Central shopping centre on McLeod St.

The airport is about 7km north of the city centre, just south of the Barron River estuary.

### Maps
Absells Chart & Map Centre (☎ 4041 2699, @ absells@iig.com.au, Andrejic Arcade, 55 Lake St) sells an impressive range of topographic, nautical and area maps, including detailed maps of Cape York.

## INFORMATION
There's no shortage of tourist information in Cairns, and you'll need it because the choices are awesome. There are dozens of privately run 'information centres' in Cairns (which are basically tour-booking agencies) while most places to stay, including backpackers hostels, also have tour-booking desks. Some, but not all, will be pushing the tours that give them the best commission (minimum of 10%). However, they'll also be offering you tours that suit your budget or your adventure threshold.

Most places to stay will implore you to book tours through them – simply said, they want the extra commission dollars (sometimes staff are paid a percentage of the tour commissions). If you've looked at a range of tour options (including diving courses) and you're happy with your accommodation and the service you've received, by all means book through them. If you're not, book elsewhere (and find somewhere else to stay while you're at it).

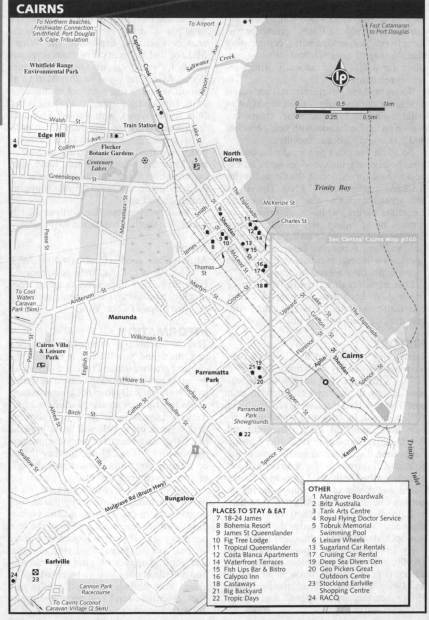

# CAIRNS

To Northern Beaches,
Freshwater Connection
Smithfield, Port Douglas
& Cape Tribulation

To Airport

Fast Catamaran
to Port Douglas

Whitfield Range
Environmental Park

Saltwater Creek

Trinity Bay

See Central Cairns map p360

Edge Hill

Flecker
Botanic Gardens

Centenary
Lakes

North
Cairns

McKenzie St

Charles St

To Cool
Waters
Caravan Park (5km)

Manunda

Cairns Villa
& Leisure
Park

Parramatta
Park

Cairns

Trinity Inlet

Parramatta
Park Showgrounds

Bungalow

Earlville

Cannon Park
Racecourse

To Cairns Coconut
Caravan Village (2.5km)

**PLACES TO STAY & EAT**
7 18-24 James
8 Bohemia Resort
9 James St Queenslander
10 Fig Tree Lodge
11 Tropical Queenslander
12 Costa Blanca Apartments
14 Waterfront Terraces
15 Fish Lips Bar & Bistro
16 Calypso Inn
18 Castaways
21 Big Backyard
22 Tropic Days

**OTHER**
1 Mangrove Boardwalk
2 Britz Australia
3 Tank Arts Centre
4 Royal Flying Doctor Service
5 Tobruk Memorial
   Swimming Pool
6 Leisure Wheels
13 Sugarland Car Rentals
17 Cruising Car Rental
19 Deep Sea Divers Den
20 Geo Pickers Great
   Outdoors Centre
23 Stockland Earlville
   Shopping Centre
24 RACQ

## Tourist Offices

Two of the more useful information centres in Cairns are:

**Tourism Tropical North Queensland** (☎ 4031 7676, fax 4051 0127, **W** www.tnq.org.au) 51 The Esplanade. This information centre is government run, and can book tours and give you info on the local area.

**AccomCairns** (☎ 4051 3200, fax 4031 1813, **e** robyn@holidaycairns.com.au) 127 Sheridan St. This is a reputable holiday accommodation booking agency that can find you a bed from backpacker budget to five star. It also specialises in accessible tourism information.

## Money

All the major banks have branches in central Cairns, most have foreign exchange sections. ATMs are located throughout the city and Cairns Central shopping centre There's a Thomas Cook (☎ 4031 3040) at 13 Spence St and American Express Travel (☎ 4051 8811) has a branch upstairs in Orchid Plaza on Abbott St (accessible also via Lake St).

## Post & Communications

The main Australia Post office (corner of Grafton and Hartley Sts) is open on weekdays 8.30am till 5pm. There are also Australia Post branches in Orchid Plaza, accessible via either Abbott or Lake Sts, and in Cairns Central shopping centre. The Grafton St post office has the only poste restante service.

Many hostels now offer Internet access, either free or for around $3 to $4 an hour. In Cairns, Abbott St is the Internet cafe Mecca, with most places opening around 8.30am and closing around 11.30pm. Expect to pay around $3 to $5 an hour. Many also offer cheap international calls. A few include:

**Call Station** (☎ 4052 1572) 123 Abbott St
**Global Gossip** (☎ 4031 6411) 125 Abbott St
**Traveller's Contact Point** (☎ 4041 4677) 1st floor, 13 Shields St

## Travel Agencies

Recommended travel agencies include:

**Backpackers Travel Centre** (☎ 4051 1500, **e** cairns@backpackerstravel.net.au) Corner of Shields St and The Esplanade. Recommended

by readers, it does the usual local and national tour bookings. It also has French-speaking staff.
**Gulf Savannah Tourist Organisation** (☎ 4051 4658) 74 Abbott St
**Rendez-Vous Futé** (☎ 4031 3533, **e** pascalegerson@dingoblue.net.au) 28 Spence St. This French-speaking travel agency can book local and national tours and tickets.
**STA Travel** (☎ 4031 4199, **e** shield@statravel .com.au) 9 Shields St
**Trailfinders** (☎ 4041 1199, fax 4041 1339) Hides Corner, Lake St

## Useful Organisations

For more than the usual tourist information, try these places:

**Community Information Service** (☎ 4051 4953, **W** www.cisci.org.au) Tropical Arcade, Corner of Shield and Abbott Sts. It has info on local activities.
**Queensland Parks & Wildlife Service** (QPWS; ☎ 4046 6600) 10 McLeod St. Dealing with national park camping permits, including permits for Frankland and Lizard Islands, and walking trail information, it's open from 8.40am to 4.30pm Monday to Friday.
**Royal Automobile Club of Queensland** (RACQ; ☎ 4033 6711) 520 Mulgrave St, Earlville. RACQ is a good place to get maps and information on road conditions, especially if you're driving up to Cape York. It also has a 24-hour recorded road report service (☎ 1300 130 595).
**The Wilderness Society** (☎ 4051 8967) 69 Grafton St. The society has a Cape York campaign office and welcomes volunteers.

## Bookshops

Walker's Bookshop (☎ 4031 1433, Cairns Central shopping centre) has a good range of titles, but for specialist titles on Australia's natural landscape we recommend you head to Australian Geographic (☎ 4041 6211), located at Shop 3, Ground Level, Pier Marketplace.

At the popular Exchange Bookshop (☎ 4051 1443, 78 Grafton St) books can be bought, sold and exchanged.

## Cultural Centres

Alliance Française is based at the travel agency, Rendez-Vous Futé (see Travel Agencies earlier in this entry).

## Photography

For all your photography needs, head to Garricks Camera House (☎ 4031 8466, Cairns Central shopping centre) or Smiths Camera & Video (☎ 4051 2125, 86 Lake St).

## Laundry

Most places to stay have laundry facilities, but if you need a laundrette, try Cairns City Laundromat (☎ 4051 9413) at 49 Grafton St.

## Left Luggage

Cairns airport has storage lockers and most places to stay will also store baggage while you head off elsewhere.

## Medical Services

Cairns City 24 Hour Medical Centre (☎ 4052 1119), on the corner of Florence and Grafton Sts, is a full emergency, general, diving and travel medical service. The Cairns Base Hospital (☎ 4050 6333) is on the Esplanade, just north of the centre, and has a casualty ward. A free Sexual Health Clinic (☎ 4050 6205) also operates from the hospital.

## Emergency

If you need the police, an ambulance or the fire department in an emergency, dial 000, ask the operator for the service you need and wait to be connected. This is a 24-hour, free call, which can be traced. Other numbers are:

**Cairns Rape Crisis Service** (24 hours)
  ☎ 4031 3590
**Police** (local) ☎ 4030 7000

## Dangers & Annoyances

Theft can be an infrequent problem in some budget places to stay, although it's generally only an issue in places that can be entered from one street and exited from another; use safes if they're available.

Private security guards patrol the Esplanade, but it's best not to walk alone along the northern end late at night. Munro Martin Park is also somewhere to avoid at night.

One thing you should keep aware of is the likelihood of sea sickness on reef trips, as one reader thunderously discovered.

I boarded…a boat out of Cairns to make the 2½-hour journey to the Great Barrier Reef. About an hour from land, I found myself standing on the lower deck at the back of the boat trying to keep my breakfast down, when someone from the top deck threw up on someone below on the lower deck! The guy next to me saw that and threw up too! I saw him get sick and promptly threw up as well. Chain reaction! The moral of the story: Anyone taking a reef trip…should take a seasickness tablet.

**Karli de Vries**

## Gay & Lesbian Travellers

Cairns' gay and lesbian scene generally livens up before and after Sydney's Gay & Lesbian Mardi Gras. A good initial contact is the Gay & Lesbian Recorded Information Service (☎ 4041 6146) and the free what's on magazine *Bar Fly*, which has a Gay Fly section.

The Gay Men's Tour Company (☎ 4031 5011, e michael@boyzbrickroad.com.au, w www.boyzbrickroad.com.au) can provide travel information.

## THINGS TO SEE & DO

Cairns itself has relatively few attractions. The **Esplanade Walking Trail** follows the foreshore for almost 3km north from the centre of town. It makes for a peaceful (or energetic) stroll, with views over to the mountains across the estuary. If you're up early and the tides are right, you'll often see locals netting for prawns.

The booming developments of the 1980s and '90s have engulfed most of Cairns' older buildings. The oldest part of town is the **Trinity Wharf** area, but even this area has been redeveloped. There are still some imposing neoclassical buildings from the 1920s on Abbott St, and the frontages around the corner of Spence and Lake Sts date from 1909 to 1926.

The **Cairns Regional Gallery** *(☎ 4031 6865, w www.cairnsregionalgallery.com .au, Cnr Abbott & Shields Sts; admission $4, children under 10 free; open 10am-6pm Mon-Fri, 1pm-6pm Sat & Sun)* is housed in a cleverly restored historic building. Changing exhibitions focus on work by FNQ and international artists.

Right in the centre of town, the **Cairns Museum** *(☎ 4051 5582, Cnr Lake & Shields Sts; adult/child $4/2; open 10am-3pm Mon-Sat)* is housed in the 1907 School of Arts building. The museum has Aboriginal artefacts, a display on the construction of the Cairns to Kuranda railway, the contents of a now-demolished Grafton St Chinese temple and exhibits on the Palmer River and Hodgkinson River goldfields.

The **Pier Marketplace** *(☎ 4051 7244; open 9am-9pm)* is a glossy shopping plaza with expensive boutiques, souvenir shops, a food hall, cafes and restaurants. On weekends the **Mud Markets** are held here, with a wide range of stalls selling food and local arts and crafts. Also here is **Undersea World** *(☎ 4041 1777; adult/child $12.50/7; open 8am-8pm Mon-Sun)*, a small aquarium. If you didn't get a chance to snorkel or dive while in FNQ, a visit here will only fill you with regret! Shark feeding takes place four times daily.

The markets at **Rusty's Bazaar** *(Between Spence & Shields Sts; open 6am-6pm Fri, 6am-2pm Sat & Sun)* are great for people-watching and browsing among the dozens of stalls that sell fruit and vegies and bric a brac.

The **Flecker Botanic Gardens** *(☎ 4044 3398, Collins Ave, Edge Hill; open 7.30am-5.30pm Mon-Fri, 8.30am-5.30pm Sat & Sun)* are 4km north-west from the centre of Cairns. The gardens have various sections, including an interesting Aboriginal plant-use area and there are guided walks through the gardens every weekday at 1pm *(adult/child $5/free)*. The Botanic Gardens Restaurant is a fine place to stop for lunch (see the later Places to Eat entry for more information). Over the road from the gardens, a boardwalk leads through a patch of rainforest to **Saltwater Creek** and **Centenary Lakes**.

Near the gardens is the entrance to the **Mt Whitfield Range Conservation Park**, the last remnant of Cairns rainforest and once home to a small cassowary population. The **Red Arrow Trail** (one hour) and the **Blue Arrow Trail** (3½ hours) both offer good views over the city and coast. You can get to the botanic gardens with Sunbus or Cairns Discovery Tours.

The **Tanks Arts Centre**, *(☎ 4032 2349, 46 Collins Ave, Edge Hill)*, just north of the Botanic Gardens, is one of Cairns' most interesting art spaces. These circular cement and iron WWII naval supply tanks have been transformed into an exhibition and function centre.

Also in Edge Hill is the regional office of the **Royal Flying Doctor Service** *(RFDS; ☎ 4053 5687, 1 Junction St; adults $5.50/2.75; open 9.30am-4.30pm Mon-Sat)*. At the Visitors Centre you'll learn about the origins and workings of this unique remote-area medical service, which first flew in 1928. Take bus No 5A, 6 or 6A from Lake St and ask the driver to let you off at the nearest stop to the RFDS.

Heading out of Cairns towards the airport, you'll discover Cairns' best-kept secret (perhaps because it's free!), an elevated **mangrove boardwalk**. Signs explain the ecological complexities of mangrove forests, and there's a small observation platform. It's off Airport Ave, about 200m before the airport. Take a taxi, the airport bus or walk.

Kamerunga Rd, off the Cook Hwy just north of the airport turn-off, leads inland to the pretty Kuranda Scenic Railway stop of **Freshwater Connection** *(☎ 4055 222, open 7am-5pm)*. It has a museum, gardens and a *restaurant* with meals from $3.50 to $10, but it closes at 2pm. It's 10km from the centre of town. Just beyond Freshwater is the turn-off south along Redlynch Intake Rd to **Crystal Cascades**, a popular destination 22km from Cairns, with waterfalls and swimming holes.

**Tjapukai Cultural Park** *(☎ 4042 9999, W www.tjapukai.com.au, Kamerunga Rd, Carevonica; adult/child $66/37.75 including transfers from Cairns or Palm Cove, $27/13.50 without transfers; open 9am-5pm daily)* is a fascinating complex that incorporates a cultural village and a traditional dance theatre, as well as a museum. The history theatre discusses the experiences of Aboriginal people following white contact. The park is beside the Skyrail terminal at Smithfield, just off the Captain Cook Hwy, about 15km north of the centre.

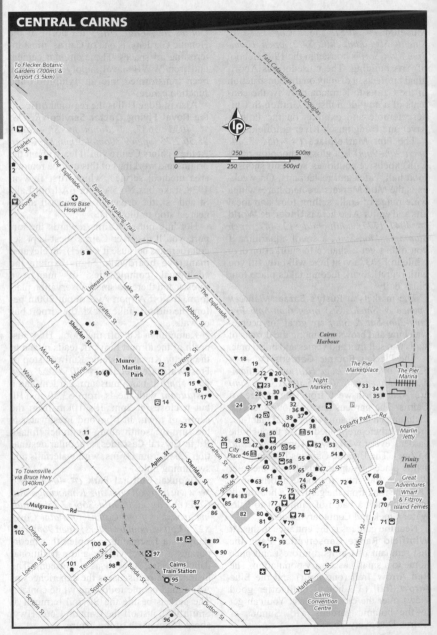

CENTRAL CAIRNS

To Flecker Botanic
Gardens (700m) &
Airport (3.5km)

Fast Catamaran to Port Douglas

Charles St

The Esplanade

Esplanade Walking Trail

Grove St

Cairns Base
Hospital

Upward St

Lake St

Grafton St

Sheridan St

McLeod St

Minnie St

Water St

Munro
Martin
Park

Florence St

The Esplanade

Abbott St

Cairns
Harbour

The Pier
Marketplace

The Pier
Marina

Night
Markets

Fogarty Park Rd

Marlin
Jetty

Trinity
Inlet

Aplin St

Grafton St

City
Place

Sheridan St

Shields St

Spence St

Wharf St

Great
Adventures
Wharf
& Fitzroy
Island Ferries

To Townsville
via Bruce Hwy
(340km)

Mulgrave Rd

McLeod St

Draper St

Loeven St

Terminus St

Bunda St

Cairns
Train Station

Scott St

Severn St

Dutton St

Hartley St

Cairns
Convention
Centre

0        250        500m
0        250        500yd

## CENTRAL CAIRNS

**PLACES TO STAY**
2  Coral Cay Villas
3  Floriana Guesthouse
5  The Balinese
7  Cascade Gardens Apartments
8  Caravella Backpackers 149
9  Poinsettia Motel
16  Cairns Girls Hostel
19  All Seasons Esplanade
20  YHA On The Esplanade;
     The Chapel Cafe
21  Hostel 89
29  Il Palazzo
30  Royal Harbour Tradewinds
31  Jimmy's On The Esplanade
32  Caravella Backpackers 77
35  Radisson Plaza Hotel
36  International Hostel;
     Rattle 'n' Hum Pub
54  Quality Hotel, Pacific
     International
57  Global Palace
60  Club Crocodile Hides Hotel;
     PJ O'Briens
62  Inn Cairns
67  The Great Northern
89  Macleod St Youth Hostel
98  Travellers Oasis
99  Gecko's Backpackers
100  Dreamtime Travellers Rest
101  Ryan's Rest

**PLACES TO EAT**
18  Chapter One Cafe
22  Meeting Place
25  Yanni's Greek Taverna
27  Java Joe's
33  Coffee Bean
34  Pesci's
64  Lillipad
68  Mondo
73  Midori Noodles Bar
79  Yama
83  Beethoven Cafe

84  La Fettucina
85  Red Ochre Grill
87  Mediterraneo
91  Taj
93  Tiny's Juice Bar

**OTHER**
1  Blue Mango Cafe Wine Bar
4  Cock & Bull
6  Billabong Car Rentals
10  Accom Cairns
11  Sheridan Rent A Car
12  Cairns City 24 Hour Medical
     Centre
13  Budget Rent A Car; All Day
     Bike Hire
14  Theatre
15  Leisure Wheels
17  Mike Ball Dive Expeditions
23  Johno's Blues Bar
24  Cairns Library
26  Cairns City Cinemas
28  Gulf Savannah Tourist
     Organisation
37  Backpackers Travel Centre
38  Tusa Dive
39  Air Niugini; Tropical Arcade;
     Community Information
     Service
40  Pro-Dive
41  Cairns Dive Centre
42  Call Station; Global Gossip
43  Taxi Stand
44  Bandicoot Bicycles
45  City Place Disposals
46  Cairns Museum
47  City Place Amphitheatre
48  Walker's Bookshop;
     All Bar One
49  Qantas & Sunstate Airlines
50  Wool Shed Chargrill & Saloon
51  Cairns Regional Gallery;
     Perrotta's at the Gallery
52  Court House Hotel

53  Tourism Tropical North
     Queensland
55  Woolworths
56  Traveller's Contact Point;
     STA; It's Extreme
58  Lake St Transit Centre
59  Smiths Camera & Video
61  Trailfinders
63  Exchange Bookshop
65  Orchid Plaza; Post Office;
     American Express; Sushi
     Express
66  Reef Teach
69  Cairns Yacht Club
70  Great Adventures Booking
     Office
71  Trinity Wharf; Transit Centre
72  Reef Casino
74  Thomas Cook &
     Ansett
75  Tropo's; Fox & Firkin
76  Underdog Hotel; White Car
     Coaches Terminus
77  Rendez-Vous Futé;
     It's Extreme
78  Sports Bar
80  Wilderness Society
81  Cairns City Laundromat
82  Rusty's Bazaar
86  Northern Disposals
88  Taxi Stand
90  Queensland Parks & Wildlife
     Service
92  Nu-Trix
94  Playpen International;
     Millennium Club
95  Cairns Train Station; Queens-
     land Rail Travel Centre;
     Kuranda Scenic Railway
96  Travellers Auto Barn
97  Cairns Central; Post Office;
     Central Cinemas; Garricks
     Camera House
102  Down Under Dive

## ACTIVITIES

There is a huge range of activities on offer leaving from Cairns, and this list is but a small sample.

### White-Water Rafting, Kayaking, Canoeing & Sailing

Three of the rivers flowing down from the Atherton Tableland make for some excellent white-water rafting. Most popular is a day in the rainforest gorges of the Tully River, 150km south of Cairns.

Day trips on the Tully leave daily from Cairns; Raging Thunder (☎ 1800 079 092, 4030 7990) and R'n'R (☎ 4051 4777) charge $145; there are cheaper half-day trips on the Barron River ($83) that run down to Cairns from Kuranda. There are also two-day ($450) or five-day ($815) expeditions (run by R'n'R) on the North Johnstone River.

Foaming Fury (☎ 4032 1460) offers white-water rafting ($145) on the Russell River south of Wooroonooran National Park, and half-day trips on the Barron River for $83.

The Adventure Company (☎ 4051 4777) has one-day wilderness canoe paddles on the Musgrave River ($110).

Cairns Yacht Club (☎/fax 4031 2750, Wharf St) has sailing sessions open to who-ever turns up on a Wednesday afternoon at 12.30pm. The price is a hefty $3 (for a bar-becue afterwards).

### Bicycle Tours

Bandicoot Bicycle Tours (☎ 4055 0155, 59 Sheridan St) offers a day-long bicycle tour of the Tableland for $98 each Monday, Wednesday and Friday.

Dan's Mountain Biking (☎ 4033 0128, W www.cairns.aust.com/mtb) has an ad-venturous range of tour destinations (in-cluding a night ride) from $59.

### Horse Riding

Blazing Saddles (☎ 4093 4493, Captain Cook Hwy, Palm Cove) and Springmount Station (☎ 4093 4493, Springmount Rd, Mutchilba), based near Mareeba, both offer a range of horse trail rides around Cairns, including half-day rides for around $88.

### Other Activities

At Smithfield, 15km north of the city centre, you can bungee jump from a steel tower with sensational views or try the lat-est heart-pumper, a jungle swing known as 'minjin', with AJ Hackett (☎ 4057 7188). Bungee jumping is $109, including trans-fers, and minjin solo/twin rides are $79/118.

Skydive Cairns (☎ 4035 9667) and Paul's Parachuting (☎ 4051 8855, W www .paulsparachuting.com.au) both have tandem skydiving from $228, or for air travel at a more leisurely pace, there are three balloon-ing outfits, all flying over Mareeba, with half-hour ($126) and one-hour flights ($186), including transfers and breakfast. Contact Raging Thunder (☎ 4030 7990), Hot Air (☎ 4039 2900, W www.hotair.com.au) or Champagne Balloon Flights (☎ 4058 1688, W champagneballoons.com.au).

Jet boat trips are on offer from Tropical Jet (☎ 4035 6599, The Pier) from $65, while Cairns Parasail Watersports Adven-ture (☎ 4031 7888, The Pier) does parasail-ing trips from $72.

Cairns Heli-Scenic (☎ 4031 5999) has a range of scenic flights from $140 to $340, in-cluding a half-hour flight over Cairns, Green Island, Yarrabah and the fringing reefs.

### DIVING COURSES

Cairns is one of the scuba-diving capitals of the Barrier Reef and one of the most popular places for PADI open-water certification.

There are a wide range of courses on offer, from no-frills, four-day courses (that com-bine pool training with a few day-trips to the reef, and start from about $280), to five-day courses that include two days of pool and theory, three days on a boat (known as a live-aboard) with multiple reef pleasure dives, in-cluding at least one night dive; these start from about $549. Unless you are particularly short on time or money, it's worth paying a little more for one of the longer courses – safety standards will generally be higher.

Divers who are already certified could consider taking advanced specialty courses. Many of these are on offer on live-aboard tours. See Diving Trips under Organised Tours later for more information, or contact any of the schools listed here. A selection of reputable dive schools in Cairns include:

**Down Under Dive** (☎ 1800 079 099, W www .downunderdive.com.au) 287 Draper St
**Deep Sea Divers Den** (☎ 4031 2223, W www.divers-den.com.au) 319 Draper St
**Cairns Dive Centre** (☎ 1800 642 591, 4051 0294, W www.cairnsdive.com.au) 121 Abbott St
**Pro-Dive** (☎ 4031 5255, W www.prodive-cairns .com.au) Corner of Abbot and Shields Sts
**Tusa Dive** (☎ 4031 1248, W www.tusadive .com) Corner of Shields St and The Esplanade

If you want to learn about the reef before you dive, Reef Teach (☎/fax 4031 7794, Boland's Centre, 14 Spence St) offers an entertaining and educational lecture nightly (except Sun-day) from 6.15pm to 8.30pm for $13. The lectures get rave reports from travellers.

## ORGANISED TOURS

As you'd expect, there are hundreds of tours available from Cairns. Some are specifically aimed at backpackers, with adventure the focus, while others offer more laid-back days out. Most tours on offer in Cairns are good value, with friendly guides. You can make bookings direct, through your accommodation or at travel information centres.

### Cairns

Some worthwhile tours of Cairns itself include:

**Cairns Discovery Tours** (☎ 4053 5259) Guided by horticulturalists, this tour takes in Cairns city, Flecker Botanic Gardens, the Royal Flying Doctor Service and Palm Cove. Tickets are $49/26 per adult/child and it leaves at 12.30pm.
**SS Louisa Paddlewheeler** (☎ 4054 1145) This delightfully tacky paddlewheeler travels the mangroves of Trinity Inlet and Admiralty Island, where you'll have a chance to do some croc spotting. The 2½-hour tour leaves Marlin Jetty at 10am and 1pm and costs $22/$8.80 for adults/children.

### Atherton Tableland

Tours to the high, green plateau of the Tableland include:

**On the Wallaby** (☎ 4050 0650) One-/two-/three-day tours are $70/130/150. Expect a lively guided tour of the Tableland, including wildlife-spotting and canoeing.
**Peach's off the Beaten Track** (☎ 4033 0242, W www.iig.com.au/peachy) This genuine 4WD trip journeys through disused logging tracks in World Heritage–listed areas west of Cairns. Tours are $105 for adults.
**Uncle Brian's Tours** (☎ 4050 0615) These tours of the Babinda-Josephine Falls-Lake Eacham area are always popular (despite their name) and cost $75/55.
**Tropical Horizons Day Tours** (☎ 4058 1244, W www.tropicalhorizonstours.com.au) Tours head to various areas of the Tableland, including Kuranda, and cost from $46.

### Wooroonooran National Park

For tours to the peaceful rainforest of Wooroonooran National Park, or a day walk along the 19km **Goldfield Trail** call Wooroonooran Safaris (☎ 4031 0800, W www.wooroonooran-safaris.com.au). German- and Italian-speaking guides are available; French- and Spanish-speaking guides will be available from April 2002. Tours cost from $119/99.

### Daintree River & Cape Tribulation

Daintree River and Cape Tribulation is one of the most popular destinations for day trips and there is a regular onslaught of vehicles that head there daily. Most operators use 4WD vehicles to give a 'safari feel' to the whole experience, but don't be misled into thinking that you can't do this trip yourself by rental car with ease – the well-signposted road is bitumen until just before Cape Trib Beach House and it's impossible to get lost! Most tours include an over-hyped Daintree River cruise (cruises along Trinity Inlet in Cairns and Dixon Inlet in Port Douglas are just as interesting).

**Trek North Safaris** (☎ 4051 4328) Trek North heads to Cape Trib stopping at Port Douglas, Mossman Gorge and Daintree Village for $120/82 per adult/child. It also has a tour to Daintree Village only ($99/60) with more of an emphasis on wildlife viewing.
**Native Guide Safari Tours** (☎ 4098 2206) This is an Aboriginal tour company running informative tours of the local area. They charge $130/90 from Cairns and $120/80 from Port Douglas.
**Jeni's Tours** (☎ 4036 3272) This small operator has tours to Cape Tribulation staying at a farmstay for $99 (two days) or $115 (three days).

### Cooktown

A good-value overnight 4WD-tour is Wilderness Challenge (☎ 4055 6504). It goes to Cooktown via **Split Rock Galleries**, an Aboriginal rock-art site outside Laura, and returns via the **Bloomfield Track**, for $330 to $365.

### Barrier Reef & Islands

There are dozens of options for day trips to the reef. Most tours include morning and afternoon tea, lunch and snorkelling gear. As a general rule, the outer reefs provide better diving – so check the trip's destination with the agent when you book. The majority of cruise boats depart from Trinity Wharf, Marlin Jetty or the Pier Marina at around 8am and return at around 6pm. All offer introductory dive and certified dive options. In addition to the list here, there are many, many boats and operators, so shop around.

**Great Adventures** (☎ 1800 079 080) This company has a wide range of combination cruises, including a day trip to either Norman or Moore Reefs, and Fitzroy or Green Islands. The trip includes rides in a semi-submersible and a glass-bottom boat (adult/child from $148/76, maximum 350 passengers).

**Compass** (☎ 1800 815 811, 4050 0666, W www .reeftrip.com) Compass heads out to Hastings Reef and Breaking Patches, and includes boom netting (adult/child $60/40, maximum 100 passengers).

**Noah's Ark Cruises** (☎ 4041 0036) A backpackers' favourite, Noah's Ark heads to Hastings Reef and Michaelmas Cay for a $70 day trip.

**Cairns Dive Centre** (☎ 1800 642 591, 4051 0294, W www.cairnsdive.com.au) The MV *Seakist* stops at Moore, Milln or Briggs Reefs ($71, maximum 38 passengers).

**Down Under Dive** (☎ 1800 079 099, 4052 8344) The MV *Super Cat* sails to Norma, Moore or Saxon Reefs and offers half-day and full-day cruises from $75.

**Sunlover** (☎ 1800 810 512, 4031 1055) Sunlover sails to Arlington Reef, and a semi-submersible and glass-bottom boat tour is included in the package (adult/child $126/63, maximum 250 passengers).

**Falla** (☎ 4031 3488) *Falla*, an old converted pearl lugger (maximum 35 passengers), and the catamaran *Passions of Paradise* (☎ 4050 0676, maximum 65 passengers) are both smaller operators that sail to the fringing reefs of Upolo Cay and Paradise Reef. Trips cost around $70/35 for adults/children.

## Diving Trips

Apart from the popular day trips to the reef, quite a few operators offer day trips and longer live-aboard trips for certified divers who want to explore the reef in more depth, and include night dives. Many also offer advanced diving courses. They include the following:

**Cairns Dive Centre** (☎ 1800 642 591, W www .cairnsdive.com.au) Dives at Moore, Milln and Briggs Reefs cost $275 overnight or $385 for a three-day live-aboard.

**Coral Sea Diving Company** (☎ 4041 2024, W www.coralseadiving.com.au) This company offers a four-day live-aboard trip to Holmes Reef from $1110.

**Explorer Ventures** (☎ 4031 5566, W www .explorerventures.com) This trip dives the Ribbon Reef and the Cod Hole and costs from $845 for 3½ days or $1690 for seven days (both live-aboard). The trip ends at Lizard Island, where you'll return to Cairns by plane.

**Mike Ball Dive Expeditions – Cairns** (☎1800 643 216, 4031 5484, W www.mikeball.com) The boat dives the Cod Hole for a cost of $963 for a four-day live-aboard tour; Mike Ball comes well recommended.

**Pro Dive** (☎ 4031 5255, W www.prodive-cairns .com.au) Three-day live-aboard trips to Milln and Flynn Reefs cost from $510.

**Tusa Dive Charters** (☎ 4031 1248, W www .tusadive.com) Tusa dives the outer reef on day trips only for $175.

## Cruises

There are a quite a few cruises on offer that offer good value (the fares include all meals and activities except diving) and the opportunity to see remote parts of the Great Barrier Reef. See also the Cruises entry under Organised Tours in the Cape York chapter for cruises to the 'tip of the top'.

**Captain Cook Cruises** (☎ 4031 4433, W www .captcookcrus.com.au) This five-day cruise departs Cairns on Monday and stops at Fitzroy Island, Cooktown, Two Isles, Lizard Island and Ribbon Reef. Adult prices are $1460 to $2000.

**Coral Princess** (☎ 1800 679 545 or 4721 1673, W www.coralprincess.com.au) *Coral Princess* does four-day cruises between Cairns and Townsville twice a week, via Hinchinbrook, Dunk, Pelorus and Orpheus Islands, and Sudbury and Thetford Reefs. You can board at either end and prices start at $1233.

## Chillagoe & Mt Mulligan

Tours of Chillagoe only run from the town itself, so you'll have to make your own way there, or take a tour with the *Savannahlander* train (see Train under the later Getting There & Away section). There are also off-the-beaten-track owner-operator tours of Mt Mulligan Cattle Station and Tyrconnel Historic Gold Mine (see the Mareeba to Chillagoe entry in the Atherton Tableland section later for details).

### Gulf Savannah & Undara Lava Tubes

Several companies run tours to the Gulf Savannah, including the Undara lava tubes, Tallaroo Springs and Karumba. You can also link up with the *Gulflander* and the *Savannahlander*. Contact the Gulf Savannah Tourist Organisation (☎ 4051 4658), at 74 Abbott St, for more information.

**Undara Experience** (☎ 4097 1411, W undara .com.au) These two-day bus trips out to the Undara lava tubes include accommodation, meals and a tour of the vast lava tubes, and cost from $339 to $393.
**The Adventure Company** (☎ 4051 4777, 13 Shields St) Book ahead for a place on the popular *Survivor II* outback tour, which goes to Goshen Station, Blencoe Falls, Herbert River, the 'Kucha Camp' and 'Tribal Council' area! It costs $1590.

### Cape York Peninsula

See Organised Tours in the Cape York chapter for 4WD tour information, or for something completely different, go on the outback mail run with Cape York Air (☎ 4035 9399, W www.capeyorkair.com.au, Cairns airport). Each weekday, the postie heads to remote stations and, space permitting, accepts paying passengers ($236 to $472). It also runs a Top of the Cape Tour from late May to November, which flies to the tip of Cape York and returns via several outback stations. It leaves Tuesday and Saturday and costs $670 per person (minimum of five passengers), including lunch.

### PLACES TO STAY

The accommodation business is extremely competitive in Cairns and prices go up and down with the seasons. Lower weekly rates are par for the course, as are stand-by rates for mid-range and top-end options. Prices quoted here are peak season prices (1 June to 31 October). In the low/shoulder season (1

November to 31 May), prices will drop dramatically for mid-range and top-end places.

### PLACES TO STAY – BUDGET
### Camping Grounds & Caravan Parks

There are about a dozen caravan parks in and around Cairns. If you want to camp by the beach, the nearest option is at Yorkey's Knob, about 20km north from the centre of Cairns. A little further north Ellis Beach has the best beachfront camping you'll find. Alternatively head south to Bramston Beach.

***Cairns Coconut Caravan Village*** (☎ 4054 6644, fax 4054 7591, 21 Anderson Rd) Unpowered/powered sites $24/28, cabins $58, self-contained units $78. Off the Bruce Hwy, about 8km south of the centre, is this huge and modern caravan and camping village. Sunbus No 1B (Monday to Friday) or 1G/1H (Saturday and Sunday) runs from the Lake St Transit Centre to the van park.

***Cairns Villa & Leisure Park*** (☎ 4053 7133, e info@cairnsvilla.com.au, 28 Pease St). Unpowered/powered sites $16/18, budget cabins from $39.50, Queenslander cabins $65. Only 4km from the city centre and set on 4 hectares, the park has good facilities in a relaxed setting.

***Coolwaters Caravan Park*** (☎ 4034 1949, Cnr Brinsmead & View Sts) Unpowered/powered sites $18/22, units from $55. This is a nice camping ground 7km from central Cairns, near Freshwater. Take the No 5 bus if you're on foot.

### Hostels

The city attracts swarms of backpackers, and there are plenty of decent hostels and guesthouses to choose from – and plenty of Third-World-style dives to avoid. A pretty standard set-up is dorm rooms (often with bunks), communal kitchens, shared bathrooms and leafy outdoor areas centred on a pool. Most hostels also have TV rooms, Internet facilities and coin-operated laundries. Some have a bar and restaurant.

There are two main accommodation areas, the Esplanade and the area behind Cairns Central shopping centre. The Esplanade has a reputation as the livelier place to stay – if you want to party, head there. Hostels away from the centre offer much more breathing space and are generally quieter, better maintained and better value for money; however, depending on the location, you'll have to rely on an hourly courtesy bus into town, or else make the 15- to 25-minute walk yourself.

**The Esplanade** Heading north along the Esplanade from the corner of Shields St, the first place you come to is the big, multilevel *International Hostel (☎ 4031 1424, fax 4031 3804, 67 Esplanade)* which has beds in a five- to six-bed dorm from $17, and singles/doubles from $25/35. This place is popular with partygoers, but the atmosphere is impersonal and some of the rooms could do with a good scrub and some air freshener. If you can wear the dirt, head there.

*Caravella Backpackers 77 (☎ 4051 2159, fax 4031 6329,* e *info@caravella.com.au, 77 The Esplanade)* Beds in 6-8–bed dorm with fan $15, beds in 4-bed dorm with aircon and en suite $20, singles/doubles from $30/43. A big, rambling place, this is one of the longest established Cairns hostels and has basic rooms, a TV room and pool table.

*Jimmy's on the Esplanade (☎ 4031 6884, fax 4041 5900, 83 The Esplanade)* Beds in 4-bed dorm with en suite $18, doubles $44, with bathroom $55. Jimmy's is a reasonably modern place with clean air-con dorms.

*Hostel 89 (☎ 1800 061 712, 4031 7477, fax 4031 4924, 89 The Esplanade)* Beds in 4-bed dorm $20, singles/doubles from $40/48. This is probably the best-maintained hostel on the Esplanade. It's smallish, spotlessly clean and all rooms have air-con. Security is good.

*YHA on the Esplanade (☎ 4031 1919, fax 4031 4381, 93 The Esplanade)* Dorm beds $19 with air-con and en suite, doubles $44, share bathroom with fans (nonmembers pay an extra $3.50). The location is the big selling point here. It has the usual facilities, but no pool.

Three blocks further along the Esplanade there's another cluster of backpackers hostels.

*Caravella Backpackers 149 (☎ 4031 5680,* e *info@caravella.com.au, 149 The Esplanade)* Beds in 10-bed/4-6–bed dorm $16/19, doubles & twins $40. This is another big, busy popular hostel. Some dorm rooms have en suite and air-con.

**Around Town** There are plenty of budget places further out from the city centre.

*Global Palace (☎ 1800 819 024, 4031 7921, fax 4031 3231, City Place, Cnr Lake & Shields Sts)* Dorm beds/twins/doubles $21/46/50. A new place with top-class facilities and, best of all, no bunk beds. The building's facade has been restored to its original design, while the interior is cutting edge. It has a great timber balcony overlooking City Place.

*Cairns Girls Hostel (☎ 4051 2767, fax 4051 2016, 147 Lake St)* Dorm beds per day/week $16/90. The name's pretty bad, but the place isn't. Catering to women only, it has a relaxed, home-away-from-home feel.

*Big Backyard (☎ 4031 3133,* e *bigbackyard@one.net.au, 34 Martyn St)*. Dorm beds/doubles $18/35. Set in three adjoining Queenslanders, and with a no bunk bed policy, this place rocks! It has a pool (like most hostels), but it also has an adjoining volleyball court. It's clean and well run, but on the downside, it's not in the most central location.

*Gecko's Backpackers (☎ 1800 011 344, 4031 1344, fax 4051 5150, 187 Bunda St)* Dorm beds/singles $18/25, doubles/doubles with air-con $40/45. Gecko's, set in a converted Queenslander, is a great place to chill. The rooms are comfortable with polished floorboards and painted furniture. It also has disabled facilities.

*McLeod St Youth Hostel (☎ 4051 0772, fax 4031 3158, 20-24 McLeod St)* Beds in 6-bed dorm with fan/air-con $18/19, twins/doubles $44 (non-members pay $3.50 extra). This YHA hostel has a helpful tour desk, good facilities and car parking.

*Castaways (☎ 4051 1238, 207 Sheridan St)* Beds in 3-bed dorm $18, singles $32, doubles & twins $38. A friendly and well-maintained place that offers free Internet, bike hire and a courtesy bus.

*Calypso Inn (☎ 1800 815 628, fax 4051 7518, 5-9 Digger St)* Dorm beds $18, singles/doubles $28/38. Located behind the

Cock & Bull tavern in a renovated Queenslander, this is a party-hostel. It has its own bar and restaurant (you know when you're in a backpackers when the blackboard advertising the $5 all-you-can-eat-buffet says, 'meals must not be shared'!). Rooms are simple and clean.

***Bohemia Resort*** (☎ *1800 155 353, fax 4041 7292, 231 McLeod St)* Beds in 4-bed dorm with fan/air-con $18/20, singles/doubles $20/40. Newly opened, this large-scale 'resort' is a soulless place, but its rooms are clean and modern. It's at least a 20-minute walk from the city centre and runs an hourly courtesy bus.

### Guesthouses
These guesthouses cater for budget travellers, but their emphasis is on rooms rather than dorms (although most do have dorms). They are generally quieter, smaller and a bit more personalised than the hostels.

***Dreamtime Travellers Rest*** (☎ *4031 6753, fax 4031 6566, e dreamtime@iig .com.au, 4 Terminus St)* Beds in 3-4-bed dorm $18, twins & doubles $40. Housed in a renovated Queenslander, this small guesthouse is run by a friendly young couple.

***Ryan's Rest*** (☎ *4051 4734, 18 Terminus St)* Singles/doubles & twins $40/45. This is a cosy, calm place with brightly painted rooms.

***Tropic Days*** (☎ *4041 1521, fax 4031 6576, 26-28 Bunting St)* Camping/dorm beds/doubles $11/18/42. Set in a lovely tropical garden, Tropic Days is in a quiet spot that is a hike from the Esplanade, but there's a courtesy bus. It's run by a friendly young couple and has good facilities (no bunk beds). Camping is also an option here.

***Travellers Oasis*** (☎ *1800 621 353, fax 4052 1634, 8 Scott St)* Dorm beds/singles/doubles $18/30/40. A low-key place in a converted Queenslander, offering free Internet and no bunks. It's in the area behind Cairns Central shopping centre.

***Floriana Guesthouse*** (☎ *4051 7886, fax 4051 3056, 183 The Esplanade)* Singles/doubles from $35/48, doubles with en suite $55-85. This quiet guesthouse is ideal for families and has a range of options, including self-contained units with TVs that

can sleep up to four people, and somewhat shabby singles and doubles without en suite. It has a communal kitchen (which is locked after 9.30pm).

## PLACES TO STAY – MID-RANGE
### Motels
Motels are fairly pricey in Cairns, but there's some good options about.

***Poinsettia Motel*** (☎ *4051 2144, fax 4051 2144, 169 Lake St)* Singles/doubles $55/65. In a central location, this budget motel has decent rooms.

***All Seasons Esplanade*** (*Lyon's Motel;* ☎ *4051 2311, fax 4031 1294, Cnr The Esplanade & Aplin Sts)* Doubles $62. Behind its tower block, the All Seasons has a budget motel section. Rooms are clean, with standard motel facilities, and the location is right in the thick of things.

***Club Crocodile Hides Hotel*** (☎ *4051 1266, fax 4031 2276, Cnr Lake & Shields Sts)* Hotel room without/with bathroom $79/99, motel room $119. This renovated pub, with well-maintained rooms without views, has a timber balcony overlooking City Place – right among all Cairns' amazingly frenetic bird-life.

***The Great Northern*** (☎ *1800 804 910, 4051 3090, e sales@greatnortherncairns .com, 69 Abbott St)* Singles/doubles/suites $75/85/119. In the centre of town, it's a good-value option. All rooms have TVs and en suites.

***The Balinese*** (☎ *4051 9922, fax 4051 9822, e info@balinese.com.au, 215 Lake St)*. Singles/doubles $75/94. A small-scale, super-friendly place to stay. Rooms are very comfortable, but don't expect views.

***Figtree Lodge*** (☎ *4041 0000, fax 4041 0001, 253 Sheridan St)* Doubles $89, self-contained suites $125. This is about a 20-minute walk from the town centre, but the facilities are impressive and include a bar and restaurant.

### Self-Contained Apartments
Holiday flats are well worth considering, especially for a group of three or four people who are staying a few days or more. Expect pools, air-con, cooking and laundry facilities

in this category. Holiday flats generally supply all bedding, cooking utensils etc.

**Costa Blanca Holiday Apartments** (☎/fax 4051 3114, 241 The Esplanade) 1-bedroom/2-bedroom units from $66/77. This is one of the few affordable places on the waterfront. The self-contained rooms aren't flash, but they're clean and comfortable, and sleep four people. The upstairs units have mountain views, and there's a big old pool.

**Tropical Queenslander** (☎ 4031 1666, fax 4031 1491, 287 Lake St) Doubles $86. Built in Colonial Australian-style, it has two pools and spas. Rooms have kitchenettes and all the standard facilities.

**Coral Cay Villas** (☎ 4046 5100, fax 4031 2703, e info@coralcay.com.au, 267 Lake St) Singles/doubles $75/85. This is a leafy place to stay, with barbecue facilities, pool and spa, and fully self-contained units.

**Cascade Gardens Apartments** (☎ 4051 8000, fax 4052 1396, 175 Lake St) Studio apartments from $98, 1-bedroom apartments $112. These apartments are modern and self-contained.

**James St Queenslander** (☎ 4058 1009, fax 4041 0790, 3 James St) 1-bed units $70, 3-bed house $100. This place is well set up and good value.

## Gay & Lesbian Accommodation

There are fairly limited options for dedicated gay and lesbian accommodation.

**18-24 James** (☎ 1800 621 824, 4051 4644, fax 4051 0103, 18-24 James St) Beds in 4-bed room $60, singles/doubles $87/137, including breakfast. This relaxed place to stay is exclusively gay and lesbian. If only more of the straight places could be like this!

## PLACES TO STAY – TOP END

There are some superb places here.

**Inn Cairns** (☎ 4041 2350, fax 4041 2420, 71 Lake St) Twins & doubles $144. This is a very well-run, spacious boutique hotel in the city centre. Room facilities are top notch.

**Il Palazzo** (☎ 4041 2155, fax 4041 2166, 62 Abbott St) Doubles $195. A stylish boutique hotel, all units have balconies and are fully self-contained.

**Waterfront Terraces** (☎ 4031 8333, fax 4031 8444, e res@cairnsluxury.com, 233 The Esplanade) 1-bedroom/2-bedroom suites $160/198. At the quiet northern end of The Esplanade, this is a comfortable boutique hotel. All rooms are fully self-contained and have ocean views.

**Quality Hotel, Pacific International** (☎ 4051 7888, fax 4051 9716, 43 The Esplanade) Doubles $225. This is one of Cairns' original hotels. It's a bit smaller and more laid-back than some of the newer places.

**Royal Harbour Tradewinds** (☎ 4080 8888, fax 4041 4522, 73-75 The Esplanade) Doubles from $176. This hotel is in a great position and all rooms have ocean views, spa bath, TV, video and stereo.

## PLACES TO EAT

Cairns is certainly well stocked with eateries of all types, and you shouldn't have too much trouble finding something to satisfy your cravings or your budget. There are a lot of eateries on the Esplanade, but if you venture beyond it you'll find that the quality improves, even if the price remains the same.

### Restaurants

Gourmands should be reasonably sated by the choice of international cuisine on offer.

**Pesci's** (☎ 4041 1133, Pier Marketplace) Dishes $13.50-32.50. Open 9am-9pm. On the eastern side of the Pier complex, this relaxed bar and eatery overlooks the marina. The cuisine is mod Oz and the coffee is damn fine.

**Yama** (☎ 4052 1009, 45 Spence St) Lunch sets $11, dinner around $20. One of the best Japanese places in town, by night it's an izzakaya (bar-eatery), where you can order from a range of small, tasty dishes, that go perfectly with large glasses of beer.

**Sushi Express** (☎ 4041 4388, Orchid Plaza) Sushi plates $2-4. Open 1pm-3pm & from 5pm Mon-Sat. This almost authentic kaiten-sushi (sushi wheel) eatery is an excellent find.

**Midori Noodles Bar** (☎ 4031 1892, Village Lane, Abbott St) Dishes $6-10. Steaming bowls of ramen are served up at this casual little place.

*Taj* (☎ 4051 2228, 61 Spence St) Mains $13-17.50. Open for dinner Mon-Sun. Taj serves pretty good north Indian food, and is BYO (no beer).

*All Bar One* (☎ 4051 6060, 92A Lake St). Lunch $6.60-12.80, dinner $12.90. Next to Walker's Bookshop, this lively little alfresco Italian restaurant is always busy.

*Red Ochre Grill* (☎ 4051 0100, 43 Shields St) Mains $25-30. Stylish bush tucker is the go here.

*La Fettuccina* (☎ 4031 5959, 43 Shields St) Mains $19-24. Open daily for dinner. This atmospheric Italian restaurant serves up excellent homemade pasta.

*Mediterraneo* (☎ 4051 4335, 74 Shields St) Mains $16.50-23.80. Mediterraneo is a newish BYO trattoria cooking up voluptuous Sicilian cuisine.

*Yanni's Greek Taverna* (☎ 4041 1500, Cnr Aplin & Grafton Sts) Mains $16.50-24.90. Yanni's has a classy candlelit interior and old fashioned Queenslander exterior. It serves up a tasty range of char grills and seafood.

*Fish Lips Bar & Bistro* (☎ 4041 1700, 228 Sheridan St) Meals $10.50-32. Open noon-2pm & 6pm-10pm. A lip-smacking seafood experience is in store, but make sure you book.

## Cafes & Delis

Make the most of the warm climate at Cairns' many alfresco cafes.

*Coffee Bean* (☎ 4051 3688, Pier Marketplace) Dishes $7-10. Working on the same theme as Starbucks, it has a huge array of coffees (and tea), and simple panini rolls.

*Mondo* (☎ 4052 5780, Wharf St) Mains $8-19.50. Open lunch & dinner daily. Open-air, casual, tables on the edge of Trinity Inlet and excellent food – now this is paradise! Try the char-grilled tuna with warm Vietnamese salad ($16.50).

*Perrotta's at the Gallery* (☎ 4031 5899, 38 Abbott St) Meals $3.50-23.90. Open 8.30am-10pm daily. Adjoining Cairns Regional Gallery, this breezy cafe and bar is perfect at any time of the day – try ricotta pancakes for brekky or a hazelnut martini to get the evening rolling.

*Night Markets* (The Esplanade) Dishes $7-14. In the thick of it, this is a soulless hawker-style food court, but it does have plenty of eating options.

*Meeting Place* (☎ 4031 5081, 5 Aplin St) Dishes $7-14. Around the corner from the Night Markets, the Meeting Place has a good range of international food stalls.

*Tiny's Juice Bar* (☎ 4031 4331, 45 Grafton St) Meals $2.50-5.60. Near the Spence St corner, this is a yummy little lunch spot. It has a great range of fresh juices and smoothies, as well as healthy filled rolls.

*Lillipad* (☎ 4051 9565, 72 Grafton St) Open 7am-5pm. A comfy cafe run by a young couple, it serves up breakfasts (including a backpacker breakfast for $4.50), salads, filled rolls and does a tasty gluten- and wheat-free buckwheat burger.

*Beethoven Cafe* (☎ 4051 6988, 105 Grafton St) Meals $4-10. Open 7am-5pm Mon-Fri, 6am-1pm Sat. Worlds collide at Beethoven's – a popular alfresco breakfast and lunch spot serving up German pastries and continental deli rolls – it's right next door to the Crown Hotel, one of Cairn's rowdiest pubs.

*Java Joe's* (☎ 4041 6679, 143 Abbott St) Open 7am-4.30pm. Meals $4-10. This friendly place serves up fresh food and offers free Internet access for 30 minutes.

*Chapter One Cafe* (☎ 4031 3505, fax 4031 5538, 92 Abbott St) Mains $5.50-8.80. This is an excellent little cafe that's worth checking out if you're staying nearby. It serves up generous brekkies and lunches.

*Botanic Gardens Restaurant* (☎/fax 4053 7087, Collins Ave, Edge Hill) Meals $7-13.50. Surrounded by calming greenery, the licensed restaurant is worth heading to for a quiet lunch.

## ENTERTAINMENT

The best starting point for entertainment is the free what's on magazine, Son of Barfly. It appears weekly and is available in cafes and shops all over town. Quite a few of the pubs have live music, as well as kitchens serving up good pub grub. The pub and nightclub scene is notoriously wild in

Cairns, especially in the early hours of the morning – be prepared!

## Pubs & Bars

Take your pick from a huge range of drinking holes ranging from boorish to stylish.

*Cairns Yacht Club (☎/fax 4031 2750, 4 Wharf St)* One of the few surviving reminders of old Cairns, it's a great place for a gin and tonic and a bucket of prawns at dusk. It has meals from $8.50 to $15.

*Woolshed Chargrill & Saloon (☎ 4031 6304, 24 Shields St)* The phenomenally popular Woolshed is right in the heart of the action, with party games, backpacker theme nights and other wild stuff. It also serves meals from $9 to $14.

*The Chapel Cafe (☎ 4041 4222, Level 1, 91 The Esplanade)* Cocktails from $10.50. Open 5pm-2am. Tucked away above the Esplanade is this low-key cafe and bar, serving up mod Oz cuisine (mains from $18), with live acoustic music some nights.

*Court House Hotel (☎ 4031 4166, 38 Abbott St)* Originally the city's courthouse, the hotel is now a swish bar, serving Mediterranean cuisine (meals $6 to $19).

*Cock & Bull (☎ 4031 1160, 6 Grove St)* Open for lunch and dinner. A popular English-style tavern, it's just the spot for homesick Brits. It has a good range of draught beers on tap and the meals are suitably stodgy (dishes $5 to $12).

*Blue Mango Cafe Wine Bar (☎ 4031 6297, 209-217 The Esplanade)* Featuring sax and acoustic guitar from Tuesday to Sunday night, Blue Mango is a relaxed alfresco bar. The menu is small but good, with dishes priced between $6.50 and $20.50.

*PJ O'Briens (☎ 4031 5333, 87 Lake St)* On the corner of Shields St, this mock-Irish pub satisfies the punters.

*Sports Bar (☎ 4041 2533, 33 Spence St)* Nightclub admission $5.50 Tues, Thur, Fri & Sat. Open 6pm-late Sun-Thur, 6pm-5am Fri & Sat. It's a busy, hip nightclub, with DJs and live music.

*Johno's Blues Bar (☎ 4051 8770, Cnr Abbott & Aplin Sts)* Admission changes nightly, free entry before 9pm. Open until 1am-3am

Mon-Thur & Sun, until 4am-5am Fri & Sat. This long-running bar has blues, rock, and rhythm and blues bands every night until late.

The *Fox & Firkin (☎ 4031 5305, Cnr Spence & Lake Sts)* has live music (in the form of cover bands) from Tuesday to Sunday nights, and the downmarket *Underdog Hotel (☎ 4051 2490, 48 Spence St)* has live music on Sunday afternoon and evening, and DJs for the rest of the week.

## Nightclubs

It's a fine line between pubs and nightclubs in Cairns, but there are some dedicated nightclubs.

*Tropo's (☎ 4031 2530, Upstairs, Cnr Spence & Lake Sts)* Admission $5.50, free before 10pm. Cheap drinks and Top 40 tunes are what you'll find here. It caters to a local crowd.

*Playpen International (☎ 4051 8211, Cnr Lake & Hartley Sts)* General admission $5.50, free early. This huge nightclub often has big-name bands – so keep an eye out. On Friday and Saturday night, it has a dance club, *Millennium Bar*, open till 5am.

*Fitzroy Island Resort (☎ 4051 9588)* runs 'party nights' at the *Raging Thunder Beach Bar* on the island. It departs Cairns at 7pm ($15) and returns at midnight, making for a concentrated drinking session!

*Nu-Trix (☎ 4051 8223, Spence St)* is a gay venue that opens late and parties hard.

## Cinemas

If you're tired of the heat and want some time out, Cairns' air-con cinemas are a welcome option. *Cairns City Cinemas (☎ 4031 1077, 108 Grafton St)* and *Central Cinemas (☎ 4052 1166, Cairns Central shopping centre)* both show mainstream, new-release flicks.

## SHOPPING

It seems like every second shopfront in Cairns is a tourist information centre and every third one is a didgeridoo shop! If you want to find a good-quality instrument, you may need some stamina, because there are a lot of machine-made (as opposed to termite-made) instruments on sale.

Didgeridoos are priced on their sound quality – look for a didg with a deep, resonant sound, which is able to move sharply between rhythmic patterns or tones – avoid a piece that can only make a dull continuous drone. Look for a mouthpiece that isn't too big, otherwise too much air will escape. The end of the didg, however, should bell outwards. Feel inside the didg – termites leave the inside of didgs smooth – so if you find chiselling, it's bound to be man-made. Also look out for bamboo didgs. These will be really light. Painted decoration can also be used to mask manufactured didgs (and bamboo), so feel the full length of the didg, you may find a steel ring used to piece two sections of wood together. Prices range from $100 to $300, and most places can arrange air-freight in a special didg box for around $50 worldwide.

A great option if you're serious about didgeridoos is to make your own. Mt Mulligan Station (☎ 1800 359 798, 4094 8360, fax 4092 2147), west of Cairns, runs overnight bush experience tours. For the price of a didg in Cairns, you can see some wild country *and* learn the craft of didg making.

South Sea pearls are also popular souvenirs. Look out for the colour, lustre and shape, and ask whether it's a genuine pearl or merely pearl shell.

If you're looking for local crafts, try the *Mud Markets* at the Pier Marketplace, or wait until you travel to Tolga and elsewhere in the Tableland. Avoid the Night Markets; the most you'll find here is junky souvenirs and shopkeepers with pained, bored expressions on their face.

Cairns is a good place to shop for camping and outdoor gear if you're heading bush. For budget-priced gear, try *City Place Disposals (☎ 4051 6040, Cnr Grafton & Shields Sts)* or *Northern Disposals (☎ 4051 7099, 47-49 Sheridan St). It's Extreme (☎ 4051 0344, 32 Spence St; 13 Shield St)* has two shopfronts in Cairns and is a one-stop spot for camping, walking and rock climbing gear, and comfortable but edgy travelling clothes. If you want to buy a hat or rashie (a light UV-resistant fitted top worn in the water) to protect yourself from the north's fierce sun, there are some good *surfwear shops* in the Pier Marketplace.

## GETTING THERE & AWAY
### Air
Qantas (☎ 13 13 13, 4050 4000) is on the corner of Shields and Lake Sts. Air Niugini (☎ 4051 4177) is at 4 Shields St.

**Domestic Services** Qantas has daily full economy flights between Cairns and Alice Springs ($560), Brisbane ($505), Darwin ($538), Melbourne ($768), Sydney ($685) and Townsville ($250).

For shorter hops within Queensland, Qantas flies to Thursday Island ($374 one way) and Weipa ($212 one way). Skytrans (☎ 1800 818 405) flies to Cooktown ($101 one way). Macair (☎ 13 15 28, 4035 9722) flies to Lizard Island ($251) and Dunk Island ($165). Cheaper advance fares are available.

**International Services** Regular flights leave Cairns airport for Auckland (Air New Zealand), Kuala Lumpur (Malaysian Airlines and Air Niugini), Hong Kong (Cathay Pacific), Port Moresby, Singapore and Manila (Air Niugini) and Tokyo (Japan Airlines).

### Bus
Expect a welcoming party – a crowd of touts from backpackers hostels normally meets and greets arriving buses.

The bus companies operate from the Transit Centre at Trinity Wharf. McCafferty's/Greyhound runs six buses a day up the coast from Brisbane and Townsville to Cairns: Brisbane ($182, 27 hours); Rockhampton ($122, 16 hours); Mackay ($97, 12 hours); and Townsville ($49, six hours).

Coral Coaches (☎ 4031 7577) runs services from Cairns to Port Douglas ($16, 1½ hours, eight a day); Mossman ($23, two hours, eight a day); Daintree Village ($30, 2½ hours, two a day); Cape Tribulation ($37, four hours, two a day); and Cooktown, via the inland route ($64, 6½ hours, three a week) or the coast road ($64, eight hours, two a week, June to October only). It also runs a service to Karumba ($150, 12 hours, three a week) and a drop-off at the turn-off to the Undara lava tubes ($60, 4½ hours) – you'll have to arrange pick-up from there with your accommodation (see the Gulf Savannah chapter for more information on the lava tubes).

See the Atherton Tableland section later for details on White Car Coaches (☎ 4091 1855) bus services from Cairns.

## Train

Two trains run up and down the coast from Brisbane, the *Queenslander* (from $163 one way, 29 hours, one a week) and the *Sunlander* (from $163, 30 hours, three a week).

The most interesting train journey is the *Savannahlander*, which runs between Cairns and Forsayth (adult/child $95/48 one way, one a week), stopping along the way at Almaden, Lappa Junction and Mt Surprise. You can take add-on bus tours along the way to Chillagoe, the Undara lava tubes and Cobbold Gorge. The fare doesn't include meals, accommodation or tours.

From Cairns, the Kuranda Scenic Railway climbs to Kuranda daily (see the Getting There & Away entry under Kuranda in the later Atherton Tableland section).

Queensland Rail's Cairns Travel Centre (☎ 1800 620 324) at Cairns railway station is open 8am to 5pm from Monday to Friday and 7am to 1pm Saturday.

## Car & 4WD

A hire vehicle is the best way to explore areas beyond and around Cairns. As well as the major rental firms, there are dozens of smaller, reliable local operators offering good deals. Generally, small cars cost from around $49 per day.

Note that most Cairns rental firms specifically prohibit you from taking their vehicles to Cooktown or Chillagoe. If you ignore this prohibition, you risk losing your deposit. If you're planning to tackle one of these routes, you'll need to hire a small 4WD, which are widely available for around $75 per day. See also Getting There & Away in the Cape York chapter for details of dedicated 4WD rental firms in Cairns.

**Car Rental** As well as those listed below, Thrifty, Avis, Hertz and Budget have counters at Cairns airport and offices in town. All companies stock a wide range of vehicles to suit all budgets and requirements.

**Billabong Car Rentals** (☎ 4051 4299, **W** www.billabongrentals.com.au) 132 Sheridan St
**Budget Rent A Car** (☎ 4051 922) 153A Lake St
**Cruising Car Rentals** (☎ 4041 4666, **e** cruising@cairns.net.au) 196A Sheridan St
**Leisure Wheels** (☎ 4051 8988, **e** sales@leisurewheels.com.au) 314 Sheridan St & 147c Lake St
**Sheridan Rent A Car** (☎ 4051 3942) 36 Water St at Florence St
**Sugarland Car Rentals** (☎ 4052 1300, **e** sales@sugarland.com.au) 252 Sheridan St

**Campervan Rental** Campervans are a hugely popular way to travel – giving you plenty of freedom.

**Britz Australia** (☎ 4032 2611, **W** www.britz.com) 411 Sheridan St. Britz has campervans and 4WD campervans (which contain stove, fridge, linen etc).
**Travellers Auto Barn** (☎ 1800 674 374, 4041 3722, **W** www.travellers-autobarn.com.au) 123 Bunda St. On the corner of Spence St, this budget operation has offices interstate, so you can organise one-way hire. The campervans come supplied with most of the gear you'll need on the road.

## Boat

The daily *Quicksilver* (☎ 4099 5500) fast catamaran service links Cairns with Port Douglas (one way/return adult $22/32, child $11/16, 1½ hours), departing from the Pier Marina in Cairns at 8am and from Port Douglas at 5.30pm.

## GETTING AROUND
## To/From the Airport

The approach road to the Cairns airport (domestic and international flights) leaves the main highway about 3.5km north of the centre. The shuttle bus Australia Coach (☎ 4048 8355) meets all incoming flights and runs a regular pick-up and drop-off service (adult/child $7/3). Black & White taxis (☎ 13 10 08) charge about $10.

## Bus

Sunbus (☎ 4057 7411 Ⓦ www.sunbus.com
.au) runs the local bus services in and
around Cairns. Schedules for most routes
are posted at the main city stop (known as
the Lake St transit centre) in City Place.
Buses run from early morning to late
evening. Useful destinations include: Edge
Hill (Nos 6, 6A, 7), Flecker Botanic Gardens (7), Machans Beach (7), Holloways
Beach (1C, 1H), Yorkey's Knob (1C, 1D,
1H), Trinity Beach (1, 1A, 2X), Clifton
Beach (1, 1B) and Palm Cove (1, 1B, 2X).
All are served by the 24-hour night service
(N) on Friday and Saturday. Heading south,
bus No 1 goes as far as Gordonvale.

## Taxi

Black & White taxis (☎ 13 10 08) offer incredibly prompt service. There are taxi
ranks on the corner of Lake and Shields Sts
(near Cairns Museum) and outside Cairns
Central shopping centre.

## Bicycle

Some of the hostels have bikes for hire –
expect to pay $10 to $15 per day. Other-
wise, check out Bandicoot Bicycle Tours &
Rental (☎ 4055 0155) at 59 Sheridan St or
All Day Bike Hire (☎ 4031 3348) at 151
Lake St, next door to Budget Rent A Car.

# Islands off Cairns

Off the coast from Cairns are Green Island
(a coral cay) and Fitzroy Island (a continental island). Both of these very pretty islands attract hordes of day-trippers. South
of Cairns, the Frankland Islands group is a
cluster of undeveloped national park islands. You can go on a day trip to the Frank-
lands or camp overnight or longer.

## GREEN ISLAND NATIONAL
## PARK

Green Island, 27km north-east of Cairns, is
a coral cay only 660m long by 260m wide.
Although a national park, a multimillion dollar resort takes up a substantial proportion of
the island. Nevertheless, a 10-minute stroll

from the resort to the far end of the island
will remind you that the beach is beautiful,
the snorkelling good and the fish prolific.

Captain Cook named the island after the
chief astronomer on the *Endeavour*. The island was home to a beche-de-mer boom;
from the 1870s most of the trees were logged
for firewood to boil up the sea cucumbers.

The resort has a separate section for day-
trippers, with impressive facilities, including
a pool, a bar, *Emeralds* restaurant and the
*Canopy Grill* for light lunches, and water-
sports gear for hire. **Marineland Melanesia**
*(☎ 4051 4032, adult/child $9/4)* is worth a
visit, with its aquarium of fish, turtles,
stingrays, limpet sharks and crocodiles, and
a collection of Melanesian artefacts.

*Green Island Resort (☎ 4031 3300,
fax 4052 1511)* has reef suite doubles for
$555 and island suite doubles for $455. The
reef suites at this luxury island resort are split-
level and have their own private balcony. The
island suites sleep up to four people.

## Getting There & Away

Great Adventures (☎ 4051 0455) has regular services to Green Island by fast catamaran ($46 return). It also has a day package,
which includes snorkelling and lunch ($92).
Other operators include the Big Cat (☎ 4051
0444), with a day cruise for adult/child
$52/29 or $62/36 including lunch.

## FITZROY ISLAND NATIONAL
## PARK

About 6km off the coast and 26km east of
Cairns, Fitzroy is a large continental island
that is hugely popular with day-trippers. The
small resort pool area and fish and chip kiosk
may blight your first impression , but beyond
it are coral shores and picturesque walking
tracks across the island, including a reasonably strenuous hike to its highest point.

Captain Cook named the island after the
Duke of Grafton, a noted politician of the
era. In 1877 it was made a quarantine station for Chinese immigrants bound for the
north Queensland goldfields, and a number
of unmarked Chinese graves remain from
that period. The island also supported a
beche-de-mer business for a time.

## Things to See & Do

Day-trippers can use the resort facilities. Water-sports equipment hire is available, including snorkelling and diving gear, and sea kayaks. The resort also runs diving courses and sea kayak tours. The most popular snorkelling spot is around the rocks at the coral-covered Nudey Beach (1.2km from the resort).

There are two walking trails on the island: the 20-minute **Secret Garden Walk**, where you're likely to see 30cm-long lizards known as Major's skinks, and the steep, two-hour **Lighthouse & Summit Trail**. From the lighthouse, there's a short, rocky trail to a lookout, where you can see the jewel-like Little Fitzroy Island below. On the trail you'll step over the unlikely grave of 'The Good Dog Rastus', who was sadly buried here in 1949!

## Places to Stay & Eat

*Fitzroy Island Resort* (☎ *4051 9588, fax 4052 1335*) Beds in 4-bed unit $31 or $124 for whole room, double $116 (shared kitchen & bathroom), double/family villa units $220/250. This resort has hostel-style dorms, with shared kitchen, bathroom, laundry facilities, and cottages by the water.

The resort has a *kiosk* by the pool, serving salads and toasted sandwiches. There is also a *bar*, open from 10am to 5.30pm. A waterfront *restaurant* opens at 5pm for resort guests, with seafood and pasta meals from $6 to $20.

On Friday and Saturday nights, the resort runs party nights at the bar, including transfers from Cairns ($15, 7pm).

## Getting There & Away

Fitzroy Island Ferries (☎ 4030 7907) runs excursions to the island ($36/18 return, 45 minutes, three daily).

Sunlover Cruises (☎ 1800 810 512) has a day trip to Moore Reef that stops at Fitzroy Island (adult/child $142/71), as well as an overnight tour ($232/110).

## FRANKLAND ISLANDS

The Frankland Islands form a beautiful, untouched national park about 12km offshore

from the mouth of the Mulgrave River, south of Cairns. Named by Captain Cook after Admiral Sir Thomas Frankland, the continental islands consist of High Island to the north and four smaller islands – Normanby, Mabel, Round and Russell Islands – to the south. The islands have fine, sandy beaches, stunning fringing coral and excellent snorkelling opportunities. On day trips from Cairns, island time is spent on Normanby Island, which takes about eight minutes to walk around, while divers go to Round Island.

Campers can be dropped off on High or Russell Islands, but must come totally equipped. Usually campers go to Russell Island; High Island drop-offs are only made at peak periods when Russell is full. A maximum of 15 campers is allowed on each island and permits are available from Cairns QPWS.

## Getting There & Away

Frankland Islands Cruise & Dive (☎ 4031 6300) run a good-value tour. You're taken by bus from Cairns to Deeral, where you cruise down the Mulgrave River, with stunning views of Walshs Pyramid in the background, past the isolated community of Russell Heads and out to the open ocean. It costs $138/69 per adult/child. Introductory dives/certified dives ($90/60) are also on offer, as well as a campers' drop-off ($144 return).

# Atherton Tableland

Inland from the coast between Innisfail and Cairns, the land rises sharply then rolls gently across the lush Atherton Tableland towards the Great Dividing Range. The Tableland's altitude, more than 900m in places, tempers the tropical heat, and the abundant rainfall and rich volcanic soil combine to make this one of the greenest places in Queensland. In the south are Queensland's two highest mountains – Bartle Frere (1657m) and Bellenden Ker (1591m).

The Tableland is a region of beautiful scenery, with lakes and waterfalls, national parks and state forests, small villages and busy rural centres. The area has some excellent B&Bs and lush camping grounds.

West of the Tableland are the historic mining towns of Herberton and Irvinebank.

Little more than a 100 years ago, this peaceful, pastoral region was still wild jungle. The first pioneers came in the 1870s, looking for a repeat of the Palmer River gold rush further north. As elsewhere in Queensland, the Ngadjonji tribe, of the wider language group the Djirbal, was violently opposed to this intrusion but was soon tragically overrun.

Mining spurred the development of roads and railways, though farming and timber felling soon became the chief activities.

## Getting There & Around

There are bus services to the main towns from Cairns, but not to all the interesting areas around the towns, so hire car is the best way to get around.

From south to north, the three major roads from the coast are the Palmerston Hwy from Innisfail to Millaa Millaa and Ravenshoe; the Gillies Hwy from Gordonvale past the lakes of Tinaroo, Barrine and Eacham to Yungaburra and Atherton; and the Kennedy Hwy from Cairns to Kuranda and Mareeba. Heading north from Mareeba, the Peninsula Developmental Rd runs through Mt Molloy to Mossman.

White Car Coaches (☎ 4091 1855) has regular bus services connecting Cairns with the Tableland, departing from outside the Underdog Hotel at 48 Spence St. There are services to Mareeba ($16.80, one hour) and Atherton ($22, 1¾ hours) at 8.30am, 3.15pm and 5.30pm Monday to Friday, 9.30am and 1pm on Saturday and 1pm on Sunday. There are also services to Herberton ($25.20, two hours, 8.30am and 3.15pm Monday to Friday, 9.30am and 1pm Saturday, and 1pm Sunday) and Ravenshoe ($30.40, 2½ hours, 8.30am and 3.15pm Monday to Friday). Five daily services run to Kuranda ($7.40, 30 minutes, 8.30am, 9.30am, 1.30pm, 3.15pm and 5.30pm).

**Organised Tours** There are plenty of companies offering day trips and tours from Cairns. See Organised Tours in the Cairns and Port Douglas sections for details.

## KURANDA
postcode 4872 • pop 670

Kuranda's fame was earned by its spectacular rainforest scenery, alternative culture and its original craft markets. These days, the scenery is still spectacular but the pretty mountain village has been swallowed-up by its own popularity. Commercialism, some appalling tourist developments (such as a shooting gallery) and cheap imports rather than locally made crafts are what you'll be confronting these days. On nonmarket days, and in the afternoon and evening, Kuranda reverts, in some small part, to the laid-back atmosphere it was once known for.

Seventh Day Adventists founded the Mona Mona Mission near Kuranda in 1912. At the time, the state government's policy was to house Aboriginal people in missions and reserves. The mission was closed in 1962 and many of the people who once lived there, and their descendants, now live in or near Kuranda.

Kuranda Visitor Information Centre (☎ 4093 9311) in Centenary Park is open 10am to 5pm daily.

### Things to See & Do

The **Kuranda markets** are held every Wednesday, Thursday, Friday and Sunday, although things quieten down after about 2pm. The best spot to find genuine crafts is at the **Kuranda Arts Co-op** (☎/fax 4093 9026, **W** www.artskuranda.asn.au, 24 Coondoo St). It also has Internet access.

Kuranda has a number of 'attractions', and if you have some time to spare, it's worth checking out one or two. The **Kuranda Wildlife Noctarium** (☎ 4093 7334, Coondoo St; adult/child $9.90/4.50; open 10am-3pm), gives you the opportunity to see wide-awake nocturnal rainforest animals, such as sugar gliders, fruit bats and echidnas at very close range. You'll definitely see more than on a guided night-walk in Cape Tribulation!

**The Aviary** (☎ 4093 7411, 8 Thongon St; adult/child $11/5; open 10am-3.30pm) has a free-flight native parrot and finch enclosure, and a smattering of reptiles.

Within the market area, **Birdworld** (☎ 4093 9188, Heritage Markets; adult/child $11/4;

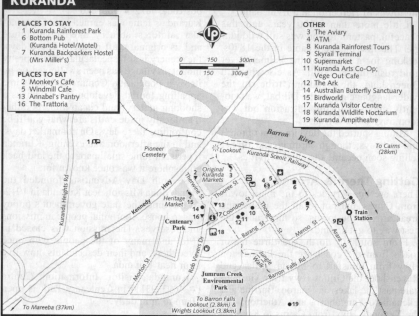

## KURANDA

**PLACES TO STAY**
1  Kuranda Rainforest Park
6  Bottom Pub
   (Kuranda Hotel/Motel)
7  Kuranda Backpackers Hostel
   (Mrs Miller's)

**PLACES TO EAT**
2  Monkey's Cafe
5  Windmill Cafe
13  Annabel's Pantry
16  The Trattoria

**OTHER**
3  The Aviary
4  ATM
8  Kuranda Rainforest Tours
9  Skyrail Terminal
10  Supermarket
11  Kuranda Arts Co-Op;
    Vege Out Cafe
12  The Ark
14  Australian Butterfly Sanctuary
15  Birdworld
17  Kuranda Visitor Centre
18  Kuranda Wildlife Noctarium
19  Kuranda Ampitheatre

open 9am-4pm) is a canopied garden with over 30 species of birds, including non-native species. Near the market area, the **Australian Butterfly Sanctuary** (☎ 4093 7575, 8 Rob Veivers Dr; adult/child $12/5; open 10am-4pm Mon-Fri) has regular guided tours. If the weather's rainy, the butterflies won't be very active, so save your money and don't bother going in.

Over the footbridge behind the train station, Kuranda Rainforest Tours (☎ 4093 7476) runs peaceful 45-minute cruises along the Barron River for $12/6 adult/child. They depart hourly from 10.30am to 2.30pm, but the service often closes during the Wet due to river flooding, so call beforehand to check.

There are several signposted walks through the market, and a short walking track through **Jumrum Creek Environmental Park**, off the Barron Falls Rd, 700m from the bottom of Thongon St. The park has a big population of fruit bats.

Further down, the Barron Falls Rd divides: The left fork takes you to a **lookout** over the falls, while a further 1.5km along the right fork brings you to **Wrights Lookout**. A walking trail leads down to another lookout from here.

## Places to Stay

There are several small B&Bs around Kuranda – check with the tourist office for contact details and information.

**Kuranda Rainforest Park** (☎ 4093 7316, Kuranda Heights Rd) Camp sites $15 (2 people), single/double backpacker cabins $15/32, on-site cabins from $66. Located in a quiet, chilled setting close to the Barron River, night walks are a feature; pick-up from Kuranda station is available.

**Kuranda Backpackers Hostel** (Mrs Miller's; ☎ 4093 7355, 6 Arara St) Dorm beds $16, singles/doubles $28/38. This agreeably rambling, rustic place has a huge garden. It's a quiet, relaxing place to stay.

*Bottom Pub* *(Kuranda Hotel/Motel;*
☎ *4093 7206, Cnr Coondoo & Arara Sts)*
Singles/doubles $45/55, with ceiling fans.
Remaining doggedly downmarket, it has 12
clean, basic motel rooms. The *Garden Bar
& Grill* (dishes $7-12.60) in the pub's back-
yard is a surprisingly pretty spot. It serves
up counter lunches of the steak and sanger
variety.

## Places to Eat

There's some good food on offer in the market's *food stalls* – fresh juices, Thai stir-fries
and Indian curries. There's a *supermarket* in
Coondoo St if you're self-catering, and the
excellent bakery *Annabel's Pantry* on Therwine St has a large range of pastries.

*Windmill Cafe* (☎ *4093 9466, Condoo St)*
Meals $5-12.50. Open 7am-5pm. One of the
best places for breakfast, coffee or lunch, it
serves up pancakes, savoury muffins, bagels
and burgers.

*Monkey's Cafe* (☎ *4093 7451, 1 Therwine St)* Dinner mains $13-15.50. Open
10am-3pm, Wed-Fri & Sun. Tucked away at
the bottom of Therwine St, near the markets, this cafe offers generous, healthy fare.

*Vege Out Cafe* (☎ *4093 8483, Shop 5, 24
Condoo St)* Meals $4.40-10. Open 10am-
4pm daily. In the Red House, next to the
'The Ark', it specialises in wholesome
vegetarian dishes.

*The Trattoria* (☎ *4093 8733, Rob Vievers Dr)* Meals $7-17.60. Open lunch & din-
ner Tues-Sun. Expect tasty pizza, pasta and
calzone.

## Getting There & Away

Getting to Kuranda is all part of the experience, whether you come via the scenic railway or the Skyrail over the rainforest. It's
worth trying both options, though you'll
have to take the train or bus if you have a
backpack in tow – the Skyrail has baggage
restrictions and only allows daypacks to be
carried on-board.

The Kuranda Scenic Railway (☎ 4036
9288) winds 34km from Cairns to Kuranda.
The line, which took five years to build, was
opened in 1891 and goes through 15 tunnels,
climbing more than 300m in the last 21km.

The trains operate daily from Cairns train
station on Bunda St ($29.60/48 one way/
return, 1¾ hours, 8.30am & 9.30am Sunday
to Friday, 8.30am Saturday). Trains depart
Kuranda at 2pm and 3.30pm from Sunday to
Monday and 3.30pm Saturday.

The Skyrail Rainforest Cableway (☎ 4038
1555) is a 7.5km gondola cableway that runs
from Smithfield, a northern suburb of Cairns,
to Kuranda, with two stops along the way. It
operates daily from 8am to 5pm (last departure from Cairns and Kuranda at 3.30pm);
fares are $30/45 one way/return for adults,
$15/22.50 for children aged 4+, and $75/
112.50 for families (two adults, two or more
children). A number of day-tour packages
combine travel on both the train and the cableway for about $73.80, including return
transfers to Cairns.

White Car Coaches (☎ 4091 1855) has
buses five times daily from outside the
Underdog Hotel, at 48 Spence St, Cairns
($7.40 one way).

## KURANDA TO MAREEBA

It's 37km (30 minutes) from Kuranda to
Mareeba, along the Kennedy Hwy. The first
section of the drive continues to twist and
climb through the green mountains, but the
road soon levels out as you enter the flatter,
drier farmlands to the west of the Tableland.

There's an intriguing accommodation possibility along this route: *Cedar Park Rainforest Resort* (☎ *4093 7022, fax 4093 7044,
1 Cedar Park Rd)*. The turn-off to this resort
is about 14km from Kuranda, and then it's
another 6km of dirt road. It can only be described as quirky – a blend of raw timber
poles, medieval brick arches and tacky 1970s
architecture. The resort charges $100 for
doubles and also has a *restaurant*, but the
best part is its rainforest environment.

About 23km south-west of Kuranda is
the turn-off to **Davies Creek National Park**.
It's another 7km of gravel road to this small
but pretty park of eucalypt forest. It's a
great spot for bushwalking. There's a self-
registration *camping ground* with toilets,
fireplaces and picnic tables, and several
walking tracks lead to the creek, a waterfall
and a lookout.

## MAREEBA

**postcode 4880 • pop 6870**

In the far corner of the Tableland, Mareeba is the centre of a rich farming area. Tobacco, cattle, macadamia nuts and sugar are traditionally the area's money-earners, although coffee, mango wine and a stunning waterbird reserve are bringing tourist dollars to the town. Mareeba Rodeo, held each July, is one of Australia's biggest rodeos.

The Information Centre & Museum (☎ 4092 5674), in Centenary Park near the Kuranda turn-off on the highway, is open from 8am to 4pm daily.

### Things to See & Do

**Mareeba Wetlands** (☎ 4093 2514, W www .mareebawetlands.com, adult/child $8/5; open 8.30am-4pm Wed-Sun) is top of the list. It's a 20 sq km reserve of timbered savannah grasslands, with 12 lakes that attract waterbirds as well as marsupials and reptiles. At different times of the year, you'll see ospreys, black swans, brolgas, pelicans and jabirus, just to name a few. The Visitor Centre has a *cafe* and runs a range of guided walks and electric boat tours. There are also several long self-guided walking trails, and canoes for hire ($11). To reach the wetlands, take the Pickford Rd turn-off from Biboohra, 7km north of Mareeba. It may be closed during the wet season – ring beforehand to check.

**Granite Gorge** (admission $2), on private land 12km south-west of Mareeba, is famous for its large population of rock wallabies. There are also walking trails and waterfalls around the huge granite formations and a *camping ground*. To reach it, follow Chewco Rd out of Mareeba for 7km; there's a turn-off to your right from there.

The **cattle saleyards**, just north of town on the road to Mt Molloy, are a fascinating place to visit on Tuesday mornings at the crack of dawn – you'll see more Akubra hats and bowed legs than you ever thought possible!

There are a few coffee tour options around town. Head to **Coffee Works** (☎ 4092 4101, 136 Mason St; adult/child under 12 $5/free; open 9am-4pm), a coffee roaster that runs tasting tours, or the heart-warming **Bruno's Coffee Plantation at Paddy's Green** (☎ 4093

2269, Dimbulah Rd; admission free), where you'll learn about one man's determination to make the perfect brew.

It's also worth dropping by **Golden Pride Winery** (☎ 4093 2750) in Bilwon for a taste of its sweet mango wines. Head north on the road to Mt Molloy for 11km and turn right at Bilwon Rd. It's another 2km to the winery.

About 5km south of Mareeba, some will find the **Beck Museum** (☎ 4092 3979, Kennedy Hwy; adult/child $11/6; open 10am-4pm) worthy of a visit. It has the biggest military and aviation collection in Queensland, including P39 American fighter planes used over the Coral Sea during WWII.

### Places to Stay & Eat

**Riverside Caravan Park** (☎/fax 4092 2309, 13 Egan St) Unpowered/powered sites $11/14. On the Barron River, this is good place to stop for the night. Turn right from the highway at the Noble Service Station and follow the signs.

**Ant Hill Hotel** (☎ 4092 1011, fax 4092 2147, 79 Byrnes St) Dorm beds/singles/doubles $10/36/46. This renovated pub in the centre of town has funky 1950s-inspired rooms upstairs, none with en suite. It also has a *bistro*. If you're looking for agricultural work, it's a good contact point.

**Jackaroo Motel** (☎ 4092 2677, fax 4092 3837, 340 Byrnes St) Singles/doubles $60/70. This is a modern motel with top-notch facilities, including disabled facilities.

**Arriga Park Farm Stay** (☎ 4093 2114, fax 4093 2114, Dimbulah Rd) Adult/child $60/30 per person, including full breakfast. Surrounded by fruit trees and sugarcane, this modern colonial homestead has comfortable, if chintzy, rooms.

An old-style milk-bar, **Nastasi's** (☎ 4092 2321) on the main street, has vegie burgers, foccacia and chicken dishes. It also has Internet access. Also on the main drag, **Ali Baba's Takeaway** (☎ 4092 5166), near the corner of Atherton St, has Turkish sweets, falafel rolls and kebabs.

## MAREEBA TO CHILLAGOE

The Burke Developmental Rd leaves the Kennedy Hwy at Mareeba and heads west all the way across to Karumba and Normanton on the Gulf of Carpentaria. Most of the route is unsealed and passes through some of the most remote and inhospitable parts of the state. It is only suitable for well-equipped, self-sufficient and experienced 4WD adventurers, preferably travelling with a companion vehicle. Caution is advised during the wet season; check road conditions with the Chillagoe police.

However, the first section of the route, the road to Chillagoe (141km from Mareeba, three hours), is well within the reach of the average day-tripper. If you have the time, it's worth veering north at Dimbulah to Tyrconnel Historic Gold Mine and Mt Mulligan Station. This once-rich mining area of the Hodgkinson goldfields is the very reason for the establishment of Cairns and Port Douglas.

Heading west from Dimbulah to Chillagoe, a former mining town surrounded by countryside of towering karst, all but the last 25km of the route is on sealed roads, which won't present a problem for 2WD vehicles during the dry season. If you're travelling by rental car, however, you'll need to hire a small 4WD (see Car & 4WD Rental under the Cairns Getting There & Away section).

## Tyrconnel Historic Gold Mine & Mt Mulligan Station

Once a busy town of 10,000 people, the old gold mine at Tyrconnel, 32km north of Dimbulah, has been restored and is now a working museum offering tours and accommodation. *Tyrconnel Historic Gold Mine* (☎ 4093 5177, fax 4093 5177, W www .tyrconnell.com.au) has camping for $5 and self-contained cottages from $50 per person. It also offers a two-day/one-night tour for $266, and a three-day/two-night tour for $411; both include meals and transfers from Cairns. Mining tours ($12/6) and night cemetery tours ($10/5) are also available.

A further 17km north, Mt Mulligan was the site of Queensland's worst mining disaster in 1921 when 75 men were killed; the mountain itself is an eerie and spectacular formation. There isn't much left of the old township, but it's an interesting area to explore. The town's former hospital, a big, old

Queenslander, is now the homestead of this large cattle station set on 260 sq km. *Mt Mulligan Station* (☎ 1800 359 798, 4094 8360, fax 4092 2147) has two-day/one-night tours for $110, and three-day/two-night tours for $145; both include pick-up from Cairns and all meals. There is also a self-drive tour for $50 that includes meals, and 'bush experience' tours from Cairns that include bushwalking, swimming, horse riding ($20) and didgeridoo-making ($50).

The unsealed road to Tyrconnel and Mt Mulligan is rough in patches; 4WDs are recommended during the wet season (ring beforehand to check the road condition), although you can make it easily in a 2WD vehicle during the dry season.

## Irvinebank

At Petford, 79km south-west of Mareeba, there's a turn-off that leads south and then west across to Herberton, via the old mining township of Irvinebank. This road is gravel for 13km.

Established in 1883, there are still about 100 people kicking on in this once-wealthy mining town, living in an interesting collection of restored old houses and cottages. Tin, copper and silver were the main mining targets here.

The **Loudoun House Museum** (☎ 4096 4020, McDonald St; open 10am-noon & 1pm-4pm Fri-Wed) is set in the former home of John Moffat, one of Queensland's most successful mining pioneers. Built in 1884, it's said to be the oldest two-storey timber and iron building in north Queensland.

*Irvinebank Tavern* (☎ 4096 4176, McDonald St) offers singles/doubles for $25/45. The rooms in this friendly pub all have en suites and TVs. You can also camp in the backyard of the pub and use the showers and loos for no charge – just make sure you have a few drinks in the pub to repay the hospitality!

## Petford to Chillagoe

Back on the road to Chillagoe, it's another 7km west from Petford to the tiny, almost nonexistent town of **Lappa**, which was once a Cobb & Co stop. Today it has what must be the only BYO pub in the world, the ramshackle tin **Espanol Hotel**, built by a Spaniard in 1901. If you plan to stop by this friendly pub, Dimbulah is your last chance to buy beer and crisps, or wine and tapas (or close to) and imbibe in style! There's a small **museum** and *camping* area here – entry to both is by donation, so dig deep.

Some 25km on is **Almaden**, and the *Almaden Pub (Railway Hotel; ☎/fax 4094 8307)* charges $55 per person including dinner and breakfast; book ahead. It's a ferny oasis to stop for a drink or stay overnight, although there's not anything to do here. The beauty of the town is that it's unfenced, so horses and Brahman cattle roam around on the town's streets. The *Savannahlander* stops here and you can transfer by bus to Chillagoe.

Beyond Almaden the gravel sections of the road begin, and the distinctive outback landscape of red earth and termite hills emerges, rising among sparse woodland, jagged outcrops and rocky hills.

## CHILLAGOE
### postcode 4871 • pop 200
It may only be three hours' drive from the coast, but it's a long way from the commercialisation of Cairns or the glam of Port Douglas. A visit to the mining village of Chillagoe, established by William Atherton in 1888 against fierce opposition from the local Aboriginal tribe, offers a glimpse into life in the outback. Aboriginal rock-art galleries exist at nearby Mungana.

There are plenty of mining relics, and today some marble is still quarried in the area. Of more interest than mining is Chillagoe's spectacular landscape of limestone pinnacles and dark caves, abuzz (literally) with bats, birds and pythons. The limestone developed from coral reefs deposited over 400 million years ago – and today, it truly is extraordinary scenery.

On the main street, Queen St, you'll find a small general store and one or two tacky souvenir shops. If you don't have a vehicle, and want to go visit the rock-art galleries, a number of places to stay offer reasonably priced tours.

## Things to See & Do
The extensive cave systems and limestone peaks of **Chillagoe-Mungana Caves National Park** can take a few happy days to explore. Drop by the QPWS (☎ 4094 7163, Queen St) for detailed maps and information on self-guided cave trails. The rangers run interesting guided tours of **Donna Cave** ($5.50, one hour, 9am), **Trezkinn Cave** ($5.50, 30 minutes, 11am) and **Royal Cave** ($8.25, 1¼ hours, 1.30pm). The Donna and Trezkinn Caves are both electrically lit, with steep steps taking you through their delicate formations. The Royal Cave is a larger, more open cave system with small daylight chambers; expect to walk among large colonies of bats and nesting white-rumped swiftlets.

A 3.5km walking trail links the Royal Arch Cave section with the Donna and Trezkinn Caves carpark, taking you through a harsh, craggy landscape via the must-see **Balancing Rock**, where a 4m-tall boulder balances (somehow!) on a much smaller rock. About 2km north-west of town are the moonscape ruins of the **Chillagoe Smelters**, which were built at the turn of the 20th century and operated until 1943. An interpretive walk takes you through the rusting remains. The **Aboriginal rock-art** galleries are in the national park near the ghost town of Mungana, about 15km from Chillagoe.

The **Chillagoe Heritage Museum** (☎ 4094 7109, Hill St; admission $3; open 8.30am-5pm) is only of interest to local history buffs. It's also the tourist information centre.

## Places to Stay & Eat
*Chillagoe Tourist Village (☎/fax 4094 7177, Queen St)* Tent sites $6 per person, single/double cabins $35/40, units $45/60. The self-contained cabins are modern and comfortable, with a TV. There's also a pool, a classy marble barbecue and a *restaurant* on site.

*Post Office Hotel (☎ 4094 7119, 37 Queen St)* Singles/doubles with fan $11/33, singles/doubles with air-con $33. This is a classic country pub with a huge timber balcony overlooking the town. The iron beds in the fan rooms may be about the narrowest thing you'll sleep in, at least in this lifetime!

More modern bedding is also available in very nice air-con rooms. Simple and wholesome *pub food* is available.

*Chillagoe Bush Camp & Eco Lodge* (☎ 1800 447 155, ☎/fax 4094 7155, Hospital Ave) Singles/twins $20/33, doubles from $50. About 1km from the centre of town, near the railway station, this is a former miners' village with accommodation in dongas and cabins. Reasonably priced *meals* and tours are available.

*Chillagoe Cabins* (☎/fax 4094 7206, Queen St) Singles/doubles $82.50/93.50. The comfortable modern cabins are modelled on old miner's huts. It also runs 4WD tours.

*Chillagoe Creek Homestead* (☎ 4094 7160) Camping $5.50, singles/doubles from $40/71.50. Just out of town by the airstrip, this is a small B&B by Chillagoe Creek.

There's a small general store on Queen Street if you're self-catering.

### Getting There & Away
To reach Chillagoe, take a White Car Coach to Mareeba to connect with the Chillagoe Bus Service (☎ 4094 7155). The service departs Mareeba on Monday and Friday at 10.15am, 1pm and 3pm, and on Wednesday at 11.30am ($31.25, two hours). It departs Chillagoe at 7.30am and 9.30am (Monday, Wednesday and Thursday).

The *Savannahlander* is also another good way to reach Chillagoe. The train stops at Almaden, on its way to Forsayth, and is met by the Chillagoe Bus Service. See Train under the Getting There & Away section under Cairns.

### TOLGA
Tolga, a small township 5km north of Atherton, is a good place to stop for lunch. It has the **Tolga Woodworks Gallery & Café** (☎ 4095 4488), a woodworking centre that sells oh-so beautiful handcrafted furniture and kitchenware made from native timbers. The *cafe* has a delicious range of goodies, soups and sandwiches.

You can turn east at Tolga to reach **Danbulla Forest Drive**, which technically starts at Tinaroo Falls 13km north-east of here (see the later Lake Tinaroo entry for details).

Just south of town is a turn-off to *The Homestead* (☎ 4095 4266, fax 4095 4801, Beantree Rd). This avocado farm has an up-market restaurant serving mod Oz cuisine (lunch/dinner from $15/20), as well as some basic motel units (singles/doubles $70/80, including breakfast).

Also nearby is *Lavender Hill B&B* (☎ 4095 8384, fax 4095 8084, 1 Favier Rd, Kairi) with doubles/suites from $99/120. Right on the Barron River front, this Tuscan-style B&B is a great place to unwind.

### ATHERTON
postcode 4883 • pop 5690
Atherton is the major township in the Tableland. It's a busy commercial and farming centre that isn't overly geared towards attracting tourists.

The **Old Post Office Gallery** (☎ 4091 4222, e info@athertontableland.com; open 9am-5pm), on the Herberton Rd, houses the Tableland Information Centre, a small art gallery and museum.

The Forestry section of the Department of Natural Resources (☎ 4091 1844, 83 Main St; open 9am to 5pm weekdays) is the place to come for camping and 4WD permits and information on the Tableland's state forests.

If you want to hire a car, head to Simon's Vehicle Hire (☎ 4091 2739, 43 Robert St), opposite the swimming pool. It has 2WD and 4WD vehicles. Atherton Blue Gum B&B (☎ 4091 5149) runs tours on demand.

### Things to See & Do
At the southern end of town is Platypus Park, the starting point for the **Railco Scenic Heritage Steam Railway** (☎ 4091 4871, Platypus Park Station, Herberton Rd; return trips adult/child $27.50/13.75; departs 10.30am Wed, Sat & Sun), which runs from Atherton to Herberton (1½ hours). The 1927 C17 class steam locomotive climbs the Herberton Range, stops in Herberton for 1½ hours, then returns to Atherton at 2.30pm. There's a nice little *cafe* with an outdoor deck at the park that's open 8am to 4pm Wednesday to Monday.

There are plans to restore Atherton's Chinatown. The **Hou Wang Temple**, behind the Old Post Office Gallery, once sat among a busy village of shops and houses. Today it sits alone, facing an interpretive walk through grasslands.

On the main street, **Crystal Caves** (☎ *4091 2365, Main St; adult/child $11/5.50; open 8.30am-5pm Mon-Fri, 10am-4pm Sat & Sun)* is a mineralogical museum in an artificial cave setting straight out of *The Flintstones.*

At the eastern end of Main St, **Rainforest Arts** (☎ *4091 3371; open 8.30am-5pm Mon-Fri, 8.30am-noon Sat)* has a great selection of local arts and handcrafted timber pieces.

## Places to Stay & Eat

*Woodlands Tourist Park* (☎ *4091 1407, fax 4091 3449, Herberton Rd)* Unpowered/powered sites $14/18, single/double on-site cabins from $40/45. At the southern entrance to town, it has bushland camp sites and mini-Queenslander cabins.

*Atherton Travellers Lodge* (☎/fax *4091 3552,* e *athertonbackpack@hotmail.com, 37 Alice St)* Dorm beds from $15, singles/doubles $22/36. Near the town centre, this is a quiet, friendly hostel. It's signposted off the main road into town from Yungaburra, just before it meets the Kennedy Hwy. Agricultural work in the area can be arranged.

*Atherton Blue Gum Bed & Breakfast* (☎ *4091 5149, 36 Twelfth Ave)* Singles/doubles $75/85. On Halloran's Hill in town, this friendly B&B has sweeping views from its timber deck. Tours and transfers are available.

*Grand Hotel* (☎ *4091 4899, fax 4091 3565, Cnr Main and Vernon Sts)* Bunk beds/singles $25/36, doubles $45-75, includes continental breakfast. This renovated old pub has nice rooms, some with en suites and great views. It also has a *bistro* open for lunch and dinner.

## LAKE TINAROO

From Atherton, Tolga or Yungaburra it's a short drive to picturesque Lake Tinaroo with over 200km of sheltered shoreline, which was created for the Barron River hydroelectric power scheme. Tinaroo is a popular bird-watching, swimming and water-sports

spot, and is one of the best barramundi fishing spots in Australia – barramundi fishing is open year-round.

Tinaroo Waters Birds & Barra (☎ 4095 8425) offers personal bird-watching or fishing tours for $165/275 per half-day/full-day.

## Danbulla Forest Drive

Drop by the Department of Natural Resources in Atherton for the *Danbulla Forest Drive* brochure, which highlights the main camping grounds and sights on the circuit drive around the lake.

The drive starts at **Tinaroo Falls**, a sleepy village at the north-western corner of the lake. *Lake Tinaroo Holiday Park* (☎ *4095 8232, fax 4095 8808, Dam Rd)* is a pleasant camping ground by the lake. It has unpowered/powered sites for $13/18 and cabins from $52.

If you're up for something different, houseboats can be rented through *Tinaroo Tropical Houseboats* (☎ *4095 8322, fax 4095 8460)*. Economy and luxury houseboats sleeping four to six start from $340 for two days.

Three kilometres south of the caravan park is *Tinaroo Haven Holiday Lodge* (☎ *4095 8686, Lot 42, Wavell Dr, Tinaroo Waters)* Sleeping eight people, this comfortable timber pole-house has stunning views, and also has disabled facilities. It charges $132 for a double, plus $22 for each extra person.

Just out of town there's a lookout over the powerful waters of **Tinaroo Falls Dam**. Nearby is *Pensini's Café & Restaurant* (☎ *4095 8242, Lake Tinaroo Lookout)*, a modern bar and bistro with great views, and dishes from $6 to $26.50. It's open 10am to 5pm daily; later on Saturday.

Once you're past the dam, the road turns to dirt and the Danbulla Forest Drive officially starts. The drive is a pot-holed but beautiful 31km circuit of the lake, finally emerging on the Gillies Hwy at Boar Pocket Rd, 4km north of Lake Barrine. It passes several stunning lakeside self-registration *camping grounds* ($3.85 per person per night) with showers and toilets.

One of the most pleasant of these is the first along the drive, **Platypus Creek**.

There's a great camping ground with shady pine trees and a boat ramp. Further on, just after **Kauri Creek**, another superb camping ground, you pass the 4WD tracks of Mt Edith Rd, Tinaroo Creek Rd and Kauri Creek Rd, which, depending on the route you take, can lead you north through the hills all the way to Mareeba. The tracks have some great views along the way, but you need a permit from the Department of Natural Resources in Atherton, who can also provide a mud map. The road can be closed during the Wet.

About halfway around the circuit, **Lake Euramoo** is in a double volcanic crater; there's a short botanic walk around the lake. There is another crater at **Mobo Creek**, a 600m circuit-walk off the drive. Then, 25km from the dam, it's a short walk to the 500-year-old **Cathedral Fig**, a gigantic strangler fig tree shouldering epiphytes nesting in its branches.

## YUNGABURRA
### postcode 4872 • pop 985

This pretty village of National Trust–classified buildings is 13km east of Atherton along the Gillies Hwy. It's right in the heart of the Tableland. The **Yungaburra Markets** (☎ 4095 2111) are held in the centre of town on the fourth Saturday of every month, and there are several signposted **galleries** in town that are worth checking out. There's no bank in town, although Eftpos is available from the hotel, which can also cash travellers cheques.

For a chance to see the elusive platypus, there's a viewing area off the main street on Petersen Creek, as well as at Platypus Park.

About 2km south of Yungaburra on the road to Malanda is the 500-year-old **Curtain Fig Tree**, a 50m-high strangler fig whose aerial roots form a beautiful 20m-high hanging screen. A viewing platform snakes around the tree and you'll see brush turkeys foraging about.

### Places to Stay

**On the Wallaby** (☎ 4095 2031, 34 Eacham Rd) Camp sites $10 (in backyard), dorm beds/doubles $18/40. This is an excellent,

comfy, clean backpackers hostel. It has a $70 package that includes return bus from Cairns, accommodation and a canoe trip.

**Lake Eacham Hotel** (☎ 4095 3515, fax 4095 3202, Gillies Hwy) Singles/doubles $49.40/55. This fine, old Federation-era pub has a magnificent timber dining room, a *bistro* and comfortable modern en suite rooms.

**Kookaburra Lodge** (☎/fax 4095 3222, Cnr Oak St & Eacham Rd) Doubles $80. A small peaceful place with bright, modern units. There's a pool and small reading room with a potbelly stove.

**Gumtree Getaway** (☎ 4095 3105, Gillies Hwy) Doubles $98. This quiet place, with en suite cabins, is just outside town on the Atherton Rd.

**Eden House** (☎ 4095 3355, fax 4095 3377, 20 Gillies Hwy) Doubles from $128. Eden House has private garden units, and its bar and *restaurant* (meals $18 to $25, open 11am to 2pm Saturday and Sunday, 6pm till late Tuesday to Sunday) is in a renovated, heritage homestead.

There are some gorgeous B&B options around Yungaburra including **Mt Quinkan Crater Retreat** (☎/fax 4095 2255, Peeramon Rd) where a three-night stay starts from $500 per person, including breakfast. The self-contained tree-houses are positioned at the very top of a volcanic cinder cone and offer awesome views, privacy and everything else you could want – including double-headed showers! Follow the road between Yungaburra and Peeramon to the signposted turn-off.

### Places to Eat

**The Gem Gallery** (☎ 4095 3455, 21 Eacham Rd) Meals $1-4.50. The small coffee shop next to the gallery does no-frills breakfasts and sandwiches and also has Internet access.

**Keddie's** (☎ 4095 3265, Gillies Hwy) Dishes $4-16. Open 8.30am-7.30pm. On the main street, Keddie's has an outdoor deck and serves up breakfast, falafel rolls, pizza and fast food.

**Burra Inn** (☎/fax 4095 3657, 1 Cedar St) Mains around $22. Open 6pm-late Wed-Mon.

This is a charming little BYO gourmet restaurant opposite the pub.

*Nick's Swiss-Italian Restaurant & Yodeller's Bar* (☎ 4095 3330, Gillies Hwy) Meals $10.50-28.50. Open 11am-3.30pm Fri-Tues, 6pm-11pm Thur-Tues. This chalet-style place serves up rösti, pasta and mod Oz cuisine. Brace yourself for the Swiss music complete with mooing cows piped through the toilets! Again with the cows!

## CRATER LAKES NATIONAL PARK & AROUND

Part of the World Heritage Area, the two mirror-like crater lakes, **Lake Barrine** and **Lake Eacham**, are off the Gillies Hwy just east of Yungaburra. Lake Eacham (Bana Yidyam) was an assembly place for the Ngadjonji and Yidinyji Bama Aboriginal people. The area, like much of the Tableland, was felled for timber in the 1880s. In 1934 it became a national park.

The lakes are reached by paved roads and make peaceful swimming and bird-watching spots. There are walking tracks around their perimeters – 6km around Lake Barrine (best avoided when Japanese tour groups use a loudspeaker to blast their commentary across the lake!) and 4km around Lake Eacham. Camping is not permitted around either lake.

At Lake Barrine, the *Lake Barrine Rainforest Cruise & Tea House* (☎ 4095 3847, Gillies Hwy), established in 1927, serves breakfast, Devonshire tea and lunch daily from 9am to 5pm. From the tea house, you can take a 40-minute **cruise** (adult/child $9.95/5.50; 10.15am, 11.30am, 1.30pm, 2.30pm & 3.35pm). A short hop from the tea house, there are two neck-tilting, 1000-year-old **Kauri pines**.

Lake Eacham is quieter and more beautiful, and makes an excellent place for a swim in clear water.

Within Gadgarra State Forest, 12km from Yungaburra, and accessed from either lake, is the breathtaking **Gadgarra Red Cedar**. The tree is the largest red cedar remaining in FNQ. Seeing it gives some perspective on what the landscape was like before non-Indigenous settlement. It's a 600m walk to the tree from the carpark.

## Places to Stay

*Lake Eacham Caravan Park* (☎ 4095 3730, Lakes Dr) Unpowered/powered sites $10/15.40, cabins $49.50. Less than 2km down the Malanda Rd from Lake Eacham, this is a pretty camping ground with nice en suite cabins.

*Chambers Wildlife Rainforest Lodge* (☎/fax 4095 3754, Eacham Close) Singles/doubles from $85/99. Surrounded by national park, the lodge caters for bird-watchers and nature groups. All units are self-contained.

*Crater Lakes Rainforest Cottages* (☎ 1800 992 322, ℮ jenny@craterlakes .com.au, Eacham Close, Off Lakes Dr) Doubles $150, including breakfast. These comfortable self-contained timber cottages are lovely – the decor in each has an individual touch.

## PEERAMON

The tiny village of Peeramon is tucked into the hills midway between Malanda and Yungaburra on the Peeramon Rd, and its main attraction is its atmospheric, old country pub. *Peeramon Hotel* (☎ 4096 5873, Main St) has dongas for $10, comfortable singles/doubles for $40/50 and *pub grub* for $7 to $11.

## MALANDA

**postcode 4885 • pop 860**

About 15km south of Lake Eacham, Malanda is a small town with some historic buildings, such as the gargantuan timber Malanda Hotel. Malanda also has a huge dairy. The helpful Malanda Falls Visitors Centre (☎ 4096 6957, Atherton Rd; open 10am till 4pm) has thoughtful displays on the area's human and geological history. There's a National Australia Bank on James St, the main street. There are a few shops in town selling local crafts that are worth exploring.

## Things to See & Do

The Visitors Centre runs guided **rainforest walks** ($5) led by a Ngadjonji tribal elder at 10.30am and 2pm Wednesday to Sunday.

On the outskirts of town, beside the Johnstone River crossing, **Malanda Falls** drop into a big pool, surrounded by lawns and forest. It's a popular swimming spot, and a 1km walking trail passes through the forest nearby.

If you're staying in the town, the **Majestic Theatre** (☎ 4096 5726, **W** www .majestictheatre.com.au, Eacham Place), built in 1922, is a cinematic experience. It still has canvas chairs, and screens crowd-pleaser flicks on Friday and Saturday nights.

A couple of kilometres west of Malanda is **Bromfield Swamp**, an important waterbird sanctuary. A viewing platform beside the road overlooks an eroded volcanic crater.

## Places to Stay & Eat

**Malanda Falls Caravan Park** (☎ 4096 5314, fax 4096 6188, 38 Park Ave) Tent sites $13.20, cabins $33-60.50. Located right next to Malanda Falls, you'll probably see more wildlife in its spacious grounds than you will around Cape Tribulation! The cabins are all good value.

**Malanda Hotel** (☎ 4096 5101, fax 4096 5102, Cnr James & English Sts) Single/ double pub rooms $22/44, motel rooms $33/55. Right in the centre of town, this huge, old timber pub has rooms and a **dining room** with a good reputation serving meals for $7 to $15.

**Tree Kangaroo Café** (☎ 4096 6658) Meals $2.50-10. Open 9am-4.30pm. Next to the Malanda Falls Visitors Centre, the cafe has a yummy selection of sandwiches and light meals.

For self-caterers, there's a **supermarket** on English St.

## AROUND MALANDA

There are also a couple of good places to stay in the hills around Malanda.

**Fairdale Farmstay** (☎/fax 4096 6599, Hillcrest Rd) Cottages from $121 (family of 4), doubles from $95. In a scenic setting, guests can get involved in the farm activities or just enjoy the location. It's 3km south of Malanda.

**Platypus Forest Lodge** (☎ 4096 5926, 12 Topaz Rd) Singles/doubles $45/55. This is a good-value B&B with a creek running through the property. Take the Malanda–Lake Barrine Rd, and turn right at Topaz Rd.

**Rose Gums** (☎ 4096 8360, fax 4096 8230, Land Rd, Butcher's Creek) Doubles $150. Rose Gums overlooks Wooroonooran National Park, 17km from Malanda, and has self-contained and very private timber and pole chalets.

Ten kilometres from Malanda on the Millaa Millaa Rd is the small village of Tarzali. It has yet another gorgeous Tableland B&B, **Fur 'n' Feathers** (☎ 4096 5364, fax 4096 5380, Hogan Rd, Tarzali, via Malanda), with doubles for $220. On pristine rainforest rich with wildlife, its riverfront treehouses are all self-contained (including a barbecue on the deck!).

Nearby is **The Roundyard** (☎ 4096 5115, Millaa Millaa Rd, Tarzali). Decked out in natural timbers, this cheerful eatery serves plain but good lunches and dinners (dishes $7 to $15).

## MILLAA MILLAA
**postcode 4886 • pop 320**

Set in what was recently the heart of dairy country until government deregulation, the tiny township is 24km south of Malanda. A large number of artists live in the area, attracted by the meditative countryside, and there's a push within Millaa Millaa to open up its diverse artistic community to travellers. The Falls Holiday Park acts as the tourist information centre; it also has Internet access. A few kilometres west of Millaa Millaa, the East Evelyn Rd passes the **Millaa Millaa Lookout**, with its superb panoramic view.

## Places to Stay & Eat

**The Falls Holiday Park** (☎ 4097 2290, Malanda Rd) Unpowered/powered sites $13/15, bunkhouses $12, cabins from $26 without en suites. Set on 2.8 hectares rich in wildlife, the park has basic cabins and a **restaurant**.

**Millaa Millaa Hotel** (☎ 4097 2212, fax 4097 2990, 15 Main St) Singles/doubles $45/55. The original grand timber pub, built in 1922, burnt down in 1998. Its replacement is modern and bland, but it does have very comfortable motel units. The pub also has a **bistro**.

**The Falls Tea House** (☎ 4097 2237, Palmerston Hwy) Meals $6-10. Just outside the township is this lovely, timber 1930s homestead. Meals have a Mediterranean twist and charming **B&B** accommodation (doubles $85-95) is also an option.

*Iskanda Park Farmstay (☎/fax 4097 2401, Nash Rd)* Rooms $110-125, with breakfast. About 7km north of Millaa Millaa, on the road between Malanda and Millaa Millaa, this working cattle farm has gorgeous vistas, comfortable accommodation and extroverted hosts!

## WATERFALLS CIRCUIT
The start of this 16km circuit is a little way east of Millaa Millaa, and passes some of the most picturesque falls on the Tableland. You enter the circuit by taking Theresa Creek Rd, 1km east of Millaa Millaa on the Palmerston Hwy. **Millaa Millaa Falls**, the first you reach, are the most spectacular; surrounded by tree ferns and flowers, the waterfall forms a perfect white foam of water falling from a drop of about 12m. These falls have the best swimming hole and a grassy area perfect for picnics.

Continuing around the circuit, you reach **Zillie Falls**, where a short walking trail leads to a lookout beside the falls. Further on you come to **Ellinjaa Falls**, with a 200m walking trail down to a swimming hole at the base of the falls, before returning to the Palmerston Hwy just 2.5km out of Millaa Millaa.

A further 5.5km down the Palmerston Hwy there's a turn-off to **Mungalli Falls**, 5km off the highway, where you'll also find *Mungalli Falls Outpost (☎ 4097 2358, Junction Rd)* with double/four-bed cabins for $50/60 with communal cooking facilities. There is also a *kiosk* and horse trail rides ($50, 2½ hours). The Palmerston Hwy continues through Palmerston National Park to Innisfail.

Back at Millaa Millaa, take the Old Palmerston Hwy, which is the scenic route to Ravenshoe and **Millstream Falls**. Follow this road for about 10km and turn left at Middlebrook Rd. Continue for about 4km, until you reach **Souita Falls**. Head back to the Old Palmerston Hwy towards Ravenshoe and after a kilometre or so, you'll reach **Pepina Falls**, which is a good platypus-viewing area.

## MT HYPIPAMEE NATIONAL PARK
The Kennedy Hwy between Atherton and Ravenshoe passes the eerie Mt Hypipamee crater after 26km. The **bird-watching** in this little rainforest park is good – look for the golden bowerbird on the walking trails. It's a scenic 800m-return walk from the carpark, past **Dinner Falls** (which ultimately becomes the Barron River) to the narrow, 138m-deep crater with its moody lake, covered in a green crust of duckweed, far below. Back at Dinner Falls there's a nice swimming area.

## HERBERTON
**postcode 4872 • pop 990**
On a slightly longer alternative route between Atherton and Ravenshoe, the historic tin-mining town of Herberton is surrounded by picturesque hills. The town was founded at the headwaters of the Wild River in 1880 when a tin-lode was discovered. Dozens of mines opened in the area, and hotels and public buildings were erected, although the town was already in decline when the railway from Cairns, built to service the tin-mining industry, finally reached it in 1910. The town's establishment decimated the local Aboriginal tribe, the Mbabaram; in later years, many were relocated to Mona Mona Mission.

As you enter town from Atherton, you'll pass **Herberton Historical Village** *(☎ 4096 2271, 6 Broadway; adult/child $10/5; open 10am-4pm)*. This is a unique collection of historic buildings, transported from the surrounding area to form a little township complete with a blacksmith and bootmaker.

Herberton is also one of the departure points for the **Railco Scenic Heritage Steam Railway** to Atherton (see the Atherton section earlier for information).

If you're feeling adventurous, you can also head 28km west from Herberton to the old mining township of Irvinebank, eventually linking up with Petford, on the road to Chillagoe – see the earlier Mareeba to Chillagoe section.

### Places to Stay & Eat
*Wild River Caravan Park (☎ 4096 2121, Holdcroft Dr)* Unpowered/powered sites

$6/16.50, cabins $38. On the edge of town, the park has new, fully self-contained cabins.

**The Australian Hotel** (☎ 4096 2263, fax 4096 2099, 44 Grace St) Rooms $25/50. Located in the centre of town, the pub has clean, motel-style rooms. It also serves up *counter lunches* and *dinners* from $6.50.

**Green Springs Holiday Farm** (☎ 4096 2292, fax 4096 3154, Off Wieland Rd, Wondecla) Doubles/family rooms $88/99, including breakfast. About 6km out of town on the Longlands Gap Rd (Ravenshoe Rd), this mixed farm in a 1930s homestead specialises in family farm-stays, including donkey rides and animal feeding.

**Risley's** (☎ 4096 2111, 55 Grace St) Meals $7.50-25. Open 11am-late Wed-Sat, 11am-4pm Sun. Opposite the pub, Risley's is a surprisingly cosmopolitan little eatery to find in the surrounding meat-and-three-veg culture!

**Jake's Takeaway Foods** on Grace St is the best place for a cheap meal.

## RAVENSHOE
postcode 4872 • pop 870

At 904m altitude, Ravenshoe was once a busy timber town and is now something of a green energy centre. The excellent Ravenshoe Visitor Centre (☎/fax 4097 7700, **W** toptown@ledanet.com.au, 24 Moore St) provides local maps and also information on the local Jirrdal tribe before non-Indigenous settlement. **Win's Gallery** (☎ 4097 6522) on the main street, sells pretty landscape paintings and handcrafted timber pieces.

The town's new attraction is the spectacular **WindyHill Wind Farm** – 20 wind turbines that provide a green energy supply. The wind farm is on Windy Hill, 3km from Ravenshoe, reached either from the Kennedy Hwy from Ravenshoe or from Millaa Millaa along the winding, scenic Old Palmerston Hwy.

**Little Millstream Falls** are 2km south of Ravenshoe on the Tully Gorge Rd, and **Tully Falls** are 24km south. About 6km past Ravenshoe and 1km off the road are the 13m-high **Millstream Falls**, said to be the widest in Australia. About 34km (one hour) from Ravenshoe, **Koombooloomba Dam** is a little-known camping and fishing spot.

Train enthusiasts can take a ride on the **Railco Scenic Heritage Steam Railway** (☎ 4097 6006; adult/child $11.50/5.50; departs 2.30pm Sat & Sun), a historic steam train that runs 7km north to Tumoulin, returning to Ravenshoe at 4pm. The railway closes from February to March.

### Places to Stay & Eat

**Kool Moon Motel** (☎/fax 4097 6407, 6 Moore St) Units $41/52.80. It's not flash, but it's cheap and clean.

**Millstream Retreat** (☎ 4097 6785, McHugh Rd) Doubles $105. Off the Kennedy Hwy about 12km from Ravenshoe, this place has nice cottages overlooking the Millstream.

**The Popular Cafe** (☎ 4097 6857) Meals $3-8. Open 9am-late Tues-Sun. A replica of the original 1940s cafe that burnt down in 1991, the cafe has good coffee, smoothies and healthy fare, such as quiche and salad. The owner also has a *homestay*.

---

### Wind Farm-o-Rama

In the 1980s Ravenshoe was one of the timber communities most opposed to the World Heritage listing of the Wet Tropics, determined that its future lay in nonrenewable resources. In late 2000, however, it became the site of Australia's largest wind farm, Windy-Hill, which generates enough green energy in the form of electricity to supply more than 3500 homes per year.

The 20 wind towers, each standing 46m tall, are an impressive sight on the gently sloping hills of the surrounding farmland. Standing close to one of these towers at the viewing area, you'll be surprised by the quiet generating capacity of their 22m turbine-blades – all you'll hear is a soothing susurration.

Wind energy is one of the cheapest renewable technologies, and one of the cleanest. The use of wind, rather than conventional energy sources such as coal, to generate electricity at WindyHill prevents the release of more than 25,000 tonnes of carbon dioxide into the Earth's atmosphere per annum.

There are also several other excellent B&Bs and farm-stays in the area; it's worth getting a full list from the Ravenshoe Visitor Centre.

## RAVENSHOE TO UNDARA OR CHARTERS TOWERS

The Kennedy Hwy (part of Australia's Hwy 1 at this point) continues south-west from Ravenshoe for 114km, where it forks. The road south goes to Charters Towers and is paved road all the way; to the west is the Gulf Developmental Rd to Croydon and Normanton via the Undara lava tubes.

### Innot Hot Springs

About 32km west of Ravenshoe is the small township of Innot Hot Springs, where a hot spring measuring 73°C heats up the cool waters of the town's Nettle Creek. The spring water is said to be therapeutic, and after a steaming, sandy soak you'll certainly feel relaxed! The art is in creating a sand bath with enough cool water that you can safely lounge in it.

You can also 'take the waters' at *Innot Hot Springs Village* (*☎/fax 4097 0136*), which has unpowered/powered sites for $15/17.50 and single/double cabins from $30/40. It pumps the water into outdoor and indoor pools of varying temperatures, rather like a Japanese *onsen* (hot-spring resort), but not quite as atmospheric! Guests have free use of the pools, while nonguests pay ($5.50/3.00 for adults/children). It's open 8am to 6pm.

The Village is the best place to stay, with a camping area and some cabins fronting Nettle Creek. There's a pub, the *Hot Springs Hotel*, on the other side of the creek.

Heading to Mt Garnet, the landscape starts thinning out, with peaked termite mounds changing colour from rich red to sand to earthy brown.

### Mt Garnet

The small, neat mining town of Mt Garnet, 15km west of Innot Hot Springs, comes alive one weekend every May when it hosts one of Queensland's top outback race meetings. *Mt Garnet Hotel* (*☎ 4097 9210*) has a cool, leafy beer garden and does *counter meals*.

Spectacular **Blencoe Falls**, the setting for the second US *Survivor* series, is 84km south-east of Mt Garnet on the unsealed Gunnawarra Rd. The first waterfall drop is a massive 91m. It's an excellent spot for *bush camping*.

About 60km past Mt Garnet, the Kennedy Hwy passes through **Forty Mile Scrub National Park**, where the semi-evergreen vine thicket is a descendant of the vegetation that covered much of the Gondwana supercontinent 300 million years ago – before Australia, South America, India, Africa and Antarctica drifted apart. Just past the park is the turn-off to the **Undara lava tubes** (a must-see) and the Gulf Savannah.

# Cairns to Port Douglas

The Bruce Hwy, which runs nearly 2000km north from Brisbane, ends in Cairns, but the coastal road, the Captain Cook Hwy, continues for another 110km north through Mossman to Daintree, with a turn-off to Port Douglas. This final stretch is one of Queensland's most scenic coastal drives, along the Marlin Coast.

## NORTHERN BEACHES

postcodes 4878, 4879 • pop 14,770

North along the highway is a string of coastal suburbs – Cairns' northern beaches. Some, like Machans and Clifton Beaches, are residential and sleepy and others, like Trinity Beach and Palm Cove, are gaudy and lumbering under the weight of inappropriate beach developments. Machans, Holloways, Trinity and Palm Cove are the best for a short beach trip from Cairns. See Getting Around in the Cairns section for bus details.

### Machans Beach

Small houses along the waterfront wallow in the ocean breeze at this quiet, residential community. There's no swimming beach here, which explains why there are no ugly hotel high-rises either. Off Machan St, a block back from the Esplanade, the road to the wide mouth of the Barron River is sign-posted. It's a popular fishing spot. There are a few choices food-wise, but no places to stay.

*Juice & Jam Cafe (☎ 4055 5039, O'Shea Esplanade)* Dishes around $10. Open 8.30am-3pm Tues-Sun, 6pm-late Thur-Sat, BYO. Right on the waterfront, this old, timber double-storey place, serving up simple meals, is a find.

*Little Italy (☎ 4055 9967, Machan St)* Mains $12-25. Veal is the chef's speciality at this adorable, little vine-cloaked restaurant.

Just around the corner from Juice & Jam Cafe, on Machan St, is the Fishnet Web Lounge (☎ 4037 0099).

## Holloways Beach
The waters of Holloways Beach seem to be more mud than water (thanks to dredging down south) – still it's fine to swim and there is a Surf Life Saving Club and a stinger net. The beachfront *Strait on the Beach (☎ 4055 9616, 100 Oleander St)* is a breezy spot for an alfresco coffee. Just next door is *Coolum's on the Beach (☎ 4055 9200, Cnr Hibiscus & Oleandar Sts)*. Time your visit to this cafe for Sunday afternoon, when live jazz sessions are on and people spill onto the beach from the bar. If you're not Australian, it'll make you want to emigrate!

*Pacific Sands (☎ 4055 0277, 4055 0899, 1-19 Poinciana St)* has double self-contained units for $120, just a short walk to the beach.

## Yorkey's Knob
Yorkey's Knob has what must be one of the most – um – interesting names for a beach in the world. Its knob, a rocky outcrop, sits at the northern end of the white stretch of beach, and a stinger net is set up during the summer. The impressive Yorkey's Knob Boat Club & Marina is around the headland. There's an ATM at the boat club.

If you're staying here, Half Moon Bay Sailing School (☎ 4055 7820) offers a full range of sailing courses.

**Places to Stay & Eat** Yorkey's Knob is a low-key place that has a few accommodation options.

*Yorkey's Knob Beachfront Van Park (☎ 4055 7201, fax 4055 3982, 69-73 Sims Esplanade)* Unpowered/powered sites $18/22, on-site vans $38. This park offers the closest beachfront camping to Cairns.

*Yorkey's Beach Bures (☎ 4055 7755, fax 4055 7776, 23 Sims Esplanade)* Doubles $79 (minimum 3-night stay). This super-relaxed, Fijian-style lodge has open-air timber cabins in a leafy setting.

*Green Tree Frog (☎ 4055 8188, 9 Albion St)* Doubles $80, including breakfast. At the southern end of the beach, one street back from the water, this spacious B&B is an easy place to feel at home.

Food options are sparse, but there's a little *takeaway* on the Esplanade, or try *Blue Moon Grill (☎ 4055 8333, Yorkey's Knob Boat Club & Marina, 25 Buckley St)*. Open from noon to 9pm daily, this is an alfresco eatery serving grills, pasta, burgers and sashimi. It also does a 'BLT & beer' lunch special ($6.50).

## Trinity Beach
Trinity is one of the prettiest of Cairns' northern beaches, but unfortunate high-rise developments have destroyed the castaway ambience the area once had. The beach is a long stretch of sand sheltered by a high headland at the southern end, and there's a stinger net here over summer. Water-sports equipment is for hire at the beach.

Billabong Car Rentals (☎ 4057 7466, 8 Trinity Beach Rd) has an office here.

**Places to Stay** There are a few accommodation options, and around the next bay is Kewarra Beach, a residential area with a large resort.

*Amaroo Beach Resort (☎ 4055 6066, fax 4057 7992, 92 Moore St)* Mountain view $75, ocean view $99 (minimum 3-night stay). At the northern end of Trinity Beach, near the pub, this budget resort has tennis courts, a pool and spa.

*Casablanca Domes (☎ 4055 6339, fax 4055 6319, 47 Vasey Esplanade)* Single/double units $80/85. This is a quirky set of nine white concrete domes, each housing a somewhat shabby self-contained unit, complete with '70s decor. Apparently the architect was a 'genius' – decide for yourself!

***Tropic Sun*** (☎ *4057 8888, fax 4057 6577, 46 Moore St)* Doubles $85. While you won't have views, you'll only be a 50m walk from the beach, and the price is right. All units are fully self-contained.

**Places to Eat & Drink** There are several eateries on the waterfront, though head to the Trinity Beach Hotel to mix it with the locals. There's also a ***supermarket*** on Trinity Beach Rd, a few kilometres back from the beach.

***Blue Waters at the Beach*** (☎ *4055 6194, 77 Vasey Esplanade)* Dishes $6-16.50. Open 6.30am-9pm. A cheap and sometimes cheerful eatery that also has Internet access.

***L'unico Trattoria*** (☎ *4057 8855, 75 Vasey Esplanade)* Dishes $8.50-20. Open 7am-10pm daily. Delicious pasta and pizza are on offer at this breezy trattoria.

***Trinity Beach Hotel*** (☎ *4055 6106, Moore St)* Dishes $6.50-15. Bistro open for lunch daily, dinner Sat & Sun. Perched high on a hill overlooking the water, the pub is a popular watering hole. It has a beer garden with a small bistro and incredible views.

## Clifton Beach

Another 3km north of the Trinity Beach turn-off is Clifton Beach, a laid-back residential community. There's a stinger net at the northern end of the beach, and a number of places to stay and eat.

***Paradise Gardens Caravan Resort*** (☎ *4055 3712, Cnr Captain Cook Hwy & Clifton Rd)* Unpowered/powered sites $20/21, cabins $45-70. It's not by the beach, but the cabins are good value.

There are a couple of holiday apartments along the beachfront.

***Clifton Palms*** (☎ *4055 3839, fax 4055 3888, 35 Upolu Esplanade)* Doubles $88, self-contained cabins $66. The two-bedroom apartments are ideal for families.

***Clifton Sands Holiday Units*** (☎ *4055 3355, 81-87 Guide St)* Units $65 (minimum 3-night stay) or $85 (1 night). A block or two back from the beach, these fully self-contained units are excellent value (maximum four people).

***Clifton Capers Bar & Grill*** (☎ *4055 3355, 14 Clifton Rd)* Mains around $17.50. The chef is German, so expect some traditional and modern dishes.

## Palm Cove

Since the mid-1980s, Palm Cove has developed from a sleepy, little beach community into a wannabe-chic resort town, and still manages to be a pretty spot despite all the development. The beach has a stinger net in summer, plenty of shady melaleuca trees, and views of the small, privately owned Double Island.

The town's jetty is regarded by local anglers as the area's best fishing spot and is a great place for a stroll. *Quicksilver* and *Sunlover* stop at the jetty for pick-ups on the way out to the reef. There are no banks here, but the Paradise Village complex in the centre of Williams Esplanade has a post office and ATM, while the Village Store (☎ 4059 0244) also in the complex, has Eftpos and cashes travellers cheques. Cyberjam (☎ 4055 3035), opposite the Village Store, has Internet access.

If you have still haven't seen enough Australian wildlife, head to **Wild World, the Tropical Zoo** (☎ *4055 3669, Captain Cook Hwy; adult/child $20/10; open 8.30am-5pm)*.

**Places to Stay** The waterfront has a pleasant range of accommodation options.

***Palm Cove Camping Ground*** (☎/*fax 4055 3824, 149 Williams Esplanade)* Unpowered/ powered sites $11.40/15.95. Just south of the jetty, this is a dedicated beachfront camping ground run by the local council.

***Palm Cove Retreat*** (☎ *4055 3630, Captain Cook Hwy)*. Tent site $6 per person, beds in 4-bed dorm overnight/weekly $12/70. What a bargain! Opposite the Palm Cove turn-off on the mountain side of the highway, the Retreat has all the usual facilities and is about a 20-minute walk to the beach. It's a good place to stay long-term if you've found work in Cairns.

***Palm Cove Accommodation B&B*** (☎ *4055 3797, 19 Vievers Rd)* Doubles $70. This is a small, basic B&B, although the owner has plans to build a second storey.

*Paradise Village Resort* (☎ *4055 3300, fax 4055 3991, Williams Esplanade)* Doubles $100, 1-bed unit $130. Behind Apres Beach, all rooms have balconies overlooking the pool.

*Silvestor Palms* (☎ *4055 3831, fax 4055 3598, 32 Vievers Rd)* Doubles $99. Set in tropical gardens, all units are fully self-contained.

*Melaleuca Resort* (☎ *4055 3222, fax 4055 3307, 85 Williams Esplanade)* Doubles $168. This modern resort has fully self-contained units, all with ocean views.

*Angsana Resort & Spa* (☎ *4055 3000, fax 4055 3090, 1 Vievers Rd)* Pool view /ocean view 1-bed unit $374/446. This is an impressive resort hotel right on the beachfront, with three pools, a spa and the excellent *Far Horizons* restaurant.

*Novotel Palm Cove Resort* (☎ *4059 1234, Coral Coast Dr)* Rooms and apartments $150-270; substantial discounts for Accor 'Advantage Plus' card holders. This sprawling four-star complex, complete with 10 pools (!), tennis courts, gym and 11-hole golf course, is the mothership of Palm Cove resorts. It's five minutes from the beach, and is popular with families as it not only has a crocodile-slide swimming pool, but also child-minding facilities. Some rooms are looking a bit tired though. It contains the *Canecutters* restaurant for buffet dinners and the classier *Paperbark* restaurant.

*Villa Paradiso* (☎ *1800 683 773, 4055 3533, fax 4055 3946, 111 Williams Esplanade)* 1-3–bedroom apartments $195-378. Well located, these upmarket apartments have full kitchen and laundry facilities and balconies with sea views.

**Places to Eat & Drink** There are eateries for all budgets in Palm Cove.

*Cocky's at the Cove* (☎ *4059 1691)* is a good, casual eatery for a quick breakfast or lunch, and *Cairns Surf Life Saving Club* (☎ *4059 1244)* is good for a cheap dinner. There are also a few other places worth checking out.

*Il Forno Pizzeria* (☎ *4059 1666, Paradise Village)* Dishes $13-16. Open 5.30pm-10pm. This is a small, stylish BYO pizzeria.

*Golden Cane Bar* (☎ *4055 3999, Courtyard Marriot, Cnr Vievers Rd & Williams Esplanade)* Meals $6.50-17. Seafood chowder and other filling dishes are on offer at this good-value eatery.

*Far Horizons* (☎ *4055 3000, 1 Vievers Rd)* Mains $15-28. Open for breakfast, lunch and dinner. The setting and design is pure tropics, while the cuisine is creative mod Oz. Book ahead for seafront tables.

*Apres Beach Bar & Grill* (☎ *4055 3300, Williams Esplanade)* Dishes $8-28. Open 6.30am-late. In front of Paradise Village Resort, this is a popular spot for a drink or casual meal during the day; slightly more formal meals are served in the evening.

## Ellis Beach

Round the headland past Palm Cove and Double Island, the highway meets the coast at pretty Ellis Beach. It's a sheltered, white, sandy beach, complete with a stinger net and lifeguard in summer, and has one excellent accommodation option, with camp sites right on the beach: *Ellis Beach Oceanfront Bungalows* (☎ *1800 637 036, 4055 3538, fax 4055 3077, Captain Cook Hwy)*. This place has unpowered/powered sites for $19/24, cabins from $60 and bungalows for $140.

Across the road, *Ellis Beach Bar 'n' Grill* is fine for a quick stop, but don't miss the friendly *Ellis Beach Surf Life Saving Club* (☎ *4055 3695)* for a drink.

## ELLIS BEACH TO PORT DOUGLAS

The Ellis Beach to Port Douglas section of the Captain Cook Hwy follows the coastline for much of its length. Soon after Ellis Beach and 40km north of Cairns, **Hartleys Creek Crocodile Farm** (☎ *4055 3576,* Ⓦ *www .hartleyscreek.com, Capt Cook Hwy; adult/child $13/7; open 8am-5pm Mon-Fri; free tour 11am)* has a collection of Australian wildlife, including dingoes. There are shows throughout the day, but make sure you're there at crocodile-feeding time (3pm).

North of Cairns (38km) is *Thala Beach Lodge* (☎ *4098 5700, fax 4098 5837, Oak Beach)* with singles/doubles with mountain views for $223/293, and with ocean views for $290/377. Overlooking the ocean, its timber bungalows are comfortable enough, but the panoramic design of its *restaurant*, which is open to nonguests, is stunning.

*Turtle Cove Resort (☎ 4059 1800, fax 4059 1969, Off Captain Cook Hwy)* has singles/doubles from $120/140. About 45km north of Cairns this is an exclusive gay and lesbian beachfront resort. It has comfortable cabins, its own restaurant, a great swimming pool and spa, and access to a private beach.

# Port Douglas to Cape Tribulation

## PORT DOUGLAS
### postcode 4871 • pop 3640

Port Douglas certainly outclasses Cairns in the hip stakes. It's a genuine reef resort with a long stretch of beach backed by palm trees, and an atmosphere far different from its southern rival Cairns. Its streets are lined with expensive eateries and clothes shops, and exclusive resorts. Despite its development and upmarket allegiances, the town has a relaxed village feel about it, especially on the weekend when the down-at-heel beer gardens of its pubs fill up with drinkers and its outdoor Sunday markets take over Anzac Park. You can make trips to the Low Isles, the Great Barrier Reef, Mossman Gorge, the Tableland and Cape Tribulation from here.

### History

Port Douglas was founded in 1877 as the port town for the Hodgkinson River goldfields. The town flourished at the outset, but its prosperity came to a grinding halt in the mid-1880s when Cairns was chosen ahead of it as the terminal for the new rail line from Kuranda and Mareeba. A disastrous cyclone in 1911 destroyed most of the town's buildings, and Port remained a sleepy coastal village until the mid-1980s. The now infamous entrepreneur Christopher Skase, saw the town's potential and backed the development of the Sheraton Mirage complex. Up went multimillion dollar resorts, a golf course and heliport, hovercraft services

from Cairns, a marina and shopping complex, and an avenue of palms lining the road from the highway to Port Douglas. Within a few years, Skase's model resort had burgeoned into a huge money-making machine, though Skase fled to Majorca leaving behind massive debts. After years of legal brawling with the Australian government, Skase died in Majorca in 2001 without ever returning to Australia.

### Orientation

It's 6km from the highway along a long, low spit of land to Port Douglas. The Sheraton Mirage resort occupies a long stretch of Four Mile Beach. The main entry road, Davidson St, ends in a T-intersection with Macrossan St; to the left is the town centre with most of the shops and restaurants. The beach is to the right, and there are fine views over the coastline and sea from Flagstaff Hill lookout.

The Marina Mirage is the departure point for most of the reef trips.

### Information

There are several tour booking agents, including the Port Douglas Tourist Information Centre (☎ 4099 5599, 23 Macrossan St), which is open 9am to 6pm daily, and Port Douglas Accom-Holiday Rentals (☎ 4099 4488, W www.portdouglasaccom.com.au, corner of Macrossan and Owen Sts), also open daily.

The ANZ has a branch with an ATM on Macrossan St, and there's a Commonwealth Bank agency inside the post office on Owen St. There's a cluster of public telephone booths on Macrossan St between Grant and Owen Sts. Cyberworld (☎ 4099 5661; open 9am to 8pm), behind the eatery Lime on Macrossan St, has Internet access.

The Jungle Bookshop (☎ 4099 4203, 46 Macrossan St) has a good range of books. If you have small children, there's even a casual day-care centre, called Tropical Tots (☎ 4099 3392, 336 Port Douglas Rd), which is open 7.30am to 5.30pm from Monday to Friday.

### Things to See

Port's **Sunday Markets**, held every weekend in Anzac Park, always attract a good crowd

# PORT DOUGLAS

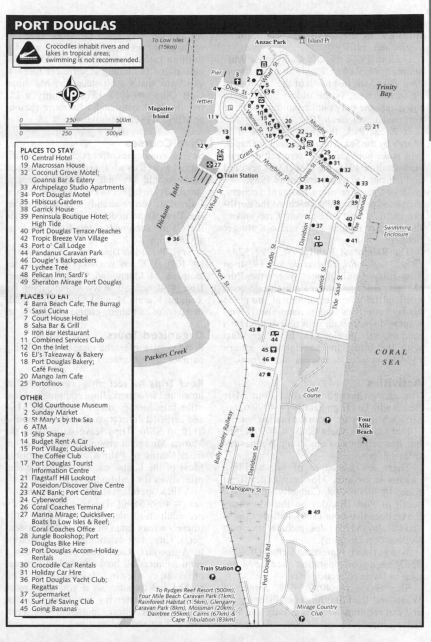

Crocodiles inhabit rivers and lakes in tropical areas; swimming is not recommended.

**PLACES TO STAY**
10 Central Hotel
19 Macrossan House
32 Coconut Grove Motel;
   Goanna Bar & Eatery
33 Archipelago Studio Apartments
34 Port Douglas Motel
35 Hibiscus Gardens
38 Garrick House
39 Peninsula Boutique Hotel;
   High Tide
40 Port Douglas Terrace/Beaches
42 Tropic Breeze Van Village
43 Port o' Call Lodge
44 Pandanus Caravan Park
46 Dougie's Backpackers
47 Lychee Tree
48 Pelican Inn; Sardi's
49 Sheraton Mirage Port Douglas

**PLACES TO EAT**
4 Barra Beach Cafe; The Burragi
5 Sassi Cucina
7 Court House Hotel
8 Salsa Bar & Grill
9 Iron Bar Restaurant
11 Combined Services Club
12 On the Inlet
16 EJ's Takeaway & Bakery
18 Port Douglas Bakery;
   Café Fresq
20 Mango Jam Cafe
25 Portofinos

**OTHER**
1 Old Courthouse Museum
2 Sunday Market
3 St Mary's by the Sea
6 ATM
13 Ship Shape
14 Budget Rent A Car
15 Port Village; Quicksilver;
   The Coffee Club
17 Port Douglas Tourist
   Information Centre
21 Flagstaff Hill Lookout
22 Poseidon/Discover Dive Centre
23 ANZ Bank; Port Central
24 Cyberworld
26 Coral Coaches Terminal
27 Marina Mirage; Quicksilver;
   Boats to Low Isles & Reef;
   Coral Coaches Office
28 Jungle Bookshop; Port
   Douglas Bike Hire
29 Port Douglas Accom-Holiday
   Rentals
30 Crocodile Car Rentals
31 Holiday Car Hire
36 Port Douglas Yacht Club;
   Regattas
37 Supermarket
41 Surf Life Saving Club
45 Going Bananas

to its dozens of stalls selling fresh tropical fruits and ice creams, fresh coconut juice, vegies and crafts.

Built in 1879, the **Old Courthouse Museum** *(☎ 4099 4635, Wharf St; open 10am-1pm Tues-Sat)*, just north of the Macrossan St intersection, is the oldest building in town, and the only public building to have survived a cyclone in 1911.

In Anzac Park, the stunning vistas of **St Mary's by the Sea**, a tiny white timber chapel, will make you wish you were getting married. Built in 1911, the chapel was restored and relocated to its present site in 1989.

If you're after more postcard scenery, then head to **Four Mile Beach**. At the northern end is a Surf Life Saving Club and in the summer months there's also a stinger net here.

The **Rainforest Habitat** *(☎ 4099 3235, Port Douglas Rd; adult/child $20/10; open 8am-5.30pm daily)*, near where the Port Douglas Rd meets the main highway, is an artificial rainforest environment, home to birds, butterflies and marsupials. If you want to do more with your muesli (and be a total tourist!), go along and have 'breakfast with the birds' in the Habitat's aviary *($34/17 includes admission, 8am-11am)*.

## Activities

You can go paragliding over Four Mile Beach with Get High Parafly (☎ 4099 6366, $65), which departs from the marina hourly.

Port Douglas Yacht Club (☎ 4099 4386) has free sailing sessions every Wednesday from 4.30pm.

There are a couple of horse riding ranches in the area. Mowbray Valley Trail Rides (☎ 4099 3268, Connolly Rd), based south of Port Douglas on the Mowbray River, does two-hour ($66), half-day ($88) and full-day ($125) rides (includes transport to/from Port Douglas).

Wonga Beach Equestrian Centre (☎ 4098 7583) has a good reputation – see the Mossman to Daintree section later.

Ship Shape (☎ 4099 5621, corner of Wharf and Inlet Sts) hires out fishing gear and can recommend good estuary and reef fishing trips.

Golfers will be pleased to hear that the Mirage Country Club (☎ 4099 5888) is open to the general public. The not-so-thrilling catch is that it costs $145 an 18-hole round (including electric car hire). If you think that's a bit steep, the Mossman Golf Club (☎ 4098 1570) is only a 15-minute drive away and a lot more reasonably priced ($25, 18-hole round).

## Dive Courses

Several companies offer open-water certification, as well as advanced dive certificates. Some would say that safety and general standards are higher in Port Douglas than in Cairns. (If you're already a certified diver, see Dive Trips under Organised Tours in the Cairns section for details of the live-aboard trips.)

Try Poseidon/Discover Dive Centre (☎ 4099 4772, W wwww.poseiden-cruises .com.au, 34 Macrossan St) or Quicksilver Dive (☎ 4099 5050, W www.quicksilverdive .com.au, Marina Mirage). Quicksilver holds two days of its training course in Palm Cove.

## Organised Tours

Port Douglas offers the same overwhelming number of tour options as Cairns.

**Reef Trips** All reef trips provide a buffet lunch and free snorkelling equipment. Most offer introductory dives for around $180 and certified dives (two dives) from around $110 to $170. Trips leave daily from the Marina Mirage at around 8.30am; pick-up from Cairns or Palm Cove is an option. Most of the boats heading out to the reef offer dives for certified divers.

A slick operation is offered by *Quicksilver* (☎ 4099 5500). The cost is $150/77.50 per adult/child, departures at 10am daily (there's a maximum of 310 or 440 passengers). Huge fast catamarans do daily trips to Agincourt Reef. The trip includes a semi-submersible boat ride and underwater observatory viewing. It can all be a bit rushed and frenetic, so if you want more time in the water try the smaller boats, which offer more personalised reef, snorkelling and diving trips:

*Haba* (☎ 4099 5254) Adult/child $120/75. Heads out to Tongue Reef and Opal Reef (maximum 40 passengers).

*Aristocat* (☎ 4099 4727) Adult/child $139/88. Heads out to St Crispins and Agincourt Reefs (max 45).

*Calypso* (☎ 4099 3377) Adult/child $110/90. Heads out to Opal, Tongue or Chinaman's Reef (max 49).

*Poseidon* (☎ 4099 4772) Adult/child $125/90. Heads out to Agincourt Reef (max 48).

*Wavelength* (☎ 4099 5031) Adult/child $123/83. This is a snorkelling cruise only and heads out to Opal, Sister or Chinaman's Reef.

*Quicksmart* (☎ 4087 2100) Adult/child $110/85. Heads out to Agincourt Reef (max 80).

**Low Isles** There are also cruises out to the Low Isles, only 15km offshore. The fine, little coral cay is surrounded by a lagoon and topped by an old lighthouse. Several smaller sailing catamarans offer snorkelling day trips:

*Shaolin* (☎ 4099 4929) Adult/child $110/55 daily. A refitted Chinese junk, the *Shaolin* has snorkelling cruises to Blue Lagoon.

*Sail Away* (☎ 4099 5599) Adult/child $99/49.

*Wavedancer* (☎ 4099 5500) Adult/child $105/55 full package, $65/35 boat trip and transfers only.

**River Cruises** The *Lady Douglas Paddle-wheeler* (☎ 4098 8077) runs cruises down the Dixon Inlet.

**Other Tours** There are numerous operators offering day trips to Cape Tribulation, some via Mossman Gorge. Many of the tours out of Cairns also do pick-ups from Port Douglas – book with one of the agencies in town.

Bike N Hike (☎ 4099 4000, 62 Davidson St) Half-day/full-day $65/90. Bike N Hike, based in the Port Douglas Reef Club, does excellent mountain bike day trips to the Mowbray Valley and also has bike hire.

Reef and Rainforest Connections (☎ 4099 5599) This operator has a huge combination of day tours to the Atherton Tableland, including Mareeba Wetlands & Skyrail (adult/child $149/95), and also trips up to Cooktown (adult/child $118/59).

Fine Feather Tours (☎ 4094 1199) Full-day bird safari $165 (Monday, Wednesday, Friday),

half-day wildlife or half-day Daintree River cruise $110 (Sunday, Tuesday, Thursday). Fine Feathers specialises in bird and wildlife safaris, including a bird-watching tour of Julatten and the Mt Carbine area.

## Places to Stay – Budget

There's a shortage of budget accommodation in Port Douglas, and plenty of pricey places to stay.

### Camping Grounds & Caravan Parks

Port Douglas offers a good choice of options for campers.

*Tropic Breeze Van Village (☎/fax 4099 5449, 24 Davidson St)* Unpowered/powered sites $17/20.30, on-site cabins (no en suite) $70. Next door to the IGA supermarket, this park is a short walk from the beach. The tent sites are shady.

*Pandanus Caravan Park (☎ 4099 5944, fax 4099 4034, 97-107 Davidson St)* Unpowered/powered sites $16/19, cabins $55-72. About 1km further south from Tropic Breeze, this place is well set up.

*Four Mile Beach Caravan Park (☎ 4098 5281, fax 4099 3814, 2 Reef St)*. Unpowered/powered sites $17.50/20, cabins $66. Almost 4km south of the centre, off Barrier St, this park has beach frontage and good camping areas.

*Glengarry Caravan Park (☎ 4098 5922, fax 4099 3158, Mowbray River Rd)* Unpowered sites $17, powered sites from $21, cabins $70. By the Mowbray River about 8km south-west of Port Douglas, off the highway, this is a pleasant family-run park.

### Hostels

There are less backpacker options in Port Douglas than Cairns, but the standards are generally higher here.

*Port o' Call Lodge (☎ 4099 5422, fax 4099 5495, Cnr Port St & Craven Close)* Beds in 4-bed dorm with en suite $19.50 (nonmembers $21.50), doubles from $85. This YHA-associate hostel has modern dorms with bathrooms, and air-con motel units. There's a pool, cooking facilities and a *bar & bistro*. The hostel also offers a free courtesy coach to and from Cairns (Monday, Wednesday, Saturday).

***Dougie's Backpackers*** (☎ *1800 4099 6200, 4099 6200, fax 4099 6047, 111 Davidson St*) Unpowered/powered sites $12/13 per person, dorm beds $20, doubles $60. Dougie's is well maintained, friendly and has a good kitchen, and a nice garden and pool. There's also a camping area at the rear.

## Places to Stay – Mid Range

**Motels** There are quite a few good, central motel options.

***Coconut Grove Motel*** (☎ *4099 5124, fax 4099 5144, 58 Macrossan St*) Singles/doubles $60/82.50. A relaxed environment and budget rooms are on offer at this central place, next door to the Goanna Bar & Eatery.

***Central Hotel*** (☎ *4099 5271, fax 4099 4112, 9 Macrossan St*) Doubles $85.50. This old pub has basic motel units out the back. The pub has reasonably good ***bistro*** meals.

***Port Central*** (☎ *4051 6722, 36 Macrossan St*) Singles/doubles from $65/76. Above the ANZ Bank, there's no reception desk here – just a phone. Rooms have en suites and one or two have balconies overlooking the main street.

***Port Douglas Motel*** (☎ *4099 5248, fax 4099 5504, 9 Davidson St*) Doubles $88. It has standard motel rooms, definitely without views, but in a convenient location near the beach.

***Pelican Inn*** (☎ *4099 5266, fax 4099 5821, 123 Davidson St*) Doubles $115. The motel's rooms are spacious and modern with full kitchen facilities.

**Self-contained Apartments** Rates for self-contained apartments are generally cheaper by the week. There are literally dozens of these in Port Douglas, so check accommodation agencies for many more listings than we can possibly give here.

***Macrossan House*** (☎ *4099 4366, 4099 4377, 19 Macrossan St*) Doubles $157. Right in the middle of Port, these self-contained apartments have a nice breezy feel.

***Port Douglas Terrace/Beaches*** (☎ *4099 5397, fax 4099 5206, 17 The Esplanade*) Apartments from $150. The Port Douglas Terrace/Beaches has self-contained one- and two-bedroom apartments (the more expensive ones with sea views).

***Garrick House*** (☎ *4099 5322, fax 4099 5021, 11-13 Garrick St*) 1-2–bedroom apartments $150-195. The modern, airy apartments all overlook the pool.

***Hibiscus Gardens*** (☎ *4099 5315, fax 4099 4678, Cnr Mowbray & Owen Sts*) Studio/ 1-bedroom units from $125/165. Hibiscus Gardens is a modern resort with stylish Balinese decor and a large pool.

***Lychee Tree*** (☎ *4099 5811, fax 4099 5175, 95 Davidson St*) Units $115-140. Spacious one- and two-bedroom units sleeping from one to five people are on offer here.

## Places to Stay – Top End

***Peninsula Boutique Hotel*** (☎ *4099 9100, fax 4099 5440, 9-13 The Esplanade*) Poolside/ocean suites $280/320, including breakfast. You'll never want to leave this designer hotel. The self-contained apartments are definitely a 'couples escape'.

***Rydges Reef Resort*** (☎ *4099 5577, fax 4099 5559, Port Douglas Rd*) Singles/doubles $180, 2-bedroom villas $240. The villas are good value – the one price covers from one to four people.

***Sheraton Mirage Port Douglas*** (☎ *4099 5888, fax 4099 4424, Davidson St*) Doubles with garden/lagoon view from $590/685. In a league of its own, this place rates as one of the best resort hotels in Australia. Even if you can't afford to stay here, at least drop in and have a drink.

## Places to Eat

You'll definitely have trouble choosing where to eat when you stay at Port Douglas – there are so many excellent options. For self-caterers, there are a few ***supermarkets*** in town, including one in Port Village on Macrossan St and one next to the Tropic Breeze Van Village.

**Restaurants** Restaurants are generally pricey in Port Douglas, though lunch is generally a more affordable option.

***On the Inlet*** (☎ *4099 5255, 3 Inlet St*) Meals $16.50-110. Open noon-late. A smart seafood restaurant and bar, its best meal would have to be its late-afternoon bucket of prawns and a beer deal ($15) by the bar overlooking the inlet.

*Mango Jam Cafe* (☎ *4099 4611, 24 Macrossan St)* Meals $8.50-16. Always busy and always good, Mango's speciality is gourmet, wood-fired pizza.

*Portofinos* (☎ *4099 5458, 31 Macrossan St)* Pizzas $8.50-21. Open lunch & dinner. This is a casual licensed bistro with gourmet pizza and salads.

*Iron Bar Restaurant* (☎ *4099 4776, 5 Macrossan St)* Mains around $25. Open 10am-2am. Wedged between two pubs, this creation (or is that abomination?) is decked out like an outback wool shed and its menu is a meat-fest of beef, croc, roo and emu. The bar has *live music* from Wednesday to Sunday night and *cane toad races* (yes, cane toad races!) run on Tuesday and Wednesday from 8.30pm.

*Sardi's* (☎ *4099 6585, 123 Davidson St)* Mains $14-27. Open 5pm-10.30pm Mon-Sat. Try what the chef does best: chargrilled calamari.

*Salsa Bar & Grill* (☎ *4099 4922, 26 Wharf St)* Mains $10-25. This smart place serves up Tex-Mex cuisine.

*Sassi Cucina* (☎ *4099 6100, Cnr Wharf & Macrossan Sts)* Open 7.30am-late. Dinner mains $21-32. Why not come here just for dessert and go all gooey over the basil and macerated prune ice cream!

*High Tide* (☎ *4099 9100, 9-13 The Esplanade)* Breakfast $5-11, lunch $11-19, dinner $16-24. Part of the Peninsula Boutique Hotel, this intimate eatery serves quality produce simply.

**Cafes & Takeaways** For takeaways, there's a couple of places in Grant St clustered around the corner of Grant and Macrossan Sts.

*EJ's Takeaway & Bakery* does fish and chips, and burgers; the *Port Douglas Bakery* has pies, breads and pastries; and *Café Fresq* does foccacia and other more substantial meals. Across the road, the pleasant, breezy *Café Macrossan* has a varied menu, ranging from snacks (from $8) and coffee to delicious lunch and evening meals ($18 to $26); it's fully licensed. *Barra Beach Cafe*, by the water, does the usual takeaways as well as gourmet prawn rolls ($8.50). The *bistro* at Port o' Call Lodge is also worth checking out.

*The Coffee Club* (☎ *4099 5409, Macrossan St)* Dishes $6-10. This popular place in Port Village serves standard cafe fare and breakfasts.

*Goanna Bar & Eatery* (☎ *4099 4333, 58 Macrossan St)* Dishes $7-20. Goanna is an open-air eatery that's always crowded.

**Pubs & Clubs** If you're after a pub lunch or dinner, there are a few decent options.

*Court House Hotel* (☎ *4099 5181, Cnr Macrossan & Wharf Sts)* Meals $9-11. The Court House Hotel has an outdoor garden bistro. It also has live bands in the beer garden on weekends.

*Combined Services Club* (☎ *4099 5553)* Lunch from $3.30, dinner from $6.50. A locals' alternative to the pubs, the old tin-and-timber club is down on the waterfront near the marina. The bistro meals, while pretty uninspiring, are good value.

*Regattas* (☎ *4099 4386, Port Douglas Yacht Club, Wharf St)* Meals $9.50-16. Expect great water views and cheap healthy meals, such as spinach salad or beer-battered fish and chips.

**Entertainment**

A few of the pubs and restaurants in Port Douglas have live music, including the Court House Hotel and the Iron Bar Restaurant. There are also several *bars* upstairs in the Marina Mirage, and a few other places in town.

*The Burragi* (☎ *4099 6114)* Moored by Anzac Park, this former Sydney Harbour ferry is now a bar.

*Going Bananas* (☎ *4099 5400, 87 Davidson St)* Retro without a touch of irony, this restaurant-bar is best for a drink and run – before the owner orders you an Orgasm. It's open for dinner Monday to Saturday (mains $25 to $71).

*Sheraton Mirage* If you'd rather drink in more opulent surrounds, the bars here are open to nonguests.

## Getting There & Away

**Bus** The Coral Coaches office (☎ 4099 5351) is in the Marina Mirage, while the bus terminal is in the marina's carpark. There are about eight buses a day between Cairns and Port Douglas ($16, 1½ hours), about 13 buses a day from Port Douglas to Mossman ($6, 30 minutes), and twice-daily buses to Daintree Village ($14, one hour) and Cape Tribulation ($20, 2½ hours). Buses to Cooktown via the Bloomfield Track run on Tuesday and Saturday ($45, about six hours), plus Thursday from June to October.

**Boat** The daily *Quicksilver* (☎ 4099 5500, one way/return $20/30, 1½ hours) fast catamaran service between Cairns and the Marina at Port Douglas; departs Cairns at 8am and Port Douglas at 5.30pm.

## Getting Around

**To/From the Airport** The Airport Shuttle (☎ 4099 5950) does regular trips to Cairns airport (one way/return $22/44) and Coral Coaches (☎ 4098 2600) has 15 daily services ($27, 6am to 9.15pm).

**Bus** The Port Douglas Bus Service (☎ 4099 5351) runs in a continuous loop from the Rainforest Habitat (near the Captain Cook Hwy turn-off) to the Marina, stopping regularly (7.30am-midnight). Flag the driver down at the marked bus stops ($1.10 to $3 one way).

**Car** Budget Rent A Car (☎ 4099 4778) has an office at 7 Warner St, and there are also some local operators including Crocodile Car Rentals (☎ 4099 5555), 2/50 Macrossan St, and Holiday Car Hire (☎ 4099 4999), which has mokes, sedans and 4WDs.

**Taxi** Call ☎ 4099 5345 for a taxi.

**Bicycle** Port Douglas is very compact and the best way to get around is by bike. You can hire bikes at the Port o' Call Lodge and Dougies Backpackers, while Port Douglas Bike Hire (☎ 4099 5799, 40 Macrossan St) rents out mountain bikes for $14 per day.

# MOSSMAN
**postcode 4873 • pop 1920**

Shadowed by Mt Demi, Mossman is at the centre of Queensland's most northerly sugar-growing district, and is also a tropical fruit-growing area. It's a pleasant, unpretentious country town that is largely unaffected by the frenzied tourist activity that surrounds it. The main attraction is Mossman Gorge, 5km west of the town centre.

The Mossman QPWS (☎ 4098 2188) is in Mt Demi Plaza on the corner of Front and Johnston Sts, near the main turn-off to the Gorge. Mossman Newsagency, opposite the school on the main street, has Internet access.

## Mossman Gorge

Mossman Gorge is in the Southern Section of Daintree National Park and forms part of the traditional lands of the Kuku Yalanji Aboriginal people. Carved by the Mossman River, the gorge is a boulder-strewn river valley. There are some great swimming holes here, with crystal-clear water tumbling over giant boulders, all shaded by the rainforest. The gorge, however, can be treacherous after heavy rains, and people have drowned here, so swim with care. Beyond the swimming spots, a suspension bridge takes you across the river to a 2.4km circuit trail through the lowland rainforest.

The upper reaches of the park are also accessible, but this area is only suitable for fit and experienced bushwalkers. There is no camping in the Mossman Gorge Section of the national park unless you're on an extended bushwalk at least four hours from the carpark. Mossman QPWS issues permits for overnight **bush camping** in the national park ($3.85 per person), and a pamphlet and map are available.

Excellent guided walks are run by the Aboriginal-run Kuku-Yalanji Dreamtime Walks (☎ 4098 2595; adult/child $16.50/8.25) Monday to Friday at 10am, noon and 2pm.

Coral Coaches (☎ 4098 2600) runs regular bus services from Mossman and Port Douglas out to the Gorge and back. The cost is $6 from Mossmann and $16 from Port Douglas.

## Places to Stay & Eat

*Demi-View Motel* (☎ *4098 1277, fax 4098 2102, 41 Front St)* Singles/doubles $55/66. This is a friendly budget motel, with a *restaurant* out the front.

*White Cockatoo Cabins* (☎ *4098 2222, fax 4098 2221, 9 Alchera Dr)* Single/double cabins $66/82. About 1km south of the centre, White Cockatoo has spacious self-contained timber cabins, centred on a pool.

*Mossman Gorge B&B* (☎ *4098 2497, Mossman Gorge Crescent)*. Singles $60-80, doubles $60-110. Off the road to the gorge, this timber B&B has stunning views over the gorge.

*Goodies Cafe* (☎ *4098 1118, 33 Front St)* Next to the National Australia Bank, this small cafe makes fresh juices and healthy meals, such as homemade lasagne.

*Lynne's Pizza & BYO Family Restaurant* (☎ *4098 1458, Capt Cook Hwy)* Meals $8-14. Open dinner Mon-Sun. About 1.5km south of the centre, this is a laid-back pizza and pasta joint with dine-in and takeaway sections.

## Getting There & Away

Coral Coaches (☎ 4098 2600), based at 37 Front St, runs regular daily bus services to and from Port Douglas ($6), Cairns ($23), Newell Beach ($8), Wonga Beach ($8), Daintree ($10), Cape Tribulation ($19) and Cooktown ($44), among other places.

## MOSSMAN TO MT MOLLOY

Just south of Mossman is the turn-off to Mt Molloy, which links up with the inland route to Cooktown. For 33km the Rex Hwy climbs and winds through some very pretty and productive tropical fruit farms and cattle farms.

At **Julatten**, about 20km from the turn-off, there are a few interesting accommodation options, such as the lovely, quiet camping ground of *Julatten Tableland Caravan Park* (☎ *4094 1145, 1045 Rex Hwy)* with unpowered/powered sites for $6/15.

There's also a bird-watchers' lodge, in a serene garden setting. *Kingfisher Park* (☎ *4094 1263, fax 4094 1466, Lot 1, Mt Kooyong Rd)* has camp sites for $18.80 and single/double self-contained units for $93/104.

And if you feel like treating yourself, head to the *Mountain Retreat & Spa* (☎ *4094 1282, fax 4094 1582, English Rd, via Euluma Creek Rd)* with single/double B&Bs from $72/110, self-contained cabins for $143 (up to four people), and one-night/two-night pamper packages for $209/330 (per person; twin share) that include massage, mud bath and meals. The Retreat is yet another FNQ B&B where you'll experience separation anxiety when it's time to leave! It specialises in mud baths, massage and general chilling out in its private timber cabins. It also has a day-visit option for $132.

## MOSSMAN TO DAINTREE

It's another 36km north from Mossman to the village of Daintree. The road passes through cane fields and farms, with turn-offs en route to **Newell Beach**, **Wonga Beach** and Cape Tribulation. If you have a little time, there are a few potentially interesting detours along here – exotic fruit farms, a spectacular open-air theatre and some accommodation possibilities.

A couple of kilometres north of Mossman you'll see the turn-off to *Silky Oaks Lodge* (☎ *4098 1666, fax 4098 1983, Finleyvale Rd)*, upmarket spa retreat overlooking the Mossman River with chalets for $440, including breakfast. Its breezy *Treehouse Restaurant* is open to nonguests (mains $18 to $30).

Five kilometres from Mossman, Newell Beach is a quiet, palm-fringed beach. *Newell Beach Caravan Park* (☎*/fax 4098 1331)* has tent sites for $15 and units with/without air-con for $60/55. This is a friendly spot to stay, right on the water.

At Miallo, about 8km north-west of Mossman, is the **Karnak Playhouse & Rainforest Sanctuary** (☎ *4098 8194, Whyanbeel Rd, via Miallo)*. This amphitheatre has a magical setting – the open-air seats look down onto a timber stage set beside a small lake, and a backdrop of rainforest-covered hills surrounds the whole set-up. It has varied performances including theatre, dance and a high-tech laser show, *Creations*, which includes a performance by Aboriginal children. The Karnak is open from

April/May to November, and bookings are essential. It's also best to call ahead to see what's on.

Just next door is the **High Falls Fruit Farm** (*☎ 4098 8148, Lot 1, Old Forestry Rd, Whyanbeel*), which has tropical fruit tasting for $4 and a tour and tasting for $9. It also has a *restaurant* (mains $5 to $22) that uses tropical fruit in every dish!

The turn-off to Wonga Beach is 22km north of Mossman. A further kilometre on is *Pinnacle Village Holiday Park* (*☎ 4098 7566, fax 4098 7813, Vixies Rd*) with unpowered/powered sites for $18/20 and cabins from $55 to $77. It's a well-grassed park, fronting a long, sandy beach. Another good place is *Wonga Beach Caravan Park* (*☎ 4098 7514, fax 4098 7704*) with unpowered/powered sites for $13.20/14.30. It's quiet, simple and right on the water.

Just north of the Wonga Beach turn-off is **Wonga Beach Equestrian Centre** (*☎ 4098 7583; $75 per person, including pick-up from Port Douglas; trail rides 8.30am and 3pm; 2½ hours*). These horse rides follow trails through the surrounding cane fields, rainforest and beaches.

Further on is the turn-off to the Daintree River ferry crossing and Cape Tribulation; continue straight on for another 11km to get to Daintree Village. The *Big Croc Cafe* (*☎ 4098 7608*) is right by the ferry crossing.

## DAINTREE VILLAGE

The highway continues 36km beyond Mossman to the village of Daintree, passing the turn-off to the Daintree River ferry crossing after 24km. The ferry crossing is a short punt across the river.

Established as a logging town, with timber cutters concentrating on the prized red cedars that were so common in this area, Daintree is now hyped as a centre for river cruises along the Daintree River. During the wet season it's a quiet village, but come the tourist season, the town is buzzing with busloads of tourists itching to see a crocodile along the farmland banks of the Daintree river.

Many visitors mistakenly believe that Daintree Village is the centre of the Wet Tropics World Heritage Area. In fact, it's not within the area that's listed, and much (but not all) of the surrounding area is cleared farmland. There are a couple of souvenir shops and cafes, and several excellent B&Bs in the area. The public ferry wharf is 400m north of the ferry crossing.

## Organised Tours

About a dozen tours offer river trips on the Daintree from various points between the ferry crossing and Daintree Village. In the cooler months (April to September) crocodile sightings are more common, especially on sunny days when the tide is low and they sun themselves on the exposed banks. There are tour booking agencies in and around Daintree.

There are several operators that offer more individual tours for smaller groups.

Chris Dahlberg's Specialised River Tours (☎ 4098 6169, Daintree Village) has two-hour tours for $35 that leave at 6.30am (winter) or 6am (summer). These tours are run by an enthusiastic bird-watcher and knowledgeable guide.

Peter Cooper's Mangrove Ecosystem Tours (☎ 4098 2066, Public Wharf) leave hourly and cost $20/10 per adult/child. Peter's tours specialise in the plant life of the Daintree.

Electric Boat Cruises (☎ 1800 686 103, Daintree Rd) takes groups of 12 in quiet, eco-friendly, electric-powered boats for 1½-hour daybreak cruises (8am, adult/child $28/14, including breakfast), sundown cruises ($50/25) or one-hour cruises (10.30am, 11.30am, 12.30pm, 1.30pm, 2.30pm, 4pm, 5pm, $17/8). Book ahead.

If you're travelling with kids, they'll probably love Daintree Rainforest River Trains (☎ 1800 808 309, 4090 7676, Ferry Crossing). It has one-hour cruises for $17/8.50 per adult/child (9.30am and 4pm), 1½-hour cruises for $22/11 (10.30am and 1.30pm) and 2½-hour cruises for $28/11 (10.30am).

The longest-established operator is Daintree Connection (☎ 1800 658 833) It has 1½-hour cruises from Daintree Village ($20/7) and popular 2½-hour cruises to the mouth of the Daintree, including a walk along the beach at Cape Kimberley ($28/13).

## Bush Tucker Goes Upmarket

Before non-Indigenous settlement, the rainforest Aborigines of Far North Queensland (FNQ) lived a life totally in balance with the natural world. They followed seasonal cycles, moving to the drier Tableland in the wet season. In their relationship to their food sources, they followed pure ecological reasoning: After mating seasons when certain species were pregnant or birthing, those animals would not be hunted – thereby protecting and enriching that particular food source. The fruits of the rainforest were eaten only in season and only after long and complex treatments to remove toxins, such as crushing and rinsing with water. Nuts were also eaten; sometimes they were roasted and then chewed while still hot to form a damper, which was then cooked.

A number of restaurants in FNQ serve, in combination with standard Australian produce, what is known as bush tucker or native cuisine. It's a whole new eating experience, and Baaru House restaurant in Daintree is a good place to go to sample some of this bush tucker – its head chef is an Australian Aborigine who has used knowledge passed down from his family, elders and Aboriginal friends, to develop the intrinsic tastes and possibilities of native foods.

Bush tucker uses native meats such as wallaby, emu and kangaroo, accompanied by bush herbs and fruits, and enhanced with bush ingredients such as bush honey, Kakadu plums, Illawarra plums, bush tomatoes and wild ginger.

Crocodile might be rolled in ground wattle seed, which tastes like coffee-chocolate-hazelnut, and then transformed into ravioli. Camel fillets might be served with a roasted bunya nut and Kahlua cream sauce – bunya nuts have a starchy, white flesh with a yellow central stalk, and a taste similar to chestnut, but with a subtle pine-flavoured overtone. The desserts might use gumleaf oils, wild limes, bush honey, green ants and the tart berry-and-rhubarb flavour of wild rosella flowers.

And while not necessarily native ingredients, quite a few eateries in FNQ do fab things with the tropical fruits grown locally. Wallaby rump might be served with a warm tropical fruit salsa, while homemade ice creams use mangosteen, rambutan, dragon fruit and the sensational, chocolate-flavoured black sapote as their flavour base.

## Places to Stay

There are several excellent B&Bs in the village and the surrounding farmland. Many are off unsealed roads, but all are signposted.

*Red Mill House* (☎ 4098 6233, Stewart St) Singles $40-60, doubles $66-88, including breakfast. This excellent B&B, in the centre of the village, has comfortable rooms; lovely, spacious gardens and a pool.

*Kenadon Homestead Cabins* (☎/fax 4098 6142, Dagmar St) Singles/doubles $70/80. The self-contained cabins are fairly basic.

*Vistas of the Daintree* (☎/fax 4098 6118, Stewart Creek Rd) Singles/doubles $110/120, including breakfast. This modern villa has great views of the river and surrounding pastureland.

*River Home Cottages* (☎/fax 4098 6225, Upper Daintree Rd) Doubles $120, including breakfast. This working cattle property is a fine place to experience bush hospitality (and a drop of home-brew). All the cottages are fully self-contained with sweeping views. Night walks and tours (to pristine rainforest on the property) are available gratis.

*Daintree Valley Haven* (☎ 4098 6206, fax 4098 6106, Steward Creek Rd) Doubles $110, including breakfast. This is a quiet getaway, 8km from the village. All cabins are fully self-contained and overlook a waterway.

*Daintree Eco Lodge & Spa* (☎ *4098 6100, fax 4098 6100, 20 Daintree Rd)* Singles/doubles from $437/476. Set in the rainforest, 3.5km south of the village, this impressive lodge has spacious timber lodges and to-die-for spa treatments.

## Places to Eat

There are a couple of eateries in the centre of the village.

*Jacanas Restaurant* Meals $4.50-17.50. This is a casual cafe and takeaway with an outdoor section.

*Daintree Tea House Restaurant* (☎ *4098 6161, Daintree Rd)* Meals from $13. Open 9am-6.30pm. About 3km south of Daintree, by Barratt Creek, the Tea House specialises in wild barramundi and light meals.

*Baaru House* (☎ *4098 6100, 20 Daintree Rd)* Lunch mains from $9, dinner mains $18-21. Open early-9pm Mon-Sun. Part of the Daintree Eco Lodge & Spa, the restaurant is open to nonguests and is reasonably priced, so make the most of it! The chef uses native produce.

## Getting There & Away

See the Bus entry under Getting There & Away in the Cairns section earlier for details.

## CAPE TRIBULATION AREA

Part of the Wet Tropics World Heritage Area, Cape Tribulation is famed for its superb scenery, with long beaches stretching north and south and a backdrop of the rugged, forest-covered mountains of Thornton Peak (1374m) and Mt Sorrow. It's an incredibly beautiful stretch of coast, and is one of the few places in Australia where tropical rainforest meets the sea. These rainforests, dry woodlands and coastal mangroves are home to a host of unique flora and fauna, including rare and threatened species such as Bennett's tree kangaroo. Most, but not all, of this region is national park – Cow Bay and Cape Tribulation are loosely termed villages, but the whole Cape Tribulation Rd is just a scattering of places to stay, restaurants, tiny general stores, and national park boardwalks.

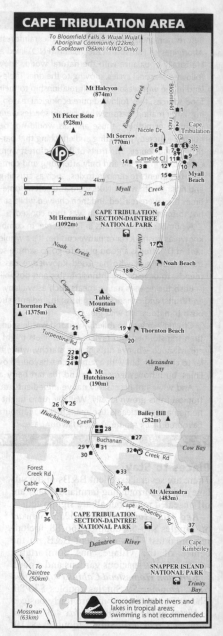

**CAPE TRIBULATION AREA**

To Bloomfield Falls & Wujal Wujal Aboriginal Community (22km), & Cooktown (96km) (4WD Only)

Mt Halcyon (874m)

Mt Pieter Botte (928m)

Mt Sorrow (770m)

Nicole Dr

Cape Tribulation

Camelot Cl

Myall Beach

Enmagoen Creek

Bloomfield Track

0     2     4km
0   1    2mi

Myall    Creek

Mt Hemmant (1092m)

**CAPE TRIBULATION SECTION-DAINTREE NATIONAL PARK**

Noah   Creek

Oliver Creek

Noah Beach

Cooper    Creek

Thornton Peak (1375m)

Table Mountain (450m)

Turpentine Rd

Thornton Beach

Mt Hutchinson (190m)

Alexandra Bay

Bailey Hill (282m)

Hutchinson   Creek

Buchanan

Cow Bay

Creek Rd

Forest Creek Rd

Cable Ferry

Mt Alexandra (483m)

Cape   Kimberley   Rd

**CAPE TRIBULATION SECTION-DAINTREE NATIONAL PARK**

Daintree   River

Cape Kimberley

To Daintree (50km)

**SNAPPER ISLAND NATIONAL PARK**

Trinity Bay

To Mossman (63km)

Crocodiles inhabit rivers and lakes in tropical areas; swimming is not recommended.

## CAPE TRIBULATION AREA

**PLACES TO STAY**

1 Cape Trib Beach House
4 Cape Trib Farmstay
5 Cape Tribulation
  Retreat
6 Tropical Paradise B&B
9 PK's Jungle Village
11 Ferntree Rainforest
  Resort
13 Cape Trib Rainforest
  Hideaway
14 Jungle Treehouse
16 Coconut Beach Rainforest
  Resort; Long House
17 Noah Beach Camping Area
21 Heritage Lodge
22 Daintree Deep Forest
  Lodge

24 Lync-Haven
27 Crocodylus Village
30 Rainforest Retreat
  Motel
31 Cow Bay Hotel Motel
35 Daintree Manor B&B
37 Club Daintree

**PLACES TO EAT**

8 Boardwalk Cafe
12 Dragonfly Gallery Cafe
19 Cafe On Sea
25 Fan Palm Boardwalk
  Café
26 Daintree Ice Cream
  Company
29 The Waterhole Café
36 Big Croc Cafe

**OTHER**

2 Kulki Boardwalk; Carpark
3 Rangers Station
7 Bat House
10 Dubuji Boardwalk
15 Mason's Store
18 Marrdja Botanical Walk
20 Cooper Creek Wilderness
  Cruises
23 Wundu Trailrides
28 Cow Bay Airstrip
32 Cow Bay Service Station &
  General Store
33 Daintree Rainforest
  Environmental Centre;
  Jindalba Boardwalk
34 Alexandra Range
  Lookout

Once known as a quiet idyll, the booming tourism industry to the south and sealed access roads has made Cape Trib one of the most popular day trips from Port Douglas and Cairns. Whereas once you'd pass the occasional 4WD or battered old station wagon, nowadays there's a steady stream of tour operators and independent visitors heading up to the area.

From the Daintree cable ferry, it's another 34km to Cape Trib. You can get fuel at two or three places between Mossman and Cooktown along the coastal route.

### History

Cape Tribulation was named by Captain Cook, as it was north of here that the *Endeavour* struck a reef. Mt Sorrow was also named by Cook. The Kuku Yalanji Aboriginal people called the area Kulki. Because of its steep mountainous terrain, the area west and north of Cape Tribulation is one of the few in FNQ that have never been cleared for agriculture. The first European to settle permanently was the father of the present owner of Mason's Store in 1928. In WWII, troops from the Women's Land Army came to the area to grow food for the war effort. After the war, saw-milling and then cattle grazing became the area's main sources of income.

The first cable ferry service across the Daintree River began in 1956. By the 1970s,

a trickle of visitors had started to arrive, and Cape Trib started to gain a reputation for its remote beauty. The area became something of a hippie outpost, and settlements such as the alternative Cedar Bay community in the rainforests north of Cape Trib grew.

In 1981 recognition of the unique natural values of this area led to the declaration of the Cape Tribulation National Park (now known as the Cape Tribulation Section of Daintree National Park). The park stretches from the Daintree River to the Bloomfield River, with the mountains of the McDowell Range providing the western boundary. The area around Cow Bay is freehold land and not part of the national park. As part of the Wet Tropics Area, Cape Trib was also granted World Heritage listing in 1988 (see the boxed text 'World Heritage Listing – What Does It Guarantee?' earlier in this chapter).

### Information

There isn't an official information centre here, although the Bat House and the Daintree Rainforest Environmental Centre are both good sources of information. See the Things to See & Do entry later.

There's a rangers station (☎ 4098 0052) on the main road just before the turn-off to Cape Trib beach. It's staffed only between 9am and 11am; for information at other times, contact Mossman QPWS (☎ 4098 2188).

Note that accommodation at Cape Tribulation is often booked out during the high season – ring before you arrive to make sure there's a bed!

**Money** Most accommodation, places to stay and eat, and the general stores have Eftpos, but there are no banking facilities here. The closest banks are in Mossman.

**Fuel & Supplies** You can get fuel, bait and limited groceries at Cow Bay Service Station and General Store (☎ 4098 9127, Buchanan Creek Rd), open 7.30am to 6pm daily, and Rainforest Village (☎ 4098 9015), 5km north of the Cow Bay turn-off. Mason's Store (☎ 4098 0070), just off the main road about 1.5km south of the Cape, is open every day from 8.30am to 5pm. It sells groceries, film and alcohol, and also fuel. A **swimming hole** near the store is open to the general public during daylight hours.

## Things to See & Do

About 3km past the Daintree River crossing, Cape Kimberley Rd turns off the main road and heads east down to **Cape Kimberley beach**, near the estuary of the Daintree River. Crocodylus Village (☎ 4098 9166, Buchanan Creek Rd) organises overnight sea-kayaking expeditions out to **Snapper Island**, which is just offshore from the Cape, for $179. The island has a national parks camping ground at West Point.

About 9km from the ferry, just after you cross the spectacular **Heights of Alexandra Range**, is the **Alexandra Range Lookout**, with panoramic views out over the Daintree River estuary and the national park.

Further on is the **Daintree Rainforest Environmental Centre** (☎ 4098 9171, Cape Tribulation Rd; adult/child $11/5.50; open 9am-5pm) This is a great place to learn more about rainforests, with knowledgeable staff, interactive displays and a 25m tower that stretches up into the jungle canopy. The **Jindalba Boardwalk** snakes through the rainforest behind the centre.

About 12km from the ferry you reach Buchanan Creek Rd, which is the turn-off

for **Cow Bay** (5.5km) and the Crocodylus Village hostel.

After crossing Hutchinson Creek the road swings sharply inland, and on the left is the **Daintree Ice Cream Company** (open noon-5pm, Mon-Sat), which sells heavenly ice creams made from exotic fruits like black sapote, macadamia, jackfruit and wattle seed – the chocolate-flavoured black sapote is divine. Further on, the road strikes the shore at **Thornton Beach**. The **Marrdja Botanical Walk** at Oliver Creek is an interesting 800m interpretive boardwalk which follows the creek through the rainforest and mangroves to a lookout over Noah Creek. At the northern end of Noah Beach there's a very pleasant **picnic ground**.

Opposite PK's Jungle Village, the **Bat House** (☎ 4098 0063, Cape Tribulation Rd, 🖳 www.austrop.org.au; admission by donation; open 10.30am-3.30pm) is a small rainforest information and education centre. Volunteers from AUSTROP, a local conservation organisation, run the centre. As the name suggests, it's also a nursery for fruit bats, and you may have the chance to see and touch one close up.

The **Dubuji Boardwalk** area was once zoned for a resort, but was saved thanks to the Daintree Rescue Program, and it's now a 1.8km circuit walk down to Myall Beach through rainforest and mangroves. Further north is the **Kulki Boardwalk**; the 400m walk leads to a platform overlooking the beach. To get to Myall Beach from here, walk over the saddle west of the headland.

For something more strenuous, there's the **Mt Sorrow Ridge Walk** (7½ hours return), but walkers should be well prepared with wet-weather gear and first seek local advice. The trail leaves from just beyond the ranger's office.

The road heading north becomes progressively rougher beyond Cape Trib Beach House, leading to the Bloomfield Track.

## Organised Tours

If you want to do more than relax on the beach or by the pool, there's a good range of tours on offer including fishing and rainforest walks.

**Guided Walks** If you're taking a guided walk, don't expect too many night critters to be dropping by to say Hi. Jungle Adventures (☎ 4099 5651) runs night walks at 7.30pm guided by qualified zoologists (from $28).

Mason's Tours (☎ 4098 0070), based at Mason's Store, runs four-hour daytime walks ($32), 2½-hour night walks ($32) and 4WD trips along the Bloomfield Track.

**Reef Trips** The other attraction in Cape Tribulation is the reef, which is only 45 minutes away by fast launch. Only one operator offers trips out to the reef: The catamaran *Rum Runner* (☎ 1800 686 444) has reef cruises for $109 ($89 stand-by); certified and introductory dives are possible.

**Sea Kayaking** One small operator with worthwhile sea-kayaking trips is Tropical Paradise B&B (☎/fax 4098 0072) costing $30 for two hours, $65 for a half day and $140 for a full day.

**River Cruises** Cooper Creek Wilderness Cruises (☎ 4098 9052), based just south of Cafe on Sea, takes small groups on one-hour cruises (adult $17) up Cooper Creek, which meets the ocean a little way south of the kiosk. Departure times depend on the tides. It also does 1½-hour night cruises. Book ahead to reserve a place.

**Horse Riding** Wundu Trailrides (☎ 4098 9156), on the main road about 5km north of

---

## Cassowaries – the Vital Rainforest Link

The flightless cassowary, standing up to 1.8m in height, is one of the largest birds in the world. It is only found in Australia in the tropical lowland rainforest habitats of the Gold Coast and north Queensland and to a lesser degree in northern Cape York Peninsula. The cassowary is an endangered species – its biggest threat is loss of habitat, and while adult cassowaries probably have no natural enemies, their eggs and chicks, protected by the male cassowary, are vulnerable to dogs, feral cats and wild pigs. The birds are also frequently hit by cars – heed road signs warning of cassowary habitat areas. The most important habitats are Mission Beach, Cape Tribulation, Wallaman Falls on the Gold Coast and the MacAllister Range in Cape York.

In 1993 a CSIRO report estimated that only 54 adult cassowaries remained in the study area north of the Daintree River to Cape Tribulation; recovery programs including wildlife corridors linking habitats are slowly being established. The report emphasised the vital role played by the cassowary in rainforest ecology. It is perhaps the only 'dispersal agent' for some 70 species of plant in the rainforest, as well as the main dispersal agent for another 30 species. Cassowaries carry out this crucial role by swallowing fruits and berries whole – the seeds are later deposited in their droppings elsewhere in the rainforest (see **W** www.csiro.com.au for more information).

The Daintree Cassowary Care Group (☎ 4090 7663) asks that visitors report cassowary sightings. Report the location, the shape of the bird's casque (its headpiece) and the colour of its wattle (the fleshy lobe hanging from its neck).

The Mission Beach area has an estimated population of about 50 to 60 adult cassowaries. The C4 (Community for Coastal Cassowary Conservation; ☎ 4068 7197) has an info centre next to the tourist office in Mission Beach.

If you are lucky enough to see a cassowary in the forest, take care – people are sometimes chased and attacked. And one more thing – just like the dingoes on Fraser Island and native animals anywhere – don't feed them. They need to find their own tucker.

the Cow Bay turn-off, has three- to four-hour horse rides at 8.40am and 2.40pm (only one per day during the wet season) for $52. You ride through the local tea plantation and along steep rainforest tracks.

**Joy Flights** Gondwana Aviation (☎ 4098 9054), based at the airstrip just north of the Cow Bay turn-off, offers joy flights in a light plane over Cape Trib and the reef from $65 per person.

## Places to Stay

Ten or so years ago, camping or backpacker hostels used to be the only accommodation options available, but as the Cape Trib area becomes more and more well known, boutique resorts and B&Bs have become increasingly popular.

## Places to Stay – Budget
### Daintree River to Cape Tribulation
The Cape Kimberley area offers the first budget option across the river.

*Club Daintree* (☎ 4090 7500, *Cape Kimberley Beach*) Camp sites $8.80 per person, dorm beds $16.30, cabins $107.80. On the beachfront, with views of Snapper Island, Club Daintree has a big camping area and reasonable cabins. There's a casual *restaurant* and bar. Cape Kimberley is on the lowlands of the Daintree River estuary, so mosquitoes are sometimes a problem here.

Snapper Island is just offshore from Cape Kimberley and has *camp sites* ($3.85). You'll need to get a permit from Mossman QPWS (☎ 4098 2188) before heading out there. There are toilets on the island, but wood fires are banned so take a fuel stove, as well as water. You should also note that because it's so close to the Cape, it's a crocodile habitat.

*Lync-Haven* (☎ 4098 9155, *fax 4098 9189, Cape Tribulation Rd*) Unpowered/powered sites $8/15 per person, cabins from $95. About 5km north of the Cow Bay, this 16-hectare property, on the main road, has basic cabins (some with en suite), walking trails, a rather small *grocery store* and a licensed *cafe*.

*Crocodylus Village* (☎ 4098 9166, *Buchanan Creek Rd*) Beds in 16–20-bed

dorm $18 ($20 for nonmembers), double cabins $65 (1 double bed, 6 bunks and bathrooms) plus $10 for each extra person. This YHA-associate hostel is about 2.5km off the main Cape Trib Rd. Its canvas-cabin accommodation has the feel of a school camp, but on the plus side, it has a swimming pool and great outdoor *bar-cafe*. The hostel runs guests down to Cow Bay beach and organises tours, including guided forest walks, half-day horse rides ($55), a three-hour sunrise paddle-trek ($45) and a two-day sea-kayaking trip to Snapper Island ($179 with everything supplied).

**Cape Tribulation** Cape Trib has the better choice of budget options.

At Noah Beach there's the QPWS self-registration *Noah Beach Camping Area* (☎ *4098 0052*) with camp sites for $3.85 per person. This site has 16 shady sites set 100m back from the beach. There are toilets, a cold-water shower and water is available. Depending on the weather, it may be closed during the wet season.

*Cape Trib Beach House* (☎ *4098 0030, fax 4098 0120*) Limited tent sites $8 per person, beds in 4-bed dorm/en suite dorm $25/32, doubles $70-109, some with en suites. This is by far the best budget place to stay in Cape Trib, right on the beach. Dorms are in small cabins with decks, surrounded by rainforest. There's a good *bar-cafe* here also.

*PK's Jungle Village* (☎ *4098 0197*) Camp sites $11, beds in 8-bed cabin $24, doubles $65 (no en suite). Close to the excellent Myall Beach, this is well set up with log cabins, a pool, a lively *bar* and a *restaurant* with cheap meals. PK's has a reputation as a party place, which has its consequences.

## Places to Stay – Mid-Range
### Daintree River to Cape Tribulation
There are cheaper mid-range motel options in this area.

*Cow Bay Hotel Motel* (☎ *4098 9011, fax 4098 9022, Cape Tribulation Rd, Cow Bay*) Doubles $66, including breakfast. Back on the Cape Trib Rd, just south of the Cow Bay turn-off, this pub has modern motel units and a pleasant *bistro* with mains from $7.

*Rainforest Retreat Motel (☎ 4098 9101, fax 4098 9120, Cape Tribulation Rd)* Singles/doubles $66/77. This low-key place has budget, self-contained motel units centred on a swimming pool.

*Daintree Deep Forest Lodge (☎ 4098 9162, fax 4098 9242, Cape Tribulation Rd, Thornton Peak)* Singles/doubles $60/99, family units $150 (sleeps 5). About 5km north of the Cow Bay turn-off, at the base of Thornton Peak, this friendly place has self-contained units in a peaceful setting.

*Daintree Manor B&B (☎ 4090 7041, Forest Creek Rd)* Doubles from $85. About 1km north of the ferry crossing, Daintree Manor is an elevated Queenslander with panoramic views.

**Cape Tribulation** Cosy hideaway B&Bs are the best options in this area.

*Tropical Paradise B&B (☎/fax 4098 0072, 23 Nicole Dr)* Singles/doubles $70/110, including breakfast. This B&B is in a great spot with views of the Coral Sea and Mt Sorrow. It also runs excellent sea-kayaking tours.

*Cape Tribulation Retreat (☎ 4098 0028, W www.capetribretreat.com.au, 19 Nicole Dr)* Doubles $100. Signposted from PK's, at the end of Nicole Drive, this gorgeous B&B has rainforest literally in the backyard. The elevated timber home has cathedral ceilings and features rainforest timbers.

*Rainforest Hideaway (☎ 4098 0108, 19 Camelot Close)* Singles/doubles $70/90, including breakfast. Past the Dragonfly Gallery Cafe, this small, open-plan timber cottage has handcrafted furniture.

*Jungle Treehouse (☎ 4099 5651, fax 4099 5293, Camelot Close)* Singles/doubles $85/120, including breakfast. On 28 hectares of pristine rainforest, this tall pole-house has comfortable rooms, and runs night walks and tours.

*Cape Trib Farmstay (☎ 4098 0042, Cape Tribulation Rd)* Doubles $77. This tropical fruit orchard has private timber cottages with views of Mt Sorrow.

## Places to Stay – Top End
### Daintree River to Cape Tribulation
Turpentine Rd runs inland near Thornton Beach, and about 2km along is this secluded and low-key resort.

*Heritage Lodge (☎ 4098 9138, fax 4098 9004, Turpentine Rd)* Doubles $176, including breakfast. The Lodge has comfortable timber cabins, a pool and a wonderful swimming hole on Cooper Creek. The *bar-restaurant* has a small but varied menu, with Thai curries, vegetarian dishes and seafood from $14 to $26.

**Cape Tribulation** About 3km south of the Cape is Cape Trib's most pricey accommodation.

*Coconut Beach Rainforest Resort (☎ 4098 0033, fax 4098 0047)* Double units/villas $230/345, including breakfast. The resort has pools, a *restaurant* and can arrange a wide range of activities.

*Ferntree Rainforest Resort (☎ 4098 0000, fax 4053 1200, Camelot Close, Cape Tribulation)* Doubles from $230. The plush Ferntree Rainforest has luxury cabins, two pools, a *restaurant* and bar. The breezy timber restaurant is open to nonguests and serves meals from $20.

## Places to Eat
There are a few good restaurants, cafes and kiosks along Cape Tribulation Rd.

*The Waterhole Cafe (☎ 4098 9133, Cow Bay)* Meals around $13. Open 5pm-late Mon-Fri, noon-late Sat & Sun. Just south of the Cow Bay turn-off, this relaxed bar and cafe serves simple Thai and Mediterranean dishes. It has live music and DJs on the weekends.

*Fan Palm Boardwalk Cafe (☎ 4098 9119, Cow Bay)* Lunch $5.50-13.50, dinner $12.50-16.50. Open 9am-5pm daily, dinner Thur-Sun, live music Fri & Sat night. This open-air licensed cafe has its own boardwalk through the rainforest and serves up generous vegetarian and Middle Eastern dishes and gourmet burgers.

*Cafe on Sea (☎ 4098 9718, Thornton Beach)* Meals $8-11. Open 8.30am-5pm Mon-Sun. A relaxed, beachfront licensed cafe and takeaway, serving up delicious food, such as Thai fish burgers.

*Boardwalk Cafe* Open 7.30am-7pm Mon-Sun. Opposite PK's, this is a handy takeaway that serves cheap breakfasts, burgers and sandwiches.

**Dragonfly Gallery Cafe** (☎ *4098 0121, Lot 9, Camelot Close*) Mains around $12.50. Open 10am-10pm. This timber pole-house has garden views, decent food and a relaxed Internet area upstairs in the loft.

**Long House** (☎ *4098 0033, Coconut Beach Rainforest Resort*) Lunch mains $11-16, dinner mains $31-55. The Long House restaurant is quite a spectacular Melanesian-style building, with its own turtle pond and a bar overlooking the pool (and the food's good!).

### Getting There & Away
Coral Coaches travel to Cape Tribulation. See the Getting There & Away entries in the Cairns and Port Douglas sections for details. You can also take organised tours to the area (see Organised Tours in the Cairns section). The cable ferry across the Daintree River operates every 15 minutes or so from 6am to midnight ($16 return for cars, $7 return for motorbikes, $2 return for bicycles/ pedestrians, two minutes). It's also reasonably easy to hitch, since beyond the Daintree ferry all vehicles must head to Cape Trib – there's nowhere else to go!

### Getting Around
Apart from Coral Coaches passing through, there are no scheduled transport services here. You may be able to hire a bike from your accommodation.

# North to Cooktown

There are two routes to Cooktown from the south: the 4WD Bloomfield Track from Cape Tribulation (known as the 'coast road') and the Peninsula Developmental Rd/Cooktown Developmental Rd (known as the 'inland route').

## CAPE TRIBULATION TO COOKTOWN – THE COAST ROAD
The controversial Bloomfield Track carves its way through mountains and dense rainforest for almost 80km before linking up

with the Cooktown Developmental Rd, 28km south of Cooktown. During the wet season this road may be closed – check with Cooktown police (☎ 4069 5320) before heading off.

The Track was built back in 1983, when the local Douglas Shire Council decided to bulldoze a gravel road through the forest from just north of Cape Tribulation to the Bloomfield River. The proposal was vigorously opposed by local conservationists who were concerned about its impact on the local environment, and Cape Trib became the scene of a classic 'greenies versus bulldozers' blockade. Several months and numerous arrests later, the road builders won and the Bloomfield Track was opened, despite serious concerns that soil runoff from the track would wash into the ocean and damage the Great Barrier Reef.

## Cape Tribulation to Bloomfield River
It's 5km from Cape Trib to **Emmagen Creek**, which is the official start of the Bloomfield Track. Just before you reach Emmagen Creek, the road passes a huge strangler fig. From beside the tree, a **walking path** leads down to a pretty crescent-shaped beach. A little way beyond this crossing, the road begins to climb a series of hills. With a combination of very steep climbs and descents, sharp corners, and fine, slippery bull dust, this is the most challenging section of the drive, especially after rain. The Bloomfield River is a tidal crossing, so you'll need to check with locals about the best times to cross.

The road then follows the broad Bloomfield River, before crossing it 30km north of Cape Trib. The **Wujal Wujal Aboriginal Community** (pop 293) is on the northern bank of the river. Contact the Wujal Wujal Aboriginal Land Council (☎ 4060 8155) for permit details if you want to visit. A mustsee here is **Bloomfield Falls** (turn left after crossing the bridge).

About 10km beyond Wujal Wujal is the small hamlet of **Ayton**, (otherwise known as **Bloomfield**) where you can stop for fuel and snacks at the *general store*. There are also a couple of places to stay.

*Bloomfield Cabins & Camping (☎ 4060 8207, fax 4060 8187, 20 Bloomfield Rd, Ayton)* Tent sites $9 per person, cabins $49. Just north of Ayton this place has a great setting, with tall, shady gum trees and Weary Bay only a 400m-walk away. There's a *bar* and casual *restaurant*. Reef and river trips can be organised from here.

*Bloomfield Rainforest Lodge (☎ 4035 9166, fax 4035 9166, Weary Bay)* Packages from $640 per person twin share for 2 nights, including air transfer, meals and activities. Close to the mouth of the Bloomfield River, this remote resort is on Weary Bay. It's only accessible from the sea, and the tariff includes air transfer and all meals. The lodge offers river cruises, guided rainforest walks, local fishing, reef trips and 4WD safaris.

### Bloomfield River to Cooktown

North of Bloomfield, the road passes through the **Cedar Bay National Park**, which stretches inland a short distance. There are no facilities here, and access into the park is either by boat or by walking along the numerous small tracks through the bush. If you want to stop in this area there are a few options.

*Home Rule Rainforest Lodge (☎ 4060 3925, fax 4060 3902, Rossville)* Camp sites $8 per person, bunk beds $18, double cabins $36. The turn-off to this lodge is signposted from Rossville, 33km north of the Bloomfield River crossing. At the end of a very long and bumpy driveway, this place has a peaceful setting, with a *bar*, cheap *meals* and good cooking facilities. There's a two-hour walk to a nearby **waterfall**. Ring from Rossville for a pick-up.

*Lion's Den Hotel (☎ 4060 3911, fax 4060 3958, Helensvale)* Camp sites $5. Open 8am until midnight. At Helenvale, 9km further north, slap-bang in the middle of what seems like nowhere, this once-infamous bush pub dates back to 1875. With its corrugated, graffiti-covered tin walls and slab-timber bar, it attracts a steady stream of travellers and local characters. It has a *restaurant* that serves up excellent budget meals, including pizza and lasagne for around $8. Plans are afoot to build safari lodges.

*Mungumby Lodge (☎ 4060 3158, fax 4060 3159)* Doubles $195. This verdant little oasis of lawns and mango trees, with timber cabins scattered around, has straightforward and comfortable cabins, with en suites. Bushwalking and 4WD tours are offered.

Around 4km further on the road meets the Cooktown Developmental Rd.

### CAIRNS TO COOKTOWN – THE INLAND ROUTE

The main route between Cairns and Cooktown is 332km long (4½ to five hours' drive time). The road is open to conventional 2WD vehicles and shouldn't present any major problems in the Dry, although the second half is over unsealed roads, which tend to be rough, corrugated and mighty dusty – all part of the challenge of getting to Cooktown! The scenery is in dramatic contrast to the lush rainforest that surrounds the coastal road. This route is more like an outback trip, passing through dry eucalypt forests.

As with the coast road, this inland route may be closed during the Wet – check with the Cooktown police (☎ 4069 5320) before heading off.

### Cairns to the Palmer River Roadhouse

After heading north out of Cairns, take the turn-off to Kuranda and climb over the Atherton Tableland. At Mareeba you meet the Peninsula Developmental Rd, which takes you north, and about 40km further on the small township of **Mt Molloy**.

James Venture Mulligan, the man who jump-started both the Palmer River and Hodgkinson River gold rushes, is buried in the **Mt Molloy cemetery**. Mt Molloy Trail Rides (☎ 4094 1382) offers trail rides to the ruins of an old copper smelter and to Rifle Creek. You can camp out or stay overnight at the pub in town.

The *National Hotel (☎ 4094 1133, Main St)* offers cheap accommodation (singles/doubles $30/50) and is also a pleasant place for a drink or a *meal* (meals $6 to $14). It's open for lunch and dinner.

For genuinely (believe it or not) authentic Mexican, head to *Mt Molloy Licensed*

*Cafe & Takeaway (☎ 4094 1187, Main St)* which has dishes for $5 to $15. Otherwise known as Lobo Loco, it has inexpensive, home-cooked burritos and enchiladas, as well as award-winning hamburgers.

Just past Mt Molloy is the evocatively named **Abattoir Swamp Environment Park**, a lotus flower–covered wetland with a sheltered bird-hide.

The former wolfram-mining town of **Mt Carbine**, 30km north-west of Mt Molloy, consists of a pub, a *roadhouse* and a handful of houses. Located just south of the town, a former mining village has been transformed into a scenic, if somewhat, solitary van park. *Mt Carbine Village & Caravan Park (☎/fax 4094 3160)* has unpowered/powered sites for $13/15 and double cabins from $45.

The **McLeod River** crossing, 14km west of Mt Carbine, is one of the best spots to *camp* along this section of road and it is popular with travellers. Further north the road climbs through the DeSailly Range and there are panoramic views from **Bob's Lookout** that are worthy of a quick photo stop.

At the **Palmer River** crossing, 85km north-west of Mt Carbine, you'll find the solitary *Palmer River Roadhouse (☎ 4060 2020)* which has unpowered/powered sites for $6.50/12.50. It's open 7am till late. There's an interesting collection of paintings inside, including James Baines' *River of Gold*, which depicts the times and characters of the Palmer River gold rush. There's a basic *camping area* behind the roadhouse.

The bitumen finishes a couple of kilometres beyond the roadhouse. There are a couple of sealed sections further on, but the majority of the trip from here to Cooktown is along unsealed roads of varying standards.

## Palmerville & Maytown

The 1873 to 1883 gold rush, for which the Palmer River is famous, happened about 70km west of the Palmer River Roadhouse. Its main towns were Palmerville and Maytown, of which very little is left today, but the area is protected as a historic reserve and, if you have a 4WD and a little time, a visit to the former goldfields can make for an interesting side trip. There is another

road into the area from the Burke Developmental Rd, north of Chillagoe.

The turn-off from the Peninsula Developmental Rd is about 17km south of the Palmer River Roadhouse, just before the White's Creek crossing – it isn't signposted, but there's a tree with a painted circle of colour, which marks the turn-off west.

Bear in mind that this is wild, remote country. Good maps, a companion vehicle, local advice and proper preparation are essential. Contact the QPWS office in Cairns, Mossman or Chillagoe for information, a camping permit, maps and current track details.

## Lakeland to Cooktown

It's another 30km from the Palmer River Roadhouse to Lakeland, a hamlet at the junction of the Peninsula Developmental Rd and the Cooktown Developmental Rd. Head west and you're on your way to Laura and Cape York; continue straight north-east and you've got another 82km of often-unsealed and bumpy road to Cooktown. The local RACQ rep is Chris Engineering (☎ 4060 2010), on the main road, about 6km before Lakeland.

There are a few places to stay and eat, all with Eftpos facilities.

*Lakeland Caravan Park (☎ 4060 2008, fax 4060 2179)* Unpowered/powered sites $8/14 per person. This is a friendly park with open fireplaces set up for convivial evenings.

*Lakeland Downs Hotel-Motel (☎ 4060 2142, fax 4060 2114, Peninsula Developmental Rd)* Dongas $16.50, single/double motel rooms for $55/66. The rooms are comfortable and the pub also serves up big *meals* at lunch and dinner for $3 to $13.

*Lakeland Coffee House (☎ 4060 2040)* Open 6.30am-6.30pm. This place sells sandwiches and locally grown (but tragically brewed) coffee. It's also a grocery store and service station.

The *Lakeland Roadhouse (☎ 4060 2188)* is open from 7am to 9pm.

The next major point of interest is the **Annan River Gorge**, which is about 52km past Lakeland. It's well worth stopping here and walking downstream a little way – the river has carved, in pick-axe fashion, an impressive gorge through solid rock, and you'll soon come to a waterfall that is equally impressive, especially during the wet season.

A little further down the road is the turn-off to **Helenvale** and the Lion's Den Hotel (see the Bloomfield to Cooktown section earlier).

Continuing to Cooktown, the road soon passes **Black Mountain National Park**, with its thousands of stacked, square, black, granite boulders that look unnervingly precarious, as though they might tumble down with the slightest movement. The mountain is known to Aboriginal people as Kalcajagga, or Place of the Spears and is home to unique species of frogs, skinks and geckoes. It was formed 260 million years ago by a magma intrusion below the surface, which then solidified, and was gradually exposed by erosion. Black Mountain marks the northern end of the Wet Tropics World Heritage Area. From here, it's another 28km to Cooktown.

## COOKTOWN
postcode 4871 • pop 1410

Cooktown is just far enough away from Cairns, and just difficult enough to reach, to have remained relatively untouched by mass tourism. The pristine Endeavour River is geographically much as Cook and his crew found it, its three remaining pubs are full of interesting characters (a pub crawl along Charlotte St is recommended) and the James Cook Historical Museum, housed in an old convent hidden in the back streets, is worth checking out.

Cooktown seems determined to trade on its history, but the surrounding countryside shouldn't be underestimated. It has diverse habitats of wetlands, mangroves, rainforest and long, lonely beaches. With a 4WD vehicle, you can use the town as a base for visiting Trevethan Falls, Walker's Bay and Archer Point, all south of Cooktown, and to the north, the Split Rock galleries near Laura or even Lakefield National Park.

### History

On 17 June 1770 Cooktown became the site of Australia's first non-Indigenous settlement, however transient, when Captain James Cook beached his barque, the *Endeavour*, on the banks of its river. The *Endeavour* had earlier struck a reef offshore from Cape Tribulation, and Cook and his crew spent 48 days here while they repaired the damage. During this time, Joseph Banks the chief naturalist, and botanist Daniel Solander studied the flora and fauna along the banks of the Endeavour River, while the artist Sydney Parkinson illustrated their finds. Banks collected 186 plant species and wrote the first European description of a kangaroo. Remarkably, the northern side of the river has scarcely changed since that time.

While Cook had amicable contacts with the local Aboriginal people, race relations turned sour a century later when Cooktown was founded and became the unruly port for the 1873–83 Palmer River gold rush, 140km south-west. Hell's Gate, a narrow pass on the track between Cooktown and the Palmer River, was the scene of frequent ambushes as Aborigines tried to stop their lands being overrun. Battle Camp, about 60km inland from Cooktown, was the site of a major battle between European settlers and Aborigines.

In 1874, before Cairns was even thought of, Cooktown was the second biggest town in Queensland. At its peak there were no less than 94 pubs and the population was over 30,000. As much as half of this population were Chinese, and their industrious presence led to some wild race riots.

Cooktown's glory was short-lived and as the gold ran out, the population dwindled. Two cyclones and an evacuation in WWII came close to killing the town. It wasn't until the James Cook Historical Museum opened in 1970 that visitors started arriving and Cooktown's steady decline was somewhat halted. Fortunes will no doubt change again for Cooktown, when the sealing of the Peninsula Development Rd is completed in 2005.

### Orientation & Information

Cooktown is on the inland side of a headland sheltering the mouth of the Endeavour River. Charlotte St runs south from the wharf, and along it are three pubs, a post office, a heritage bank and several cafes and restaurants. Overlooking the town from the northern end of the headland is Grassy Hill, and east of the town centre are the Cherry Tree and Finch Bays, the Botanic Gardens and Mt Cook National Park. The airfield is 10km west of the town centre along McIvor Rd.

Cooktown hibernates during the wet season (known to locals as the dead season) and reduced hours or closure applies to the town's museums and cruises. Call beforehand to check on opening times.

The Cooktown Travel Centre (☎ 4069 5446, fax 4069 6023, e cooktowntravel@ bigpond.com) in the Charlotte Street Centre, opposite the West Coast Hotel, has walking

trail maps and Trevethan Falls access information. Cooktown QPWS (☎ 4069 5777), on Webber Esplanade, can provide information on the surrounding national parks, including walking trails. If you're heading up to Cape York, you can also organise camping permits here and pick up extra information. The office is open from 8am to noon weekdays, although if you drop by in the afternoon there may be someone around.

There's a Westpac agency in the post office, and an ATM outside the post office. For Internet access head to Cooktown Library (☎ 4069 5009) on Helen St. The local

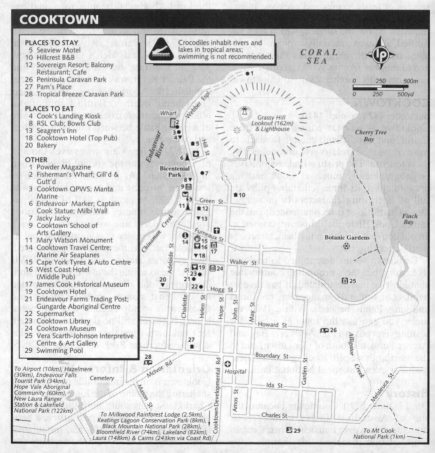

# COOKTOWN

**PLACES TO STAY**
5 Seaview Motel
10 Hillcrest B&B
12 Sovereign Resort; Balcony Restaurant; Cafe
26 Peninsula Caravan Park
27 Pam's Place
28 Tropical Breeze Caravan Park

**PLACES TO EAT**
4 Cook's Landing Kiosk
8 RSL Club; Bowls Club
13 Seagren's Inn
18 Cooktown Hotel (Top Pub)
20 Bakery

**OTHER**
1 Powder Magazine
2 Fisherman's Wharf; Gill'd & Gutt'd
3 Cooktown QPWS; Manta Marine
6 Endeavour Marker; Captain Cook Statue; Milbi Wall
7 Jacky Jacky
9 Cooktown School of Arts Gallery
11 Mary Watson Monument
14 Cooktown Travel Centre; Marine Air Seaplanes
15 Cape York Tyres & Auto Centre
16 West Coast Hotel (Middle Pub)
17 James Cook Historical Museum
19 Cooktown Hotel
21 Endeavour Farms Trading Post; Gungarde Aboriginal Centre
22 Supermarket
23 Cooktown Library
24 Cooktown Museum
25 Vera Scarth-Johnson Interpretive Centre & Art Gallery
29 Swimming Pool

Crocodiles inhabit rivers and lakes in tropical areas; swimming is not recommended.

*CORAL SEA*

Grassy Hill Lookout (162m) & Lighthouse

*Cherry Tree Bay*

Wharf

*Endeavour River*

Bicentenial Park

*Chinaman Creek*

Green St

Furneaux St

Walker St

Hogg St

Howard St

Boundary St

Ida St

Charles St

*Finch Bay*

Botanic Gardens

*Alligator Creek*

To Airport (10km), Hazelmere (30km), Endeavour Falls Tourist Park (34km), Hope Vale Aboriginal Community (60km), New Laura Ranger Station & Lakefield National Park (122km)

Cemetery

McIvor Rd

Mason St

Hospital

Cooktown Developmental Rd

To Milkwood Rainforest Lodge (2.5km), Keatings Lagoon Conservation Park (8km), Black Mountain National Park (28km), Bloomfield River (74km), Lakeland (82km), Laura (148km) & Cairns (243km via Coast Rd)

To Mt Cook National Park (1km)

RACQ depot is Cape York Tyres & Auto Centre (☎ 4069 5233) on the corner of Charlotte and Furneaux Sts.

## Things to See & Do

Cooktown's major attraction is **James Cook Historical Museum** *(☎ 4069 5386, Cnr Helen & Furneaux Sts; adult/child $7/2.50; open 9.30am-4pm Sun, Mon, Wed, Fri; 9am-4pm Tues, Thur, Sat)*. Built as a convent in 1889, the museum has a fascinating collection of displays relating to all aspects of Cooktown's past – its Aboriginal history, Captain Cook's life and voyages, the Palmer River gold rush and the Chinese community.

Nearby, is the idiosyncratic **Cooktown Museum** *(☎ 4069 5680, Cnr Helen & Walker Sts; admission $5; open 8.30am-5pm)*, which focuses on Cape York's maritime history.

Charlotte St has a number of interesting **monuments** starting with one to the tragic Mary Watson (see the Lizard Island section later) opposite the Sovereign Resort. Towards the wharf stands a **cannon** that was sent from Brisbane in 1885 along with three cannonballs, two rifles and one officer in response to Cooktown's plea for defences against a feared Russian invasion (note the inscribed 'fire this way' arrow!). Further on there's a much-photographed **bronze statue** of Cook, and right by the waterside, a monument marks the spot where the *Endeavour* was careened.

Next to this is the **Milbi Wall (Story Wall)** built by the Gungarde Aboriginal Community – a snaking, tiled mosaic wall that holds more interest than the concrete cairns dedicated to 19th-century explorers found elsewhere in Bicentennial Park. The **Gungarde Aboriginal Centre** *(☎ 4069 6522)*, south of the Cooktown Hotel, has a small selection of work by local Aboriginal artists.

The **Cooktown School of Arts Society Gallery**, beside the post office, houses a small collection of local art works, and on the opposite side of the road is **Jacky Jacky**, a small, timber building with a window display of interesting historical photos.

A short walk along Webber Esplanade past the wharf brings you to the **old powder magazine**. It dates back to 1874, making it one of the first brick buildings to be built in Cape York.

The **Grassy Hill Lookout** has sensational 360-degree views of the town, river and ocean. Captain Cook climbed this hill looking for a passage out through the reefs. At the top sits a compact, corrugated, 19th-century iron lighthouse. A **walking trail** leads from the summit down to the beach at Cherry Tree Bay.

It's a 1½-hour trek to the summit of 431m **Mt Cook**, which has even better views. The trail starts by the Mt Cook National Park sign on Melaleuca St, beyond the swimming pool.

The **Cooktown Cemetery** on McIvor Rd has a walking trail leading to the Jewish and Chinese sections, giving an indication of the earlier multicultural nature of the town. A tall palm tree marks the site of Mary Watson's grave.

The pleasant **Botanic Gardens**, off Walker St, were first planted in 1886 and restored in 1984. Two **walking trails** lead from the gardens to the beaches at Cherry Tree Bay and Finch Bay.

The gardens now house the impressive **Vera Scarth-Johnson Interpretive Centre and Art Gallery** *(☎ 4069 6011)*. Scarth-Johnson (1912–99), a local artist, made it her life's work to paint the native plant species of the Endeavour River as described by Banks and Solander in 1770.

Off the Peninsula Development Rd, 8km from Cooktown, is **Keatings Lagoon Conservation (Mulbabidgee) Park**, a woodland with wet melaleuca swamps covered in lilac water lilies. Pick up a walking trail pamphlet from Cooktown QPWS. You can hitch out there easily if you don't have a car.

## Organised Tours

Tours can be booked directly or through the tourist office.

Cooktown Cruises (☎ 4069 5712) has a two-hour scenic cruise up to the head of the Endeavour River (adult/child $25/12), departing daily at 1pm (Easter to December).

Cooktown Tours (☎/fax 4069 5125) offers 1½-hour town tours ($20/12) and half-day trips to Black Mountain and the Lion's Den Hotel ($55/23); both depart daily at 9am.

There are also 4WD trips to the Split Rock galleries at Laura, and Lakefield National Park ($120/80), and trips to Coloured Sands (an area of spectacular sand dunes) via the Hope Vale Aboriginal Community ($90/60).

Taxi Tours (☎ 4069 5387) run tours of the town, down to the Bloomfield Falls or up to Coloured Sands – you choose where you'd like to go ($50 per hour).

Munbah Aboriginal Culture Tours (☎ 4060 9173) is operated by the local Aboriginal community. The 4WD tour ($110/120 day/overnight) heads to Cape Flattery and includes guided walks. The art of spear making is also covered. Pick-up from Cooktown can be arranged and the tour only runs on demand.

One part boat and one part plane, Marine Air Seaplanes (☎ 4069 5915) next to the tourist office, offers scenic reef flights ($85 to $210) and an extraordinary Lizard Island tour ($245), which lands in Watson's Bay by seaplane. Cape Air Transport (☎ 4069 5007) at Milkwood Rainforest Lodge offers scenic flights of the area, right up to the Tip.

## Special Events

The Cooktown Endeavour Festival, commemorating Captain Cook's landing in 1770, is held over the Queen's Birthday weekend every June, and includes a re-enactment of Cook's landing, a gala ball, a parade, various sporting events and a fishing competition.

The Cooktown Amateur Turf Club holds two-day race meetings twice a year (usually June and August). These are popular events and the town is crowded with people from the stations as far away as Weipa for the sport and socialising.

## Places to Stay

If you want to venture a bit further afield, head to the *Endeavour Falls Tourist Park*, 34km west of Cooktown. Also in a bush setting, it's a peaceful place to stop. See the Cooktown to Musgrave via Lakefield National Park section in the Cape York chapter.

## Places to Stay – Budget

*Tropical Breeze Caravan Park* (☎ 4069 5417, fax 4069 5740, Cnr Charlotte St &

McIvor Rd) Tent sites $14, self-contained units with/without en suites $76/50. This place has very good facilities including a small shop and two swimming pools.

*Peninsula Caravan Park* (☎ 4069 5107, fax 4069 5255, Howard St) Tent sites $7.70 per person, self-contained single/double cabins $55/60.50. On the outskirts of the town at the eastern end of Howard St, this place has a lovely bush setting, with stands of big, old paperbark and gum trees.

*Pam's Place* (☎ 4069 5166, fax 4069 5964, Cnr Charlotte & Boundary Sts) Bunk bed $16.50, singles/doubles $35/45 (nonmembers pay $1 extra). This is a comfortable, YHA-associate hostel with a pool, leafy garden and an assortment of neurotic parrots! Fab 4WD tours of Archer's Point and Walker's Bay are sometimes on offer (beg if you have to!).

## Places to Stay – Mid-Range & Top End

*Hillcrest B&B* (☎ 4069 5305, fax 4069 5893, 130 Hope St) Room $50, including breakfast. This is an old-style guesthouse with shared bathroom facilities.

*Hazelmere* (☎/fax 4069 5466) Double $66, including breakfast. Homestead rooms are on offer at this beef cattle property 30km north-west of Cooktown, via the McIvor Rd.

*Seaview Motel* (☎ 4069 5377, fax 4069 5807, Webber Esplanade) Singles/doubles from $60/70. This pleasant little motel overlooks the Endeavour River.

*Sovereign Resort* (☎ 4069 5400, fax 4069 5582, Cnr Charlotte & Green Sts) Singles/doubles from $115/130. This impressive place is in the middle of town and has a superb pool and a range of accommodation, with well-appointed rooms. It also has a swish cafe-bar and restaurant.

*Milkwood Rainforest Lodge* (☎ 4069 5007, fax 4069 5834, Annan Rd) Doubles $94. About 2.5km south of town off the main road, this lodge offers spacious timber pole-cabins in a rainforest setting. It also has 4WD vehicles for hire.

## Places to Eat

If you're planning to do your own cooking, you'll find a *supermarket* in town, as well as a *bakery*. If you're after a takeaway meal, there are a few places on Charlotte St.

*Cook's Landing Kiosk* (☎ 4069 5101, *Webber Esplanade).* Just south of the wharf, it has outdoor tables overlooking the river and is a pleasant spot for breakfast, lunch or a bottomless coffee.

*Gill'd & Gutt'd (Fisherman's Wharf, Webber Esplanade)* Meals $5-10. This is a mighty fine fish and chippery, serving up barramundi over the counter.

If you're after something cheap and cheerful for lunch or dinner, try the *Bowls Club* (☎ 4069 5819), the *RSL* (☎ 4069 5780) or the *Cooktown Hotel (Top Pub;* ☎ 4069 5308), all on Charlotte St. All serve up standard pub fare and all have nice beer gardens.

There's also a couple of classier places.

*Seagren's Inn* (☎ 4069 5357, *Charlotte St).* Mains $16-28. Eat mod Oz cuisine in smart city decor. It also has a good wine list.

*Sovereign Resort* (see Places to Stay) Lunch mains $6.50-15, dinner mains $19-32. The resort has the excellent *Balcony Restaurant* upstairs with tables overlooking the river (open 7pm-late) and downstairs it has the *Café Bar* (11am-7pm).

### Getting There & Away
Cooktown's airfield is 10km west of town on the road to Hope Vale. Skytrans (☎ 1800 818 405) flies to Cooktown from Cairns ($101 one way).

Coral Coaches (☎ 4031 7577) travels between Cairns and Cooktown via the Cooktown Developmental Rd ($64, 6½ hours, three a week), or the coastal road ($64, eight hours, two a week, June to October only). For details and return bookings contact the agent in Cooktown, the Endeavour Farm Trading Post (☎ 4069 5723) on Charlotte St.

You can also get to Hope Vale on Monday and Thursday with Coral Coaches ($20 one way).

### Getting Around
Cooktown is small enough to cover on foot, if you have the time and energy. Otherwise Cooktown Car Hire (☎ 4069 5007), at Milkwood Rainforest Lodge, rents out small 4WD jeeps from $90 per day, with 150km

free, or you can hire a tinnie (small boat) from Manta Marine (☎ 4069 5601) for $55 (half-day) and tour the river on your own.

For a taxi call (☎ 4069 5387).

See the Organised Tours entry in the Cairns section for details of an overnight 4WD tour of the area.

## LIZARD ISLAND
Lizard Island, the furthest north of the Barrier Reef resort islands, is about 100km from Cooktown and 240km from Cairns. Lizard is a continental island with a dry, rocky and mountainous terrain – far removed from the tropical paradise of swaying palm trees that some people seem to expect. Nevertheless, the island has superb beaches and is a great place for swimming, snorkelling and diving, and has some good bushwalks and great views from Cook's Look (368m), the highest point on the island. Almost the entire island is national park, which means it's open to anyone who makes the effort to get here.

### History
Captain Cook and his crew were the first non-Indigenous people to visit Lizard Island. Having successfully patched up the *Endeavour* in Cooktown, they sailed north and stopped on Lizard Island, where Cook and the botanist Joseph Banks climbed to the top of Cook's Look to search for a way through the Barrier Reef maze and out to the open sea. Banks named the island after its large lizards, known as Gould's monitor, which are from the same family as Indonesia's Komodo dragon. Eventually, other crew members found a safe route out to deeper water, and the *Endeavour* continued its journey. The Dingaal Aboriginal people, many of whom now live at Hope Vale, north of Cooktown, are the traditional owners of the island, which they call Jigurru, and consider a sacred place.

### Things to See & Do
Lizard Island's **beaches** are nothing short of sensational, and range from long stretches of white sand to idyllic little rocky bays. The water is crystal clear and magnificent

## When Worlds Collide

The Dingaal people see Jigurru (Lizard Island) as a sacred place, and shell middens found here date back 3000 years, proving a long physical relationship. Their spiritual relationship with the island is also strong – male initiation ceremonies and meetings between elders of neighbouring tribes once took place here. During Cook's visit Aboriginal huts were sighted in the south-eastern area of the island, as well as piles of shells the inhabitants had feasted on. Banks reported, 'The Indians had been here in their poor embarkations', and later visitors also noted that Aborigines visited the island.

In 1881 Robert and Mary Watson settled on the island to collect beche-de-mer, a noted Chinese delicacy. They built a small, granite cottage overlooking the southern end of what is now Watson's Bay. In September of that year, Robert Watson left the island to search for new fishing grounds, leaving Mary Watson with her baby, Ferrier, and two Chinese servants, Ah Sam and Ah Leong. In October a group of Dingaal people arrived on the island and attacked the group, killing Ah Leong and wounding Ah Sam. The following day Mary Watson fled the island and, with a few supplies, her baby and Ah Sam, paddled away in a beche-de-mer boiling tank.

For 10 days they drifted from coral cay to island to reef to mangrove swamp, signalling unsuccessfully to passing steamers, all the while suffering from dehydration. Their bodies were found on No. 5 Howick Island, east of Cape Flattery, in January 1882. During this ordeal Mary Watson kept a diary, now held in the Queensland Museum in Brisbane, which reveals a brave and surprisingly calm reaction to her situation. The ruined walls of the stone cottage can still be seen on the island.

---

coral surrounds the island – snorkelling here is superb.

Immediately south of the resort are three postcard beaches – Sunset Beach, Pebbly Beach and Hibiscus Beach. Watson's Bay to the north of the resort is a wonderful stretch of sand with great snorkelling at both ends and a giant clam field in the middle. There are also plenty of other choices right around the island.

The island is noted for its **diving**. There are good dives right off the island, and the outer Barrier Reef is less than 20km away, including what is probably Australia's best-known dive, the **Cod Hole**. The resort offers a full range of diving facilities to its guests, and some live-aboard tours from Cairns dive the Cod Hole.

Lizard is also famed among anglers, particularly its **heavy-tackle fishing** – from September to December black marlin come to feed on the outer reef.

The climb to the top of **Cook's Look** is a great walk (three hours return). Near the top there are traces of stones marking an **Aboriginal ceremonial area**. The trail, which starts from the northern end of Watson's Bay near the camp site, is clearly signposted and,

although it can be steep and a bit of a clamber at times, it's easy to follow. The views from the top are sensational, and on a clear day the opening in the reef where Cook made his thankful escape is visible.

The privately funded **Lizard Island Research Station** (☎ 4060 3977) researches topics as diverse as marine organisms for cancer research, the deaths of giant clams, coral reproductive processes, sea bird ecology, and life patterns of reef fish during their larval stage. The station runs tours on Monday and Friday at 9.30am for lodge guests and 11am for campers.

Lizard has plenty of **wildlife**. There are 11 different species of lizards, including Gould's monitors, which can be up to 1m long. More than 40 species of birds have also been recorded on the island and a dozen or so actually nest there, including the beautiful little sunbirds with their long, hanging nests. Bar-shouldered doves, crested terns, Caspian terns and a variety of other terns, oystercatchers and the large sea eagles are other resident species. Seabird Islet in the Blue Lagoon is a popular nesting site for terns, and visitors should keep away from the islet during the summer months.

## Places to Stay

The choice is extreme – camping or five-star luxury! There is a national park *camping ground* at the northern end of Watson's Bay. For a permit ($3.85 per person), contact Cairns QPWS (☎ 4053 4533). The camping ground has toilets, gas barbecues, tables and benches, and fresh water is available from a pump about 250m from the site. For everything else, campers must be totally self-sufficient (the resort is open only to guests). Naturally, you'll need to take your garbage with you when you leave.

*Lizard Island Resort (☎ 4060 3999, fax 4060 3991, Anchor Bay)* Singles/doubles from $800/1200 with all meals. Expect isolation and an enviable location, less than 20km from the outer edge of the reef. The resort itself is low-scale and downright stunning – expect comfortable designer rooms and suites. Facilities include a tennis court, swimming pool, sea kayaks, windsurfers and outboard dinghies, and – of course – your choice of pillow!

## Getting There & Away

**Air** Macair (☎ 13 15 28) flies to Lizard Island ($251 one way) from Cairns, and Aussie Airways (☎ 1800 620 022, 4055 9088, **W** www.amitytours.com.au) has a good day trip from Cairns for $385 per person, including lunch and snorkelling gear.

Marine Air Seaplanes (☎ 4069 5915), next to the tourist office in Cooktown, has fantastic day tours to Lizard Island ($245), flying into Watson's Bay and walking to the top of Cook's Look. The tour includes lunch and snorkelling gear; camping drop-off can also be arranged.

**Boat** A number of cruise boats stop at Lizard Island, including Captain Cook Cruises (see the Cruises entry under the Cairns section earlier in this chapter) and Kangaroo Explorer Cruises, which stops on its way from Cairns to Thursday Island and Cape York. See the Cruises entry under Organised Tours in the Cape York chapter.

## ISLANDS AROUND LIZARD ISLAND

There are four other smaller islands in the Lizard group. **Osprey Island**, with its nesting birds, is right in front of the resort and can be waded to. Around the edge of Blue Lagoon, south of the main island, are **Palfrey Island** with an automatic lighthouse, **South Island** and **Seabird Islet**.

There are a number of continental islands and small cays dotted around Lizard Island and south towards Cooktown. *Camping* is permitted on a number of the islands with a permit. Contact Cairns QPWS (☎ 4046 6600) for more information.

# Cape York Peninsula

Cape York Peninsula, one of the last great frontiers of Australia, is bordered on the east by the Coral Sea and the Pacific Ocean and on the west by the Gulf of Carpentaria. Most of the peninsula is a low-lying patchwork of tropical savannah overlaid by wild snaking rivers and streams, while along its eastern flank is the elevated northern section of the Great Dividing Range, which ends in Dauan, a remote outer island of Torres Strait – the northernmost tip of Australia's Great Dividing Range.

Covering an area totalling around 207,000 sq km, Cape York has a population of around 15,000 people, and approximately half are Aborigines or Torres Strait Islanders. The largest towns in the region are Cooktown, on the south-eastern coast, Weipa, a large mining community on the central-western coast, Bamaga at the top end, and Thursday Island in Torres Strait. A handful of smaller towns and cattle stations make up the remainder of the communities throughout the Cape.

The peninsula has some of the least developed land in Australia and much of it is protected in spectacular national parks, all of which are jointly managed with their traditional Indigenous owners, as well as Aboriginal land, for which you'll need a permit to visit. The peninsula also has an extreme climate of two seasons only – the dry season from June to October and the wet season from November to May.

This predominantly undeveloped landscape, its isolation and climatic extremes make for stunning wilderness scenery, including the rugged peaks and deep valleys of the last old growth tropical rainforests in Australia in Mungkan Kandju National Park, wetlands that rival those of Kakadu with their rich bird-life, the sand dune systems of Cape Flattery and Cape Bedford, and 16 wild undammed river catchments. Offshore the Great Barrier Reef Marine Park stretches over thousands of square kilometres.

It's wild country and once you've visited, you'll itch to come back.

## Highlights

- Visit Lakefield National Park – your best chance to see a crocodile in the wild.

- See superb Aboriginal rock-art at Split Rock galleries, south of Laura.

- Soak up the casual Torres Strait atmosphere of Thursday Island.

## History

Before non-Indigenous settlement a large number of Aboriginal tribal groups occupied and used the land throughout the Cape. These same groups continue to live in Cape York Peninsula. A unique group of people inhabited the islands dotted across the Torres Strait that separates mainland Australia from Papua New Guinea. Torres Strait Islanders came from Melanesia and Polynesia about 2000 years ago and are culturally distinct from the Aborigines.

Non-Indigenous history in Australia can be traced back to the early-17th-century Dutch navigators, Willem Jansz in 1606 and Abel Tasman in 1644, who were the first Europeans to report seeing the Great South Land. In 1606 during Jansz' exploration of the Gulf of Carpentaria, Aboriginal warriors killed members of the *Duyfken* crew.

Captain James Cook mapped the eastern coast of Australia in 1770, and stepped ashore at Possession Island claiming the continent, encompassing hundreds of Aboriginal nations, for Britain. Over the next hundred years other British navigators, including Bligh, Flinders and King, mapped sections of the coast.

Ludwig Leichhardt was the first explorer to journey over a section of the Cape during his 1845 expedition. Edmund Kennedy and his party had a difficult time in 1848 heading up the eastern coast along the Great Dividing Range. Aborigines fatally speared Kennedy among the swamps and waterways of the Escape River, south-east of Cape York.

In 1863 Frank Jardine and his brother led cattle from Rockhampton to the new government outpost at Somerset. They were resisted all the way by Aboriginal warriors and the party shot at least 30 Aborigines at the Battle of Mitchell River, before making it to the top. This was to be the start of the Jardine legend on Cape York, with Frank Jardine dominating the top of the Cape until his death in 1919, and earning the reputation as a ruthless murderer among local tribes.

The discovery of gold in the Palmer River in 1873 was the great catalyst for the development of Cooktown, Laura and, later, Cairns.

In 1887 the Overland Telegraph Line from near Somerset to Palmerville and Cooktown was finally completed, linking the northernmost outpost with Brisbane. This is the route most travellers to Cape York follow today.

During WWII, Cape York Peninsula was a major staging post for the battles against the Japanese in New Guinea and the Coral Sea. The Cape was evacuated, and people of Japanese descent who had made their home on Thursday Island were interned in camps in NSW and Victoria. Some 10,000 troops were stationed all over the peninsula, including Iron Range and Portland Roads, on the mid-eastern coast; Horn Island in Torres Strait, Mutee Heads and Jackey Jackey airfield (then called Higgins Field) at the northern tip of Cape York; as well as around Cooktown. Many relics of those

days can still be seen, including wrecks of some of the 160-odd aircraft that were reported lost over the region.

In the late 1940s, Torres Strait Islanders from Saibai established the townships of Bamaga and Seisia a few kilometres from Injinoo, and people from Lockhart River set up the township of Umagico.

In the 1950s bauxite was discovered along the coast near Weipa and mining began, but not without disgraceful upheaval to the Aboriginal community when, in 1963, Aboriginal people from Mapoon were forcibly removed by police at gunpoint to New Mapoon near Bamaga. Their homes, schools and church were then torched. The Queensland government apologised in March 2001, and the Weipa agreement was signed, recognising native title rights of the traditional owners, and allowing for consultation over future mining operations.

In 1996 the Cape York Heads of Agreement (Land Use) was co-signed by pastoralists, traditional owners and environmental groups. It recognised that the natural and cultural values of the peninsula should form the basis of future development. This agreement will hopefully ensure a sustainable future and protection of this unique wilderness environment.

## Orientation

From Cairns to the top of Cape York is 952km via the shortest and most challenging route. However, there are a host of worthy diversions from this route, including Lakefield and Iron Range National Parks, and these will add considerably to the total distance covered.

From Lakeland you can travel straight up the heart of the Cape or go via Cooktown and through Lakefield National Park to Laura or Musgrave. Initially, the corrugated Peninsula Developmental Rd cuts its way through the middle, turning west for the mining town of Weipa 29km from the Archer River. As you head further north of the Weipa turn-off the real adventure begins along the Telegraph Rd (or Overland Telegraph Track – OTL) to Cape York – the creek crossings become more numerous and

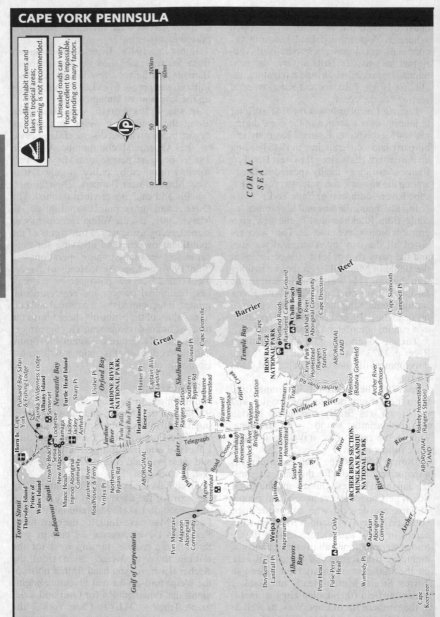

# CAPE YORK PENINSULA

Crocodiles inhabit rivers and lakes in tropical areas; swimming is not recommended.

Unsealed roads can vary from excellent to impassable, depending on many factors.

*Torres Strait*
Horn Is
Thursday Island
*Prince of Wales Island*
*Endeavour Strait*
Loyalty Beach
Seisia
Lockerbie
New Mapoon
Mutee Heads
Injinoo Aboriginal Community
Bamaga
Jackey Jackey Airfield
Jardine River Roadhouse & Ferry
Vrilya Pt
Northern Bypass Rd
Somerset
Cape York
Punsand Bay Safari & Fishing Lodge
Pajinka Wilderness Lodge
Albany Island
Newcastle Bay
Turtle Head Island
Orford Bay
Usher Pt
Jardine River
*JARDINE RIVER NATIONAL PARK*
Twin Falls
Fruit Bat Falls

*Gulf of Carpentaria*

Port Musgrave
Mapoon Aboriginal Community
Dulhunty River
*ABORIGINAL LAND*
Telegraph Rd
Road Closed
Agnew Homestead
Bertiehaugh Homestead
Wenlock River
Moreton Telegraph Station

Duyfken Pt
Landfall Pt
Weipa
Napranum
*Albatross Bay*
Pera Head
False Pera Head
Worbody Pt
Mission River
Batavia Downs Homestead
Sudley Homestead
*ARCHER BEND SECTION - MUNGKAN KANDJU NATIONAL PARK*
Aurukun Aboriginal Community
Watson River
Coen River
*ABORIGINAL LAND*
Archer River
Rokeby Homestead (Rangers Station)
Archer River Roadhouse

Heathlands Rangers Station
Heathlands Reserve
Southern Bypass Rd
Shelburne Homestead
Bramwell Homestead
Hunter Pt
Captain Billy Landing
Round Pt
*Shelburne Bay*
Cape Grenville
Olive Creek
Frenchman's Track
King Park Homestead
Wenlock (Batavia Goldfield)
Archer River Rd
Wenlock River

*Great Barrier Reef*

*Temple Bay*
Fair Cape
*IRON RANGE NATIONAL PARK*
Portland Roads
Rainforest Camping Ground
Chilli Beach
Lockhart River Aboriginal Community
*Weymouth Bay*
Cape Direction
Cape Sidmouth
Campbell Pt

*CORAL SEA*

0   30   60mi
0   50   100km

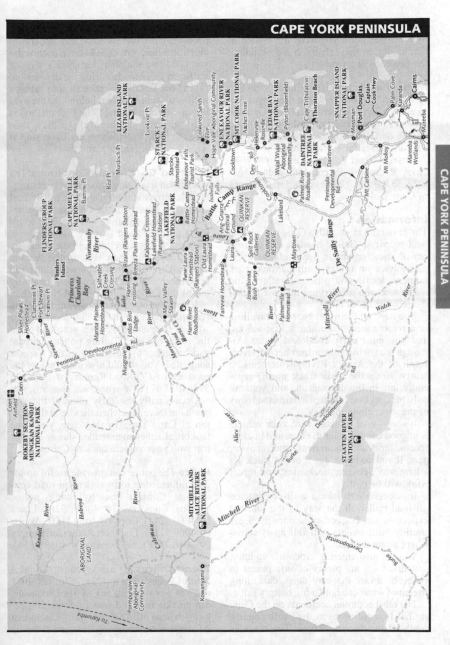

CAPE YORK PENINSULA

more challenging – this is pure 4WD territory. Further north you have the choice of continuing on the Telegraph Rd or taking the newer bypass roads.

**Maps** The Hema maps *Cape York* and *Lakefield National Park* and the Royal Automobile Club of Queensland (RACQ) maps *Cairns/Townsville* and *Cape York Peninsula* are the best. See Books in the Facts for the Visitor chapter for useful guides.

Absells Chart & Map Centre (☎ 4041 2699, e absells@iig.com.au, Andrejic Arcade, 55 Lake St, Cairns) sells detailed maps of Cape York.

## Information

The important issue with a Cape trip is to be well prepared. Before heading off to each new destination on the peninsula, seek expert advice on routes from national park rangers, locals and other travellers, and make sure you're carrying at least one of the recommended maps.

You need all the usual gear for travelling in a remote area, including a first-aid kit, and you *must* carry food and water. Although you will cross a number of rivers south of the Archer River, water can be scarce along the main track north, especially late in the dry season, and you can only pick up basic food provisions at many of the stops along the way.

It's also vital to make sure your vehicle is in good condition for the trip, and to carry spares, tools and equipment, and recovery gear. If you do break down or get stuck it's a long way between mechanics, and repair work will be costly.

It is possible to take a well-constructed off-road trailer all the way to the top, but expect to get bogged occasionally. Less sturdily built trailers will fall apart somewhere along the track.

You are also entering crocodile country, so while there are plenty of safe places to swim, be aware that any deep, dark, long stretch of water can hold a big hungry saltie.

The most common accidents on the Cape are head-on collisions in the heath country south of the Jardine River. The track is

narrow here with many blind corners; people often travel too fast, and sometimes they meet head-on. Deaths have occurred – you need to remember that there's a lot of traffic on these roads during the dry season.

And one last thing – take all your rubbish with you – don't leave it behind for the next person to camp among! The best method is crush all cans and burn all rubbish, then take the remains with you until you stop at a roadhouse or ranger station.

**When to Go & Road Conditions** The wet season from November to May restricts vehicle movement on Cape York. The best time to go is early in the dry season, generally from the beginning of June. The country is greener, there is more water around, there are fewer travellers and the roads are less chopped up than later in the season. The peak travel period is between June and September, with the last travellers generally out of the Cape by around mid-November.

If you plan to visit very early or late in the season, it pays to check with locals to see what is happening weather-wise and what the roads are like. Calling police, national park rangers or roadhouses in the Cape is suggested. You should also make use of the recorded RACQ Road Reports (☎ 1300 130 595, 4033 6711, w www.racq.com.au).

Occasionally the early rains of the Wet catch out travellers when they're at the very top of Cape York. In that case, you'll be looking at either an extended stay or a barge trip with your vehicle back to Cairns.

**Police** The police can provide useful up-to-date information to travellers on road conditions. Contact the following police stations: Cooktown (☎ 4069 5320); Laura (☎ 4060 3244); Coen (☎ 4060 1150); Weipa (☎ 4069 9119); Lockhart River Community (☎ 4060 7120); or Bamaga (☎ 4069 3156).

**Tourist Offices** In Cairns, Tourism Tropical North Queensland (☎ 4031 7676, fax 4051 0127, w www.tnq.org.au), 51 The Esplanade, can provide tour and travel information before you head off. There are no official tourist information centres along the route to the tip

## 4WD – the One and Only Way to Get to the Tip

It's a common perception that Cape York is only accessible for well-equipped and experienced 4WD adventurers – and it's a perception that is totally valid. You may well see numerous 2WD vehicles on the roads, but these are the vehicles that generally keep the mechanics in Weipa and Bamaga (if they make it that far) in business. Without a 4WD you'll have to stick to the main road, which means you'll miss out on the most spectacular parts of the Cape, such as the national parks.

While the roads on the Cape are all unsealed the majority are reasonably well maintained in the dry season. Expect varied sections of smooth dirt, soft sand, and rocky and corrugated sections. The conditions of the roads can, however, also vary substantially depending on a number of factors, including how recently they have been graded, the time of year and how much water is about, the effects of recent rain, and the amount of traffic using the roads.

The main route to Weipa along the Peninsula Developmental Rd is used by mining company vehicles and is virtually a dirt highway. It is certainly *possible* to drive as far as Weipa in a 2WD vehicle (without detouring), but it's not advisable. North of Weipa, the road conditions deteriorate rapidly and the numerous river crossings north of the Wenlock River make it total bravado to attempt it in a 2WD vehicle.

of Cape York, although you'll find information readily available from the many helpful locals in the roadhouses, towns and camping grounds along the way.

**Money** Banking facilities are very limited on Cape York, and full banking facilities are only available at Cooktown, Weipa and Thursday Island.

Credit cards, such as MasterCard and Visa, are accepted widely for most services, although cash advances on credit cards may be difficult to access. Eftpos is readily available in roadhouses, general stores and some places to stay.

**Useful Organisations** You should visit Cairns Queensland Parks and Wildlife Service (QPWS; ☎ 4046 6600) at 10 McLeod St before your visit.

**Medical Services** Hospitals on Cape York Peninsula include: Cooktown (☎ 4069 5433), Weipa (☎ 4069 9155) and Bamaga (☎ 4069 3166). There are also medical clinics in Laura (☎ 4060 3320) and Coen (☎ 4060 1166).

**Permits** Once you are north of the Dulhunty River you will need a permit to camp on Aboriginal land, which in effect is nearly all the land north of the river. The Injinoo

people are the traditional custodians of much of this land, along with other Aboriginal communities at Umagico and New Mapoon. Please respect the signs and by-laws of the community councils.

Designated camping grounds are provided in a number of areas, including Seisia, Pajinka, Loyalty Beach and Punsand Bay. Camping elsewhere in the area requires a permit from the Injinoo Community Council (☎ 4069 3252). You can organise this when you get to the Injinoo-owned and operated ferry across the Jardine River. The crossing fee includes the permit fee and the cost of camping at a number of pleasant, isolated sites.

Travelling across Aboriginal land elsewhere on the Cape may require a permit. It is best to contact the relevant community council stating the reason for your visit and dates. Allow plenty of time for an answer. The Balkanu Cape York Development Corporation (W www.balkanu.com.au) has an excellent Web site featuring all the Cape York Aboriginal communities.

**Radio Frequencies** A CB radio is recommended for travelling in Cape York although, unless you are doing something way out of the ordinary, a High Frequency (HF) radio is not a necessity. Contact the Royal

Flying Doctor Service (RFDS; ☎ 4053 5687) in Cairns for details of emergency frequencies covering the Cape.

### RACQ Services, Towing & Spare Parts

The centres listed operate towing and RACQ services, which could prove extremely useful. Many of the roadhouses along the main route also offer minor vehicle repairs and welding.

**Mt Molloy Service Centre** (☎ 4094 1260) 8 Brown St, Mt Molloy
**Chris Engineering & RACQ Service Depot** (☎ 4060 2010) Peninsula Developmental Rd, Lakeland (about 8km before the township)
**Cape York Tyres & Auto Centre** (☎ 4069 5233) Corner Charlotte and Furneaux Sts, Cooktown
**Weipa Service Centre & RACQ Service Depot** (☎ 4069 7277) Boundary Rd, Rocky Point, Weipa. This centre offers towing and mechanical repairs anywhere on Cape York.
**Weipa 4WD Spares** (☎ 4069 7877) Evans Landing, Weipa. It sells 4WD parts and accessories, as well as camping gear.

**Fuel** Diesel, unleaded and super are generally readily available along the route to the Cape, but there is no LPG after the Hann River Roadhouse until Bamaga and Seisia.

**Camping Equipment Rental** Geo Pickers Great Outdoors Centre (☎ 4051 1944, 270 Mulgrave Rd, Cnr Brown St, Parramatta Park, Cairns), has a range of camping equipment and accessories for hire.

### Organised Tours

Cairns and the Tablelands have a host of tour operators who can organise part, or all, of your trip to the Cape.

**4WD** Trips generally range from six to 16 days, travelling by 4WD with five to 12 passengers, and take in Cooktown, Laura, the Split Rock art galleries, Lakefield National Park, Coen, Weipa, the Eliot River System (including Twin Falls etc), Bamaga, Somerset and Cape York itself. Most 4WD trips also visit Thursday Island (often an optional extra).

Most companies offer a range of travel options, such as to fly or sail from either Cairns or Cape York and travel overland the other way, and some offer camping or accommodated tours. Prices are inclusive of all meals, accommodation, and airfare/cruise fare from Cairns.

**Billy Tea Bush Safaris** (☎ 4032 0077, W www.billytea.com.au) Nine-day fly/drive tours $2100 and 14-day overland tours $2200. The nine-day trip takes in Cooktown, the Quinkan art sites, Lakefield National Park, Weipa, the Telegraph Rd, Twin Falls, Thursday Island (optional) and the Tip.
**Exploring Oz Safaris** (☎ 0500 502 688, 4093 8347, W www.exploring-oz.com.au) Six-day to 12-day tours $1200 to $1699. The six-day trip flies to Horn Island, takes in Thursday Island, tours the Tip, heads to Twin Falls, Wenlock River, Mary Valley Station, and the Split Rock art galleries.
**Heritage 4WD Tours** (☎ 4038 2628, W www.heritagetours.com.au) Six-day to 15-day tours $1450 to $2295. Its six-day tour starts from Cape York and takes an interesting route back, stopping at Thursday Island, Twin Falls, Archer River, Lakefield National Park and the Bloomfield Track.
**Jowalbinna Bush Camp** (☎ 4060 3236, 4051 4777, fax 4051 4888, W www.adventures.com.au) Four-day tour $745. This tour takes in the the in the Split Rock art galleries, Jowalbinna Bush Camp, Lakefield National Park, Cooktown and the Bloomfield Track.
**Oz Tours Safaris** (☎ 1800 079 006, 4055 9535, W www.oztours.com.au) Six-day fly/drive to 16-day $2195 to $2240. Its six-day tour is for those who want to travel the peninsula, but don't want to camp – there's guesthouse accommodation each night of the journey. Its longer trips all offer camping.
**Wilderness Challenge** (☎ 4055 6504, W www.wilderness-challenge.com.au) Eight-day camping $1825, 12-day cruise/drive from $3175. This award-winning company has a huge range of camping and accommodated options (stopping at Lotus Bird Lodge among other places).

**Motorcycle** A company that comes well recommended is Weipa Motorcycles (☎/fax 4069 9712, e capebikes@bigpond.com.au). It has tours flying from Cairns to Weipa, then riding overland for three days up to the Tip, stopping at Punsand Bay. Tours then return overland to Weipa ($2750 all inclusive).

**Guide Services** A popular way to see the Cape is in the company of a tag-along operator. The cost doesn't include a vehicle, but if you need to hire one they can organise it for you.

A well-recommended company is Guides to Adventure (☎ 4091 1978, W www.guidestoadventure.com.au), which travels to (among other places) Cape York (12-day/16-day/22-day trips $1056/1408/1991 per person).

**Air** Based in Cairns, Cape York Air (☎ 4035 9399, W www.capeyorkair.com.au) operates the Peninsula Mail Run, the world's longest mail run to remote Cape York communities. See Organised Tours under Cape York in the Cairns section of the Far North Queensland chapter.

**Cruises** If you're more interested in the ocean than the earth, cruise up to Cape York.

Kangaroo Explorer (☎ 4032 4000, W kangarooruises.com.au) runs a range of cruises between Cairns and Cape York. On the seven-day trip, which costs $1895 to $2595 per person, the cruising catamaran stops at Cooktown, Outer Reef, Pixies Pinnacles, the Cod Hole, Lizard Island, Forbes Island, Cape York and Thursday Island. The cost includes all meals and activities excluding diving (available only for certified divers).

## Special Events

The best time for festivals in Cape York is June to September.

**Laura Aboriginal Dance Festival** Held on the banks of the Laura River, it brings together Aborigines from all over Cape York and Australia for three excellent days. The festival is held in June of odd-numbered years. Contact the Ang-Gnarra Aboriginal Corporation (☎ 4060 3214, W www.laurafestival.com).

**Laura Races and Rodeo** Held in the last weekend of June, locals from the surrounding cattle stations show off their skills.

**Coming of the Light** This festival is celebrated annually on Thursday Island on 1 July to commemorate the London Missionary Society landing on Darnley Island in 1871. The town is full of Christian youth groups at this time.

**Hope Vale Show & Rodeo** Staged in July or August each year. Contact the Hope Vale Community Council (☎ 4060 9185) for more information.

**Pormpuraaw Croc Races** Held at the end of July each year, the races raise money for the RFDS. You'll need to arrange a permit if you're thinking of going.

**Bamaga Annual Show** Run in August or September each year, the show features rodeo events, horse races, carnival stalls and an amusement fair.

## Getting There & Around

**Air** Qantas flies daily from Cairns to Thursday Island ($374 one-way) and Weipa ($212 one-way).

Skytrans (☎ 1800 818 405, e info@ skytrans.com.au), based in Cairns, has flights from Coen to Lockhart River ($108) and Yorke Island to Horn Island ($193), while from Cairns it flies to Lockhart River ($308, five a week), Coen ($308, four a week), Aurukun ($308, four a week), Yorke Island ($376, five a week) and Horn Island ($369, five a week). All prices are one-way.

A number of smaller airlines operate flights and charter services from Thursday Island around the islands of the Torres Strait and to Cape York; see the Thursday Island section for information.

**4WD** The following companies are based in Cairns but there are also 4WD car-hire agents in Cooktown, Weipa and Bamaga.

**Britz Australia** (☎ 4032 2611, W www.britz.com) 411 Sheridan St. Britz has 4WDs and 4WD-campervans. Four-wheel drives cost from $231 per day, and 4WD-campervans start from $194.

**4WD Hire Service** (☎ 4031 3094, W www.4wdhire.com.au) 440 Sheridan St. Toyota Landcruisers are available for $177 a day (minimum of ten days), and Zelt Cruisers, which come with full camping gear, for $204 per day.

**Cruising Car Rental** (☎ 4041 4666, e cruising@ cairns.net.au) 196A Sheridan St. Small 4WD vehicles are available to take as far as Lakefield National Park and Laura, but not right up to the Tip ($169 per day, minimum of 14 days).

**Boat** A number of shipping companies cruise the coast of Cape York. While many can transport vehicles, only a couple actually take passengers.

**Gulf Freight Services** (☎ 1800 640 079, 4069 8619, **W** www.riversidemarine.com.au) Weekly barge services between Weipa and Karumba in the Gulf (from $284.50 per person, vehicles extra, 36 hours). The service is popular, so book as far in advance as possible. At the time of writing, Gulf Freight is also trialling a run that includes a stop at Nhulunbuy in the Northern Territory.
**Seaswift** (☎ 4035 1234, **W** www.seaswift.com.au) Weekly cargo ferry to Thursday Island and Bamaga, which takes up to 48 passengers. It departs Cairns every Friday and reaches Thursday Island on Sunday. The trip costs from $325/625 one-way/return (five days) and includes all meals.

## COOKTOWN TO MUSGRAVE VIA LAKEFIELD NATIONAL PARK (275km)

This route is a great alternative to the main road north, taking you on a short sidetrack to Hope Vale through the Lakefield National Park via Battle Camp. Battle Camp was the site of a major battle during the Palmer River gold rush when, in 1873, a large group of Aborigines attacked a party of diggers and police, but were overpowered by gunfire.

This route is very isolated, without any facilities or fuel stops along the way. You must be prepared to carry enough water to get between the permanent water points.

### Cooktown to Hope Vale

The McIvor Rd heads west out of Cooktown, taking you past the cemetery and racecourse. The bitumen soon ends, and 10km west of town you cross the **Endeavour River** before passing the Cooktown airfield.

*Endeavour Falls Tourist Park (☎/fax 4069 5431, McIvor Rd)* has unpowered/ powered sites for $13/16.50 and double self-contained units $55. Just 33km northwest of Cooktown, this park is surrounded by palm trees and **Endeavour Falls** is a short walk away. The falls make a good swimming hole year-round. The park has a small grocery store and fuel.

At the 36km mark is the turn-off for Battle Camp and Lakefield. Continue straight on

(north) to get to the **Hope Vale Aboriginal Community**. You'll need a permit from the Hope Vale Aboriginal Community to visit **Coloured Sands** north of Elim, which are impressive layered sand cliffs of different hues. For further information, contact the Hope Vale Community Council (☎ 4060 9133).

Munbah Aboriginal Culture Tours (☎ 4060 9173) is operated by the local Aboriginal community. The 4WD tour ($110/$120 day tour/overnight tour) heads to McIvor Beach and Cape Flattery and includes guided walks. Pick-up from Cooktown can be arranged and the tour runs only on demand.

### Hope Vale to Musgrave

The turn-off to Battle Camp and Lakefield is back along the Cooktown-Hopevale Rd, 36km north-west of Cooktown. Turn to the north-west, and about 5km further on there is a stony river crossing; just downstream is **Isabella Falls**. This is a magic spot – it's worth a stop and even a swim.

Keep left at the next junction 2.5km up the road. From here the road begins to climb the range and patches of rainforest begin.

The **Normanby River** is crossed 66km from Cooktown. Early in the dry season this river will be flowing, but by the end of the season it is just a sandy bed. There are pools upstream and downstream.

Keep on the main track heading west across undulating country with numerous gates, and 18km from the river crossing you pass the turn-off to **Battle Camp Homestead**. The mountains to the south are the rugged Battle Camp Range. Less than 3km further on you enter Lakefield National Park.

There are a large number of *camping grounds* spread along the rivers and billabongs of the park. You will often see tracks leading to these as you travel along the main track. If you want to camp here, you'll need to get a permit. The ranger will let you know the best spot to camp. The ranger station is at New Laura Homestead, 51km from the park boundary.

The **Laura River** is crossed 25km from the park boundary (112km from Cooktown). This crossing can be a little tricky early in the dry season, but by the end of the season

## Lakefield National Park

Lakefield National Park is the second-largest national park in Queensland and covers more than 537,000 hectares. It encompasses a wide variety of country around the flood plains of the Normanby, Kennedy, Bizant, Morehead and Hann Rivers.

During the wet season these rivers flood the plains, at times forming a small inland sea. As the dry season begins, the rivers gradually retreat to form a chain of deep waterholes and billabongs. Along these rivers, rainforest patches are in stark contrast to the surrounding grass plains and eucalypt woodland.

### Flora & Fauna

In the north of the park, around Princess Charlotte Bay, mud flats and mangroves line the coast and the estuaries of the rivers. It might be an area full of sandflies, mosquitoes and crocodiles, but it's also the nursery for rich marine life.

As the dry season progresses bird-life begins to congregate around permanent water, and at times thousands of ducks and geese create an unholy noise but a spectacular sight. Groups of brolgas dance on the open plain, and tall stately jabirus stalk their way through the grass. Birds of prey soar on the thermals looking for a meal, while in the deepest, darkest patches of the rainforest, pheasant coucals and Torres Strait pigeons can be found. In all, over 180 species of birds have been identified in the park.

Agile wallabies are probably the most commonly seen mammals in the park, but bats make up the largest group of mammals. The large flying foxes are an impressive sight as they burst from their roosting spots in the thousands, on their evening search for nectar and fruit. You won't forget the sight, smell or damage they can do to the trees in which they roost.

### Crocodiles

Both the freshwater (top) and saltwater or estuarine (bottom) crocodile are found in Lakefield National Park. The park is one of only six key areas in Queensland for estuarine crocodile conservation, and for many people it offers the best chance of seeing one in the wild.

### Fishing

Lakefield is one of the few national parks in Queensland where you are allowed to fish, and barramundi is the prize catch. The season is closed between 1 November and 31 January; at other times there's a bag limit of five fish per day, but the rangers recommend that a self-imposed limit of two fish per day is followed to avoid over-fishing. Line fishing is the only permitted method of fishing.

### Camping

There are 28 camp sites ($3.85 per person per night) in the park, with many adjacent to rivers and waterholes. In order to camp, a permit or a self-registration form must be obtained from the park's rangers or you can book by mail six to 12 weeks in advance (Ranger, Lakefield National Park, PMB 29, Cairns Mail Centre, Qld 4871). However, at the time of writing, plans are under way for a new self-registration camping system to operate throughout the national park from the various entry nodes into the park.

The contact details for the ranger stations are: New Laura (☎ 4060 3260), Bizant (☎ 4060 3258) or Lakefield (☎ 4060 3271). Permits and self-registration forms can also be obtained from QPWS Cooktown (☎ 4069 5777).

CAPE YORK PENINSULA

it is generally no problem. The **Old Laura Homestead** on the far bank is worth a good look around. Pioneer settlers lived here and in places like this throughout the Cape. The homestead was restored with the help of Operation Raleigh in 1986.

Just past the homestead and within 1km of the river crossing, you reach a T-junction. Turning left here will take you south to Laura, 28km away. This is the nearest place for fuel and supplies if you have decided to stay in the park for longer.

To continue to Musgrave and deeper into the Lakefield National Park, turn right at the T-junction. The QPWS rangers station (☎ 4060 3260) at New Laura Homestead is 25km north of the junction.

Heading north from here, you pass across vast grass plains, bordered by trees lining the rivers. Termite hills tower above the gold of drying grass and occasionally you'll see a shy wallaby skip across the road, or a mob of wild pigs. After travelling 33km, you pass the ranger station at **Lakefield Homestead**. About three kilometres before the ranger station is a turn-off for **Kalpowar Crossing**, a good *camping ground* with lots of bird-life.

The turn-off to **Bizant**, another QPWS ranger station (☎ 4060 3258), is 15km past the Lakefield Ranger Station, with yet another turn-off 10km further on. Just a few hundred metres past this track junction is the **Hann Crossing** of the North Kennedy River. The crossing itself demands a little care as it is potholed and rough.

Just downstream from the crossing there are a couple of waterfalls that drop into a large pool. The river is tidal to the base of the falls and we wouldn't advise swimming here (nor anywhere else in the park). If you want to see how many crocodiles can inhabit a small stretch of water, take a spotlight down and check the pool at night – count the eyes and divide by two!

There is some excellent *camping* upstream from the crossing. The sites are numbered and at peak periods the place is booked out. The **Morehead River** is crossed 13km from the Hann crossing and is normally an easy crossing. The turn-off to **Low Lake**, a spectacular bird habitat, especially at the

end of the dry season, is found 15km further on. Continue straight ahead and in less than 2km you'll reach **Saltwater Creek Crossing**; it is sandy but generally no problem. You can camp around here, but it isn't as good as Kalpowar Crossing.

The road swings south-west as it begins to head towards Musgrave. Keep left at the next few track junctions, as the tracks on the right lead to Marina Plains Station. You leave the national park 16km west of Saltwater Creek.

Stick to the main track heading westward and 34km later you will hit the Peninsula Developmental Rd, opposite Musgrave.

*Lotus Bird Lodge* (☎ *1800 674 974, 4059 0773, fax 4059 0703,* e *lotusbird@iig .com.au*) has accommodation in comfortable, timber cabins ($192.50 per person, including all meals and tours). This small resort about 26km before Musgrave, on a huge area of land, has plenty to keep you busy, including an in-house naturalist and guided bushwalks. The lodge also has a four-star chef. There are fly-in packages available from Cairns (three-day/four-day $847/995.50). The lodge operates only in the dry season.

## LAKELAND TO MUSGRAVE (200km)
### Lakeland to Laura

From Lakeland you're on your way to Laura and Cape York on a formed dirt road and this is about as good as the run north to the top gets.

About 45km from Lakeland just after the Kennedy River crossing, the *Ang-Gnarra Festival Ground* (☎ *4060 3200*) has self-registration camping ($10 per car), with hot showers and a camp kitchen. The place is overflowing during the Laura Festival.

The turn-off to the **Split Rock Aboriginal art site** is about 7km further north. From the carpark, just off the road, there is a looped walking trail (see the boxed text 'Quinkan Art').

### Laura

About 12km on from the Split Rock galleries is Laura, a hospitable little town in which to enjoy a beer at the pub, or to use as a base to explore the surrounding area.

From here, you can easily visit Lakefield National Park, the Split Rock galleries, and Jowalbinna Bush Camp, a wilderness reserve 40km west of Laura.

The *Laura Store & Post Office* (☎ 4060 3238) is open from 7am to 6pm weekdays. Next to the pub, this place sells a good range of groceries including fresh fruit and vegies, gas refills for camping bottles and fuel.

**Organised Tours** Located 42km west of Laura by 4WD, Jowalbinna Bush Camp (☎ 4060 3236, 4051 4777, fax 4051 4888, W www.adventures.com.au, Maytown Track) offers excellent guided day walks to some of the magnificent rock-art sites in the area (half-day/full-day $75/100). Camp sites are $8 per person, safari cabins $80.

**Places to Stay & Eat** Apart from camping near the Laura River, you have a choice of staying at the *pub* or in the *caravan park.*

*Quinkan Hotel* (☎/fax 4060 3255) Unpowered/powered sites $5/8 per person,

---

## Quinkan Art

Quinkan is one of the great art styles of northern Australia. Vastly different to the X-ray art of Arnhem Land in the Northern Territory, or the Wandjina art of the Kimberley in Western Australia, Quinkan art is named after the human-shaped spirit figures with unusually shaped heads, called Quinkans, which appear often in the art of the region.

Over 1200 galleries have been discovered in the escarpment country south of Laura. The rock-art is difficult to date, although Aboriginal people have been living in the Laura area for at least 33,000 years. However, most of the paintings that exist today are probably comparatively young. Interpretation of the images is based on the legends of surrounding tribes as the Quinkan artists were all killed by settlers or disease during the 1873 gold rush.

The rock-art galleries contain many fine paintings of native animals, while others depict tools such as boomerangs and axes. Rock engravings are also found in small numbers, and in a couple of galleries images of horses echo the European invasion.

Only the Split Rock and Guguyalangi (the Northern Art sites) galleries are open to the public. There are a number of overhangs in the Split Rock group of galleries, and while Split Rock itself is the most visually stunning, within 100m there are smaller galleries containing flying foxes, tall Quinkans and hand stencils. The Guguyalangi group of galleries consists of over a dozen overhangs adorned with a vast array of figures, animals and implements.

A walking trail leads from the carpark at Split Rock, past the galleries in this group and then up onto the plateau to a lookout at Turtle Rock. The view from here is stunning. From this point the trail wanders through the open forest of the plateau for 1km to the Guguyalangi group. If you're going to do this walk, save it for the late afternoon or early morning – the plateau bakes in the midday sun. Take some water and food and enjoy the wild solitude of this place.

The **Giant Horse galleries**, across the road from the Split Rock and Guguyalangi sites, are a little harder to see and consist of five shelters depicting many animals, including a number of horses. These galleries can only be visited with a guide, see the ranger or the Ang-Gnarra Visitor Information Centre in Laura.

Percy Trezise, a pilot, artist, historian and amateur archaeologist opened the sites up to the world in the 1960s. Trezise established the wilderness reserve, Jowalbinna Bush Camp, which specialises in guided walking trips to the Quinkan galleries.

If you want more information on Quinkan art around Laura, visit the Ang-Gnarra Visitor Centre (☎ 4090 3200).

There is a fee of $5 to visit Split Rock, and $10 to do the entire loop (there's a box by the rangers station). No videos or cameras are allowed in the galleries and you should not touch the painted and engraved surfaces.

dorm beds $13, singles without/with breakfast $28/39 (share bathrooms). This historic corrugated-iron pub is jammed with character, and has clean, simple rooms and good-value meals . There's a camping ground next to the pub. Cane toad racing sometimes takes place during the busy dry season.

*Laura Cafe (☎/fax 4060 3230, Peninsula Developmental Rd)* Open 7am-9pm. Dishes $5.50-15.50. On the main north-south road the Laura Cafe sells fuel, a few groceries, takeaways and meals; Eftpos is available.

## Laura to Musgrave

The road continues to be well-formed dirt as it heads north from Laura. Most of the creek crossings are dry, but early in the dry season some may have water in them. Some of these creek and river crossings provide a welcome spot to *camp*. The Little Laura River, 12km north of Laura, and the Kennedy River, 32km north, are two such spots.

On the banks of the Hann River, 76km north of Laura (1 hour), another pleasant place to stop is the *Hann River Roadhouse (☎ 4060 3242, fax 4060 3394, Peninsula Developmental Rd)*. The roadhouse sells fuel and LPG, does minor vehicle repairs, has grocery supplies, takeaways and a licensed restaurant. It's a pleasant spot to camp (tent sites and powered sites $6 per person) and the nearby permanently flowing Hann River has good barramundi fishing.

Twenty kilometres from the Hann River Roadhouse, there's a turn-off east for 6km to *Mary Valley Station (☎ 4060 3254)*, a cattle property offering camp sites ($5 per person), and single ($25) and double ($40) homestead rooms. Breakfast ($6), lunch ($8) and dinner ($15) are available but must be booked ahead. The station has one of the largest colonies of little red flying foxes in the world estimated at around 10 million – it's an amazing sight in the late evening to see and hear them fly out for the night. The station also does guided bird-watching walks, as well as 'bow and arrow' pig shooting (which could perhaps become a new Olympic event).

From here to Musgrave it's 61km (one hour). A few bad creek crossings and nasty dips will keep your speed down. About the only spot worth camping at is the **Morehead River**, 29km north of the Hann River.

## MUSGRAVE

There is only one main building in Musgrave, the historic *Musgrave Telegraph Station (☎/fax 4060 3229, Peninsula Development Rd)*. Built in 1887, it's now a licensed cafe (kitchen closes at 8pm) and fuel stop. It sells a few basic groceries and takeaway food. Its rooms (singles/doubles $30/48) are simple and its camp sites ($6 per person) have showers.

From near here, tracks run east to the Lakefield National Park or west to Edward River and the **Pormpuraaw Aboriginal Community**. If you're heading that way, you must report to the Pormpuraaw Aboriginal Community Council (☎ 4060 4175, fax 4060 4130) on arrival in town and arrange camping permits. There's a **crocodile farm** here.

## MUSGRAVE TO COEN (106km)

The road to Coen is little different to what you have experienced before – there may be a few more bull dust patches.

About 95km north of Musgrave you meet a road junction. The better, newer road leads left to Coen, while the older, rougher road swings right, crossing the **Stewart River** twice before reaching Coen. With little traffic, the first crossing of the Stewart River makes a fine *camp site*.

The old road gives access to the road to **Port Stewart** on the eastern coast of the Cape, with reasonable *camping* and good fishing.

## COEN

Coen is the 'capital' of the Cape, and unless you take the turn-off into Weipa, it is the biggest town you'll see north of Cooktown. People have some entertaining times in this place, all of course in and around the pub. There is a choice of places to buy food and fuel and even a couple of places offering accommodation.

### Information

The QPWS ranger (☎ 4060 1137) is worth visiting if you require any information about Cape York's national parks.

Groceries, fuel and gas refills for camping bottles can be found at *Clark's General Store* (☎ 4060 1144, Regent St), open daily.

*Ambrust & Co General Store* (☎ 4060 1134) also has a good range of groceries, and doubles as the post office with a Commonwealth Bank agency. Fuel and camping gas are available.

Next door to Clark's General Store is the Great Divide Trading Workshop (☎ 4060 1120, Regent St), which does mechanical repairs, welding and towing.

## Places to Stay & Eat

You'll find slightly more options here than on most other stops heading to the Tip.

*Coen Camping Ground* (☎ 4060 1134) Unpowered/powered sites $6/7 per person. Run by Ambrust General Store, the camping ground has hot showers and toilets.

*Exchange Hotel* (☎ 4060 1133, fax 4060 1180, Regent St) Single/double pub rooms $38.50/49.50, motel rooms $55/66. The pub has basic air con pub rooms with share bathrooms or motel rooms with en suite. Its dining room serves breakfast ($13.20) and three course dinners ($25).

*Homestead Guest House* (☎ 4060 1157, fax 4060 1158, Regent St) Singles/twin share $38.50/27.50 per person. Just down from the pub, this guesthouse has simple, clean and comfortable rooms with ceiling fans and share bathroom facilities. Home-cooked breakfasts are available.

## COEN TO ARCHER RIVER (66km)

About 3km north of Coen, the main road north parallels the **Coen River** for a short distance. There is some good *camping* along the river, and while it is a popular spot, there is generally no problem in finding a place to throw down the swag or erect a tent.

For the first 23km north of Coen the road is very well maintained, but once you pass the Coen airfield the road quickly returns to its former standard. About 2km past the airfield you reach the main access track to **Mungkan Kandju National Park**. This park consists of two large sections and straddles much of the Archer River and its tributaries.

The **Rokeby section** takes in much of the country from the western edge of the Great Dividing Range almost to the boundary of the Archer Bend section of the same park. It has excellent bush camping on a number of lagoons and along the banks of the Archer River.

In order to access the more remote **Archer Bend section**, you'll need to organise a permit (or self-register) with the ranger station (☎ 4060 3256), which will only let you proceed if you're in a group of at least two vehicles. The ranger station, **Rokeby Homestead**, is about 70km west from the Peninsula Developmental Rd, or visit the district ranger based in Coen.

Further north, the main road continues as before, until about 50km north of Coen where the road becomes more like a roller coaster.

## ARCHER RIVER

Just down the hill from the roadhouse is the magnificent Archer River. During the dry season this river is normally just a pleasant stream bordered by a wide, tree-lined sandy bed. It is an ideal spot to *camp*, although at times space is at a premium. As with many of the permanent streams on the Cape, the banks are lined with varieties of paperbarks, or melaleucas. Growing to more than 40m tall, these often stout, flaky-barked trees offer shade; and when in flower they attract hordes of birds and fruit bats that love the heavy, sweet-smelling nectar.

The Archer River crossing used to be a real terror, but now, with its concrete causeway, is quite easy. However, any heavy rain in the catchment will quickly send the water over the bridge, cutting access to Weipa and places further north.

*Archer River Roadhouse* (☎/fax 4060 3266, Peninsula Developmental Rd) has singles/doubles/quads for $38.50/55/66. It's open from 7am till 10pm. This is a great place to stop and enjoy a cold beer and the famous Archer Burger. Basic food supplies, takeaway food and fuel can be purchased. Campers can pitch a tent in the camping ground ($6 per person) and have a hot shower, and there are also good, clean units with share bathrooms.

## ARCHER RIVER TO IRON RANGE NATIONAL PARK (128km)

About 20km north of the Archer River Roadhouse, the Archer River Rd turns off east for Iron Range National Park. It's another 110km to the ranger station at **King Park Homestead**. An alternative route to the park is via **Frenchman's Track**, which heads east from the Telegraph Rd, 2km north of the Batavia Downs to Weipa road. From there it's around 50km (2 hours) to where it meets the Archer River Rd, crossing the sandy Wenlock River and the rough and rocky Pascoe River crossing (which is best walked first), then another 30km to King Park Homestead.

The Iron Range National Park is of world significance and conserves the largest area of lowland tropical rainforest in Australia. Daintree National Park doesn't compare to this one, which is wilder, with more endemic animals and plants. There is a rich variety of vegetation, from heathland to dense rainforest.

Bird-life in the area is rich and includes the southern cassowary – this is one of the only habitats where the bird isn't endangered. Look out also for the spotted and the grey cuscus – a monkey-like marsupial with a prehensile tail. Some 10% of Australia's butterfly species also reside in this park; of these, 25 species are found no further south and the park is their stronghold.

There are only a couple of *camp sites* in the park. Near the East Claudie River and Gordon Creek is the Rainforest camping ground. The other is at the northern end of Chilli Beach. This is where most travellers set up camp. While it's a nice spot, it would be even better if the south-east trade winds would stop blowing! Register with the ranger (☎ 4060 7170), based at King Park Homestead, when you visit.

**Portland Roads**, 135km east of the track, is a small fishing community with no facilities for the traveller, except a telephone and a boat ramp. The fishing offshore, if you have a small boat, is excellent. Camping is not encouraged here.

Forty kilometres south of Portland Roads, Lockhart River Mission was established in 1922 and the Lockhart River Aboriginal Council became a local government in 1987. A permit to visit the community is not required but visitors are asked to respect the community's privacy; the use of cameras and videos is not permitted.

The *General Store (☎ 4060 7192)* can supply most food items as well as fuel. The Lockhart River Aboriginal Council (☎ 4060 7144) runs the post office, and has a Commonwealth Bank agency. There is also a police station here.

The community-run **Lockhart River Arts & Culture Centre** (☎/fax 4060 7341) is home to the Lockhart River Art Gang, a successful group of artists. You can meet the artists while they're at work creating screenprints, lithographs, batik, paints, woodwork, jewellery and weaving.

## ARCHER RIVER TO WEIPA (145km)

The road north of the Archer is good all the way to Weipa. The Northern Access Route to Weipa via Stones Crossing is now closed, while the Southern Access Route is via the continuation of the Peninsula Developmental Rd, which leaves the Telegraph Rd 48km north of the Archer River.

Just over halfway, at the 74km mark, a track which leaves the Telegraph Rd at Batavia Downs, south of the Wenlock River, joins up with the Peninsula Developmental Rd at Sudley Homestead, 71km east of Weipa. This track is often chopped up and a couple of the creek crossings are muddy early in the dry season. This route gives people another option to leave or join the route to the Tip.

As you get closer to Weipa, the mining activities increase and the road improves. Heed all the warning signs, especially where the road crosses the mine haulage ways.

## WEIPA

**postcode 4874  •  pop 2500**

Weipa is a bauxite-mining town of red clay, coconut palms, mounds of mined earth and intermittent danger signs. Leased by Comalco, the mine works the world's largest deposits of bauxite (the ore from which

A dirt road through frontier country

Stunning Twin Falls, Cape York Peninsula

Aerial view of open country in Aurukun, Cape York Peninsula

OLIVER STREWE

OLIVER STREWE

OLIVER STREWE

Flame grevillea

King of the road: one of Queensland's road trains

The top tip of Australia, Cape York Peninsula

Bush race meeting at Laura

Bush tucker

aluminium is processed). In the vicinity there's interesting country to explore, good fishing and some pleasant camp sites in a little-visited corner of Australia.

## History
The Weipa Peninsula is rich in shellfish and there are around 500 midden mounds, up to 13m high and consisting mainly of cockle shells, along the Hey, Mission, Embley and Pine Rivers. These sites are protected under the Queensland Cultural Record Act.

In 1955 a geologist, Harry Evans, led an expedition to Cape York in search of oil. Almost by chance, he discovered a large outcrop of bauxite near Weipa. He collected a number of ore samples, which were later analysed and found to be high grade and, within a few years, Comalco commenced mining operations. Its first trial shipment of bauxite was sent to Japan in 1961.

## Information
In the suburb of Nanum, there's a credit union and ATM, post office and supermarket. At Rocky Point, you'll find the police, hospital, a health centre and the Hibberd Centre, which houses the noteworthy **Cape York Collection** of books and documents. There are numerous mechanical service centres around town.

Weipa Camping Ground operates as the town's informal tourist office, and can book mining and fishing tours, and it can also provide permits for the camping grounds on Napranum, Mapoon and Aurukun Aboriginal lands, including False Pera Head, 100km north of Aurukun.

## Things to See & Do
Around Weipa and the areas north there is some excellent fishing, due to the big river systems nearby. Fishing safaris, scenic flights and 4WD tours can be booked from Weipa Camping Ground, as can Town and Mine Tours (adult/child $19/7, 9am & 1pm). The two-hour tours run daily during the dry season and tour Comalco's mining operations.

Weipa also has the **Carpentaria Golf Club** (☎ 4069 7332), which is open to the public. It has a relaxed bar area overlooking the green (though the stuffed croc on the wall isn't looking too chilled).

There are a number of short walks through the enjoyable **Uningan Nature Reserve**, which protects mangrove wetlands and large middens.

## Places to Stay & Eat
***Weipa Camping Ground*** (☎ 4069 7871, fax 4069 8211, e ianandgail@bigpond.com.au) Unpowered/powered sites $18/20. Cabins with share bathroom/fully self-contained $60/85. By the waterfront, this relaxed camping ground also operates as an informal tourist office. There are also comfortable cabins and a pool and hire boats. Disabled facilities are available.

***Albatross Hotel Resort*** (☎ 4069 7314, fax 4069 7130, e albatrosshotel@bigpond. com, Duyfken Crescent) Singles/doubles $82.50/93.50. Meals $8-28. By the waterfront, the rooms are nice enough and there's a pool and good beer garden. Meals, including vegetarian lasagne and barramundi salad, are served in ***Trawlers***.

***Heritage Resort*** (☎ 4069 8000, fax 4069 8011, e heritage.resort@bigpond.com, Nanum) Rooms $105. This new upmarket motel doesn't have upmarket views, though it's modern, spacious and has a pool and restaurant, the ***Barra Bar & Grill***. Mains $18.50-27. It serves up local Weipa mud crab.

***Weipa Snack Shack*** (☎ 4069 7495) is a small takeaway by Evan's Landing. There's a ***supermarket*** in the suburb of Nanum.

## Getting There & Away
Qantas (☎ 13 13 00) has a daily flight from Cairns to Weipa ($212).

Gulf Freight Services (☎ 1800 640 079, 4069 8619, Humbug Wharf) operates weekly barge services between Weipa and Karumba (see the Boat entry under Getting There & Away earlier in this chapter).

## Getting Around
Weipa Rent-A-Car (☎ 4069 7311, fax 4069 7435), based at the airport, has 2WD and 4WD vehicles available for touring around Weipa and for going to the Tip, from $140 to $180 per day.

## ARCHER RIVER TO WENLOCK RIVER (117km)

After the turn-off to Weipa, which is 48km north of the Archer River, the road heading north quickly deteriorates and becomes more of a track, although it's still reasonably well maintained.

On the left of the road is **Batavia Downs Homestead**, which marks the second major turn-off to Weipa, 48km north of the first, southernmost one. The final 22km to the Wenlock River is along a road that is sandy and rough in places.

The Wenlock River was once a major water challenge on the way north to the Cape, but much to the surprise of locals and tour operators a one-lane bridge was built in late 2000. It's a bridge that has been built to last, with sturdy concrete ramparts. Raised about 6m above the river, it still floods in the wet season (when the waters might reach 14m), but it means that the Cape is more accessible earlier in the wet and later in the Dry.

*Moreton Telegraph Station (☎ 4060 3360, Peninsula Development Rd, Wenlock River)* has camp sites for $6/18 per person/family and homestead accommodation $25. Just north of Wenlock is this old place, which provides homestead accommodation, camping (with hot showers) and very limited stores. It can supply dinner and breakfast, but you'll need to book in advance. It also does minor mechanical and welding repairs. There's a pay phone out the front.

## WENLOCK RIVER TO JARDINE RIVER (155km)
### Telegraph Road

The 155km from the Wenlock River to the Jardine River is the best part of the trip, with some great creek crossings and excellent *camp sites*. Take your time and enjoy all the delights the Cape has to offer.

The challenge of following the rough track along the historic Overland Telegraph Line means that the trip will take at least a very long day, even if all goes well. A newer and easier route, known as the Southern and Northern Bypass Rds, avoids much of the Telegraph Rd and bypasses most of the creeks and rivers between the Wenlock and Jardine Rivers. This route is covered later in the section on Bypass Roads.

Most of the major creek crossings on the Telegraph Rd have water in them; however, it's not the water that is the problem but the banks on each side. Take care. The track is reasonable for the first 40km north of the Wenlock, until the first of the bypass roads leaves the old track. The turn-off for Bramwell Homestead is 26km north of the Wenlock River.

*Bramwell Homestead (☎ 4060 3237)* has camp sites for $5.50 per person and single/twin share homestead rooms for $33/27.50. Located on the eastern side of the road, it offers very pleasant and reasonably priced accommodation and camping, and meals are available.

The first of the major bypass roads, the **Southern Bypass Rd**, turns off the Telegraph Rd 40km north of the Wenlock. Staying on the Telegraph Rd, Palm Creek, 43km north of the Wenlock, is followed by Ducie Creek, South Alice Creek and North Alice Creek, before you reach the **Dulhunty River**, 70km north of the Wenlock. This is a popular spot to *camp*. There are also some lovely places to swim, and the falls beside the road make a pleasant natural spa.

After crossing another major stream, a road leaves the Telegraph Rd 2km north of the Dulhunty and heads for **Heathlands Ranger Station** (☎ 4060 3241), the base for the Jardine River National Park ranger. This road also bypasses the **Gunshot Creek crossing**. This crossing, just 15km past the track junction, requires care.

About 2km north of the Gunshot crossing, a track heads east to Heathlands Station. The vegetation changes again. No longer is it dominated by straggly eucalypts such as ironbarks and bloodwoods, but instead the country is covered in tall heathland.

After Gunshot Creek the track is sandy until you come to the **Cockatoo Creek crossing**, 94km north of the Wenlock River. Once again the actual riverbed is no drama, although it is rocky and rough; it's the banks that are the problem. In this case it is the northern bank that often has a long haul of soft sand. The Injinoo people have a permanent camp set up at Cockatoo Creek.

For the next 24km the road improves slightly. A couple more creek crossings follow and 14km past Cockatoo Creek the Southern Bypass Rd joins up with the Telegraph Rd.

Just 9km further on, the second major bypass, the **Northern Bypass Rd**, heads west away from the Telegraph Rd to the Jardine River ferry crossing. Stick to the Telegraph Rd at this point and keep heading north, even though the track north does deteriorate a little. There are other tracks that lead back to the Northern Bypass Rd and the ferry.

Within 200m a track heads off to the east, taking travellers to **Fruit Bat Falls**. Camping is not allowed here but it is a good spot to stop, have lunch and enjoy the waters of the **Eliot River System**.

The turn-off to **Twin Falls** is 6.5km north of the previous track junction to Fruit Bat Falls. The track leads less than 2km to an excellent *camping ground*. This is the most popular camping spot on the trip north, and although it gets crowded, it's still very enjoyable. A camping permit is required.

Back on the Telegraph Rd, over the next 10km there are Canal, Sam, Mistake, Cannibal and Cypress Creeks to cross. All offer their own sweet challenges. Just south of **Mistake Creek** a track heads west to join up with the Northern Bypass Rd, which in turn leads to the ferry across the Jardine River.

From Cypress Creek it is a 7.5km run to **Logan Creek**. From here the road is badly chopped up and often flooded in places. You are now passing through the heart of an area the early settlers called the 'wet desert' because of the abundance of water but lack of feed for their stock.

About 5.5km further on is **Bridge Creek**, or Nolan's Brook, which once had a bridge, and when you get to it you'll know why. It is an interesting crossing, and though it is short it does demand a lot of care. Less than 2km north of here the last track to the ferry heads west, while just 4km past this junction the main track veers away from the Telegraph Rd to the right and winds for 2km through tall open forest to the Jardine River.

## Bypass Roads

As an alternative to sticking to the old Telegraph Rd, the Southern and Northern Bypass Rds avoid most of the creeks and rivers between the Wenlock and Jardine rivers. Both sections of this road are corrugated and people travel too fast on them. Each year a number of head-on accidents occur in the first two months of the Dry, most on the Southern Bypass Rd – be careful!

**Southern Bypass Rd** This road leaves the Telegraph Rd 40km north of the Wenlock River crossing and heads east and then north. The turn-off east to Shelburne Homestead is 24km north of the junction, while another 35km will find you at the junction to Heathlands Ranger Station, 14km to the west.

When you reach a large patch of rainforest, 11km north of the Heathlands turn-off, the bypass road swings north-west, while a track to Captain Billy Landing, on the eastern coast, continues straight ahead. You can *camp* at Captain Billy Landing, although there is no water. Keep on the bypass road for the next 45km to rejoin the Telegraph Rd 14km north of Cockatoo Creek.

**Northern Bypass Rd** This road leaves the Telegraph Rd 9km north of where the Southern Bypass Rd rejoins the Telegraph Rd, north of Cockatoo Creek.

This route heads west away from the Telegraph Rd and for 50km winds through tropical savannah woodland to the Jardine River ferry. At the 18km and 30km marks, tracks head east to the Telegraph Rd.

On the southern bank of the river, the ***Jardine River Ferry & Roadhouse*** (☎ *4069 1369*) is open from 8am till 5pm daily. The ferry crossing is run by the Injinoo Community Council and operates only during the dry season ($88 return, plus $11 for trailers). The fee includes a permit, which allows you to bush camp in the area north of the Jardine River, including Mutee Heads, Somerset and the mouth of the Jardine. The roadhouse sells fuel and cold drinks and has a camping ground with toilets and hot showers for $10 per camp.

## JARDINE RIVER

The Jardine River has some magical *camp sites* along its southern bank, west of the old treacherous vehicle ford. There are no facilities here, and a camping permit is required from the ranger at Heathlands Station.

The Department of Environment and the Injinoo community ask that all travellers use the ferry crossing at Jardine River and avoid driving across the river at the vehicle ford. See the Bypass Roads entry later for more information on the ferry.

Remember, estuarine crocodiles inhabit the Jardine River, and although you might not be able to see them they are definitely there. In December 1993 a crocodile killed a man while he was swimming to the ferry at the ferry crossing, not far downstream from the vehicle ford.

Fishing upstream of the old crossing is not allowed. Downstream from this point there is no problem and at times the fishing can be good, although closer to the mouth is better again.

## JARDINE RIVER TO CAPE YORK (69km)

From the ferry crossing to the Tip it is less than 70km and for most of the way the track is in good condition. Once you have crossed the Jardine, the track swings to the east, joining up with the old Telegraph Rd, before heading north to the Tip.

A number of minor tracks in this area lead back down to the river and some reasonable *camp sites*. The best is on the northern bank where the telegraph line crosses the river; an old linesman's hut marks the spot.

At the next T-junction, 17km north of where you came onto this major dirt road, turn right. After a further 5km, turn right again, which will lead to the coast at the old wartime port of **Mutee Heads**, just north of the Jardine River.

Just 7km past the junction there is a small carpark beside a fenced area that encloses the remains of a **WWII DC3 aeroplane wreck**. The plane ploughed in heading to PNG. It's a curious tourist 'sight', and there are a few more scattered around the main airfield, which is just a stone's throw away.

At the carpark there is a second T-junction. Right will lead to the main airfield, while left will lead to Bamaga.

Less than 5km from the second T-junction, a signposted road heads off to the right leading to Cape York, Somerset and places close to the Tip. This is the road you will require, but most travellers will need fuel and other supplies, and will continue straight ahead to Bamaga.

### Bamaga

In 1947, Chief Bamaga Ginau decided to move his community to the mainland from Saibai Island, just 8km from Papua New Guinea, to escape flooding and a lack of fresh water. Bamaga is the largest community in northern Cape York Peninsula, with all the facilities most travellers need. There is a hospital, police station, supermarket, bakery, newsagency and service station. There is no camping ground at Bamaga, head to Seisia (Red Island Point), Umagico, Punsand Bay Safari and Fishing Lodge and Pajinka Wilderness Lodge at the Tip.

**Information** The Bamaga Service Centre (☎ 4069 3275) is open Monday to Friday, and Saturday and Sunday mornings. It has fuel available and can provide mechanical repairs, along with ice and camping-gas refills. The post office is also the Commonwealth Bank agency. Resort Bamaga has 4WD vehicles for hire from $165 per day.

**Places to Stay & Eat** For camping, head to Seisia, otherwise there are some pricier options in Bamaga.

*Resort Bamaga* (☎ *4069 3050, fax 4069 3653,* e *bamaga@resortbamaga.com.au)* Rooms $150. Overlooking Mosby Creek, by the main thoroughfare into town, this place is new, with very good facilities, including a saltwater pool. The *restaurant* (mains $11.50 to $20) is open for breakfast, lunch and dinner and has a interesting menu. The resort also runs *The Bungalow* nearby, which has en-suite rooms for $65 a double.

*The Bakehaus* (☎ *4069 3168)* Open 7am-2pm Mon-Sat. A few blocks from the resort, on the main street, this would have to be the busiest bakery in Australia. It bakes rye, wholemeal and grain bread, croissants, pizzas and delicious cakes. There's a *takeaway* next door.

A reasonably well-stocked *supermarket* is open seven days a week during the tourist season, with limited trading hours on the weekend. Beer and wine can be purchased from the *Bamaga Canteen*. There is also a *snack bar* and a *bakery*.

## Seisia

The Islander town of Seisia was established at Red Island Point around the same time as fellow Saibai Islanders set up at Bamaga. The name is derived from the first initials of the father and brothers of the founder, Mugai Elu: Sagaukaz, Elu, Isua, Sunai, Ibuai and Aken. Five kilometres north-west of Bamaga, it's an idyllic spot for the weary traveller to relax after the long journey to the Tip. There is an excellent foreshore *camping ground*, a *kiosk* and *service station*, and the nearby jetty is a great place for fishing.

**Information** Seisia Holiday Park is the booking agent for all tours, the ferry and taxi service, and anything else available. You can get up-to-date fishing information and maps, along with general tourist information.

Top End Motors (☎ 4069 3182), Tradesmans Way, is the place to go for all mechanical and welding repairs to your vehicle. Top Form Engineering (☎ 4069 3230), next door, can supply LPG.

The Seisia Palms Service Station (☎ 4069 3133) is Australia's northernmost service station and can supply petrol, diesel and marine fuels.

**Organised Tours** Seisia Holiday Park is the booking agent for all tours, which include guided fishing trips, pearl farm tours to Roko Island Pearl Farm, croc spotting, half or full day 4WD tours of the Tip and scenic flights.

Among the boat operators, John Charlton's Cape York Boat Adventures (☎ 4069 3302) has an excellent reputation and can organise island cruises, Thursday Island trips and fishing charters.

Peddells' Ferry & Tour Bus Service (☎ 4069 1551) runs a Horn Island WWII package, including lunch and guided tours of both Horn and Thursday Island, which costs $145.49/72.20 (adult/child). The ferry can also pick you up from Punsand Bay.

**Places to Stay & Eat** Seisia has some comfortable accommodation options.

*Seisia Holiday Park* (☎ 1800 653 243, 4069 3243, fax 4069 3307, e seisiaresort@ bigpond.com) Camp sites $8.80 per person. Overlooking the islands of Torres Strait, this is the most central place to camp at the Tip, and is only a minute's walk from the ferry wharf. On the waterfront in leafy grounds, it has standard van park facilities.

*Seisia Seaview Lodge* Single/double units $85/105.60, villas $185 (sleeps six). Within the Seisia Holiday Park, these comfortable units have share kitchens, while the villas are fully self-contained double-storey cabins.

*Seisia Kiosk*, within the camping ground, is open daily and has meals and takeaways.

**Getting There & Around** Peddells' Ferry Services runs regular ferries between Seisia and Thursday Island – see the Thursday Island section later in this chapter for details.

A taxi service (☎ 4069 3333) operates out of Seisia.

## Loyalty Beach

The new *Loyalty Beach Campground* (☎ 4069 3372, fax 4069 3770, e fishcapeyork@c130.aone.net.au), 3km north of Red Island Point, has camp sites ($8 per night), cabins ($66 a double) and a house ($198; sleeps six). It has beachfront sites, modern facilities and a *kiosk*.

## Injinoo Aboriginal Community

The small township of Injinoo is 8km south-west of Bamaga. For any information regarding permits phone the Injinoo Community Council (☎ 4069 3252).

## Umagico

Limited facilities, including a *general food store* and *canteen*, are available from this small community.

## Bamaga to Cape York

From Bamaga, turn north towards the Tip along a well-formed dirt road. The ruins of Jardine's outstation, **Lockerbie**, are 16km north. The galvanised iron and timber building is a more recent residence, built by the Holland family in 1946. Nearby are mango trees and paths established by Jardine. There is usually a *small store* at the Lockerbie site and visitors are welcome to stop for refreshments, souvenirs and information.

Just north of Lockerbie a track heads west to **Punsand Bay**, about 11 bumpy, sandy kilometres away. A few kilometres later the main track north begins to pass through an area of rainforest called the **Lockerbie Scrub**. This small patch of rainforest, only 25km long and between 1km and 5km wide, is the northernmost rainforest in Australia.

About 7km from Lockerbie a Y-junction in the middle of the jungle gives you a choice of veering right for Somerset or left for the top of Australia. Less than 3km from this point on the way to the Tip, a track on the left will lead you 7km to **Punsand Bay Safari and Fishing Lodge**.

A further 7km brings you to the **Pajinka Wilderness Lodge** and the *camping ground*. There is a small *kiosk* to service the camping ground. From near the kiosk, a walking track leads through the forest bordering the camping ground at Pajinka to the beach near the boat ramp. From the beach you can head overland on the marked trail, or when the tide is low you can head around the coast to the northern tip. Both routes are relatively easy walks of an hour or so.

The islands of Torres Strait are just a stone's throw away. Swimming is not recommended: The fishing, though, can be pretty good.

## Punsand Bay

Punsand Bay, on a north-facing beach just a few kilometres west from the tip of Cape York, is one of the best, friendliest and most scenic spots on the Cape.

**Punsand Bay Safari and Fishing Lodge** (☎ *4069 1722, fax 4069 1403)* Camp sites $9 per person, on-site safari tents $115, cabins $155, includes three generous meals. This place is very well set up, with a camping ground, on-site tents, cabins, hot showers, a laundry and above-ground pool. Its licensed restaurant is open for breakfast, lunch and dinner. Tours include 4WD Tip tours ($98), and airport transfer ($40) is possible.

## Pajinka

Run by the Injinoo Aboriginal Community, **Pajinka Wilderness Lodge** (☎ *1800 802 968, 4031 3988, fax 4069 2110,* W *www.pajinka .com)* has camp sites for $7 per person and cabins for singles/doubles/children $297/275/ 110 per person (1-3 nights), including all meals (prices fall in the wet season). Only 400m from the northernmost tip of mainland Australia, this is a great place to reward yourself for making it to the top. There are cabin-style rooms, a swimming pool, an open-sided *restaurant* and a bar. The rooms, all with bathroom, are simple and airy, with a small verandah. The lodge also has its own camping ground. A licensed kiosk supplies limited stores and takeaway food. The lodge also runs guided walks for its guests.

# Thursday Island & Torres Strait

There are a number of islands scattered across the reef-strewn waters of Torres Strait, running like stepping stones from the top of Cape York to the southern coast of Papua New Guinea, about 150km north of the Australian mainland. The islands are politically part of Australia, although some are only a few kilometres from Papua New Guinea.

The islands of the Torres Strait exhibit a surprising variety in form and function. There are three main types: the rocky, mountain-top extension of the Great Dividing Range makes up the western group that includes Thursday Island and Prince of Wales Island; the central group of islands that dot the waters east of the Great Barrier Reef are little more than coral cays; while the third type of islands are volcanic in origin and are in the far east of the strait, at the very northern end of the Great Barrier Reef. These Murray Islands are some of the most spectacular and picturesque in the area.

While Thursday Island (or 'TI' as it's casually known) is the 'capital' of Torres Strait, there are 17 inhabited islands, the northernmost being Saibai and Boigu Islands, a couple of kilometres from the New Guinea coast. The population of the islands is around 8700 and the people are Melanesians, racially related to the peoples of Papua New Guinea.

## History

The inner islands are the traditional lands of the Kaurareg people, who are Aboriginal rather than Islander and have strong links to the traditional owners of northern Cape York. The Kaurareg lived primarily on Prince of Wales Island (Muralag) until they were removed to Hammond Island early in the 20th century.

In 1606 two explorers became the first Europeans to pass through Torres Strait. Jansz sighted the western coast of Cape York from his ship the *Duyfken*. He led a party ashore and could have claimed the honour of being the first European to set foot on Australia, except that he thought he was still on Papua New Guinea. Meanwhile Spanish explorer Luiz Vaez Torres was approaching the strait from the eastern side with his ship the *San Pedrico*. He had set out from Peru as part of an expedition to search for *Terra Australis Incognita*, the Great South Land, but the two ships were separated. Torres continued east and was swept through the straits by the prevailing winds and current. He landed on several islands before continuing around Papua New Guinea, eventually reaching the Philippines.

The Spanish, however, did not reveal Torres' historic discovery and for the next two centuries the straits remained a rumour until Captain Cook confirmed their existence in 1770.

In 1868 rich oyster beds were discovered in the strait, and within months a pearling rush had begun. Around the same time missionaries arrived, and today Islanders are still one of the most church-going populations in Australia.

In WWII Torres Strait and the islands formed part of Australia's front line in the battle against the Japanese. Horn Island was bombed a number of times in 1942, but Thursday Island never had a bomb dropped on it.

In early 2001, there has been a claim for native title sea rights over Torres Strait, with locals claiming that mainland commercial fishing operators are destroying and denying access to traditional fishing grounds.

## THURSDAY ISLAND

**postcode 4875 • pop 2300**

No visit to the top of the Cape would be complete without a visit to fascinating, multicultural Thursday Island. The view sailing into the island is unlike anything you'll see elsewhere in Queensland. The timber spires of the 19th-century Sacred Heart Mission Church and the corrugated roof of the old Federal Hotel mark the skyline, as do two huge wind turbines that make good use of the trade winds – all surrounded by pure turquoise waters.

## Orientation & Information

The island is little more than 3 sq km in area, with the town of Thursday Island on its southern shore. There are a few stores, including a general store, fruit barn, chemist, a post office and a branch of the National Australia Bank (with an ATM). Thursday Island also has a police station (☎ 4069 1520) and a hospital (☎ 4069 1109). For tourist information head to Peddells' Ferry Island Tourist Bureau (☎ 4069 1551), Engineers Wharf.

## Organised Tours

Peddells' Ferry & Tour Bus Service (☎ 4069 1551, fax 4069 1365, W www.peddellsferry .com.au) offers bus tours of Thursday Island (adult/child $14.50/6.50), taking in the major tourist sites including the All Souls Quetta Memorial Church and Green Hill Fort and museum. You can also do a Two-Island Tour, which includes the Horn Island tour (see the Horn Island section) for $70, including lunch. You can also take these tours from the mainland (see the Seisia section).

CAPE YORK PENINSULA

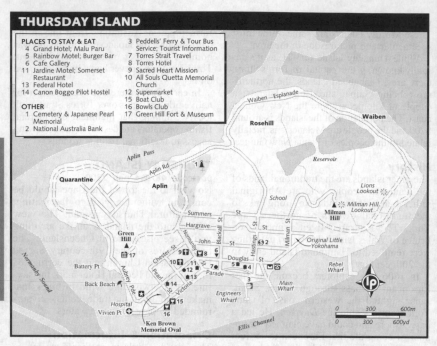

# THURSDAY ISLAND

**PLACES TO STAY & EAT**
4 Grand Hotel; Malu Paru
5 Rainbow Motel; Burger Bar
6 Cafe Gallery
11 Jardine Motel; Somerset Restaurant
13 Federal Hotel
14 Canon Boggo Pilot Hostel

**OTHER**
1 Cemetery & Japanese Pearl Memorial
2 National Australia Bank

3 Peddells' Ferry & Tour Bus Service; Tourist Information
7 Torres Strait Travel
8 Torres Hotel
9 Sacred Heart Mission
10 All Souls Quetta Memorial Church
12 Supermarket
15 Boat Club
16 Bowls Club
17 Green Hill Fort & Museum

## Things to See

There are some fascinating reminders of Thursday Island's rich history around town. The **All Souls Quetta Memorial Church** was built in 1893 in memory of the shipwreck of the *Quetta*, which struck an uncharted reef in the Adolphus Channel in 1890, with 133 lives lost. Today its walls are adorned with curious memorabilia, including a porthole recovered from the *Quetta* in 1906, which is encrusted with marine growth.

The Japanese section of the town's cemetery is crowded with hundreds of *kanji*-inscribed graves of pearl divers who died from decompression sickness. The **Japanese Pearl Memorial** is dedicated to them. **Green Hill Fort**, on the western side of town, was built in 1893, in response to fears of a Russian invasion. There's a small **museum** here.

## Places to Stay

Thursday Island has a real shortage of reasonably priced accommodation, however,

there are a number of inexpensive hostels in town operated by Aboriginal Hostels Limited set up to accommodate Indigenous Australians. They officially can't take non-Indigenous guests, but it's worth asking – they might bend the rules for a night (or two). Try the ***Canon Boggo Pilot Hostel*** (☎ 4090 3246, Cnr Douglas & Pearl Sts).

***Rainbow Motel*** (☎ 4069 2460, fax 4069 2714, Douglas St) Singles/doubles $66/90. Easily missed because of its miserable-looking facade, the motel has basic rooms with air-con and share bathroom.

***Federal Hotel*** (☎ 4069 1569, Victoria Parade) Singles/doubles $93.50/132. The Federal's motel-style rooms are modern and comfortable. There's also a ***restaurant*** (lunch noon till 2pm, dinner 6pm till 7.15pm).

***Grand Hotel*** (☎ 4069 1557, fax 4069 1327, Upper Victoria Parade) Singles/doubles from $110/150. Located on a hill behind the wharf, the Grand Hotel was rebuilt after it burned down in 1997. It has comfortable, modern rooms, and there are facilities for disabled guests.

*Jardine Motel (☎ 4069 1555, fax 4069 1470, e stay@jardinemotel.com.au, Victoria Parade)* Singles/doubles $130/150, includes continental breakfast. The rooms here are much the same as the Federal, but they do have telephones. The motel also has a pool and bar.

## Places to Eat
The main street is door-to-door fried chicken and fish and chip takeaways.

*Burger Bar (Down a lane next to the Rainbow Motel, Douglas St)* Dishes $5-10. Open 10am-2pm & 6pm-9pm Mon-Fri, 10am-2pm Sat. This is one of the best places to try.

*Cafe Gallery (☎ 4069 2617, Cnr Douglas & Blackall Sts)* Dishes $5-10. Open 8am-5pm Mon-Tues & Thur-Sat, 8am-8pm Wed, 10am-2pm Sun. If a fry-up doesn't appeal, this breezy (and low-fat) place serves up good coffee, sandwiches and salads. Its fan-cooled timber balcony is a great spot to chill, and its small **art gallery** has some impressive contemporary art on display.

*Federal Hotel (☎ 4069 1569, Victoria Parade)* Meals $6-15. Lunch noon-2pm, dinner 6pm-7.15pm. The Federal serves up decent counter meals.

*Malu Paru (☎ 4069 1557, fax 4069 1327, Upper Victoria Parade)* Mains $16-40. The restaurant at the Grand, the Malu Paru, which means 'ocean view', has a balcony area with sweeping views (and sweeping trade winds!). The chef focuses on fresh seafood dishes and, if you're cashed-up, it's worth trying the grilled cray tail ($40), a local specialty.

*Somerset Restaurant (☎ 4069 1555, fax 4069 1470, Victoria Parade)* Mains $19.50-39.50. At the Jardine Motel, the Somerset has a classic Australian menu, served up a notch. It specialises in seafood, including Carpentaria Gulf barramundi.

## Entertainment
The Federal, the Torres, and the Grand are all popular local pubs.

*Boat Club (Torres Strait Water Sports Club; ☎ 4069 1915, Victoria Parade)* For

## Diving for Pearls

Discovery of pearl shell in the waters of the Torres Strait during the 1860s led to an invasion of boats and crews in search of this new form of wealth. It was a wild and savage industry with murder and blackbirding – a form of kidnapping for sale into slavery – common. Many pearlers made a regular practice of raiding Islander and Aboriginal camps, to kidnap men and children to dive for pearls and women to entertain their crews. The strait was on the frontier, and all those who plundered its resources were beyond the reach of the law.

During the first half of the 20th century the pearling industry was still the lifeblood of the area. It was dangerous work, as there was little knowledge of the physiological aspects of deep diving, and death from 'the bends', or decompression sickness, was common. Poor equipment and cyclones were also perils divers and crews faced – a cyclone in March 1899 devastated the industry and killed hundreds.

While a number of nationalities made up the working population, the Japanese were considered by many to make the best divers. The Japanese community lived north-east of the main wharf in an area known as Little Yokohama. A wander round the Thursday Island cemetery will show the price they paid for their expertise: over 500 are buried there, most of whom died while diving for pearls.

After WWII plastics took over where pearl shell left off. A number of cultured pearl bases, such as the one at Roko Island, still operate around the waters of Thursday Island, but the 100 or more pearl luggers that once worked the beds have long since disappeared.

drinks with a view head to this place right on the waterfront. The Boat Club's big night is Friday, when locals come all the way from Horn Island for the club's cheap and cheerful barbecue.

*Thursday Island Bowls Club (☎ 4069 2339, Victoria Parade)* The Bowls Club also has a great beer garden looking across to Muralug Beach on Prince of Wales Island.

## Getting There & Away

**Air** The airport is on Horn Island. See the Air entry under the introductory Getting There & Away section earlier in this chapter. On Thursday Island the Qantas/Sunstate office is at Torres Strait Travel (☎ 4069 1264) on the corner of Victoria Parade and Blackall St, and this is also where you complete check-in for outgoing flights. The air fare includes a shuttle across the harbour between Horn and Thursday Islands.

**Boat** See the Boat entry under the introductory Getting There & Away section earlier in this chapter.

There are regular ferry services between Seisia, on the mainland, and Thursday Island run by Peddells' Ferry Service (☎ 4069 1551, **w** www.peddellsferry.com.au) on Thursday Island. From June to October it has two daily services from Monday to Saturday ($40/75 one-way/return, 1 hour) and from November to May it operates only on Monday, Wednesday and Friday. In the dry season it also has a service between Punsand Bay, Pajinka and Thursday Island ($40/75 one way/return). These are basically day trips, leaving in the morning and returning from Thursday Island in the evening.

## Getting Around

Horn Island Ferry Service (☎ 4069 1011) operates between Thursday Island and Horn Island. The ferries run roughly hourly between 6am and 6pm ($6 one-way, 15 minutes).

Around Thursday Island there are plenty of taxis (including water taxis), and Peddells' also runs bus tours on demand ($17.40).

## HORN ISLAND

During WWII, Horn Island became a battle zone, suffering eight Japanese air raids. Among the 5000 troops stationed on the island was the 830-strong Torres Strait Light Infantry Battalion (TSLIB). Today the Island, and its small town of Wasaga, is deathly quiet and undeveloped.

## Organised Tours

Run by the Gateway Torres Strait Resort (☎ 4069 2222), the Horn Island Tour (adult with/without lunch $39.40/23.20) focuses on the role played by Horn Island and Torres Strait during WWII, and also includes a visit to the museum. You can combine the tour with a Thursday Island tour.

## Things to See & Do

Within the Gateway Torres Strait Resort is the **Torres Strait Heritage Museum & Art Gallery** (☎ 4069 2222, 24 Outie St; adult/child $5.50/2.75; open on request). You could easily spend hours here. It has extensive displays on Horn Island's little known WWII transformation, pearl diving, the internment of people of Japanese descent during WWII, as well as Islander carvings, art and traditional stories.

## Places to Stay & Eat

As with Thursday Island, you'll find only overpriced accommodation.

**Elikiam Holiday Park** (☎ 4069 2222, 1 Miskin St) Nightly/weekly from $71.50/177, air-con extra. Run by Gateway Torres Strait Resort, the 'holiday park' resembles a prison compound! It has self-contained bunkhouses and cabins (with bathroom). Don't expect a pool.

**Gateway Torres Strait Resort** (☎ 4069 2222, fax 4069 2211, **e** gtsr@bigpond.com, 24 Outie St) Singles/doubles $109/135, includes full breakfast. 'Resort' is used loosely here – the self-contained units have a fan and TV, but as with Elikiam, don't expect to have a splash about in a pool. There's also a **restaurant**, serving buffet dinners from 7pm to 9pm ($13.80 to $16.80), and lunch only during the dry season.

There's a small **supermarket** near the wharf.

## Getting There & Away

See the Thursday Island section for details.

## OTHER TORRES STRAIT ISLANDS

The inhabited outer islands are not too difficult to visit, but you must plan well in advance. These tropical islands, some of them sitting on their own coral reefs, have virtually no tourist infrastructure, and very small populations. To visit any of the islands other than

Thursday Island or Horn Island, you usually need a permit or permission from the island's council. Contact the Torres Strait Regional Authority (☎ 4069 1247, fax 4069 1879, W www.tsra.gov.au, Victoria Parade).

The islands of **Coconut** (Poruma), **Darnley** (Erub) and **Warraber** all have guesthouses and, at the time of writing, welcome travellers.

## Getting There & Away

Most inhabited islands have an airstrip and quite a few airlines operate light aircraft in the strait. Many have scheduled services and most won't allow you to book a ticket until you have permission from the council to visit the island.

The following airlines operate in the Torres Strait:

**Aero-Tropics** (☎ 4035 9138)
**Cape York Air** (☎ 4069 2973)
**Northern Air Services** (☎ 4069 2777)
**Skytrans Airlines** (☎ 4069 2033)
**Torres Strait Airlines** (☎ 4069 2121)

Although it's only a few kilometres away, you cannot travel to Papua New Guinea from the northern islands of the Torres Strait. Under the Torres Strait Treaty between Australia and Papua New Guinea, only traditional inhabitants with a special pass are permitted to cross the border for traditional business.

# Gulf Savannah

The Gulf Savannah is a vast, flat and empty landscape of bushland, saltpans and savannah grasslands, all cut by a huge number of tidal creeks and rivers that feed into the Gulf of Carpentaria. It's a remote, hot, tough region with excellent fishing and a large crocodile population.

The coastline of the Gulf is mainly mangrove forests, which is why there is so little habitation – only a few thousand people live in the area, scattered among a handful of small towns, lonely pubs and roadhouses, isolated cattle stations, and Aboriginal communities.

The Gulf's two major natural attractions are at opposite ends of the region. The Lawn Hill National Park is a virtual oasis in the midst of the arid north-west: a stunning river gorge harbouring a verdant remnant of rainforest and the superb Riversleigh fossil field. The second major attraction is the spectacular Undara lava tubes, a collection of ancient and enormous volcanic lava tubes, which are near the eastern end of the Gulf Developmental Rd.

The Gulf's main towns – Burketown, Normanton and Karumba – still have the feel of frontier settlements. There are plenty of interesting fossicking areas in the area, including the rich gem fields around the old mining towns of Croydon, Georgetown and Mt Surprise.

## History

The coastline of the Gulf of Carpentaria was charted by Dutch explorers long before Cook's visit to Australia. Willem Jansz sailed the *Duyfken* into the Gulf in 1606; in 1644 Abel Tasman named it the Gulf of Carpentaria after the then-governor of Batavia.

In 1802 Matthew Flinders sailed into the Gulf during his historic circumnavigation of the Australian continent, stopping at Sweers Island (among other places) where he is said to have dug a well.

The first European to pass through this area was Ludwig Leichhardt, the eccentric

## Highlights

- Cool down in the oasis of Lawn Hill – emerald-green river, tropical palms and soaring red cliffs.
- Marvel at the scope of the ancient Undara lava tubes and be informed and entertained by the Gulf Savannah Guides.
- Take a plunge in the river at the beautiful black basalt gorge at Einasleigh.
- View outback life from a train window, rattling 'n' rolling across the Savannah on the Gulf's two quirky, characterful trains, the *Gulflander* and the *Savannahlander*.
- Rodeos, canoe races, barra comps, wilderness camping, beer swilling, solitude seeking – the Gulf country has something for enthusiasts of all persuasions.

Prussian explorer who skirted the Gulf on his 1844 trek from Brisbane to the newly settled Port Essington (near Darwin). After Leichhardt came the ill-fated Burke and Wills expedition. Burke, Wills, King and Gray camped a little way west of Normanton in February 1861. Because of the thick mangroves that line the coast here they didn't actually reach the sea, but knew they

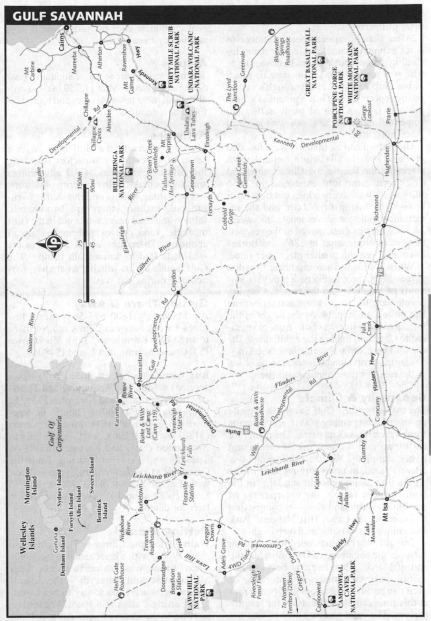

# GULF SAVANNAH

GULF SAVANNAH

were close to it because of the tidal movement of the rivers.

After their disappearance a number of other explorers came looking for them, including the intrepid William Landsborough, who was responsible for opening up much of the Gulf region. Landsborough's enthusiastic reports of the Gulf's potential as fine pastoral land motivated many settlers to come to the area in the 1860s with herds of sheep and cattle.

Burketown and Normanton were founded in the 1860s, well before better-known places on the Pacific coast like Cairns and Cooktown came into existence. In 1866 Burketown was nearly wiped out by a fever brought by a ship from Java, and the remaining population was evacuated to Sweers Island. Many of them moved to the new settlement of Normanton in 1867 and Burketown has been the smaller place ever since.

When gold was discovered near Croydon in the 1880s, the ensuing rush brought thousands of hopefuls into the region. Croydon developed into a major town, and at one time had more than 30 pubs. At the height of the rush, a railway line was built from Normanton to Croydon, linking the goldfields to the coast. These days the anachronistic *Gulflander* train trip along this short route is one of the region's most popular attractions.

## Geography & Climate

The majority of the Gulf Savannah is made up of the vast, empty plains and saltpans from which it takes its name. The plains are cut by an intricate network of creeks and rivers; during the Wet these fill up and frequently flood, at times turning parts of the region into an immense inland lake. In the north-western region, the escarpments of the Barkly Tableland rise – encompassing the spectacular Lawn Hill National Park and unique fossil fields of Riversleigh.

Travel is not recommended in the region between the beginning of December and the end of March, when extreme heat and humidity make conditions uncomfortable or even dangerous. Apart from that, heavy rain at this time can close the roads for lengthy periods. The most pleasant time to visit the Gulf is during the winter months, when you will encounter cool mornings, warm days and balmy evenings.

### Maps

The best road guide to use is Sunmap's *Gulf Savannah* Tourist Map (1:750,000), available from most newsagencies and tourist information centres.

### Activities

Most travellers to the Gulf come with a sense of adventure; prospectors searching for gold or gemstones, 4WD adventurers and anglers make up the majority of visitors.

The fishing here is nothing short of sensational. Inshore, there are barramundi, salmon and mud crabs, while out in the Gulf mackerel, tuna, cod and red emperor are all abundant. There are several lodges in the area dedicated to barramundi fishing. The Gulf is also a bird-watcher's paradise, particularly during the Wet.

### Getting There & Away

**Air** Macair (☎ 1800 677 566) flies a few times a week between Cairns and Normanton ($347), Karumba ($385), Burketown ($460) and Mornington Island ($480).

**Bus** Coral Coaches (☎ 4031 7577) has a service on Monday, Wednesday and Thursday between Cairns and Karumba ($150, 12 hours) via Undara ($60, 4½ hours), Georgetown ($84), Croydon ($110) and Normanton ($138). From Mt Isa, Coral Coaches goes to Normanton ($98) and Karumba ($111) on Tuesday and Friday (departing from the Campbell's Coaches terminal; you can book with Campbell's: ☎ 4743 2006); and to Lawn Hill National Park – see that section later for details.

### Getting Around

**Train** Plying the Cairns to Forsayth route since 1960 – with a brief hiatus in the 1990s when its route was restricted to that between Mt Surprise and Forsayth – the *Savannahlander* is a laid-back way to head west.

Departing Cairns at 6.30am Wednesday, arriving at the Forsayth terminal at 5.45pm on Thursday afternoon, the *Savannahlander* then departs Forsayth early on Friday morning, arriving back in Cairns on Saturday (Cairns-Forsayth one-way adult/child $95/48). For bookings ring ☎ 1800 620 324. If you don't want to do the whole trip, a popular excursion is to pick up the train in Mt Surprise, stay the night at Forsayth, five hours and 120km south-west, then return to Mt Surprise the next morning. Travelling this leg is a great way to see the red rugged landscape around Einasleigh, with its stunning gorge of black basalt and turquoise-coloured water. The one-way adult/child fare is $40/20.

The quaint, snub-nosed *Gulflander* runs just once weekly in each direction between Normanton and Croydon, alongside the last stretch of the Gulf Developmental Rd. There are connecting bus services from Cairns and Mt Isa to Croydon and Normanton. See the *Gulflander* section later for details.

**Car & Motorcycle** This chapter is divided into sections that basically follow the routes of the major roads through the Gulf.

From Queensland's eastern coast, the Gulf Developmental Rd takes you from the Kennedy Hwy, south of the Atherton Tableland, across to Normanton and Karumba.

If you're coming from the Northern Territory, the unsealed Gulf Track takes you across the top of the Gulf country to Burketown and on to Normanton. From Burketown you have two options if you're heading south: You can take the unsealed road to Camooweal, via Gregory Downs and the Lawn Hill National Park; or the Nardoo-Burketown Rd, which cuts across to meet the Burke Developmental Rd at the Burke & Wills Roadhouse.

The other major route is the Burke Developmental Rd, a good sealed highway that takes you south from Normanton to the Burke & Wills Roadhouse. From here, you can continue south to Cloncurry, or head south-east to Julia Creek.

There aren't too many options apart from these major routes, particularly if you don't have a 4WD. Even if you do, remember that this is remote country and the going can be

This warning sign is found throughout Gulf Savannah.

rough once you get off the beaten track. If you're thinking of attempting other routes, such as the continuation of the Burke Developmental Rd, which takes you east from between Normanton and Karumba to Mareeba via Chillagoe, you'll need to be well prepared and carry good maps, plenty of water and preferably a radio.

And a note on cattle, kangaroos and the monsters called road trains, trucks up to 60m long. Most of the roads in this area are very narrow – more like a single lane – dirt roads at various stages of corrugation: If there's a road train coming your way, just pull over and wait for it to pass by. Cattle and kangaroos can suddenly appear on the road as if from nowhere, and hitting one will probably kill the animal and ruin your car for good; driving at twilight and night is to be avoided.

Olé!

# Eastern Gulf Region

The Gulf Developmental Rd is the main route into the Gulf from the east. It leaves the Kennedy Hwy 66km south of Mt Garnet, passing through Georgetown and Croydon en route to Normanton. The first section of the highway is paved and in reasonably good condition. After Georgetown the surface alternates between sections of sealed and unsealed highway; this section of the route is sometimes impassable during the Wet. The region crossed by this road has many ruined gold mines and settlements.

## UNDARA VOLCANIC NATIONAL PARK

Just 17km past the start of the Gulf Developmental Rd is the turn-off to the Undara lava tubes, one of inland Queensland's most fascinating natural attractions. An impressive tourist complex has been built here to cater for visitors; there's a good range of accommodation, from restored railway carriages to tents. Tours of the tubes and surrounding countryside are taken by Savannah Guides, whose extensive knowledge of the area, peppered with local lore and dry humour, makes for a fascinating experience. These massive lava tubes were formed around 190,000 years ago following the eruption of a single shield volcano. The eruption continued for three months. The huge lava flows drained towards the sea, following the routes of ancient river beds, and as the lava cooled it formed a surface crust – just like skin on a custard. The hot lava continued to flow through the centre of the tubes, eventually leaving huge hollow basalt chambers.

## Organised Tours

Savannah Guides (☎ 4097 1411) offers full-day tours for $93/$46 adult/child including lunch; half-day tours for $74/37 adult/child including lunch, $63/31 without and a two-hour tour for $33/16. The full-day tour departs at 8.30am, the half-day at 8.30am and 1pm, and two-hour tours at various times throughout the day. Leaving the lodge by bus, the tours are a highly informative, entertaining journey through the landscape and enormous caves – much of which is covered by boardwalks. During quieter times tours are less frequent so it's worth ringing ahead to check.

## Places to Stay & Eat

*Undara Lava Lodge* (☎1800 990 992, 4097 1411, fax 4097 1450, e info@undara .com.au, w www.undara.com.au) Camp sites $5.50 per person, camp-o-tels $16 per person, bed in 4-bed Wilderness Lodge $16 (linen hire $5); B&B with dinner at Lava Lodge adult/child $76/38. Plenty of camp sites (only some powered) are scattered throughout the pretty bush; excellent facilities include barbecues, hot showers and laundries. The Wilderness Lodge offers share accommodation, and the camp-o-tels are semi-permanent tents with beds and lights. Top of the range are the beautifully restored old railway carriages; rooms are small but quaint and comfortable (though the walls are thin), with shared bathroom facilities.

The lodge has a souvenir shop, a bar and a restaurant serving breakfast, lunch and dinner, open to everyone. There's no kiosk, so if you're self-catering stock up before you come. Each evening there's a free Savannah Guides' campfire activity, including a slide show on the area's flora and fauna.

## Getting There & Away

The lodge and lava tubes are along 15km of well-maintained dirt road off the main highway.

Coral Coaches (☎ 4031 7577) on its run from Cairns to Karumba on Monday, Wednesday and Thursday, can drop you off at the main turn-off from where someone from the lodge will collect you. The one-way fare is $60. (See Organised Tours in the Cairns section of the Far North Queensland chapter for details of tours to Undara.)

## MT SURPRISE

Back on the Gulf Developmental Rd, 39km past the Undara turn-off, you'll find the small township of Mt Surprise, with its pub, train station and two roadhouses. In the centre of rich cattle country, the town was founded in 1864 by Ezra Firth, a stonemason and gold-miner turned sheep farmer. You can read his strange story in the cafe at the BP Roadhouse.

**O'Brien's Creek Gemfields**, 42km northwest of town, is one of Australia's best topaz fields.

The **Old Post Office Museum** (☎ 4062 3126; adult/child $2/0.50; open 7am-5pm daily) has a small and quirky display of local history items.

The Mobil Service Station & General Store (☎ 4062 3115) is the local Royal Automobile Club of Queensland (RACQ) depot. It also has Eftpos facilities.

## Places to Stay & Eat

*Mt Surprise Tourist Van Park & Motel* (☎ 4062 3153, fax 4062 3162) Unpowered/powered sites $12/15, double on-site vans $35/44, motel units $66/72. This park and motel are set amid lush gardens, with an extensive gem and mineral display; a cafe next door serves a good range of meals.

*Bedrock Village* (☎ 4062 3193, fax 4062 3166) Unpowered/powered sites $9/15, cabins with/without en suite $46/35. This is a good place if you want to get away from the main road. Activities offered here include a tour of a nearby cattle station.

*Mt Surprise Hotel* (☎ 4062 3118) Singles/doubles $25/50. There are very basic rooms upstairs, and meals are served any time the pub is open.

The *Mobil Service Station & General Store* sells groceries and takeaway meals.

## Getting There & Away

Coral Coaches (☎ 4031 7577) stop at Mt Surprise en route to Karumba (see the Getting There & Away section at the beginning of the chapter).

## EINASLEIGH & FORSAYTH

About 32km west of Mt Surprise, you can take an interesting, slow detour off the highway through the old mining townships of Einasleigh and Forsayth. You can also visit them on the *Savannahlander* train.

The turn-off to Einasleigh from the Gulf Developmental Rd is poorly marked and easy to miss: From the road it looks like just another gate and cattle grid leading off into nowhere. It's a 150km loop from here back to Georgetown – a diversion well worth the effort and time. The road is unsealed and fairly rough in sections, but is passable for normal vehicles during the dry season; there is one wide, rocky, though straightforward, river crossing. Until 2001 the Kidston goldmine, the largest open-cut goldmine in the country, operated 45km south of Einasleigh.

Einasleigh, a former copper-mining centre and railway siding, is set in a rugged landscape of low, flat-topped hills. There's hardly anything to it today, but for a few houses and the pub – and, of course, the beautiful black basalt gorge. The *Einasleigh Pub* (☎ 4062 5222, fax 4062 5221, Daintree St) has singles and doubles for $33; some of the upstairs rooms in this old, largely corrugated iron pub have been tastefully renovated, and open up on to the east-facing veranda and sunrise views of the Einasleigh Gorge. The bar downstairs is simple and has a real outback feel to it; snacks are available. In another room the publican has a collection of beautifully made miniatures – have a peek.

Forsayth is 67km further west. It's a bit bigger than Einasleigh, and has a train station, a post office and a phone booth. There are a couple of places to stay; the *Goldfields Hotel* (☎ 4062 5374, fax 4062 5426, First St) has basic donga (a prefabricated transportable cabin) singles/doubles for $30/50, or B&B with dinner for $63 per person. Bathrooms are shared, and meals are available, as is fuel and a few groceries. If you're camping or towing a van, the best place would be *Forsayth Homestay & Van Park* (☎ 4062 5386, fax 4062 5464, Fourth St). Unpowered/powered sites cost $11/14, a double on-site van is $45, and B&B with dinner is $64/130 for singles/doubles.

You can also drive from Forsayth to the **Agate Creek Gemfields**, which are 75km south-west, although the road conditions are fairly rough and you'll need a good map (or ask at the pub for directions). Remember to get a fossicking licence before you head out.

If you're driving on to Georgetown, be sure to turn right just *before* the pub: It's quite easy to miss the sign to Georgetown and end up in the middle of nowhere, opening and closing cattle gates as the sun slowly sets.

## COBBOLD GORGE

This scenic oasis, with swimming hole, rugged cliffs and gorges and an abundance of wildlife, is 45km south of Forsayth. Savannah Guide tours include a boat cruise (adult/child $31/15) up the gorge and a half-day cruise and walk (adult/child $66/33). You can stay 3km away at the *Cobbold Camping Village* (☎ *4062 5470, fax 4062 5453)* which has camp sites (adult/child $6/3) and cabins (single/double $70/35). Bookings for the gorge tours can be made here, and if you're travelling on the *Savannahlander* the operators will pick you up from Forsayth.

## MT SURPRISE TO GEORGETOWN

Back on the Gulf Developmental Road, 40km west of Mt Surprise, is the turn-off to the **Tallaroo Hot Springs** *(☎/fax 4062 1221; adult/child $10/6, open 8.30am-5pm Easter-Sept)*, where you can soak in a pool fed from five naturally terraced hot springs. If you want to stay overnight here there are camp sites (unpowered/powered $5/7) by the river.

## GEORGETOWN

During the days of the Etheridge River gold rush, Georgetown was a bustling commercial centre, but these days things are pretty quiet. The tourist information centre is in the library (☎ 4062 1485), where there's free Internet access 8.30am to 4.30pm Monday to Friday. Georgetown has fuel, a post office, food (including a good bakery selling smoothies and fresh juices – rarities in this part of the world) and accommodation. There's also a pub (of course) and a tyre repair outfit.

### Places to Stay & Eat

*Midway Caravan Park & Service Station* (☎ *4062 1219, fax 4062 1227)* Camp sites $10, single/double cabins $33/44. On the highway, this place also has a cafe and take-away section, and has Eftpos facilities.

*Latara Resort Motel (☎ 4062 1190, fax 4062 1262)* Air-con singles/doubles $58/76. On the highway 1km west of Georgetown, this is by far the best place to stay with modern units, and meals are available.

*Savannah Bakery (☎ 4062 1195)*. This bakery has good pies and pastries plus fresh juices and an ebullient baker.

There's also a *produce store* selling fresh fruit and vegies.

## CROYDON

postcode 4871 • pop 150

Connected to Normanton by the *Gulflander* train, this old gold-mining town was once the biggest in the Gulf. Gold was discovered here in 1885, and within a couple of years there were 8000 diggers living here. It's reckoned there were once 5000 gold mines in the area, reminders of which are scattered all around the countryside. Such was the prosperity of the town that it had its own aerated water factory, a foundry and coach-builders, gas street lamps, and more than 30 pubs.

The town's boom years were during the 1890s, but by the end of WWI the gold had run out and Croydon became little more than a ghost town. There is a handful of interesting **historic buildings**, some beautifully restored: The shire hall on Samwell St is a great old timber building topped by a clock tower. The old courthouse, the mining warden's office, the general store, the butcher shop and the Club Hotel also date back to the mining days.

**Lake Belmore**, 4km from the town centre and bred up with barramundi, is a popular fishing spot – though you'll need to get a permit from the shire offices. On the way out to the lake are the Chinese Temple and cemetery ruins; at the time of writing plans were under way to improve access to this area.

### Information

Croydon's information centre (☎ 4745 6125), museum and craft shop are housed in the historic police station on the corner of Samwell and Aldridge Sts. It's open 8am to 5pm daily Monday to Friday, November to March. The *Croydon General Store (☎ 4745 6163)* sells fuel (and just about everything else), does most repairs and is the local RACQ depot. Next door there's a small **museum** with a collection of photos, tools, rocks and records, all fairly well hidden under a blanket of dust. Of particular interest are some old newspaper cuttings about Leonore Gregory, a young woman from Tasmania who came to Croydon by herself in 1930 – certainly no mean feat – to resurrect a defunct printing press; single-handedly she wrote, edited, published and distributed her newspaper throughout the Gulf country for several years, until travelling to London to take up a job on Fleet St.

## Organised Tours
The information centre's Chris Weirman leads one-hour walking tours (☎ 4745 6125, adult/child $5/free) of the town's historic precinct at 8am, 10am, 2pm and 4pm. Chris points out historic points of interest, as well as relaying local lore and tales of Croydon's early pioneers.

## Places to Stay & Eat
**Golden Caravan Park** (☎ 4745 6238, Cnr Brown & Alldridge Sts) Unpowered/powered sites $10/13. The town's only camping ground is run by the council; it's small and bleak, though tempered by a few trees.

**Club Hotel** (☎ 4745 6184, Cnr Brown & Sircom Sts) Beds in enclosed veranda or dorm $15, singles/doubles $35/45, motel-style dongas with shared bathrooms $40/55. The pub rooms are basic but have plenty of character, with bare timber floors and corrugated iron walls; relatively characterless motel units are in a donga out the back, separated from the pub by lush lawn and a swimming pool. The bar, decorated with a mass of stickers (do you laugh or cry?), is friendly, and the beer's on tap.

## THE *GULFLANDER*
The Normanton to Croydon railway line was completed in 1891 with the aim of linking the booming gold-mining centre with the port town at Normanton.

Normanton's train station is a lovely old Victorian-era building with a small souvenir shop and a **railway museum**. When it's not running, the *Gulflander*, a weird-looking, snub-nosed little train, rests under the arch-roofed platform.

The *Gulflander* travels the 153km from Normanton to Croydon and back once a week, leaving Normanton on Wednesday at 8.30am and returning from Croydon on Thursday at 8.30am. It's one of the Gulf's most popular attractions – if you have the time, don't miss it. The trip takes a leisurely four hours, with a couple of stops at points of interest along the way; most people stay overnight in Croydon at the Club Hotel, returning to Normanton the next day. The one-way adult/concession fare is $40/20, return $75/40. From mid-June to mid-September, it also does a two-hour 'tea and damper' trip at 9am every Saturday, and a 'Sunset Sizzle' at 4pm on Thursday; each costs $25 (no concessions). For bookings, phone the Normanton train station on ☎ 4745 1391.

## NORMANTON
postcode 4090 • pop 500
Established on the banks of the Norman River back in 1868, Normanton is now the Gulf's major town. Its boom years were during the 1890s, when it acted as the port town for the gold rush around the Croydon goldfields.

Since the heady days of gold ended, the town has existed as a major supply point for the surrounding cattle stations, and as the shire centre.

It's a busy little town with three pubs, a motel and a caravan park. Some of the **historic buildings** still in use include the shire offices and the large Burns Philp & Co Ltd store (down towards the river end of the town), the Westpac Bank and the simple Normanton train station.

Travellers may also be interested in the Normanton Rodeo and Gymkhana held in June, the area's biggest social and sporting event of the year. The Normanton Races are also held in June.

As a base for fishing, Normanton is hard to beat, with the Norman River producing some magic-sized barramundi; each Easter weekend the Barramundi Classic draws a big crowd.

GULF SAVANNAH

## Information

The Gulf Service Station (☎ 4745 1221), on Landsborough St, sells fuel, is the local RACQ depot and does repairs, welding and 24-hour towing.

Carpentaria Shire Offices (☎ 4745 1166), on the corner of Haig and Landsborough Sts, has a small information section with brochures and a collection of old photos. The library (☎ 4745 1065) is on Landsborough St; Internet access is available here 2pm to 6pm Tuesday and Thursday, and 9am to noon Saturday.

Normanton has a Westpac Bank and the post office has a Commonwealth Bank agency. Next door to the post office there's a laundrette, open daily.

## Organised Tours

Norman River Fishing & Cruises (☎ 4745 1347, e normfish@tpg.com.au, PO Box 290, Normanton 4890) offers sunset cruises (adult/child $15/5) and fishing trips ($55 per person). The *Savannah Queen* 1½-hour sunset tour is probably the best bet if you want to spot a croc. These tours receive positive reviews from many travellers; ring ahead to make a booking.

## Places to Stay & Eat

*Gulfland Motel* (☎ 4745 1290, fax 4745 1138, 11 Landsborough St) Unpowered/powered sites $7/18, single/double motel units $77/88. On your left as you come from Croydon, this is a well-kept motel with a licensed restaurant and a good swimming pool.

*Normanton Caravan Park* (☎ 4745 1121, Brown St) Unpowered/powered sites $6/14. This is a *very* basic camping ground.

*Albion Hotel/Motel* (☎ 4745 1218, fax 4745 1675, Haig St) Motel-style rooms $55/60. There are eight air-con rooms out the back of this friendly pub, just off the main road. Good pub meals are available and there's a shady balcony next to the bar.

*Central Hotel* (☎ 4745 1215, fax 4745 1692, Cnr Haig & Landsborough Sts) Single/double motel-style rooms $55/60; donga-style $25/40. Known as the 'barracks', the budget rooms here have shared bathroom, and are set back from the pub.

*National Hotel* (☎ 4745 1324, fax 4745 1675, Landsborough St) Single/double motel units $55/60, upstairs pub rooms $20 per person. Purple stands out anywhere at the best of times; a double-storey purple pub on the main drag of an outback town is no exception. The budget rooms are upstairs in the pub, while motel-style en suite rooms are out the back and not purple.

There are a few *takeaways* along the main street, serving the usual outback range of burgers, sandwiches, fried chicken, and fish and chips.

## Getting There & Away

Macair has regular flights from Mt Isa to Normanton ($340) and from Cairns to Normanton ($350). There are also regular bus services from Mt Isa and Cairns to Karumba, via Normanton – see Getting There & Away at the beginning of the chapter.

## NORMANTON TO KARUMBA (72km)

Heading out of town, the Burke Developmental Rd soon crosses the Norman River and, less than 29km up the road, a major tributary of the river, Walker Creek. At the 30km mark from the centre of town, you come to a major intersection. Veer left here, sticking to the bitumen, and the road quickly swings almost due west.

Traversing these great plains, it is not hard to imagine that, during the torrential rains of the wet season, this area becomes one huge lake. At times, with king tides backing up the waters of the rivers, the floods isolate towns like Normanton for weeks at a time.

The birdlife is rich and varied – this region is the best in Australia to see the stately brolga, magpie-coloured jabiru and sarus crane – a recent natural invader from South-East Asia.

## KARUMBA

postcode 4891 • pop 500

Karumba, 70km north of Normanton, lies at the point where the Norman River meets the Gulf of Carpentaria. The town actually has two separate sections – Karumba itself is on the banks of the Norman River, while

Karumba Point is a couple of kilometres north (as the crow flies) on the shores of the Gulf. The main reason for driving out here is to *see* the Gulf, and to fish.

Established as a telegraph station in the 1870s, Karumba became a stopover for the flying boats of the Empire Mail Service in the 1930s. The discovery of prawns in the Gulf in the 1960s brought Karumba alive, and today the prawning and barramundi industries keep the town humming.

Karumba has a supermarket, a couple of pubs, caravan parks and holiday units, all of which mainly cater for those going fishing. The town lives and breathes fish and fishing, prawns and prawning. If you aren't interested in these things, you won't stay long. Once you've seen the sea at Karumba Point, and enjoyed a prawn or two at the pub, there's not much else to hold your attention. You could always fly to Mornington or Sweers islands out in the Gulf, but once again, these are favoured fishing haunts and you need to *love* fishing to fully appreciate these wild, remote places.

Note that while the beach at Karumba Point may look rather inviting, don't even *think* about having a swim in the Gulf – if the sharks don't get you, the crocs will.

### Information
The Westpac Bank, in the Transtate Travel Agency & Post Office on Yappar St, is open 9.30am till 1.00pm and 2pm till 4.00pm Monday to Friday, and there is a also a Commonwealth Bank agency at the post office, which keeps post office hours (9.00am till 1.00pm and 2.00pm till 5.00pm).

If you don't have your own boat, there are several places where you can hire one. Karumba Boat Hire (☎ 4745 9393), at Karumba Point, has a variety of dinghies.

### Organised Tours
Ferryman Cruises (☎/fax 4745 9155) offers a two-hour Gulf Sunset tour (adult/child $22/10). The tour provides the quintessential Gulf experience – the chance to be *in* the sunset, *on* the water. Other special focus tours, like bird-watching and croc-spotting, leave either early morning or at dusk.

Karumba Air (☎ 4745 9354, fax 4745 9259) runs a Sweers Island/Mornington Island/Burketown day trip for $250 per person. This tour in a six-seater plane covers a lot of ground: morning tea on Sweers, lunch on Mornington and a tour of Burketown, finishing up in the pub.

### Places to Stay
*Gulf Country Caravan Park* (☎/fax 4745 9148, Cnr Yappar St & Massey Dr) Unpowered/powered sites $14/15, cabins from $58. This shady caravan park, with pool and all the usual amenities, is a block back from the pub and the boat ramp.

*Matilda's End Holiday Units* (☎ 4745 9368, fax 4745 9319, 62 Yappar St) Self-contained single/double units $50/61, $10 extra person. This row of rather old and plain, one, two and three-bedroom units is right on the main street.

*Karumba Lodge Hotel* (☎ 4745 9143, fax 4745 9379, PO Box 19, Karumba 4891) Singles/doubles 72/83. This two-storey row of motel-style units is on the Norman River. Rooms are plain, a bit tawdry, and there's no stopping the afternoon sun from pouring in.

There are more places to stay out at Karumba Point.

*Ash's Holiday Units* (☎ 4745 9132, fax 4745 9134, Cnr Palmer & Ward Sts) Single/double self-contained units $60/66, $5 extra person. These small, spic and span on-site vans offer comfortable en suite accommodation. The pool is surrounded by the zaniest paving in the Gulf.

*Savannah Shores* (☎ 4745 9126, fax 4745 9077, The Esplanade) Singles & doubles $61, $5.50 extra person. These bland, prim cabins are right on the foreshore – though they lack views; breakfast costs $5.50.

### Places to Eat
*Ash's* (☎ 4745 9132, Karumba Point) Open 7am-7.30pm daily. They *really* know how to do fish and chips here. Barra straight from the sea is deliciously battered, sandwiched, grilled, rissolled, you name it.

*Karumba Cafe* (☎ 4745 9187, Yappar St) Mains $10-14. Open 6am-8.30pm Mon-Fri, 7am-8.30pm Sat & Sun. This busy little cafe churns out the usual breakfasts and mixed grills.

***Karumba Recreation & Golf Club*** (☎/fax 4745 9100) Open 5pm-late Wed-Sat. Coming in from Normanton this club is about 3km before you get to Karumba. It's a good alternative to the pubs in town if you're looking for a quieter atmosphere; it has a small bar, and meals are usually available.

***Sunset Tavern*** (☎ 4745 9183, The Esplanade, Karumba Point) Lunch $9-18, dinner $14-23. Open 10am-midnight daily. This is another barn-like pub with a fantastic location on the point. The menu here is extensive and mostly expensive.

There's also a ***supermarket*** in town, open seven days a week.

### Getting There & Away

**Air** Macair has regular flights from Cairns to Karumba ($385).

**Bus** Coral Coaches (☎ 4031 7577) has services from Cairns to Karumba three times a week, and from Mt Isa to Karumba on Tuesday and Friday (book with Campbell's ☎ 4743 2006).

**Boat** Gulf Freight Services (☎ 4745 9333) has regular weekly barge services from Karumba to Weipa on the Cape York Peninsula, transporting freight, people and vehicles. See Getting There & Away at the start of the Cape York Peninsula chapter for more details.

# Western Gulf Region

## NORTHERN TERRITORY BORDER TO BURKETOWN (228km)

This route is part of the historic Gulf Track, which stretches from Roper Bar in the Northern Territory's Top End to Normanton. The entire route is along unsealed roads, although a 4WD vehicle isn't normally required during the dry season unless you plan to take the track that leads to the coast from Hell's Gate. Traffic along this route varies from none in summer to an average of about 30 vehicles a day at the height of the winter tourist season. Travel isn't recommended between the beginning of December and March, when extreme heat and humidity make conditions uncomfortable or even dangerous. Heavy rains at this time can also close the roads for lengthy periods.

The country has little going for it in the way of scenery, being mainly flat and covered with scrubby vegetation. In fact, apart from Hell's Gate and the Gregory River, there is little reason to linger in this section.

### Hell's Gate

About 52km east of the border you arrive at ***Hell's Gate Roadhouse*** (☎ 4745 8258, fax 4745 8225, PMB 45, Mt Isa, 4825) set among low outcrops of grey conglomerate that rise from the surrounding bush. It offers unpowered sites ($6 per person; plus $10 per site for power), en-suite motel units with aircon (singles/doubles $55/88) and dongas with fan (singles/doubles $50/30). In the droving days the police from Turn-Off Lagoon, on the Nicholson River, escorted westbound travellers as far as these rocks, after which they were on their own.

The roadhouse has a good licensed ***restaurant*** that serves breakfast, lunch and dinner, and a Sunday night barbecue. The roadhouse is open 7am to 10pm (or later) daily. Bookings are recommended for accommodation.

Bill Olive, the owner of the roadhouse, runs two-hour/half-day/full-day 4WD tours ($30/50/100 per person) for groups of five or more, taking in spectacular escarpment landscapes and lagoons rich in birdlife. Bookings are preferred.

### Kingfisher Camp & Bowthorn Homestead

There are a couple of other places to stay in this part of the area.

***Kingfisher Camp*** (☎ 4745 8212) Camp sites $7 per person, single rooms $20 per person; day pass $3. Between Hell's Gate and Doomadgee there's a signposted turn-off to this camping ground beside a 5km-long hole on the banks of the Nicholson River. Facilities include hot showers, toilets and laundry, and firewood is supplied. Boats can be hired and there's a small kiosk selling basic supplies.

***Bowthorn Homestead** (☎ 4745 8132, fax 4745 8202, W www.ozemail.com.au/ ~bowthorn, Bowthorn Station, PMB 75, Mount Isa, 4825)* B&B with dinner $75 per person. This homestead offers a great opportunity to stay on a working cattle station. Accommodation is in the Big House, and there's a craft room with local goods for sale. Bowthorn is operated by the McGinnis family, who also runs the Kingfisher Camp; Kerry McGinnis' autobiography *Heart Country* is a fascinating account of life in the Gulf country. Bowthorn is 33km south of Kingfisher Camp; you can head east 72km and join up with the Gulf Track east of the Nicholson River, or head south 100km or so to Lawn Hill National Park. Bookings are essential.

### Doomadgee

Other than patches of open forest along occasional creek lines, there is little break in the mallee and paperbark scrub that lines the track for the 80km between Hell's Gate and the Doomadgee turn-off. Doomadgee is an Aboriginal community of about 1300 residents. While you are welcome to shop at the store, camping on the community's land is subject to permission being obtained from the council.

The well-stocked ***Doomadgee Retail Store** (☎ 4745 8265)* sells fuel, meat, groceries and a limited range of hardware items. It's open 9am to 4.30pm Monday to Friday (from 10.30am on Tuesday) and 9am to noon on Saturday.

### Doomadgee to Burketown

About 4km past Doomadgee you arrive at the **Nicholson River** crossing. The river is about 600m across, and in the dry season its bed of solid rock presents a desolate picture.

In remarkable contrast, the **Gregory River**, 53km further on, presents a lush picture of running water crowded with tropical vegetation. Herons stalk the shallows, and the milky water holds promise of feasts of yabbies. However, motorists must exercise extreme care here, as the single-lane concrete crossing has a sharp bend in it and you can't see the other side.

On the other side is the deserted Tirranna Roadhouse, and 8km later there's a major road junction – turn right for the Gregory Downs Hotel (90km) and left for Burketown.

## BURKETOWN

**postcode 4831 • pop 170**

For many, Burketown is 'on the Gulf', but in reality it is over 30km from the waters of the Gulf of Carpentaria. Even so, it sits precariously on the very flat plains that border the waters of the Gulf, just a few metres above the high-tide mark. Just a stone's throw from the waters of the Albert River, Burketown operated as a port – ships travelled up the muddy waters of the river to service the town and hinterland.

Founded in 1865, Burketown almost came to a premature end a year later when a fever wiped out most of the residents. In 1887 a huge tidal surge almost carried the town away and, while nothing so dramatic has occurred since, the township is often cut off from the rest of Australia by floods.

Once (by all accounts) the wildest township in Australia, Burketown today is much more peaceful and friendly. Not only is it the administrative centre for a vast region dotted with huge cattle properties, it is also a supply centre for travellers heading to, from or along the Gulf.

There are a few **historic sites** to see including the old wharves, the boiling-down works (where meat, hooves and hides were processed) and, not far away, the tree emblazoned by the explorer Landsborough. Like many historic sites, this one is fast decaying under the onslaught of the weather and white ants. The cemetery is also interesting.

Besides declaring itself as the 'barramundi capital of Australia', Burketown is also home to a phenomenon known as 'Morning Glory' – weird tubular cloud formations, extending the full length of the horizon, which roll out of the Gulf in the early morning, often in lines of three or four. This only happens from September to November.

## Information

The Burketown and Gulf Regional Tourist Information Centre (☎ 4745 5111) can supply information and make arrangements for local tours on the Albert River and elsewhere. The Burketown General Store (☎ 4745 5101) on Beames St sells fuel. It also has Eftpos, as does the pub.

## Special Events

The Burketown Rodeo, held in the second weekend of July, guarantees a good crowd, and there's a barramundi fishing competition each Easter. The Burketown Show takes place on the second weekend of September.

## Places to Stay & Eat

**Burketown Pub** (☎ 4745 5104, fax 4745 5146, Beames St) Singles/doubles $44/55; comfortable, air-con motel-style dongas from $72/94. This pub is the heart and soul of Burketown. Originally built as the local customs house, it's the oldest building in town – all its contemporaries have been blown over or washed away! Motel/donga units are far away enough from the pub to be quiet, and there's a lovely, though cane-toad infested, beer garden. It's a friendly, well-run outback pub and definitely worth a visit. The pub serves a good range of meals.

**Burketown Caravan Park** (☎ 4745 5101, Sloman St) Unpowered/powered sites $13/16, cabins $44/55. There's nothing too flash about these grounds, though there is some shade.

The **Burketown General Store** has a supermarket, a licensed restaurant and a takeaway food section.

## Getting There & Away

Macair has regular flights to Burketown from Mt Isa ($284) and Cairns ($454).

## BURKETOWN TO NORMANTON (233km)

From Burketown the Gulf Track improves as it sweeps across the flat plains of the Gulf to Normanton. The road, which follows the original coach route between Darwin and Port Douglas, was known as the Great Top Rd.

This route is open to conventional vehicles throughout the dry season, and shouldn't present too many problems if you take it easy; however, the higher clearance of a 4WD will certainly make for an easier trip. As you head south on the Burketown road, most of the creek crossings of any note have been upgraded to a bitumen causeway. How bad the road is depends on when the graders have been out and how bad the preceding wet season has been – sometimes it can be little better than a track, while at other times it is a wide, graded road interspersed with a few corrugations, potholes and bull dust.

Heading south out of Burketown you'll pass the 100-year-old artesian bore on the right, just on the outskirts of town. At Harris Creek, 15km from the centre of town, the dirt begins. The bull dust on these vast, flat plains is finer, deeper and seemingly more enveloping than anywhere else in Australia.

## Floraville Station

The turn-off to Floraville Station is found at the 73km mark, on the right. A 'Historic Site' sign indicates that this is more than a station track, and it is worth the 1.3km diversion to check the plaque and monument to Frederick Walker, who died here in 1866. He was a wild lad in his time, but a fine explorer, who had been sent out to find Burke and Wills. Although he didn't find them, he did discover their Camp 119, from which they made their final push to the Gulf.

**Walker's Monument** is through the gate, heading towards the station. Keep left at the first track junction, about 400m from the road, and turn left again a little later. Now you should be able to see the monument, down the rise a little, across a narrow creek. Please respect the privacy of the station people and stay away from the nearby homestead.

## Leichhardt Falls

Just 1km after the turn-off to Floraville, the road drops down the bank of the Leichhardt River and winds its way across the rock bar that makes up the wide bed of the river here. A narrow, short bridge crosses the stream in one spot.

The best place to pull up for a short wander, and probably the best *camp* on the run between Burketown and Normanton, is at the small, sandy, tree-covered island on the left – about halfway across the river's rocky bed, just past the narrow bridge. From here it is only a short walk downstream to the spectacular Leichhardt Falls. There are pools of water to cool off in (don't swim in the big stretch of water above the road crossing – there are crocs), the trees offer shade and the birdlife is rich and varied. In a big flood, there is so much water coming down the river that the falls are barely a ripple. These sorts of floods occur every 10 years or so.

## Leichhardt Falls to Normanton

Once you have climbed the eastern bank of the Leichhardt River, the road winds a short distance and crosses a causeway before reaching a road junction, which can be easy to miss. You are less than 4km from the Floraville Station turn-off, less than 2km from the eastern bank of the Leichhardt and a total of 77km from Burketown. You need to turn left here for Normanton. Heading south on the better-looking road will take you to the Burke & Wills Roadhouse, 146km away on the Wills Developmental Rd.

Turn left at the junction, go through a gate, and 500m later you will begin crossing the very rocky and rough bed of the **Alexandra River**.

After the Alexandra, the road continues in a north-easterly direction, crossing the occasional creek (some have a causeway) and ploughing through bull dust and across corrugations. The turn-off to **Wernadinga Station** is 16km from the Alexandra River crossing, while the track into **Inverleigh Station** is 85km from the road junction.

You cross the **Flinders River** 28km past the Inverleigh turn-off, and then 3km later the **Big Bynoe River**. The **Little Bynoe River** is crossed 2.5km further east. Just up the top of the eastern bank, 500m from the river, is a track heading south (right); it leads less than 2km to **Burke and Wills' Camp 119**. This is a good spot to have a brew, and if

you want to camp, a track leads a short distance back to the edge of the Little Bynoe.

Camp 119 was the northernmost camp of the Burke and Wills expedition. Leaving their companions, Gray and King, to mind the camels and their equipment at Cooper Creek (near present-day Innamincka in South Australia), Burke and Wills pushed north across the wet and flooded country to try to reach the waters of the Gulf. While the water was salty and they observed a rise and fall in the tide, they were disappointed that the barrier of mangroves and mud kept them from seeing the coast. They turned back around 9 February 1861.

Returning to Camp 119, they planned their dash back to Cooper Creek. No longer was it an exploratory expedition with mapping and observing a prime consideration, but a dash south for survival. In the end, only King made it back alive.

Camp 119 is marked by a ring of trees and a centre one blazed by Burke and Wills. A couple of monuments also mark the spot.

All the rivers previously mentioned are home to estuarine crocodiles, so swimming is not advisable. A huge number of cattle use these places for drinking and cooling off, so unless the river is flowing, it's not recommended for drinking either.

Continuing eastwards you reach the bitumen at a road junction 32km east of the turn-off to Camp 119. Turn left here and 5km later you'll be in Normanton.

## BURKETOWN TO CAMOOWEAL (334km)

The road from Burketown to Camooweal via Gregory Downs is the most direct way for people heading to the Lawn Hill National Park, although for conventional vehicles the longer route via the Burke & Wills Roadhouse provides much easier access, as it is sealed for most of the way. This road is unsealed dirt all the way, and while there are no major river crossings to negotiate, it's quite rough in patches and a 4WD vehicle is recommended. Having said all that, it is *possible* to drive this route in a conventional vehicle, particularly if the road has been recently graded. On the other hand, conditions can quickly deteriorate after heavy rain, so either way it's important to check on local conditions before heading out.

From Burketown it's 117km south to Gregory Downs, which is the main turn-off to Lawn Hill. **Gregory Downs** consists of a busy (by outback standards) pub and a friendly general store. *Gregory Downs Hotel (☎ 4748 5566)* has single/double motel-style units for $60/70, and air-con dongas for $25 per person. You can also camp behind the pub on the riverbank. The pub sells meals and fuel, and can handle emergency repairs. *Billy Hangers General Store (☎ 4748 5540)* is jam-packed with just about everything you might need. You can also fix your tyres and rent canoes here for $5/25 per hour/day.

Every Labour Day weekend in May, the pub hosts the famous **Gregory Canoe Races** – a great event, and not to be missed if you're around at this time of year.

From Gregory Downs, it's another 217km to Camooweal. About 40km south the road turns from dirt to gravel as you start to move into a series of low hills. This section gets pretty bumpy, with stony patches and sand drifts competing for your attention, and the occasional (and sudden) sharp dip to keep you on your toes. About 69km south of Gregory Downs, you pass the second turn-off to Lawn Hill – this route is only open to 4WD vehicles.

The next section of the road resembles a dirt roller coaster, and it's a real boneshaker in sections. About 126km south of Gregory Downs the road splits in two. The left-hand branch heads south for another 58km before meeting the Barkly Hwy, and this is the route you'll take if you're heading for Mt Isa. The right-hand branch continues south-west for another 91km, meeting the Barkly Hwy 2km west of Camooweal.

## LAWN HILL NATIONAL PARK

Amid arid country 100km west of Gregory Downs, the Lawn Hill Gorge is an oasis of gorges, creeks, ponds and tropical vegetation that the Aboriginal people have enjoyed for perhaps thirty thousand years. Their paintings and old camp sites abound.

Two rock-art sites have been made accessible to visitors. There are freshwater crocodiles – the inoffensive variety – in the creek.

In the southern part of the park is the amazing World Heritage-listed **Riversleigh fossil field**. The field contains fossils ranging from 15 million to a mere 50,000 years old, making it one of the world's pre-eminent fossil sites. The fossils include everything from giant snakes to carnivorous kangaroos to small rodents. The Riversleigh Fossils Interpretive Centre in Mt Isa has fossils on display and is well worth a look if you can't get out to the park.

There are 20km of walking tracks as well as a great *camping ground* with showers and toilets at Lawn Hill; it's very popular and sites ($3.85 per person) must be booked well in advance with the park rangers (☎ 4748 5572, fax 4748 5549). Canoes can be hired and paddling up the emerald green river with the red cliffs towering above is an experience not to be missed; swimming up near the waterfalls is also a real treat.

Ten kilometres east of the park entrance, *Adels Grove (☎/fax 4748 5502, e adelsgrove@bigpond.com)* is a camping ground set amid trees close to the Lawn Hill Creek. In addition to camp sites (family/adult/child $21/8/4), there are several permanently set-up tents ($60/22/11), with beds and linen; B&B with dinner costs $62/31 per adult/child. Fuel and basic groceries are also available.

From 1920 to the early 1950s, the lease of this land was held by Albert de Lestang (contracted to Adels), a French Botanist apparently commissioned by the government of the day to experiment with tropical horticulture; eventually de Lestang established a wonderful botanic garden here, comprising over one thousand species of trees and shrubs. However, with time, and fire, the gardens were destroyed – though there are still a few remnants to be seen.

Getting to Lawn Hill is the problem – it's a beautiful, pristine place that's miles from anywhere. There are a couple of different ways of getting here, and, as mentioned previously, the easiest route for conventional vehicles is to come via the Burke & Wills

Roadhouse. If you're coming along the Camooweal to Burketown road, 4WD vehicles are recommended.

Campbell's Tours & Travel (☎ 4743 2006) in Mt Isa do a three-day safari (adult/child $451/275) out to Lawn Hill and Riversleigh on Wednesday and Saturday, with accommodation and meals provided at Adels Grove. Alternatively, you can buy a return Mt Isa-Adels Grove ticket ($150), and do all your own catering; a return lift out to the park from Adels Grove costs $15 per person.

## CLONCURRY TO NORMANTON (375km)

The major road into the Gulf from the south is the Burke Developmental Rd, which runs from Cloncurry to Normanton. This is the last section of the route known as the Matilda Hwy, which starts way down south at Cunnamulla near the Queensland/New South Wales border. The highway is bitumen all the way and in excellent condition.

**Quamby**, 43km north of Cloncurry, was once a Cobb & Co coach stop and a centre for gold mining that helped develop the region. Quamby now has nothing but the historic *Quamby Hotel* (☎/fax 4742 5952) The pub offers simple accommodation (singles/doubles $15/25) and serves meals. Note that at the time of writing no fuel was available at Quamby.

Continuing north across the rolling hills dotted with low, spindly gums, you reach the turn-off to **Kajabbi**, 29km north of Quamby. Once the focus of the area, Kajabbi has been all but forgotten. The town was once the railhead for this part of the Gulf's cattle industry and the nearby copper mines, but all that has long since disappeared. The *Kalkadoon Hotel* (☎/fax 4742 5979) is Kajabbi's focal point, for locals and visitors alike. Single/twin/double rooms go for $28/39/44. Battle Mountain, the site of the last stand of the local warlike Kalkadoon people, who resisted the white invasion in bloody battles during the 1880s, is about 30km south.

Just before you get to the Burke & Wills Roadhouse along the Burke Developmental Rd, 180km north of Cloncurry, the Wills Developmental Rd from Julia Creek joins the road you are on from the right.

*Burke & Wills Roadhouse (☎ 4742 5909, fax 4742 5958)* Unpowered/powered sites $5/9 per person, single/double air-con dongas $39/50. Open 7am-10pm daily. Nearly everyone stops here, where there's a little shade, some greenery at any time of the year, meals, ice creams from the well-stocked store and, if you really need it, fuel.

From the roadhouse you can strike northwest along the Wills Developmental Rd to the fabulous Gregory River and the *Gregory Downs Hotel* (see the Burketown to Camooweal section). For those travelling on to Normanton, the route continues in a more northerly direction towards the Gulf. The country remains reasonably flat, but once you get to **Bang Bang Jump-up** and descend about 40m to the Gulf plains proper, you really know what 'flat' means. This near-sheer escarpment vividly marks where the high country ends, 80km north of the roadhouse.

From this point the road stretches across vast, billiard-table-flat plains covered in deep grass, which in the Dry is the colour of gold. Dotted here and there are clumps of trees, and wherever there is permanent water or shade there are cattle. In this country the cattle stand out – during the day. At night, as everywhere in outback Queensland, they can make driving on the roads very hazardous.

## WELLESLEY ISLANDS

There are numerous islands scattered in the Gulf of Carpentaria north of Burketown, most of which are Aboriginal communities and are not open to visitors. There are, however, a couple of places set up specifically to cater to people wanting to fish the abundant waters of the Gulf.

### Mornington Island

The largest of the Gulf islands, Mornington Island has an Aboriginal community administered from Gununa, on the southwestern coast.

*Birri Fishing Resort (☎ 4745 7277, fax 4745 7297, ℮ dibbywithers@bigpond.com.au, ☒ www.birri.com.au; lodge open last week Mar-end Oct)* Seven-night package deal $2860 per person. On the north-western coast of the island is this remote lodge catering for anglers. The tariff includes accommodation, all meals, boats etc.

There are regular flights to the island from Karumba and you can also fly there from Burketown – see those sections for details.

## Sweers Island

The smaller Sweers Island, midway between Burketown and Mornington Island, became the headquarters of the Gulf district after an outbreak of fever in Burketown in 1865, but because of its remoteness Normanton later took over as the administrative centre. Today, Sweers Island also has its own fishing resort.

*Sweers Island Resort* (☎ *4748 5544, fax 4748 5644*) $210 per person per night. Cabins cater for families, and have shared bathroom facilities; the tariff includes all meals, boat hire, fuel, bait and hand lines. You'll need to book during the peak Spanish mackerel season (June to August).

There are flights to the island from Karumba and Burketown; Savannah Aviation (☎ 4745 5177) also has day trips to the resort from Burketown for $300 for up to five people.

# Outback Queensland

This chapter covers Queensland's vast outback region. Stretching westward beyond the Great Dividing Range, the legendary outback is truly, in the well-worn words of Dorothea Mackellar, 'a sunburnt country, a land of sweeping plains, of rugged mountain ranges, of droughts and flooding rains'.

The outback has some outstanding attractions, including the Australian Workers Heritage Centre in Barcaldine, the Stockman's Hall of Fame & Outback Heritage Centre in Longreach, and the Birdsville Working Museum. But this country isn't really about attractions or sights, it's essentially about experiences – the characters you meet in pubs and roadhouses; the exhilaration of being in the middle of nowhere in the shimmering heat, surrounded by silence, spinifex and sand; the acute boredom of sitting behind the wheel watching the unchanging landscape for hour after hour after hour...

There are plenty of reminders of the outback's history out here, from the old stone and timber buildings bleached by the sun of a hundred summers, to the fascinating tales of the early explorers and pioneers who opened up the region to white settlement.

Remember that this is harsh, unforgiving country; as the locals say, you should never underestimate the outback. No matter how safe you feel sitting in your air-con 4WD, expect the unexpected. The combination of extreme temperatures, scarcity of water and isolation makes it one of the few places in the world where your survival is in your hands. There is no substitute for good preparation.

## History

Ludwig Leichhardt crossed the outback's Western Plains on his way to Port Essington in the Northern Territory in 1844. Over the next 20 years, some of Australia's greatest explorers, including Thomas Mitchell (later knighted for his achievements), the doomed Robert Burke and William Wills, William Landsborough, Augustus Gregory and John McKinlay, crisscrossed the vast plains and

## Highlights

- Visit the huge Mt Isa mine – it never fails to impress.
- Make the (long!) pilgrimage to the must-see Stockman's Hall of Fame in Longreach.
- Head for remote Birdsville in the state's far south-west for the annual race meeting.

low rugged ranges of outback Queensland. In the process, they opened up this land to the sheep and cattle graziers who quickly followed.

## Geography

The area 'out back' of the Great Dividing Range is a vast, semi-arid region known as the Western Plains. Beneath these endless, grassy plains lies the Great Artesian Basin, an enormous underground water supply that supports the outback's sheep and cattle stations. The arid south-western corner of the state (Channel Country) is cut by innumerable rivers and creeks that remain dry most of the year until they are filled to overflowing by waters running from the north during the Wet.

As well as the plains, there are several low mountain ranges in the region, including the

OUTBACK QUEENSLAND

461

OUTBACK QUEENSLAND

ancient Selwyn Range east of Mt Isa, the Aramac Range north of Barcaldine, and the Grey Range, which stretches from near Blackall down to the New South Wales border.

The outback's major river systems include the Diamantina, Thomson, Barcoo, Bulloo and Warrego.

## Climate

Summer isn't a great time to visit the outback. Average temperatures are over 35°C and frequently soar towards 50°C, and travelling in such heat can be hazardous. Summer is also the time of the Wet, when monsoon rains in the north fill the region's hundreds of rivers and creeks, sometimes flooding vast areas of the Channel Country and cutting off many outback roads.

Conditions are much more favourable in the cooler months between April and October, with generally mild to warm days and temperatures seldom topping 30°C. However, it can be bitterly cold at night in winter – temperatures below freezing are not uncommon.

Rain is a rare occurrence in the outback, with the southern areas averaging around 150mm a year. Rainfall is slightly heavier north of the tropic of Capricorn, particularly in summer.

## Getting There & Away

**Air** Qantas (☎ 13 13 13) flies from Brisbane to Roma and Charleville.

Macair, a Qantas affiliate, (☎ 13 15 28, 1800 677 566) flies between Brisbane and Birdsville via Charleville, Quilpie and Windorah; from Birdsville to Mt Isa with stops at Bedourie and Boulia; from Brisbane to Mt Isa via Cloncurry; and from Townsville to Mt Isa via Hughenden, Richmond, Julia Creek and Cloncurry. Macair also flies direct between Mt Isa and Townsville, and between Townsville and Longreach via Winton.

Macair also services the north-western corner of the state, connecting Mt Isa to Cairns via Doomadgee or Burketown, Mornington Island and Normanton. Airlines of South Australia does a weekly mail run from Port Augusta to Bedourie and Boulia on Saturday, and back via Birdsville on Sunday.

**Bus** There are three major bus routes through the outback – from Townsville to Mt Isa via Hughenden, from Rockhampton to Longreach via Emerald, and from Brisbane to Mt Isa via Roma and Longreach. McCafferty's/Greyhound services all three routes; buses continue from Mt Isa to Threeways in the Northern Territory, from there you can head north to Darwin or south to Alice Springs.

**Train** Similarly, there are three train services from the coast to the outback, all running twice weekly: The *Spirit of the Outback* runs from Brisbane to Longreach via Rockhampton, with connecting bus services to Winton; the *Westlander* runs from Brisbane to Charleville, with connecting bus services to Cunnamulla and Quilpie; and the *Inlander* runs from Townsville to Mt Isa.

**Car & Motorcycle** The outback, although sparsely settled, is well serviced by major roads – the Flinders Hwy connects northern Queensland with the Northern Territory, meeting the Barkly Hwy at Cloncurry; the

Capricorn Hwy runs along the tropic of Capricorn from Rockhampton to Longreach; and the Landsborough and Mitchell Hwys run from the New South Wales border south of Cunnamulla right up to Mt Isa.

However, off these major arteries roads deteriorate rapidly; services are extremely limited: You need to be completely self-sufficient with spare parts, fuel and water. With the right preparation, you can make the great outback journeys down the tracks connecting Queensland with South Australia – the Strzelecki and Birdsville tracks.

## The Art of the Drive-By Wave

Driving the outback's long, remote roads gives you plenty of time to contemplate life, loneliness and the transient nature of contemporary existence. In the days of yore when the pace of the world was gentler, travellers would have time to stop and chat, and exchange news and information, such as which inns had the softest beds, the best meals, the coldest beer. Nowadays all this has been compressed into a split-second greeting as two vehicles zoom past each other at combined speeds of over 200km/h, on smooth black-topped highways.

The incidence of drive-by waves rises in direct proportion to the remoteness of the road being travelled. Closer to the coast and larger cities, hardly anyone acknowledges other drivers, but as you head into the outback you'll start noticing passing drivers waving at you. At first you might think these waves are identical, but a closer study will reveal subtle but significant variations: from the four-finger greeting, to the nonchalant one- or two-finger wave usually practised by seasoned outback travellers – and poorly imitated by novices.

At the other extreme is the full-hand wave, where the right hand actually leaves the steering wheel. Those practising this potentially dangerous method are probably deeply lonely, insecure people, desperate for a fleeting moment of on-the-road acceptance that they can never hope to achieve back in urban society.

OUTBACK QUEENSLAND

# Charters Towers to Camooweal – the Flinders & Barkly Highways

The Flinders Hwy, which stretches 775km from Townsville to Cloncurry is the major route across the top of outback Queensland. From Cloncurry, the Barkly Hwy picks up where the Flinders Hwy leaves off and takes you on to Mt Isa, Camooweal and into the Northern Territory.

As a scenic drive, this is probably the most boring route in Queensland, although there are a few minor points of interest along the way to break the monotony. Apart from the Charters Towers to Torrens Creek section, which passes through the Great Dividing Range, the terrain is flat as a pancake – a seemingly endless landscape of dry, grassy plains. There is little visual relief until you pass Cloncurry and reach the low, red hills that surround Mt Isa.

The two highways are sealed all the way and are generally in good condition, although north-west of Mt Isa the road deteriorates in sections to a narrow, poorly engineered and dangerous single-lane strip of bitumen. The inland railway line runs beside the highway for the majority of the route.

McCafferty's/Greyhound operates daily services along the Townsville to Mt Isa route and on to the Northern Territory. The *Inlander* train follows an almost identical route twice weekly, with stops at most towns along the way.

## CHARTERS TOWERS TO HUGHENDEN

It's 246km from Charters Towers to Hughenden. This route is a former Cobb & Co coach run. It's dotted with tiny townships along the way that were originally established as stopovers for the coaches. The theory is that the towns are evenly spaced, with roughly a day's run for the coach horses between each.

The first section, from Charters Towers to Torrens Creek, passes through the Great Dividing Range. Beyond, the land becomes flatter and drier, trees become a rarity and the flat, grassy plains begin.

It's 105km to the small settlement of **Pentland**, and another 94km to the aptly-named town of **Prairie**, which consists of a small cluster of houses, a railway station and the quiet little *Prairie Hotel (☎/fax 4741 5121, Flinders Hwy)*. Here you can camp out the back ($11), stay in the pub (singles/doubles $22/38.50) or rent a motel room ($49.50/60.50). First licensed in 1884, this historic pub was originally a Cobb & Co coach stop. It's filled with atmosphere and memorabilia, and even has a resident ghost – ask at the bar for his written story.

## HUGHENDEN
**postcode 4821 • pop 1650**

Hughenden is on the banks of the Flinders River, in the same spot where explorer William Landsborough camped in 1862 during his fruitless search for survivors from the Burke and Wills expedition. Today Hughenden is a busy commercial centre servicing the surrounding cattle, wool and grain industries.

The town bills itself as the home of beauty and the beast. The 'beauty' is the **Porcupine Gorge National Park**, 65km north; the 'beast' is imprisoned in the **Dinosaur Display & Museum**, at the rear of the town's information centre in Gray St.

Inside is a replica skeleton of *Muttaburrasaurus*, one of the largest and most complete dinosaur skeletons ever found in Australia. It was discovered by a grazier in 1961 in a cattle holding yard at Muttaburra, 206km south of Hughenden. The centre also has a few locally found fossils and other historic relics on display.

### Information

The Hughenden visitor information centre (☎ 4741 1021, 34 Gray St; museum entry $2; open 9am to 5pm daily) is very helpful. Caltex Flinders Star Service Station (☎ 4741 1626) is the local Royal Automobile Club of Queensland (RACQ) depot. The Shire of Flinders Library (☎ 4741

DUNCAN SUTHERLAND

Undara Volcanic National Park

ANDREW MARSHALL & LEANNE WALKER

The Pyramid, Porcupine Gorge National Park

ROSS BARNETT

Corys Range, south-west of Winton

JOHN BANAGAN

Colony wattle

SARA-JANE CLELAND

An outback windmill

River red gums on Cooper Creek, Australia's most famous inland river

Dramatic red rock formations near Mount Isa

Harsh country south of Mt Isa

1817, corner of Gray and Brodie Sts; open 10.30am to 5pm weekdays and 9am to 11.45am on Saturday) provides Internet access at $2.20 an hour.

## Places to Stay

*Allan Terry Caravan Park* (☎/fax 4741 1190, Resolution St) Camp sites/cabins $10/40. Opposite the train station and next to the pool, this park has a large grassed area, some shade, and good clean cabins, but the railway yard can be noisy.

*Grand Hotel* (☎/fax 4741 1588, 25 Gray St) Singles/doubles $15/30, $35 with aircon. The Grand is a classic, old two-storey timber pub occupying a prominent corner in town. It has basic rooms upstairs with sagging floors and clean shared amenities, but the beds are starting to show their age. You can get good country-style tucker in the bar.

*Royal Hotel-Motel* (☎ 4741 1183, fax 4741 1731, e royal100@tpg.com.au, 21 Morun St) Singles/doubles from $55/66. This is one of the better motels in town, offering a choice between large, spotless older-style motel units, and smaller, brand new ones.

## PORCUPINE GORGE NATIONAL PARK

If the weather has been dry, and you have a vehicle, head out to Porcupine Gorge National Park. It's an oasis in the dry country north of Hughenden, off the mostly unpaved Kennedy Developmental Rd.

The best spot to go is **Pyramid Lookout**, about 70km north of Hughenden. You can *camp* here and it's an easy 30-minute walk into the gorge, with some fine rock formations and a permanently running creek. Few people come here and there's a fair bit of wildlife. Also in the area are the **White Mountains** and **Great Basalt Wall National Parks**.

The Kennedy Developmental Rd, a well-maintained (though often corrugated) dirt route, takes you to the turn-off to the Undara lava tubes and eventually to Ravenshoe and the Atherton Tableland. It's reasonably scenic, but is not recommended after heavy rain.

## RICHMOND
### postcode 4822 • pop 800

Like most of the towns out here, Richmond exists primarily to service the local cattle and sheep industries, but lately it's been getting tourism mileage from its location in the fossil-rich former inland sea. It's a progressive little place that's working hard to raise its tourism profile.

The town is set on the Flinders River and was a Cobb & Co stopover. There's a restored Cobb & Co **mail coach** in a cage beside the town's caravan park – it's worth stopping here and considering what it would have been like travelling in these things over unpaved roads through the heat and dust.

The area around Richmond is abundant in sandalwood, and a factory in the town processes the wood for export to Asia, where it is used for incense and joss sticks.

## Information

Kronosaurus Korner (☎ 4741 3429, 91 Goldring St; open 8.30am to 4.45pm) is Richmond's tourist information centre. Out the front it has a huge model of a crocodile-like prehistoric creature, an advertisement for an impressive **fossil museum** (adult/child $8/3) inside, which includes an almost-complete 4.25m Pliosaur skeleton.

Richmond Motors (☎ 4741 3420) is the RACQ agent, and the Richmond library (☎ 4741 3077, 50 Goldring St) has free Internet access for the first hour.

## Places to Stay & Eat

*Richmond Caravan Park* (☎ 4741 3772, fax 4741 3308, 109 Goldring St). Unpowered/powered sites $11/14, twin cabins $16.50 per person, units $50. This is a council-run park that is obviously considered a worthwhile asset. It's well run and has an immaculate amenities block, pleasant camping areas and small, but spotless budget cabins.

*Federal Palace Hotel* (☎ 4741 3463, fax 4741 3099, 64 Goldring St) Singles/doubles $25/45 with shared bathrooms. There are well-maintained air-con rooms with new beds and cupboards in this friendly place, and it also serves a good range of *bistro* meals.

*Aminite Inn (☎ 4741 3932, fax 4741 3934, 88 Goldring St)* Singles/doubles $71.50/82.50. The Aminite Inn is a brand new motel, built to cater to a growing tourist market. As you would expect, it has spacious, upmarket rooms, and a good *restaurant* and *bar*.

## JULIA CREEK

It's another flat and featureless 144km from Richmond to Julia Creek, a small pastoral centre specialising in selling and transporting cattle.

About 4km west of Julia Creek, the sealed Wills Developmental Rd heads north to the Burke & Wills Roadhouse (235km). From the roadhouse you can continue north to Normanton and Karumba; you can also reach Burketown this way. See the Gulf Savannah chapter for more details.

The town's accommodation options include a fairly cheap, basic *caravan park* and the *Julia Creek Hotel (☎ 4746 7175, fax 4746 7311, 33 Goldring St)*, which has surprisingly good upstairs rooms (singles/doubles $31/50). The modern *Julia Creek Villas (☎ 4746 7468, fax 4746 7328, 2 Burke St)* has clean units at $55/66 for singles/doubles.

## CLONCURRY

postcode 4824 • pop 3900

Cloncurry's major claim to fame is as the birthplace of the Royal Flying Doctor Service. The town was the centre of a copper boom in the 19th century, and was the largest copper producer in the British empire in 1916. Today it's a busy little pastoral centre with a couple of attractions for passing tourists. The Burke Developmental Rd, which heads north from Cloncurry, is paved all the way to Normanton (376km) and Karumba (449km), near the Gulf of Carpentaria. Burketown is 425km from Cloncurry. See the Gulf Savannah chapter for details.

## Information

The Mary Kathleen Park & Museum (see Things to See & Do) on the eastern side of town acts as a tourist information centre. East Side Panel Repairs (☎ 4742 1158) is the local RACQ agent. The Cloncurry Library (☎ 4742 1588, 19 Scarr St; 2.30pm to 5.30pm Monday to Friday, but 10am to 1pm Wednesday) provides Internet access at $2.75 for half an hour.

## Things to See & Do

The **John Flynn Place** museum and art gallery *(☎ 4742 1251, Cnr Daintree & King Sts; adult/child $7/3; open 8am-4.30pm Mon-Fri, 9am-3pm Sat & Sun, Apr-Oct)* commemorates Flynn's work in setting up the invaluable Royal Flying Doctor Service. It's an interesting, easy-to-follow exhibition, and the building incorporates a quality art gallery.

The **Mary Kathleen Park & Museum** *(☎ 4742 1361, McIlwraith St; adult/child $7/3; open 8am-4.30pm Mon-Fri)* is partly housed in buildings transported from the former uranium-mining town of Mary Kathleen. The collection includes relics of the Burke and Wills expedition and a big array of local rocks and minerals.

## Places to Stay & Eat

*Gilbert Park Tourist Park (☎ 4742 2300, fax 4742 2303, e gilpark@topend.com.au, 2 McIlwraith St)* Camp sites $6.60 per person, units $64.50. Gilbert Park is a new and neat tourist park set amid desert vegetation and hillocks of red rock. It has pretty cheap camp sites and pretty dear, modern, self-contained units.

*Central Hotel (☎ 4742 1418, fax 4742 2290, 46 Scarr St)* Singles/doubles $28/39. There are decent, tidy timber-lined pub rooms here, with air-con and shared toilets and showers. The amenities could do with some maintenance though.

*Wagon Wheel Motel (☎ 4742 1866, fax 4742 1819, 54 Ramsay St)* Singles/doubles from $54/69. Recently renovated, the rooms here are clean and comfortable, the new owners friendly and there is a good *restaurant* that serves superb pasta (mains $8-26).

*Gidgee Inn (☎ 4742 1599, fax 4742 2431, e gidgeeinn@bigpond.com.au, Matilda Hwy)* Rooms from $104. This is an interesting and attractive upmarket motel built from rammed red earth and trimmed with corrugated iron. The rooms are modern and spotless, and there is an excellent **bar and grill** here (mains $10-25).

## CLONCURRY TO MT ISA

After Cloncurry, the terrain finally starts to change as you leave the plains behind and pass into the low, rocky, scrub-scattered red hills surrounding Mt Isa.

This 124km stretch of the Barkly Hwy has several interesting stops. Beside the **Corella River**, 44km west of Cloncurry, there's a memorial cairn to the Burke and Wills expedition, which passed here in 1861. Another 1km down the road is the **Kalkadoon & Mitakoodi Memorial**, which marks an old Aboriginal tribal boundary (see the boxed text 'Last Stand of the Kalkadoons' in this section). Unfortunately both have been vandalised, but are still worth a stop.

Another 9km on you pass the (unmarked) former site of **Mary Kathleen**, a uranium-mining town from the 1950s to 1982, now completely demolished.

The turn-off to **Lake Julius**, Mt Isa's reserve water supply, is 36km past Mary Kathleen. The lake is on the Leichhardt River, 90km of unsealed road from the highway. It is a popular spot for fishing, canoeing, sailing and water-skiing, and the excellent

**Lake Julius Recreation Camp** (☎ *4742 5998, 4742 2186, fax 4742 5110, Lake Julius Rd*) offers a cheap getaway, with camping ($2.60), dorm beds ($5.50) and eight-bed self-contained units ($32.60 for four, extras $6.30).

Near here is **Battle Mountain**, which was the scene of the last stand of the Kalkadoon people in 1884.

## MT ISA

**postcode 4825 • pop 22,190**

Mt Isa owes its existence to an immensely rich copper, silver, lead and zinc mine, whose massive 270m lead smelter exhaust stack dominates the skyline. 'The Isa', as it is known locally, is inland Queensland's major town.

It's a rough-and-ready but prosperous place, and the job opportunities here have attracted people from about 60 different ethnic groups. Aesthetically and geographically, Mt Isa is a long way from anywhere, but it's definitely worth staying a few days. Apart from anything else, descending into one of the world's largest underground mines is an experience not to be missed.

Prospector John Campbell Miles discovered the first deposits here in 1923, and gave Mt Isa its name – a corruption of Mt Ida, a

---

### Last Stand of the Kalkadoons

Before European settlement, the arid, rocky hills north-west of Mt Isa were home to the Kalkadoons, a fierce and bellicose Aboriginal tribe. The Kalkadoons were one of the last tribes to resist white settlement, and from the mid-1870s fought an ongoing battle against pastoralists and the Native Police.

They were a formidable and feared opponent who often used guerrilla tactics to attack settlers and troops. Warriors decorated themselves with body-paint and feathers, and used pole clubs, razor-sharp tomahawks and knives made from local stone for weapons.

In 1884 the authorities sent Frederic Urquhart, the sub-inspector of police, to the region to take command, but the Kalkadoons continued to ambush and attack the invaders. In September of that year, Urquhart gathered his heavily-armed troops and local squatters and rode to the rocky hill that came to be known as Battle Mountain.

When they saw the mounted troops, the Kalkadoons formed themselves into ranks and made a series of disciplined but suicidal charges down the hill. Armed with only spears they stood no chance against the troopers' carbines, and were mown down in waves until they were practically wiped out. Only a handful survived and the massacre marked the end of the region's Aboriginal resistance.

A memorial beside the Barkly Hwy, 45km west of Cloncurry, is inscribed: 'You who pass by are now entering the ancient tribal lands of the Kalkadoon/Mitakoodi, dispossessed by the European. Honour their name, be brother and sister to their descendants'.

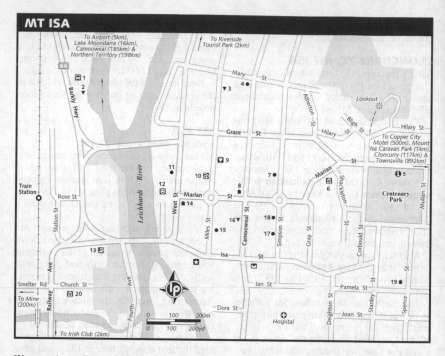

**MT ISA**

To Airport (5km),
Lake Moondarra (16km),
Camooweal (185km) &
Northern Territory (198km)

To Riverside
Tourist Park (2km)

Lookout

To Copper City
Motel (500m), Mount
Isa Caravan Park (1km),
Cloncurry (117km) &
Townsville (892km)

Centenary
Park

Train
Station

Leichhardt River

Smelter Rd

To Mine
(200m)

To Irish Club (2km)

Hospital

0   100   200m
0   100   200yd

Western Australian goldfield. Since the ore deposits were large and low grade, working them required the sort of investment only a company could afford. Mt Isa Mines (MIM) was founded in 1924. Life was predictably rough and tough in Mt Isa's early days and the Isa Hotel had a 'bullring' in its backyard for men to sort out their personal differences. It was during and after WWII that Mt Isa really took off; today it's among the world's top three producers of silver and the top 10 of copper and zinc – the ore is railed 900km to Townsville on the coast. The company's importance to the town is undeniable – its activities support around 5000 jobs and it spends some $300m a year in wages and payments to local contractors and suppliers. Over the past five years, MIM has invested about $1 billion in the town's mining operations.

## Information

The Riversleigh Fossils Museum and Tourist Information Centre (☎ 4749 1555,

19 Marian St; open 8.30am to 5pm weekdays, 9am to 2pm weekends) is in Centenary Park, east of the centre.

The Mt Isa Newsagency (☎ 4743 9105, 25b Miles St) has 10 Internet terminals available for $6.60 an hour. The city library (☎ 4744 4266, 23 West St) has four terminals and charges $2 for 15 minutes.

Book Country is an excellent bookshop with a good travel section in Isa Square in Simpson St.

Power Automotive (☎ 4743 2542, 13 Simpson St) is the RACQ agent, while the Environmental Protection Agency (EPA; ☎ 4744 7888, corner of Mary and Camooweal Sts) can provide information on the area's national parks, including Lawn Hill and Camooweal Caves.

## The Mine

The town's major attraction is undoubtedly the mine (☎ 4749 1555; underground tour $60, surface tour adult/child $17.60/8.80;

## MT ISA

**PLACES TO STAY**
8   Mercure Hotel Mt Isa
14   Hotel Boyd
19   Travellers Haven

**PLACES TO EAT**
2   Rafles
3   Lunch Box Cafe
16   Los Toros Mexican Restaurant

**OTHER**
1   Campbell's Coaches Terminal
4   EPA Office
5   Riversleigh Fossils Museum & Tourist
     Information Centre
6   Frank Aston Museum
7   Book Country
9   Switches Nightclub
10   Mt Isa Newsagency
11   Mt Isa Library
12   Civic Centre
13   Swimming Pool
15   Ansett
17   Four Wheel Drive Hire Service
18   RACQ
20   John Middlin Mining Display &
     Visitors Centre

*underground tours 7.30am & 10.30am Mon-Fri, surface tours 9am & 1pm Mon-Sat).* There are two tours available and both require advance bookings. The eye-opening four-hour underground tour, for which you don a hard hat and miners suit, is one you shouldn't miss. It takes you down into some of the 1000km of dark, humid tunnels up to 1km under the surface, where you're transported in a specially-built 4WD. You must be over 16 for this tour.

Campbell's Coaches runs the rewarding two-hour surface tour, which takes you right through the major workshops and mine site. You must wear enclosed shoes, so no sandals or thongs (flip flops).

### John Middlin Mining Display & Visitors Centre

This centre (*☎ 4749 1429, Church St; adult/child $3/1; open 9am-4pm daily, closed Sat & Sun Nov-Mar)* provides an interesting insight to mining operations. The displays include an informative audio-visual

program, ore and mineral samples, and even a 'simulated underground experience', complete with the sensation of descending a shaft in a cage.

### Other Attractions

The **Frank Aston Museum** (*☎ 4743 0610, Cnr Shackleton & Marian Sts; adult/child $6/1; open 9am-4pm daily)* is an informal, partly underground complex on a hill close to the town centre. You follow a meandering path through a range of diverse exhibits, including old army vehicles and Aboriginal culture displays, before descending 70 steps down a vertical shaft to an extensive gemstone collection.

At the tourist office, the **Riversleigh Fossils Museum** features an important collection of fossils spanning 25 million years, which have revealed much about the evolution of Australia's unique wildlife. The fossils were found on a station near Lawn Hill National Park, 250km north-west of Mt Isa (the site now has World Heritage listing) and the centre has dioramas featuring some of the creatures discovered.

A short drive or climb off Hilary St is the **City Lookout** – coming up here certainly puts things into perspective. You can see virtually the whole town, sprawled out across a flat valley, backed by a series of low hills and watched over by the huge, dark, brooding mine. If you don't mind a rough climb, there's another excellent lookout at the eastern end of Pamela St.

**Lake Moondarra**, 16km north of town, is a popular spot for swimming, boating, waterskiing, fishing and birdwatching. There are barbecue facilities at the lake and at Warrina Park, which is just below the dam wall.

### Organised Tours

There's a large range of tours and activities that can be booked through the tourist office.

Look-About Trips (*☎ 4743 9523)* does day tours to Kajabbi and Lake Julius ($60), a night town tour ($10) and a half-day town tour ($15).

Between April and October, Campbell's Tours & Safaris (*☎ 4743 2006)* runs a three-day camping safari to Lawn Hill National

Park and the Riversleigh fossil sites ($451, with all meals and equipment supplied).

Air Mt Isa (☎ 4743 2844), the local mail run operator, runs tours to the area's more remote reaches, including Adels Grove at Lawn Hill National Park ($205), Kingfisher Camp on the Nicholson River ($225) and a gulf day tour ($270). Each requires a minimum of four people.

## Special Events
Held every August, the Mt Isa Rotary Rodeo is one of the biggest in Australia, with serious prize money up for grabs. It is held at Kalkadoon Park on the Barkly Hwy. The Mt Isa Show is held each June.

## Places to Stay – Budget
*Riverside Tourist Park (☎ 4743 3904, fax 4743 9417, 195 West St)* Camp sites/cabins $14/61. This large, palm-lined park is about 2km north of the centre. It's well set out, with a row of neat new cabins at the front, clean amenities and pleasant, shaded lawn sites.

*Mount Isa Caravan Park (☎ 4743 3252, fax 4743 3100, ℮ mtcvpark@austarnet .com.au, 112 Marian St)* Camp sites/on-site vans/cabins $13.50/33/55. An orderly and well-established park on the highway in the east of town, this friendly place has a big pool and plenty of trees and grass.

*Travellers Haven (☎ 4743 0313, fax 4743 4007, ℮ kimisa@one.net.au, 75 Spence St)* Dorm beds/singles/doubles $17/30/40. The clean Travellers Haven is the main budget accommodation option for travellers. It's generally quiet – save for the odd noisy weekend episode – and all the rooms have air-con and a fridge. There's a good pool, bikes for hire and a courtesy bus.

*Hotel Boyd (☎ 4743 3000, fax 4743 4090, 16 West St)* Rooms $30. There's not a lot of pub accommodation around, but this place offers the usual basic old-style rooms upstairs. They're satisfactory and pretty clean, with a double bed and air-con, and shared toilets and showers.

*West Leichhardt Station (☎ 4743 8947, fax 4743 3595, Lake Julius Rd)* Unpowered/ powered camp sites $10/12.50, powered caravan sites $25, rooms $77; meal prices

on application. This 1250 sq km cattle station, about half an hour's drive north-east of Mt Isa, can give you a taste of life in the sticks. It offers air-con rooms, limited camping and caravan sites, a barbecue area on the lawn and a tennis court.

## Places to Stay – Mid-Range & Top End
*Copper City Motel (☎ 4743 2033, fax 4743 2290, 105 Butler St)* Singles/doubles $65/75. The Copper City Motel is tucked away in a quiet spot east of the centre, and offers a good-value, mid-range option. It has simple modern rooms, hospitable owners and the entire place is spotlessly clean.

*Mercure Hotel Mt Isa (☎ 4743 3024, fax 4743 8715, ℮ tahlmerc@bigpond.com .au, Cnr Marian & Camooweal Sts)* Rooms from $115. This 4½-star place is the choice if you want to splash out. It has three storeys of modern, upmarket rooms (some with spectacular views of the mine lit up at night), a pool and an excellent licensed restaurant downstairs (see Places to Eat later).

## Places to Eat
*Lunch Box Cafe (☎ 4743 5454, Miles St)* Meals $3-10. For snacks, sandwiches and hot takeaways, this is the pick of the cafes.

*Keane's Bar & Grill (☎ 4743 2577, Nineteenth Ave)* Lunch $8-13, dinner $10-21. The Irish Club, 2km south of the centre, has this excellent, bistro-style place that serves generous helpings, from salmon stacks and garlic prawns to veal medallions and coral trout.

*Rafles (☎ 4743 3219, 17 Barkly Hwy)* Mains $15-22. On the banks of the Leichhardt River, Rafles is proof a rough mining town can have a soft underbelly. The decor whispers elegance, and the menu offers unusual treats like home-made Camooweal sausages.

*Los Toros Mexican Restaurant (☎ 4743 7718, 79 Camooweal St)* Mains $10-16. This lively Mexican-style eatery serves good sangria and a range of spicy dishes, including paella, burritos, chilli con carne and spicy chorizo. It also does takeaways.

*Verona Restaurant (☎ 4743 3024, Cnr Marian & Camooweal Sts)* Mains $16-27.

Located in the Mercure Hotel, the classy Verona Restaurant has an imaginative menu featuring seafood and Italian cuisine.

## Entertainment

*Switches Nightclub* (☎ *4749 0388, 26 Miles St)* Admission $5. Open until 5am Wed-Sat. A favourite with the younger crowd, Switches is a huge swanky club with a spacious dance area downstairs, and a restaurant and bar overlooking it.

*Irish Club* (☎ *4743 2577, Nineteenth Ave)* The bountiful Irish Club offers a variety of good entertainment. Live bands often play in Keane's Bar & Grill, while downstairs there's a popular neon-lit nightclub – 'The Rish' – and a karaoke bar.

*Civic Centre* (☎ *4744 4244, 23 West St)* Mt Isa's civic centre includes a theatre and a 1000-seat auditorium, and is the town's major venue for live concerts, plays, and balls.

## Getting There & Away

**Air** Macair flies to Brisbane ($520), Townsville ($369) Birdsville ($291) and Cairns ($528) from Mt Isa. See the Getting There and Away section at the start of the chapter for details of stops on each of these routes.

**Bus** The Campbell's Coaches terminal (☎ 4743 2006), at 29 Barkly Hwy, is the main McCafferty's/Greyhound depot. There are daily services between Townsville and Mt Isa ($108, 11½ hours), continuing on from Mt Isa to Tennant Creek in the NT ($97, seven hours). From Tennant Creek you can head north to Darwin ($216 from Mt Isa) or south to Alice Springs ($188). The company also has daily buses southeast to Brisbane ($144, 25 hours) through Winton ($64) and Longreach ($77).

Coral Coaches (☎ 4031 7577) travel to Normanton ($98) and Karumba ($111) twice weekly from the Campbell's Coaches terminal. You can book through Campbell's.

**Train** The *Inlander* operates twice weekly between Townsville and Mt Isa, via Charters Towers, Hughenden and Cloncurry. The full journey takes about 20 hours and costs

$96/134/204 for an economy seat/economy sleeper/1st-class sleeper.

## Getting Around

There are no local bus services. If you want a taxi, call ☎ 4743 2333.

There are several car hire firms in Mt Isa, including Avis (☎ 4743 3733), Hertz (☎ 4743 4142) and Thrifty (☎ 4743 2911).

Four Wheel Drive Hire Service (☎ 4743 6306, 4743 6581, 7 Simpson St) has Toyota Hiluxes (from $100 per day) and Landcruisers (from $115) both with 300km free per day. Camping packages, including vehicle, tent and equipment, are available for $160 per day.

## CAMOOWEAL

**postcode 4828 • pop 230**

Camooweal, 13km east of the Northern Territory border, is either your first or last chance to get fuel or food in Queensland, depending on which way you're headed. Be warned that the fuel here is fiendishly expensive – up to $0.20 more *per litre* than in Mt Isa.

The town was established in 1884 as a service centre for the vast cattle stations of the Barkly Tablelands, and is the turn-off for the Camooweal Caves National Park. You can also turn off here for Lawn Hill National Park, Gregory Downs and Burketown (see the Gulf Savannah chapter for details). There are a couple of historic buildings – the **Shire Hall** (1922) and **Freckleton's General Store**, an old corrugated-tin building on the main street. The Shell Roadhouse (☎ 4748 2155) is the local RACQ agent.

The *Post Office Hotel* (☎ *4748 2124, fax 4748 2125, Barkly Hwy)* has budget rooms, motel units and counter meals Monday to Saturday, and you can camp cheaply behind the Shell Roadhouse, although there's not much grass. For a home away from home, try the *Rainbow Hostel* (☎ *4748 2011, Barkly Hwy)*, with comfortable, private bedrooms ($15), a garden, laundry and resident canine.

## CAMOOWEAL CAVES NATIONAL PARK

Beneath the surface of this small national park is a network of unusual caves with sinkhole openings. The largest, the Great Nowranie Cave, is 70m deep and almost 300m long. The caves can be explored, but only if you're an experienced caver and have all the right equipment. For the average punter, the park can be dangerous to wander around in and it's extremely isolated.

If you are planning to visit, check with the local police and the EPA office in Mt Isa (☎ 4744 7888) first. The caves are usually flooded during the wet season, so the middle of the year is the best time to visit – at other times you can expect extremely high temperatures and the usual precautions apply.

The park entrance is 8km south of Camooweal along a rough, unsealed road. There are several creek crossings; the road is usually impassable after rain. There's a self-registration camping ground with toilets.

## CAMOOWEAL TO THREEWAYS

There's nothing much for the whole 460km from Camooweal to the Threeways junction in the Northern Territory. *Barkly Homestead* (☎ 08-8964 4549, fax 8964 4543, Barkly Hwy), 260km west of Camooweal, has unpowered/powered sites for $5/21 and single/double motel-style rooms for $75/90.

# Cloncurry to Cunnamulla – The Matilda Highway

The Matilda Hwy is the best and most popular north-south route through outback Queensland. This bitumen highway starts at the Queensland–New South Wales border south of Cunnamulla and runs north for over 1700km, ending in Karumba on the Gulf.

The Matilda Hwy takes you through most of the outback's major towns and to some of its best tourist attractions, including the Australian Workers Heritage Centre in Barcaldine and the Stockman's Hall of Fame in Longreach.

The Matilda Hwy is in fact the name given to a route made up of several roads and highways. It consists of sections of the Mitchell Hwy, the Landsborough Hwy and the Burke Developmental Rd. Only the Cloncurry to Cunnamulla section is covered in this chapter – see the Gulf Savannah chapter for details of the northern section of the route.

### Maps

The Department of Natural Resources Queensland has produced a map called *The Matilda Highway*; it can be purchased from Sunmap agencies, service stations and bookshops.

## CLONCURRY TO WINTON

About 14km east of Cloncurry, the narrow Landsborough Hwy turns off the Flinders Hwy and heads south-east to Winton via the one-pub towns of McKinlay and Kynuna.

The first section of this 341km route, from Cloncurry to McKinlay, passes through a rugged and rocky landscape of low, craggy hills; these gradually give way to the flat plains that characterise most of the outback.

### McKinlay

McKinlay is a tiny settlement that would probably have been doomed to eternal insignificance were it not home to the **Walkabout Creek Hotel**, which featured in the amazingly successful movie *Crocodile Dundee* starring Paul Hogan. Stills from the film and other Dundee memorabilia clutter the walls of the pub, but unfortunately recent renovations have subtracted substantially from its knockabout charm. A better stopover is down the road at Kynuna's Blue Heeler Hotel.

*Walkabout Creek Hotel* (☎ 4746 8424, fax 4746 8768, Landsborough Hwy) has some small and simple units with air-con (singles/doubles $42/52) a block west of the pub, or there's a basic camping ground (sites $6 per person) out the back.

### Kynuna

Kynuna, another 74km south-east, isn't much bigger than McKinlay. It's home to **Magoffin's Matilda Expo** (☎ 4746 8401, Landsborough Hwy; admission variable), a simultaneously gaudy and ramshackle 'museum' that claims to have the real story behind Australia's unofficial anthem 'Waltzing Matilda' told in curling photographs and documents pinned to the walls. Its colourful owner, Richard Magoffin, is a real outback character. He does live musical renditions of the song, two-hour shows at night, and promises a peek at what he says is the original hand-written composition penned by Banjo Patterson in 1895. Whether you believe it or not, it's well worth a visit (there's a variable 'exit fee') and is a stark contrast to the flashy Waltzing Matilda Centre at Winton.

There's a lot to like about the historic little **Blue Heeler Hotel** (*☎ 4746 8650, fax 4746 8643,* e *blueheelerhotel@bigpond.com, Landsborough Hwy*), from its walls covered with scrawled messages and signatures, to its unquestionably essential Surf Life Saving Club. It's a friendly place with good meals, pub rooms ($33), spotless air-con motel units ($55), and camp sites ($3) in the adjacent Jolly Swag-van Park.

The nearest beach may be almost 1000km away, but each August the Blue Heeler hosts its own surf life-saving carnival. The locals carry a surf boat up the main street, compete in surfboard relays and a tug of war, and top it all off with an evening beach party.

## Kynuna to Winton (165km)
The turn-off to the **Combo Waterhole**, which Banjo Paterson is said to have visited in 1895 before he wrote 'Waltzing Matilda', is signposted off the highway about 12km east of Kynuna. The waterhole is on Dagworth Station.

## WINTON
### postcode 4735 • pop 1200
Winton is a cattle- and sheep-raising centre, and also the railhead from which the beasts are transported after being brought from the Channel Country by road train. The town has two major claims to fame: the founding of Qantas airlines in 1920, and the regionally inspired verse of one of Australia's most famous poets, Banjo Paterson. Both are commemorated inside the impressive Waltzing Matilda Centre on the main street.

The North Gregory Hotel holds its place in history as the venue where 'Waltzing Matilda' reportedly was first performed on April 6 1895, although the original building burnt down in 1900.

Winton is a friendly, laid-back place with some interesting attractions and characters, and is a good place for a stopover if you're not in a hurry.

## Information
The modern Waltzing Matilda Centre (see Things to See & Do later) is also the tourist information centre.

Winton Fuel & Tyre Centre (*☎ 4657 1305*) is the local RACQ depot. The town library (*☎ 4657 1188, 75 Vindex St*) has Internet access at $3 an hour; so does the Winton Neighbourhood Centre (*☎ 4657 1287, 19 Cork St*).

## Things to See & Do
Winton's biggest attraction is the **Waltzing Matilda Centre** (*☎ 4657 1466, 50 Elderslie St; adult/child $14/12; open 8.30am-5pm*). There's a surprising amount here for a museum devoted to a song, including an indoor billabong, complete with a squatter, troopers and a jolly swagman; a hologram display oozing nationalism; and the **Jolly Swagman** statue – a tribute to the unknown swagmen who lie in unmarked graves in the area. The centre also houses a gallery and the **Qantilda Pioneer Place**, which has a huge collection of fascinating artefacts as well as displays on the founding of Qantas.

The **Corfield & Fitzmaurice Building** (*☎ 4657 1486, 63 Elderslie St; adult/child $5/1; open 9am-5pm Mon-Fri, 9am-12.30pm Sat*) is a former general store now classified by the National Trust. It has been restored to house a craft cooperative centre with a huge gem and mineral collection, and a life-size recreation of a dinosaur stampede that occurred at what is now Lark Quarry, south-west of Winton (see the South of Winton section later in this chapter).

The **Royal Theatre**, at the rear of the Gift and Gem Centre (*☎ 4657 1296, 73 Elderslie St*) in the centre of town, is a wonderful open-air theatre with canvas-slung chairs,

## 100 Years of Waltzing Our Matildas

Written in 1895 by Banjo Paterson, 'Waltzing Matilda' is widely regarded as Australia's unofficial national anthem.

While not many can sing the official national anthem, 'Advance Australia Fair', without a lyric sheet, just about every Aussie knows the words to the strange ditty about a jolly swagman who jumped into a billabong and drowned himself rather than be arrested for stealing a jumbuck (sheep). But what the hell does it mean?

The Waltzing Matilda Centenary festival, held in Winton in April 1995, created a raging controversy among local historians over the origins and meaning of the famous tune, with first Winton, then Kynuna, claiming to be the true 'birthplace' of 'Waltzing Matilda'.

To understand the song's origins, it has to be seen in the political context of its time. The 1890s were a period of social upheaval and political change in Queensland. Along with nationalistic calls for the Australian states to amalgamate and form a federation, economic crisis, mass unemployment and severe droughts dominated the decade. An ongoing battle between pastoralists and shearers led to a series of strikes that divided the state and led to the formation of the Australian Labor Party to represent workers' interests.

In 1895 Paterson visited his fiancée in Winton, and together they travelled to Dagworth Station south of Kynuna, where they met Christina McPherson. During their stay there went on a picnic to the Combo Waterhole, a series of billabongs on the Diamantina River, where Paterson heard stories about the violent 1894 shearers' strike on Dagworth Station. During the strike rebel shearers had burned seven woolsheds to the ground, leading the police to declare martial law and place a reward of £1000 on the head of their leader, Samuel Hofmeister. Rather than be captured, Hofmeister drowned himself in a billabong near the Combo Waterhole.

Paterson later wrote the words to 'Waltzing Matilda' to accompany a tune played by Christina McPherson on a zither. While there is no direct proof he was writing allegorically about Hofmeister and the shearers' strikes, a number of prominent historians have supported the theory and claimed the song was a political statement. Others maintain it is just an innocent but catchy tune about a hungry vagrant, but the song's undeniable antiauthoritarianism, and the fact that it was adopted as an anthem by the rebel shearers, weigh heavily in favour of the former argument.

corrugated tin walls and a star-studded ceiling. It has a small museum in the projection room (admission $2) and screens 'nostalgia nights' on Wednesdays from April to October, featuring old favourites like Laurel and Hardy, and Abbott and Costello.

**Arno's Wall** is Winton's quirkiest attraction – a 70m-long work-in-progress featuring a huge range of household items ensnared in the mortar, from televisions to motorbikes. It's in Vindex St, behind the North Gregory Hotel.

### Organised Tours

Diamantina Outback Tours (☎ 4657 1514) offers day trips to the Lark Quarry Environmental Park and Merton Gorge ($85 with lunch included).

QOTS Air Charter (☎ 4657 1340) takes a three-day flying tour of the outback, including Lake Eyre, Innamincka and Birdsville. There's a minimum of five people per flight, and the cost is $1200 per person, with all meals, accommodation and tours included. There are also day trips to Lawn Hill National Park ($475), or you can inquire about other destinations including Uluru, Alice Springs and Carnarvon Gorge.

You can also take a day trip to Carisbrooke Station – see the South of Winton section for details.

### Special Events

Winton holds the five-day Outback Festival in September every second (odd) year. It features crayfish races, a dunny derby, ironman and ironwoman competitions, country music, bush bands and buskers.

The annual Bush Poetry Festival, in July, attracts entrants from all over Australia keen to perform some verse for a prize. It culminates in the announcement of the winner of the Bronze Swagman Award for written poetry.

The town also hosts Easter in the Outback annually, along with Longreach, Ilfracombe and Barcaldine. It's a four-day festival involving all four towns, beginning with a race meeting in Barcaldine, and including exhibitions, motorcycle races and celebrations of bush poetry.

## Places to Stay

*Matilda Country Tourist Park (☎/fax 4657 1607, e matpark@tpg.com.au, 43 Chirnside St)* Camp sites $12 a double, cabins $60. If you're camping, this place in the northern end of town is a good choice. It has lawn sites and good barbecue facilities, and puts on regular campfire meals, complete with bush poetry and yarns.

*North Gregory Hotel (☎ 1800 801 611, 4657 1375, fax 4657 0106, e northgregoryhotel@yahoo.com.au, 67 Elderslie St)* Singles/doubles from $33/44 (2nd night half price). The epitome of the big, friendly country pub, the North Gregory has dozens of comfortable old-fashioned air-con rooms upstairs with spotless shared facilities.

*Pelican Waters Motel (☎ 4657 1211, fax 4657 1331, Elderslie St)* Singles/doubles $75/86. For something more up-market, Pelican Waters offers large, modern rooms with all the trappings. There's a good saltwater pool, and the tariff includes a free continental breakfast.

## Places to Eat

*North Gregory Hotel* Mains $10-18. You can eat good bistro meals here, in the bar or the dining room next door. It's the usual fare of steak, fish and chicken, but the pub prides itself on big, old-fashioned serves, so you won't go hungry.

*Tattersalls Hotel (☎ 4657 1309, 78 Elderslie St)* Mains $10-18. The dining room

here is decorated with weathered corrugated iron, rusty old saws and iron wheels, and two old car doors frame the entrance. You can eat good pub food in here, or alfresco on the footpath.

*Mulga Bill's Steakhouse (☎ 4657 1211, Elderslie St)* Mains $17-30. Located at the Pelican Waters Motel, this place is kind of pricey, but you can get good value for money with a massive 500g rump steak.

## Getting There & Away

Winton is on the main Brisbane to Mt Isa bus route, and you can get here with McCafferty's/Greyhound.

There are also connecting bus services between Winton and Longreach that meet up with the twice-weekly *Spirit of the Outback* train.

Macair flies to Winton from Townsville ($259) and Longreach ($78).

## SOUTH OF WINTON

The country around Winton is rough and rugged, with much wildlife, notably brolgas. There are also Aboriginal sites with paintings, carvings and artefacts.

It's a bit out of the way, but the **Lark Quarry Environmental Park**, where hundreds of dinosaur footprints are preserved in the rock, is worth the trip. The park is well-signposted 110km south-west of Winton, and it takes about 90 minutes to drive there, but the mostly dirt road is impassable in wet weather. Once a prehistoric lake, the area was the scene of a stampede of small dinosaurs startled by a large predator. It is now protected by a sheltered walkway, although there are no other facilities here other than a toilet and a rainwater tank. Contact the Waltzing Matilda Centre at Winton for more information. Alternatively, Diamantina Outback Tours (☎ 4657 1514) runs day trips from Winton to Lark Quarry for $85 per person (minimum of four).

*Carisbrooke Station (☎/fax 4657 3984, Cork Mail Rd)* offers accommodation in camp sites for $5, shearers' quarters or a cottage for $28, or a self-contained unit for $33 (all per-person rates). Set amid spectacular escarpment country 85km south-west of

Winton, this is an interesting place that features a wildlife sanctuary, an old opal mine, Aboriginal paintings and bora rings (ceremonial grounds). The station offers day tours (with advance notice) starting from Winton ($110 per person, minimum of four).

The **Opalton Mining Field**, 112km south of Winton, is a remote gemfield where the unique boulder opals can be found. Unlike opals from places like Lightning Ridge and Coober Pedy, which are found in clay, boulder opals are attached to a host rock that has to be ground away to free the opal. The name relates more to the host rocks than to the size of the opals. There are few facilities here, and the road is unsealed and slow going.

## LONGREACH
**postcode 4730 • pop 4500**
This prosperous outback town was the home of Qantas early last century, but these days it's equally famous for the Australian Stockman's Hall of Fame & Outback Heritage Centre, probably the biggest attraction in outback Queensland.

Longreach's human population is vastly outnumbered by more than a million sheep, and there are a fair few cattle too.

## Information
The tourist information office (☎ 4658 3555, 99 Eagle St; open 9am to 5pm weekdays, 9am to 1pm weekends) is in the centre of town. The local RACQ depot is Slade's Smash Repairs (☎ 4658 1609) at 146 Crane St. The Longreach library (☎ 4658 4104, 96a Eagle St, open half days on Tuesday, Thursday and Saturday from 9am, and Wednesday and Friday from 12.30pm) has free Internet access. The Queensland Parks and Wildlife Service (QPWS; ☎ 4652 7333, Landsborough Hwy) has an office in a group of government buildings just east of the Hall of Fame. It offers a range of information about the area's national parks.

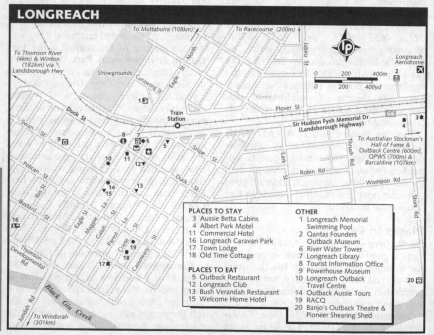

LONGREACH

**PLACES TO STAY**
3 Aussie Betta Cabins
4 Albert Park Motel
11 Commercial Hotel
16 Longreach Caravan Park
17 Town Lodge
18 Old Time Cottage

**PLACES TO EAT**
5 Outback Restaurant
12 Longreach Club
13 Bush Verandah Restaurant
15 Welcome Home Hotel

**OTHER**
1 Longreach Memorial Swimming Pool
2 Qantas Founders Outback Museum
6 River Water Tower
7 Longreach Library
8 Tourist Information Office
9 Powerhouse Museum
10 Longreach Outback Travel Centre
14 Outback Aussie Tours
19 RACQ
20 Banjo's Outback Theatre & Pioneer Shearing Shed

OUTBACK QUEENSLAND

## The Origins of Qantas

Qantas, the Queensland & Northern Territory Aerial Service, had humble beginnings as a joy flight and air taxi service in Queensland's outback – and at times it seems every second outback town has claimed to be the birthplace of Australia's major airline.

The idea to establish the airline came about when two former Flying Corps airmen, Hudson Fysh and Paul McGuinness, travelled through outback Queensland to prepare the route for the famous London to Melbourne Air Race. They saw the potential for an air service to link remote outback centres and established an airline with the financial backing of local pastoralists.

The fledgling company was registered for business at Winton on 16 November 1920, and the first official board meeting was held in the Winton Club. Soon afterwards it was decided to move the company headquarters to Longreach, where the first office was opened in Duck St, and Longreach remained the headquarters of Qantas until it moved to Brisbane in 1930.

Qantas' first regular air service, begun on 22 November 1922, was between Cloncurry and Charleville. Its first overseas passenger flight occurred on 17 April 1935 between Brisbane and Singapore. It took four days. After that, steady expansion saw the headquarters move to Sydney in 1938, and following WWII Qantas rebuilt and modernised its fleet.

By 1958 the flying kangaroo symbol was a familiar sight at airports in 23 countries. The acquisition of Boeing 707s in 1959, then 747s in 1971, saw the airline expand further.

In 1993, British Airways bought 25% of Qantas for $665 million.

Today the airline operates 145 aircraft, flies to 35 countries and transports 19 million passengers a year. It has a proud safety record, although in the past few years there have been some well-publicised hiccups, most notably the September 1999 accident at Bangkok airport, when a London-bound Qantas Boeing 747 slid off the end of the runway.

## Things to See & Do

**Australian Stockman's Hall of Fame & Outback Heritage Centre** (☎ *4658 2166, Landsborough Hwy; family/adult/child $44/18.70/8.80; open 9am-5pm daily*) is housed in a beautifully conceived building, 2km east of town towards Barcaldine. The centre was built as a tribute to the early explorers and stockmen, and also commemorates the crucial roles played by the pioneer women and Aboriginal stockmen, although the section on the latter is pathetically brief.

It's well worth visiting the Hall of Fame, as its excellent displays give a fascinating insight into this side of the European development of Australia. There are dozens of static exhibits featuring stories of the outback's characters and some excellent audiovisual displays like the **Talking Drover** – a computerised recreation of an old drover reminiscing in a stockman's bush camp at dusk.

There is a good bookshop, plus a souvenir shop and a cafe. The admission ticket is valid for two days, so allow yourself at least half a day to take it all in.

**Qantas Founders Outback Museum** (☎ *4658 3737, Landsborough Hwy; family/adult/concession/student $30/15/12/8; open 9am-5pm*) houses a life-size replica of an Avro 504K, the first aircraft owned by the fledgling airline, along with interactive multimedia and working displays, and permanent and temporary exhibitions. The museum tells the pioneering history of Qantas and outlines the challenges that were overcome to build the airline into what it is today. In March 2001, construction began on a massive new stage of this museum next to the original Qantas hangar, where six DH-50 biplanes were assembled in 1926.

**Powerhouse Museum** (☎ *4658 3933, 12 Swan St; adult/child $5/2; open 2pm-5pm daily Apr-Oct, varying days & hours Nov-Mar*), in Longreach's former powerhouse, houses the huge old diesel and gas-vacuum engines that were used until 1985 when a new power station on the edge of town was opened. Hard hats are supplied.

## Organised Tours

**Day Tours** There are several places along Eagle St that can organise a surprising variety of tours. You'll get pretty similar options at all of them, but the Longreach Outback Travel Centre (☎ 4658 1776, 115a Eagle St) tends to be more affordable. It offers a Longreach Lookabout tour (adult/child $80/40) that takes in the town's sites and ends with a dinner cruise on the Thomson River. There's also a tour to a merino station ($30/25), and outings to Barcaldine and the Australian Workers Heritage Centre ($80/55), Winton ($95/60) and Ilfracombe ($40/35).

Outback Aussie Tours (☎ 1300 787 890, 124b Eagle St) offers a Dinosaur Matilda Winton tour that includes Carisbrooke Station and Lark Quarry ($125/89).

**River Cruises** Yellowbelly Express (☎1800 641 661, 4658 2360) does popular river trips on the nearby Thomson River, including a two-course dinner (adult/child $35/19).

Billabong Boat Cruises (☎ 4658 1776) offers three-hour 'Sunset and Stars' dinner cruises, with live entertainment and a campfire meal under the stars (adult/child $30/17).

**Stations** You can also visit one or more of the area's sheep stations. They include: **Toobrack** (☎ 4658 9158), 68km south; **Oakley** (☎ 4658 3555), 15km north; and **Avington** (☎ 4657 5952, fax 4657 5025, e dexterja@ bigpond.com), 75km west of Blackall. Some of these places are open only for day trips while others offer accommodation and a range of activities. Avington, for example, has camp sites for $10 as well as homestead rooms for $137.50 per person ($60.50 per child), including B&B and dinner. Activities include trail-bike riding, canoeing, golf and barge cruises on the Barcoo River. Remember to phone ahead before visiting a station – don't just turn up unannounced.

## Special Events

Longreach, along with Winton, Barcaldine and Ilfracombe, holds Easter in the Outback

annually. In May, Longreach holds the Outback Muster Drovers Union & National Outback Performing Arts Show; and in July there are the Diamond Shears Shearing Championships and the Starlight Stampede Festival.

## Places to Stay

**Longreach Caravan Park** (☎ 4658 1770, fax 4658 0775, 180 Ibis St) Unpowered/ powered sites $11/13.20, on-site vans $27.50, self-contained villa vans $49.50. This is a neat, unassuming little place that has a pleasant, shady camping area, and its owners are hospitable and helpful. There's also a well-kept toilet/shower block and a good barbecue area.

**Commercial Hotel** (☎ 4658 1677, fax 4658 1798, 102 Eagle St) Singles/ doubles $27.50/38.50, motel $49.50/60. The small, modern pub rooms here are lacking somewhat in character, but they have air-con and are suitably clean and tidy. There are shared toilets and showers.

**Aussie Betta Cabins** (☎ 4658 3811, fax 4658 3812, 63 Sir Hudson Fysh Memorial Dr) Singles/doubles $58.30/67.10. This neat complex of 16 self-contained cabins is set amid palms and other greenery near the Hall of Fame. Each has two bedrooms and air-con, and sleeps up to five people. There is also a pool, outdoor garden and barbecue area here.

**Old Time Cottage** (☎ 4658 1550, 4658 3555, fax 4658 3733, 158 Crane St) Doubles $65, extras $7. This quaint little place is a good choice for a group or family as it sleeps up to six. Set in an attractive garden, it's a fully furnished, self-contained, old-style timber cottage with a polished wood floor and air-con.

**Town Lodge** (☎ 4658 1516, 161 Crane St) $33 per person, $44 with breakfast. The Town Lodge is an unusual place offering good-value accommodation. It has fairly small but spotless air-con rooms with all linen supplied, clean shared bathrooms, and will supply breakfast on request.

**Albert Park Motel** (☎ 1800 812 811, 4658 2411, fax 4658 3181, Sir Hudson Fysh Memorial Dr) Singles/doubles $75/85. The upmarket Albert Park Motel, on the highway east of the centre, has large, modern and well-appointed rooms. The complex also has a good pool, spa and a licensed *restaurant*.

## Places to Eat
There are several cafes and takeaways along Eagle St, and the pubs offer the usual suspects.

*Welcome Home Hotel* (☎ 4658 1361, 128 Eagle St) Lunches $5.50. This pub on the main street has cheap daily lunch specials, as well as the standard steak and chicken options.

*Bush Verandah Restaurant* (☎ 4658 2448, 120 Galah St) Mains $14-25. Open Tues-Sat. This is a small, licensed eatery with rustic decor and a country-style a la carte menu featuring beef, poultry and seafood dishes. It looks a bit run down from the outside, but that's apparently part of the bush theme.

*Outback Restaurant* (☎ 4658 1088, 84 Galah St) Mains $10-24. Open for dinner daily. The Outback Restaurant is a wise choice if you're looking for something above the ordinary. Located at the Longreach Motor Inn, it's a licensed place offering international cuisine – pasta, seafood and grills – and some vegetarian dishes.

*Longreach Club* (☎ 4658 1016, 31 Duck St) Meals $10-13. Open lunch & dinner.

---

### Captain Starlight

Longreach was the starting point for one of Queensland's most colourful early crimes. In 1870 Harry Redford and two accomplices stole 1000 head of cattle from Mt Cornish, north of Longreach, and drove them down the Thomson River and its continuation, Cooper Creek, to the present site of Innamincka. From there he followed the Strzelecki Creek south, finally selling his ill-gotten gains to a station owner north of Adelaide.

His exploit opened up a new stock route south, and when he was finally brought to justice in Roma in 1873, he was found not guilty by the adoring public! Rolf Boldrewood's novel *Robbery Under Arms* later immortalised Redford as 'Captain Starlight'.

---

The relaxed Longreach Club's restaurant is recommended for its range of cheap specials, including smorgasbords, roasts and beef stroganoff, while its huge seafood platter is a speciality ($46 for two). There is also has an a la carte menu.

## Entertainment
*Banjo's Outback Theatre & Pioneer Shearing Shed* (☎ 4658 2360, Stork Rd) Adult/child $14/9, with meal $26/15. This is a ramshackle place with two-hour shows most Saturday evenings and Tuesday and Thursday morning; shows include bush poems, songs, yarns and skits, as well as shearing, wool classing and spinning.

## Getting There & Away
**Air** Macair flies to Longreach from Townsville ($299).

**Bus** McCafferty's/Greyhound has daily services to Winton ($28, two hours), Mt Isa ($77, eight hours) and Brisbane ($107, 17 hours), and two services a week to Rockhampton ($68, 9½ hours). Buses stop at the Outback Travel Centre (☎ 4658 1776) at 115a Eagle St.

**Train** The twice-weekly *Spirit of the Outback* connects Longreach with Brisbane via Rockhampton ($181/273, 24 hours in an economy/1st-class sleeper); there are connecting bus services between Longreach and Winton ($31).

## LONGREACH TO WINDORAH – THE THOMSON DEVELOPMENTAL ROAD
The 310km Thomson Developmental Rd, which roughly follows the Thomson River from Longreach to Windorah, is the most direct way to Birdsville (via the Diamantina Development Rd) from Longreach. The route's first section, from Longreach to Jundah (215km), is over a narrow sealed road; the second leg, from Jundah to Windorah (95km), is over unsealed roads of dirt and gravel, and then soft red sand – this section is slower going and is often closed during the Wet.

On the way you'll come across the tiny settlement of **Stonehenge**, with half a dozen tin houses and the **Stonehenge Hotel** (☎ 4658 5944, fax 4658 5927, Stafford St), which has rooms from $30, daily meals and sells fuel.

Further on, **Jundah** has a **general store**, roadhouse, a cheap **caravan park** and the **Jundah Hotel-Motel** (☎/fax 4658 6166, Dickson St) with clean, tidy air-con rooms at $30/50 for singles/doubles.

## LONGREACH TO BARCALDINE
### Ilfracombe
This tiny little township 28km east of Longreach modestly calls itself 'the Hub of the West' and boasts a railway station, **general store**, swimming pool, golf course and a good pub.

The **Ilfracombe Machinery and Heritage Museum** (Landsborough Hwy; admission free; open permanently), on the northern side of the highway in the town centre, features a brightly painted collection of old tractors and farm machinery, carts and buggies, and several historic buildings, including claustrophobic old jail cells.

### Places to Stay & Eat
**Wellshot Hotel** (☎ 4658 2106, fax 4658 3926, Landsborough Hwy) Unpowered/powered sites $5/11, singles/doubles $16.50/33. The charming Wellshot Hotel has an eclectic collection of memorabilia, including walls lined with stencilled woolpacks, old stockman's hats and a bar made from old wool presses. There's even a wall entirely covered with a long poem called The Wellshot & The Bush Pub's Hall of Fame by Robert Raftery. The pub also has accommodation: clean, simple rooms with shared facilities out the back, and a basic camping ground next door. There are also quality country-style meals available.

## BARCALDINE
postcode 4725 • pop 1800
Barcaldine (pronounced Bar-**call**-din) lies at the junction of the Landsborough and Capricorn Hwys, 575km west of Rockhampton via Emerald, and is surrounded by sheep and cattle stations. It's known as the 'Garden City of the West', with good supplies of artesian water nourishing orchards of citrus fruits (in 1887 Barcaldine was the first town in Australia to realise its underground bounty).

Established in 1886 when the railway arrived, Barcaldine gained a place in Australian history in 1891 when it became the headquarters of the historic shearers' strike, during which more than 1000 men camped in and around the town. That confrontation saw troops called in, and the formation of the Australian Workers' Party, the forerunner of today's Australian Labor Party. The **Tree of Knowledge**, a ghost gum near the station, was the organisers' meeting place, and still stands as a monument to workers and their rights.

The Australian Workers Heritage Centre is one of the outback's major attractions and, although it doesn't quite have the stature of Longreach's Hall of Fame, it's impressive and worthwhile in its own way.

On the main street is **The Artesian Memorial**, a giant windmill dedicated to the pioneers who explored the Artesian Basin.

**BARCALDINE**

**PLACES TO STAY**
10  Shakespeare Hotel
13  Blacksmith's Cottage
14  Homestead Caravan Park
17  Landsborough Lodge Motel

**PLACES TO EAT**
3  Commercial Hotel
4  Cullen's Café
9  Witch's Kitchen/Union Hotel
18  3Ls Bar & Bistro

**OTHER**
1  McCafferty's/Greyhound Bus Stop
2  RACQ
5  Radio Theatre
6  Tourist Information Centre; Artesian Memorial
7  Tree of Knowledge
8  Swimming Pool
11  Barcaldine Library
12  Australian Workers Heritage Centre
15  Barcaldine & District Folk Museum
16  Mad Mick's

OUTBACK QUEENSLAND

## Information

Barcaldine's tourist information centre (☎ 4651 1724, Oak St) is next to the train station.

The local RACQ depot is Whyte's Service Centre (☎ 4651 1677).

Cullen's Café (☎ 4651 1588, 115 Oak St) offers Internet access on three terminals at $2 an hour; the library (☎ 4651 1170, 71 Ash St, open varying hours Monday to Saturday) has one terminal for $2.20 an hour.

## Australian Workers Heritage Centre

Built to commemorate the role played by workers in the formation of Australian social, political and industrial movements, the Australian Workers Heritage Centre (☎ 4651 2422, Ash St; adult/concession/child $9.90/ 7.70/5.50; open 9am-5pm Mon-Sat, 10am-5pm Sun) was opened during the Labor Party's centenary celebrations in Barcaldine in 1991.

Set in landscaped grounds around a central billabong, the centre includes the impressive **Australian Bicentennial Theatre**, a huge, circular big top that toured Australia in 1988 as part of the Bicentennial celebrations. A theatre inside regularly screens the short film *Celebration of a Nation*, and there is an interesting display here tracing the history of the shearers' strike.

The **Torrens Creek schoolhouse** is an old-fashioned classroom with timber desks, slates, pupils and an original school bell. It also has the classic 'Good Manners' poster, which instructed students to 'Be Honest, Truthful and Pure' and 'Do Not Bully; Only Cowards Do This'.

Other displays include a replica of an **Old Hospital Ward**, a **Powerhouse** contrasting the old generators with the power supplies of the future, a replica of Queensland's Legislative Assembly, and the **Workers Wall**, a photographic montage of prominent Labor Party members.

This centre is a major achievement and offers a fascinating look into Australian history. The entrance gate is at the western end of the complex and the ticket is valid for seven days.

## Other Attractions

The **Barcaldine & District Folk Museum** (☎ 4651 1310, 70 Gidyea St; admission $3; open 7am-5pm) is in the town's former National Bank. Built in 1906 and a museum since 1973, it is crammed with a fascinating collection of memorabilia, and offers mini-steam train rides.

**Mad Mick's** (Funny Farm or Slab Hut; ☎ 4651 1172, 84 Pine St; adult/concession/ child $8.50/7.50/5) is open most mornings between April and September – check with the information centre. It is a ramshackle, cluttered farmlet with a collection of historic buildings, art studios, shearers' quarters and dray sheds. There's also a small fauna park with emus, possums, peacocks and wallabies.

The **Radio Theatre** (☎ 4651 2488, 4 Beech St; adult/child $8/6, open Thur-Sun) is a dilapidated old building that offers an old-fashioned movie-going experience, complete with old-style canvas seats. It shows recent releases in the evenings.

## Organised Tours

Artesian Country Tours (☎ 4651 2211) offers several day tours taking in Barcaldine (adult/child $99/50), or Longreach and Ilfracombe ($129/60). Then there's the Aramac and Gracevale tour ($129/60), which takes you to Aboriginal Dreamtime sites, lava blowholes, caves and desert springs. There are also five- and six-day package deals (from $742), which include all three tours plus accommodation, meals and entry fees.

## Special Events

Regular celebrations in Barcaldine include the May Day long weekend and Labour Day march, the Tree of Knowledge race meeting (May), the Artesian Festival (sporadically) and the Bougainvillea Garden Competition. The town also co-hosts Easter in the Outback annually.

## Places to Stay

*Homestead Caravan Park* (☎/fax 4651 1308, 24 Box St) Unpowered/powered sites from $9/12, on-site vans from $27.50, cabins from $38.50. This neat, friendly place behind the Ampol service station puts on free billy tea and damper for guests in the late afternoons. It has plenty of room for campers, and a good amenities block.

**Shakespeare Hotel** (☎ *4651 1610, fax 4651 1331, e shakehtl@tpg.com.au, 95 Oak St)* Singles/doubles $16.50/27.50, backpacker rooms $10 per person. Polished boards and fresh paint upstairs, along with tidy rooms and friendly hosts, make for a pleasant pub stay. There are also clean, simple backpacker rooms and cooking facilities.

**Blacksmith's Cottage** (☎ *4651 1724, fax 4651 2243, 7 Elm St)* Singles/doubles $50/60 (extras $5). This quaint, turn-of-the-19th century B&B is an unusual accommodation experience. Period furniture and old-style rugs feature throughout, coupled with the modern conveniences of a microwave and electric stove. The tariff includes a light, self-serve breakfast.

**Landsborough Lodge Motel** (☎ *4651 1100, fax 4651 1744, 47 Box St)* Single/double motel units $64/75, budget units $49.50/55. South of the centre, Landsborough Lodge is a large, modern colonial-style place with spacious, comfortable rooms. It also has a row of small, brand-new 'budget' units at the rear.

### Places to Eat

**Commercial Hotel** (☎/fax *4651 1242, 119 Oak St)* Lunch $5-7, mains $12. Head here for a good pub feed, including crumbed barramundi and prawn kebabs, as well as daily specials.

**Cullen's Café** (☎ *4651 1588, 115 Oak St)* Lunch $3-7. This friendly cafe has a good range of fresh rolls and sandwiches, and you can check your emails here too.

**Witch's Kitchen** (☎ *4651 2269, 61 Oak St)* Lunch $5-8.50, mains $9-15.50. This little bistro at the Union Hotel serves a range of tasty, generously proportioned dishes. You can eat either in the pleasant dining area, or chatting with the bar staff.

**The 3Ls Bar & Bistro** (☎ *4651 2311, 72 Box St)* Mains $14-16. Located at the Iron Bark Inn, the rustic 3Ls offers an open barn-style dining experience, with wooden bench tables, stockmen's ropes on the walls and

(hopefully) a cool breeze. It serves country-style fare, including large steaks, pork chops and barramundi.

### Getting There & Away

Barcaldine is on the main Brisbane–Mt Isa bus route, and McCafferty's/Greyhound has daily services to Brisbane ($99, 9½ hours), Longreach ($17, one hour) and Mt Isa ($96, 9½ hours). You can also get to Rockhampton twice a week ($67, eight hours). Buses stop at the BP Roadhouse at the intersection of the Landsborough and Capricorn Hwys.

The *Spirit of the Outback* between Rockhampton and Longreach stops in Barcaldine twice weekly.

## BARCALDINE TO HUGHENDEN

From Barcaldine you can head north through the small but interesting towns of **Aramac** and **Muttaburra** to Hughenden, 357km from Barcaldine. The unsealed road from Muttaburra passes through flat country and can be a bit rough in places, but is usually quite manageable in a conventional vehicle with sufficient ground clearance if driven carefully.

## BARCALDINE TO ALPHA – THE CAPRICORN HIGHWAY

The Capricorn Hwy starts in Barcaldine and runs 136km across to Rockhampton on the coast.

Midway between Barcaldine and Alpha is the small township of **Jericho**, with a train station, pub and a *cafe*. There's a strange, interesting **sculpture** called *The Crystal Trumpeters* in the centre of town opposite the old town hall. Inspired by the trumpeters who blew down the walls of Jericho, it's an abstract work of large, clay trumpets surrounded by obelisk-like boulders.

The town has a *pub* with budget accommodation, and the local RACQ depot is Pearce's Garage (☎ 4651 4237).

## ALPHA

Alpha, 136km east of Barcaldine, has an interesting and growing collection of murals that was started by a group of local artists in 1991. The murals are on a number of public buildings along Shakespeare St, the main street, including the bakery, stock and station agent, railway station and school. There's even a great bush camping scene on the toilet block in front of the rail yards.

## Places to Stay & Eat

*Criterion Hotel (☎/fax 4985 1215, Shakespeare St)* Rooms $15/30. On the main street, the two-storey Criterion Hotel offers simple pub-style rooms upstairs with shared bathrooms, and serves *counter meals* daily.

*Alpha Hotel-Motel (☎ 4985 1311, fax 4985 1173, Shakespeare St)* Singles/doubles $49.50/60.50. If you're after something a little more comfortable, this place, further up the street, has neat air-con motel units.

There are also a couple of *caravan parks* in town.

## BLACKALL

postcode 4472 • pop 1800

Blackall claims to be the site of the mythical black stump – according to outback mythology, anywhere west of Blackall was considered to be 'beyond the black stump'.

Gazetted in 1868, Blackall is named after the second governor of Queensland, Samuel Blackall. The town is a pleasant spot to stop, and fuel and supplies are available from a good range of outlets.

Blackall prides itself on the fact that it was near here, at Alice Downs station, that legendary shearer Jackie Howe set his world record of shearing 321 sheep in less than eight hours with a set of hand shears (see the boxed text 'The Fastest Shears in the West' in the Darling Downs chapter). After his shearing days were over, Jackie ran one of the hotels in Blackall, where he's buried.

Blackall is also famous as the site of the first artesian well to be drilled in Queensland, although the well didn't strike water at first and when it did the product was undrinkable. After you use the bore water for washing or whatever, you'll probably agree with most travellers and say it stinks a little. Locals say it's got 'body'.

## Information

The Blackall Historic Woolscour & Tourist Office (☎/fax 4657 4637, Short St) is open 8.30am to 5pm weekdays and 9am to 3pm on weekends.

The local RACQ depot is Blackall Motors (☎ 4657 4136) and there's Internet access at $2.20 per half hour at the town library (☎ 4657 4764, 108 Shamrock St; open varying hours Tuesday to Saturday).

## Things to See & Do

The **Blackall Woolscour** *(☎ 4657 4637, Evora Rd; adult/concession/child $6.60/5.50/3.30; open 8am-4pm)*, the only steam-driven scour (wool-cleaner) left in Queensland, is 4km north-east of Blackall. Built in 1908, it operated until 1978 and all the machinery is intact and still in working order. This ramshackle complex is still in its formative stages, but incorporates a shearing shed, a wool-washing plant and a pond fed by an artesian bore. Book at the tourist office.

The bronze **Jackie Howe Memorial Statue** has pride of place in the town centre on the corner of Short and Shamrock Sts. When Jackie retired in 1900, he bought Blackall's Universal Hotel. The original pub was demolished in the 1950s, but the facade of the **New Universal Garden Centre & Gallery** *(☎ 4657 4344, 53 Shamrock St)*, built on the original site, reflects the old pub's design. The gallery houses a recently upgraded display of Jackie Howe memorabilia and souvenirs.

For a dip with a difference, try the **Blackall Aquatic Centre** *(☎ 4657 4975, Salvia St)*. The pool and spa are filled with artesian water which, despite the accompanying aroma, is clean and, some say, therapeutic.

The black stump display, explaining how the mythology came about, is on Thistle St.

## Special Events

Annual events in Blackall include the Claypan Bogie Country Music Festival (March) and the Black Stump Camel Races (July).

## Places to Stay & Eat

*Blackall Caravan Park (☎ 4657 4816, fax 4657 4327, ⓔ ahcarr@ozemail.com, 53 Garden St)* Unpowered/powered sites $12/15 a double, on-site vans from $28, units/cabins from $25/43 a double. This orderly little park is tucked into a quiet corner off the main street. It's a pleasant place to stay, with good camp sites, friendly owners and a clean, though small, amenities block.

***Prince of Wales Hotel** (☎ 4657 4731, fax 4657 4994, 63 Shamrock St)* Rooms without/with air-con $11/16. In terms of pub accommodation, this is the best value of an average lot. It has very basic rooms.

***Acacia Motor Inn** (☎ 4657 6022, fax 4657 6077, 110 Shamrock St)* Singles/doubles $68/79. The immaculate Acacia is right in the centre of town, near the Jackie Howe statue. It's a quality four-star motel with a licensed *bistro*, and modern, spacious rooms.

## ISISFORD

A small historic township 90km south of Ilfracombe and 125km west of Blackall, Isisford was established in 1877 by the Whitman brothers, two travelling hawkers who broke a wagon axle while crossing the Barcoo River and decided to stay. Kerry Packer's **Isis Downs Station**, with the largest shearing shed in Australia, is 20km east of Isisford.

Built in 1875, ***Clancy's Overflow Hotel** (☎ 4658 8210, fax 4658 8007, St Mary St)*, an archetypal timber pub, has bare budget accommodation downstairs ($20) and more comfortable rooms upstairs (singles/doubles $45/50), all of which have been recently renovated. It serves three *meals* daily.

There is a pleasant, free *camping area (☎ 4658 8900, fax 4658 8950)* on the banks of the river, east of the township. Toilets and showers are a short walk away, behind the shire office in St Mary St.

## IDALIA NATIONAL PARK

This remote national park off the Blackall-Emmet road 112km south-east of Blackall is only accessible with 4WD vehicles. In the rugged escarpment country of the Gowan Range, the park includes the headwaters of the Bulloo River and its numerous tributaries, with a predominantly mulga scrub landscape.

There are no facilities here and visitors need to be totally self-sufficient. Camping permits are required in advance; contact the park office (☎ 4657 5033) or the QPWS in Longreach (☎ 4652 7333) for more information on the area.

## BLACKALL TO CHARLEVILLE
### Barcoo River

Continuing south-east, the Landsborough Hwy crosses the Barcoo River 42km from Blackall and there is an excellent spot to stop and camp east of the road.

The Barcoo is one of western Queensland's great rivers and must be the only river in the world that becomes a creek in its lower reaches. It flows north-west past Blackall, then swings south-west through Isisford and into the Channel Country of south-western Queensland, where it becomes Cooper Creek, probably the most famous of Australia's inland rivers.

While Mitchell had waxed lyrical about this river in 1846, thinking it was a route to the Gulf, it was left to his second-in-command Edmund Kennedy (later of Cape York fame) to discover the river's real course and name it in 1847.

Both Banjo Paterson and Henry Lawson mention the Barcoo in their writings. The name has also entered the Australian idiom, appearing in the *Macquarie Dictionary* as the 'Barcoo salute' (waving to brush flies from the face).

### Tambo
**postcode 4478 • pop 400**
On the banks of the Barcoo River, Tambo is surrounded by perhaps the best grazing land in western Queensland, and has some of the region's earliest historic buildings. The main street boasts timber houses dating back to the town's earliest days in the 1860s, while the 'new' post office has been operating since 1904. The 'old' **post office**, built in 1876, and at the time the main repeating station for south-western Queensland, is now a museum.

The visitor information centre is at the Old Telegraph Museum (☎ 4654 6133, 12 Arthur St; open 10am to 5pm weekdays, 10am to 2pm Saturday). The RACQ depot is Rick's Tyre Centre (☎ 4654 6276).

Tambo promotes itself as 'the friendly town of the west' and each year horse races are held at the local track, a tradition dating back to the formation of the Great Western Downs Jockey Club in 1865.

It also has a flourishing teddy bear-making industry, and road signs on the main street warn motorists of crossing bears.

From Tambo you continue southwards on the Matilda Hwy, but for a good excursion, there is access to the **Salvator Rosa** section of Carnarvon National Park. Salvator Rosa is 120km east of Tambo via the Dawson Developmental Rd and Cungelella station, generally a 4WD route. See the Capricorn Coast chapter for more information on the Carnarvon National Park.

**Places to Stay** Both the *pubs* in the main street have basic budget rooms, and there is a rather rundown *caravan park* on the highway west of the centre. At the time of writing there were council plans for a new caravan park on the banks of the Barcoo River. There's also a motel.

*Tambo Mill Motel (☎ 1651 6166, fax 6151 6497, 34 Arthur St, ✉ tambomillmotel@ bigpond.com)* Singles/doubles $63/76. This attractive and beautifully maintained modern motel has spacious, comfortable lodgings and a good pool.

## Augathella

Augathella is 116km south of Tambo and 5km north of the junction of the Mitchell Hwy and the south-eastern route to Brisbane via Morven. Travellers heading north to Mt Isa, the Gulf or the Northern Territory often join the Matilda Hwy at this point.

Surveyed in 1880, Augathella began as a bullock team camp beside the Warrego River. Today, it services the sheep properties that dot the surrounding countryside.

The Boadicea Arts & Craft Centre (☎ 4654 5116, Main St; open 9am to 4pm weekdays, 10am to noon Saturday) can provide tourist information. The centre houses an extensive array of local pottery, woodcraft and artwork.

The town has a *pub* and the well-maintained *Augathella Motel & Caravan Park (☎ 4654 5177, fax 4654 5353, Matilda Hwy)* with camp sites for $6.60 and double motel rooms $66.

## CHARLEVILLE
**postcode 4470 • pop 3500**

One of outback Queensland's largest towns, Charleville is situated on the Warrego River, 760km west of Brisbane. Edmund Kennedy passed this way in 1847 and the town was gazetted in 1868, six years after the first settlers had arrived. By the turn of the 19th century the town was an important centre for the outlying sheep stations.

Cobb & Co built coaches here between 1893 and 1920, and Charleville is also linked to the origins of Qantas: The airline's first regular route was between Charleville and Cloncurry in 1922.

Charleville was one of the towns hardest hit by the devastating Channel Country floods of 1990. As the Warrego River rose the floodwaters swept through town at around 70km/h; houses were carried away like toys, and the streets opened up and swallowed cars. There are photos and books on the floods in the town's tourist office and a red line almost 2m up the wall shows the high water mark.

### Information

The tourist information centre (☎ 4654 3057, Sturt St; open 9am to 5pm daily from April to October, and weekdays from November to March) is in the Graham Andrews Parklands on the southern side of Charleville.

The Queensland Parks and Wildlife Service (QPWS) office (☎ 4654 1255, 1 Park St; open 8.30am to 4.30pm weekdays) is just off the Warrego Hwy and across the railway line.

The local RACQ depot is South West Ford (☎ 4654 1477), while the Charleville library (☎ 4654 1296, 69 Edward St, open 8.30am-4pm Mon-Fri, 9am-noon Sat) has Internet access for $7 an hour.

### Things to See & Do

The **Historic House Museum** (☎ *4654 1170, 91-93 Alfred St; admission $3; open 9am-5pm daily*) is an old Queenslander that was originally the Queensland National Bank, and later became a private residence, then a guesthouse. Nowadays it's a folk museum with an impressive collection of memorabilia and old machinery.

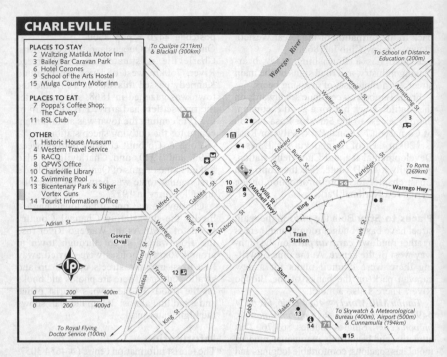

## CHARLEVILLE

**PLACES TO STAY**
2 Waltzing Matilda Motor Inn
3 Bailey Bar Caravan Park
6 Hotel Corones
9 School of the Arts Hostel
15 Mulga Country Motor Inn

**PLACES TO EAT**
7 Poppa's Coffee Shop;
 The Carvery
11 RSL Club

**OTHER**
1 Historic House Museum
4 Western Travel Service
5 RACQ
8 QPWS Office
10 Charleville Library
12 Swimming Pool
13 Bicentenary Park & Stiger
 Vortex Guns
14 Tourist Information Office

The QPWS office operates a captive breeding program and has an **aviary** and a **fauna display** where you can see several endangered species – such as yellow-footed rock wallaby, bridle nail-tail wallaby and the elusive bilby – in small enclosures. The centre also conducts fascinating bilby night tours ($5 per person). Bookings are essential.

At the front of a small park in Sturt St, you can see two of the **Stiger Vortex Rainmaker Guns** used in a futile drought-breaking attempt on 26 September 1902 (the damaged gun exploded during testing). See the boxed text 'The Meteorologist and the Drought-Buster Guns' later.

The **Skywatch** observatory (☎ 4654 3057; *Off Airport Dr; family/adult/child $22/8.80/6.60; open Mon, Wed & Sat nights, nightly Apr-Aug, unless cloudy)* is next door to the Meteorological Bureau, 2km south of the centre. Here you can tour the night sky with an expert guide through high-powered telescopes. The 90-minute sessions start soon

after sunset. There are two sessions a night in the cooler months. Book at the tourist office or through most accommodation houses.

The office of the **Meteorological Bureau** also opens for free guided tours depending on staff numbers.

You can visit the vital facilities at the **Royal Flying Doctor Service base** (☎ *4654 1233, Old Cunnamulla Rd; adult/child $2.50/0.5; open 9am-5pm)*, and the **School of Distance Education** (☎ *4654 1341, Parry St; tours $2; 9.15am & 11am Mon-Fri)* conducts guided tours.

### Organised Tours

Outback Airtours (☎ 4654 3033) offers three- and four-day tours taking in the outback's sights and characters. The all-inclusive adventures start from $1280 per person.

### Special Events

Charleville hosts the Great Matilda Camel Races & Festival in late July each year. As

## The Meteorologist and the Drought-Buster Guns

Charleville was the site of one of the more bizarre episodes in meteorological history. In 1902 meteorologist Clement Wragge proposed importing from Germany six Stiger Vortex guns in an attempt to break the 'great drought', which since 1896 had devastated large areas of Queensland.

Wragge had seen vignerons in northern Italy firing guns at storm clouds to try and reduce hailstones into raindrops. He theorised that the guns could be used in the outback as sure-fire drought-busters.

When they arrived the conical, 5m-high guns were assembled and installed around the town. On 26 September 1902, Wragge poured gunpowder into the guns and detonated them with fuses.

Horses bolted at the deafening noise and two of the guns exploded. Fortunately, no one was injured. Rain continued not to fall and Wragge left town the next day.

You can see two of the original guns on display in front of Bicentennial Park in Sturt St.

well as camels, racing is open to yabbies, goats and other beasts, and the festival includes a rodeo and ball.

### Places to Stay

*Bailey Bar Caravan Park* (☎ *1800 065 311, 4654 1744, fax 4654 3740, 196 King St)* Single/double camp sites $8/14 ($14/16 powered), on-site vans from $28, self-contained cabins from $45. Bailey Bar is the better of the town's two caravan parks. It's well kept, with plenty of grass and eucalypts, immaculate communal facilities and a regular bush poet who does evening recitals during winter.

*School of the Arts Hostel* (☎ *4654 2599, Cnr Edward & Wills Sts)* $16 per person. Dating back to 1924, the School of the Arts building was burnt out and flooded in 1990, before being renovated by the local Bidjara Aboriginal Community. It now operates as a clean, friendly hostel with single rooms and dormitories.

*Hotel Corones* (☎ *4654 1022, fax 4654 1756, 33 Wills St)* Singles/twins from $20/40, with en suite $50/55, motel units from $45/55. Dominating one of Charleville's main intersections, Corones is one of Queensland's grand old country pubs. Its charmingly preserved interior includes a huge public bar (now a cafe), leadlight windows, open fires and timber floors, and upstairs there are dozens of good rooms, only the cheapest of which have no air-con.

*Waltzing Matilda Motor Inn* (☎ *4654 1720, fax 4654 3049, e waltzin@tpg.com .au, 125 Alfred St)* Singles/doubles $44/55,

backpacker units $15. This is a good-value motel, with tidy little units arranged around a central courtyard. There's also a pool, spa and two small but brand-new backpacker units at the rear.

*Mulga Country Motor Inn* (☎ *4654 3255, fax 4654 3381, e mcminn@tpg.com.au, Cunnamulla Rd)* Singles/doubles $76/87. Charleville's top-of-the-range motel is a stylish, modern place on the highway south of the centre. It has upmarket rooms, a *restaurant* and *bar* open six nights and a good pool.

### Places to Eat

*RSL Club* (☎ *4654 1449, 30 Watson St)* Mains $10.50-16, specials from $8. Well established and popular, the RSL Club serves tasty, generous-sized meals, with a frequently changing specials menu.

*The Carvery* (☎ *4654 1022, 33 Wills St)* Soup & main course $14. Open for dinner Mon-Sat, depending on demand. Inside the Hotel Corones, the Carvery has been recommended for a filling, affordable meal.

*Poppa's Coffee Shop* Dishes $5-12. In the Hotel Corones bar, this place is reminiscent of a good city street cafe, with open doors spilling a lively atmosphere into the night. Apart from its appealing ambience, it serves quality cheap feeds for lunch and dinner.

### Getting There & Away

Western Travel Service (☎ 4654 1260, 94 Alfred St) can handle all bus, train and plane reservations and ticket sales. Macair flies from Brisbane to Charleville ($303).

OUTBACK QUEENSLAND

McCafferty's/Greyhound buses run daily between Brisbane and Charleville ($67), but to get further north you must now catch the daily Brisbane to Mt Isa service from either Morven ($106) or Augathella ($102). At the time of writing there were no connecting services from Charleville.

The twice-weekly *Westlander* runs from Brisbane to Charleville; one-way fares are $78/117 for an economy seat/sleeper and $184 for a 1st-class sleeper. There is a connecting bus service to Cunnamulla.

## CHARLEVILLE TO CUNNAMULLA (194km)

There's nothing much along this entire section of the Mitchell Hwy, save for the odd station homestead and railway siding, and the tiny community of **Wyandra**, 104km south of Charleville. The route parallels the Warrego River and the old railway line, and passes through mostly flat country clothed in mulga, a low tree of the wattle family.

## CUNNAMULLA

**postcode 4490 • pop 1500**

The southernmost town in western Queensland, Cunnamulla is on the Warrego River 120km north of the Queensland–New South Wales border.

The town was gazetted in 1868, and in 1879 Cobb & Co established a coach station here. In the 1880s an influx of farmers opened up the country to sheep farming and today millions of sheep graze the open plains around Cunnamulla. The railway arrived in 1898 and since then Cunnamulla has been a major service centre for the district; in good years it is Queensland's biggest wool-loading rail yard.

## Information

Cunnamulla's tourist information centre (☎ 4655 2481, Jane St) is based in the Shire Hall in Centenary Park.

The local RACQ depot is Bill's Auto (☎ 4655 1407), and you can access the Internet at the town library (☎ 4655 2052, 16 John St, open 9am to 5pm weekdays) for $4.70 an hour.

## Things to See & Do

The **Bicentennial Historical Museum** (☎ 4655 2052, 16 John St; admission $1; open 9am-5pm Mon-Fri) has an eclectic mix of memorabilia from old phone exchanges to farming equipment; and the **Robber's Tree**, at the southern end of Stockyard St, is a reminder of a bungled 1880s robbery.

Another tree at the civic centre takes some importance from the fact that it is a yapunyah tree, floral emblem of the Paroo Shire – and this one was planted by royalty.

## Organised Tours

Travel West (☎ 4655 2222, 50 Stockyard St) organises a range of local tours, including a 90-minute 'gossip tour' ($12) and the Innamincka, Oil and Skywatch Experience over six days. The $955 per person (twin share) price tag includes all accommodation, meals and entrance fees.

## Special Events

In late August the town celebrates the Cunnamulla-Eulo World Lizard Races – a three-day festival with arts and crafts, and a parade and ball at Cunnamulla. It culminates with lizard racing at nearby Eulo.

## Places to Stay & Eat

*Cunnamulla Caravan Park (☎/fax 4655 1421, Watson St)* Unpowered/powered sites $13.20/15.40, double cabins from $33. This large, informal park has some pleasant, grassy camp sites, and makes up for its distance from the town centre with a handy milk bar across the road.

*Warrego Hotel-Motel (☎ 4655 1737, fax 4655 2015, 9 Louise St)* Hotel singles/doubles $28/38, motel singles/doubles $59/65, backpacker rates $15 (if booked through Travel West). The basic pub rooms here are well maintained and have shared facilities, while the motel rooms are standard but comfortable. The pub has an excellent *restaurant* open for lunch and dinner.

*Country Way Motor Inn (☎ 4655 0555, fax 4655 0455, 17 Emma St).* Singles/doubles $59/69. The Country Way is Cunnamulla's new kid on the block, with smallish, but cosy, well-equipped rooms in neat surrounds.

## Getting There & Away

There are bus services connecting Cunnamulla with the twice-weekly *Westlander* train service from Charleville to Brisbane. There is also a bus service between Bourke and Cunnamulla; book through Travel West.

# The Channel Country

The remote and sparsely populated southwestern corner of Queensland, bordering the Northern Territory, South Australia and New South Wales, takes its name from the myriad channels that crisscross the area. In this inhospitable region it hardly ever rains, but water from the summer monsoons further north pours into the Channel Country along the Georgina, Hamilton and Diamantina rivers and Cooper Creek. Flooding towards the great depression of Lake Eyre in South Australia, the mass of water arrives on this huge plain, eventually drying up in water holes or salt pans.

Only on rare occasions (the early 1970s, 1989, 1995 and again in 2000) has the vast amount of water actually reached Lake Eyre and filled it. For a short period after each wet season, however, the Channel Country becomes fertile and cattle are grazed here.

## Getting There & Around

Some roads from the east and north to the fringes of the Channel Country are paved, but during the October to May wet season even these can be cut – and the dirt roads become quagmires. In addition, the summer heat is unbearable, so a visit is best made in the cooler months, from May to September.

Visiting this area requires a sturdy vehicle (4WD if you want to get off the beaten track) and some experience of outback driving. If you're travelling anywhere west of Cunnamulla or Quilpie, always carry plenty of fuel and drinking water and notify the police, so that if you don't turn up at the next town, the necessary steps can be taken.

The main road through the Channel Country is the Diamantina Developmental Rd that runs south from Mt Isa through Boulia to Bedourie and then turns east through Windorah and Quilpie to Charleville. In all it's a long and lonely 1340km, about two-thirds of which is sealed.

The paved Kennedy Developmental Rd runs from Winton to Boulia and has a fuel and accommodation stop along the way.

## MT ISA TO BOULIA (295km)

This section of the Diamantina Developmental Rd is the northern access route into the Channel Country. This first section is over narrow, sealed bitumen. The only facilities along the route are at **Dajarra**, a small railway siding with a *pub* and roadhouse 150km south of Mt Isa.

## BOULIA

postcode 4829 • pop 300

Boulia is the 'capital' of the Channel Country, and home to a mysterious supernatural phenomenon known as the Min Min. Said to resemble a car's headlights, this 'earthbound UFO' has been terrifying locals for years, hovering a metre or so above the ground before vanishing and reappearing elsewhere. Now the tiny town is hoping to make some tourism mileage out of its ghostly resident.

The new **Min Min Encounter** complex (☎ 4746 3386, fax 4746 3387, Herbert St; adult/child $11/7.70; open 8.30am-5pm Mon-Fri, 9am-noon Sat & Sun) features sophisticated robotics, imaginative sets and eerie lighting and effects in its hourly show that attempt to convert the nonbelievers. It's well worth a visit. The complex is on the main street, and doubles as the town's tourist information centre.

The town's other, less sophisticated attraction is the **Boulia Stone House Museum** (☎ 4746 3013, Pituri St; admission $2.20; open 7am-noon, Mon-Fri) contained in a National Trust building built in 1888.

You can get Internet access ($2 an hour) at the town library (☎ 4746 3408, Burke St; open 8.30am to 5pm weekdays), while the Shell Roadhouse (☎ 4746 3131, fax 4746 3392, Herbert St) is the contact point for the town's basic *caravan park*, and the local RACQ depot.

*Australian Motel/Hotel* (☎ *4746 3144, fax 4746 3191, Herbert St)* Singles/doubles $33/38, motel units $50/60. The air-con pub rooms here are basic and fairly comfortable, with small but clean shared amenities. There is a good *bistro* with generous serves downstairs.

*Desert Sands Motel* (☎ *4746 3000, fax 4746 3040, Herbert St)* Singles/doubles $66/71.50. This motel has sprung up only recently, and caters for the more indulgent accommodation market. As you would expect, it's a modern place with spacious, pleasant rooms, all with air-con.

## BOULIA TO WINTON

The Kennedy Developmental Rd links Boulia with Winton, 360km away. The only fuel stop along here is 192km east of Boulia at **Middleton**, which started out as staging post for Cobb & Co coaches. The *Middleton Hotel* (☎/*fax 4657 3980, Kennedy Development Rd)* serves meals daily and rents out simple dongas for $40.

## BEDOURIE

Almost 200km south of Boulia is Bedourie. First settled in 1880 as a Cobb & Co depot, Bedourie is now the administrative centre for the huge Diamantina Shire. You can get tourist information from the council offices (☎ 4746 1202, Herbert St), where there's a good rest stop with a shaded picnic and barbecue area and toilets.

The *Royal Hotel* (☎ *4746 1201, fax 4746 1101, Herbert St)*, a charming adobe brick building, was built in 1880 and is still in operation, both as a pub and a post office agency. It also has some accommodation in the form of two stone-built motel-style units with air-con out the back (singles/doubles $50/60). Despite the mess outside, they're clean, tidy and comfy.

There's also a caravan park and fairly expensive motel units at the *Simpson Desert Oasis* (☎ *4746 1291, fax 4746 1208, Herbert St)*, which incorporates a fuel stop, *supermarket* and *restaurant*. It's open 6.30am-8pm daily.

Bedourie hosts a **horse race meeting** on the second weekend in September.

## BIRDSVILLE
**postcode 4482 • pop 120**

The most remote place in Queensland, tiny Birdsville possesses one of Australia's most famous pubs – the Birdsville Hotel.

Birdsville, only 12km from the South Australian border, is at the northern end of the 517km Birdsville Track, which leads to Marree in South Australia. In the late 19th century, Birdsville was quite a busy place as it was here a customs charge was made on each head of cattle being driven to South Australia from Queensland. With Federation the charge was abolished and Birdsville almost became a ghost town. Recently, a thriving cattle industry and a growing tourism profile have revitalised the town; its big moment is the annual Birdsville Races on the first weekend in September, when up to 6500 racing and boozing enthusiasts converge on the town.

Birdsville gets its water from a 1219m artesian well that delivers the water at close to 100°C.

## Information

You can get tourist information from the Wirrarri Centre (☎ 4656 3300, Billabong Blvd; open 8.30am to 6pm weekdays, 9am to 5pm weekends from April to October, 8.30am to 4.30pm weekdays from November to March). It also provides Internet access at $16.50 an hour. The QPWS office (☎ 4656 3272, 4656 3249) is on the corner of Billabong Blvd and Jardine St.

The only banking facilities are at the Commonwealth Bank agency at the post office, which is at Birdsville Fuel Service (☎ 4656 3236, Adelaide St; open 7am to 6pm daily) opposite the pub, although most places now have Eftpos. Birdsville Auto (☎ 4656 3226, Frew St; open 8am to 6pm daily) is the local RACQ depot and can handle towing, mechanical repairs and has some spare parts. It also sells groceries. Both places sell fuel (the most expensive in Queensland), take all major credit cards, and will also open for after-hours fuel.

## Things to See & Do

One of Birdsville's highlights is the **Birdsville Working Museum** (☎ *4656 3259,*

*Macdonald St; adult/child $6/4; open 8am-6pm daily Apr-Oct, tours 9am, 11am, 3pm & 5pm).* It just looks like a big tin shed, but inside is one of the most impressive private museums you'll see. The diverse collection ranges from old tobacco tins and road signs through to shearing equipment, wool presses and mule-driven rounding yards out the back. Just about everything works, and the owner, John Menzies, will take you on a private tour with demonstrations.

Opposite the pub are two **stone memorials** to several expeditions that crossed the Simpson Desert with camels in the 1930s, while opposite Birdsville Auto are the ruins of the **Royal Hotel**, built in 1883 and converted to a hospital in 1923. It is on the National Trust's list for restoration and preservation.

On the first weekend in September, the annual **Birdsville Races** put this tiny community well and truly on the map. More than 6000 dedicated punters come to the town for a weekend of racing, relaxation and refreshments (the three Rs). While here they consume a plethora of beer and generally enjoy the carnival atmosphere (see the boxed text 'The Birdsville Races').

## Organised Tours

Birdsville Town & Country Tours (☎ 4656 3298, ⓔ lyn_rowlands@bigpond.com.au) offers a number of worthwhile tours – one taking in the town, racecourse and the Big Red sandhill ($132), and another exploring the Simpson Desert, lake lands and Eyre Creek ($369). Tour prices are on a sliding scale and drop dramatically per person the larger the group.

## Places to Stay & Eat

**Birdsville Caravan Park** *(☎ 4656 3214, fax 4656 3214, Florence St)* Camp sites $5.50 ($5.50 extra per vehicle for power), single/double cabins $44/60.50. This caravan park has nine new units at the rear, overlooking the nearby Diamantina River. The units are simple but comfortable, with beds, air-con, fridge and a TV. For campers, the park doesn't have much grass or shade, but there's a big clean amenities block, and barbecues.

**Birdsville Hotel** *(☎ 4656 3244, fax 4656 3262, ⓔ birdsvillehotel@bigpond.com.au, Adelaide St)* Single/double motel units $60/84. The Birdsville Hotel stands at the western edge of town, facing into the Simpson Desert like some final sentinel of civilisation. Built from sandstone in 1884, the pub is the town's most famous icon, full of outback characters and attracting tourists from far and wide. Its colourful history includes fire and cyclone, and nowadays it is tastefully renovated with whitewashed walls and slate floors. It has a spacious bar full of memorabilia, and 18 modern motel units with reverse-cycle air-con, bathrooms and phones (no TV). Breakfast, lunch and dinner are served in the licensed restaurant (lunch $5-10, dinner $13-16) or there are cheaper meals in the main and lizard bars. Culinary treats include a coat of arms double: kangaroo fillet or emu fan fillet.

## Getting There & Away

**Air** Birdsville has its own sealed airstrip. Aviation fuel is available through the hotel.

Airlines of South Australia (☎ 08-8642 3100) has a weekly mail-run service leaving Port Augusta in South Australia on Saturday and arriving in Birdsville on Sunday, with an overnight stop in Boulia ($281 one way). It returns to Port Augusta on Sunday evening.

Macair flies to Birdsville from Brisbane ($514) and Mt Isa ($291). See the Getting There and Away section at the start of this chapter for details of stops along these routes.

**Car & Motorcycle** There are two roads into Birdsville from Queensland: the north-south Eyre Developmental Rd from Bedourie and Boulia, and the east-west Birdsville Developmental Rd from Windorah and Betoota.

Both are mostly rough and unsealed (the bitumen begins 117km from Windorah) and, while a conventional vehicle will do, you'd be better off in a 4WD. The surfaces vary from gravel and dirt to soft red sand with frequent cattle grids and potentially perilous dry creek beds (slow down for these). Another hazard is the sharp rocks; it's advisable to carry at least two spare tyres, plenty of drinking water and spare parts.

## The Birdsville Races

The famous Birdsville Races, held on the first weekend in September, are by far Birdsville's biggest event. In the past, the meeting has been well known as an opportunity to get acquainted with the amber liquid, and while there's still an undeniable element, the races have developed into a good-natured gala rather than just a wild grog-fest.

Held annually since 1886, the Birdsville Races take place at the racetrack east of town, and kick off the three-week Simpson Desert Racing Carnival, with subsequent meetings at Bedourie and the one-man town of Betoota.

Visitors flock to Birdsville by road, air or bus, swelling the population from 120 to 6500 – an amazing sight to see. More than 420 planes of all shapes and sizes fly into town, and many people set up camp under the wings, accommodation fondly known as the 'Birdsville Hilton'.

Most punters bring a swag or tent to stay in, either at the airport (where there's amenities and food stalls), the caravan park or down on the mighty Diamantina River.

With the influx of visitors comes an influx of food and other stalls, with vendors bringing in all sorts of palate-tempting delights. For the townsfolk, that means no cooking and plenty of eating out – for the kids it means lots of sweet treats.

The races also bring a rodeo to town, along with Fred Brophy's boxing tent, where alcohol and/or the whole carnival atmosphere encourages some to get in the ring for 'a round or two for a pound or two'.

Meanwhile, souvenir T-shirt sellers do a roaring trade, especially long-time races regular Dirty Pierre, who donates much of his proceeds to charity. Speaking of charity, the Royal Flying Doctor stall is a must, with a great variety of things to buy, and all funds raised helping keep the doctors in the sky.

In fact, the whole race weekend is Birdsville's contribution to the Royal Flying Doctor Service, and the punters tend to give generously, particularly at the 'giant auction' held after the races on Saturday outside Brophy's tent.

And for those who feel like a jig, a ringers' dance is held on the Friday evening, and the race ball is a must on the Saturday night.

## AROUND BIRDSVILLE

Off the Simpson Desert Rd about 35km west of Birdsville is **Big Red**, a massive, wave-like sandhill popular among 4WD travellers. Off the road to Bedourie, about 15km north of Birdsville, is a patch of rare **waddi trees** that only grow in central Australia and isolated pockets of South Africa. A further 65km north are the sun-bleached ruins of the ill-fated Cacoory homestead, abandoned in 1906 because of continual drought.

### Birdsville Track

To the south, the Birdsville Track passes between the Simpson Desert to the west and Sturt Stony Desert to the east. The first stretch from Birdsville has two alternative routes, but only the longer, more easterly Outside Track is open these days. It crosses sandy country at the edge of the desert.

While it is no longer necessary to register with the Birdsville police before tackling the track, it's a good idea to keep friends or relatives informed of your movements so they can notify the authorities should you fail to report in on time. Contact the Wirrarri Centre (☎ 4656 3300) for road conditions.

### Simpson Desert National Park

The waterless Simpson Desert occupies a massive 200,000 sq km of central Australia, and stretches across the Queensland,

Northern Territory and South Australian borders. The Queensland section, in the state's far south-western corner, is protected as the Simpson Desert National Park and adjoins South Australia's Simpson Desert Conservation Park and Simpson Desert Regional Reserve.

The park is a remote, arid landscape of long, high parallel sand dunes, and limited vegetation of spinifex, canegrass and various shrubs.

While 2WD cars can tackle the Birdsville Track quite easily, the Simpson crossing requires a 4WD and far more preparation. Official advice is that crossings should only be undertaken by parties of at least two 4WD vehicles, and that you should have a suitable two-way radio to call for help if necessary. Alternatively, you can hire a satellite phone from Birdsville police (☎ 4656 3220) for $22 a day, which can be returned to Oodnadatta police in South Australia. These are more reliable than a radio, and must be booked at least a month in advance.

Temperatures are extreme, ranging from over 35°C in summer to freezing on some winter mornings. Travel in summer is not recommended.

There are no facilities, so you need to be totally self-sufficient and equipped with adequate supplies of water, food, fuel and spare parts. The park boundary is 80km west of Birdsville; from the boundary, it's another 80km to Poeppel Corner, the intersection of the three states.

Permits are required and you should advise family and friends of your intended movements. Permits are available from the QPWS office in Birdsville or from the town's service stations. For more information, contact the QPWS in Birdsville or Longreach (☎ 4652 7333). You also need a separate permit to travel into the park's South Australian sections – these are available through the South Australian National Parks & Wildlife Service (☎ 1800 816 078) in Port Augusta.

## BETOOTA (POP 1)
The old pub that constituted the 'township' of Betoota, 164km east of Birdsville, closed its doors for good in September 1997. The retired publican and sole resident, Simon Remienko, no longer offers facilities to passing motorists, meaning there are no fuel stops between Birdsville and Windorah (395km). Motorists out this way should carry extra fuel.

## WINDORAH
Windorah has a pub, a general store and a basic caravan park. *Gordon's General Store* (☎ 4656 3145) is open daily, and will open after hours if you need fuel. It also sells a range of groceries and takeaway meals, has Eftpos and takes all major credit cards.

Opposite the store, the *Western Star Hotel* (☎ 4656 3166, fax 4656 3110, 15 Albert St) has good single/double pub rooms for $35/44, and four brand-new motel units for $77/85. North of the centre *Cooper Cabins* (☎ 4656 3101, 11 Edward St), on a bare red-earth block, has self-contained units for $55.

## QUILPIE
postcode 4480 • pop 620
Quilpie is an opal-mining town and the railhead from which cattle, grazed here during the wet season, are railed to the coast. The name Quilpie comes from an Aboriginal word for stone-curlew, and all but two of the town's streets are named after birds.

The Quilpie Museum & Visitors Centre (☎ 4656 2166, 51 Brolga St) on the main street can provide you with tourist information, and there are regular opal-cutting demonstrations here.

The local RACQ agent is the John Crawley Service Station (☎ 4656 1344), while the Quilpie library (☎ 4656 1133, 48 Brolga St, open varying hours Monday to Saturday) provides Internet access.

### Places to Stay & Eat
*Channel Country Caravan Park* (☎ 4656 2087, fax 4656 1585, Chipu St) Camp sites $6 per person, single/double budget rooms $30/35, cabins $50/55. A friendly, young couple runs this well-maintained park on the town's western edge. They also run tag-along tours to the opal fields every Tuesday ($25).

The wind pump dots the horizon wherever you travel in outback Queensland.

There are grassed sites here and the modern cabins have air-con.

*Quilpie Motor Inn* (☎ *4656 1277, fax 4656 1231, 80 Brolga St)* Singles/doubles $60/70. This tidy, modern motel west of the centre has decent rooms with en suites and air-con. There's also a licensed dining room, and the kitchen can provide pre-packed lunches if you're going out fossicking.

There are several *farm-stays* in the Quilpie area; ask at the tourist office for details.

## Getting There & Away

There are bus services connecting Quilpie with the twice-weekly *Westlander* train service from Charleville to Brisbane. Macair flies to Quilpie from Brisbane ($382) and Birdsville ($242) via the stops listed in the Getting There and Away section at the start of this chapter.

## QUILPIE TO CHARLEVILLE

There are a couple of small townships along this 210km section of the Diamantina Developmental Rd: **Cheepie**, 76km east of Quilpie, has an old post office and a phone booth, while **Cooladdi** 45km further east has a *motel* and *general store*. See the earlier Matilda Hwy section for information about the Charleville region.

## CUNNAMULLA TO INNAMINCKA

Heading west from Cunnamulla 640km to Innamincka, the all-bitumen Bulloo Developmental Rd takes you through the small settlements of Eulo and Thargomindah to Noccundra. You can take a northern detour to the Yowah Opal Fields and, if you have a 4WD, you can continue west from Noccundra to Innamincka in South Australia on the Strzelecki Track.

### Eulo

Eulo, 68km west of Cunnamulla, is on the Paroo River close to the Yowah Opal Fields. In late August/early September the town hosts the **World Lizard Racing Championships**. Next to the Eulo Queen Hotel is the **Destructo Cockroach Monument**, erected in memory of a racing cockroach who died when a punter stood on it. This tiny granite plinth must be the only cockroach memorial in the world.

*Eulo Queen Hotel* (☎/fax 4655 4867, Leo St) Single/twin rooms $16.50/27.50, cabins $55/60. The pub has mediocre air-con pub rooms with shared facilities at the rear, and two comfortable, new, self-contained cabins on the block next door.

There is also a small *caravan park* resembling a paddock, while the *Eulo Store* (☎ *4655 4900)* sells fuel and supplies.

## Yowah

Yowah is a tiny opal-mining settlement about 40km north-west of Eulo. It's a popular fossicking field where the unique Yowah opal nut is found. Inside, if you're lucky, you'll find a rare ironstone matrix opal.

Yowah has a *caravan park*, free *camping ground*, *general store*, *motel* and a *museum*, and mine tours can be arranged. For tourist information call ☎ 4655 2481.

About 100km further north from Yowah is the **Duck Creek Opal Field**.

## Thargomindah

On the banks of the Bulloo River, Thargomindah is almost 200km south of Quilpie and almost 200km west of Cunnamulla. The road from Cunnamulla is good sealed bitumen; most of the route to Quilpie is unsealed. The town was gazetted back in 1874 and camel trains used to cross from here to Bourke in New South Wales.

The tourist information centre (☎ 4655 3055, Frew St) is on the main street, and you can get fuel and groceries daily in the town. Crawfo's Motors Roadhouse (☎ 4655 3178, Stafford St) is the RACQ agent, and also sells decent takeaway pizzas.

For accommodation, there's a *pub* with counter meals, a *motel* and an elementary *caravan park*. Alternatively, *Dr Becker's Guest House (☎/fax 4655 3143, Frew St)*,

has budget accommodation in air-con twin rooms ($33 per person) or a simple bunkhouse ($27). Both tariffs include a light breakfast.

## Noccundra

Noccundra, 145km further west on the Wilson River, was once a busy little community. It now has just a hotel.

Built in 1882, the *Noccundra Hotel (☎ 4655 4317, fax 4655 3097)* is an appealing, isolated sandstone pub on the Wilson River. It has five rooms including doubles, twins and a four-bed bunk room (singles/doubles/triples $30/40/60). The friendly staff serve breakfast and cheap dinners daily, sell all fuels, and do some emergency repairs.

Continuing on from Noccundra, head 20km north back to the Bulloo Developmental Rd, which continues west for another 75km through the Jackson Oil Field to the Naccowlah Oil Field. The sealed road ends here but you can continue across to Innamincka on the Strzelecki Track in South Australia via the site of the **Dig Tree**, of Burke and Wills fame (see History in the Facts about Queensland chapter). This route is particularly rough and stony with frequent creek crossings, and is only recommended for 4WD vehicles. The road is usually closed during the Wet. If you are heading this way, check at the pub for directions.

# Glossary

**award wage** – minimum pay rate

**banana bender** – resident of Queensland
**bastard** – general form of address which can mean many things, from high praise or respect ('He's the bravest bastard I know') to dire insult ('You rotten bastard!'). Avoid using if unsure!
**beche-de-mer** – sea cucumber
**beyond the black stump** – back of beyond, middle of nowhere
**billabong** – water hole in a dried-up riverbed; more correctly, an ox-bow bend cut off in the dry season by receding waters
**billy** – tin container used to boil tea in the bush
**bitumen** – surfaced road
**bluey** – *swag*; woollen workers coat; nickname for a red-haired person
**boogie board** – half-sized surfboard
**boom netting** – riding through the surf on nets in the front or rear of a travelling boat
**boomerang** – curved, flat, wooden implement traditionally used by Aboriginal people for hunting
**bottle shop** – liquor shop
**box jellyfish** – species of deadly jellyfish; also known as sea wasp, box jelly, sea jelly, stinger
**brekky** – breakfast
**bug** – Moreton Bay bug, a small edible crustacean
**bull dust** – fine and sometimes deep dust on outback roads; bullshit
**bunyip** – mythical *bush* animal or spirit
**bush tucker** – native foods, usually in the outback
**bush, the** – countryside, usually covered with trees or shrubs; anywhere away from the city
**bushranger** – Australia's equivalent of the outlaws of the Wild West (some goodies, some baddies)

**camp-o-tel** – semi-permanent tent with beds and lights
**chook** – chicken

**counter meal** – pub meal, usually eaten at the bar

**dag** – dirty lump of wool at back end of a sheep; affectionate or mildly abusive term for an unfashionable or socially inept person
**damper** – bush loaf made from flour and water and cooked in a fire or camp oven
**didgeridoo** – cylindrical wooden musical instrument traditionally played by Aboriginal men
**donga** – sugar-cane cutters cabin (archaic); prefabricated transportable cabin
**Dry, the** – dry season in northern Queensland (June to October)
**dunny** – outdoor lavatory

**flake** – shark meat, often served in fish-and-chip shops
**fossicking** – hunting for gems
**freshie** – freshwater crocodile

**galah** – noisy cockatoo; noisy idiot
**grazier** – large-scale sheep or cattle farmer
**grog** – general term for alcoholic drinks
**gum tree** – eucalypt tree

**homestead** – residence of a *station* owner or manager

**jackaroo** – young male trainee on a *station*
**jillaroo** – young female trainee on a *station*
**jumper** – sweater; pullover

**Kanaka** – South Pacific islander, especially one abducted to work in Queensland in the 19th century
**Kiwi** – New Zealander

**lamington** – square of sponge cake covered in chocolate icing and coconut
**larrikin** – a playfully mischievous person
**lay-by** – put a deposit on an article so the shop will hold it for you
**live-aboard** – cruise or dive boat offering accommodation

**Mexican** – anyone from south of the Queensland border

**milk bar** – general store

**mod Oz** – modern Australian cuisine, influenced by a wide range of foreign cuisines, but with a definite local flavour

**mozzies** – mosquitoes

**mulga** – *outback* tree or shrub; large area covered by same

**Murri** – collective term used to identify Aboriginal people from Queensland

**outback** – remote part of the bush

**paddock** – fenced area of land, usually intended for livestock

**pastoralist** – large-scale farm owner

**pokies** – poker machines

**Pom** – English person

**postie** – postal worker

**Queenslander** – traditional raised timber dwelling

**rashie, rash-top** – UV-resistant, skin-tight vest worn by surfers

**road train** – a truck pulling a number of linked trailers (semitrailer-trailer-trailer)

**saltie** – saltwater or estuarine crocodile

**savannah** – areas of grassland with scattered trees or shrubs

**scrub** – *bush*; trees, shrubs and other plants growing in an arid area

**sea wasp** – deadly *box jellyfish*

**sealed road** – hard-surfaced or *bitumen*-covered road

**shout** – buy a round of drinks (as in 'It's your shout')

**squatter** – pioneer farmer who occupied land as a tenant of the government

**station** – large farm

**stinger** – deadly *box jellyfish*

**Stolen Generations** – generations of Indigenous children forcibly removed from their parents

**stubby** – 375ml bottle of beer

**swag** – canvas-covered bed-roll used in the *outback*; a large quantity

**swagman** – (archaic) vagabond; itinerant labourer

***terra nullius*** – legal concept that Australia was uninhabited at the time of British colonisation

**thongs** – flip-flops (footwear)

**tinny** – 375ml can of beer; small, aluminium fishing dinghy

**Tip, the** – Cape York Peninsula

**togs** – swimming costume

**truckie** – truck driver

**tucker** – food

**two-up** – traditional heads-or-tails gambling game

**vegie** – vegetable; vegetarian

**walkabout** – lengthy walk away from it all

**wattle** – Australian acacia species with furry, yellow flowers

**Wet, the** – rainy season in the north (November/December to April/May, especially between January and March)

**yabbie** – freshwater crayfish

## ACRONYMS & ABBREVIATIONS

**ACT** – Australian Capital Territory

**ALP** – Australia Labor Party

**Anzac** – Australian and New Zealand Army Corps

**BYO** – bring your own (a type of restaurant licence which permits customers to drink alcohol they have purchased elsewhere)

**Eftpos** – electronic funds transfer at point of sale (method of paying for goods or services, or withdrawing cash)

**EPA** – Environment Protection Agency (government department responsible for national parks and wildlife)

**NSW** – New South Wales

**NT** – Northern Territory

**QPWS** – Queensland Parks and Wildlife Service (parks division of the *EPA*)

**RACQ** – Royal Automobile Club of Queensland

**RSL** – Returned Servicemen's League

**WA** – Western Australia

# Lonely Planet Guides by Region

**L**onely Planet is known worldwide for publishing practical, reliable and no-nonsense travel information in our guides and on our Web site. The Lonely Planet list covers just about every accessible part of the world. Currently there are 16 series: Travel guides, Shoestring guides, Condensed guides, Phrasebooks, Read This First, Healthy Travel, Walking guides, Cycling guides, Watching Wildlife guides, Pisces Diving & Snorkeling guides, City Maps, Road Atlases, Out to Eat, World Food, Journeys travel literature and Pictorials.

**AFRICA** Africa on a shoestring • Botswana • Cairo • Cairo City Map • Cape Town • Cape Town City Map • East Africa • Egypt • Egyptian Arabic phrasebook • Ethiopia, Eritrea & Djibouti • Ethiopian Amharic phrasebook • The Gambia & Senegal • Healthy Travel Africa • Kenya • Malawi • Morocco • Moroccan Arabic phrasebook • Mozambique • Namibia • Read This First: Africa • South Africa, Lesotho & Swaziland • Southern Africa • Southern Africa Road Atlas • Swahili phrasebook • Tanzania, Zanzibar & Pemba • Trekking in East Africa • Tunisia • Watching Wildlife East Africa • Watching Wildlife Southern Africa • West Africa • World Food Morocco • Zambia • Zimbabwe, Botswana & Namibia
**Travel Literature:** Mali Blues: Traveling to an African Beat • The Rainbird: A Central African Journey • Songs to an African Sunset: A Zimbabwean Story

**AUSTRALIA & THE PACIFIC** Aboriginal Australia & the Torres Strait Islands •Auckland • Australia • Australian phrasebook • Australia Road Atlas • Cycling Australia • Cycling New Zealand • Fiji • Fijian phrasebook • Healthy Travel Australia, NZ & the Pacific • Islands of Australia's Great Barrier Reef • Melbourne • Melbourne City Map • Micronesia • New Caledonia • New South Wales • New Zealand • Northern Territory • Outback Australia • Out to Eat – Melbourne • Out to Eat – Sydney • Papua New Guinea • Pidgin phrasebook • Queensland • Rarotonga & the Cook Islands • Samoa • Solomon Islands • South Australia • South Pacific • South Pacific phrasebook • Sydney • Sydney City Map • Sydney Condensed • Tahiti & French Polynesia • Tasmania • Tonga • Tramping in New Zealand • Vanuatu • Victoria • Walking in Australia • Watching Wildlife Australia • Western Australia
**Travel Literature:** Islands in the Clouds: Travels in the Highlands of New Guinea • Kiwi Tracks: A New Zealand Journey • Sean & David's Long Drive

**CENTRAL AMERICA & THE CARIBBEAN** Bahamas, Turks & Caicos • Baja California • Belize, Guatemala & Yucatán • Bermuda • Central America on a shoestring • Costa Rica • Costa Rica Spanish phrasebook • Cuba • Cycling Cuba • Dominican Republic & Haiti • Eastern Caribbean • Guatemala • Havana • Healthy Travel Central & South America • Jamaica • Mexico • Mexico City • Panama • Puerto Rico • Read This First: Central & South America • Virgin Islands • World Food Caribbean • World Food Mexico • Yucatán
**Travel Literature:** Green Dreams: Travels in Central America

**EUROPE** Amsterdam • Amsterdam City Map • Amsterdam Condensed • Andalucía • Athens • Austria • Baltic States phrasebook • Barcelona • Barcelona City Map • Belgium & Luxembourg • Berlin • Berlin City Map • Britain • British phrasebook • Brussels, Bruges & Antwerp • Brussels City Map • Budapest • Budapest City Map • Canary Islands • Catalunya & the Costa Brava • Central Europe • Central Europe phrasebook • Copenhagen • Corfu & the Ionians • Corsica • Crete • Crete Condensed • Croatia • Cycling Britain • Cycling France • Cyprus • Czech & Slovak Republics • Czech phrasebook • Denmark • Dublin • Dublin City Map • Dublin Condensed • Eastern Europe • Eastern Europe phrasebook • Edinburgh • Edinburgh City Map • England • Estonia, Latvia & Lithuania • Europe on a shoestring • Europe phrasebook • Finland • Florence • Florence City Map • France • Frankfurt City Map • Frankfurt Condensed • French phrasebook • Georgia, Armenia & Azerbaijan • Germany • German phrasebook • Greece • Greek Islands • Greek phrasebook • Hungary • Iceland, Greenland & the Faroe Islands • Ireland • Italian phrasebook • Italy • Kraków • Lisbon • The Loire • London • London City Map • London Condensed • Madrid • Madrid City Map • Malta • Mediterranean Europe • Milan, Turin & Genoa • Moscow • Munich • Netherlands • Normandy • Norway • Out to Eat – London • Out to Eat – Paris • Paris • Paris City Map • Paris Condensed • Poland • Polish phrasebook • Portugal • Portuguese phrasebook • Prague • Prague City Map • Provence & the Côte d'Azur • Read This First: Europe • Rhodes & the Dodecanese • Romania & Moldova • Rome • Rome City Map • Rome Condensed • Russia, Ukraine & Belarus • Russian phrasebook • Scandinavian & Baltic Europe • Scandinavian phrasebook • Scotland • Sicily • Slovenia • South-West France • Spain • Spanish phrasebook • Stockholm • St Petersburg • St Petersburg City Map • Sweden • Switzerland • Tuscany • Ukrainian phrasebook • Venice • Vienna • Wales • Walking in Britain • Walking in France • Walking in Ireland • Walking in Scotland • Walking in Spain • Walking in Switzerland • Western Europe • World Food France • World Food Greece • World Food Ireland • World Food Italy • World Food Spain **Travel Literature:** After Yugoslavia • Love and War in the Apennines • The Olive Grove: Travels in Greece • On the Shores of the Mediterranean • Round Ireland in Low Gear • A Small Place in Italy

# Lonely Planet Mail Order

**L**onely Planet products are distributed worldwide. They are also available by mail order from Lonely Planet, so if you have difficulty finding a title please write to us. North and South American residents should write to 150 Linden St, Oakland, CA 94607, USA; European and African residents should write to 10a Spring Place, London NW5 3BH, UK; and residents of other countries to Locked Bag 1, Footscray, Victoria 3011, Australia.

**INDIAN SUBCONTINENT & THE INDIAN OCEAN** Bangladesh • Bengali phrasebook • Bhutan • Delhi • Goa • Healthy Travel Asia & India • Hindi & Urdu phrasebook • India • India & Bangladesh City Map • Indian Himalaya • Karakoram Highway • Kathmandu City Map • Kerala • Madagascar • Maldives • Mauritius, Réunion & Seychelles • Mumbai (Bombay) • Nepal • Nepali phrasebook • North India • Pakistan • Rajasthan • Read This First: Asia & India • South India • Sri Lanka • Sri Lanka phrasebook • Tibet • Tibetan phrasebook • Trekking in the Indian Himalaya • Trekking in the Karakoram & Hindukush • Trekking in the Nepal Himalaya • World Food India **Travel Literature:** The Age of Kali: Indian Travels and Encounters • Hello Goodnight: A Life of Goa • In Rajasthan • Maverick in Madagascar • A Season in Heaven: True Tales from the Road to Kathmandu • Shopping for Buddhas • A Short Walk in the Hindu Kush • Slowly Down the Ganges

**MIDDLE EAST & CENTRAL ASIA** Bahrain, Kuwait & Qatar • Central Asia • Central Asia phrasebook • Dubai • Farsi (Persian) phrasebook • Hebrew phrasebook • Iran • Israel & the Palestinian Territories • Istanbul • Istanbul City Map • Istanbul to Cairo • Istanbul to Kathmandu • Jerusalem • Jerusalem City Map • Jordan • Lebanon • Middle East • Oman & the United Arab Emirates • Syria • Turkey • Turkish phrasebook • World Food Turkey • Yemen **Travel Literature:** Black on Black: Iran Revisited • Breaking Ranks: Turbulent Travels in the Promised Land • The Gates of Damascus • Kingdom of the Film Stars: Journey into Jordan

**NORTH AMERICA** Alaska • Boston • Boston City Map • Boston Condensed • British Columbia • California & Nevada • California Condensed • Canada • Chicago • Chicago City Map • Chicago Condensed • Florida • Georgia & the Carolinas • Great Lakes • Hawaii • Hiking in Alaska • Hiking in the USA • Honolulu & Oahu City Map • Las Vegas • Los Angeles • Los Angeles City Map • Louisiana & the Deep South • Miami • Miami City Map • Montreal • New England • New Orleans • New Orleans City Map • New York City • New York City Map • New York City Condensed • New York, New Jersey & Pennsylvania • Oahu • Out to Eat – San Francisco • Pacific Northwest • Rocky Mountains • San Diego & Tijuana • San Francisco • San Francisco City Map • Seattle • Seattle City Map • Southwest • Texas • Toronto • USA • USA phrasebook • Vancouver • Vancouver City Map • Virginia & the Capital Region • Washington, DC • Washington, DC City Map • World Food New Orleans **Travel Literature:** Caught Inside: A Surfer's Year on the California Coast • Drive Thru America

**NORTH-EAST ASIA** Beijing • Beijing City Map • Cantonese phrasebook • China • Hiking in Japan • Hong Kong & Macau • Hong Kong City Map • Hong Kong Condensed • Japan • Japanese phrasebook • Korea • Korean phrasebook • Kyoto • Mandarin phrasebook • Mongolia • Mongolian phrasebook • Seoul • Shanghai • South-West China • Taiwan • Tokyo • Tokyo Condensed • World Food Hong Kong • World Food Japan **Travel Literature:** In Xanadu: A Quest • Lost Japan

**SOUTH AMERICA** Argentina, Uruguay & Paraguay • Bolivia • Brazil • Brazilian phrasebook • Buenos Aires • Buenos Aires City Map • Chile & Easter Island • Colombia • Ecuador & the Galapagos Islands • Healthy Travel Central & South America • Latin American Spanish phrasebook • Peru • Quechua phrasebook • Read This First: Central & South America • Rio de Janeiro • Rio de Janeiro City Map • Santiago de Chile • South America on a shoestring • Trekking in the Patagonian Andes • Venezuela **Travel Literature:** Full Circle: A South American Journey

**SOUTH-EAST ASIA** Bali & Lombok • Bangkok • Bangkok City Map • Burmese phrasebook • Cambodia • Cycling Vietnam, Laos & Cambodia • East Timor phrasebook • Hanoi • Healthy Travel Asia & India • Hill Tribes phrasebook • Ho Chi Minh City (Saigon) • Indonesia • Indonesian phrasebook • Indonesia's Eastern Islands • Java • Lao phrasebook • Laos • Malay phrasebook • Malaysia, Singapore & Brunei • Myanmar (Burma) • Philippines • Pilipino (Tagalog) phrasebook • Read This First: Asia & India • Singapore • Singapore City Map • South-East Asia on a shoestring • South-East Asia phrasebook • Thailand • Thailand's Islands & Beaches • Thailand, Vietnam, Laos & Cambodia Road Atlas • Thai phrasebook • Vietnam • Vietnamese phrasebook • World Food Indonesia • World Food Thailand • World Food Vietnam

**ALSO AVAILABLE:** Antarctica • The Arctic • The Blue Man: Tales of Travel, Love and Coffee • Brief Encounters: Stories of Love, Sex & Travel • Buddhist Stupas in Asia: The Shape of Perfection • Chasing Rickshaws • The Last Grain Race • Lonely Planet ... On the Edge: Adventurous Escapades from Around the World • Lonely Planet Unpacked • Lonely Planet Unpacked Again • Not the Only Planet: Science Fiction Travel Stories • Ports of Call: A Journey by Sea • Sacred India • Travel Photography: A Guide to Taking Better Pictures • Travel with Children • Tuvalu: Portrait of an Island Nation

# LONELY PLANET

You already know that Lonely Planet produces more than this one guidebook, but you might not be aware of the other products we have on this region. Here is a selection of titles that you may want to check out as well:

**Australia**
ISBN 1 74059 065 1
US$25.99 • UK£15.99

**Outback Australia**
ISBN 0 86442 504 X
US$21.95 • UK£13.99

**Australian phrasebook**
ISBN 0 86442 576 7
US$5.95 • UK£3.99

**Cycling Australia**
ISBN 1 86450 166 9
US$21.99 • UK£13.99

**Walking in Australia**
ISBN 0 86442 669 0
US$21.99 • UK£13.99

**Healthy Travel Australia,
NZ & the Pacific**
ISBN 1 86450 052 2
US$5.95 • UK£3.99

**Aboriginal Australia & the
Torres Strait Islands**
ISBN 1 86450 114 6
US$19.99 • UK£12.99

**Watching Wildlife Australia**
ISBN 1 86450 032 8
US$19.99 • UK£12.99

**Islands of Australia's
Great Barrier Reef**
ISBN 0 86442 563 5
US$14.95 • UK£8.99

**Australia Road Atlas**
ISBN 1 86450 065 4
US$14.99 • UK£8.99

**Diving & Snorkeling
Australia's Great Barrier Reef**
ISBN 0 86442 763 8
US$17.95 • UK£11.99

**Available wherever books
are sold**

# Index

## Text

**Bold** indicates maps.

**Bold** indicates maps.

Bold indicates maps.

# Boxed Text

# MAP LEGEND

## BOUNDARIES

| | |
|---|---|
| —·—·— State | —··—··— International |
| —— —— Disputed | ++++++ Cliff |

## AREA FEATURES

| | |
|---|---|
| Aboriginal Land |
| Beach |
| Building |
| Campus |
| + + + Cemetery |
| Mall |
| ⊕ Park, Gardens, Path |
| Urban Area |

## HYDROGRAPHY

| | |
|---|---|
| Coastline |
| River, Creek |
| Dry River, Creek |
| Lake |
| Dry Lake; Salt Lake |
| ⊙ ⟶ Spring; Rapids |
| ⊛ ⊣⊢ ⊰ Waterfalls |
| Swamp |

## REGIONAL ROUTES

| | |
|---|---|
| ═══ Tollway, Freeway |
| ═══ Primary Road |
| ——— Secondary Road |
| ——— Minor Road |

## CITY ROUTES

| | |
|---|---|
| **Fwy** Freeway |
| **Hwy** Primary Road |
| **Rd** Secondary Road |
| **St** Street |
| **La** Lane |
| ═══ On/Off Ramp |
| ==== Unsealed Road |
| → One Way Street |
| ▭▭▭ Pedestrian Mall |
| ) ── Tunnel |
| ▭▭▭ Footbridge |

## POPULATION SYMBOLS

| | |
|---|---|
| ◎ **Capital** National Capital |
| ◉ **Capital** State Capital |
| ● **City** City |
| ○ **Town** Town |
| ○ Village Village |

## TRANSPORT ROUTES & STATIONS

| | |
|---|---|
| ├──○── Train | ├──┼──⊞ Cable Car, Chairlift |
| ·+·+·+· Underground Train | ─────▯ Ferry |
| ──Ⓜ── Metro | ────⚐ Walking Trail, Head |
| ───── Tramway | ·········· Walking Tour |
| ···─···─ Monorail | ────── Pier or Jetty |

## MAP SYMBOLS

| | | |
|---|---|---|
| ▪ Place to Stay | ▼ Place to Eat | ● Point of Interest |

| | | | | | | |
|---|---|---|---|---|---|---|
| 区 ✚ Airport, Airfield | ⊠ Dive Site | ▣ Parking | 🏛 Stately Home |
| ✕ Airplane Wreck | ◘ Embassy/Consulate | ⊙ Petrol Station | 🏊 Swimming Pool |
| ⊖ Bank/ATM | ◐ Golf Course | ⊛ Picnic Area | ⊠ Taxi |
| ▯ ▯ Bus Stop, Terminal | ⊕ Hospital/Clinic | ⊞ Police Station | ☎ Telephone |
| ⟍ Bird Sanctuary/Park | 🔳 Internet Cafe | ▭ Post Office | ⊟ Theatre |
| ⬛ Camping | ⚓ Lighthouse | ⊡ Pub or Bar | ⊟ Transport |
| ⏏ Caravan | ☀ Lookout | ⬛ Ruins | ○ Toilets |
| ⌂ Cave | ▲ Monument | ✕ Shipwreck | ❶ Tourist Information |
| ▦ ✚ Church | ▲ Mountain/Range | ⊠ Shopping Centre | ◢ Windsurfing |
| ⊞ Cinema | 🏛 Museum/Gallery | ◉ Snorkelling | 🍷 Winery |
| ⊛ Disabled Access | 🔲 National Park | ⟨ Surfing | 🔲 Zoo/Wildlife Park |

*Note: not all symbols displayed above appear in this book*

---

# LONELY PLANET OFFICES

**Australia**
Locked Bag 1, Footscray, Victoria 3011
☎ 03 8379 8000  fax 03 8379 8111
email: talk2us@lonelyplanet.com.au

**UK**
10a Spring Place, London NW5 3BH
☎ 020 7428 4800  fax 020 7428 4828
email: go@lonelyplanet.co.uk

**USA**
150 Linden St, Oakland, CA 94607
☎ 510 893 8555  TOLL FREE: 800 275 8555
fax 510 893 8572
email: info@lonelyplanet.com

**France**
1 rue du Dahomey, 75011 Paris
☎ 01 55 25 33 00  fax 01 55 25 33 01
email: bip@lonelyplanet.fr
www.lonelyplanet.fr

**World Wide Web: www.lonelyplanet.com** *or* **AOL keyword: lp**
**Lonely Planet Images: www.lonelyplanetimages.com**